W9-CHH-157

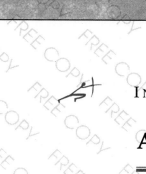

INTRODUCTION TO
Physical Anthropology

INTRODUCTION TO
Physical Anthropology

SIXTH EDITION

ROBERT JURMAIN

Department of Anthropology
San Jose State University
San Jose, California

HARRY NELSON

Emeritus
Department of Anthropology
Foothill College
Los Altos, California

West Publishing Company
Minneapolis/St. Paul   New York
Los Angeles   San Francisco

Design: Janet Bollow
Copy editor: Stuart Kenter
Illustrations: Alexander Productions, Paragon 3, Sue Sellars
Cover art: Sue Sellars
Composition: Janet Hansen, Alphatype

West's Commitment to the Environment

In 1906, West Publishing Company began recycling materials left over from the production of books. This began a tradition of efficient and responsible use of resources. Today, up to 95 percent of our legal books and 70 percent of our college and school texts are printed on recycled, acid-free stock. West also recycles nearly 22 million pounds of scrap paper annually—the equivalent of 181,717 trees. Since the 1960s, West has devised ways to capture and recycle waste inks, solvents, oils, and vapors created in the printing process. We also recycle plastics of all kinds, wood, glass, corrugated cardboard, and batteries, and have eliminated the use of styrofoam book packaging. We at West are proud of the longevity and the scope of our commitment to the environment.

Production, Prepress, Printing and Binding by West Publishing Company.

COPYRIGHT © 1979,
1982, 1985, 1988, 1991   By WEST PUBLISHING COMPANY
COPYRIGHT © 1994   By WEST PUBLISHING COMPANY
610 Opperman Drive
P.O. Box 64526
St. Paul, MN 55164-0526

All rights reserved

Printed in the United States of America

00 99 98 97 96 95 94   8 7 6 5 4 3 2 1 0

Library of Congress Cataloging-in-Publication Data

Jurmain, Robert.
  Introduction to physical anthropology / Robert Jurmain, Harry Nelson.—6th ed.
      p.   cm.
  Nelson's name appears first on the 5th ed.
  Includes bibliographical references (p.   ) and index.
  ISBN 0–314–02778–5 (soft)
  1. Physical anthropology.   I. Nelson, Harry.   II. Title.
  [DNLM: 1. Anthropology, Physical.]
GN60.N44 1994
573—dc20   93–45032
                                                                CIP

Credits

Chapter 1:   Fig. 1-1 Courtesy Peter Jones; Fig. 1-2 Bettmann Archive; Fig. 1-3(a) Institute of Human Origins. (b) Harry Nelson; (c) Lynn Kilgore; (d) George E. Jones/Photo Researchers; Fig. 1-4 Institute of Human Origins; Fig. 1-5 R. Jurmain; Fig. 1-6 Courtesy Judith Regensteiner/Michael Whitney; Fig. 1-7(a) Bonnie Pedersen/Arlene Kruse; (b) R. Jurmain; Fig. 1-8(a) Lynn Kilgore; (b) R. Jurmain; Fig. 1-9 Courtesy Lorna Pierce/Judy Suchey.

Chapter 2:   Fig. 2-2 Courtesy of Wayne Savage. Photomicrography by Mark Cunningham; Figs. 2-3, 2-4 University of California Medical Center.

Chapter 3:   Fig. 3-1 Harry Nelson.

(*continued following Index*)

Contents

CHAPTER FIVE

Approaches to Human Variation 109

CHAPTER SIX

Human Adaptability: Meeting the Challenge of the Environment 137

CHAPTER SEVEN

Evolutionary History

CHAPTER EIGHT

Living Primates

CHAPTER NINE

Fundamentals of Primate Behavior

229

CHAPTER TEN

Primate Models for Human Evolution

265

CHAPTER THIRTEEN

Plio-Pleistocene Hominids   349

CHAPTER FOURTEEN

Plio-Pleistocene Hominids: Organization and Interpretation   385

CHAPTER SEVENTEEN

Homo Sapiens Sapiens   467

Preface

We began the research and writing of *Introduction to Physical Anthropology* in 1977, and the first edition was published in 1979. Thus, we now have been working together on this project for more than 15 years. Over this time, physical anthropology has undergone a great deal of change, not just as the result of new discoveries, but also owing to the incorporation of new methodologies. Over the years, we have attempted to keep pace with both these changing data and these new perspectives. In this edition, for example, new genetic approaches in the Human Genome Project, new interpretations of *Homo habilis*, new finds of Chinese *Homo erectus*, and new dating estimates for early modern *Homo sapiens* from Israel are included. Moreover, the changing perspectives relating to use of mitochondrial DNA as a tool for reconstructing recent human evolution are incorporated into our discussion in Chapter 17.

In addition to the kinds of data analyzed by physical anthropologists and the various methodologies used to gather such information, there is a further conceptual basis that is essential in order to understand this field of knowledge. Most fundamentally, there are the basic scientific principles that structure how we *think* about our discipline, what questions we ask, and how we verify the various potential answers. In other words, understanding the way physical anthropologists organize our discipline as a *scientific* process also is a necessary component of an introductory course in this field. Accordingly, the nature of the scientific perspective, as it relates to the development of critical thinking skills, is also a focus of our presentation—especially in the chapter-opening issues.

In addition, and as a further aid to students, we have continued with a series of successful pedagogical aids and other features, including: (1) a running glossary with highlighted terms defined in the margin (as well as included in a glossary at the end of the text); (2) boxed features that incorporate interesting biographical information or supplemental, more detailed, technical details; (3) newly formatted maps, as well as photo layouts showing anatomical features of fossil hominids; (4) guest essays (also new to this edition) from physical anthropologists pursuing widely diverse research interests; and (5) two appendices reviewing comparative primate anatomy and forensic anthropology.

An introductory course in physical anthropology can be a challenge for instructors and students alike. Frequently, as a general education offering, the course attracts students with widely different backgrounds and expectations. Moreover, as an offering sometimes satisfying a *science* general education requirement, the material can be "heavy" for some students. Our text tries to address these concerns and potentially varied audiences. The pedagogical aids are expressly designed to help students get through the more difficult material. Nevertheless, there are components of the field (such as basic cell biology, principles of genetics, principles of evolution, details of human paleontology) that are not entirely amenable to simplistic treatment. Nor should they be. If some of the material proves difficult, that is because we live in a complex universe and our understanding of it is far from complete.

Nevertheless, the journey into our discipline, into the very roots of what it means to be human, can be an exciting adventure. As the guest essayists so eloquently discuss their own individual journeys of discovery, so we hope you, too, come away from this text with something you consider of permanent value. Our fifteen-plus years of presenting physical anthropology has certainly been part of our journey of discovery. And it is to our many students and colleagues that we owe thanks for showing us the way.

Over the years, the constructive comments of all the reviewers of previous editions have been of great assistance in our attempts to improve this text, and we are grateful to all our colleagues who have provided comments and critiques. For this edition, we are especially indebted to all the current reviewers: Leon H. Albert (Los Angeles Valley College); Janice Austin (Santa Monica College); David H. Dye (Memphis State University); Barbara J. King (College of William and Mary); H. Gill-King (University of North Texas); Andrew Kramer (University of Florida); John P. Marwitt (University of Akron); Andrew Nelson (UCLA); Donald W. Rogers (Fulton-Montgomery Community College—SUNY); John E. B. Stewart (University of North Texas); Robert G. Tague (Louisiana State University); H. Lyn White-Miles (University of Tennessee, Chattanooga); Linda D. Wolfe (East Carolina University); Stephen L. Zegura (University of Arizona). In addition, we are most grateful to Michael Cummings for his careful review of the chapters dealing with human genetics.

We are also most appreciative to the many friends and colleagues who have generously provided photographs: C. K. Brain, Gunter Bräuer, Desmond Clark, Jean DeRousseau, Denis Etler, David Frayer, Diane France, David Haring, Ellen Ingmanson, Richard Ingraham, Fred Jacobs, Carol Lofton, John Oates, Lorna Pierce, David Pilbeam, Judith Regensteiner, Wayne Savage, Elwyn Simons, Meredith Small, Fred Smith, Judy Suchey, Li Tianyuan, Phillip Tobias, Alan Walker, Milford Wolpoff, and Xinzhi Wu.

We also wish to acknowledge Pat McGrath; Shirley McGreal, Dieter Steklis, and Thomas Wolfie for invaluable assistance with the Issues for Chapters 8 and 9. In addition, we are also indebted to those colleagues who have contributed guest essays to this text: Alice Brues, Russel Ciochon, Nancy Lovell, Mary Ellen Morbeck, Donald Ortner, Merideth Small, Judy Suchey, Erik Trinkaus, and Stephen Zegura. We also thank Biruté Galdikas and John Oates for contributing other sections. We are also indebted to Ben Singer who has helped to keep us up to date with his many current newspaper items and popular magazine articles. Lynn Kilgore wrote several portions of this book, including Issues and other materials borrowed from her sections of *Understanding Physical Anthropology and Archeology*, 5th Ed. These contributions have greatly improved this edition, and we are also indebted to her for precise and critical editing as well as contributing numerous photographs.

In the production of this book, we are most appreciative of our editors at West Educational Publishing for their constant help and encouragement: Clyde Perlee, Denise Simon, and Denis Ralling; and to those who directly assembled this and all previous editions, Janet Bollow (text designer), Stuart Kenter (copy editor), and Janet Hansen (compositor), we remain grateful for their skill and patience.

Robert Jurmain
Harry Nelson

Chapter 1

Contents

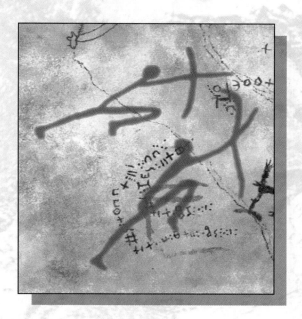

Introduction to Physical Anthropology

At the beginning of each chapter throughout the book, you will find a brief discussion of one of an assortment of contemporary topics. Some of these subjects, such as the question of the existence of Bigfoot or extraterrestrials, are not conventionally covered in textbooks. However, we feel it is important to address such issues, as scientists should not simply dismiss those views or ideas of which they are skeptical. Similarly, you should be reluctant to *accept* a view based solely on its personal appeal. Accepting or rejecting an idea based on personal feelings is as good a definition of "bias" as one could devise. Science is an approach —indeed, a *tool*—used to eliminate (or at least minimize) bias.

Scientific approaches of evaluation are, in fact, a part of a broader framework of intellectual rigor that is termed *critical thinking*. The development of critical thinking skills is an important and lasting benefit of a college education. Such skills enable people to evaluate, compare, analyze, critique, and synthesize information so that they will not accept all they hear and read at face value, but will be able to reach their own conclusions. Critical thinkers are able to assess the evidence supporting their own beliefs (in a sense, to

step outside of themselves) to identify the weaknesses in their own positions. They recognize that knowledge is not merely a collection of facts but an ongoing process of examining information to expand our understanding of the world.

In scientific inquiry, individual facts must be presented clearly, with appropriate documentation. That is the purpose of bibliographic citation, as exemplified throughout the body of this textbook. Once "facts" are established, scientists attempt to develop explanations concerning their relationships. First, a *hypothesis* is formed. A hypothesis is a provisional statement of the relationships of facts. Once a hypothesis receives further confirmation and can be seen to explain a broad array of phenomena, it can be called a *theory*. A theory, then, is a statement of relationships that has some firm basis. As such, it not only helps organize current knowledge but, ideally, should also *predict* how new facts may fit into the established pattern.

Of course, hypotheses might well prove inadequate and would thus require modification or rejection. Likewise, theories that might initially seem useful may eventually require considerable modification. Newton's Theory of Gravitation was substantially altered by Einstein's Theory of Relativity. The old theory of a "missing link" (a kind of halfway compromise between modern humans and modern apes) preceded modern evolutionary thinking, but is now seen as simplistic, misleading, and, at a practical level, of no value.

In scientific inquiry (and everyday life), much of the information we use is assembled in *quantified* form. A baseball fan is bombarded with a deluge of statistical data, such as won/lost percentage, batting average, on-base percentage, earned run average, etc., etc. Advertisers frequently use quasinumerical information to induce one to buy a product. You can hardly watch an evening newscast without seeing some commercial claiming, "Four-out-of-five doctors recommend . . ." (one wonders, "Which four doctors are they referring to?"). We are also inundated with the results of polls that cover everything from political preferences to teenage attitudes about premarital sex. Life is full of such information. How can it be assessed for *accuracy* and *reliability*?

Throughout this text you will see presented the results of numerous studies. For example, it might be stated that female chimps eat more insects than male chimps, or that Neandertal males were bigger than females, or that the gene for cystic fibrosis is more common in European populations than in other groups. First of all, you should always be cautious of generalizations. What is the specific nature of the argument? What data support it?

Can these data be quantified? If so, how is this information presented? (Note: *always* read the tables in textbooks or articles.)

Regardless of what discipline is ultimately studied, at some point in his or her academic career, a student should take a course in statistics. Many universities now make statistics a general education requirement (sometimes under the category, "quantitative reasoning"). Whether you are required to take such an offering or elect to do so, we strongly encourage it. To students, statistics often seems to be a very dry subject, and many are intimidated by the math. Nevertheless, perhaps more than any other skill you will acquire in your college years, quantitative *critical* reasoning is a tool you will be able to use every day of your life.

Another critical thinking skill is to be able to identify statements that are *tautologies*, that is, statements that are always true. For example, you may come across a statement that in a particular fossil form the front teeth are large, due either to chewing (dietary) stress or to some other (nondietary) stress. This statement *has to be true*—there is no way to test it. In science, a useful hypothesis is one that is testable—that is,

that can be proven or disproven. Viewpoints, propositions, stories, and scenarios that cannot be tested are of little or no value in science.

The topics discussed in the chapter-opening issues are those that intrigue the authors and, it is hoped, will also stimulate students. Some subjects, such as the Scopes trial (Chapter 4) or the Piltdown hoax (Chapter 13) are of historical interest. Others, such as the speculations regarding the existence of Bigfoot (Chapter 11) or extraterrestrials (Chapter 12) are examples of "pop science" sometimes promulgated in the popular press. In addition, we also address several topics that relate to recent advances in scientific knowledge, as exemplified by recombinant DNA research (Chapter 2) or developments in genetic testing (Chapter 3). Here, in addition to challenging you to grasp the basic scientific principles involved, we also ask you to consider the *social implications* of scientific/technological advances.

A responsibility of educated members of the public in a democracy is to be both informed and vigilant. The knowledge we possess and attempt to build upon is neither "good" nor "bad"; however, the uses to which knowledge may be put have highly charged moral and ethical implications. Thus, a goal of the chapter-opening issues is to stimulate your interest and provide you with a basis to reach your own conclusions. Some useful questions to ask in making critical evaluations of these issues or any other controversial scientific topic follow:

1. What facts are presented?
2. What conclusions are presented, and how are they organized (as tentative hypotheses or as more dogmatic assertions)?
3. Are these views individual opinions of the authors, or are they supported by a larger body of research?
4. What are the research findings? Are they adequately documented?
5. Is the information consistent with information that you already possess? If not, can the inconsistencies be explained?
6. Are the conclusions (hypotheses) testable? How might one go about testing the various hypotheses that are presented?
7. If presentation of new research findings is at odds with previous hypotheses (or theories), must these hypotheses now be modified (or completely rejected)?
8. How do your own personal views bias you in interpreting the results?
9. Once you have identified your own biases, are you able to set them aside so as to evaluate the information objectively?
10. Are you able to discuss *both* the pros and cons of a scientific topic in an even-handed manner?

Introduction

One day, perhaps at the beginning of the rainy season some 3.5 million years ago, two or three individuals walked across a grassland savanna in what is now northern Tanzania. These individuals were early members of the taxonomic family **Hominidae**, the family that also includes ourselves, modern *Homo sapiens*. Fortunately for us (the living descendants of those distant travelers), a record of their passage on that long-forgotten day remains in the form of fossilized footprints, preserved in hardened volcanic deposits.

As chance would have it, shortly after heels and toes were pressed into the dampened soil and volcanic ash of the area, a volcano, some 12 miles distant, erupted. The ensuing ashfall blanketed everything on the ground surface, including the footprints of the **hominids** and those of numerous other species as well. In time, the ash layer hardened into a deposit, which preserved a quite remarkable assortment of tracks and other materials that lay beneath it (Fig. 1-1).

These now-famous Laetoli prints, named for the Laetoli Beds in which they were discovered, indicate that two hominids, one smaller than the other, perhaps walked side by side, leaving parallel sets of tracks. But, because the prints of the larger individual are obscured, possibly by those of a third, it is unclear how many actually made that journey so long ago. What is clear

Hominidae The taxonomic family to which humans belong; also includes other, now extinct, bipedal relatives.

Hominids Members of the family Hominidae.

Figure 1-1

Early hominid footprints at Laetoli. The tracks to the left were made by one individual, while those to the right appear to have been formed by two individuals, the second stepping in the tracks of the first.

from the prints is that they were left by an animal that habitually walked **bipedally** (that is, on two feet). It is this critical feature that has led scientists to consider these ancient passersby as hominids.

In addition to the preserved footprints, scientists at Laetoli and elsewhere have discovered numerous fossilized skeletal remains of what most now call *Australopithecus afarensis*. These fossils, and the prints, have volumes to say about the beings they represent, provided we can learn to interpret them.

What, then, have we actually gleaned from the meager evidence we possess of those creatures who beckon to us from an incomprehensibly distant past? Where did their journey take them that far-gone day, and why were they walking in that particular place? Were they foraging for food within the boundaries of their territory? Were they simply walking to a nearby water source? Did the two (or three) indeed travel together at all, or did they only use the same route within a short period of time?

We could ask a myriad questions about these individuals, but we will never be able to answer them all. They walked down a path into what became their future, and their immediate journey has long since been ended. It remains for us to sort out what little we can know about them and the species they represent. In this sense, their greater journey continues.

From the footprints and from fossilized fragmentary skeletons, we know the early australopithecines walked in an upright posture. They thus were, in some respects, anatomically similar to ourselves, but their brains were only about one-third the size of ours. Although they may have used stones and sticks as tools, much as modern chimpanzees do, there is no current evidence to suggest they manufactured stone tools. In short, these early hominids were very much at the mercy of nature's whims. Compared to many of their contemporaries, they were not strong. They certainly could not outrun predators, and their lack of large projecting canine teeth rendered them relatively defenseless.

Modern chimpanzees often serve as living models for our early ancestors but, in fact, the australopithecines occupied a different habitat, exploited different resources, and probably had more to fear from predators than do chimpanzees. However much we may be tempted to compare early hominids to living species, we must constantly remind ourselves that there is no living form that adequately represents them. Just like every other living thing, they were unique.

On July 20, 1969, a television audience numbering in the hundreds of millions watched as two human beings stepped out of a spacecraft and onto the surface of the moon. To anyone born after that date, this event is taken more or less for granted, even though it has hardly been repeated often. But the significance of that first moonwalk cannot be overstated, for it represents humankind's presumed mastery over the natural forces that govern our presence on earth. For the first time ever, people actually walked upon the surface of a celestial body that (as far as we know) has never given birth to biological life.

As the astronauts gathered geological specimens and frolicked in near weightlessness, they left traces of their fleeting presence in the form of footprints in the lunar dust (Fig. 1-2). On the atmosphereless surface of the moon where no rain falls and no wind blows, the footprints remain undisturbed to this day. They survive as mute testimony to a brief visit by a medium-sized, big-brained creature who presumed to challenge the very forces that had created it.

We humans uncovered the Laetoli footprints, and we question the nature of the animal who made them. Perhaps one day, creatures as yet unimagined

Bipedally Walking habitually on two legs—the single most distinctive feature of the Hominidae.

Figure 1-2

Human footprints left on lunar surface during Apollo mission.

Primate   The order of mammals that includes prosimians, monkeys, apes, and humans.

Culture   Culture involves all aspects of human adaptation, including technology, traditions, language, social roles, and so forth. Culture is learned and transmitted from one generation to the next by nonbiological means.

Biocultural evolution   The mutual, interactive evolution of human biological structure and human culture. The concept that biology makes culture possible and that developing culture further influences the direction of biological evolution. The single most crucial organizing concept in understanding the unique components of human evolution.

by nature will ponder the essence of the being that made the lunar footprints. What do you suppose they will think?

We humans, who can barely comprehend a century, can only grasp at the enormity of 3.5 million years. We want to understand the essence of those creatures who traveled that day across the savanna. By what route did an insignificant but clever bipedal **primate** give rise to a species that would, in time, walk on the surface of a moon some 230,000 miles from earth? How did it come to be that, in the relatively short span (in geological time) of 3.5 million years, an inconsequential savanna dweller evolved into the species that has developed the ability to dominate and destroy much (if not all) of life on the planet?

How did it happen that *Homo sapiens*, a result of the same evolutionary forces that produced all other life on this planet, gained the power to control the flow of rivers and alter the very climate in which we live? As tropical animals, how were we able to leave the tropics and disperse over most of the earth's land surfaces, and how did we adjust to local environmental conditions as we so expanded? How could our species, which numbered less than 1 billion individuals until the mid-nineteenth century, come to number over 5.6 billion worldwide today, and, as we now do, add another billion every 11 years?

These are some of the many questions physical or biological anthropologists attempt to answer, and these questions are largely the focus of the study of human evolution and adaptation. These issues, and many more, are the topics covered directly or indirectly in this text, for physical anthropology is, in part, human biology seen from an evolutionary perspective. However, physical anthropologists are not exclusively involved in the study of physiological systems and biological phenomena. When such topics are placed within the broader context of human evolution, another factor must also be considered: the role of **culture**.

Culture is an extremely important concept, not only as it pertains to modern human beings, but also in terms of its critical role in human evolution. It has been said that there are as many definitions of culture as there are people who attempt to define it. Quite simply, culture can be said to be the strategy by which humans adapt to the natural environment. In this sense, culture includes technologies that range from stone tools to computers; subsistence patterns ranging from small hunting and gathering bands to industrialized cities; housing types, from thatched huts to skyscrapers; and clothing, from animal skins to high-tech synthetic fibers (Fig. 1-3). Because religion, values, social organization, language, kinship, marriage rules, gender roles, inheritance of property, and so on, are all aspects of culture, each culture shapes peoples' perceptions of the external environment, or world view, in particular ways that distinguish that culture from all others.

One fundamental point to remember is that culture is *learned* and not biologically determined. Culture is transmitted from generation to generation independently of biological factors (that is, genes). For example, a young girl of Vietnamese ancestry raised in the United States from infancy will biologically be Asian. However, if raised by English-speaking parents, English will be her native language. She will eat Western foods with Western utensils and will wear Western clothes. In short, she will be a product of Western culture, because that is the culture she has learned. We are all products of the culture in which we are socialized, and since much of human behavior is learned, it clearly is also culturally patterned.

As biological organisms, humans have been and are subject to the same evolutionary forces as all other species. Upon hearing the term *evolution* most

(a)

(b)

(c)

(d)

people think of the appearance of new species. Certainly, new species formation is one consequence of evolution; however, biologists see evolution as an ongoing biological process with a precise genetic meaning. Quite simply, evolution is a change in the genetic makeup of a population from one generation to the next. It is the accumulation of such changes, over considerable periods of time, that can result in the appearance of a new species. Thus, evolution can be defined and studied at different *levels*: that of the population (*microevolution*) or the species (*macroevolution*). Evolution, as it occurs at both these levels, will be addressed in this text.

One critical point to remember is that the human predisposition to assimilate a particular culture and to function within it is influenced by biological factors. In the course of human evolution, as you will see, the role of culture increasingly assumed an added importance. Over time, culture and biology interacted in such a way that humans are said to be the result of **biocultural evolution**. In this respect, humans are unique among biological organisms.

Figure 1-3

(a) *An early stone tool from East Africa. This artifact represents the oldest type of stone tools found anywhere.*

(b) *Assortment of implements available today in a modern hardware store.*

(c) *A Samburu woman building a simple, traditional dwelling of stems, plant fibers, and mud.*

(d) *A modern high-rise apartment complex, typical of industrialized cities.*

Biocultural interactions have not only resulted in such anatomical, biological, and behavioral changes as increased brain size, reorganization of neurological structures, decreased tooth size, and development of language in humans, to list a few, but they continue to be critical in changing disease patterns as well. As a contemporary example, rapid culture change (particularly in Africa) and changing social and sexual mores, may have influenced evolutionary rates of HIV, the virus that causes AIDS. Certainly, these cultural factors influenced the spread of HIV throughout populations in both the developed and developing worlds.

The study of many of the biological aspects of humankind, including **adaptation** and evolution, could certainly be the purview of human biologists and, indeed, it frequently is. However, particularly in the United States, when such research also considers the role of cultural factors, it is placed within the discipline of **anthropology**.

What Is Anthropology?

Stated ambitiously but simply, anthropology is the study of humankind. (The term *anthropology* is derived from the Greek words *anthropos*, meaning human, and *logos*, meaning word.) Anthropologists are not the only scientists who study humans, and the goals of anthropology are shared by other disciplines within the social, behavioral, and biological sciences. For example, psychologists and psychiatrists investigate various aspects of human motivation and behavior, while developing theories that have clinical significance. Historians focus upon recorded events in the human past and, therefore, their research is limited to, at most, a few thousand years. The main difference between anthropology and such related fields is that anthropology integrates the findings of many disciplines, including sociology, economics, history, psychology, and biology.

The focus of anthropology is very broad indeed. Like other disciplines, anthropology is divided into numerous subfields, but, in general, anthropologists study all aspects of what may loosely be termed *human nature*, or what it means to be human.

In the United States, anthropology comprises three main subfields: cultural or social anthropology, archeology, and physical or biological anthropology. Additionally, large departments at some universities include anthropological linguistics as a fourth area. Each of these subdisciplines, in turn, is divided into more specialized areas of interest. Following is a brief discussion of the three main subdisciplines of anthropology.

Cultural Anthropology

Cultural anthropology is the study of all aspects of human behavior. It could reasonably be argued that cultural anthropology began with Aristotle, or even earlier. But, for practical purposes, the beginnings of cultural anthropology are found in the nineteenth century, when Europeans became increasingly aware of what they termed "primitive societies" in Africa and Asia. Likewise, in the New World, there was much interest in the vanishing cultures of Native Americans.

The interest in traditional societies led numerous early anthropologists to study and record lifeways that unfortunately are now mostly extinct. These

Adaptation Functional response of organisms or populations to the environment. Adaptation results from evolutionary change (specifically, as a result of natural selection).

Anthropology The field of inquiry that studies human culture and evolutionary aspects of human biology; includes cultural anthropology, archeology, and physical anthropology.

studies produced many descriptive **ethnographies** that became the basis for later comparisons between groups. These ethnographies emphasized phenomena such as religion, ritual, myth, use of symbols, subsistence strategies, technology, gender roles, child-rearing practices, dietary preferences, taboos, medical practices, how kinship was reckoned, and so on.

The focus of cultural anthropology has shifted several times over the course of the twentieth century. The more traditional ethnographic perspectives just discussed, wherein anthropologists live for several months among a non-Western society, are still practiced productively today by numerous researchers. Indeed, physical anthropologists have frequently worked closely with cultural anthropologists in order to investigate more fully the biocultural adaptations of contemporary societies. Such research is also used by governments and international aid agencies to assess the impact of development upon traditional societies.

Ethnographic techniques can also be used today to gain information about various subcultures in, for example, urban areas. One goal of this type of research is to facilitate better relationships among the various racial and ethnic groups that today characterize most large cities in the United States and elsewhere. The type of cultural anthropology that deals with issues of the inner city is called, appropriately, *urban anthropology*.

Many cultural anthropologists today are involved in gender studies. Such studies may focus upon gender norms, how gender roles are learned, and specific cultural factors that lead to individual development of gender identity. For example, there is an interest in how one gender is perceived versus the other. In most cultures, females are viewed in many ways as being inferior to males because higher value is frequently placed upon activities generally perceived as appropriate for males. In this regard, it is valuable to examine the cultural consequences if and when gender norms are violated.

Cultural anthropologists are also interested in development and aging. This field of study is particularly relevant in industrialized nations where the proportion of elderly individuals in populations is higher than ever before. As populations age, the needs of the elderly, particularly in the area of health care, become a social issue that requires more and more attention.

One other relevant area for cultural anthropologists today is assisting in resettlement of refugees in many parts of the world. To develop plans that properly accommodate the needs of displaced peoples, governments can find the special talents of cultural anthropologists of considerable benefit.

Medical anthropology is a subfield of cultural anthropology that explores various aspects of the relationship between health and medical care on the one hand and culture on the other. One area of interest here is how different groups view disease processes and how these views affect treatment, or willingness to accept treatment. Another focus is childbirth techniques as they relate to pre- and postpartum stress. When a medical anthropologist focuses upon the social dimensions of disease, physicians and physical anthropologists may also collaborate.

Archeology

Archeology is the recovery, analysis, and interpretation of **material culture** from past civilizations. The roots of modern archeology are found in the fascination of nineteenth-century Europeans with the classical world (particularly Greece and Egypt). This interest was primarily manifested in the exca-

Ethnography The study of a human society. In cultural anthropology, ethnography is traditionally the study of non-Western societies.

Material culture The physical manifestations of human activities; includes tools, house structures, etc. As the most durable aspects of culture, material remains make up the majority of archeological evidence of past societies.

vation (sometimes controlled, sometimes not) and removal of thousands of treasures and artifacts, destined for the museums and private collections of wealthy Europeans.

New World archeology has long focused on the pre-Columbian civilizations of Mexico and Central and South America (the Aztecs, Maya, and Inca). In North America, archeological interest was sparked particularly by the large earthen burial mounds found throughout much of the southeast. Thomas Jefferson conducted one of the first controlled excavations of a burial mound on his Virginia plantation in 1784. Importantly, his goal was not simply the recovery of artifacts, but he specifically wished to address the question of how the mound was constructed.

Today, archeology is very much aimed at answering specific questions. Sites are not excavated simply because they exist or for the artifacts they may yield; excavation is conducted for the explicit purpose of gaining information about human behavior. Research questions may pertain to such topics as the development of agriculture, the rise of cities, or why certain civilizations collapsed. They may focus upon specific localities or peoples and attempt to identify aspects of social organization or subsistence patterns. Or, questions may be much broader and reflect a particular interest, such as how ecological setting influences settlement patterns and social organization in human cultures in general. The dispersal of human settlements across a landscape and the distribution of cultural remains within them are reflections of human behavior. By identifying the pattern of human behavior on a larger scale, archeologists can assist in recognizing those conventions shared by all groups; that is, those behaviors that are termed *cultural universals*.

Archeology is a discipline that requires precise measurement, description, and excavation techniques, for it must be remembered that when a site is dug, it is also destroyed. Errors in excavation or recording result in the permanent loss of valuable information. Therefore, the science of archeology is much more than simply digging up artifacts, as many people think of it. Rather, archeology is a multidisciplinary approach to the study of human behavior as evidenced by cultural remains.

For many projects, the specialized expertise of many disciplines is called upon. Among others, these can include: palynologists, chemists, geologists, physicists, paleontologists, and physical anthropologists. In some cases, even the remote sensing capabilities of NASA have been called upon, in which sophisticated satellite technologies were employed to locate archeological sites.

Archeological techniques are used to identify and excavate not only remains of human cities and settlements, but also paleontological sites containing remains of extinct species, including everything from dinosaurs to early hominids. Together, prehistoric archeology and physical anthropology form the core of a joint science called *paleoanthropology*, which is described in the next section.

Physical Anthropology

Physical anthropology, as has already been stated, is the study of human biology within the framework of evolution, with an emphasis on the interaction between biology and culture. Physical anthropology is composed of several subdisciplines or areas of specialization, the most significant of which are briefly described in the following paragraphs.

The origins of physical anthropology arose from two principal areas of interest among nineteenth-century scholars. First, there was increasingly avid concern among many scientists (at the time called *natural historians*) regarding the mechanisms by which modern species had come to be. In other words, increasing numbers of intellectuals were beginning to doubt the literal, biblical interpretation of creation. Instead, scientific explanations emphasizing natural, rather than supernatural, phenomena came to predominate. Although few were actually prepared to believe that humans had evolved from earlier forms, discoveries of several Neandertal fossils in the 1800s began, for some scientists, to raise questions regarding the origins and antiquity of the human species.

The sparks of interest in biological change over time were fueled into flames by the publication of Charles Darwin's *Origin of Species* in 1859. Today, **paleoanthropology**, or the study of human evolution, particularly as evidenced in the fossil record, is one of the major subfields of physical anthropology (Fig. 1-4). There are now thousands of specimens of human ancestors housed in museum and research collections. Taken together, these fossils cover a span of close to 4 million years of human prehistory and, although incomplete, they provide us with significantly more knowledge than was available even 10 years ago. It is the ultimate goal of paleoanthropological research to identify the various early hominid species and establish a chronological sequence of relationships among them. Only then will there emerge a clear picture of how and when humankind came into being.

A second nineteenth-century interest that had direct relevance to anthropology was racial variation, particularly as seen in skin color. Enormous effort was aimed at describing and explaining the biological differences among various human populations. Although many endeavors were mis-

Paleoanthropology   The interdisciplinary approach to the study of earlier hominids—their chronology, physical structure, archeological remains, habitats, etc.

Figure 1-4

Paleoanthropological research at the Hadar, Ethiopia, during a recent field session in 1993.

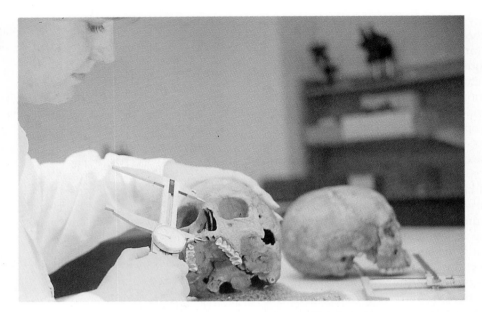

Figure 1-5

Anthropology student taking facial measurements on a human cranium using sliding calipers.

Anthropometry Measurement of human body parts, most especially measurement of skeletal elements.

Genetics The study of gene structure and action and the patterns of inheritance of traits from parent to offspring. Genetic mechanisms are the underlying foundation for evolutionary change.

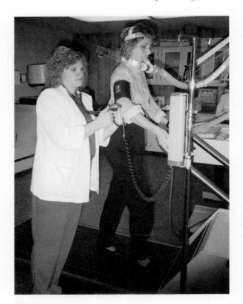

Figure 1-6

Researcher using treadmill test to assess a subject's heart rate, blood pressure, and oxygen consumption.

guided and indeed racist, they gave birth to literally thousands of body measurements that could be used to compare people. Physical anthropologists use many of the techniques of **anthropometry** today, not only in the study of living groups, but also to study skeletal remains from archeological sites (Fig. 1-5). Moreover, anthropometric techniques have considerable application in the design of everything from airplane cockpits to office furniture.

Anthropologists today are concerned with human variation primarily because of its *adaptive significance*. In other words, traits that typify certain populations, as compared to others, are seen as having evolved as biological adaptations or adjustments to local environmental conditions. Examining biological variation between populations of any species provides valuable information as to the mechanisms of genetic change in groups over time, which is precisely what the evolutionary process is all about.

Modern population studies, with a different focus from the traditional racial approach, also examine other important aspects of human variation, including how various groups respond physiologically to different kinds of environmentally induced stress (Fig. 1-6). Such stresses may include high altitude, cold, or heat. Moreover, many physical anthropologists conduct nutritional studies, investigating such issues as the relationship between various dietary components and certain aspects of health and disease.

It would be impossible to study evolutionary processes, and therefore adaptation, without a knowledge of genetic principles. For this reason and others, **genetics** is a crucial field for physical anthropologists. Modern physical anthropology would not exist as evolutionary science were it not for advances in the understanding of genetic principles.

Not only does genetics allow us to explain how evolutionary processes work, but today anthropologists use recently developed genetic technologies to investigate evolutionary distances between living primate species (including humans). Moreover, genetic theories have been used (with much debate) to explain, among other things, the origins of modern *Homo sapiens*.

Primatology, the study of nonhuman primates, has become increasingly important since the late 1950s for several reasons (Fig. 1-7). Behavioral stud-

(a)
(b)

Figure 1-7

(a) *Yahaya Alamasi, a member of the senior field staff at Gombe National Park, Tanzania. Mr. Alamasi is recording behaviors in free-ranging chimpanzees.* (b) *Oakland Zoo docent uses a laptop computer to record behaviors of a captive chimpanzee.*

ies, especially those conducted on free-ranging groups, have implications for numerous scientific disciplines. Perhaps more importantly, animal **ethology** in general has assumed greater importance in the past few decades because of the rapidly declining numbers of many species.

The behavioral study of any species provides a wealth of data pertaining to adaptation. As nonhuman primates are our closest living relatives, the identification of underlying factors related to social behavior, communication, infant care, reproductive behavior, and so on, aids in developing a better understanding of the natural forces that have shaped so many aspects of modern human behavior.

Moreover, from a less species-centric perspective, it should be pointed out that nonhuman primates are important to study in their own right (particularly true today because the majority of species are threatened or seriously endangered). Only through study will scientists be able to recommend policies that can better ensure the survival of many nonhuman primates and thousands of other species as well.

Primate paleontology, the study of the primate fossil record, has implications, not only for nonhuman primates, but also for hominids. Virtually every year, fossil-bearing beds in North America, Africa, Asia, and Europe yield important new discoveries. Through the study of fossil primates, we are able to learn much about factors such as diet or locomotion in earlier forms. By comparisons with anatomically similar living species, primate paleontologists can make reasoned inferences regarding behavior in earlier

Primatology The study of the anatomy and behavior of nonhuman primates (prosimians, monkeys, and apes).

Ethology The study of the behavior of nonhuman animals.

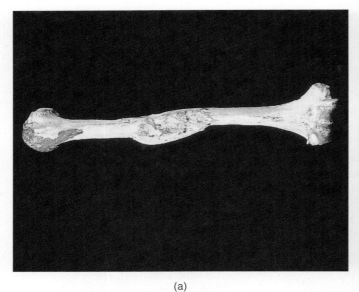

(a)

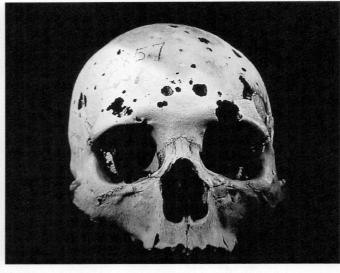

(b)

Figure 1-8

(a) *Healing fracture of humerus (upper arm bone) in a skeleton from Nubia.* (b) *Cranial lesions, probably resulting from metasticized cancer.*

Osteology   The study of skeletons. Human osteology focuses on the interpretation of the skeletal remains of past groups. The same techniques are used in paleoanthropology to study early hominids.

Paleopathology   The branch of osteology that studies the traces of disease and injury in human skeletal (or, occasionally, mummified) remains.

Forensic anthropology   An applied anthropological approach dealing with matters of law. Physical anthropologists use their expertise to assist coroners and others in the analysis and interpretation of human remains.

groups as well. Moreover, we hope to be able to elucidate general information about evolutionary relationships between extinct and modern species, including ourselves.

Osteology, the study of the skeleton, is central to physical anthropology. Indeed, it is so important that when many people think of physical anthropology, the first thing that comes to mind is bones. The emphasis upon osteology exists in part because of the concern with the analysis of fossil material. Certainly, a thorough knowledge of the structure and function of the skeleton is critical to the interpretation of fossil material.

Bone biology and physiology are of major importance to many other aspects of physical anthropology, in addition to paleontology. Many osteologists specialize in metric studies that emphasize various measurements of skeletal elements. This type of research is essential, for example, to the identification of stature and growth patterns in archeological populations.

One subdiscipline of osteology is the study of disease and trauma in archeologically derived skeletal populations. **Paleopathology** is a prominent subfield that investigates the incidence of such entities as trauma, certain infectious diseases (including syphilis and tuberculosis), nutritional deficiencies, and numerous other conditions that leave evidence in bone (Fig. 1-8). In this area of research, a precise knowledge of bone physiology and response to insult is required.

A field directly related to osteology and paleopathology is **forensic anthropology**. Technically, this approach is the application of anthropological (usually osteological and sometimes archeological) techniques to the law (Fig. 1-9). Forensic anthropologists are commonly called upon to help identify skeletal remains in cases of disaster or other situations where a human body has been found.

Forensic anthropologists have been instrumental in a number of cases having important legal and historic consequences. They assisted medical examiners in the identification of burned human remains at the Branch Davidian compound in Waco, Texas. They have also been prominent in the identification of remains of possible missing American soldiers in Southeast Asia and the skeletons of most of the Russian Imperial Family, executed in

1918. Forensic anthropology is very appealing to many, but it should be remembered that lengthy, specialized training is essential for everyone entering this field, inasmuch as they are often called upon to provide crucial testimony as expert witnesses in court cases.

Anatomical studies comprise another important area of interest for physical anthropologists. Thorough knowledge of soft tissue anatomy is essential to the understanding of biomechanical relationships involved in movement. Such relationships are important to the development of conditions, such as arthritis, which are frequently encountered in paleopathology. Moreover, accurate assessment of the structure and function of limbs and other components in fossilized remains requires expertise in anatomical relationships. Obviously, in the living organism, bone and dental structures are intimately linked to the soft tissues surrounding and operating upon them. For this reason and others, many physical anthropologists specialize in anatomical studies. In fact, several physical anthropologists hold professorships in anatomy departments at universities and medical schools.

From this brief overview, it can be seen that physical anthropology is the subdiscipline of anthropology that focuses upon many varied aspects of the biological nature of *Homo sapiens*. Humans are a product of the same forces that produced all life on earth. As such, we represent one contemporary component of a vast *biological* **continuum** at one point in time. In this regard, we are not particularly unique. Stating that humans are part of a continuum does not imply that we are at the peak of development on that continuum. Depending upon which criteria one uses, humans can be seen to exist at one end of the continuum or the other, or somewhere in between. But, humans do not necessarily occupy a position of superiority over any other species.

There is, however, one dimension in which human beings are truly unique, and that is intellect. After all, humans are the only species, born of earth, to stir the lunar dust. Humans are the only species to develop complex culture as a means of buffering the challenges posed by nature, and by so doing, eventually gain the power to shape the very destiny of the planet.

It has been said that humans created culture and that culture created humans. This statement is true in that the increased brain size and reorgani-

Continuum   A set of relationships in which all components fall along a single integrated spectrum. All life reflects a single *biological* continuum.

Figure 1-9

Physical anthropologists Lorna Pierce (to left) and Judy Suchey (to right) working as forensic consultants. The dog has just located a concealed human cranium during a training session.

zation of neurological structures that typifies much of the course of human evolution would never have occurred if not for the complex interactions between biological and behavioral factors (that is, biocultural evolution). In this sense, then, it is neither unreasonable nor presumptuous to say that we have created ourselves.

We hope the ensuing pages will help you develop an increased understanding of the similarities we share with other biological organisms and also of the processes that have shaped the traits that make us unique. We live in what may well be the most crucial period for our planet in the last 65 million years. We are members of the one species that, through the very agency of culture, has wrought such devastating changes in ecological systems that we must now alter our technologies or face potentially unspeakable consequences. In such a time, it is vital that we attempt to gain the best possible understanding of what it means to be human. We believe the study of physical anthropology is one endeavor that aids in this attempt, and that is indeed the goal of this text.

Summary

In this chapter, we have introduced the field of physical anthropology and have placed it within the overall context of anthropological studies. Anthropology as a major academic area within the social sciences also includes archeology and cultural anthropology within its major subfields.

Physical anthropology itself includes aspects of human biology (emphasizing evolutionary perspectives), the study of nonhuman primates, and the hominid fossil record. Especially as applied to the study of early hominids (as incorporated within the interdisciplinary field of paleoanthropology), physical anthropologists work in close collaboration with many other scientists—from archeology, geology, chemistry, and so forth.

Questions for Review

1. What is anthropology? What are the major subfields of anthropology?
2. How does physical anthropology differ from other disciplines interested in human biology?
3. What is meant by biocultural evolution and why is it important in understanding human evolution?
4. What are some of the primary areas of research within physical anthropology? Give two or three examples of the types of research pursued by physical anthropologists.
5. What is meant by the term, "hominid?" Be specific.
6. What fields, in addition to physical anthropology, contribute to paleoanthropology?

Contents

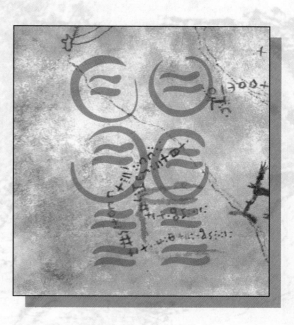

The Biological Basis of Life

Owing to the success of Steven Spielberg's movie *Jurassic Park*, based upon Michael Crichton's best-selling novel, the American public has become greatly intrigued by certain potential applications of DNA research. The basic premise of *Jurassic Park* (for the benefit of those few readers who somehow avoided exposure to that particular manifestation of pop culture) is briefly, as follows: A Silicon Valley biotechnology firm develops a method of extracting 150 million-year-old dinosaur DNA from mosquitoes preserved in amber, or fossilized tree sap. Prior to being trapped in tree sap, the mosquitoes had ingested minute quantities of dinosaur blood, a few cells of which remained in the insects' digestive tracts. From the dinosaur DNA, embryos are produced, inserted into genetically engineered plastic eggs, and incubated. The resulting animals, resurrections of several dinosaur species, become the central attraction of an island theme part—Jurassic Park.

Farfetched? Probably. Or is it just possible that someday, science will develop the technology to accomplish at least some of the *Jurassic Park* achievements? Consider that in 1992 a group of scientists at California Polytechnic State University and the University of California at Berkeley cloned (or produced copies of) DNA fragments obtained from a bee trapped in amber 25 million years ago. Does this feat mean that scientists will soon be able to produce a bee that has been extinct for 25 million years? Certainly not with today's technology, for the ancient DNA extracted from fossil species represents only a minute sample of the entire DNA sequence of an organism. But, by cloning DNA sequences from extinct species and comparing them to the DNA of their presumed descendents, scientists are able to estimate *rates* of genetic change within lineages. This achievement in itself is remarkable; the rest may well remain the stuff of fantasy. However, perhaps we should not completely rule out even some of the more preposterous scenarios, particularly in view of the remarkable developments that have occurred in genetic research since the inception of the biotechnology industry in 1976.

The techniques used in genetic engineering today are highly complex, but the basic principles are fairly straightforward, certainly for those with a grasp of the basic principles of genetics. Anyone who has ever snipped a cutting off a plant and rooted it has produced a clone (a genetically identical copy of a plant or animal), but current techniques have taken us far beyond the simplicity of "taking cuttings." Beginning with research in the 1950s, the possibility of using cloning procedures to increase the frequency of desirable traits in domesticated species has approached reality.

Cells from a single plant can be cultured to produce masses of cells, which are then induced to develop roots and shoots, resulting in large numbers of plants, all identical to the original. Variations of these techniques have been applied to a species of pine, the loblolly, with the goal of producing forests of genetically identical, disease-resistant, fast-growing trees with high wood content. Moreover, the entire forest would mature at the same time, and harvesting could be predictably scheduled. The result has obvious benefits for the lumber industry and could perhaps also allow for the setting aside of natural forests for preservation.

However, it is important to consider that such cloned forests would not be natural. For one thing, they could possess an unforeseen susceptibility to certain infectious organisms and parasites. Additionally, because they would lack many other types of plants, they would not provide the necessary habitat for most animal species provided by natural forests. These high-tech solutions could be acceptable as long as such tree stands are seen simply as tree farms, and providing that sufficient primary and secondary forests are left standing in the interests of species preservation. But these solutions do challenge traditional views of what constitutes a forest. And we must bear in mind that in terms of biodiversity, such forests of the future run the risk of being little more than sterile wastelands.

The cloning of animals is more complicated, but it is now being practiced (at least to a limited extent) in cattle and other domesticates. The technology was developed in the 1970s and early 1980s and involves the removal of cells from a developing embryo composed of 16 to 32 cells. These cells and the DNA they contain are then inserted into egg cells (harvested from other females) from which nuclei have been removed. The result is several genetically identical fertilized eggs, which are then artificially implanted into hormonally prepared surrogate mothers and allowed to develop.

Such cloning techniques have enormous implications for the livestock industry. Theoretically, breeders will be able to produce quantities of animals all possessing—to the same degree—whatever traits are deemed desirable. This capability could mean that cattle with uniformly higher milk yield or increased muscle mass, and sheep that produce more and better quality wool, may be on the horizon. But, again, such genetic homogeneity could certainly render such strains of livestock highly susceptible to the introduction of disease organisms, and with no genetic variation to offer resistance, entire herds could potentially be lost.

Because of the universality of the genetic code, it is possible to transfer DNA from one species to another (recombinant DNA). For example, recombinant DNA technology permits the insertion of human genes into bacterial cells, which subsequently possess an altered genetic makeup.

Insertion of foreign DNA into bacteria or other organisms is possible due to the discovery of *restriction enzymes* in the mid 1970s. These enzymes (over 300 are currently known) are used to snip out base pair sequences that are then spliced into circular strands of bacterial DNA called *plasmids*. The introduced strand of DNA is sealed into place by other enzymes called *DNA ligases*. The recombinant plasmid then serves as a vector, or carrier, for transferring the foreign DNA into cultured bacterial cells. As these cells divide, the plasmid, including its introduced segment, replicates with the rest of the cell's DNA. Thus, entire colonies of altered cells serve as manufacturing plants for the gene products specified by the human genes inserted into the plasmid vector (that is, insulin, clotting factor, growth hormone, and so on).

Genetic engineering has enormous potential for the treatment of disease. Because bacterial cells divide rapidly, ever-increasing numbers are capable of producing commercial quantities of beneficial gene products. For example, insulin for use by patients with insulin-dependent diabetes was formerly derived from nonhuman animals. But, since 1982, insulin produced by genetically altered bacteria has helped lower the costs of therapy for the over 2 million Americans who suffer from insulin-dependant diabetes.

In the same manner, numerous other products, such as blood clotting factors (for hemophiliacs), growth hormone, and various other hormones can now be produced. Previously, these products were derived through blood donations and tissues from human cadavers. Unfortunately, as we are all aware, recipients of products derived in these ways can be exposed to several infectious agents. Therefore, the use of artificially produced substances not only lowers the cost to the patient in many cases, but also greatly reduces the threat of contamination.

When recombinant DNA research was in its infancy in the early 1970s, scientists were concerned about potential hazards. The bacterium used in this research is *Escherichia coli*, which is ubiquitous in the human gut. Fears were aroused that altered bacteria (for example, bacteria carrying certain cancer genes) could cause disease in humans if ingested. Moreover, there was concern over the possibility that experimental bacteria could be released from the confines of the laboratory and infect literally millions of people. However, the *E. coli* strains used in laboratories have themselves been genetically altered so they cannot survive in the human gut. Addition-

ally, they can only live within a very narrow temperature range and are killed by sunlight. Therefore, for all practical purposes, these bacteria simply cannot survive outside their laboratory environment.

But, in 1975, several scientists were sufficiently concerned that, in an unprecedented move, they contacted government officials and gathered at Asilimar, California, to set up guidelines regulating the use of recombinant DNA. These were published by the United States government. Initially, there was governmental concern over the possible risks of such research, but most restraints have now been lifted, and, indeed, the government now issues patents on genetically engineered plants and animals (and does not even require FDA testing of several genetically engineered plant food products).

By changing the genetic structure of other organisms, we are indeed creating new life forms and potential new species. (It would certainly seem that such capabilities would put to rest any doubts about the reality of biological evolution.) Following are a few examples of how humans are now capable of manipulating biological processes in other organisms.

Pig embryos have received, and incorporated into their own DNA, genes for human growth hormone, in attempts to produce faster-maturing pigs. Researchers at Harvard University have developed a genetically engineered mouse that carries a gene rendering it highly susceptible to several types of cancer. The resultant strain of mice is now being used in laboratories to test cancer-resistant compounds and also the possible carcinogenic effects of various substances.

Genes conferring resistance to insect pests are now being experimentally introduced into numerous food crops. Plant geneticists are also developing methods of increasing the amino acid content of vegetables and grains normally low in protein. The gene that causes tomatoes to soften when ripe has been manipulated so that this fruit can be allowed to ripen on the vine before being picked and shipped to market. (Do we dare hope that this could result in store-bought tomatoes with a flavor resembling that of the home grown variety?) And, lastly, genetically altered bacteria, sprayed on strawberries and other crops, can protect such crops from devastating frost buildup even at temperatures some 10 to 12 degrees Fahrenheit below freezing.

Other applications of recombinant DNA technology include a genetically altered bacterium that can digest crude oil. If effective, this could be of limitless benefit during oil spill cleanups. Indeed, this method was used in Prince William Sound after the 1989 Exxon *Valdez* oil spill, and although helpful, the results were not as encouraging as had been hoped.

Today, archeologists and physical anthropologists, aided by geneticists, biochemists, and molecular biologists, can examine DNA fragments recovered from mummified tissues in individuals who died over 8000 years ago. The freeze-dried body of the now-famous "Iceman," who died over 5000 years ago in the Italian Alps, has yielded well-preserved DNA fragments that will eventually be sequenced for study. Researchers have even sequenced DNA recovered from 50,000-year-old Neanderthal bone, albeit with poor results due to inadequate DNA preservation.

By comparing the DNA of earlier people with that of modern humans, presumably their descendants, it may be possible to ascertain micro-evolutionary processes that have occurred. Furthermore, it may be possible in the future to use DNA extracted from bone to determine the sex of skeletons with a degree of accuracy not possible with currently available techniques, although as yet, such attempts have not met with success. It will undoubtedly be possible also to examine DNA from preserved intestinal parasites and even bacteria to help ascertain not only what health problems people faced but also to examine evolutionary change in the disease-producing organisms themselves. Clearly DNA analysis of prehistoric remains is still developing, but it holds the promise of rich rewards and, already, it is providing us with very tantalizing glimpses of earlier lifestyles.

The field of genetic engineering is in its infancy, and we are tempted to believe that these new technologies will offer solutions to many contemporary medical and nutritional problems. Moreover, as we discussed, these genetic technologies can help reveal the mechanisms of biological evolution. With such promise and such tools at our disposal, it is also to be hoped we use these powerful new techniques wisely.

SOURCES

Crichton, Michael, *Jurassic Park*. New York: Ballantine Books, 1990.

Cummings, Michael R., *Human Heredity, Principles and Issues*. St. Paul: West Publishing Co., 1991.

Ross, Philip E., "Eloquent Remains," *Scientific American*, **266**(5):114–125, 1992.

Introduction

This text is about human evolution, and evolution is grounded in the basic mechanisms of life. Such basic life processes involve cells, the replication of cells, the replication and decoding of genetic information, and the transmission of this information between generations. These processes are fundamental to all life on earth, obviously including humans. In order to present human evolution in the broad sense, we must first examine how life is organized at the cellular and molecular levels.

The Cell

The first step in discussing genetic and evolutionary principles is to understand cell function. Cells are the basic units of life in all organisms, and they are the smallest entities capable of self-reproduction.

In some forms—such as bacteria, amoebae, and paramecia—a single cell constitutes the entire organism. However, more complex *multicellular* forms—such as plants, insects, birds, and mammals—are composed of billions of cells. An adult human is made up of perhaps as many as 1000 billion (1,000,000,000,000) cells, all functioning in complex ways to promote the survival of the individual.

Life first appeared on earth at least 3.7 billion years ago, in the form of **prokaryotic** cells. Prokaryotes are single-celled organisms, represented today by bacteria and blue-green algae. Structurally more complex cells appeared approximately 1.2 billion years ago and are referred to as **eukaryotic** cells. Because all multicellular organisms are composed of eukaryotic cells, they are the focus of the remainder of this discussion. In spite of the numerous differences among various life forms and the cells that comprise them, it is important to understand that the cells of all living organisms share numerous similarities as a result of their common evolutionary past.

In general, a eukaryotic cell is a three-dimensional entity composed of *carbohydrates*, *lipids*, *nucleic acids*, and *proteins*. It contains a variety of structures called *organelles* within a surrounding membrane, the *cell membrane* (also called the plasma membrane) (see Fig. 2-1). One of these organelles is the **nucleus** (pl., nuclei), a discrete unit, surrounded by a double-layered nuclear membrane. Within the nucleus are molecules that contain the genetic information that controls the cell's functions. This critically important molecule is composed of **deoxyribonucleic acid (DNA).**

Surrounding the nucleus is the **cytoplasm**, which contains numerous other types of organelles involved in various cellular functions, such as breaking down nutrients and converting them to other substances (*metabolism*); storing and releasing energy; eliminating waste; and manufacturing proteins (**protein synthesis**).

Two of these cytoplasmic organelles—mitochondria and ribosomes—require further mention. The mitochondria (sing., mitochondrion) are responsible for energy production in the cell and are thus the structural "engines" that drive the cell. Mitochondria have membranes composed partly of proteins, which in turn are produced by coded messages from DNA molecules contained within. This DNA, called mitochondrial DNA (mtDNA), is distinct from that contained inside the nucleus (nuclear or chromosomal DNA). Because these mtDNA molecules are considerably shorter

Prokaryotic   Cells without nuclei, as found in bacteria and blue-green algae.

Eukaryotic   Cells with nuclei, as seen in many single-celled organisms and all multicelled organisms.

Nucleus   A structure (organelle) found in all eukaryotic cells. The nucleus contains chromosomal DNA.

Deoxyribonucleic acid (DNA)   The double-stranded molecule that contains the genetic code. DNA is the main component of chromosomes.

Cytoplasm   The portion of the cell contained within the cell membrane, excluding the nucleus. The cytoplasm consists of a semifluid material and contains numerous structures involved with cell functions.

Protein synthesis   The assembly of chains of amino acids into functional protein molecules. The process is directed by DNA.

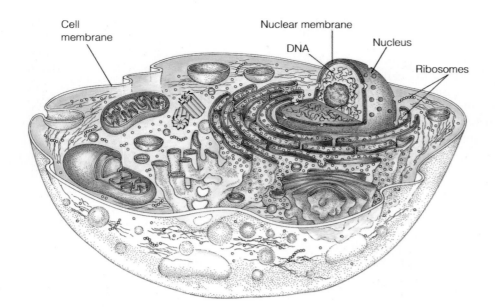

Cell membrane

Nuclear membrane

DNA

Nucleus

Ribosomes

Figure 2-1

Structure of a generalized eukaryotic cell illustrating the cell's three-dimensional nature. Although various organelles are shown, for the sake of simplicity most are not labeled.

Ribosomes   Structures (organelles) in the cytoplasm, made up of RNA and proteins, where protein synthesis takes place.

Somatic cells   Basically, all the cells in the body, except those involved with primary reproduction.

Sex cells   Those reproductive cells that produce gametes. Gametes are also sometimes referred to as sex cells.

Gametes   Reproductive cells (eggs and sperm in animals) developed from precursor cells (primary sex cells) in the ovaries or testes.

Zygote   A fertilized egg. The cell immediately following conception, containing the full set of chromosomes.

Interphase   That portion of the cell cycle when visible division is not obvious (that is, chromosomes cannot be seen). However, DNA and all other structures assorted in cell division are replicated during interphase.

Chromatin   The loose, diffuse form of DNA seen during interphase. When condensed, chromatin forms into chromosomes.

Chromosomes   Discrete structures composed of DNA and protein found only in the nuclei of cells. Chromosomes are only visible under magnification during certain portions of cell division.

and encode less information than those of nuclear DNA, they have attracted considerable interest in the last few years. (We will return to this topic, especially in Chapter 17, when we discuss the origins of modern *Homo sapiens*.)

Ribosomes are roughly spherical in shape and are the most common type of cytoplasmic organelle. They are made up partly of RNA (ribonucleic acid), ribosomal RNA (rRNA), and are segmented into two subunits. Ribosomes are centrally important in the synthesis of proteins (see p. 29).

There are two basic types of eukaryotic cells: **somatic cells** and **sex cells**. Somatic cells are the cellular components of bodily tissues, such as muscle, bone, skin, nerve, heart, brain, and so on. Sex cells, or **gametes**, are specifically involved in reproduction and are not important as structural components of the body. In animals, there are two types of gametes: *ova* (sing., *ovum*), or egg cells, produced in the ovaries in females; and *sperm*, which develop in male testes. In plants, the gametes are referred to as ovules and pollen grains, respectively. The sole function of a sex cell is to unite with a gamete from another individual to form a **zygote**, which has the potential of developing into a new individual. By so doing, gametes act to transmit genetic information from parent to offspring.

Chromosomes

Much of a cell's existence is spent in **interphase**, the portion of its life cycle during which it is involved with metabolic processes and other activities. During interphase, the cell's DNA exists as an uncoiled, noncondensed, and filamentous substance called **chromatin**. (Incredibly, there are an estimated six feet of DNA in the nucleus of every one of your somatic cells!) However, at various times in the life of most types of cells, interphase is interrupted, activities cease, and the cell divides.

Cell division is the process that results in the production of new cells, and during this process the chromatin becomes tightly coiled and is visible under a light microscope as a set of discrete structures called **chromosomes** (Fig. 2-2). Thus, it is possible to observe chromosomes only in cells that are actively dividing.

In eukaryotes, a chromosome is composed of a DNA molecule and associated proteins. During normal cell function, if chromosomes were visible, they would appear as single-stranded structures. However, as they become visible during the early stages of cell division, they are made up of two identical strands, each composed of a DNA molecule, joined together at a constricted area called the **centromere**. There are two strands because the DNA molecules *replicated* during interphase before condensation. Every species is characterized by a specific number of chromosomes in somatic cells. In humans, there are 46. Chimpanzees and gorillas possess 48. In all eukaryotic species, chromosomes occur in pairs, thus human somatic cells contain 23 pairs. One member of each pair is inherited from the father (paternal), and the other member of each pair is inherited from the mother (maternal).

Members of chromosomal pairs are said to be **homologous** in that they are alike in size and position of the centromere and they carry genetic information influencing the same *traits* (for example, ABO blood type is governed by a segment of DNA on the ninth chromosome). This does not imply that homologous chromosomes are genetically identical. It simply means that the characteristics they govern are the same. (This topic will be discussed in more detail in Chapter 3.)

There are two basic types of chromosomes: **autosomes** and **sex chromosomes**. Autosomes carry genetic information that governs all physical characteristics except primary sex determination. The two sex chromosomes are the X and Y chromosomes. In mammals, the Y chromosome carries genetic information directly involved with determining maleness. The X chromosome, although termed a "sex chromosome," is larger and functions more like an autosome in that it is not actually involved in primary sex determination and does influence a number of other traits.

Among mammals, all genetically normal females have two X chromosomes (XX) and they are female simply because the Y chromosome is not present. All genetically normal males have one X and one Y chromosome (XY). In other classes of animals, such as birds or insects, primary sex determination is governed by differing chromosomal mechanisms.

It is extremely important to note that *all* autosomes occur in pairs. Normal human somatic cells have 22 pairs of autosomes and one pair of sex chromosomes. It should also be noted that abnormal numbers of autosomes are almost always fatal to the individual, usually soon after conception. Although abnormal numbers of sex chromosomes are not usually fatal, they may result in sterility and frequently have other consequences as well (see p. 34 for further discussion). Therefore, in order to function normally, it is essential for a cell to possess both members of each chromosomal pair, or a total of 46 chromosomes, no more no less.

One method frequently used to examine single chromosomes, or an array of chromosomes, in an individual is to produce what is termed a **karyotype**. (An example of a human karyotype is shown in Fig. 2-3.) Chromosomes used in karyotypes are obtained from dividing cells. (You will remember that chromosomes are visible as discrete entities only during cell division.) For example, white blood cells, because they are easily obtained, may be cultured, chemically treated, and microscopically examined to identify those that are dividing. These cells are then photographed through a microscope to produce *photomicrographs* of intact, double-stranded chromosomes. Homologous chromosomes are then matched up and the entire set is arranged in descending order by size so that the largest (number 1) appears first. In addition to overall size, position of the centromere also aids in identification of indi-

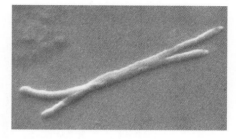

Figure 2-2

Scanning electron micrograph of a human chromosome during cell division. Note that this chromosome is composed of 2 strands, or 2 DNA molecules.

Centromere   The constricted portion of a chromosome. After replication, the two strands of a double-stranded chromosome are joined at the centromere.

Homologous   Refers to members of chromosome pairs. Homologous chromosomes carry genes that govern the same traits. During meiosis, homologous chromosomes pair and exchange segments of DNA. They are alike with regard to size, position of centromere, and banding pattern.

Autosomes   All chromosomes except the sex chromosomes.

Sex chromosomes   In animals, those chromosomes involved with primary sex determination. The X and Y chromosomes.

Karyotype   The chromosomal complement of an individual or that typical for a species. Usually displayed as a photomicrograph, often using special stains to highlight the bands or centromeres.

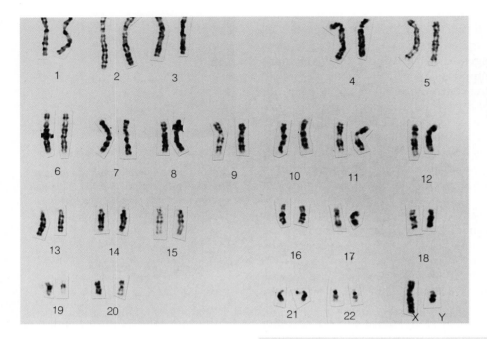

Figure 2-3

A karyotype of a male with the chromosomes arranged by size and position of the centromere, as well as by the banding patterns.

Figure 2-4

Human chromosomes as seen under a microscope with special staining to highlight the banding patterns.

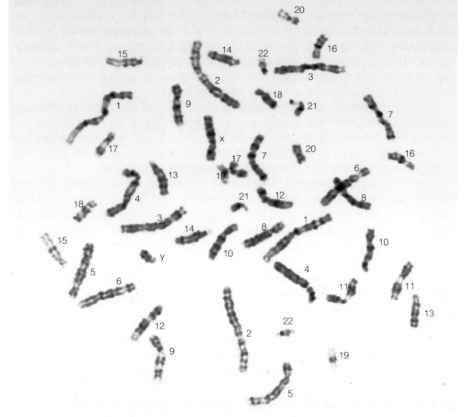

vidual chromosomes, as centromere position is characteristic of each specific chromosome.

Prior to the early 1970s, human chromosomes could only be grouped into fairly broad categories (such as 1 through 3 or 6 through 12). With the development of special techniques to highlight DNA segments that differentially

Table 2-1   Standard Chromosomal Complement in Various Organisms

Organism	Diploid Number (2n)	Haploid Number (n)
Human (*Homo sapiens*)	46	23
Chimpanzee (*Pan troglodytes*)	48	24
Gorilla (*Gorilla gorilla*)	48	24
Dog (*Canis familiaris*)	78	39
Chicken (*Gallus domesticus*)	78	39
Frog (*Rana pipiens*)	26	13
Housefly (*Musca domestica*)	12	6
Onion (*Allium cepa*)	16	8
Corn (*Zea mays*)	20	10
Tobacco (*Nicotiana tabacum*)	48	24

SOURCE: Michael R. Cummings, *Human Heredity: Principles and Issues*, 2nd ed. St. Paul: West Publishing Co., 1991, p. 16.

take up various colored stains, it is now possible to identify every chromosome on the basis of specific *banding patterns* (see Fig. 2-4).

An important aspect of a karyotype is that for each species the number and arrangement of chromosomes is constant. As already shown, humans have 46 chromosomes, while chimpanzees and gorillas have 48. It is interesting to note there are numerous highly similar regions (banding patterns) common among humans, chimps, and gorillas. The similarities in overall karyotype, as well as the marked biochemical and DNA similarities indicated by banding patterns (discussed in Chapter 9) underlie the extremely close *genetic* relationship among these three species. The standard chromosomal number for a variety of species is shown in Table 2-1.

Cell Division: Mitosis

Cell division in somatic cells is called **mitosis**. Mitosis occurs during growth of the individual. It also acts to promote healing of injured tissues and to replace older cells with newer ones. In short, it is the way somatic cells reproduce. For instance, in rapidly dividing somatic cell lines, such as those within bone marrow where red blood cells are constantly produced, mitosis is a continuous process. It has been estimated that, in humans, 2 million red blood cells are produced every second!

In the early stages of mitosis, a somatic cell possesses 46 chromosomes. Remember, each of these is double-stranded because of DNA replication during interphase, and one strand is an exact copy of the other. The chromosomes, now visible under a light microscope, line up in random order along the center of the cell (Fig. 2-5c). The chromosomes then split apart at the centromere so that the strands are separated from one another. As this separation occurs, the two strands begin to move apart and travel toward opposite ends of the dividing cell (Fig. 2-5d). At this point, each is now a separate chromosome, *composed of one DNA molecule*. Once this separation occurs, the cell membrane pinches in and becomes sealed so that two new cells are formed, each with a full complement of DNA, or 46 chromosomes. Most standard biology texts subdivide the continuous process of mitotic cell divi-

Mitosis   Simple cell division; the process by which somatic cells divide to produce two identical daughter cells.

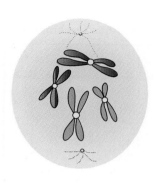

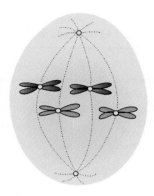

(a) Cell is involved in metabolic activities. DNA replication occurs, but chromosomes are not visible.

(b) Nuclear membrane disappears and double-stranded chromosomes are visible.

(c) Chromosomes align themselves at center of cell.

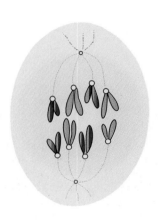

(d) The chromosomes split at the centromere and the strands separate and move to opposite ends of the dividing cell.

(e) The cell membrane pinches in as the cell continues to divide.

(f) After mitosis is complete, there are two identical daughter cells. The nuclear membrane is present and chromosomes are no longer visible.

Figure 2-5

Mitosis.

sion into four phases: prophase, metaphase, anaphase, and telophase. The major characteristics of each phase are listed in Table 2-2.

Mitosis is referred to as "simple cell division" because a somatic cell divides one time to produce two daughter cells (which are genetically identical to each other and genetically identical to the original cell). In mitosis, the original cell possesses 46 chromosomes, and each new daughter cell inherits

Table 2-2   The Stages of Mitosis

Stage	Characteristics
Interphase	Replication of chromosomes takes place
Prophase	Chromosomes become visible as threadlike structures; later, as they continue to condense, they are seen to be double, with condensed DNA molecules joined at a single centromere
Metaphase	Chromosomes become aligned at equator of cell
Anaphase	Centromeres split and chromosomes move toward opposite poles
Telophase	Chromosomes uncoil, nuclear membrane forms, cytoplasm divides

SOURCE: Michael R. Cummings, *Human Heredity: Principles and Issues*, 2nd ed. St. Paul: West Publishing Co., 1991, p. 22.

an exact copy of all 46. This arrangement is made possible by the ability of the DNA molecule to replicate. Thus, it is DNA replication that ensures that the quantity and quality of the genetic material remains constant from one generation of cells to the next. In fact, for all descendant cells in a cell line such cell reproduction could well be termed *cloning*.

Cell Division: Meiosis

While mitosis produces new cells, **meiosis** leads to the development of new individuals, for meiosis produces reproductive cells or gametes. Although meiosis is another form of cell division, and is in some ways similar to mitosis, it is a more complicated process.

During meiosis in animals, specialized cells in male testes and female ovaries divide and develop, eventually to produce sperm or egg cells. Meiosis is characterized by *two divisions* that result in *four daughter cells*, each containing 23 chromosomes, or half the original number (Fig. 2-6). Each cell will receive just one of each chromosome pair. As we will see below, the physical arrangement of the chromosomes and their consequent distribution to daughter cells is not random, but is, rather, very precise. The full complement of chromosomes in humans (46) is called the **diploid** number, while the reduced set, found only in gametes, is termed the **haploid** number.

Reduction of chromosome number is a critical feature of meiosis, for the resulting gamete, with its 23 chromosomes, may ultimately unite with another gamete, which also carries 23 chromosomes. The product of this union, the zygote or fertilized egg, reestablishes the diploid number of chromosomes (in humans, 46). In other words, the zygote inherits the full complement of DNA (half from each parent) that it needs in order to develop and function normally. If it were not for reduction division (the first division) in meiosis, it would not be possible to maintain the correct, and, of necessity, absolutely precise number of chromosomes from one generation to the next.

During the first meiotic division (Meiosis I), all 46 chromosomes line up at the center of the cell as in mitosis, but there is a difference. In the first division, homologous chromosomes come together, forming *pairs* of double-

Meiosis Specialized cell division in the reproductive organs (in animals, ovaries or testes) which produces gametes. These daughter cells contain half the number of chromosomes of the parent cells and are not identical.

Diploid The full complement of chromosomes. Two of each pair.

Haploid A half-set of chromosomes; one of each pair. Haploid complements are found in gametes.

Figure 2-6

Meiosis.

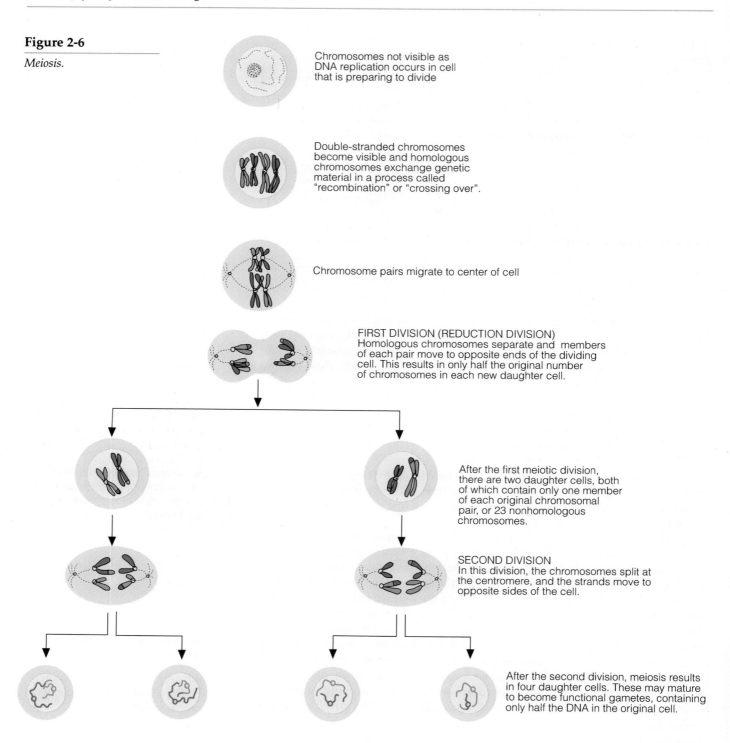

Chromosomes not visible as DNA replication occurs in cell that is preparing to divide

Double-stranded chromosomes become visible and homologous chromosomes exchange genetic material in a process called "recombination" or "crossing over".

Chromosome pairs migrate to center of cell

FIRST DIVISION (REDUCTION DIVISION) Homologous chromosomes separate and members of each pair move to opposite ends of the dividing cell. This results in only half the original number of chromosomes in each new daughter cell.

After the first meiotic division, there are two daughter cells, both of which contain only one member of each original chromosomal pair, or 23 nonhomologous chromosomes.

SECOND DIVISION In this division, the chromosomes split at the centromere, and the strands move to opposite sides of the cell.

After the second division, meiosis results in four daughter cells. These may mature to become functional gametes, containing only half the DNA in the original cell.

Recombination (crossing-over) The exchange of genetic material between homologous chromosomes during Meiosis I.

stranded chromosomes. In this way, then, pairs of chromosomes line up along the cell's equator (see Fig. 2-6).

Pairing of homologous chromosomes is highly significant, for while they are physically associated, they exchange genetic information in a process called **recombination**, or **crossing-over** (Fig. 2-7). Pairing is also important, as it facilitates the accurate reduction of chromosome number by ensuring that each new daughter cell will receive only one member of each pair.

As the cell begins to divide, the chromosomes themselves remain intact, but members of pairs disjoin and migrate to opposite ends of the cell. After the first division, there are two new daughter cells, but they are not genetically identical to each other or to the parental cell because each contains only one member of each chromosome pair, and therefore only 23 chromosomes (each of which is double-stranded). Moreover, as the result of crossing-over, each chromosome has scrambled genetic information and is thus probably different from that of either parent.

The second meiotic division (Meiosis II) proceeds in much the same way as in mitosis. In the two newly formed cells, the 23 double-stranded chromosomes align themselves at the cell's center and, as in mitosis, the strands of each chromosome separate from one another at the centromere, and move apart. Once this second division is completed, there are four daughter cells, each with 23 single-stranded chromosomes (that is, 23 DNA molecules). (See Fig. 2-8.) As in mitosis, the stages of meiosis are subdivided into phases, except here, with two divisions, the phases repeat: Prophase I, Metaphase I, Anaphase I, Telophase I, Interphase II (frequently very brief), Prophase II, Metaphase II, Anaphase II, Telophase II. (See Table 2-3 for further details.)

Meiosis occurs in all sexually reproducing organisms and is a highly important evolutionary innovation, since it increases genetic variation in populations at a faster rate than *mutation* alone can do in asexually reproducing species. Individual members of sexually reproducing species are not genetically identical clones of other individuals. Rather, they result from the contribution of genetic information from two parents. From any one human mating, an enormous number of possible offspring could result. From just the random arrangements of chromosome pairs lining up along the center of the cell in Meiosis I, each parent could produce 8 million genetically different gametes. And, given the joint probability (combination of both parents), the total number of possible genetic combinations for any human mating is about 70 trillion. It should be noted that this admittedly staggering

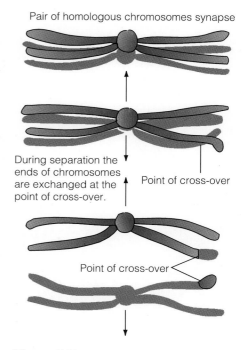

Figure 2-7

Crossing-over. During Meiosis I, homologous chromosomes pair very tightly. While paired, corresponding sections of DNA molecules of homologous chromosomes are exchanged. This event, crossing-over, results in greater variation among the gametes produced by meiosis and therefore also among the offspring of sexually reproducing organisms.

Table 2-3   The Stages of Meiosis

Stage	Characteristics
Interphase I	Chromosome replication takes place
Prophase I	Chromosomes become visible, homologous chromosomes pair (crossing-over); recombination takes place
Metaphase I	Paired chromosomes align at equator of cell
Anaphase I	Homologous chromosomes separate, members of each chromosome pair move to opposite poles
Telophase I	Cytoplasm divides, producing two cells
Interphase II	Brief pause, chromosomes uncoil slightly
Prophase II	Chromosomes recoil
Metaphase II	Unpaired chromosomes become aligned at equator of cell
Anaphase II	Centromeres split, daughter chromosomes pull apart
Telophase II	Chromosomes uncoil, nuclear membrane reforms, cytoplasm divides, meiosis is complete

SOURCE: Michael R. Cummings, *Human Heredity: Principles and Issues*, 2nd ed. St. Paul: West Publishing Co., 1991, p. 32.

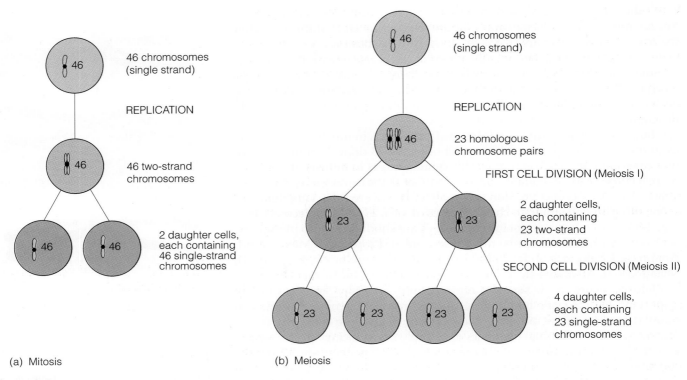

(a) Mitosis

(b) Meiosis

Figure 2-8

Mitosis and meiosis compared. In mitosis, one division produces two daughter cells, both of which contain 46 chromosomes. Meiosis is characterized by two divisions. After the first, there are two cells each containing only 23 chromosomes (one member of each original chromosome pair). Each daughter cell divides again so that the final result is four cells, each with only half the original number of chromosomes.

Random assortment The random distribution of chromosomes to daughter cells during Meiosis I. Along with recombination, the source of variation resulting from meiosis.

number is the result solely of the paired arrangements (called **random assortment**) and does not account for the many more combinations resulting from crossing-over.

The genetic uniqueness of individuals is further enhanced by recombination between homologous chromosomes during meiosis, for recombination ensures that chromosomes are not passed on unaltered from one generation to the next. Instead, in every generation, parental contributions are reshuffled in an almost infinite number of combinations thus altering the genetic composition of chromosomes even before they are passed on. Some estimates suggest that recombination (that is, crossing-over) adds to the number of genetic possibilities by another factor of up to 10^{10} (that is, 10,000,000,000 × 70,000,000,000,000), which produces a number really beyond human comprehension. Suffice it to say that, with the exception of identical twins (who are produced *after* conception), no human being is genetically identical to any other who has ever lived or who ever will live.

Natural selection acts upon genetic variation in populations. In all species, mutation is the only source of *new* genetic variation. But, in sexually reproducing species, recombination produces new *arrangements* of genetic information, which potentially provide additional material for natural selection to act upon.

Genetic variation is essential if species are to adapt to changing selective pressures. If all individuals were genetically identical, natural selection would have nothing to act upon and thus evolution could not occur. This influence on variation has been argued as the principle adaptive reason for the initial evolution of sex. You should be aware that for most of the time life has existed on this planet, reproduction has been strictly asexual. Moreover, most organisms (especially, when we include bacteria) still reproduce asexually. What is the evolutionary role of sexual reproduction? How and why did it evolve in the first place?

MEIOSIS IN MALES AND FEMALES

As discussed, meiosis involves two divisions that ultimately produce four daughter cells. However, in human females, as opposed to males, there are differences in both the distribution of materials to these cells as well as the *timing* of the process. In females, the process is called *öogenesis* and occurs in the ovaries. The first meiotic division yields one quite large cell, called the *secondary öocyte*, and it contains about 95% of the cytoplasm. The other, much smaller, cell is called a **polar body**. In the second division, there is again a markedly disproportionate distribution of the cytoplasm, so that one large, functional gamete, called the *ovum*, is produced. The other three cells—the polar bodies—receive almost no cytoplasm and cannot function as gametes.

In males, the meiotic process is called *spermatogenesis* and takes place in the testes. The primary sex cells divide to produce four haploid cells called *spermatids*. These, in turn, differentiate to yield mature sperm. It should be noted that each haploid sperm cell contains 22 autosomes and either an X *or* Y chromosome. Ova, by contrast, also contain 22 autosomes, but *always* with an X chromosome. Thus, sex determination is governed by the chromosomal complement of the sperm cell (Fig. 2-9).

Polar body A nonviable product of female meiosis (öogenesis), as it contains no cytoplasm.

Figure 2-9

Spermatogenesis and öogenesis.

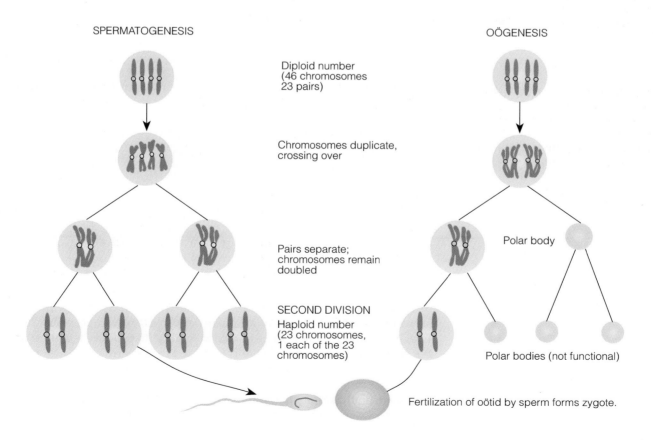

SPERMATOGENESIS

OÖGENESIS

Diploid number
(46 chromosomes
23 pairs)

Chromosomes duplicate,
crossing over

Pairs separate;
chromosomes remain
doubled

Polar body

SECOND DIVISION
Haploid number
(23 chromosomes,
1 each of the 23
chromosomes)

Polar bodies (not functional)

Fertilization of oötid by sperm forms zygote.

Alice Brues received her Ph.D. from Harvard University (Radcliffe) in 1939, the first woman to receive a doctorate in physical anthropology from Harvard. Following 18 years of teaching anatomy in the medical school at the University of Oklahoma, she moved in 1964 to the University of Colorado, where she continues her research as an emeritus professor. Dr. Brues is currently President of the Association of Senior Anthropologists and pursues her interests in bird watching as well as other aspects of natural history.

A misty memory of my childhood is hearing my father, a biology professor, say with a groan, "Oh, these students! You work so hard trying to put together an interesting lecture . . . and then at the end of the hour, there's this one student at the back of the room who raises his hand and says 'Professor Brues, will we be held responsible for this on the examination?'"

Even thus amply forewarned, I set my sights early on an academic career, perhaps because I did not know about any other kind of work. Yet I cannot recall having any particular field of interest when I entered Bryn Mawr as an undergraduate. At that time, few colleges had anthropology departments, and I had completed a major in philosophy before I really noticed anthropology. Nevertheless, I took the introductory course in anthropology in the Harvard summer school the summer after graduation, and no one batted an eye when I registered as an anthropology graduate student that fall. At that time many came into anthropology only at the graduate level, and this brought an interesting variety of points of view into the academic community.

I might note, for those of you who worry about the state of the world as you pursue an education, that I entered college almost simultaneously with the stock market crash of 1929, and graduated at the beginning of the New Deal. Then, slowly, war began to loom in Europe. You became numb to this after a while.

Naturally, perhaps, with my family background, I found myself drawn to the biological side of anthropology. Human genetics had hardly touched anthropology then, and I decided to apply it to anthropological variation. I recall my conversation with Dr. Ernest Hooton.

He said, "Well, I can't help you. I don't know anything about genetics. But it sounds like a good idea." The theory that a student should be a clone of the professor was definitely not operative in those days. I went across the street to Dr. Edward East, one of the early Mendelists in the United States, and asked his advice. He said, "Well, it's great that you want to do genetics, but of course *Homo sapiens* is the last species you should try to do it on." I thanked him kindly and embarked upon a study of genetics in family groups in the Boston area, thus circumventing the problem of financing, which was difficult at that time. All I needed for travel was a used Model A Ford, which cost me $100.

I finished my Ph.D. in 1940 and, jobs being just as iffy for new Ph.D.s as they always have been and probably will be, I was glad to fill the vacancy that arose in Dr. Hooton's bone lab, curating the large skeletal collection.

Everything was jolted in December, 1941, when the Japanese bombed Pearl Harbor. Overnight everyone asked, "What can we do to help?" The sudden expansion of the American armed forces involved specialized and often novel equipment in previously unimaginable quantities, with no time for cut-and-try design development, and the military turned to anthropologists for help. Dr. Hooton was contacted by the Air Force, and by February, 1942, he had teams of graduate stu-

There is also a notable difference in timing of meiosis in human females and males. In females, meiosis begins in fetal life and is "arrested" before birth early in Meiosis I (prophase). Years later, with sexual maturation, meiosis resumes, producing just one gamete per cycle (on average, every 28 days). Even here, Meiosis II still does not reach finality (to produce a mature ovum), but will do so only if the gamete is fertilized by a sperm cell. Thus, an ovum that is fertilized when a female is, say, 35 years old, actually began meiosis somewhat more than 35 years before. This long-term period of suspended development has been suggested as the main reason for a greater number of

dents collecting data on body and head size at various military installations across the country. In May of that year, I moved across the hall from the bone lab to the statistics lab to organize the data as they were still coming in. Eventually, these data would set size specifications for everything from gun turrets to oxygen masks. Data processing at that time consisted of punching holes in cards and then sorting and counting cards on noisy machines; computers were far in the future.

Dr. Hooton's report to the Air Force was completed in a few months, and before the end of 1942, most of the people who had worked on it moved to Wright Field in Ohio; graduate students were reincarnated as second lieutenants without a break in what they were doing. Unthreatened by the draft, I was able to remain a civilian and regard the military and its culture with a degree of detachment. Then, in 1945, the Axis surrendered and the whole world changed again. Like physical anthropologists at that time, I took a job in Anatomy. We had all taken Gross Anatomy, and, since almost the only other people who competed in the area were M.D.s, anatomy departments could save money by hiring anthropologists. I found an opening at Oklahoma, where I remained until 1964, in a place that I still look back on as one in which it was very pleasant to work and live.

In 1959 the first computers began to appear; huge mainframes filled whole rooms with heat-generating vacuum tubes and had a safety cut-off for the whole machine if the air-conditioning broke down (the computer was in danger of burning itself up otherwise). My experience with punch-card data processing made me leap at the opportunity to learn the new systems. I soon saw the possibilities of using computer techniques to simulate the processes of population genetics and published papers showing that the polymorphism of the A-B-O blood group system was maintained by heterozygote advantage.

Another event put me on a new track. One day a puzzled county sheriff appeared in the front office of the medical school with a human skull that had been accidentally unearthed in a cornfield. The receptionist recoiled slightly and then forwarded sheriff and skull to the anatomy department. Fortunately, my bone lab memories served me well: it had a cranio-facial index of nearly 100 and had to be a pre-Columbian burial, not a case for police investigation. Word got around that somebody at the medical school could identify skulls and from that time on skulls and bones came to me from all over the state, including some of what are known in the trade as "stinkers"— literally. I became one of a number of physical anthropologists who at that time were inventing forensic anthropology.

In 1965, I finally got back into official anthropology by going to the University of Colorado. The department was growing fast, and I organized a number of new courses, work which I found to be most creative and satisfying, and had the privilege of helping some fine graduate students to careers in physical anthropology. One of my new courses was "Human Races," heavy with genetics and statistics and illustrated with slides of faces from all over the world, many of them collected over a period of years from news sources. In spite of the "hard stuff," students seemed to enjoy it, and I hope I added to the small number of people who can tell an East Indian from an Afro-American and who don't think "color" is synonymous with "race." My work on this course resulted in my book, *People and Races*, published in 1977 and still in print.

Now, past retirement, with no schedules to meet, I can give my time to something I have spent 50 years putting the pieces together for: forensic identification. I still meet each year with the forensic anthropologists, who almost didn't exist in the 1940s. However, we are still using our knowledge of human variation, with its tremendous geographical detail, and the capacities of modern computers, 200 times faster than in 1959, to try and develop more versatile methods of tracking down the identity of individuals whose bones turn up in unexpected places.

meiotic problems accumulating with advanced maternal age. (See the following section.)

PROBLEMS WITH MEIOSIS

For meiosis to ensure a reasonably good opportunity for an offspring to complete normal fetal development, the process must be quite exact. The two-stage division must produce a viable gamete with exactly 23 chromosomes—with one *and only one* of each type of autosome and one sex chromosome. Moreover, this process must be precise in both male and female parents, so that two normal gametes combine to produce one normal fertilized egg, the zygote.

At birth it appears that the process has worked quite well, as more than 98% of newborns have the correct number of chromosomes. However, this statistic is misleading, for there are many genetic "mistakes" that are not detected among live-born infants. It has been estimated that one of every two pregnancies naturally terminates early as a spontaneous abortion. An estimated 70% of these miscarriages are caused by an improper number of chromosomes (Cummings, 1991). Thus, it appears that during meiosis there are frequent errors, with quite serious consequences.

The basic problem that leads to an improper number of chromosomes results from a failure during meiosis. As you will recall, during both Meiosis I and Meiosis II, the chromosomes line up along the center of the cell. If, in Meiosis I, the homologous pair fails to *disjoin* properly, then both members of the same pair may be assorted to the same gamete. Conversely, the other gamete would get neither member of the pair. This failure is called *nondisjunction*. If one of the affected gametes unites with a normal gamete containing 23 chromosomes, the resulting zygote will have either 45 or 47 chromosomes. Having only one member of a chromosome pair is referred to as *monosomy*. The term *trisomy* refers to the presence of three copies of a particular chromosome.

The far-reaching effects of an abnormal number of chromosomes can only be appreciated by remembering that the zygote will faithfully reproduce itself through mitotic division. Thus, *every* cell in the body will also have the abnormal chromosomal complement. Most problems of this type, particularly of the larger autosomes, cause such catastrophic problems that the embryo aborts quite early (frequently before the pregnancy is even recognized). Occasionally, an individual with an autosomal nondisjunction will reach full term, the most common example being *Down syndrome*, or *trisomy 21*. In this instance, as a result of a nondisjunction during meiosis, there is an extra twenty-first chromosome in every cell, and a chromosomal complement of 47.

Down syndrome, which occurs in approximately one out of a thousand live births, is the only *autosomal trisomy* that is compatible with life, which means that some affected fetuses survive to birth and can, with good medical care, attain adulthood. However, there are a number of associated developmental and health problems, including congenital heart defects (seen in about 40% of affected newborns), increased susceptibility to respiratory infection, and leukemia. Prior to the advent of antibiotic therapy in the 1940s, few individuals with trisomy 21 survived to middle age. The most widely recognized effect of trisomy 21, however, is mental retardation, which is variably expressed and ranges from mild to severe.

Trisomy 21 is associated with advanced maternal age. For example, the risk of a woman aged 20 giving birth to an affected infant is just .05% (5 in 10,000). However, 3% of babies born to mothers 45 and older are affected (a 60-fold increase). In reality, most Down syndrome infants are born to women less than 35 years old, but this statistic is only due to the fact that women in this age category give birth to the majority of babies born. The explanation for the increase in incidence with maternal age is thought to be related to the early initiation of meiosis in females and the presumed senescence of the gametic cell lines, resulting in increased risk of nondisjunction.

There are also numerous nondisjunctions that affect sex chromosomes. These syndromes can produce individuals that, for example, are: XXY (47 chromosomes); X0 (45 chromosomes); XXX (47 chromosomes); or XYY (47 chromosomes). In all these cases, the symptoms are *much* less severe than those for any abnormal number of autosomes. Geneticists explain this phenomenon by pointing to the effects of what is termed *dosage compensation,* or X chromosome deactivation.

Knowing the X chromosome contains DNA that influences many characteristics, one might well ask, How it is that both sexes can function normally when females ostensibly have twice the amount of X chromosome DNA as do males? Without going into detail, it suffices to say that in all female somatic cells, only one X chromosome is functional. The other has been "deactivated" early in embryonic development. This phenomenon accounts for the fact that females, with two X chromosomes, do not exhibit double the effects of X chromosome activity compared to males. Likewise, it explains how males function normally with only one X chromosome. In individuals who inherit additional X chromosomes, all but one are deactivated in all cells. However, in some circumstances (for example, XXY males) some problems, including sterility, arise.

DNA: Structure

Cellular functions are directed by DNA. To understand these activities and how characteristics are inherited, we must first know something about the structure and function of DNA.

In 1944, published results of a 10-year study demonstrated that the DNA molecule was the material responsible for the transmission of inherited traits, at least in some bacteria (Avery, MacLeod, and McCarty, 1944). However, the exact physical and chemical properties of DNA were still unknown. In 1953 at Cambridge University, an American researcher, James Watson, and three British scientists (Francis Crick, Maurice Wilkins, and Rosalind Franklin), developed a structural and functional model for DNA (Watson and Crick, 1953a; 1953b). For their discovery, Watson, Crick, and Wilkins were awarded the Nobel Prize in medicine and physiology in 1962. (Unfortunately, by this time, Rosalind Franklin was deceased.) The importance of their achievement cannot be overstated, for it completely revolutionized the fields of biology and medicine and forever altered our understanding of biological and evolutionary mechanisms.

The DNA molecule is composed of two chains of subunits called **nucleotides**. (A typical human chromosome has well over 50 million nucleotides.) A nucleotide, in turn, is made up of three components: a sugar molecule (deoxyribose), a phosphate, and one of four nitrogenous bases (Fig. 2-10). In DNA, nucleotides are stacked upon one another to form a chain. This chain is bonded along its bases to another, **complementary** nucleotide chain, and together the two form a helical shape. The resulting DNA molecule, then, is two-stranded and is described as forming a *double helix* that resembles a twisted ladder (Fig. 2-11). If one follows the twisted ladder analogy, it can be seen that the sugars and phosphates represent the two sides, and the nitrogenous bases and the bonds that join them are the rungs.

The secret of how DNA functions lies within the four nitrogenous bases. These are termed *adenine, guanine, thymine,* and *cytosine,* and they are frequently referred to by their initial letters A, G, T, and C. In the formation of the double helix, the joining of bases is done in a highly specific manner. Chemically, one type of base pairs or bonds with only one other. Base pairs

Nucleotides The basic subunit of DNA. Each nucleotide contains one sugar, one phosphate, and one of the four DNA bases.

Complementary Refers to the highly specific manner in which DNA bases bond with one another. Complementary base pairing is the structural basis for DNA replication.

Figure 2-10

Part of a DNA molecule. The illustration shows the two DNA strands with the sugar and phosphate backbone and the bases extending toward the center.

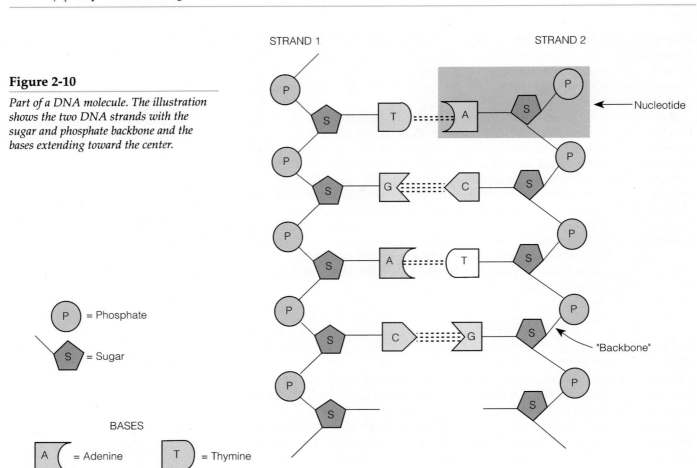

= Phosphate

= Sugar

BASES

A = Adenine   T = Thymine

G = Guanine   C = Cytosine

can form only between adenine and thymine and between guanine and cytosine (see Fig. 2-10). This pairing, both structurally and functionally, lies at the heart of the DNA molecule and is referred to as the *base-pairing rule*. This specificity is essential to the DNA molecule's unique ability to replicate.

DNA: Replication

Cells multiply by dividing through mitosis, with each new cell receiving a full complement of genetic material. As you have seen, it is essential that the DNA replicate to transmit genetic information, while at the same time allowing the original cell to retain all its DNA.

Prior to the visible beginning of cell division (that is, during interphase), specialized **enzymes** break the bonds between bases in the DNA molecule, leaving the two previously joined strands of nucleotides with their bases exposed (Fig. 2-12). This separation permits the exposed bases to attract unattached nucleotides that are free-floating within the cell nucleus.

Since, following the base-pairing rule, one base can be joined to only one other, the attraction between bases occurs in a complementary fashion. For example, if the exposed base in the original nucleotide chain is adenine, it

Enzymes Specialized proteins that initiate and direct chemical reactions in the body.

will attract a nucleotide carrying thymine, and the two nucleotides will be joined at the bases. If the next exposed base in the chain is guanine, it will bond to a nucleotide bearing cytosine, and so on. In this manner, the two previously joined parental nucleotide chains serve as models, or *templates*, for the formation of a new strand of nucleotides.

As each new strand is formed, its bases are bonded to the bases of an original strand. When the process is completed, there are two double-stranded DNA molecules exactly like the original one, and each newly formed molecule consists of one original nucleotide chain, bonded to a newly formed one. A chromosome, seen as a double-stranded structure in either mitosis or meiosis, is simply two identical DNA molecules joined together at the centromere.

Protein Synthesis

During the life of a cell, the most important function of DNA is the direction of protein synthesis within the cell. Proteins are complex, three-dimensional molecules that function through their ability to bind to other molecules. For example, the protein hemoglobin, found in red blood cells, is able to bind to oxygen and serves to transport oxygen to cells throughout the body.

Proteins function in a myriad of ways. Some are structural components of tissues. Collagen, for example, is one of the most common proteins in the body and is a major constituent of all connective tissues. Aside from mineral substances, collagen is the most abundant structural material in bone. Enzymes are also proteins, whose function is to initiate and enhance chemi-

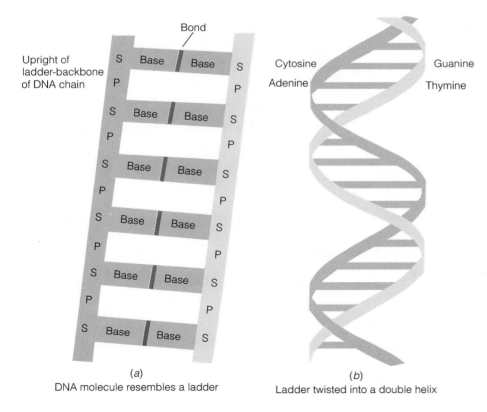

(a)
DNA molecule resembles a ladder

(b)
Ladder twisted into a double helix

Figure 2-11

(a) *DNA molecule resembles a ladder.*
(b) *Ladder twisted into a helix.*

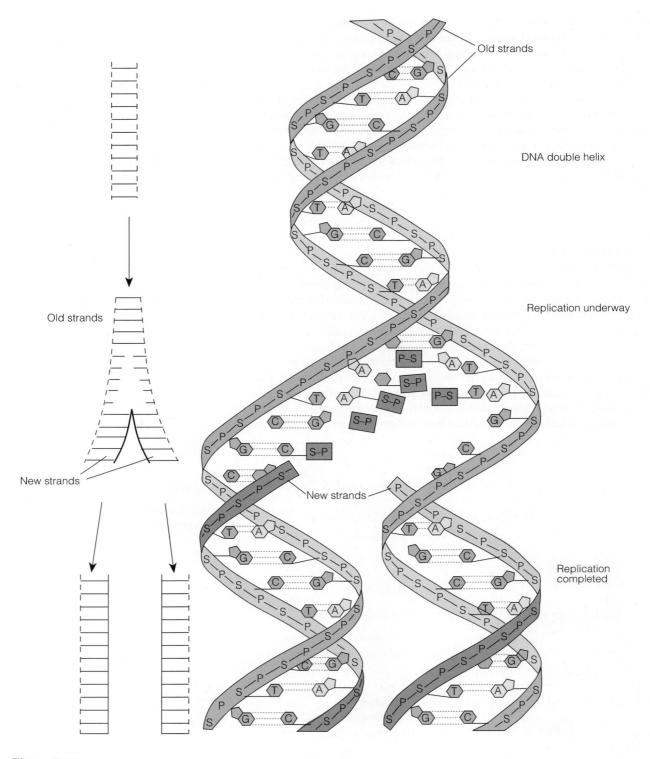

Figure 2-12

DNA replication. During DNA replication, the two strands of the DNA molecule are separated and each strand serves as a template for the formation of a new strand. When replication is complete there are two DNA molecules. Each molecule consists of one new and one old DNA strand.

cal reactions. An example of a digestive enzyme is lactase, which breaks down lactose, or milk sugar, into the two simple sugars that comprise it (see Chapter 6). Another class of proteins includes many types of **hormones**. Hormones are produced by specialized cells that release them into the bloodstream to circulate to other areas of the body, where they produce specific effects in tissues and organs. A good example of this type of protein is *insulin*, produced by cells in the pancreas. Insulin causes cells in the liver and certain types of muscle tissue to absorb glucose (sugar) from the blood.

Proteins are composed of linear chains of smaller molecules called **amino acids**. In all, there are 20 amino acids, which are combined in different amounts and sequences to produce potentially millions of proteins. What makes proteins different from one another is the number of amino acids involved and the *sequence* in which they are arranged. In order for a protein to function properly, if at all, its amino acids must be arranged in the proper sequence.

DNA serves as a recipe for making a protein, for it is the sequence of DNA bases that ultimately determines the order of amino acids in a protein molecule. In the DNA instructions, a *triplet*, or group of three bases, specifies a particular amino acid. For example, if a triplet includes the bases cytosine, guanine, and adenine (CGA), it specifies the amino acid *alanine*. If the next triplet in the chain contains guanine, thymine, and cytosine (GTC), it refers to another amino acid, *glutamine*. Therefore, a DNA recipe might look like this: AGA, CGA, ACA, ACC, TAC, TTT, TTC, CTT, AAG, GTC, etc., as it directs the cell in assembling proteins. Actually, as we will see shortly, the code does not possess "commas," so that the above sequence could even more accurately be depicted as: AGACGAACAACCTACTTTTTCCTTAAGGTC . . .

Protein synthesis is a little more complicated than the above few sentences might imply. For one thing, protein synthesis occurs outside the nucleus at the ribosomes in the cytoplasm. A logistics problem arises, as the DNA molecule is not capable of traveling outside the cell's nucleus. Thus, the first step in protein synthesis is to copy the DNA message into a form that can pass through the nuclear membrane into the cytoplasm. This process is accomplished through the formation of a molecule similar to DNA called RNA. RNA is different from DNA in that it:

1. is single-stranded
2. contains a different type of sugar
3. contains the base uracil as a substitute for the DNA base thymine—uracil is attracted to adenine, just as thymine is
4. is able to pass through the nuclear membrane into the cytoplasm

The RNA molecule forms on the DNA template in much the same manner as new strands of DNA are assembled during DNA replication. Again, DNA bases become exposed and, as this exposure occurs, free-floating nucleotides are attracted to them. However, during protein synthesis, the free-floating nucleotides are RNA (not DNA) nucleotides. As the RNA bases arrive at the DNA template, their nucleotides attach to one another in linear fashion, to produce a chain of RNA nucleotides, complementary to the DNA strand it is reading. You will recall there are two strands of DNA, and while complementary, they are not identical. Thus, at any given segment of a DNA molecule (that is, a chromosome) only one side is used to read the genetic code (Fig. 2-13).

The new RNA nucleotide chain (containing from 300 to 10,000 nucleotides) is a particular type of RNA called **messenger RNA** (mRNA). During its

Hormones   Proteins produced by specialized cells that travel to other parts of the body where they influence chemical reactions.

Amino acids   Small molecules that are the major component parts of proteins.

Messenger RNA   A form of RNA that is formed on one side (one strand) of the DNA molecule. It carries the DNA code from the nucleus (after processing) to the cytoplasm, where protein synthesis takes place.

Figure 2-13

Transcription. The two DNA strands have partly separated. Free nucleotides have been drawn to the template strand and a strand of mRNA is being made. Note that the RNA strand will exactly complement the DNA template strand except that uracil (U) replaces thymine (T).

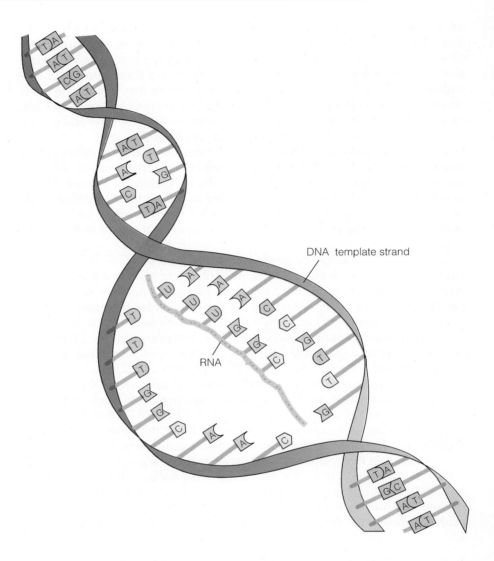

DNA template strand

RNA

Transcription   The formation of a messenger RNA molecule on a DNA template.

Translation   The process of sequencing amino acids from a messenger RNA template into a functional protein or a portion of a protein.

Codons   The triplets of messenger RNA bases that code for a specific amino acid during translation.

Transfer RNA   The type of RNA that binds to specific amino acids and, during translation, transports them to the ribosome in sequence.

assembly on the DNA model, mRNA is transcribing the DNA code and, in fact, the formation of mRNA is called **transcription**. Once the appropriate DNA segment has been copied, the mRNA strand peels away from the DNA model and travels through pores in the nuclear membrane to the ribosome. Meanwhile, the bonds between the DNA bases are reestablished, and the DNA molecule is once more intact.

As the mRNA strand arrives at the ribosome, the ribosome translates the code it contains. (This stage of the process is called **translation** because, at this point, the genetic instructions are actually being decoded and implemented.) Moreover, we are actually changing "languages" in going from a language of nucleotides to a language of amino acids. Thus, the term *translation* is a most appropriate one. Just as each DNA triplet specifies one amino acid, mRNA triplets—called **codons**—also serve this function. Therefore, the mRNA strand is "read" in codons or groups of three bases taken together.

One other form of RNA, **transfer RNA** (tRNA), is essential to the actual assembly of a protein. Each molecule of tRNA has the ability to bind to one specific amino acid. A particular tRNA molecule, carrying the amino acid matching the mRNA codon being translated, arrives at the ribosome and deposits its amino acid. As a second amino acid is deposited, the two are joined in the order dictated by the sequence of mRNA codons. In this way, amino acids are linked together to form a strand, which eventually will function as a protein or part of a protein (Fig. 2-14).

The genetic code is said to be universal in the sense that, at least on earth, DNA is the genetic material in all forms of life. Moreover, the DNA of all organisms (from bacteria to oak trees to human beings) is composed of the same molecules using the same kinds of instructions. These similarities imply biological and evolutionary relationships among, and an ultimate common ancestry for, all forms of life. What makes oak trees distinct from humans is not differences in the DNA material, but differences in how that material is arranged. In addition to its universitality, there are other general characteristics of the DNA code common to all life, including the fact that it is *commaless*, *triplet*, and *degenerate* (see Box 2-1).

Figure 2-14

Assembly of an amino acid chain in protein synthesis.

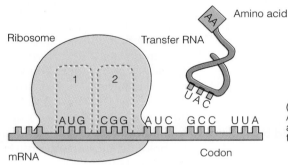

(a)
As the ribosome binds to the mRNA, tRNA brings a particular amino acid specified by the mRNA codon to the ribosome.

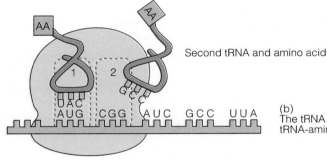

Second tRNA and amino acid

(b)
The tRNA binds to the first codon while a second tRNA-amino acid complex arrives at the ribosome.

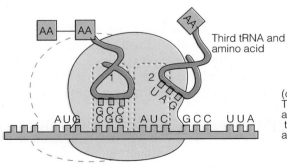

Third tRNA and amino acid

(c)
The ribosome moves down the mRNA allowing a third amino acid to be brought into position by another tRNA molecule. Note that the first two amino acids are now joined together.

Box 2-1   Characteristics of the DNA Code

1. THE CODE IS **UNIVERSAL**.

In other words, the same basic messages apply to all life forms on the planet, from bacteria to humans. The same triplet code, specifying each amino acid, thus applies to all life on earth. This commonality is the basis for the methods used in recombinant DNA technology.

2. THE CODE IS **TRIPLET**.

Each amino acid is specified by a sequence of three bases in the mRNA (the codon), which, in turn, is coded for by three bases in the DNA (a DNA "word").

3. THE CODE IS **COMMALESS** (THAT IS, WITHOUT PAUSES).

There are no pauses or other delimiters separating one codon from another. Thus, if a base should be deleted, the entire frame would be moved, drastically altering the message downstream for successive codons. Such a gross alteration is termed a *frame-shift mutation*. Note that, although the code lacks "commas," it does contain "periods." Three codons act to stop translation.

4. THE CODE IS **DEGENERATE**.

While there are 20 amino acids, there are 64 possible codons. Even considering the 3 "stop" messages, that still leaves 61 codons specifying the 20 amino acids. Thus, many amino acids are specified by more than one codon. For example, leucine and serine are each coded for by 6 different codons. In fact, only 2 amino acids (methionine and tryptophan) are coded by a single amino acid. This redundancy is referred to as *degeneracy* of the code. You should note that in evolutionary history there was little alternative. If the code were single (4^1), only 4 amino acids could be specified. If the code were double (4^2), only 16 relevant messages would be possible. With a triplet code (4^3), 64 messages are possible, meeting minimum requirements (20), but also, inevitably, yielding considerable redundancy.

Definition of the Gene

Gene The colloquial term referring to a segment of genetic material. Technically, this term has two different meanings (see *locus* and *alleles*).

Locus That portion of a chromosome responsible for the production of a polypeptide chain.

Polypeptide chain A sequence of amino acids that may act alone (or in combination) as a functional protein.

The entire sequence of bases responsible for the synthesis (or manufacture) of a protein, or in some cases, a portion of a protein, is referred to as a **gene**. Unfortunately, the term *gene* in biology has two rather distinct meanings, and is thus not a technically precise term. Geneticists prefer to use the term **locus** for a region of a chromosome responsible for a particular function (this is the first of the two meanings). Or, put another way, a locus is a segment of DNA, or sequence of DNA nucleotides, that specifies the sequence of amino acids in a particular protein.

Even more precisely, a locus codes for the production of a **polypeptide chain**. The term *polypeptide* simply refers to the multiple *peptide* bonds that unite amino acids into protein components. Some proteins, such as collagen or human growth hormone, are made up of a single polypeptide chain. Others, such as insulin or hemoglobin, are *complex* and are each made up of two different types of polypeptide chains. In other words, it requires two different loci (plural of locus) to produce either hemoglobin or insulin. A locus may comprise only a few hundred bases, or it may be composed of thousands.

If the sequence of DNA bases is altered through mutation (a change in the DNA sequence), or if it is lost, the manufacture of some proteins may not occur, and the cell (or indeed the organism) may not function properly, if at all.

Mutation: How a Gene Changes

Probably the best way to envision how the genetic material is organized is to see what happens when it changes; that is, mutates. The first clearly elucidated example of a molecular mutation in humans relates to a portion of the hemoglobin molecule. As mentioned, hemoglobin is the component of red blood cells responsible for binding to oxygen molecules and transporting them to bodily cells and tissues. Normal adult hemoglobin is made up of four polypeptide chains (two *alpha* chains and two *beta* chains) that are direct products of gene action. Each beta chain is, in turn, composed of 146 amino acids.

There are several hemoglobin disorders with genetic origins, and perhaps the best known of these is **sickle-cell anemia**, which results from a defect in the beta chain. Individuals with sickle-cell anemia inherit a gene variant from *both* parents that causes the substitution of one amino acid (*valine*) for the normally occurring *glutamic acid*. This single amino acid substitution, at the sixth position of the beta chain, results in the production of an altered and less efficient form of hemoglobin called hemoglobin S (Hb^S). The normal form is called hemoglobin A (Hb^A). In situations where the availability of oxygen is reduced, such as high altitude, or when oxygen requirements are increased through exercise, red cells bearing Hb^S collapse, roughly assuming a sickle shape. What follows is a cascade of events, all of which result in severe anemia and its consequences. Briefly, these events include impaired circulation from blocked capillaries, red cell destruction, oxygen deprivation to vital organs (including the brain), and, without treatment, death.

Sickle-cell anemia A severe inherited disease that results from a double dose of a mutant allele, which in turn results from a single base substitution at the DNA level.

Individuals who inherit the altered form of the gene from only one parent have what is termed *sickle-cell trait* and because only about 30% of their hemoglobin is abnormal, they are much less severely affected and usually have a normal life span.

The variant forms of the beta chain locus that code for these slightly different products relate to the other meaning of the term *gene* and are called **alleles**. Here, there are two alleles relevant to our discussion, Hb^A (normal) and Hb^S (sickling). Both these variants (alleles) occur *at the same locus* which is usually referred to as the hemoglobin beta (Hb) locus.

Alleles Alternative forms of a gene. Variants that occur at the same locus.

The cause of all the serious problems associated with sickle-cell anemia is a seemingly minute change in the Hb locus. Remember that both normal hemoglobin and the sickle-cell variety have 146 amino acids, 145 of which are identical. Moreover, to emphasize further the importance of a seemingly minimal alteration, consider that triplets of DNA bases are required to specify amino acids. Therefore, it takes 438 bases (146×3) to produce the chain of 146 amino acids comprising the adult hemoglobin beta chain. But, a change in only one of these 438 bases is needed to produce the cascade of life-threatening complications seen in sickle-cell anemia.

Figure 2-15 shows a possible DNA base sequence and the resulting amino acid products for both normal and sickling hemoglobin. As can be seen, a single base substitution (from CTC to CAC) could result in an altered amino acid sequence:

... proline—*glutamic acid*—glutamic acid ... to

... proline—*valine*—glutamic acid ...

Such a change in the genetic code is referred to as a **point mutation** and, in evolution, it probably is the most common and most important source of new variation in populations. Point mutations, like that for the Hb locus, proba-

Point mutation The change in a single base of a DNA sequence.

Figure 2-15

Substitution of one base at position #6 produces a sickling hemoglobin.

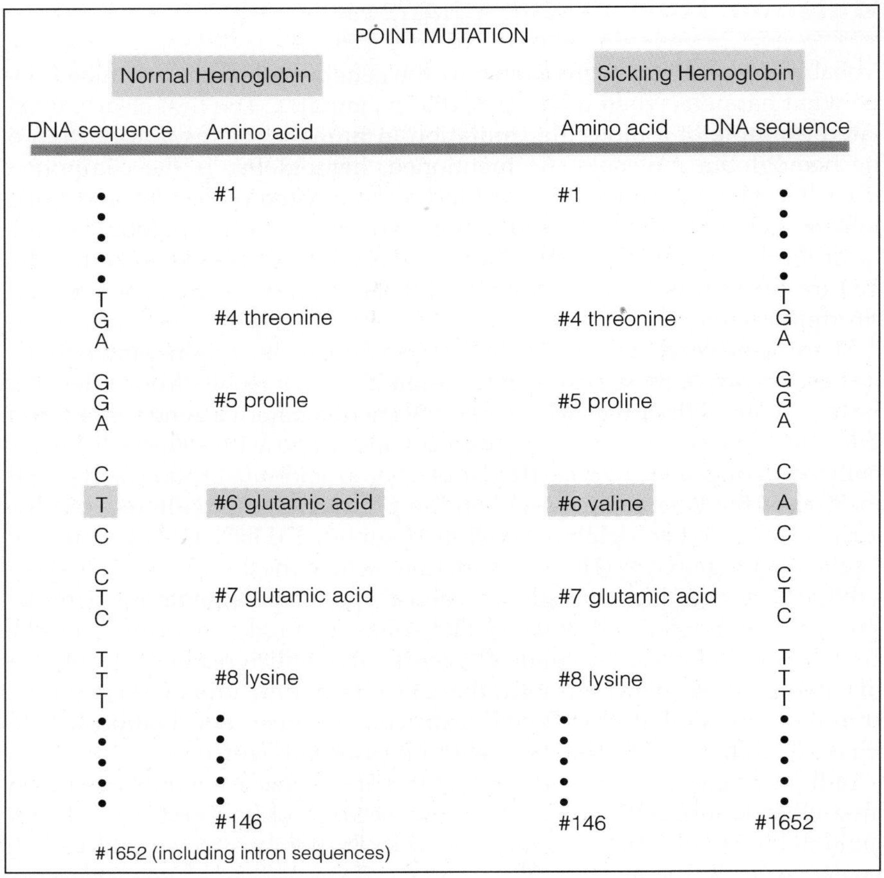

POINT MUTATION

Normal Hemoglobin			Sickling Hemoglobin	
DNA sequence	Amino acid		Amino acid	DNA sequence

• • • •	#1		#1	• • • •
T G A	#4 threonine		#4 threonine	T G A
G G A	#5 proline		#5 proline	G G A
C T C	#6 glutamic acid		#6 valine	C A C
C T C	#7 glutamic acid		#7 glutamic acid	C T C
T T	#8 lysine		#8 lysine	T T
• • • •	#146		#146	• • • • #1652

#1652 (including intron sequences)

bly occur relatively frequently during cell division, but a new mutation will have evolutionary significance only if it is passed on to offspring within the gametes. Once such a mutation has occurred, its fate in the population will depend on the other evolutionary forces, most especially, natural selection. Sickle-cell, in fact, is the best demonstrated example of natural selection acting in human beings, and this point will be considered in more detail in Chapter 4.

Sequencing Human DNA: The Ultimate Genetic Map

For many years, it has been possible to assign approximately the position of certain loci on specific human chromosomes. Initially, such assigning was possible for a few dozen loci specific to the X chromosome because of its particular mode of inheritance (as discussed in Chapter 3). Further advances during the early 1980s, especially with new techniques of cell hybridization, increased the number of mapped loci to over 400. Today, however, with greatly intensified governmental support and accumulating breakthroughs in recombinant DNA technology (see Issue, this chapter), we stand on the threshold of an entirely new era of gene mapping.

In October, 1990, the Human Genome Project officially began. This effort is a massive and highly sophisticated program aimed at ultimately sequencing all the bases in the human **genome**. Estimates suggest that for the entire genetic complement of human nuclear DNA there are as many as 3 billion nucleotides. Thus, even with highly sophisticated technology, the dimensions of the task are staggering. However, despite the modest progress to date and the enormity of the work, several authorities predict the task can be completed in the next 10 to 15 years.

Thus far, approximately 70 million nucleotides have been sequenced, and over the next decade this number is expected to double approximately every two years (Erickson, 1992). In the hopes of furthering biomedical knowledge, as well as stimulating the biotechnology industry, federal spending on the Human Genome Project has been considerable—estimated at 160 million dollars in 1992 (Erickson, 1992). Total United States government funding by the turn of the century is expected to approach 3 billion dollars (administered by the National Institutes of Health and the Department of Energy), which supports 3 governmental laboratories, 7 university centers, and another approximately 150 individual research projects. In addition, considerable further scientific and financial assistance is coordinated in an international effort with Japan, France, Great Britain, Germany, Italy, Denmark, Finland, Australia, and Canada.

There are numerous medical advances that can be realized through this research, most especially the ability (in specific families) to predict the inheritance of numerous human genetic disorders and to gain a much better understanding of the underlying causes of many of these same diseases. As a result of these studies, a more complete understanding of such disorders as Marfan syndrome and cystic fibrosis has rapidly been gained. (See Chapter 3 for further discussion of these genetic diseases.)

The techniques of DNA mapping are fairly complex. Several methods are being pursued simultaneously. At one broad level, the methods involve isolating variable DNA **markers** to specific chromosomes and then linking the pattern of inheritance (of the marker) to that of some observable trait (such as cystic fibrosis). In this way, specific (*functional*) loci can be mapped to particular human chromosomes. The next task is to locate more precisely on each chromosome where each locus resides. Another method involves isolating particular (*physical*) chromosomal areas and then obtaining nucleotide sequences for these quite small regions. Thus, in reality, different kinds of maps (functional and physical) are being assembled by various research teams. Ultimately, the goal is to merge the approaches and thus obtain a precise and complete sequence for every human chromosome.

It should also be pointed out that the quantity and complexity of the DNA data are obviously enormous. They are so far beyond the most sophisticated of current computerized data management systems that entirely new types of software will have to be developed. It has been estimated that perhaps 30% of total funding (approaching 1 billion dollars) will be used to develop a revolutionary new generation of data management software (Erickson, 1992).

As a result of this much greater precision of locating specific human loci, a molecular/genetic defect can be more accurately described and thus a more rational therapy may be adopted. At present, the full map is understood only in very rough terms. Each marker provides a new signpost but, as of yet, there are still relatively few markers known (a few thousand). By analogy, it

Genome The entire genetic complement of an individual or that characteristic of a whole species.

Marker A clearly identifiable trait that can be easily traced in pedigrees. Most markers are now ascertained at the DNA level and are mapped to specific human chromosomes. In this way, other traits (controlled by other loci) that correlate with the marker in pedigrees can also be (approximately) mapped as well.

would be like trying to find someone's house based on a map that approximated its location relative only to the interstate highway system.

With some clear advances and a real sense of optimism among many scientists and politicians, critical voices have been raised. Concerns focus upon ethical use of the data. For example, would an individual's genetic complement be used to deny health and/or life insurance? Who would store all the information, and who would have access to it? Who would receive profits from the practical applications of this technology, especially considering much of the funding comes from public sources? And, finally, concerns have been raised regarding the necessity of sampling numerous human populations—so to at least give an approximation of human genetic diversity. Many of these issues are being addressed by researchers, in particular the need to establish a human genome diversity program within the framework of the overall research (Weiss et al., 1992).

Given the level of governmental support, the advancing technologies, and the talent being marshalled, progress is inevitable. As more of the human genetic complement is sequenced, we will gain an even more powerful scientific tool. The test for scientists, policy makers, educators, and the general public is not *whether* this tool will be used, but to what ends and how wisely it will be employed.

Summary

This chapter has dealt with several concepts that are basic to understanding human variation, as well as the processes of biological evolution. (These concepts will be developed in succeeding chapters.)

Cells are the fundamental units of life. There are two basic types of eukaryotic cells: somatic cells comprise body tissues, while gametes (eggs and sperm) are reproductive cells that transmit genetic information from parent to offspring.

Cells multiply by dividing, and during cell division DNA is visible under a microscope in the form of chromosomes. In humans, there are 46 chromosomes (23 pairs). If the complement is not precisely distributed to succeeding generations of cells, catastrophic consequences will follow.

Somatic cells divide during growth, tissue repair, or to replace old, worn-out cells. Somatic cell division is called mitosis. During mitosis, a cell divides one time to produce two daughter cells, each possessing a full and identical (diploid) set of chromosomes.

Sex cells are produced when specialized cells in the ovaries and testes divide in meiosis. Unlike mitosis, meiosis is characterized by two divisions, which produce four nonidentical daughter cells, each containing only half (the haploid number) the amount of DNA (23 chromosomes) carried by the original cell.

Genetic information is contained in DNA molecules, found in the nuclei of cells. DNA is capable of replication (making copies of itself) and is the only molecule known to have this ability. Replication makes it possible for parent cells to retain a full complement of DNA while also passing on a full complement to daughter cells. The complementarity of the molecule is the key to understanding how this replication occurs.

DNA also controls protein synthesis by directing the cell to arrange amino acids in the proper sequence for each particular type of protein. Also involved in the process of protein synthesis is another, similar molecule called RNA. The DNA code for all life is universal and triplet, the latter meaning that for each three bases at the DNA level, one amino acid is coded at the protein (polypeptide) level. The full sequence of transcription and translation is best understood by following the example of the point mutation, described in this chapter for the hemoglobin beta locus.

Finally, the advances in "gene" mapping provide the potential for tremendous breakthroughs in understanding human development as the result of the Human Genome Project.

Questions for Review

1. What are the main differences between prokaryotic and eukaryotic cells?
2. What components of a eukaryotic cell are discussed in this chapter?
3. What are the two major types of eukaryotic cells? Give an example of each.
4. What are nucleotides?
5. Name the four DNA bases. Which pairs with which?
6. What is DNA replication and why is it important?
7. What are enzymes?
8. What are the building blocks of protein? How many different kinds of building blocks are there?
9. What is the function of DNA in protein synthesis?
10. What is the function of mRNA?
11. What is the function of tRNA?
12. Define *gene*. Discuss its two differing meanings.
13. Define *chromosome*.
14. What are homologous chromosomes?
15. How many cell divisions occur in mitosis, and how many chromosomes does each new cell have?
16. How many cell divisions occur in meiosis? How many daughter cells are produced when meiosis is complete? How many chromosomes does each new cell contain?
17. How does meiosis differ in females compared to males?
18. Why is reduction division important?
19. What is recombination and why is it important? When does it occur?
20. Why is the genetic code said to be universal?
21. What are the two sex chromosomes? Which two do males have? Which two do females have?

Chapter 3

Contents

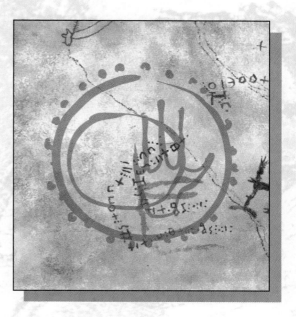

Principles
of
Inheritance

Genetic screening is used to identify individuals who possess deleterious genes that may eventually lead to debilitating illness and, perhaps, death. Screening can also identify carriers for certain recessive disorders who, though not affected themselves, can nevertheless pass a defective gene on to their offspring. The applications of genetic screening are numerous, but primarily all are aimed at decreasing the incidence of genetic disorders.

For a number of reasons, chief among which are reducing human suffering and cutting health costs, genetic screening has become a powerful diagnostic tool since the 1970s. Moreover, as new technologies are developed and as more genetic markers for disease are identified, use of such technologies in assessing individual risk will certainly continue to increase.

An estimated 10% of Americans at some point experience symptoms of an illness that is at least partly caused by genetic factors. Clearly, the benefits of genetic screening both to the individual and to society are enormous, but as with most things, they carry a price tag. The ability to identify individuals at risk for potentially fatal conditions raises numerous difficult questions never before asked. Currently, advances in genetic technology are proceeding at a rate that has far outpaced our legal and ethical systems. The purpose of this Issue is to explore some of the beneficial applications of genetic screening as well as some of the difficult choices such screening may pose.

Detection of an individual's carrier status in adults is possible for many conditions through blood testing combined with genetic counseling. Clearly, this ability is of

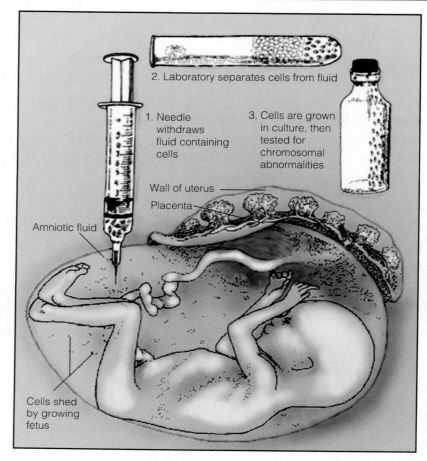

Figure 1

The amniocentesis procedure, step by step.

enormous benefit for those individuals with a family history of some recessive disorder who are making family planning decisions of their own.

The same techniques are also increasingly used today to identify persons with a genetic *predisposition* for problems associated with exposure to certain environmental agents. These results permit avoidance of potentially harmful substances when possible. Moreover, employers are increasingly screening employees to identify those who might potentially suffer from contact with particular materials in the workplace. At least 50 genetic traits have been shown to be influenced by such work-related environmental substances as lead, ozone, and nitrogen dioxide.

Newborn infants can be tested for several metabolic disorders to aid in early diagnosis and treatment. The most widespread use of newborn testing is for phenylketonuria (PKU), a recessive disorder that prevents production of the enzyme phenylalanine hydroxylase. Without this enzyme, the body cannot properly metabolize the amino acid phenylalanine, common in meat and dairy products. The accumulation of phenylalanine eventually leads to brain damage and severe mental retardation (see p. 65).

PKU testing is mandatory in most of the United States and involves a simple blood test to detect abnormal levels of phenylalanine. For those infants who test positive, the severe consequences of PKU are avoidable by strict adherance to a low phenylalanine diet when maintained throughout childhood and adolescence. What is important in this regard is that treatment depends upon early detection made available through widespread genetic screening practices.

But diagnosis of such conditions as PKU does not have to occur after birth. *Prenatal testing* permits detection of over 200 genetically determined metabolic disorders and all chromosomal abnormalities in a developing fetus. Currently, the two most commonly used methods of detecting metabolic and chromosomal defects in fetuses are *amniocentesis* and *chorionic villus sampling (CVS)*. For any given pregnancy, testing is done only to detect those disorders for which the fetus may be predisposed as a result of family background (that is, not every detectable condition is tested for in all pregnancies).

In amniocentesis, a needle is inserted through the abdominal wall into the uterus and 10 to 30 milliters of *amniotic fluid* are withdrawn (Fig. 1). Amniotic fluid contains fetal cells shed from skin and other tissues. These cells are cultured and ana-

lyzed for biochemical defects (for example, either abnormally high or low levels of certain metabolic enzymes or other substances). In addition, karyotypes are prepared to permit examination of the chromosomes themselves (see p. 23). Karyotyping ensures that the normal complement of 46 chromosomes is present and it also identifies structural abnormalities, such as breakage or deletions. Obviously, viewing the chromosomes also permits determination of fetal sex.

Although amniocentesis is a valuable diagnostic tool, there are problems associated with it. The mother's risk of infection increases slightly and there is an increased chance (less than 1%) of spontaneous abortion (miscarriage). Because of these risks, amniocentesis is recommended only if certain conditions obtain:

1. The mother is 35 years of age or older and thus has an increased likelihood of having a fetus with an autosomal trisomy, especially trisomy-21 (Down syndrome)
2. There is a family history of genetic disease for one or both prospective parents
3. If a previous pregnancy involved a genetic disorder. (For example, the incidence of recurrence of trisomies is 1 to 2%)

Another difficulty with amniocentesis is timing. Amniocentesis cannot usually be performed until week 14 to 16 of a pregnancy, and an additional 2 weeks or so are required to culture fetal cells. Therefore, if indeed the fetus does have a genetic abnormality, the mother faces the very painful decision of whether to have a middle-to-late second trimester abortion.

Chorionic villus sampling (CVS) involves the removal of a sample of cells from the chorion (the structure that gives rise to the placenta) at

about the eighth fetal week. Chorionic cells are genetically identical to fetal cells; therefore CVS can detect any condition identifiable by amniocentesis. Because it can be performed much earlier in the pregnancy (by week 8 to 10) and does not involve invasive procedures, many patients and physicians now prefer CVS to amniocentesis. However, like amniocentesis, CVS carries a risk of damage to the fetus and/or miscarriage of about 1%.

Another technique, ultrasound or sonography, is widely used to detect many developmental defects including missing or malformed limbs. Twinning and fetal sex may also be determined. During this procedure, ultrasonic waves are passed through the mother's abdomen. These waves are reflected off the developing fetus and a fetal image is projected onto a video screen. In addition to the above-mentioned application, ultrasound is used during amniocentesis to guide the needle safely through the uterine wall.

Currently there are few data regarding risks of sonography to the fetus. But the popularity of the technique (between one-third and one-half of all fetuses in the United States are now exposed to ultrasound) has prompted the National Institutes of Health to request detailed studies into possible negative effects of the procedure.

Prenatal testing is controversial for the obvious reason that test results may lead to termination of a pregnancy. Although therapeutic abortion may be the outcome, the notion that amniocentesis and chorionic villus sampling are aimed at the elimination of all abnormal fetuses is inaccurate. Not all negative findings result in abortion and, in fact, prenatal testing can be highly beneficial in preparing physicians and parents for the birth of an infant requiring special care and treatment.

Individuals must make personal decisions as to where to draw the line if they are told their fetus has a genetic disorder. Tay-Sachs (see p. 65) carriers can be identified through screening prior to beginning a pregnancy. But, if both prospective parents are carriers and they choose to conceive, they face a 25% risk of having an affected child. Because Tay-Sachs is such a devastating condition with no chance of survival beyond childhood, 80 to 90% of diagnosed pregnancies are terminated.

Likewise, the majority (but not all) of pregnancies *with a diagnosis* of trisomy-21 also end in abortion. This fact does not mean, however, that the majority of all trisomy-21 pregnancies are terminated. Most pregnant women over the age of 35 are not screened. Moreover, the majority (at least 65%) of Down syndrome infants are born to younger women who are not tested unless there are other known risk factors. Because Down syndrome is variably expressed, with many affected persons leading fairly normal, and in some cases, productive lives, the certainty of outcome is not as clear as with Tay-Sachs. Because of this uncertainty, some parents who would terminate a Tay-Sachs pregnancy would not do so in the case of a trisomy-21 diagnosis.

Other situations are even more ambiguous. Does one choose abortion if a fetus has PKU, cystic fibrosis, or sickle-cell anemia? All three are treatable to some extent, though at considerable costs (financial and otherwise).

Another serious question is faced by individuals who learn that they themselves possess a gene that will eventually cause illness and death. What does one do with such knowledge? For example, it is now possible to identify people at risk for *Huntington disease,* a fatal, degenerative disorder of the central nervous system. Huntington disease is inherited as an autosomal dominant trait and usually produces no symptoms until middle age. Symptoms include progressive degeneration of the central nervous system, involuntary twitching, mental deterioration, and eventually, after 5 to 15 years, death.

Because Huntington disease is a dominant trait, all affected people (barring new mutations) will have an affected parent (see p. 64). Moreover, anyone who has a parent with Huntington disease has a 50% chance of having symptoms by middle age. However, until the development of reliable methods of detecting genetic markers, children of affected parents could not know for certain if they had the defective gene or not. Such a test exists today, and it is possible to know if, in later life, one will succumb to this tragic condition.

Persons with a parent afflicted with Huntington disease face a most terrible dilemma. They can go untested and continue hoping, but not knowing, that they do not have the gene. Or they can be tested and either be tremendously relieved or plan the rest of their lives in anticipation of catastrophic debilitating disease and early death. Unless one has faced such an horrific decision, one cannot adequately comprehend the uncertainty and fear that must surely accompany it. Unfortunately, our technology has given us the tools with which to answer many such painful questions, but it has not prepared us for how to cope with what we may learn.

The fact that many genetic disorders are treatable (but, as yet, not curable) raises another issue: cost. The dietary management and supplementation required for PKU patients costs over $5000 per year. This dollar amount may not seem like much when one considers the consequences of severe mental retardation. However, many parents cannot afford $5000 a year, regardless of need. Therefore, the cost is borne by the state. The federal budget for PKU treatment alone is not high, and certainly it is much lower than costs of institutionalizing severely retarded PKU patients. But, with medical costs soaring out of reach for millions today, financial considerations must be addressed, and this obviously raises many deeply painful questions.

How does an individual or the state place a monetary value on a human life? Can we morally establish limits on public expenditures for the treatment of genetic diseases, when those diseases can be prevented by prenatal testing and selective abortion? On the other hand, is society obligated to bear the costs of preventable hereditary conditions?

Do people have a fundamental right to have children regardless of circumstances? Or do they have an obligation to society to be personally responsible for the financial costs of medical treatment? Does a fetus have a right to be born free of disease? If so, can an afflicted child later sue the parents for having given birth? Is it indeed desirable for society to be free of "imperfect" people? If so, who defines "perfect" and what does such a policy say about our tolerance of diversity? (One should note that a goal of the Nazi regime in Germany was to rid society of imperfection, as it was defined, and create a "master race.")

These are only a few of the many discomforting ethical questions that have accompanied advances in genetic screening and prenatal testing. There are numerous other questions and potentials for abuse as well. For example, after federal screening programs for the sickle-cell trait were instituted in 1972, indi-viduals testing positive as heterozygotes were, in some cases, reportedly denied health insurance or employment opportunities. Do employers or insurance companies have the right to refuse opportunities to people because, due to potential health problems, they ostensibly constitute an economic risk? This issue raises the question of whether or not individual rights (including rights to privacy) are violated by governmental mandates to institute genetic screening programs.

These examples illustrate the imbalances among technology, ethical standards, and the legal system. The questions raised are disturbing because they challenge traditionally held views about fundamental aspects of life. In the past, people with hereditary disorders frequently died. They still do. But now, there are treatments, however costly, for some conditions. Moreover, we now have the means to detect genetic defects or determine their risk of occurrence. How we come to terms with the ethical and legal issues surrounding our new technologies will increasingly become social, religious, and, ultimately, political concerns. Solutions will not come easily and—most assuredly—they will not please everyone.

SOURCES

Cummings, Michael R., *Human Heredity* (2nd ed.). St. Paul: West, 1991.

Edlin, Gordon, *Genetic Principles*. Boston: Jones and Bartlett, 1984.

Introduction

In Chapter 2, we discussed the structure and function of DNA within the cell. In this chapter, we shift to a somewhat broader perspective and focus on the principles that guide how characteristics are passed from parent to offspring.

Since at least 10,000 years ago, when the domestication of plants and animals was a relatively new human enterprise, people have wondered how traits were passed from parents to offspring. Although their theories were far from accurate, farmers and herders had known for millennia they could enhance favorable attributes through selective breeding. However, exactly why desirable traits were often seen in offspring of carefully chosen breeding stock remained a mystery. It was equally perplexing when offspring did not show the traits their human owners had hoped for.

From the time ancient Greek philosophers considered the problem until well into the nineteenth century, one predominant belief was that characteristics of offspring resulted from the *blending* of parental traits. Blending was accomplished by means of particles, which existed in every part of the body, and were miniatures of whatever body part (limbs, organs, etc.) they inhabited. These particles traveled through the blood to the reproductive organs and blended with particles of another individual during reproduction. There were variations on the theme—termed **pangenesis**—and numerous scholars, including Charles Darwin, adhered to certain aspects of the theory.

There were also questions as to which parent made the greater contribution to the sex and appearance of offspring. One widely accepted explanation, developed in the seventeenth and eighteenth centuries, proposed the existence in sex cells of a miniature preformed adult called an *homunculus*. Controversy arose, however, over which parent (male or female) contributed the homunculus and which primarily provided nutrition for its development.

Pangenesis   An early belief that contributions to reproductive cells came from particles within different body parts.

Gregor Mendel's Experiments with Garden Peas

It was not until an Augustinian monk, Father Johann Gregor Mendel (1822–1884), addressed the question of inheritance that the basic principles of heredity were discovered. Gregor Mendel (Fig. 3-1) grew up in a poor peasant family in the region formerly called Czechoslovakia, and at the age of 21 he was accepted as a novice at the monastery at Brno.

Mendel was attracted to monastic life because of the security it offered and because it presented opportunities for higher education. In fact, it was relatively common for young men with few other options to seek a life in the Church. Moreover, life in Brno did not fit the stereotype of cloistered monasticism, and Mendel was not isolated in some backwater village, denied contact with the rest of the world. On the contrary, at the time Brno was a center of scientific and cultural endeavor for much of southeastern Europe, and many of the monks there were involved in various areas of scientific research (Hartl, 1983).

After becoming established at Brno, Mendel left for two years to study at the University of Vienna, where he acquired scientific expertise from leading professors in botany, physics, and mathematics. Given this impressive background, perhaps it is not surprising that an obscure monk was able to unravel the mysteries of inheritance and thus achieve one of the most important biological discoveries ever made.

When Mendel returned to Brno, he resumed his former occupation as a substitute teacher in a nearby town. He also returned to work in the monastery garden, where he had been experimenting with the fertilization of flowers, hoping to develop new variations in colors. This experimentation eventually led him to attempt to elucidate the various ways in which physical traits (such as color or height) could be expressed in plant **hybrids**.

Mendel hoped that by making crosses between two strains of *purebred* plants and examining their progeny, he could determine and predict how many different forms of hybrids there were, arrange the forms by generation, and evaluate the proportion in each generation of each type represented.

CROSSES BETWEEN PLANTS: SINGLE TRAITS

Mendel chose to work with the common garden pea and he wisely decided to consider one characteristic at a time, rather than repeat what other investigators had done and examine several simultaneously. In all, he focused on seven different traits, each of which could be expressed in two different ways (Table 3-1).

In 1856, Mendel began his experiments by making 287 crosses between 70 different purebred plants, which differed with regard to a specific trait. (In all, Mendel used over 28,000 pea plants before he completed his research.) The plants used in this first cross were designated the "parental generation," or P_1. Crossing pure lines in the parental generation means that each parent (when self-crossed) produces only one kind of offspring. For example, if the trait in question were the height of the plant (tall or short), Mendel made crosses between varieties that produced *only* tall plants with varieties that produced *only* short plants. If he was interested in seed color (yellow or green), he made crosses between plants that produced only yellow seeds and those with all green seeds.

The offspring of the parental generation were designated the F_1 (first filial) generation. As the F_1 plants matured, all were tall (Fig. 3-2). Not one was short. According to blending theories, height in the F_1s should have been intermediate between the heights of the parent plants, but these theories were not confirmed by Mendel's results.

Next, since pea plants have both male and female parts, the F_1s were allowed to self-fertilize to produce a second hybrid generation (the F_2 generation). This time, all the offspring were not uniformly tall. Instead, approxi-

Figure 3-1

Gregor Mendel.

Hybrid   Offspring of mixed ancestry.

Table 3-1   The Seven Characteristics of the Garden Pea Mendel Selected

Characteristics	Dominant Expression	Recessive Expression
1. Form of the ripe seed	smooth	wrinkled
2. Color of seed albumen	yellow	green
3. Color of seed coat	gray	white
4. Form of ripe pods	inflated	constricted
5. Color of unripe pods	green	yellow
6. Position of flowers	axial	terminal
7. Length of stem	tall	dwarf

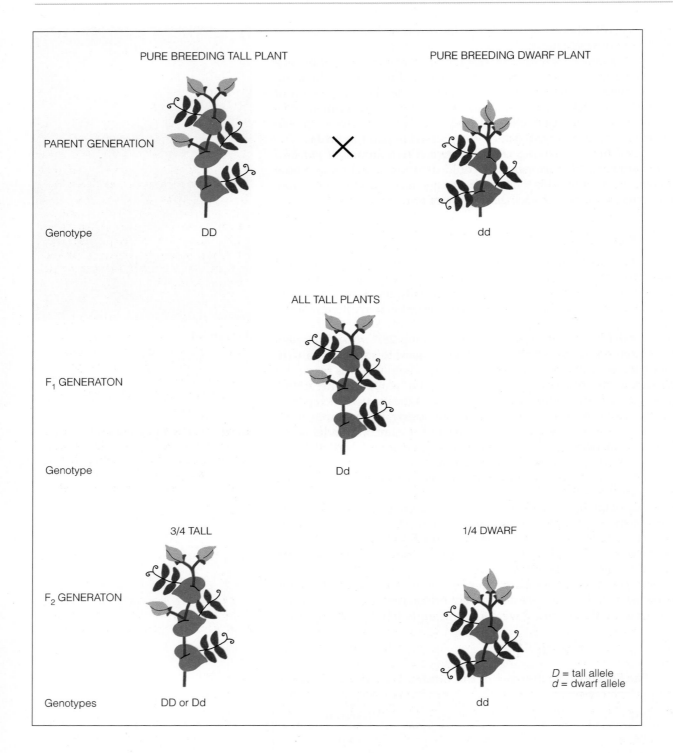

PURE BREEDING TALL PLANT

PURE BREEDING DWARF PLANT

PARENT GENERATION   ✕

Genotype   DD   dd

ALL TALL PLANTS

F₁ GENERATON

Genotype   Dd

3/4 TALL   1/4 DWARF

F₂ GENERATON

                                                    D = tall allele
                                                    d = dwarf allele

Genotypes   DD or Dd   dd

Figure 3-2

Diagrammatic representation of crosses considering only one trait at a time.

mately ¾ were tall and the other ¼ were short (dwarf) (Fig. 3-2). In one experiment, there were 787 tall plants and 277 dwarfs, which produced a good approximation of the ratio of 3 tall plants for every dwarf (3:1).

Regardless of the trait he examined, every time the experiment was done, Mendel obtained almost exactly the same results. One expression of the trait disappeared in the F_1 generation and reappeared in the F_2s. Moreover, the expression that was present in the F_1 generation was more common in the F_2s, occurring in a ratio of approximately 3:1 to the less-common expression.

These results suggested at least two important facts. First, it appeared that the various expressions of a trait were controlled by discrete *units that occurred in pairs* and that offspring inherited one unit from each parent. Mendel correctly reasoned that the members of a pair of units controlling a trait somehow separated into different sex cells and were united with another member during fertilization of the egg. This thinking comprises Mendel's *first law of inheritance*, known as the **Law of Segregation**.

Today, we know that meiosis explains Mendel's Law of Segregation. You will remember that during meiosis, homologous chromosomes and the genes they carry separate from one another and end up in different gametes. However, in the zygote, the full complement of chromosomes is restored, and both members of each chromosome pair (homologous chromosomes) are present in the offspring.

Second, Mendel recognized that the expression which was absent in the F_1s had not actually disappeared at all. It had remained present, but somehow it was masked and could not be expressed. To describe the trait manifestation which seemed to be lost, Mendel used the term **recessive**; and the one which was expressed was said to be **dominant**. Thus, the important principles of *recessiveness* and *dominance* were formulated, and they remain today as basic underlying concepts in the field of genetics.

As you already know, a *locus* (pl., loci) is a segment of DNA that controls the production of a specific protein. At numerous genetic loci, however, there may be more than one form of the gene, and these variations of genes at specific loci are what we have defined as alleles. Therefore, an allele is an alternate form of a gene which can direct the cell to produce slightly different forms of the same protein and, ultimately, different expressions of traits.

As it turns out, plant height in garden peas is controlled by two different alleles at one genetic locus. The allele determining that a plant will be tall is dominant to the allele for short, or dwarf. (It is worth mentioning that height is not governed in this manner in all plants.)

In Mendel's experiments, all the parent plants (P_1s) had two copies of the same allele, either dominant or recessive, depending upon whether they were tall or short. When two copies of the same allele are present at the same locus on homologous chromosomes, the individual is said to be **homozygous**. Thus, all the tall P_1 plants were homozygous for the dominant allele, and all the short P_1 plants were homozygous for the recessive allele. (This homozygosity explains why tall plants crossed with tall plants produced only tall offspring and short plants crossed with short plants produced all short offspring; that is, they were "pure lines" and lacked genetic variation at this locus.) However, all the F_1 plants (hybrids) had inherited one allele from each parent plant and, therefore, they all possessed two different alleles. Such individuals, who possess two different alleles at a locus, are termed **heterozygous**.

Geneticists use standard symbols to refer to alleles. Thus, uppercase letters refer to dominant alleles, or dominant traits; and lowercase letters refer to recessive alleles, or recessive traits. As a matter of convention, the initial letter of the word for the recessive expression is used, and in the case of short pea plants, the term "dwarf" describes shortness. Therefore, we get:

D = the allele for tallness

d = the allele for shortness (dwarfism)

Law of Segregation   Genes occur in pairs (because chromosomes occur in pairs). During gamete production (meiosis), the members of each gene pair separate so that each gamete contains one member of each pair. During fertilization, the full number of chromosomes is restored and members of gene pairs are reunited.

Recessive   A trait that is not phenotypically expressed in heterozygotes. Also refers to the allele that governs the trait. In order for the trait to be expressed, there must be two copies of the allele (that is, the individual must be homozygous).

Dominant   A trait governed by an allele that can be expressed in the presence of another, different allele (that is, heterozygotes). Dominant alleles prevent the expression of recessive alleles in heterozygotes.

Homozygous   Having the same allele at the same locus on both members of a pair of homologous chromosomes.

Heterozygous   Having different alleles at the same locus on both members of homologous chromosomes.

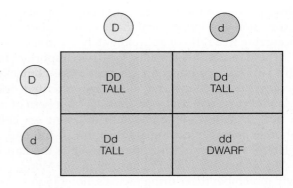

Figure 3-3

Punnett square representing possible genotypes and phenotypes and their proportions in the F₂ generation.

The circles across the top and at the left of the Punnett square represent the gametes of the F_1 parents. The four inner squares illustrate that 1/4 of the F_2s will be tall (DD); another 1/2 also will be tall but will be heterozygous (Dd); and the remaining 1/4 will be dwarf (dd). Thus, 3/4 can be expected to be tall, and 1/4 will be dwarf.

Genotype   The genetic makeup of an individual. *Genotype* can refer to an organism's entire genetic makeup, or to the alleles at a particular locus.

The same symbols are combined to describe an individual's actual genetic makeup, or **genotype**. The term *genotype* can be used to refer to an individual's entire genetic makeup or to the paired complement of alleles at a genetic locus on homologous chromosomes. Thus, the genotypes of the plants in Mendel's experiments were:

DD = homozygous tall plants
Dd = heterozygous tall plants
dd = homozygous short plants

The crosses Mendel performed are diagrammed in Fig. 3-3. You should note that the types of gametes each plant can produce are represented by circles that include the symbol for the allele they possess. Remember, each gamete can carry only one allele for each trait; in this case, height of plant. Fig. 3-3 also illustrates that *all* the gametes of individual P_1 plants must carry the same allele (either D or d), because each P_1 plant carries only one type of allele.

However, because F_1 plants are heterozygous, it is also shown that the gametes produced by F_1 plants may possess one of two alleles. The plants produce the alleles in approximately equal proportions (that is, half the F_1 gametes receive a dominant D allele and the other half receive the recessive d allele).

Figure 3-3 is what is called a *Punnett square*, and it diagrammatically represents the different ways in which the alleles can be combined when the F_1s are self-fertilized to produce an F_2 generation. In this way, the figure shows the *genotypes* that are possible in the F_2 generation, and it also demonstrates that approximately ¼ of the F_2s are DD (*homozygous dominant*); ½ are heterozygous (Dd); and the remaining ¼ are **homozygous recessive** (dd).

Homozygous recessive   A genotype that contains two recessive alleles at the same locus. Only in this genotype will recessive phenotypes be expressed.

Phenotype   The observable or detectable physical characteristics of an organism; the detectable expression of the genotype.

The Punnett square can also be used to show and predict the proportions of F_2 **phenotypes**, or the detectable physical manifestations of gene action. Here, the phenotypes are tall and dwarf. Some phenotypes could also be ascertained biochemically, as in blood types. In short, a phenotype is *any* expression beyond the DNA (genotype) that we choose to measure.

The Punnett square also illustrates why Mendel observed three tall plants for every short plant in the F_2 generation. By examining the Punnett square, you can see that ¼ of the F_2s are tall because they have the DD genotype. An additional ½, which are heterozygous (Dd), will also be tall because D is dominant to d and will therefore be expressed in the phenotype. The remaining ¼ are homozygous recessive (dd), and they will be short because no dominant allele is present. It is important to emphasize that the *only* way a recessive allele can be expressed is in combination with another recessive allele; that is, the individual is homozygous recessive at the particular locus in question. This form of expression, wherein an allele is phenotypically expressed only when it occurs in double dose (that is, on both members of a chromosome pair) defines what we mean by *recessive*.

It is shown, therefore, that ¾ of the F_2 generation will express the dominant phenotype and ¼ will show the recessive phenotype. This relationship is expressed as a **phenotypic ratio** of 3:1, and this proportion typifies heterozygous crosses in all *Mendelian traits* (characteristics governed by only one genetic locus). It must be noted, however, that this ratio relates only to loci where two alleles are involved, one of which is completely dominant to the other.

Phenotypic ratio The proportion of one set of phenotypes to other phenotypes in a specific sample. For example, Mendel observed that there were approximately three tall plants for every short plant in the F_2 generation. This situation is expressed as a phenotypic ratio of 3:1.

CROSSES BETWEEN PLANTS: TWO TRAITS TOGETHER

Mendel also made crosses in which two characteristics were considered simultaneously to determine whether there was a relationship between them. Two such characteristics were plant height and seed color.

In peas, seeds are either yellow (dominant) or green (recessive). We use the symbols G to represent the dominant allele and g for the recessive allele.

In the P_1 generation, crosses were made between tall plants with yellow seeds and short plants with green seeds (Fig. 3-4). As expected, the recessive expression of each trait was not seen in the F_1 generation: all plants were tall and all produced yellow seeds. However, in the F_2 plants, both recessive traits reappeared in a small proportion of individuals (Fig. 3-4). The Punnett square in Fig. 3-5 shows the 16 allelic combinations that can result in the F_2 generation when two traits are simultaneously considered. The phenotypic ratio for this type of cross is 9:3:3:1, meaning that out of 16 possible combinations, 9 ($\frac{9}{16}$) will be tall with yellow seeds, $\frac{3}{16}$ will be tall with green seeds, $\frac{3}{16}$ will be short with yellow seeds, and $\frac{1}{16}$ will show both recessive traits and be short with green seeds.

Although this proportional distribution may seem confusing, it serves to illustrate the point that there is no relationship between the two traits; that is, there is nothing to dictate that a tall plant must have yellow (or green) seeds—the expression (and segregation) of one trait is not influenced by the expression of the other trait. The allele for tallness (D) has equal probabilities (50–50) of ending up in a zygote with either G or g.

Mendel stated this principle as his second law of inheritance, the **Law of Independent Assortment**. The Law of Independent Assortment states that the units (alleles) that code for different traits assort independently of each other during gamete formation and recombine in offspring Today, we know this phenomenon to be true because the genetic loci controlling these two characteristics are located on different, nonhomologous chromosomes, and during meiosis, chromosomes travel to newly forming cells independently of one another.

Law of Independent Assortment Mendel's second law which states that the units (alleles) which govern one trait assort independently of the units that govern other traits.

If Mendel had used just *any* two traits, the phenotypic ratios may well have not conformed to those expected by independent assortment (9:3:3:1). The ratios came out as he predicted because the loci governing most of the

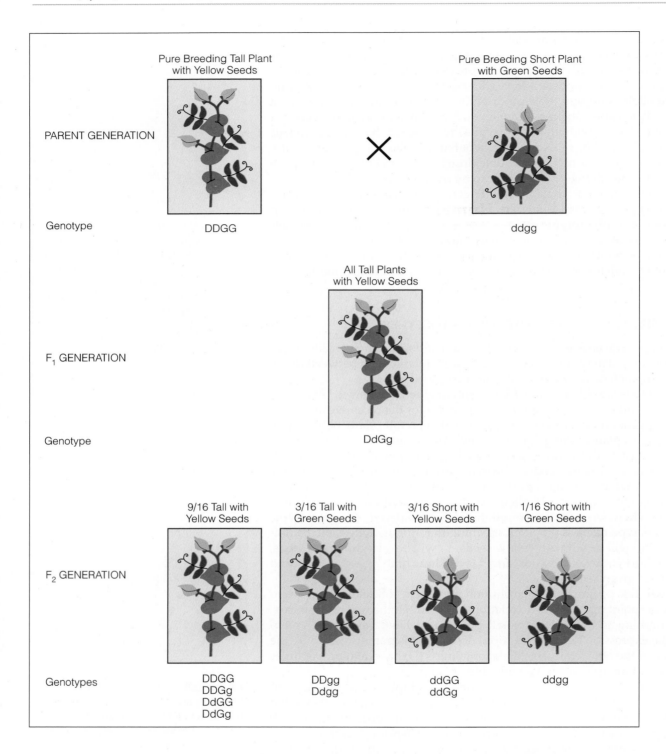

Figure 3-4

Results of crosses when two traits are considered simultaneously. It is shown that height of plant and seed color are independent of one another. Also shown are the genotypes associated with each phenotype.

traits he chose were carried on different chromosomes. (In a couple of cases, the situation was more complex.)

In 1865, Mendel presented his results at a meeting of the local Natural History Society. The following year, the Society published his report, but unfortunately, the methodology and the statistical nature of the results were beyond the thinking of the time. The scientific community was not at all prepared for Mendel's unusual approach and, consequently, the significance of his work was unappreciated.

In the latter part of the nineteenth century, several investigators made important contributions to the understanding of chromosomes and cell division. Moreover, the discovery of reduction division in meiosis provided an explanation for Mendel's discoveries. However, Mendel's research remained unknown until 1900, when three different scientists, conducting similar experiments to Mendel's, came across his paper. Unfortunately, Mendel had died 16 years earlier and never saw his work vindicated.

Mendelian Inheritance in Humans

The focus of this text is human evolution. Understanding patterns of heredity is essential, as *only* genetically influenced traits contribute to the evolutionary process. The rules of Mendelian inheritance, so elegantly described by Gregor Mendel for garden peas, also apply to humans. Indeed, the exact same principles of segregation and independent assortment as those for garden peas also account for the transmission of **Mendelian traits** in humans.

A Mendelian trait is one that is influenced by a single genetic locus and follows what is termed a *simple* pattern of inheritance. Such traits are frequently referred to as simple traits, as opposed to those traits under the influence of multiple loci (see p. 68). In 1902 (just two years after the rediscovery of Mendel's work), the first Mendelian trait (brachydactyly—see p. 63) was demonstrated in humans. Today, after almost a century of intensive research in human genetics, more than 4900 Mendelian characteristics are now documented for humans (McKusick, 1990).

Good examples of human Mendelian traits include the "blood groups," reflected as protein (antigen) specificities on the surface of red or white blood cells. The best known of the red blood cell systems is ABO. The ABO system is governed by three alleles, A, B, and O, found at the ABO locus on the ninth chromosome. (It should be noted that although three alleles are present in populations, each individual can possess only two.) These alleles determine which ABO blood type an individual has by coding for the production of antigens on the surfaces of red blood cells. If only antigen A is present, the blood type (phenotype) is A; if only B, then the individual has B blood; if both are present, blood type is AB; and when neither is present, blood type is said to be O.

The principles of dominance and recessiveness, as well as a third, **codominance**, are clearly illustrated by the ABO system. The O allele is recessive to

Mendelian traits   Traits that are under the influence of one genetic locus; also called *simple traits.*

Codominance   Refers to the expression of two alleles in the heterozygote. In this situation, neither allele is dominant or recessive, so that both are expressed in the phenotype.

Figure 3-5

Punnett square showing results of dihybrid cross in F_2 generation. Heterozygous tall plants with yellow seeds are self-crossed. Each parent produces 4 different gametes, and there are, thus, 16 different genotypic combinations.

	DG	Dg	dG	dg
DG	DDGG	DDGg	DdGG	DdGg
Dg	DDGg	DDgg	DdGg	Ddgg
dG	DdGG	DdGg	ddGG	ddGg
dg	DdGg	Ddgg	ddGg	ddgg

Table 3-2   ABO Genotypes and Associated Phenotypes

Genotype	Antigens on Red Blood Cells	ABO Blood Type (Phenotype)
AA, AO	A	A
BB, BO	B	B
AB	A and B	AB
OO	none	O

both A and B; therefore, if a person has type O blood, he or she must be homozygous for the O allele. Since both A and B are dominant to O, an individual with blood type A can have one of two genotypes: AA or AO. The same is true of type B, which results from the genotypes BB and BO (Table 3-2). However, type AB presents a slightly different situation and is an example of codominance.

Codominance is seen when two different alleles occur in heterozygous condition, but instead of one having the ability to mask the expression of the other, the products of *both* are seen in the phenotype. Therefore, when both A and B alleles are present, both A and B antigens can be detected on the surfaces of red blood cells.

Because humans obviously cannot be used in experimental breeding programs, as were Mendel's peas, a more indirect approach must be used to demonstrate patterns of inheritance. The principal technique traditionally used in human genetic studies thus requires the reconstruction of **pedigrees**. Pedigrees are charts of matings and resulting offspring shown in human families over the span of a few generations. As generation spans are long, much of the data are determined retrospectively—that is, reconstructed from memories of the descendants or, occasionally, from old medical records, family bibles, etc. Another common feature of human genetic data, when compared to the number of offspring in experimental organisms (peas, fruit flies, mice), is that human families are comparatively quite small. Accordingly, it is usually necessary to compare pedigrees from numerous families in order to generate sufficient data. Even then, for a complex animal such as humans, many ambiguities remain: the influence of culture, the very similar expression of some phenotypes (which are produced by different loci), incomplete or variable expression in phenotypes, and the question of paternity.

Pedigree A diagram showing family relationships in order to trace the hereditary pattern of particular genetic (usually Mendelian) traits.

MODES OF MENDELIAN INHERITANCE IN HUMANS

Analysis of pedigrees first of all helps determine if a trait is indeed Mendelian in nature. Second, the *mode* of inheritance can be established. As discussed in Chapter 2, genetic traits are governed by specific loci. These loci, in turn, are located on specific chromosomes, which are either autosomes or sex chromosomes. Finally, a trait is said to be either dominant or recessive. In the discussion of Mendel's pea experiments, we noted that a recessive phenotype is expressed *only* when the alleles occur in a homozygous combination (for example, aa). Conversely, a dominant trait would be expressed in either homozygous *or* heterozygous allele combinations (for example, AA or Aa). Thus, a recessive characteristic is phenotypically expressed only when the recessive allele combines in homozygous genotypes. From considerations of whether the locus influencing a trait is on an autosome or sex chromosome

Figure 3-6

Inheritance of autosomal dominant trait. Human pedigree for brachydactyly (short fingers). Spouse in all cases is normal and not shown.

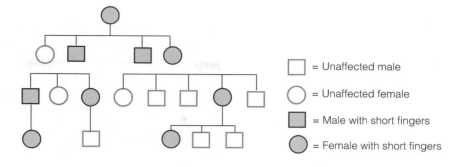

☐ = Unaffected male

○ = Unaffected female

■ = Male with short fingers

● = Female with short fingers

and whether it is dominant or recessive, five different modes of Mendelian inheritance have been described in humans:

autosomal dominant traits

autosomal recessive traits

Y-linked traits

X-linked dominant traits

X-linked recessive traits

Autosomal Dominant Traits These traits are governed by loci that are located on autosomes, that is, any chromosome other than X or Y. A good example of an autosomal dominant trait is brachydactyly (short, broad fingers). Figure 3-6 shows a partial pedigree for a family with numerous affected individuals. In this example, we are dealing with a dominant allele; therefore, an individual who is Bb is affected, whereas one who is bb is unaffected (that is, "normal"). Individuals who are homozygous dominant for rare alleles are extremely uncommon. Moreover, mutant alleles that produce abnormalities in heterozygotes cause such extreme defects in homozygotes that such fetuses frequently abort prior to reaching full term. In these cases, the pregnancy may not even have been detected, and thus these severely affected phenotypes almost never are reflected in pedigrees.

In a pedigree for an autosomal dominant trait (Fig. 3-6), we can see that the trait is always passed from an *affected* parent to the offspring without skipping generations. (Remember, if an individual inherits a dominant allele, the trait it codes for will be expressed. Therefore, all individuals who have a so-called dominant trait will have at least one affected parent.) In addition, if you count the total number of offspring of affected parents (all offspring shown) you will find 17, and of these, 8 are affected. The proportion affected ($^8/_{17}$) is very close to 50%, which is exactly what we would predict for an autosomal dominant trait where only one parent is affected. The reason for this occurrence is directly explained by Mendel's Law of Segregation. Each parent who has brachydactyly is heterozygous (Bb) and all here mate with a normal individual (not shown in the pedigree). The matings would therefore be (Fig. 3-7): Bb (affected) X bb (unaffected). Following the principle of segregation and the underlying process of meiosis, we can then predict that one-half the offspring will be brachydactylous and one-half normal. In fact, this ratio is exactly what we find (in statistical terms—$^8/_{17}$ is not appreciably different from the ½ prediction). A final observation you can easily confirm shows that no sex bias exists in affected individuals, as an equal number of males and females show the trait.

Numerous other autosomal dominant traits have been demonstrated through conclusive pedigree analysis. Among these are Marfan syndrome,

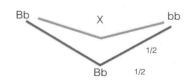

Figure 3-7

Typical mating producing offspring who are brachydactylous. An affected parent (Bb) mates with an unaffected parent (bb).

Table 3-3   Examples of Some Autosomal Dominant Traits in Humans

Condition	Incidence*	Phenotypic Effects
Achondroplasia	1/30,000	Dwarfism; short stature, broad, short limbs
Brachydactyly	Very rare	Short, deformed fingers
Familial hypercholesterolemia	1/500	Increased cholesterol levels, oftentimes leading to heart disease by middle age
Huntington disease	1/25,000	Degeneration of nervous system, early death
Marfan syndrome	1/10,000	Affects the eyes and cardiovascular and skeletal systems. Greater than average height, long arms and legs, enlargement of the aorta. Death due to rupture of the aorta is common. Abraham Lincoln may have had Marfan syndrome.
Neurofibromatosis	1/3,000	Symptoms range from abnormal skin pigmentation to large tumors resulting in gross deformities. This so-called *elephant man disease* can lead to paralysis, blindness, and death.

*Approximate.

Huntington disease, achondroplasia, and familial hypercholesterolemia (see Table 3-3).

Autosomal Recessive Traits   These traits are also influenced by loci on autosomes but show a different pattern from that for autosomal dominant traits mainly because, as we know, a recessive allele can only be expressed if the individual inherits two copies of it, one from each parent. A good example of such a trait is shown in Fig. 3-8, a pedigree for albinism, a metabolic disorder causing deficient production of a skin pigment called melanin (see Chapter 6). This disorder is phenotypically expressed as very light skin, hair, and iris of the eyes.

Actually, albinism is a group of genetic disorders each influenced by different loci. Some forms affect only the eyes, while others also involve skin and hair. The most widely known variety of albinism does influence eye, skin, and hair pigmentation, and is caused by an autosomal recessive allele. The frequency of this particular form of albinism varies widely among populations with an incidence of about 1 in 37,000 in American whites. But a much higher frequency, approaching 1 in 200, is seen among Hopi Indians. How populations have come to be so different in the frequencies of various alleles (such as that for albinism) will be a major focus of the next two chapters.

Pedigrees for autosomal recessive traits show obvious differences from those for autosomal dominant characteristics. A comparison with the pedigree for a dominant trait shows that recessive traits often "skip" generations, so that an affected offspring is produced by two phenotypically normal parents. In addition, the proportion of affected offspring from most matings is less than the 50% so frequently seen in pedigrees for autosomal dominant traits. In fact, we can demonstrate that when an albino child is born to two normal parents, the chance of having another albino child is one in four. Once

Figure 3-8

Partial pedigree for albinism, an autosomal recessive trait.

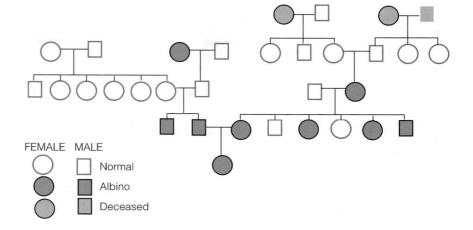

FEMALE MALE

○ □ Normal

● ■ Albino

● ■ Deceased

again, a return to the simple Mendelian principle of segregation provides the explanation. Nonaffected parents who produce an albino child are heterozygous **carriers**, while the albino child is a double recessive or homozygote (aa). We can see in Fig. 3-9 how such a mating produces both affected and nonaffected offspring in predictable proportions. If two albinos should mate (the last mating of Fig. 3-8), they will produce all albino progeny. It is readily apparent that an albino is the *only* kind of offspring they could have produced, barring any new mutation. Other recessive traits that are medically important are listed in Table 3-4.

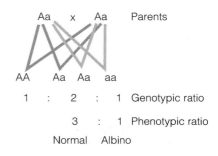

Figure 3-9

Typical mating producing albino offspring. Each parent is unaffected, but is a carrier (heterozygous) for the albino allele.

Carrier In recessive inheritance, a person who *carries* a recessive allele in single dose (that is, heterozygous). Thus, a carrier does not express the recessive trait in the phenotype.

Table 3-4   Examples of Some Autosomal Recessive Mendelian Traits in Humans

Condition	Incidence*	Phenotypic Effects
Albinism	1/37,000 in American whites; much higher in some other groups	Loss of pigment in skin, eyes, and hair. Can lead to increased risk of skin cancer.
Cystic fibrosis	1/2,000 in American whites; much lower in American blacks	Abnormal secretion of exocrine glands with pronounced involvement of the pancreas. Most patients develop obstructive lung disease, and only about half live to early adulthood.
Phenylketonuria	1/12,000	Inability to metabolize amino acid phenylalanine. If left untreated in childhood, results in severe mental retardation.
Sickle-cell anemia	1/500 in American blacks; much lower in American whites	Abnormal hemoglobin, altered shape of red blood cells, anemia and blockage of small blood vessels. Secondary infections, reduced lifespan.
Tay-Sachs disease	1/2,500 in Eastern European (Ashkenazi) Jews; much lower in most other populations	Degeneration of nervous system beginning at about 6 months of age. Death by age 4.
*Approximate.		

Sex-Linked Traits The other modes of Mendelian inheritance in humans are controlled by loci on sex chromosomes, and the term *sex-linked* simply refers to the fact they are found on the sex chromosomes. Of the more than 240 traits suspected to result from this form of inheritance, almost all are controlled by loci on the X chromosome. Only recently have any traits been traced to regions on the Y chromosome, where at least four loci have been identified. One is involved in determining maleness (the TDF locus), and one other may be involved with sperm production (the H-Y locus). Because of the scarcity of known Y-linked traits, they are not dealt with here.

The best known of the sex-linked traits is hemophilia, caused by a recessive allele at a locus on the X chromosome. This type of condition is thus referred to as an *X-linked recessive*. Hemophilia results from the lack of a clotting factor in the blood (Factor VIII), and affected individuals suffer bleeding episodes and may hemorrhage to death from incidents that most of us would consider trivial.

The most famous pedigree documenting this malady is that of Queen Victoria and her descendants (shown in Fig. 3-10). The most striking feature shown by this pattern of inheritance is that usually only males are affected. To understand this pattern, once again we have to refer to the principle of segregation, but with one important additional stipulation: we are now dealing with *sex chromosomes*.

Because they possess two X chromosomes, females show the same pattern of expression of X-linked traits as for autosomal traits. That is, the only way

Figure 3-10

Pedigree for Queen Victoria and some of her descendants, showing inheritance of hemophilia, an X-linked recessive trait in humans.

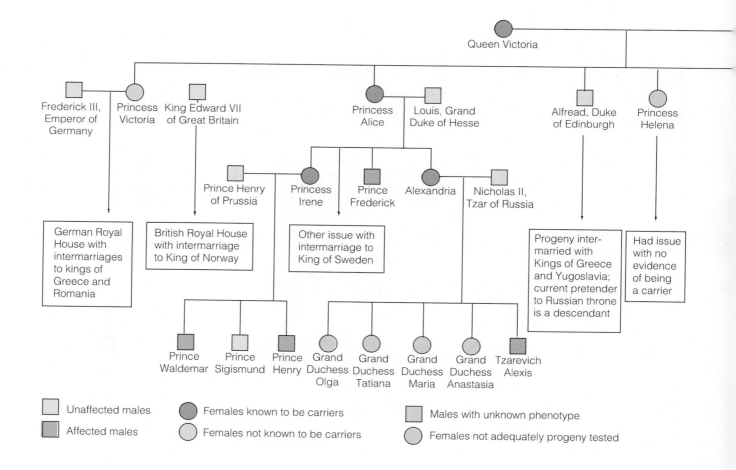

an X-linked recessive allele can be phenotypically expressed in a female is when she is homozygous for it. Therefore, we observe that females who carry the hemophilia allele in single dose (that is, they are heterozygous) are unaffected. In cases where female heterozygotes express an X-linked trait, this is precisely what then defines the trait as an X-linked dominant.

On the other hand, since males are XY and have only one X chromosome, they possess only one copy of an X-linked gene. With only one X chromosome, males can never be homozygous or heterozygous for X-linked loci, and are thus referred to as **hemizygous**. Moreover, males do not exhibit dominance or recessiveness for X-linked traits because *any* allele located on their X chromosome, even a recessive one, will be expressed.

The contrast between males and females in number of X chromosomes is directly related to the incidence of hemophilia seen in Fig. 3-10. Females who have the hemophilia allele in single dose are carriers for the trait. Although they may have some tendency toward bleeding, they are not severely affected. On the other hand, males who have the allele in single dose (on their *only* X chromosome) are severely afflicted, and prior to recent therapy, faced short and often painful lives.

A mating between a carrier female and normal male is depicted in Fig. 3-11. In this type of mating, four kinds of offspring are possible. There is a 50–50 chance of either having a daughter who is a carrier or one who is normal. That is, statistically speaking, half the daughters will be normal and half will be carriers. In a similar manner, half the sons would be expected to be

Hemizygous   *Hemi* means half. The condition in males for an allele on the X chromosome. As males have only one X chromosome, the allele is always expressed.

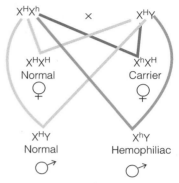

Figure 3-11

Mating producing hemophiliac offspring. Neither parent is affected. The mother is a carrier ($X^H X^h$) and the father is normal ($X^H Y$).

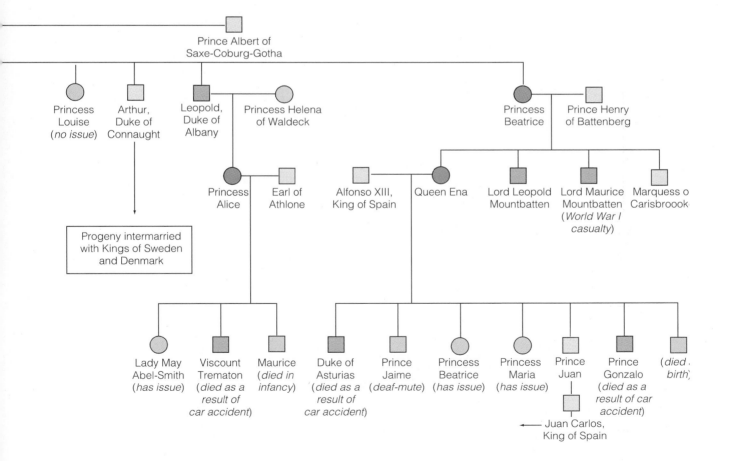

normal, while half will have hemophilia. For both sons and daughters, their status relative to the hemophilia allele depends solely upon which X chromosome they inherit from their mother.

Prior to advances in therapy, male hemophiliacs rarely lived long enough to produce offspring. In recent years, effective treatment for hemophilia has involved collecting the missing Factor VIII from donated blood (from potentially thousands of donors) and transfusing it to patients. (During the 1970s and early 1980s, before effective donor screening was available, the majority of hemophiliacs in the United States—up to 90%—were infected with HIV, the virus that causes AIDS, thus compounding the tragedy they faced.)

In addition to hemophilia (two different varieties inherited on the X chromosome), there are several other X-linked traits that have been well studied in humans, including red-green color blindness and a form of muscular dystrophy.

Polygenic Inheritance

Polygenic *Poly* means many; *genic* represents genes (that is, loci). Refers to traits that are influenced by two or more loci.

Mendelian traits are said to be *discrete*, or *discontinuous*, because their phenotypic expressions do not overlap, but rather they fall into clearly defined categories. For example, Mendel's pea plants were either short or tall, but none was intermediate in height. In the ABO system, the four phenotypes are completely distinct from one another; that is, there is no intermediate form between Type A and Type B to represent a gradation between the two. In other words, Mendelian traits do not show *continuous* variation.

However, many traits do have a wide range of phenotypic expressions that overlap to form a graded series. These are called **polygenic**, or *continuous*, traits. While Mendelian traits are governed by only one genetic locus, polygenic characteristics are influenced by alleles at *several* loci, with *each* locus making a contribution to the phenotype.

Polygenic traits actually account for most of the easily visible phenotypic variation seen in humans, and they have traditionally served as a basis for racial classification (see Chapter 5). Skin color, hair color, eye color, weight, shape of face, and fingerprints are but a few examples of polygenic inheritance. Since they exhibit continuous variation, most polygenic traits can be measured on a scale composed of equal increments. For example, height (stature) is measured in feet and inches, or meters and centimeters. If one were to measure height in a large number of individuals, the distribution of measurements would continue uninterrupted from the shortest extreme to the tallest. This is what is meant by the term *continuous traits*.

Because polygenic traits usually lend themselves to metric analysis, biologists, geneticists, and physical anthropologists treat them statistically. Although statistical analysis can be complicated, the use of simple summary statistics, such as the *mean* (average) or *standard deviation* (a measure of within-group variation), permits basic descriptions of, and comparisons between, populations. For example, one might be interested in average height in two different populations and whether or not differences between the two are significant.

Statistical manipulations are not possible with Mendelian traits simply because they cannot be measured in the same manner. They are either present or they are not. But, the fact that Mendelian traits are not amenable to statistical analysis in the same manner as polygenic characters does not mean that Mendelian traits are less informative. Indeed, for most medical applications, quite the opposite is true. The different requirements simply mean that scientists must approach the study of these two types of inheritance from different perspectives.

Mendelian characteristics can be described in terms of frequency within populations, yielding between-group comparisons regarding incidence. Even more precisely, the frequency of the *alleles* in question can be determined, providing the foundation for the science of population genetics (discussed in Chapter 5). These characteristics can also be analyzed for mode of inheritance (dominant or recessive) from pedigree data.

Finally, for many Mendelian traits, the approximate or exact position of genetic loci has been identified, thus making it possible to postulate the molecular/biochemical basis of certain genetic disorders (see Chapter 2). Because polygenic characteristics are influenced by several loci, they cannot usually be traced to specific loci and, therefore, such analyses as those just noted are not currently feasible in humans.

Genetic and Environmental Factors

From the preceding discussion it might appear that phenotype is solely the expression of the genotype, but this is not true. (Here we use the terms *genotype* and *phenotype* in a broader sense to refer to an individual's *entire* genetic makeup, and *all* observable characteristics.) The genotype sets limits and potentials for development, but it also interacts with the environment. Many aspects of the phenotype are influenced by this genetic/environmental interaction. Scientists have developed statistical methods for calculating what proportion of phenotypic variation is due to genetic or environmental components. However, it is usually not possible to identify the *specific* environmental factors that affect the phenotype.

Polygenic traits especially are influenced by environmental conditions. Adult stature, for instance, is strongly affected by the individual's nutritional status during growth and development. One study showed that children of Japanese immigrants to Hawaii were, on average, 3 to 4 inches taller than their parents. This dramatic change, seen in one generation, was attributed to environmental change, and specifically to a change in diet (Froelich, 1970).

Other important environmental factors include exposure to sunlight, altitude, temperature, and, unfortunately, increasing levels of exposure to toxic waste and airborne pollutants. All these, and many more, contribute in complex ways to the continuous phenotypic variation seen in characteristics governed by multiple genes (see Chapter 6).

Simple Mendelian traits are less likely to be influenced by environmental factors. For example, ABO blood type is determined at fertilization and remains fixed throughout the individual's lifetime regardless of diet, exposure to ultraviolet radiation, temperature, and so on.

Simple Mendelian and polygenic inheritance produce different manifestations of phenotypic variation. In the former, variation occurs in discrete categories, while in the latter, it is continuous. However, it is important to understand that, for polygenic characteristics, Mendelian principles still apply at individual loci. In other words, if a trait is influenced by seven loci, each one of those loci may have two or more alleles with one perhaps being dominant to the other, or they may be codominant. Each of the alleles, in turn, segregates during meiosis, following the same principles as for traits of simple (Mendelian) inheritance. It is the combined action of the alleles at all seven loci, interacting with the environment, that results in observable phenotypic expression.

Summary

We have seen how Gregor Mendel discovered the principles of segregation, independent assortment, and dominance and recessiveness by conducting experiments on garden peas. Although the field of genetics has progressed dramatically in the twentieth century, the concepts first put forth by Gregor Mendel remain the basis of our current knowledge on how traits are inherited.

Traits that are influenced by only one genetic locus are *Mendelian traits*. At many genetic loci, two or more alleles may interact in dominant, recessive, or codominant fashion with one another. Examples of Mendelian traits in humans include ABO blood type, sickle-cell anemia, brachydactyly, and hemophilia. These traits are oftentimes clearly demarcated in the phenotype and can be traced through several generations in a family by the construction and analysis of a pedigree. In contrast, many characteristics (such as stature and skin color) are said to be polygenic or continuous because they are influenced by more than one genetic locus and show a continuous range of expression. These more complex traits are not amenable to pedigree studies.

The expression of all traits is, to varying degrees, under genetic control. Genetics then, can be said to set limits and potentials for human growth, development, and achievement. However, these limits and potentials are not written in stone so to speak, because many characteristics are also very much influenced by environmental factors (such as temperature, diet, sunlight, etc.). Ultimately, it is the interaction between genetic and environmental factors that produces phenotypic variation in all species, including *Homo sapiens*.

Questions for Review

1. What is Mendel's Law of Segregation?
2. How does meiosis explain the Law of Segregation?
3. What is Mendel's Law of Independent Assortment?
4. Explain dominance and recessiveness.
5. Define *allele*.
6. What is a *phenotype*, and what is its relationship to a *genotype*?
7. Why were all of Mendel's F_1 pea plants phenotypically the same?
8. Explain what is meant by a phenotypic ratio of 3:1 in the F_2 generation.
9. What is codominance? Give an example.
10. If two people who have blood type A (both with the AO genotype) have children, what proportion of their children would be expected to have O blood? Why?
11. Can the two parents in question 10 have a child with AB blood? Why or why not?

12. In a hypothetical situation, a serious disorder is caused by a recessive allele (a). The dominant allele (A) produces the normal phenotype. What is the genotype of people who have the disorder? Can *unaffected* people have more than one genotype? What is/are the genotype(s) of unaffected people?

13. What are polygenic traits? Give two examples.

14. Why are polygenic traits said to be continuous?

15. What factors, other than genetics, contribute to phenotypic variation in populations?

16. What is meant by saying that in a pedigree recessive traits "skip" generations?

17. Why are males much more commonly affected by X-linked recessive traits? What is meant by the term *hemizygous*?

18. Construct a pedigree for an autosomal dominant trait, and carefully explain what basic principles you followed.

Contents

Principles of Evolution

That it shall be unlawful for any teacher in any of the universities, normals and all other public schools of the State . . . to teach any theory that denies the story of the Divine Creation of man as taught in the Bible, and to teach instead that man has descended from a lower order of animals (Section 1 of the Butler Act, March 21, 1925, State of Tennessee).

In May, 1925, several leading citizens from Dayton,Tennessee (population 1,800), were sitting around Doc Robinson's drugstore, the town's social center, discussing various and sundry topics of great import. To settle an argument, they sent for John T. Scopes, a local high school coach and teacher of algebra, physics, and chemistry. Scopes came over from his tennis game not realizing that he was about to enter the most dramatic period of his life, one he would never forget.

One of the men, a local businessman, said, "John, we've been arguing, and I said that nobody could teach biology without teaching evolution."

"That's right," said Scopes, and showed them the biology textbook that had been adopted by the state of Tennessee.

"Then, you've been violating the law," Doc Robinson said.

Although he did not teach biology, Scopes had, one day in April, substituted for the principal, who did. Technically, therefore, it could be said that he had taught biology and had thus violated the newly passed law.

As the discussion continued, and it became clear that Scopes felt strongly on the matter of academic freedom, Robinson asked him whether he would stand for a test case. Scopes said he would, whereupon Robinson called the *Chattanooga News* and reported, "This is F. E. Robinson in Dayton. I'm chairman of the school board here. We've just arrested a man for teaching evolution." The man who had been "arrested" finished his soft drink and returned to his tennis game. (Writing forty years later in 1967, Scopes suggested that the trial was deliberately planned by Dayton businessmen to put that town on the map and bring in business, which is precisely what happened.)

The "arrest" made front page news across the country. William Jennings Bryan—three times Democratic nominee for President, Secretary of State under Woodrow Wilson, famous for his Cross of Gold speech at the Democratic convention of 1896, and acknowledged leader of the crusade against Darwinism—offered his services to the prosecution as the representative of the World Christian Fundamentals Association.

With Bryan's entry into the fray, Clarence Darrow, nationally known labor and criminal lawyer, offered his services to the defense without fee or expense. The American Civil Liberties Union was in charge of the case for the defense and provided other well-known lawyers: John Randolph Neal, Arthur Garfield Hayes, and Dudley Field Malone.

In the weeks before the trial, the town of Dayton took on the atmosphere of a circus. The trial was referred to as "the monkey business." Merchants used monkey motifs in their advertising: little cotton apes were featured in store windows; pins that read "Your Old Man's a Monkey" could be purchased; and at Doc Robinson's drugstore, a monkey fizz was available for refreshment from the summer heat. Hot dog stands, lemonade peddlers, booths selling books on biology or religion, and Bryan's truck, equipped with a loudspeaker touting Florida real estate, all added spice and noise to the carnival.

The trial began on Friday, July 10, 1925, with Judge John T. Raulston on the bench, and ended on Tuesday, July 21. It was clear from the start that Scopes would be convicted. The court, strongly religious, consistently favored the prosecution and forbade the testimony of expert defense witnesses—scientists—who were prepared to prove that evolution was a valid scientific concept. The prosecution insisted that the trial was not about the validity of evolution but that the real issue was simply whether or not Scopes had violated the law.

There were magnificent speeches. On Monday, July 13, in his support of the motion to quash the indictment against Scopes, Darrow displayed his famous forensic ability, and the crowded courthouse hung on every word. If the teaching of evolution is outlawed, he argued, then:

After a while, Your Honor, it is the setting of man against man and creed against creed until with flying banners and beating drums we are marching backward to the glorious age of the sixteenth century when bigots lighted faggots to burn the men who dared to bring any intelligence and enlightenment and culture to the human mind.

On Thursday, Bryan stood up to speak against the admissibility of scientific testimony. The crowd had been waiting for this moment, but they were to be disappointed. Bryan was an old man, not the man he once was; the fire was missing. H. L. Mencken, the acidulous reporter from the *Baltimore Sun*, attended the trial and wrote:

His . . . speech was a grotesque performance and downright touching in its imbecility. Its climax came when he launched into a furious denunciation of the doctrine that man is a mammal. It seemed a sheer impossibility that any literate man should stand up in public and discharge any such nonsense. Yet the poor old fellow did it. . . . To call man mammal, it appeared, was to flout the revelation of God (Tompkins, 1965, p. 48).

Malone replied to Bryan, his former superior officer at the State Department, and his eloquence carried the day even among the spectators who fully supported Bryan. Bryan himself recognized this when he told Malone afterwards, "Dudley, that was the greatest speech I have ever heard."

The climax of the trial came on Monday afternoon, July 20, when the defense called Bryan as an expert witness on the Bible. The prosecutors immediately jumped to their feet protesting, aware of the danger inherent in the questions that might be asked and the answers that might be given. However, Bryan himself insisted on testifying, perhaps because he felt compelled to defend the Bible and "show up" the evolutionists. It was an opportunity not to be missed.

Darrow's strategy was to question Bryan about his literal interpretation of the Bible. The Bible, Bryan held, was true, every word of it, every comma. Every miracle recorded in the Bible actually happened. And it was on these points that Darrow broke Bryan, made him appear foolish, unthinking, and even a "traitor" to the cause of fundamentalism. At one point Darrow asked, "Do you think the earth was made in six days?"

"Not in six days of twenty-four hours," Bryan replied.

The crowd gasped at this heresy. The Bible read six days, and a day was obviously twenty-four hours. What was Bryan thinking of? Toward the end of the afternoon Darrow brought up the Bible story of Adam and Eve and the serpent. Had God punished the serpent by making him crawl on his belly? Bryan said he believed that. Then, Darrow asked, "Have you any idea how the snake went before that time?"

"No, sir."

"Do you know whether he walked on his tail or not?"

"No, sir, I have no way to know."

The crowd laughed and Bryan's hands nervously trembled and his lips quivered.*

The trial ended the next day. The jury (excused for most of the trial) was called back and charged to decide whether Scopes had violated the law; no other question was to be considered. The jury took but a short time and returned with their verdict—guilty! Judge Raulston fined Scopes $100 and the trial closed.

The case was appealed to the Tennessee Supreme Court, which handed down its decision on January 15, 1927. The Court upheld the Butler Act and also recommended that the state drop the indictment against Scopes on the technicality that the judge had imposed the fine, instead of the jury, as Tennessee law required. The Court thus made it impossible to appeal the case before the United States Supreme Court.

In the more than sixty years since the Scopes trial, religious fundamentalists have not ceased their attempts to remove the teaching of evolution from the public schools of the nation. Known as "creationists" because they explain the existence of the universe, energy, and life as a result of sudden creation, they are determined either to eliminate the teaching of evolution or to introduce anti-evolutionary subject matter. In a ploy developed in recent years, creationists have insisted that "creation-science" is just as much science as what they term "evolution-science." Therefore, they claim, in the interest of fair play, a balanced view should be offered to students— if evolution is taught as science, then creationism should also be taught as science.

So-called "creation-science" is not science as we know it.† Far from the spirit of science, creationists, for

---

*A diabetic and in ill health, Bryan died on Sunday, July 26, five days after the trial ended.

†See Niles Eldridge, "Creationism Isn't Science," *The New Republic*, April 14, 1981, pp. 15–20.

instance, assert that their position is absolute and not subject to error. Therefore, it is impossible for any sort of evidence to alter their position, for anything that might modify creationism is automatically rejected.

Creationists have been active in state legislatures, promoting the passage of laws mandating the inclusion of creationism in school curricula wherever evolution is taught. To this effect, creationists successfully lobbied the legislature of the state of Arkansas, which passed Act 590 in March of 1981.

The law was challenged and, on January 5, 1982, Judge William Ray Overton ruled against the state of Arkansas. He found that "creation science has no scientific merit or education value," that *"a theory that is by its own terms dogmatic, absolutist and never subject to revision is not a scientific theory"* (emphasis added), and that "since creation is not science, the conclusion is inescapable that the only real effect of Act 590 is the advancement of religion."

On June 19, 1987, the United States Supreme Court struck down (by a vote of seven to two) a Louisiana law that required the teaching of creationism if the concept of evolution were taught. The Court stated that the Louisiana law was enacted to clearly advance a religious purpose and was therefore unconstitutional.

Creationists continue their efforts to prevent the teaching of evolution in public schools and to introduce creationism as science. New approaches are being used, however, since the Supreme Court has ruled against laws mandating "equal time" for creation and evolution. One approach is for creationist teachers to claim "academic freedom" to teach creationism as science. These attempts have not been successful thus far. In 1990, a junior high school teacher in northern Illinois sued his superintendent for his "right" to teach creationism, and lost. In 1992, a high school biology teacher in California sued his district in an almost identical case, and also lost.

Because the Supreme Court decision was decided on the First Amendment grounds of the separation of church and state, another tact being tried is to avoid the use of the term "creationism" and substitute euphemisms that sound less religious. Currently, creationists are fighting evolution by promoting the teaching of "intelligent design theory" or "abrupt appearance theory." Another approach is to teach creationism ideas as "alternatives to evolution," or "evidence against evolution." From a scientific standpoint, there is no dispute about whether evolution occurred, though there is lively debate over how it occurred and through what mechanisms.

A larger problem than the teaching of creation "science" is the avoidance of evolution by teachers who seek to escape "controversy." In this situation, teachers advance neither theory, and students are left knowing nothing about evolution, one of the most important and influential of all scientific concepts.*

---

*For further information about the creation/evolution controversy, contact The National Center for Science Education, Inc., Box 9477, Berkeley, CA 94709–0477.

Introduction

The central focus of physical anthropology is the study of evolution. Fundamental to understanding the *process* of evolution is precise knowledge of evolutionary *theory*; that is, how the process works. In this chapter, we trace the development of evolutionary thought from its early beginnings to its present scientific principles.

Probably no other single factor has so influenced modern civilization in the last 500 years than the development of science as a way of understanding the universe and its component parts.

Science began its modern course in the sixteenth century with the realization that the universe was not rigidly fixed. Scientists learned that the earth is not the center of the universe; they also learned to predict the action of stars and other celestial bodies, the organization of matter, and the relationship of matter and energy. During this period, a greater scientific understanding developed regarding the organic forms that inhabit our planet, how they are related, and how they came to be.

This understanding is based entirely on the process of evolutionary change and a *consistent* theory to explain its mechanisms. This chapter details how the theory was developed and how it is used today. The remainder of this text is a practical application of evolutionary theory, specifically aimed at understanding the human organism.

The Path to Natural Selection

Charles Darwin did not arrive at his theory of evolution, published in 1859, without assistance. Looking at the intellectual climate of Europe of the Middle Ages, we find that Christianity was associated with certain views of the universe. Since the time of Ptolemy, a Greco-Egyptian mathematician, geographer, and astronomer of the second century A.D., the earth had been placed at the center of the universe, with spheres that revolved around it in perfect regularity. Similarly, the organic world was seen as stable and unchanging. It was widely believed in the Middle Ages that all species on earth had been created (according to Genesis of the Old Testament) on a progression from the simplest living forms to the most complex—humans. This progression was not evolutionary; that is, one species did not lead to or evolve into the next. The forms and sequence were permanent, each species forever linked to the next in a great chain of beings. No creatures had appeared since creation, and none had disappeared.

This progression was known as the Great Chain of Being, a belief held by Aristotle, and the plan of the entire universe was seen as the grand design; that is, God's Design. The limbs of humans and animals seemed designed to meet the purpose for which they were required. The wings of birds, the talons of eagles, the hoofs of horses, etc., all these structures were interpreted as neatly fitting the functions they were intended to perform. It was considered to be a deliberate plan of the "Grand Designer." The Grand Designer concept was supported by what is known as the "argument from design," which was stated by John Ray, one of the leading naturalists of the sixteenth century. Following is a shortened version in somewhat modern English:

> If works of art, designed for a certain purpose, infer the existence of an intelligent Architect or Engineer, then why should not Nature, which transcends human art, infer the existence of an Omnipotent and Allwise Creator?

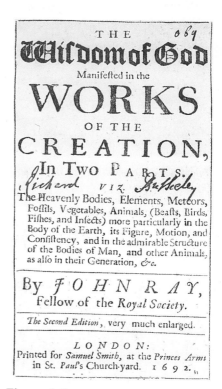

THE 064

Wisdom of God

Manifested in the

WORKS

OF THE

CREATION,

In Two PARTS.

Richard VIZ. *Sutteeley*

The Heavenly Bodies, Elements, Meteors, Foßils, Vegetables, Animals, (Beaßts, Birds, Fißhes, and Inßects) more particularly in the Body of the Earth, its Figure, Motion, and Conßistency, and in the admirable Structure of the Bodies of Man, and other Animals, as alßo in their Generation, &c.

By JOHN RAY,
Fellow of the Royal Society.

The Second Edition, very much enlarged.

LONDON:
Printed for *Samuel Smith*, at the *Princes Arms* in St. *Paul's* Church-yard. 1692.

Figure 4-1

An early (seventeenth century) version of the Argument from Design.

Fixity of species The notion that species, once created, never change. An idea diametrically opposed to theories of biological evolution.

Furthermore, the Grand Designer had completed work in quite a short time, since creation was dated at 4004 B.C. by Archbishop James Ussher (1581–1656), an Irish prelate and scholar, who gleaned the date by analyzing the "begat" chapter of Genesis.*

Until these concepts of **fixity of species** and the short timeframe were changed, it would be very unlikely that the idea of natural selection could be conceived. What, then, upset the Medieval belief in a rigid universe of planets, stars, plants, and animals? What scientific philosophy would, within the following 150 years, strike a death blow to the whole Medieval system of thought? How would the scientific method as we know it today develop and, especially with Newton and Galileo in the seventeenth century, demonstrate a moving, not unchanging, universe?

The Scientific Revolution

The change might be said to begin in the sixteenth century when Copernicus, a Polish cleric and astronomer, wrote a treatise on Ptolemy's ancient system. In it, he noted that earth, rotating on its axis, revolved around a fixed sun, not vice versa. This heresy attracted little attention at the time, but it was picked up almost a century later by the German astrologer/astronomer Johannes Kepler. Kepler, like Copernicus, was interested in motion, and formulated three laws of planetary motion that influenced later scientists.

In Italy, Galileo, a contemporary of Kepler, reintroduced Copernicus' heliocentric (sun-centered) theory and was largely responsible for making the basic law of motion a general feature of seventeenth-century science.

The seventeenth century was a beehive of scientific activity, a unique period of exceptional scholars with remarkable insights whose thinking ended almost 2000 years of dependence on the earth-centered Aristotelian view of the universe and set on course the methodology of modern science. Francis Bacon emphasized both the use of the inductive method and the need for experiment with careful, detailed observation. René Descartes contributed a new method of mathematics and also established a mechanical philosophy: bodies were explained in terms of their material composition; the *purpose* of an object or being could no longer be used scientifically as an *explanation of its form or behavior*. Teleology—the notion that the structures of organic beings were formed for specific purposes—was out, as far as science was concerned.

Probably the greatest of the seventeenth-century thinkers was the English physicist Isaac Newton. His achievements included the reorganization of the calculus, the application of mathematics to physics and astronomy, the formulation of three laws of motion, the creation of the field of optics (theory of light and color), and perhaps, most importantly, the Law of Universal Gravity.

Scientists of the seventeenth century developed methods and theories that revolutionized scientific thought and produced the foundation of modern science. They gave the intellectual milieu of their era a definite naturalistic

Figure 4-2

Nicolaus Copernicus (1473–1543), Polish astronomer whose work formed the foundation of modern astronomy.

---

*John Lightfoot, vice-chancellor of Cambridge University, declared that the final act by which man was created took place at nine o'clock on the morning of Sunday, October 23, 4004 B.C. (Bowler, 1988, p. 4). It has been said that Lightfoot chose that date because the fall term at Cambridge started on Sunday, October 23, at 9 o'clock.

basis. While still a significant factor in scientific thinking, God was being viewed increasingly as a superfluous factor in a more naturalistic view of the universe. It was becoming possible to investigate the stars, planets, animals, and plants without reference to the supernatural. The image of a static universe was challenged; nature was seen as a mechanism, functioning according to certain physical laws, and it was these laws that scientists sought to identify.

The work of naturalists of this period reflects a modern biological approach. They collected, classified, and described; they upset ancient notions and exploded old fables. Like other scientists, they adopted the mechanical model of nature to explain organic function.

The erosion of the concept of God as the center of scientific and philosophic thought continued into the eighteenth century. For some thinkers, known as materialists, nature was the sole reality, and they challenged the argument from design. For materialists,

> Everything we see in the world must be a chance product of the ceaseless activity of material nature, including the various living species and man himself. Fixed species . . . represented vestiges of the old creationist myth . . . (Bowler, 1989, p. 77).

Although materialists were seen as radicals, the trend of scientific thought continued in the direction of secularism. Inevitably, it turned toward the study of humankind, and human nature became the center of science. As Alexander Pope wrote in his famous couplet of the 1730s:

> *Know then thyself, presume not God to scan;*
> *The proper study of Mankind is Man.*

Secularization among scientists continued in the eighteenth century, a period known as the Enlightenment, but it is ironic that a Christian belief—that the order and design of the universe could be interpreted by rational minds—led to Darwin's ideas regarding natural selection. In the seventeenth century, there was an overwhelming thrust by philosopher/scientists toward examining nature in all its aspects. Thus diligently studying natural relationships was not considered an irreverent exercise, but a human duty, since such study would demonstrate the majesty and glory of God:

> It is surely one of the curious paradoxes of history that science, which professionally has little to do with faith, owes its origins to an act of faith that the universe can be rationally interpreted, and that science today is sustained by that assumption (Eiseley, 1958, p. 62).

Charles Darwin, in the nineteenth century, was heir to the thinking and ideas of these earlier naturalists and philosophers. The radical change in the intellectual climate of the seventeenth century enabled scientists of the following century to think about the universe in a manner that made the idea of evolution possible, and paved the way for Darwin (and also Wallace—see pp. 87–88).

LINNAEUS

The course to a consistent evolutionary theory was not an easy one. The notion of the fixity of species held sway among the public, as well as among most scientists. One such scientist, a leading naturalist of his day, was **Carolus Linnaeus** (1707–1778), who is best known for developing a classification system for plants and animals. First published in 1735, the system isolated

Figure 4-3

Isaac Newton, probably best known for his law concerning gravitation.

Figure 4-4

Linnaeus developed a classification system for plants and animals, and a binomial system of two names—genus and species.

Table 4-1 Examples of Linnaeus' Binomial System

Genus*	Species
Homo	sapiens
Pan	troglodytes (common chimpanzee
Gorilla	gorilla (gorilla)
Rosa	setigera (prairie rose)

*It is customary to italicize both genus and species and to capitalize genus but use lowercase for species. Genus is often indicated by the first letter, capitalized, followed by a period. Thus, *H. sapiens*.

those particular physical traits that best characterized a particular group of organisms. In plants, for instance, he used blossoms; in insects, wings; and, in fish, scales. He even included humans in his classification of animals, defying the contemporary thought that humans, made in God's image, should be considered separately, outside the animal kingdom.

Linnaeus also assigned names to animals and plants, using the simple but effective idea of assigning two Latin names to each organism. The first word was the generic term (the genus) for the organism and the second word was the specific term (the species). Thus, two words together would become a unit internationally recognized as the name for that particular form. This system of binomial (or binominal) nomenclature was widely accepted and is still in use today (see Table 4-1).

In his ideas about evolution, Linnaeus reflected the scientific thought of his time. He saw nature as a "rationally ordained system of means and ends." That is, every living thing is created perfectly adapted to the environment in which it lives. Although some scientists by this time had abandoned the notion of fixity, Linnaeus still adhered to the idea that species, once divinely created, had never changed,* and "to study nature diligently" meant assigning to every living thing its proper name.

However, there were other voices, especially in France, raised loud and clear in favor of a universe based on change and, much more to the point, of the relationship between similar forms based on descent from a common ancestor.

BUFFON

The leading advocate of this point of view was George Louis Leclerc, better known as **Count Buffon** (1707–1788). Buffon recognized the dynamic relationship of environment and nature. He was convinced that different species could develop from a common ancestor that divided into two or more groups through migration to different areas of the world. Each group was then influenced by local climatic conditions and gradually changed form. But Buffon did not believe in what he called "the transformation of species."

Buffon emphasized the variety and minute gradations of nature, which he explained in terms of "a system of laws, elements and forces." Thus, nature could be seen as functioning by *natural* means rather than through a divine mind. Buffon considered it important to see life as a dynamic system of processes instead of a static structure. He felt that the true aim of natural history was to discover and understand these processes, not simply to classify (as Linnaeus taught) their result.

Figure 4-5

Buffon recognized the influence of the environment on life forms.

ERASMUS DARWIN

In this period of the popularization of science (which saw the beginnings of archeology and the recognition that fossil bones belonged to species of animals since perished), we must take notice of a most interesting figure who saw clearly the force of evolutionary ideas.

Erasmus Darwin (1731–1802), the grandfather of Charles Darwin, was a country physician, poet, and versatile scientist. More than fifty years before his grandson was to startle Europe with his views on natural selection,

---

*In later life, Linnaeus suggested that the multiplicity of organisms had arisen through hybridization.

Erasmus had expressed such ideas as "evolution by natural and sexual selection, protective adaptation, inheritance of acquired characteristics, and even the evolution of mankind" (Francoeuer, 1965, p. 68).

Contrasting the ideas of Linnaeus with those of Buffon and Erasmus Darwin reflects on both old and new thinking. The concept of immutability of species continued to be the dominant theme among most scientists until the latter years of the eighteenth century when the voluminous writings of Buffon, Erasmus Darwin, and others had spread the ideas of mutability of species and the possibility of unlimited organic change. The doctrine of organic change was not widely accepted, but at least it was being discussed at length in intellectual circles.

Although both Buffon and Erasmus Darwin were thinking in evolutionary terms, neither one codified his beliefs into a comprehensive system. The first European scientist to do so was Jean Baptiste Pierre Antoine de Monet de **Lamarck** (1744–1829).

LAMARCK

Lamarck, unlike his predecessors, was the first major proponent of the idea of organic evolution. Earlier scholars, including Erasmus Darwin, believed in the transmutation or transformation of one species to another, but Lamarck organized his views into a system that attempted to explain how it all happened.

His theory of organic development, or evolution

> was set in the context of a **uniformitarian** geology that provided the vast expanses of time necessary for imperceptibly small changes to produce over countless generations all the different forms of life on earth (Burkhardt, 1984, p. xxiii).

Lamarck also provided a method for the origin of *new* species based on the laws of *use and disuse* of organs:

> *First law*: The more frequent and continuous use of any organ strengthens, develops, and enlarges that organ; while the permanent disuse of any organ imperceptibly weakens and deteriorates it until it finally disappears.

> *Second law*: All the acquisitions or losses wrought by nature through the *influence of the environment* are preserved by reproduction (Lamarck, *Zoological Philosophy*, 1809, 1984, p. 113). (Emphasis added.)

Thus, the permanent disuse of an organ, arising from a change of habits, causes the disappearance and even the extinction of that organ; conversely, the frequent use of any organ, when confirmed by habit, leads to its development. Applying this insight to humans, Lamarck suggested that

> if some race of *quadrumanous* [four-handed] animals were to lose the habit of climbing trees and grasping the branches with feet; and if the individuals of this race were forced for a series of generations to use their feet only for walking, there is no doubt that these quadrumanous animals would at length be transformed into *bimanous* [two-handed animals], and that the thumbs on their feet would cease to be separated from the other digits . . . (Lamarck, *Zoological Philosophy*, 1809, 1984, p. 170).*

Lamarck considered wish, desire, will, and needs as ways in which change could be motivated. More important, however, were the animal's habits,

---
*This paragraph is slightly abridged.

Figure 4-6

Erasmus Darwin, an early believer in evolution.

Figure 4-7

Lamarck believed that evolution occurred when new organs developed in adapting to a changing environment.

Uniformitarian   Also called uniformitarianism. The view that the same processes shaping the earth's surface today have also acted in the past. (See p. 83.)

which could effectively initiate change through the movements of invisible fluids, especially heat and electricity. Little by little, as habits altered the fluids' pathways, the body's form would change.

According to Lamarck, when the environment changes, there is an alteration in the needs (wishes, desires) of animals that necessitates new activities (habits). The animal is then required to use some of its organs more frequently or to make use of entirely new organs developed by the fluids. The altered organs (or the new ones) will then be passed on through heredity to the next generation and, in time, new species and more complex species will arise.

Unfortunately, motivation by needs or the actions of fluids, as Lamarck described them, is not supported by evidence. Nor can his notion of how traits are inherited—what is called the **inheritance of acquired characteristics**—be scientifically supported. As we discussed in Chapter 3, with the rediscovery of Mendel's principles (in 1900) and the development of the modern science of genetics, we know that it is impossible to have acquired characteristics passed to offspring. Furthermore, as discussed in Chapter 2, the *somatic* cell line is completely separate from the *sex* cell line. Only those genetic changes (that is, structural changes to the DNA itself) that are contained in the gametes will be transmitted to the next generation. All of the modifications of somatic tissues, such as muscle development through exercise, obviously do *not* get passed on. Despite popular misunderstanding from the time of Lamarck to this day, science is unequivocal on this point.

In fairness to Lamarck, it should be mentioned that the belief in the inheritance of acquired characteristics was so widespread in the scientific community of his day that Lamarck did not feel a need to prove it.

Lamarck developed a detailed system to account for the acquisition of new traits, how they could be transmitted, and how the environment dynamically interacted with organic forms. He brought together vast quantities of materials to support his evolutionary ideas, carrying them beyond those of his mentor, Buffon. Ernst Heinrich Haeckel, a well-known scientist of the late nineteenth century, said that to Lamarck will always belong the immortal glory of having for the first time

> worked out the Theory of Descent as an independent scientific theory of the first order, and as the philosophical foundation of the whole science of Biology (Clodd, 1897, p. 115).

On the other hand, Lamarck

> was unable to relate his broad hypotheses to factual evidence in such a way as to cause his contemporaries to treat his hypotheses as profound insights rather than unfounded speculations (Burkhardt, 1984, p. xvi).

Lamarck was Darwin's only genuine precursor, and the world of science (especially biology) owes him a great debt.

An opponent of Lamarck and evolution was **George Cuvier**, known as the father of zoology. Cuvier proposed the concept of *catastrophism*, an hypothesis based on the assumption of a series of violent and sudden catastrophes.* Areas of the world were destroyed and then restocked from unaffected neighboring areas. Like Lamarck's system, catastrophism lacks evidence and is not scientifically acceptable.

Inheritance of acquired characteristics The theory that traits acquired by an individual during its lifetime are passed on to offspring. As demonstrated by modern genetics, this idea is now known to be invalid.

Figure 4-8

Cuvier explained species change by catastrophic destruction and the creation of new species.

---

*A recent school of thought suggests that evolution can occur with sudden and rapid change. This idea (quite different from catastrophism) is known as "punctuated equilibrium" and is discussed on p. 187. Cuvier's catastrophism had no religious basis. Many creationists today mistakenly use catastrophism to support their position.

MALTHUS

Thomas Robert Malthus (1766–1834) was an English clergyman, political economist, and devotee of the natural sciences. His *An Essay on the Principle of Population* was to become a standard consulted by politicians dealing with population problems as well as a source of inspiration to both Charles Darwin and Alfred Russel Wallace (see p. 87) in their independent discovery of the principle of natural selection.

In his *Essay*, Malthus points out that if human population growth is unrestrained by natural causes, it will double every 25 years, but that the capacity for food production increases only in a straight arithmetic progression. In nature, Malthus noted, the impulse to multiply was checked by the *struggle for existence*, but humans had to apply artificial restraints. It is interesting that, in England, the middle class accepted Malthus' dire prediction of population growth and supported efforts to decrease the birth rate of the poor.

From an evolutionary point of view, it was Malthus' phrase, the "struggle for existence" that provided Charles Darwin, in 1838, with the key to the process of *natural selection* (see p. 86).

LYELL

Charles Lyell (1797–1875), the son of Scottish landowners, is considered the founder of modern geology. He was a barrister by training, a geologist by avocation, and, for many years, Charles Darwin's mentor. Before he met Darwin in 1836, Lyell had earned wide popular acclaim as well as acceptance in Europe's most prestigious scientific circles, thanks to his highly praised *Principles of Geology*, published in three volumes beginning in 1830.

In this immensely important work, Lyell argued that the geological processes observed in the present are the same as those that obtained in the past. This theory, which has come to be termed *uniformitarianism* (see p. 81), did not completely originate with Lyell. It had been proposed by another Scotsman, James Hutton, in the late 1700s, and, as we have seen, was also alluded to by Lamarck. Nevertheless, it was Lyell who convincingly demonstrated that such forces as wind, water erosion, periodic local flooding, frost, the decomposition of vegetable matter, volcanoes, earthquakes, and glacial movements all had contributed in the past to produce the geological landscape that exists in the present. Moreover, the fact that these processes could still be observed in operation indicated that geological change continued to occur, and that the forces that drove such change were uniform over time. In other words, although various aspects of the earth's surface (for example, climate, flora, fauna, and land surfaces) are variable through time, the underlying *processes* that influence them are constant.

The theory of uniformitarianism flew in the face of prevailing views of catastrophism and did not go unopposed. Moreover, and every bit as controversial, Lyell emphasized the obvious: namely, that in order for such slow-acting forces to produce momentous change, the earth must indeed be far older than anyone had previously suspected.

By providing an immense time scale and thereby altering perceptions of earth's history from a mere few thousand years to many millions of years, Lyell changed the framework within which scientists viewed the geological past. Thus, the concept of "deep time" (Gould, 1987) remains as one of Lyell's most significant contributions. This concept, coupled with theories of uniform processes, was to have a profound effect upon eighteenth-century scientific thinking and was to influence Charles Darwin tremendously as he

Figure 4-9

Thomas Malthus' essay led both Charles Darwin and Alfred Russel Wallace to a solution of the evolutionary process.

Figure 4-10

Sir Charles Lyell was a good friend and supporter of Darwin. It was from Lyell's Principles of Geology *that Darwin learned of uniformitarianism.*

wrestled with the question of biological evolution. The immensity of geological time permitted the necessary time depth for the inherently slow process of biological change.

Upon his death in 1875, and in recognition of his tremendous contributions to science, Lyell was buried in Westminster Abbey, an honor awarded only to the very select. Not only had he revolutionized the science of geology, he had also, albeit unintentionally, laid the foundation upon which concrete theories of biological evolution could be laid.

CHARLES DARWIN

Early Years   **Charles Darwin** (1809–1882), born on the same day and year as Abraham Lincoln, was the last of six children. His father, Robert, was a well-known physician, and his mother, Susannah, was the daughter of Joseph Wedgewood, of Wedgewood pottery fame. The family was well off and of the gentry class.

Darwin's boyhood was characteristic of many sons of his class in England, and he did the usual things (collecting shells, stamps, coins), but at school he displayed no special inclination for scholarship.

At age 16, Darwin accompanied his father on his rounds and seemed to enjoy the experience. This persuaded Robert Darwin to select a medical career for Charles, and he made plans to send him to Edinburgh University, the school that he and his father (Erasmus) had attended.

Darwin spent two fruitful years at Edinburgh, more interested in the natural sciences than medicine, which he loathed:

> During a particularly bad operation on a child, Darwin finally fled the room, unable to watch, and determined never again to enter an operating theater (Desmond and Moore, 1991, p. 27).

Disappointed, Robert Darwin decided that a country parsonage would suit his son since it was a profession that would allow him plenty of time to follow his interest in the natural sciences.

In 1828, Darwin, accepting his father's decision to become a clergyman, matriculated at Christ College, Cambridge. Although Darwin looked forward to becoming an Anglican cleric, field trips with J. S. Henslow, botany professor and good friend, developed his interest in plants, and his meetings with Professor Sedgewick, an eminent geologist, attracted his attention to that field, an attraction that lasted a lifetime.

Darwin was 22 when he graduated in 1832 with his divinity degree, and could look forward to a serene future as a country parson. However, that was not to be, for a letter from Professor Henslow that summer drastically changed his future.

Henslow wrote that he had recommended Darwin as the best-qualified person he knew for the position of naturalist on a scientific expedition that would chart the coast lines of South America and go on to circle the globe. Darwin was willing, even eager, for the opportunity to combine travel with the pursuit of botany, geology, and zoology. His father reluctantly gave his permission.

Darwin learned that the ship on which he would travel was the HMS *Beagle,* under the command of Captain Robert FitzRoy, who was not so much interested in taking on a naturalist as having on board ship a person he could relate to—talk to, eat with—as a friend. Darwin filled the bill nicely and was given the position of naturalist.

On December 27, 1831, Darwin set sail on a voyage that would take 5 years, where attacks of seasickness would place him in his hammock for days

Figure 4-11

Charles Darwin.

on end. Satisfied to be a country parson before the ship sailed, Darwin soon found that his true calling was natural science. Through his fossil collecting and diligent work of arranging and dissecting specimens he collected, Darwin matured from an amateur observer to a professional naturalist with doubts about the fixity of species.

As early as 1832, he noted in his diary that a snake with rudimentary hind limbs marked "the passage by which Nature joins lizards to the snakes." He came across fossils of ancient giant animals that looked, except for size, very much like forms living in the same vicinity, and wondered whether the fossils were the *ancestors* of those forms. He observed that the Andean Mountain Range constituted a natural barrier to life, and different flora and fauna were found on opposite sides of the range.

Darwin's visit to the Galápagos Islands, off the west coast of South America (see Fig. 4-12) was to become a crucial factor in his thinking on evolution. He noted that the flora and fauna of South America were similar, as if related, to those of the Galápagos Islands, yet different enough so that they were not the same. More surprising, the inhabitants of the various islands differed slightly from one another. He learned from John Gould, an ornithologist, after his return to England, that the finches on the 13 islands that resembled one another in the structure of their beaks, body form, and plumage were not merely varieties. Despite the fact that few geographic differences existed among the islands, the finches constituted separate species—but only one species existed on the mainland!

This abbreviated account of Darwin and his research on the *Beagle* does not do justice to the vital role the voyage played in Darwin's intellectual growth. He returned to England on board the *Beagle* on October 2, 1836 (just short of 5 years from the date he sailed), a more mature and serious scientist.

Figure 4-12

The route of the HMS Beagle.

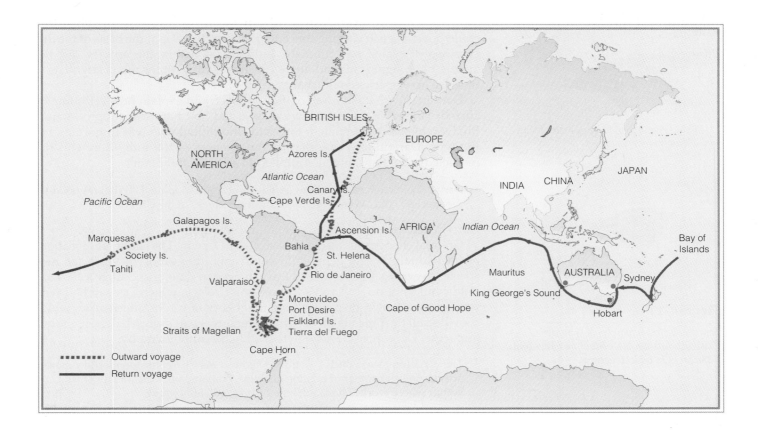

After visiting with family and friends, Darwin started work on the material he brought back from the voyage. In January, 1839, Darwin married his cousin, Emma Wedgewood, and moved to the village of Downe, about 15 miles southeast of London, where he and Emma lived for the rest of their lives.

Before moving from London, Darwin had already begun distributing his collection of animals, plants, and fossils to various scientists for analysis. To ornithologist John Gould he gave the birds from the Galápagos Islands. Shortly thereafter, in March, 1837, Gould informed Darwin that the three mockingbirds he was given came from three different islands. As with the just-noted example of the finches, the mockingbirds were not varieties as Darwin thought, but three different species! If this were true (and Gould insisted it was), Darwin could only conclude that when groups of a species are geographically separated, the separate groups develop *gradually* into separate species, an example of *evolution by common descent*.

In July of the same year, Darwin began a notebook on *transmutation*—the gradual change from one species to another. On September 28, 1838, 15 months after he started the "transmutation" notebook (Darwin wrote in his autobiography in 1858):

> I happened to read for amusement Malthus on Population, and being well prepared to appreciate the struggle for existence which everywhere goes on . . . it at once struck me that under these circumstances favourable variations would tend to be preserved, and unfavourable ones to be destroyed. The result of this would be *the formation of a new species*. Here, then, I had at last got a theory by which to work. (Emphasis added.)

Darwin deduced from Malthus that *individuals* with favorable variations were the ones who would survive to reproduce, those with unfavorable variations would not.

Before Darwin, scientists considered species as an entity—a type—that could not change. It was the concept of species that was at the basis of the discussions of plants and animals. Individuals within the species did not appear to be significant and, therefore, it was difficult for many scientists to imagine how species could change.

Darwin saw that variation of individuals could explain how selection occurred. Favorable variations were "selected" by nature for reproduction; unfavorable were eliminated. It was the individual who was important, not the type. Darwin also saw that the uniqueness of the individual was not restricted to humans, but also applied to animals and plants:

> Darwin no longer asked, as had [scientists and philosophers], "What is good for the species?" but "What is good for the individual?" (Ghiselin, 1969).

Darwin had formed his theory of natural selection.

Gradual change was also emphasized by Darwin. The slight modifications of individuals in one generation could take thousands of years for new species to evolve. For his theory, Darwin needed time, and Ussher's 4004 B.C. date would not do. In Lyell's *Principles of Geology*, which Darwin had read while on the *Beagle*, he came across the theory of uniformitarianism, which provided all the time his theory would require. Lyell's work had tremendous impact on Darwin, as he acknowledged in his autobiography:

> The very first place which I examined showed me clearly the wonderful superiority of Lyell's manner of treating geology compared with that of any other author whose works I have with me or ever read afterwards.

(a) Ground finch
Main food: seeds
Beak: heavy

(b) Tree finch
Main food: leaves, buds, blossoms, fruits
Beak: thick, short, slightly decurved

(c) Tree finch (called woodpecker finch)
Main food: insects
Beak: stout, straight

(d) Ground finch (known as warbler finch)
Main food: insects
Beak: slender

Figure 4-13

Finches' beaks. Examples of some of Darwin's finches. Note the similarities and differences in beak structure.

Figure 4 -14

The Darwin home at Downe where the Origin of Species *was written.*

In 1842 Darwin wrote a short summary of his views on natural selection and revised it in 1844. However, he was reluctant to publish his theory since he knew it would be controversial. He also knew he surely would be subjected to severe criticism.

An event occurred in 1858 that confronted him with a possibility he had always dreaded—that someone would publish his theory of natural selection before he did. Darwin had confided his theories to his good friends and highly respected scientists Sir Charles Lyell, geologist, and Joseph Hooker, botanist. They had encouraged him to publish, but Darwin declined because he believed he needed still more evidence. His friends cautioned him that someone else might publish before he did and, indeed, his friends' warning was realized in June, 1858, when A. R. Wallace sent Darwin his paper on natural selection.

WALLACE

Born 14 years after Darwin and into another social class, **Alfred Russel Wallace** (1823–1913) nevertheless reached the same key conclusions as his slightly older contemporary. A talented young man interested in collecting, Wallace sailed to the Malayan Archipelago in 1854 to continue his study and collection of bird and insect specimens, and often thought about the puzzle of the succession of species.

In 1858, on the Island of Ternate, just off the coast of the Sulawesi Islands, Wallace was in bed suffering from one of his periodic attacks of fever. Suddenly, the solution to the problem he had so long thought about flashed through his mind. Recalling the phrase "the positive checks to increase" from Malthus' *Essay*, he immediately realized that this phenomenon could apply to animals as well as human beings. Without checks, the earth would quickly be overrun by the most prolific breeders. Why, then, did some species of plants or animals perish while others survived? The answer came at once— the best adapted continued to reproduce; the less well adapted perished. Wallace promptly set his thoughts on paper and sent Darwin his essay, "On the Tendency of Varieties to Depart Indefinitely from the Original Type."

Figure 4 -15

Alfred Russel Wallace independently discovered the key to the evolutionary process.

Wallace accepted his older contemporary's views of evolution, but in the 1860s he developed doubts that natural selection was capable of producing certain characteristics and suggested that humans "do indeed possess a soul capable of existing independent of the body. . . ." His doubts were expressed in a paper entitled "The Limits of Natural Selection as Applied to Man" (Bowler, 1983, 1989, p. 230).

When Darwin read Wallace's paper, he was thoroughly depressed. He wrote Lyell, "Your words have come true with a vengeance—that I should be forestalled" (F. Darwin, 1950, p. 199). Darwin wondered whether it would be honorable to publish his own paper, and decided to let his closest friends, Lyell and Hooker, devise a formula that would be fair to both men. His friends decided that joint reading of papers by Wallace and Darwin should be done at a meeting of the Linnaean Society. Both papers were read on the evening of July 1, 1858, with Wallace in the Far East and Darwin at home where he and his wife were burying their baby child, Charles, who had died a few days earlier, apparently from scarlet fever.

To ensure credit for his theories, Darwin set to work explaining his system and completed the *Origin** within a year, in 1859. With publication the storm broke and has not abated to this day. While there was much praise for his book, there was also severe criticism. Darwin expected skepticism from many scientists, "but he had not anticipated the vehemence with which even the most respected scientists and philosophers would denounce his efforts as not being properly 'scientific'" (Hull, 1973, p. 3). Nevertheless, scientific opinion gradually came to Darwin's support. The species riddle was explained: species were not fixed, but mutable; they evolved from other species through the mechanism of natural selection. Science was never to be the same again.

Darwin's Theory of Evolution

As we have seen, Darwin did not originate the idea of evolution. Ancient Greeks, and more recently Erasmus Darwin, and especially Lamarck, wrote supporting it. Nor were the basic ideas used by Darwin completely his own invention. Struggle for existence, extinction of species, variation, adaptation—these were all known and discussed for years by many European scientists. Darwin's great contribution was bringing these divergent ideas together and adding the key idea of natural selection.

In *The Origin of Species*, Darwin explained his concept of evolution, emphasizing the following points:

1. All species are capable of producing offspring faster than the food supply increases.
2. All living things show variations; no two individuals of a species are alike.
3. Because the population grows faster than the food supply, there are more individuals than can possibly survive; there is a fierce struggle for existence and those with one or more favorable variations in size, strength, running ability, etc., will have a better chance to survive and reproduce.
4. These favorable variations are inherited and passed on to the next generation.

---

*The complete title of Darwin's book is *On the Origin of Species by Means of Natural Selection, or the Preservation of Favoured Races in the Struggle for Life.*

5. Over long periods of geologic time, the successful variations produce great differences that result in new species.

According to Ernst Mayr (1991, pp. 36–37) Darwin's evolutionary theory actually consisted of five major theories (listed below) and several minor theories (please note that a few terms used here will be explained later in the chapter):

1. *Evolution as such*   The world is not constant, not recently created, but changes steadily and organisms are transformed over time.
2. *Common descent*   Every group of organisms—including animals, plants, and microorganisms—descended from a common ancestor, and can ultimately be traced back to a single origin of life.
3. *Multiplication of species*   Species multiply either by splitting into daughter species or by "budding"; that is, geographically isolated founder populations may evolve into new species.*
4. *Gradualism*   Gradual change of populations produces evolutionary changes, not the sudden appearance of a new type (but see Punctuated Equilibrium, p. 187).
5. *Natural selection*   Evolutionary change is possible because of the abundant variation present in every generation. Because they possess a well-adapted combination of heritable characters, the relatively few survivors give rise to the next generation. (Several examples of how the process operates, especially in humans, are presented later in this chapter.)

Darwin's evolutionary theory (or theories) challenged deeply held beliefs of Victorian England. It is not surprising that Darwin hesitated to publish his views that people—especially many of his friends—would consider antisocial (even unscientific) and lead to dangerous social and political thinking. He challenged:

1. belief in a constant world
2. belief in a created world
3. belief in a divine grand design
4. belief in a created unique position of humans (Mayr, 1991, p. 38)

Darwin changed the way scientists looked at the world, and his theories of evolution have been accepted by almost all biological scientists. The evidence he brought forward to support his concept of evolution has, for the most part, held up for almost 150 years. However, he was not correct in everything he suggested. Some of the problems with his formulations are discussed in the next section.

Darwin's Failures

Darwin argued eloquently for the notion of evolution in general and the role of natural selection in particular, but he did not entirely comprehend inheritance and the mechanism maintaining variation.

As we have seen, natural selection acts on *variation* within species. Neither Darwin, nor anyone else in the nineteenth century, understood the source of

---

*Geographical speciation has not been discussed in the text, but the concept is not a difficult one. ". . . new species may originate by the gradual genetic transformation of isolated populations. These isolated populations become in the course of time geographic races or subspecies" (Mayr, 1991, p. 20) and, ultimately, if isolated sufficiently long, may become new species.

all this variation. Consequently, Darwin speculated about variation arising from "use"—an idea similar to Lamarck's. Darwin, however, was not as dogmatic in his views as Lamarck, and most emphatically argued against inner "needs" or "effort." Darwin had to confess that when it came to explaining variation, he simply did not know:

> Our ignorance of the laws of variation is profound. Not in one case out of a hundred can we pretend to assign any reason why this or that part differs, more or less, from the same part in the parents. But whenever we have the means of instituting a comparison, the same laws appear to have acted in producing the lesser differences between varieties of the same species, and the greater differences between species of the same genus. The external conditions of life, as climate and food, &c., seem to have induced some slight modifications. Habit in producing constitutional differences, and use in strengthening, and disuse in weakening and diminishing organs, seem to have been more potent in their effects (Darwin, 1859, pp. 167–168).

In addition to his inability to explain the origins of variation, Darwin also did not completely understand the mechanism by which parents transmitted traits to offspring. Almost without exception, nineteenth-century scholars were confused about the laws of heredity, and the popular consensus was that inheritance was *blending* by nature. In other words, offspring were always expected to express intermediate traits as a result of a blending of their parents' contributions. Given this view, we can see why the actual nature of genes was thus unimaginable. Without any viable alternatives, Darwin accepted this popular misconception. Unbeknownst to Darwin, Gregor Mendel, a contemporary of his, had systematically worked out the rules of heredity. As we have seen, the work of this brilliant but obscure Augustinian monk was not recognized until the beginning of the twentieth century.

Modern Theory of Evolution

By the start of the twentieth century, the essential foundations for evolutionary theory had already been developed. Darwin and Wallace had articulated the key principle of natural selection 40 years earlier, and the rediscovery of Mendelian genetics in 1900 contributed the other major component—a mechanism for inheritance. We might expect that these two basic contributions would have been joined rather quickly into a consistent theory of evolution. However, such was not the case. For the first 30 years of this century, geneticists (working with experimental animals, such as fruit flies) emphasized sharp contrasts within particular characteristics of organisms. As such, evolution was seen as a process of fairly large radical "jumps," and this "mutationist" view came to be seen as an alternative to the "selectionist" tradition.

A *synthesis* of these two views was not achieved until the mid-1930s, and we owe much of our current view of the evolutionary process to this intellectual development. (See Box 4-1.)

THE MODERN SYNTHESIS

Biologists working on mathematical models of evolutionary change in the late 1920s and early 1930s came to realize that genetic and selective processes were not opposing themes, but that a comprehensive explanation of organic evolution required *both*. Small new changes in the genetic material—trans-

Box 4-1   Development of Modern Evolutionary Theory

Theodosius Dobzhansky.

Our modern understanding of the evolutionary process came about through contributions of biologists in the United States, Great Britain, and Russia.

While "mutationists" were arguing with "selectionists" about the single primary mechanism in evolution, several population geneticists began to realize that both small genetic changes and natural selection were necessary ingredients in the evolutionary formula.

These population geneticists were largely concerned with mathematical reconstructions of evolution—

in particular, measuring those small accumulations of genetic changes in populations over just a few generations. Central figures in these early theoretical developments include Ronald Fisher and J. B. S. Haldane in Great Britain, Sewall Wright in the United States, and Sergei Chetverikov in Russia.

While the work of these scientists often produced brilliant insights (see particularly Fisher's *The Genetical Theory of Natural Selection*, 1930), their conclusions were largely unknown to most evolutionary biologists, especially in North America. It remained, therefore, for an individual to transcend these two worlds: the mathematical jargon of the population geneticists and the general constructs of theoretical evolutionary biologists. The scientist who performed this task (and to whom we owe the most credit as the first true synthesizer) was Theodosius Dobzhansky. In his *Genetics and the Origin of Species* (1937), Dobzhansky skillfully integrated the mathematics of population genetics with overall evolutionary theory. His insights then became the basis for a period of tremendous activity in evolutionary thinking that directly led to major contributions by George Gaylord Simpson (who brought paleontology into the synthesis), Ernst Mayr,* and others. In fact, the "Modern Synthesis" produced by these scientists stood basically unchallenged for an entire generation as *the* explanation of the evolutionary process. In recent years, however, some aspects of this theory have been brought under serious question.

---

*For an interesting discussion of the intellectual developments concerning the formulation of modern evolutionary theory, see Ernst Mayr and William B. Provine (eds.), *The Evolutionary Synthesis*. Cambridge, Mass.: Harvard University Press, 1980.

---

mitted from parent to offspring by strict Mendelian principles—are, in fact, the fuel for natural selection. The two major foundations of the biological sciences had thus been brought together in what Julian Huxley termed the "modern synthesis."

From such a "modern" (that is, the middle of the twentieth century onward) perspective we define evolution as a two-stage process:

1. Production and redistribution of **variation** (inherited differences between individuals).

Variation (genetic)   Inherited differences between individuals. The basis of all evolutionary change.

Natural selection   The evolutionary factor (first articulated by Charles Darwin) that causes changes in allele frequencies in populations due to differential net reproductive success of individuals.

Population   Within a species, a community of individuals where mates are usually found.

2. **Natural selection** acts on this variation (inherited differences, or variation, among individuals differentially affect their ability to reproduce successfully).

Definition of Evolution

As mentioned, Darwin saw evolution as the gradual unfolding of new varieties of life from previous forms over long periods of time. This depiction is what most of us think of as "evolution," and it is indeed the end result of the evolutionary process. But these long-term effects can only come about by the accumulation of many small evolutionary changes occurring every generation. In order to understand how the process of evolution works, we must necessarily study these short-term events. Darwin attempted this kind of study in his breeding experiments, but because the science of genetics was still in its infancy, he was not able to comprehend fully the mechanics of evolutionary change. Today, we study in various organisms (including humans) evolutionary changes occurring between generations, and are able to demonstrate how evolution works. From such a modern genetics perspective, we define evolution as *a change in allele frequency from one generation to the next*.

Allele frequencies are numerical indicators of the genetic makeup of an interbreeding group of individuals known as a **population**. (We will return to this topic in more detail in Chapter 5.) Here, let us illustrate the way allele frequencies change (that is, how evolution occurs) through a simplified example. First of all, we must look at a physical trait that is inherited, in this case human blood type (as discussed in Chapter 3). The best known of the human blood-type traits is ABO. There are, however, many similar blood-type systems controlled by different loci that determine genetically transmitted properties of the red blood cells.

An inherited trait, such as human blood type, may be of slightly different form in different individuals. As indicated, we call the variant genes that underlie these different forms of an inherited trait, alleles. The best-known blood-type alleles are A, B, and O. These different expressions of inherited traits are the results of genetic variation within a population.

Let us assume that your present class represents a population, an interbreeding group of individuals, and that we have ascertained the blood type of each member for the ABO trait. To be a population, individuals in your class must choose mates more often from *within* the group than from outside it. Of course, the individuals in your class will not meet this requirement, but for this example's sake we will make the assumption that they do. The proportions of each of the A, B, and O alleles are the allele frequencies for this trait. For example, suppose we find that the proportion of alleles in your class (population) is as follows:* A = .50; B = .40; 0 = .10.

Since the frequencies for combinations of these genes represent only proportions of a total, it is obvious that allele frequencies can refer only to whole groups of individuals; that is, populations. Individuals do not have an allele frequency, they have either A, B, or O (or a combination of these). Nor can individuals change alleles. From conception onward, the genetic composition of an individual is fixed. If you start out with blood type A, you will remain type A. Therefore, an individual cannot evolve: Only a group of individuals—a population—can evolve over time.

---

*This simplified example shows frequencies for the various gene combinations, what we have called *genotypes*. The way allele frequencies are calculated will be shown in Chapter 5.

What happens when a population evolves? Evolution is not an unusual or a mysterious process. In fact, it is incredibly commonplace, and may occur between every generation for every group of organisms in the world, including humans. Assume we measure the allele combination frequencies for the ABO blood trait 25 years later in the children of our classroom population and find the following: A = .30; B = .40; O = .30.

We can see that the relative proportions have changed: A has decreased, O has increased, while B has remained the same in frequency. Such a simple, apparently minor, change is what we call evolution. Over the short run of just a few generations, such changes in inherited traits may be only very small, but if further continued and elaborated, the results can and do produce spectacular kinds of adaptation and whole new varieties of life.

Whether we are talking about such short-term effects as our classroom population from one generation to the next, which is sometimes called **microevolution**, or the long-term effects through fossil history, sometimes called **macroevolution**, the basic evolutionary mechanisms are similar. As we will discuss in Chapter 7, however, they are not necessarily identical.

> **Microevolution** Small, short-term changes occurring over just a few generations.
>
> **Macroevolution** Large changes produced only after many generations.

The question may be asked: How do allele frequencies change? Or, to put it another way, what causes evolution? The modern theory of evolution isolates general factors that can produce alterations in allele frequencies. As we have noted, evolution is a two-stage process. Genetic variation must first be produced and distributed before it can be acted upon by natural selection.

Factors that Produce and Redistribute Variation

MUTATION

An actual alteration in genetic material is called **mutation**. A genetic locus may take one of several alternative forms, which we have defined as alleles (A, B, or O, for example). If one allele changes to another—that is, if the gene itself is altered—a mutation has occurred. As we have seen, a mutation is a molecular alteration—a change in the base sequence of DNA. For such changes to have evolutionary significance, they must occur in the sex cells, which are passed between generations. Evolution is a change in allele frequencies *between* generations. If mutations do not occur in sex cells (either the egg or sperm), they will not be passed to the next generation, and no evolutionary change can result. If, however, a genetic change does occur in the sperm or egg of one of the individuals in our classroom (A mutates to X, for instance), the offspring's blood type also will be altered, causing a change in allele frequencies of that generation. In Chapter 2, we showed how the change in a single DNA base, a *point mutation* could cause a change in hemoglobin structure (that is, from normal to sickle-cell allele). Other mutations that produce phenotypic effects (and are discussed in Chapter 3) include the albinism allele, the allele producing brachydactyly, and the alteration causing hemophilia.

> **Mutation** An alteration in the genetic material (a change in the base sequence of DNA).

Actually, it would be rare to see evolution occurring by mutation *alone*. Mutation rates for any given trait are quite low, and thus their effects would rarely be seen in such a small population as our class. In larger populations, mutations might be observed (1 individual in 10,000, say), but would, by themselves, have very little impact on shifting allele frequencies. However, when mutation is coupled with natural selection, evolutionary changes are quite possible.

Steve Zegura graduated from Stanford University with a B.A. in Anthropology and earned his M.S. and Ph.D. degrees in Human Biology from the University of Wisconsin, Madison. His specialities include anthropological genetics, evolutionary theory, and statistical applications. He has taught at the University of Arizona in Tucson since 1972 where he has grown accustomed to the Sonoran Desert flora and fauna while searching for wayward golf balls.

"Well, son, I know you would really like to be a centerfielder but we're going to have to move you to first base. You are just too big and slow for the outfield." My first "career adjustment" was not my decision—it was made by my high school baseball coach. Fortunately, the next

time I changed my area of specialization it was entirely my choice. Before I tell you why I switched from working primarily with skeletons to concentrating on genes, I'd like to give you some background information about my education and professional philosophy.

Ever since I was an undergraduate at Stanford, I have focused on the interaction of human biology and culture as an explanatory framework for understanding human variation and human evolution. Indeed, an important personal legacy as an academic has been the establishment of the widely acclaimed and extremely popular Human Biology Undergraduate Major at Stanford. As originally organized by Donald Kennedy, this major is based partly on the experimental interdisciplinary degree program that I devised with him as an undergraduate. My doctorate in Human Biology at the University of Wisconsin, Madison, was also an interdisciplinary degree. The last 20 years have served to reinforce my commitment to interdisciplinary inquiry, the pursuit of connections among diverse bodies of fact and theory, and the importance of a synthetic approach to knowledge and understanding.

My main research interest over the last 25 years has been the initial peopling of the Americas. In 1968, the same year the Alaskan North Slope oil fields were discovered east of Point Barrow, I went to the Eskimo community of Wainwright, Alaska, as part of an interdisciplinary research team sponsored by the International Biological Program. I went on the trip to collect anthropometric data on the residents of

Wainwright as part of a human adaptability study. At the time, I didn't have a clue what I would do for my dissertation project. While in Wainwright, Dr. Fred Milan, one of the organizers of the expedition, was walking along the beach when he noticed part of a skull protruding from a depression in a cliff. As the days went by, I was struck by the frequently heard comment that living conditions were particularly nice this summer. Well, true, it was not very cold; however, the mosquitos were straight out of cartoonist Gary Larson's "The Far Side" . . . rather small for bombers but quite large for maneuverable fighters. Every time I opened my mouth out on the tundra I got more than the recommended daily protein intake for an adult male. The more I went outside, the more I wanted to be back inside. I began to think about what daily living conditions must have been like hundreds or perhaps even thousands of years ago for Native Americans like our newly discovered friend who ended up stuck in a cliff.

By the time I got back to Madison I had a dissertation in mind. I wanted to find out when the first Eskimos came to the North American Arctic. I was also interested in where they had come from, who they were related to, and what ingenious cultural equipment facilitated their survival in such a generally hostile environment. The most important thing one learns about doing a Ph.D. dissertation is that one must limit the scope of one's inquiry so that one can finish *something*. In the end, I limited myself to studying the cranial variation of 609 skeletons from 12 different Eskimo and Aleut populations using a framework derived from linguistics.

Over the next decade as I continued to study Native American skeletons to try to answer my earlier questions, it became more and more clear that the ancestors of the American Indians arrived in North America long before the Eskimo-Aleut ancestors made the crossing from Asia to America. In the early 1980s, it also became evident that new dating technologies had rendered invalid all claims for human skeletal remains in the New World that predated 11,000 BP. At the same time, there were some new tantalizing clues primarily from archaeology that humans may have reached the Americas well before 11,000 BP. As I mused over this dilemma, I started to wonder if there was any other way that I could answer basic questions about the early peopling of the Americas.

I eventually concluded that often the best biological data for reconstructing evolutionary relationships were genetic data, and for over a decade now I have concentrated on the analysis and interpretation of genetic data to answer fundamental questions about population structure, history, and relationships. For instance, I collaborated with the linguist Joseph Greenberg and dental anthropologist Christy Turner to present a three-wave migration theory for the early peopling of the Americas. In addition, over the last few years I have developed a second major research commitment: a collaborative effort with Croatian scientists to elucidate the population history and structure of the Dalmatian population system of the eastern Adriatic. This goal is both personal (my father was born in Dalmatia) and practical (it represents an application of my academic expertise to solve research questions for a country with limited scientific resources and research funding).

My "conversion" to genetic approaches necessitated a substantial effort to retrain and re-educate myself. Genetics in the 1980s and 1990s is far different from what I was taught as an undergraduate and graduate student. When I was a student, recombinant DNA technology and horizontal transfer of genes from one species to another were the stuff of science fiction. Now they are routine realities, as are the extraction of genetic material from fossils, the Human Genome Project, and the discovery of the genetic causes for myriad diseases. Understanding the molecular basis of behavior (both normal and abnormal) may be the next great frontier for applied human genetics. Let us hope that our ethics are as sophisticated as our genetic technology. Indeed, as Michael Crichton cogently observed in the introduction to his best-selling cautionary tale, *Jurassic Park*: "The commercialization of molecular biology is the most stunning ethical event in the history of science, and it has happened with astonishing speed."

My most recent research project involves an attempt to relate molecular genetic variation to normal phenotypic functioning at the level of linguistic coding of basic color terminology. Once again, retraining became essential, so I spent the early part of one summer learning how to perform a variety of PCR (polymerase chain reaction) protocols so I could amplify the opsin genes ultimately responsible for human color vision. What I am doing certainly isn't as exciting as "reconstituting" dinosaurs; however, the possibility that a difference in a single nucleotide might place people in different perceptual and/or cognitive worlds may be just as important with respect to the ultimate goal of human biology: the scientific understanding of human variation and human evolution.

Mutation is the basic creative force in evolution, and in fact is the only way to produce "new" variation. Its key role in the production of variation represents the first stage of the evolutionary process. Darwin was not aware of the nature of mutation. Only in the twentieth century, with the spectacular development of molecular biology, have the secrets of genetic structure been revealed.

MIGRATION

Migration Movement of genes between populations.

The movement of genes from one population to another is called **migration** (also known as gene flow). If all individuals in our classroom population do not choose their mates from within the group, significant changes in allele frequencies could occur. For example, if four of the people who were type A married and settled outside the population, and four new individuals who were type O moved in and interbred with classroom individuals, the allele frequencies would be altered. If a change in allele frequency does take place, evolution will have occurred, this time by migration.

In humans, social rules, more than any other factor, determine mating patterns, and cultural anthropologists must work closely with physical anthropologists in order to isolate and measure this aspect of evolutionary change. Population movements (particularly in the last 500 years) have reached enormous proportions, and few breeding isolates remain. It should not, however, be assumed that significant population movements did not occur prior to modern times. Our hunting and gathering ancestors probably lived in small groups that were both mobile and flexible in membership. Early farmers also were probably highly mobile, moving from area to area as the land wore out. Intensive, highly sedentary agricultural communities came later, but even then significant migration was still possible. From the Near East, one of the early farming centers, populations spread very gradually in a "creeping occupation of Europe, India, and northern and eastern Africa" (Bodmer and Cavalli-Sforza, 1976, p. 563).

Migration between populations has been a consistent feature of hominid evolution since the first dispersal of our genus, and helps explain why speciation has not occurred in human evolution for at least the last million years. Of course, migration patterns are a manifestation of human cultural behavior, once again emphasizing the essential biocultural nature of human evolution.

An interesting application of how migration influences microevolutionary changes in modern human populations is seen in the admixture of parental groups among African Americans over the last three centuries. Blacks in the United States are largely of West African descent, but there has also been considerable influx of alleles from European stock. By measuring allele frequencies for specific genetic loci (for example, Rh and Duffy blood groups —discussed in Chapter 5) we can estimate the amount of migration: European alleles → Afro-American gene pool. By using different methods, migration rate (or the percentage of gene flow from one population into another) estimates have varied considerably, but one of the most comprehensive studies has suggested for northern cities a figure close to 20% (22% in Oakland, California, but much lower in the deep South: 4% in Charleston, South Carolina, and 11% in rural Georgia).

It would be a misconception to think that migration can occur only through such large-scale movements of whole groups. In fact, significant alterations in allele frequencies can come about through long-term patterns of mate selection. If exchange of mates were consistently in one direction over a long period of time, ultimately allele frequencies would be altered. Due to demographic, economic, and social pressures, individuals must often choose mates from outside the immediate vicinity.

Transportation factors play a crucial role in determining the potential radius for finding mates. Today, highly efficient mechanized forms of transportation make the potential radius of mate choice worldwide, but actual patterns are obviously somewhat more restricted. For example, data from Ann Arbor, Michigan, indicate marital distance of about 160 miles, which obviously includes a tremendous number of potential marriage partners.

GENETIC DRIFT

The random factor in evolution is called **genetic drift** and is due primarily to sampling phenomena (that is, the size of the population). Since evolution occurs in populations, it is directly tied not only to the nature of the initial allele freqencies of the population, but to the size of the group as well. If, in our parent population of, say, 100 individuals, two type O individuals had been killed in an auto accident before completing reproduction, their genes would have been removed from the population. The frequency of the O allele would have been reduced in the next generation, and evolution would have occurred. In this case, with only 100 individuals in the population, the change due to the accident would have altered the O frequency in a noticeable way. If, however, our initial population had been very large (10,000 people), then the effect of removing a few individuals would be very small indeed. In fact, in a population of large size, random effects, such as traffic accidents, would be balanced out by the equal probabilities of such events affecting all the other individuals with different genetic combinations (that is, different genotypes). As you can see, evolutionary change due to genetic drift is directly and inversely related to population size. To put it simply, the smaller the population, the larger the effect of genetic drift.

When considering genetic drift, we must remember that the genetic makeup of individuals is in no way related to the chance happenings that affect their lives. When applied to our example, this fact means that the genetic makeup of individuals has absolutely nothing to do with their being involved in automobile accidents. This is what is meant by a random event and why this factor is usually called *random genetic drift*. If, for example, a person had died in an auto accident caused by hereditary poor eyesight, such an event would not be genetic drift. If the individual, because of some such hereditary trait, dies early and produces fewer offspring than other individuals, this is not random genetic drift, it is natural selection.

An example of a particular kind of drift seen in modern human populations is called the **founder effect,** or after its formulator, the *Sewall Wright effect.* Founder effect operates when only an exceedingly small group of individuals contributes genes to the next generation, a kind of genetic bottleneck. This phenomenon can occur when a small migrant band of "founders" colonizes a new and separate area away from the parent group. Small founding populations may also be left as remnants when famine, plague, or war ravage a normally larger group. Actually, each generation is the founder of all succeeding generations in any population.

The cases of founder effect producing noticeable microevolutionary changes are necessarily in small groups. For example, several small and isolated Alpine villages have unusually high frequencies of albinism, and an

Genetic drift Evolutionary changes produced by random factors.

Founder effect Also called the *Sewall Wright effect.* A type of genetic drift in which allele frequencies are altered in small populations that are nonrandom samples of larger ones.

island in the South Atlantic, Tristan da Cunha, has unusually high frequencies of an hereditary eye disorder. First settled in 1817 by one Scottish family, this isolated island's native inhabitants include only descendants of this one family and a few other individuals, such as shipwrecked sailors. All in all, only about two dozen individuals constituted the founding population of this island. In 1961, the 294 inhabitants were evacuated because of an impending volcanic eruption and removed to England. Extensive medical tests were performed, which revealed four individuals with the very rare recessive disease retinitis pigmentosa. The frequency for the allele causing this disease was abnormally high in this population, and a considerable portion of the group were no doubt carriers.

How did this circumstance come about? Apparently, just by chance, one of the initial founders carried the gene in heterozygous form and later passed it on to offspring who through inbreeding occasionally produced affected individuals. Since so few individuals founded this population, the fact that one carried the allele for this disease made a disproportionate contribution to succeeding generations (Bodmer and Cavalli-Sforza, 1976).

Genetic drift has probably played an important role in human evolution, influencing genetic changes in small isolated groups. From studies of recent hunter-gatherers in Australia, the range of potential mates is limited to the linguistic tribe usually consisting of around 500 members. Given this small population size, drift could act significantly, particularly if drought, disease, etc., should reduce the population even further.

Much insight concerning the evolutionary factors that have acted in the past can be gained by understanding how such factors continue to operate on human populations today. In small populations like Tristan da Cunha, drift plays a major evolutionary role. Fairly sudden fluctuations in allele frequency can and do occur owing to the small population size. Likewise, throughout a good deal of human evolution (at least the last 4–5 m.y.*) hominids probably lived in small groups, and drift, therefore, would have had significant impact.

Joseph Birdsell, a physical anthropologist who has worked extensively in Australia, has postulated general models for human evolution from his Australian data. He suggests population size during most of the Pleistocene was comparable to the 500 figure seen in Australia. Moreover, when agriculturists became sedentary and isolated in small villages, the effects of drift may have been even greater. Indications of such a phenomenon are still operative in Melanesia, where individuals often spend their entire lives within just a few miles of their birthplace.

While drift has been a factor in human evolution from the start, the effects have been irregular and nondirectional (for drift is *random* in nature). Certainly the pace of evolution could have been accelerated if many small populations became isolated and thus subject to drift. However, by producing populations with varying evolutionary potential, drift only provides fodder for the truly directional force of evolution, natural selection.

RECOMBINATION

Since in any sexually reproducing species both parents contribute genes to offspring, the genetic information is inevitably reshuffled every generation. Such recombination does not in itself change allele frequencies (that is, cause

---

*The initials m.y. constitute an abbreviation for million years.

evolution). However, it does produce the whole array of genetic combinations, which natural selection can then act upon. In fact, we have shown how the reshuffling of chromosomes during meiosis can produce literally trillions of gene combinations, making every human being genetically unique.

Natural Selection Acts on Variation

The evolutionary factors just discussed—mutation, migration, genetic drift, and recombination—interact to produce variation and to distribute genes within and between populations. But there is no long-term *direction* to any of these factors. How then do populations adapt? A result of natural selection is a change in allele frequency relative to specific environmental factors. If the environment changes, then the selection pressures change as well. Such a functional shift in allele frequencies is what we mean by **adaptation**. If there are long-term environmental changes in a consistent direction, then allele frequencies should also shift gradually each generation. If sustained for many generations, the results may be quite dramatic. The best way to demonstrate how natural selection operates is through specific examples. However, since it is so difficult to demonstrate precisely the action of natural selection in human populations, we begin with two examples from other organisms. Later, we will return to humans with one detailed example that is quite well established.

The best historically documented case of natural selection acting in a contemporary organism deals with changes in pigmentation among peppered moths near Manchester, England. Before the nineteenth century, the common variety of moth was a mottled gray color that provided extremely effective camouflage against lichen-covered tree trunks. Also present, though in much lower frequency, was a dark variety of moth. While resting on such trees, the dark, uncamouflaged moths against the light tree trunks were more visible to birds, and were therefore eaten more often. Thus, in the end, they produced fewer offspring than the light, camouflaged moths. Yet, in 50 years, by the end of the nineteenth century, the common gray, camouflaged form had been almost completely replaced by the black variety.

What had brought about this rapid change? The answer lies in the rapidly changing environment of industrialized nineteenth-century England. Pollutants released in the area settled on trees, killing the lichen and turning the bark a dark color. Moths living in the area continued to rest on trees, but the gray (or light) variety was increasingly conspicuous as the trees became darker. Consequently, they began to be preyed upon more frequently by birds and contributed fewer genes to the next generation.

In the twentieth century, increasing control of pollutants has allowed some forested areas to return to their lighter, preindustrial conditions, with lichen growing again on the trees. As would be expected, in these areas the black variety is now being supplanted by the gray.

The substance that produces pigmentation is called *melanin*, and the evolutionary shift in the peppered moth, as well as in many other moth species, is termed *industrial melanism*. Such an evolutionary shift in response to environmental change is an excellent example of what we have defined as an *adaptation*.

This example provides numerous insights into the mechanism of evolutionary change by natural selection:

(a)

(b)

Figure 4-16

Variation in the peppered moth. In (a), the dark form is more visible to bird predators on the light (unpolluted) trees. In (b), the light form is more visible: trees are darker due to pollution.

Adaptation   Genetic changes in response to selection (environmental) factors.

1. A trait must be inherited to have importance in natural selection. A characteristic that is not hereditary (such as a change in hair pigmentation brought about by dye) will not be passed on to succeeding generations. In moths, pigmentation is a demonstrated hereditary trait.

2. Natural selection cannot occur without variation in inherited characteristics. If all the moths had initially been gray (you will recall some dark forms were present) and the trees became darker, the survival and reproduction of all moths may have been so low that the population would have become extinct. Such an event is not unusual in evolution and, without variation, would nearly always occur. *Selection can only work with variation already present.*

3. "Fitness" is a relative measure that will change as the environment changes. Fitness is simply reproductive success. In the initial stage, the gray moth was the most-fit variety, but as the environment changed, the black moth became more fit, and a further change reversed the adaptive pattern. It should be obvious that statements regarding the "most-fit" life form mean nothing without reference to specific environments.

The example of peppered moths shows how different death rates influence natural selection, for moths that die early tend to leave fewer offspring. But mortality is not the entire picture. Another important aspect of natural selection is fertility, for an animal that gives birth to more young would pass its genes on at a faster rate than those who bear fewer offspring. However, fertility is not the whole picture either, for the crucial element is the number of young raised successfully to the point where they reproduce themselves. We may state this simply as *differential net reproductive success*. The way this mechanism works can be demonstrated through another example.

In a common variety of small birds called swifts, data show that giving birth to more offspring does not necessarily guarantee that more young will be successfully raised. The number of eggs hatched in a breeding season is a measure of fertility. The number of birds that mature and are eventually able to leave the nest is a measure of net reproductive success, or offspring successfully raised. The following tabulation shows the correlation between the number of eggs hatched (fertility) and the number of young that leave the nest (reproductive success) averaged over four breeding seasons (Lack, 1966).

NUMBER OF EGGS HATCHED (FERTILITY)	2 EGGS	3 EGGS	4 EGGS
Average number of young raised (reproductive success)	1.92	2.54	1.76
Sample size	72	20	16

As the tabulation shows, the most efficient fertility number is three eggs, for that yields the highest reproductive success. Raising two is less beneficial to the parents since the *end result* is not as successful as with three eggs. Trying to raise more than three young is actually detrimental, since the parents may not be able to provide adequate nourishment for any of the offspring. An offspring that dies before reaching reproductive age is, in evolutionary terms, an equivalent of never having been born in the first place. Actually, such a result may be an evolutionary minus to the parents, for this offspring will drain their resources and may inhibit their ability to raise other offspring, thereby lowering their reproductive success even further. Selection will favor those genetic traits that yield the maximum net reproductive suc-

Figure 4-17

A frequency map of the sickle-cell distribution in the Old World.

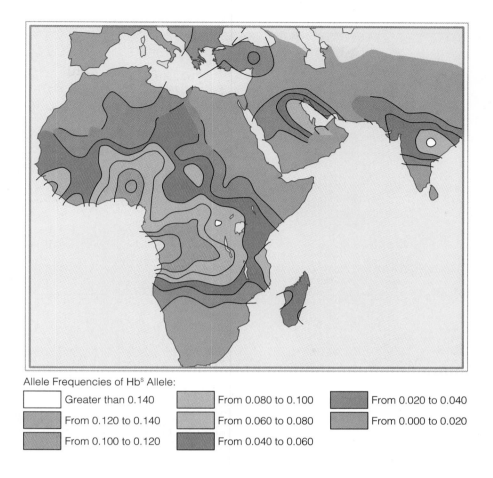

Allele Frequencies of Hbˢ Allele:

Greater than 0.140	From 0.080 to 0.100	From 0.020 to 0.040
From 0.120 to 0.140	From 0.060 to 0.080	From 0.000 to 0.020
From 0.100 to 0.120	From 0.040 to 0.060	

cess. If the number of eggs laid* is a genetic trait in birds (and it seems to be), natural selection in swifts should act to favor the laying of three eggs as opposed to two or four.

NATURAL SELECTION IN HUMANS

Human beings are neither quickly reproducing nor are they amenable to controlled laboratory manipulations. Therefore, there are few unambiguous examples of natural selection in action among contemporary human populations.

The best documented case deals with the *sickle-cell trait*, which is the result of a point mutation within the gene producing the hemoglobin beta chain. If inherited in double dose, this allele causes severe problems of anemia, circulatory disturbances, and usually early death. (See Table 4-2.) Even with aggressive medical intervention, life expectancy in the United States today is less than 20 years for victims of sickle-cell anemia. Worldwide, sickle-cell anemia causes an estimated 100,000 deaths per year, and in the United States an estimated 40,000–50,000 individuals, mostly of African descent, suffer from this disease.

*The number of eggs hatched is directly related to the number of eggs laid.

Table 4-2 Sickle-Cell Terminology

Sickle-cell allele in single dose:

= carrier, called the sickle-cell trait (not much affected; functions normally in most environments)

Sickle-cell allele in double dose:

= sickle-cell anemia or sicklemia (very severe effects, usually lethal)

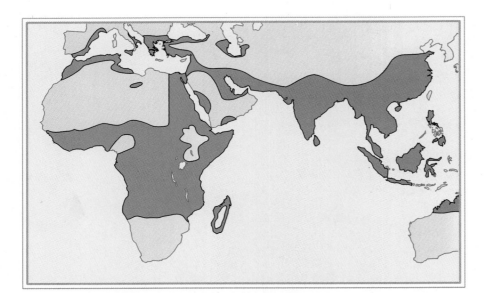

Figure 4-18

Malaria distribution in the Old World.

With such obviously harmful effects it is surprising to find the sickle-cell allele (Hb^S) so frequent in some populations. The highest allele frequencies are found in western and central African populations, reaching levels close to 20%; values are also moderately high in some Greek and Asiatic Indian populations. How do we explain such a phenomenon? Obviously the allele originated from a point mutation, but why did it spread?

The answer lies in yet another kind of disease producing enormous selective pressure. In those areas of the world where Hb^S is found in unusually high frequencies, *falciparium malaria* is also found (see Fig. 4-18). Caused by a protozoan parasite (*Plasmodium*), this debilitating infectious disease is transmitted to humans by mosquitoes. In areas that are endemically affected, many individuals suffer sharp declines in reproductive success due to high infant mortality or lowered vitality as adults.

Such a geographic correlation between malarial incidence and sickle-cell distribution is an indirect suggestion of a biological relationship. More positive evidence comes from experimental work done by the British biologist A. C. Allison. Volunteers from the Luo population of East Africa with known genotypes were injected with malaria-causing agents. After a short time the results showed that heterozygous carriers were much more resistant to malarial infection compared to homozygous "normals." (Hb^{A}Hb^A: 15 injected—14 had malarial parasites; Hb^{A}Hb^S: 15 injected—only 2 had malarial parasites.) Carriers (people with the sickle-cell trait) resist malarial infection because their red blood cells provide a less adequate environment for the *Plasmodium* parasite. Approximately 40% of carriers' hemoglobin is Hb^S; some of their red blood cells should therefore show tendencies to sickle. Under normal circumstances only about 5% would be expected to sickle, but when infected by the parasite this is greatly increased. The presence of the parasite apparently stimulates greater sickling, disrupting the cell membrane, releasing intracellular potassium and thereby killing the host cell (*and the parasite—before it can reproduce itself*) (Friedman and Trager, 1981).

The sickle-cell allele apparently has not always been an important genetic factor in human populations. In fact, human cultural modification of environments provided the initial stimulus. Before agriculture, humans rarely, if ever, lived close to mosquito breeding areas. With the development and spread to Africa of slash-and-burn agricultural practices, perhaps in just the last two thousand years, penetration and clearing of tropical rain forests occurred. As a result, open stagnant pools provided fertile mosquito breeding areas in close proximity to human settlements.

Malaria, for the first time, now struck human populations with its full impact, and as a selective force it was powerful indeed. No doubt, humans attempted to adjust culturally to these circumstances, and numerous biological adaptations also probably came into play. The sickle-cell trait is one of these, and the experimental evidence just cited demonstrates its biological value as a malarial resistant. However, there is a definite cost involved with such an adaptation. While carriers have more malarial resistance and presumably higher reproductive success, some of their offspring will be lost through the genetic disease, sickle-cell anemia. So there is a counterbalancing of selective forces with an advantage for carriers *only* in malarial environments.

Following World War II extensive DDT sprayings by the World Health Organization began systematically to wipe out mosquito breeding areas in the tropics. As would be expected, malaria decreased sharply, and also as expected Hb^S frequencies were apparently on the decline. The intertwined story of human cultural practices, mosquitoes, malarial parasites, and the sickle-cell trait is still not finished. Thirty years of DDT spraying killed many mosquitoes, but selection is acting on these insect populations also. Due to the tremendous amount of genetic diversity among insects as well as their short generation span, several DDT-resistant strains have arisen and spread over the last few years. As a result, malaria is again on the upswing, with several hundred thousand new cases reported in India, Africa, and Central America.

A genetic trait like sickle-cell that provides a reproductive advantage in certain circumstances is a clear example of natural selection in action among human populations. The precise evolutionary mechanism in the sickle-cell example is usually called a **balanced polymorphism**.

A genetic trait is called a polymorphism "when two or more alleles at a given genetic locus occur with appreciable frequencies in a population" (Bodmer and Cavalli-Sforza, 1976, p. 308). We will return to this topic in more detail in Chapter 5. By "balanced," we are referring to the interaction of selection pressures operating in malarial environments. Some individuals (mainly Hb^{A}Hb^A) will be removed by the infectious disease, malaria, and some (Hb^{S}Hb^S) will be eliminated by the inherited disease, sickle-cell anemia. Those with the highest fitness (that is, reproductive success) are the heterozygotes (Hb^{A}Hb^S), but what alleles do they carry? Obviously they are passing *both* Hb^A and Hb^S alleles to offspring, and that explains why both alleles are maintained in the population—at least as long as malaria continues to be a selective factor.

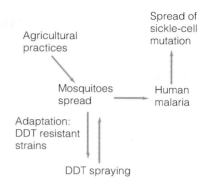

Figure 4-19

Biocultural interactions of the sickle-cell allele.

Balanced polymorphism   The maintenance of two or more alleles in a population due to a selective advantage of the heterozygote.

Review, Genetics and Evolutionary Factors

Starting in Chapter 2 with a discussion of the molecular and cellular bases of heredity, we proceeded to Chapter 3 to show how such genetic information is passed from individuals in one generation to those in the next. In this chapter we discussed the history of evolutionary theory and its current applica-

Table 4-3   Levels of Organization in the Evolutionary Process

Evolutionary Factor	Level	Evolutionary Process	Science	Technique of Study
Mutation	DNA	Storage of genetic information; ability to replicate; influences phenotype by production of proteins	Molecular biology	Biochemistry, electron microscopy, recombinant DNA
Mutation	Chromosomes	A vehicle for packaging and transmitting genetic material (DNA)	Cytogenetics	Light, electron microscope
Recombination (sex cells only)	Cell	The basic unit of life that contains the chromosomes and divides for growth and for production of sex cells	Cytogenetics	Light, electron microscope
Natural selection	Organism	The unit, composed of cells, which reproduces and which we observe for phenotypic traits	Genetics	Visual, biochemical
Drift, migration	Population	A group of interbreeding organisms. We look at changes in allele frequencies between generations; it is the population that evolves	Population genetics	Statistical

tion, emphasizing the crucial role of natural selection. It may seem that these different levels, molecular, cellular, individual, and populational, are different aspects of evolution, but they are all related and highly integrated in a way that can eventually produce evolutionary change. A step-by-step example will make this clear.

In our earlier discussion of sickle-cell hemoglobin, you will recall that the actual genetic information was coded in the sequence of bases in the DNA molecule. We started out with a situation where everyone in the population has the same hemoglobin type; therefore, initially no variation for this trait exists, and without some source of new variation evolution is not possible. How does this gene change? We have seen that a substitution of a single base in the DNA sequence can alter the code significantly enough to alter the protein product and ultimately the whole phenotype of the individual. Imagine that, several generations ago, just such an "accident" occurred in a single individual. For this mutated allele to be passed on to succeeding offspring, the gametes must carry the alteration. Any new mutation, therefore, must be transmitted during sex cell formation.

Once the mutation has occurred in the DNA, it will be packaged into chromosomes, and these chromosomes in turn will assort during meiosis to be passed to offspring. The results of this process are seen by looking at phenotypes (traits) in individuals, and the mode of inheritance is described simply by Mendel's principle of segregation. In other words, if our initial individual has a mutation in only one paired allele on a set of homologous chromosomes, there will be a 50% chance of passing this chromosome (with the new mutation) to an offspring.

Thus far, we have seen what a gene is, how it can change, and how it is passed on to offspring. But what does all this activity have to do with *evolution*? To repeat an earlier definition, evolution is a change in allele frequency in a *population* from one generation to the next. The key point here is that we are now looking at a whole group of individuals, a population, and it is the population that will or will not change over time.

We know whether allele frequencies have changed in a population where sickle-cell hemoglobin is found by ascertaining the percentage of individuals with the sickling allele (Hb^S) versus those with the normal allele (Hb^A). If the relative proportions of these alleles alter with time, evolution has occurred. In addition to discovering that evolution has occurred, it is important to know why. Several possibilities arise. First, we know that the only way the new allele Hb^S could have arisen is by mutation, and we have shown how this process might happen in a single individual. This change, however, is not yet really an evolutionary one, for in a relatively large population the alteration of one individual's genes will not significantly alter allele frequencies of the entire population. Somehow, this new allele must *spread* in the population.

One way this could happen is in a small population where mutations in one of just a few individuals and their offspring may indeed alter the overall frequency quite quickly. This case would be representative of genetic drift. As discussed, drift acts in small populations where random factors may cause significant changes in allele frequency. Due to small population size, there is not likely to be a balance of factors affecting individual survival, reproduction, etc. Consequently, some alleles may be completely removed from the population, while others may become established as the only allele present at that particular locus (and are said to be "fixed" in the population).

In the course of human evolution, drift may have played a significant role at times, but long-term evolutionary trends could only have been sustained by *natural selection*. The way this has worked in the past and still operates today (as in sickle-cell) is through differential reproduction. That is, individuals who carry a particular allele or combination of alleles produce more offspring. By producing more offspring than other individuals with alternative alleles, such individuals cause the frequency of the new allele in the population to increase slowly in proportion from generation to generation. When this process is compounded over hundreds of generations for numerous loci, the result is significant evolutionary change.

Summary

The scientific revolution of the seventeenth and eighteenth centuries hastened changes in the philosophical and scientific beliefs already challenged by Copernicus and others in the two previous centuries. The European world view from the time of Plato and Aristotle (that the universe, including the earth and all living things on it, once created had never changed) was giving way to a belief in a moving, dynamic universe.

In the late eighteenth and early nineteenth centuries, the evidence for the evolution of species and a theory to explain it were being explored. Lamarck, for example, constructed a system that explained how species could be transformed to other species, but his explanation was unsatisfactory to most people.

After his return from the voyage of the HMS *Beagle*, Charles Darwin developed his theory of evolution. Malthus' phrase, "struggle for existence" alerted Darwin to the significance of individual variation and, ultimately, to the explanation of how one species could evolve into another species.

Published in *Origin of Species* in 1859, Darwin's theory of evolution irrevocably changed the tide of intellectual thought. Gradually, scientists universally accepted Darwin's formulation of the evolutionary process as the very foundation of all the biological sciences, including physical anthropology.

Contributions from genetics in the twentieth century have allowed scientists to demonstrate the mechanics of evolution in ways unknown to Darwin and his contemporaries.

Building upon these fundamental nineteenth-century contributions and the rediscovery in 1900 of Mendel's work, further refinements later in the twentieth century have been added to contemporary evolutionary thought. In particular, the combination of natural selection with Mendel's principles of inheritance and experimental evidence concerning the nature of mutation have all been synthesized into a modern understanding of evolutionary change, appropriately termed the *modern synthesis*. In this, the central contemporary theory of evolution, evolutionary change is seen as a two-stage process: the first stage, which is the production and redistribution of variation; and the second stage, where natural selection acts on the accumulated genetic variation.

Crucial to all evolutionary change is mutation, the only source of completely new genetic variation. In addition, the factors of migration, genetic drift, and recombination function to redistribute variation within individuals (recombination), within populations (genetic drift), and between populations (migration).

Natural selection is the central determining factor influencing the long-term *direction* of evolutionary change. How natural selection works can best be explained as differential reproductive success, meaning, in other words, how successful individuals are in leaving offspring to succeeding generations. To more fully illustrate the mechanics of evolutionary change through natural selection, comprehensive and well-understood examples from other organisms (for example, industrial melanism in moths) are most helpful. The detailed history of the evolutionary spread of the sickle-cell allele provides the best-documented example of natural selection among recent human populations. It must be remembered that evolution is an integrated process, and this chapter concludes with a discussion of how the various evolutionary factors can be integrated into a single, comprehensive view of evolutionary change.

Questions for Review

1. What components of Medieval thinking had to be altered before a modern scientific view could be developed?
2. What role did Copernicus and Galileo play in this new world view? What role did Newton play?
3. Discuss the influence of Malthus' *Essay on Population* on the thinking of Darwin.
4. How would you account for the Theory of Natural Selection being independently developed by two people (Darwin and Wallace) at the same time? Discuss the major ideas that influenced both these thinkers.
5. Discuss the major contributions of Buffon and Linneaus to biological theory.
6. Why is Lamarck called the first true evolutionist?
7. What is the Theory of Acquired Characteristics? (Illustrate through an example.) Why is this idea no longer considered valid?
8. What role did Lyell play in evolutionary thinking? Specifically, what is the significance of uniformitarianism?

9. What evidence did Darwin use to explain his Theory of Natural Selection?

10. In addition to natural selection, what are the major components of Darwin's overall evolutionary theory?

11. Explain how natural selection works. (a) Illustrate through an example for nonhuman animals. (b) Illustrate through an example in humans.

12. What is the Modern Synthesis? Explain how the major components of this theory explain evolutionary change.

13. What is genetic drift? Illustrate through an example for human populations.

14. What role does variation play in the evolutionary process? Where does variation come from? (Hint: you may wish to discuss the source of variation as completely new to a species, or as it is introduced into a population *within* a species.)

15. Discuss how evolutionary change occurs as an integrated process. Illustrate through an example.

Chapter 5

Contents

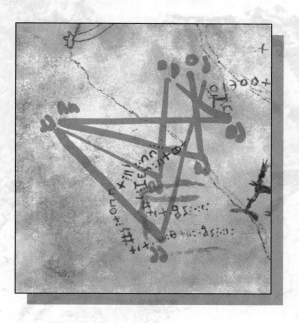

Approaches to Human Variation

The evidence to support the position that IQ (and intelligence generally) is strongly influenced by genetic factors has come from a variety of sources. For a number of years, one of the most influential of such sources came from the studies conducted by the British psychologist Sir Cyril Burt. However, his data, and indeed his scientific integrity, have recently been called into question. In following the history of this episode, apply critical thinking skills and judge how such an approach ultimately exposed Burt. Did Sir Cyril cook his figures?

Burt, who died in 1971, believed that heredity could explain the high scores achieved in intelligence tests, that mental abilities were inborn, and that intelligence was concentrated in the higher social classes. When he found an unusually high IQ among orphans or adopted children, he explained, "We commonly learned later on that the child was the illegitimate offspring of a father belonging to a superior social class." The class system, he firmly believed, was an economic reflection of a genetically determined order of human merit.

It is not surprising to learn that Burt was influenced by eugenicists, and, as a matter of fact, was acquainted with Sir Francis Galton.

Galton was the principal founder of eugenics, and believed that influencing the mating and/or fertility of individuals could improve or impair the qualities of future generations. Burt's explanation of differences in intelligence was invariably associated with social class. In 1912, he coauthored a paper in which Liverpool slum boys were compared with Oxford preparatory boys. He claimed the results were consistent with investigations of savage and civilized races!

Burt also conducted studies of separated pairs of identical twins.* His results showed a high correlation in the IQs of the separated twins, thus effectively controlling for the influence of the environment on intelligence scores.

Burt's work influenced educational legislation in England. The British Education Act of 1944 was based explicitly on his statistical reports, which established principles of educational selectivity and segregation: three types of schools established for different innate abilities—grammar schools, technical schools, and secondary schools.

In 1961, he published a major paper, "Intelligence and Social Mobility," which was a deadly attack against those who argued that the environment could affect scores achieved in intelligence tests. This paper also demonstrated a remarkable correlation between intelligence and social class.

This work has been widely quoted by geneticists and psychologists, especially those involved in IQ testing, since it appeared to be the most comprehensive study ever performed on the relation of intelligence to social class and social mobility. Burt's publications had

great impact on such men as Jensen, Eyesenck, and Herrnstein, staunch supporters of the importance of heredity on intelligence and intelligence scores. Burt was knighted in 1946 for his work on intelligence and his recommendations for educational reform.

Doubts about the validity and accuracy (as well as the honesty) of Burt's work surfaced at the time of his death in 1971. Professor Leon Kamin (1974) of Princeton questioned Burt's studies of twins. Kamin pointed out that Burt's number of separated identical twin pairs increased from 15 in 1943 to 21 in 1955, to 30 in 1957, to 42 in 1958, and in 1966 reached 53, one of the world's largest samples of an extremely rare phenomenon. Yet the correlation of intelligence of the separated twin pairs remained constant to three decimal places over this period of twenty-five years, even though the number of pairs had increased almost four times. Such a stable correlation is so unlikely that statisticians consider it impossible unless the figures were deliberately fixed.

An English journalist, Oliver Gillie (1978, 1979), tried to find the women who had collaborated with Burt in his research and publications in order to learn more of Burt's unlikely statistics. Gillie searched records at universities and psychological societies for traces of these

---

*Monozygotic twins raised from birth in separate households.

three women associates, and he also talked to friends and employees of Burt who should have known the women and something of their whereabouts. However, he found no trace of them with the possible exception of one—a Miss Howard—who, said Gillie, if she did exist, was not the person Burt said she was. It is difficult to know why Burt would fabricate such associates, or what purpose this might have served.

The most damaging report on Burt's work is probably Professor D. D. Dorfman's examination of the statistics given in Burt's 1961 report. Burt claimed he had studied 40,000 people over a period of fifty years, comparing the intelligence of children and their fathers. He illustrated his findings in tables that showed the intelligence of fathers of six social classes and, in another table, the intelligence of their children.

In results so perfect (and too good to be true), Burt found an almost perfect normal curve of intelligence among fathers and children, and the statistics for each group were almost identical. The probability of an exactly normal curve for intelligence is highly unlikely. The U.S. Army, for example, in the Alpha test scores for intelligence given to draftees in World War I, found a skewed, not a normal, curve. Other summaries of intelligence scores show similarly skewed results. That children's intelligence scores would be identical with their fathers', over a period of fifty years, is equally unlikely.

Dorfman concluded that Burt's results were precisely what they should have been according to a theoretical formula for such work, but, he added, such results do not occur in nature. "The almost perfect fit of Burt's adult and child distributions to the normal curve suggests that his 'actual' distributions were not actual distributions." Furthermore, "we may now say that, beyond a reasonable doubt, the frequency distributions of Burt's tables . . . were carefully constructed so as to [be] in agreement with the normal curve." And, finally, "these findings show, beyond any reasonable doubt, that Burt fixed the row and column totals of the tables in his highly acclaimed 1961 study."

We might ask, along with Gillie, "Why did psychologists, educationalists, and civil servants let him get away with it for so long?—for any reasonably careful inspection shows Burt's work to be careless, riddled with implausibilities, and inadequately documented? . . . Sir Cyril Burt, the supposed guardian of intellectual rigour, the hero of the educational conservatives, the defender of a future which was to be given over to the genetically pure, was one of the most formidable confidence tricksters British society has produced. . . . Sir Cyril takes his place alongside the manufacturers of the Piltdown Skull."

SOURCES:

Dorfman, D. D., "The Cyril Burt Questions: New Findings," *Science*, **201**:1177, September 29, 1978.

Gillie, Oliver, "Sir Cyril Burt and the Great IQ Fraud," *New Statesman*, **24**, November, 1978.

———, "Burt's Missing Ladies," *Science*, **204**:1035, June 8, 1979.

Jensen, Arthur R., *Bias in Mental Testing*. New York: Free Press, 1980.

Kamin, Leon, *The Science and Politics of IQ*. New York: John Wiley & Sons, 1974.

Introduction

In Chapters 2 and 3, we saw how physical characteristics are influenced by the DNA in our cells. Furthermore, we discussed how individuals inherit genes from parents and how variations in genes (alleles) can cause different expressions of traits. In Chapter 4, we discussed how evolutionary factors, especially natural selection, can play a crucial role in human variation. In this chapter, we will broaden our perspective somewhat and focus on phenotypic variability as it is expressed both within and between entire *populations* of humans.

The Concept of Race

In discussions of human variation, people typically clump together various attributes such as skin color, shape of face, shape of nose, hair color, hair form, and eye color. They then place particular combinations of these traits into categories called *races*. Furthermore, these clusters of traits have been traditionally associated with specific geographic localities.

Although we all think we know what we mean by the term "race," in reality the term is often misused, for the concept of race is a very elusive one. First of all, the term *race* is frequently misapplied to groups that differ with regard to various cultural attributes.

One often hears references to, for example, the "English race" or the "German race." In these cases, people are really referring to nationality, not biological differences between groups. Another often heard phrase is the "Jewish race." What the speaker is really talking about here is a particular ethnic and religious identity. One even occasionally hears references to the "male" or "female race." Undeniably, gender differences do exist; however, it is hardly justifiable to categorize males and females within the same groups as racially distinct.

When anthropologists, geneticists, and other researchers use the term *race* they are referring specifically to populations that differ with regard to the frequency of certain biological (that is, inherited) characteristics. However, placing biological limitations upon the concept offers little clarification, and defining race is still an enormously difficult task, as we shall see.

Polytypic Refers to species composed of several populations that differ from each other with regard to certain physical traits.

All contemporary humans are members of the same **polytypic** species, *Homo sapiens*. A polytypic species is one composed of local populations that differ from one another with regard to one or several traits. Moreover, within local populations there is a great deal of phenotypic variability among individuals. Most species are polytypic, and, thus, there is no species type to which all members exactly conform.

Geographically localized human populations that share a cluster of *biological* traits not shared by other such populations are called races. Actually, there are probably as many definitions of the term *race* as there are people who write about it. While most definitions repeat a basic theme, there is, nevertheless, no general consensus as to what a precise definition is.

E. A. Hooton of Harvard University defined race as follows:

> A race is a great division of mankind, the members of which, though individually varying, are characterized as a group by a certain combination of morphological and metrical features, principally non-adaptive, which have been derived from their common descent (Hooton, 1926).

Here is a more modern definition:

> ... a division of a species which differs from other divisions by the frequency with which certain hereditary traits appear among its members (Brues, 1990).

One of the most recent modifications of the definition of race adds the concept of a *breeding* (or Mendelian) population (Garn, 1965). Objections to this approach are based on the idea that the concept of breeding populations may be difficult to apply (Livingstone, 1964). For example, Stanley Garn (1965) applies the term *Mediterranean* to a local race (see Table 5-1) that ranges from Tangier to the Dardanelles and includes the Arabian Peninsula. However, this is a very unlikely breeding population, containing as it does a number of different nationalities and ethnic and religious groupings. Very few Christians interbreed with Muslims, or Arab Beduins with, say, Italian farmers.

The foregoing comments are not intended to discourage or confuse. However, the fact is that there exists a great deal of confusion about race among anthropologists, geneticists, and others concerned with this concept. Obviously, there *are* physical differences among human beings. No one will mistake an indigenous resident of China for a European or African. However, the matter cannot rest with this statement, for the issue is not that simple.

Physical differences distinguishing large segments of *Homo sapiens* that are easily observable include primarily skin color, hair color, facial form, and body proportions. The ready *visibility* of these features reinforces their apparent significance. Clearly, as primates, we are a visually oriented species (see Chapter 8), so it seems to most people that there *are* human races. Moreover, the characterization of these groups is seen as quite simple.

However, there are numerous complexities in grouping humans, most of which are *not* immediately apparent. It is not as though "our eyes are deceiving us," but that superficial observations are not as *biologically* informative as other, less obvious data. For example, as we will see later in this chapter, the evidence from Mendelian traits (blood groups, etc.) compared to visual observations is more precise, more clearly genetically based, and thus more easily understood in an evolutionary framework.

Another difficulty in working through the confusing aspects of racial categorization is the tendency to think **typologically**. Human brains are organized to retain information according to classes of objects. For example, there are many differences in the variety of objects we recognize as "chairs." Nevertheless, we have a mental template of what features all chairs share, and the naming of objects as "chairs" (and quite likely memory patterning as well) reflects these common features. In order to *reduce complexity* and deal effectively with our surroundings, humans subconsciously overlook variation—and, alternatively, focus on relatively broad (largely visual) cues.

Today there are billions of humans on the planet. In a large urban setting, one could easily see thousands of people in a single day. At some level, we know all these individuals differ, but we simply classify them all together as a group of "strangers." We use more precise visual cues to discriminate relatives and friends. (As a further evolutionary note, we should point out that monkeys and apes apparently recognize other group members in the same manner.) Yet, to avoid stimulus overload, particularly when grouping strangers, superficial categorization is the almost inevitable result. When trying to understand the ways in which people differ, emphasis on superficial visual cues is the human tendency, often resulting in gross superficial classification and bias.

Typology   The sorting of phenomena into simple types. Traditional racial classifications were largely based on typological thinking.

Table 5-1   Racial Classifications

Linnaeus, 1758	**Blumenbach, 1781**
Homo europaeus	Caucasian
Homo asiaticus	Mongolian
Homo afer	Malay
Homo americanus	Ethiopian
	American

E. A. Hooton, 1926

PRIMARY RACE	PRIMARY SUBRACE	COMPOSITE RACE*	COMPOSITE SUBRACE*	RESIDUAL MIXED TYPES*
White	Mediterranean	Australian	Armenoid	Nordic-Alpine
	Ainu	Indo-Dravidian	Dinaric	Nordic-Mediterranean
	Keltic	Polynesian		
	Nordic			
	Alpine			
	East Baltic			
Negroid	African Negro	Bushman-Hottentot		
	Nilotic Negro			
	Negrito			
Mongoloid	Classic Mongoloid	Indonesian-Mongoloid		
	Arctic Mongoloid	American Indian		

SECONDARY SUBRACE

Malay-Mongoloid
Indonesian

Stanley M. Garn, 1965

GEOGRAPHICAL RACES: "A collection of race populations, separated from other such collections by major geographical barriers."

Amerindian	Melanesian-Papuan	Indian
Polynesian	Australian	European
Micronesian	Asiatic	African

LOCAL RACES: "A breeding population adapted to local selection pressures and maintained by either natural or social barriers to gene interchange."

These are examples of local races; there are many, many more.

Northwest European	East African	North Chinese
Northeast European	Bantu	Extreme Mongoloid
Alpine	Tibetan	Hindu
Mediterranean		

MICRO-RACES: Not well defined but apparently refers to neighborhoods within a city or a city itself since "marriage or mating, is a mathematical function of distance. With millions of potential mates, the male ordinarily chooses one near at hand."

*Example of categories, not to be read across.

Relevant biological/genetic data are more obscure and in some ways "counterintuitive," incompatible with what our first glance so quickly infers. Consequently, a major goal of scientific inquiry is to overcome biases and more accurately understand the world (and people) around us.

To understand the difficulties the concept of race presents, it may help to summarize briefly the process of *speciation*, or the appearance of a new

species. A species is defined as a *group of interbreeding organisms that is reproductively isolated from other such groups*. As populations within a species diverge geographically, differences between them arise as each population makes biological adjustments to its own local environment. When the differences become detectable, taxonomists may classify these populations as races or subspecies. Eventually, they may become sufficiently distinct that breeding between the two is no longer possible. At that point they are considered two separate species. (See Chapter 11 for more detail.)

Populations of humans today are not on their way to becoming separate species. Although human groups have been distributed throughout the Old World long enough for regional variations to appear, we do not know exactly when the process began. More importantly, by the time humans dispersed out of Africa to Europe and Asia, they were, to some extent, adapting to the natural environment by cultural means. Since that time, we have increasingly used culture to buffer the effects of the environment. Moreover, the considerable degree of *migration* that has characterized human populations for some time ensures that no group remains isolated for long. Thus, speciation does not occur. We can say then, that biological adaptation has, to varying degrees, been shaped by cultural evolution.

Species A group of interbreeding organisms that is reproductively isolated from other such groups.

Historical Views toward Human Variation

The first step toward human understanding of natural phenomena is the ordering of variation into categories that can then be named, discussed, and perhaps studied. Historically, when different groups came into contact with one another, they offered explanations for the phenotypic variations they saw. Because skin color was so noticeable, it was one of the more frequently explained traits, and most systems of racial classification were based upon it.

The ancient Egyptians may have been the first to classify humans on the basis of skin color. Because of their military and trading successes (including the slave trade), the Egyptians were familiar with black Africans to the south and many peoples to the east. As early as 1350 B.C., they had classified groups on the basis of skin color: red for Egyptian, yellow for people to the east, white for those to the north, and black for Africans from the south (Gossett, 1963, p. 4).

The ancient Greeks referred to all black Africans as "Ethiopians," meaning "scorched ones" (Brues, 1990), implying a response to exposure to the sun. Ovid, a first century A.D. Roman poet, presents us with a Greek myth that offers an environmental explanation for the dark skin color of sub-Saharan Africans (Book Two of Ovid's *Metamorphoses*).

The sun god, Apollo, ill-advisedly allowed his adolescent son Phaeton to drive the chariot of the sun through its daily round across the sky. Feeling an unfamiliar hand upon the reins, the fiery chariot horses bolted, and in their frenzy, they plummeted toward the earth. In the end, Apollo was forced to kill Phaeton in order to keep the earth from burning and, as Ovid tells us:

> . . . that was when, or so men think, the people
> Of Africa turned black, since the blood was driven
> By that fierce heat to the surface of their bodies . . .
> (Humphries, 1973, p. 35).

Until the late fifteenth century, most Europeans were unfamiliar with people from other parts of the world. From the fall of Rome (A.D. 455) until the

Renaissance, most Europeans were pretty much isolated from the mainstream of people and events in the rest of the world.

The Arabs, who by the seventh century A.D. had expanded throughout the Mediterranean, were not so isolated. Through extensive trade routes and because they controlled the slave trade out of what is now the Sudan, the Arabs had knowledge of many peoples. Not surprisingly, they had their own explanations for how humans came to differ from area to area. Skin color was seen as a function of a type of embryonic cooking process. In northern climates, infants were pale and blond because the womb never warmed up properly, so they were not quite "done." By contrast, in hot southern areas, the contents of the womb were overdone to the point that people had their skin burned black and their hair scorched and frizzled (Lewis, 1971, *in*: Brues, 1990). The Arabs considered themselves to be intermediate between these extremes and, "To their way of thinking, only they themselves were 'done' just right" (Brues, 1990, p. 13).

In the sixteenth century, after the discovery of the New World, Europe embarked upon a period of intense exploration and colonization in both the New and Old Worlds. Resulting from this contact was an increased awareness of racial diversity.

The discovery of the New World was of major importance in shaking the complacency of Europeans, who viewed the world as static and nonchanging. In the Americas, early explorers found numerous species of previously unknown (to them) plants and animals. But the most important discovery was that these new lands were inhabited by groups of dark-skinned people who were not Christian, spoke strange languages, and by all appearances, were not "civilized." Native Americans were, at first, thought to be Asian, and since Columbus believed he had discovered a new route to India, he called them "Indians." (This term was later applied to indigenous, dark-skinned populations of Australia as well.)

By the late eighteenth century, Europeans and Americans were asking questions that posed challenges to traditional Christian beliefs and standards of morality. They wanted to know if other groups belonged to the same species as themselves; that is, were they indeed human? Were they descendants of Adam and Eve or had there been later creations of non-Europeans? If the latter were true, then they had to represent different species or else the Genesis account of creation could not be taken literally.

Europeans also wondered if it were possible for themselves and non-Europeans to interbreed and produce fertile offspring. Was mental capacity in Native Americans and the peoples of Africa, India, and elsewhere comparable to that of Europeans? Did traits such as skin color and shape of face and head contribute to character and morality?

Monogenism The nonevolutionary theory that all human races are descendants of one pair (Adam and Eve).

Polygenism Another nonevolutionary theory that states human races are not all descended from Adam and Eve and therefore are not all members of the same species.

Two schools of thought, known as **monogenism** and **polygenism**, devised responses. In the monogenist view, all races were descended from a single, original pair (Adam and Eve). Insisting on the plasticity of the human physical structure, monogenists contended that climate, environment, and local conditions modified the original form, resulting in separate races. Monogenist views were initially attractive to many, for they did not conflict with the Genesis version of creation.

The polygenist view, on the other hand, argued that races did not descend from a single, original pair, but from a number of pairs. Also, they saw such a wide gap in the physical, mental, and moral attributes between themselves and other races that they were sure that outsiders belonged to different species.

Other polygenists were dissatisfied with the concept of species and resorted to using the word *type* instead. However, they believed there had been "pure" races in the past, which through intermixture, migration, and conquest had become modified to their present condition. Nor did polygenists accept the monogenist notion of plasticity of physical traits, and they rejected the proposition that climate and environment were modifying instruments.

The first scientific attempt to describe the newly discovered variation, including human, was Linnaeus' taxonomic classification, which ordered humans into four separate categories (Linnaeus, 1758). (See Table 5-1.) Linnaeus assigned behavioral and intellectual qualities to each group, with the least complimentary descriptions going to African blacks. This ranking was typical of the period and reflected the almost universal European view that they were superior to all other peoples.

Johann Friedrich Blumenbach (1752–1840), a German anatomist, classified humans into five races: Caucasoid, Mongoloid, American, Ethiopian, and Malayan. Although Blumenbach's categories came to be described simply as White, Yellow, Red, Black, and Brown, he also used other criteria than skin color. Moreover, Blumenbach emphasized that racial categories based upon skin color were arbitrary and that many traits, including skin color, were not discrete phenomena. Rather, what we now call polygenic traits existed on a continuum and showed a wide range of expression. He pointed out that to attempt to classify all humans using such a system would be to omit altogether all those who did not neatly fall into a specific category.

Although most scientists were monogenists in the early nineteenth century, by 1850 polygenism was gaining favor. Some scientists, taking the polygenist view that certain physical traits were stable (that is, nonadaptive), began measuring the skull. (The skull was regarded as unchanging, and in order to determine racial differences fully, it was necessary to use a trait that, in their view, did not change.) Also, the skull was selected because it housed the brain, and conventional wisdom of the time erroneously held that there was a direct correlation between size and shape of the brain and intelligence and morality. There is certainly a relationship between the brain and intelligence. However, there is a wide range of normal variation regarding brain size in humans, and within that range, we now know that size is not an indicator of cognitive ability.

In 1842, Anders Retzius, a Swedish anatomist, developed the *cephalic index* as a method for describing the shape of the head. The cephalic index illustrates the ratio of head breadth to length, and Retzius used it to divide Europeans into two types: **dolichocephalics**, or those with long, narrow heads; and those with broad heads, or **brachycephalics**. Northern Europeans tended to be dolichocephalic while southern Europeans (including the French and many Germans) were brachycephalic. Not surprisingly, these results led to some heated and nationalistic debate over whether one group was superior to the other.

By the mid-nineteenth century, monogenists were beginning to reject their somewhat egalitarian concept of race in favor of a more hierarchical view. Therefore, they came to accept what was obvious to most Europeans; namely, that Europeans were superior to all other peoples. Races were ranked essentially on a scale based on color (along with size and shape of the head), with Africans at the bottom. Moreover, Europeans themselves were ranked so that northern, light-skinned populations were considered superior to their southern, more olive-skinned neighbors.

Dolicocephalic   Having a long, narrow head. A skull in which the width is less than 75% of the length.

Brachycephalic   Having a broad head or a skull in which the width is 80% or more of the length.

Biological determinism The concept that various aspects of behavior (e.g., intelligence, values, morals) are governed by biological factors (genes). The inaccurate association of various behavioral attributes with certain biological traits, such as skin color.

Eugenics The science of race improvement through forced sterilization of members of some groups and encouraged reproduction among others. An overly simplified, often racist view—now discredited.

Many non-Europeans were not Christian and were seen as "uncivilized," which implied an inferiority of character and intellect. This view was based upon a concept known as **biological determinism**, which holds that there is an association between physical characteristics and such attributes as intelligence, morals, values, abilities, and even social and economic differences between groups. In other words, cultural variations are inherited in the same manner as are biological variations. It follows then that there are inherent behavioral and cognitive differences between groups (racism), or between sexes (sexism); and, therefore, some groups are *by nature* superior to others. Following this logic, it is a simple matter to justify the persecution and enslavement of other peoples, simply because their appearance differs from what is familiar.

After 1850, biological determinism was a constant theme underlying common thinking as well as scientific research in Europe and the United States. Moreover, deterministic views (and, indeed, what we today would call racist views) were held to some extent by most people, including such notable figures as Thomas Jefferson, Georges Cuvier, Benjamin Franklin, Charles Lyell, Abraham Lincoln, Charles Darwin, and Oliver Wendell Holmes. Commenting upon this usually deemphasized characteristic of notable historical figures, Stephen J. Gould (1981, p. 32) of Harvard University emphasizes that, "All American culture heroes embraced racial attitudes that would embarrass public-school mythmakers."

At the same time, some scientists were becoming frustrated over their inability to define racial groups. Many shared the opinion that race was merely a hypothetical concept because it was rare that an individual possessed all the traits characteristic of his or her race. However, in spite of these sentiments, the predominant view was that races existed and culturally determined characteristics were inherited.

Francis Galton (1822–1911), a cousin of Charles Darwin, shared an increasingly common fear among Europeans that civilized society was being weakened by the failure of natural selection to eliminate unfit and inferior members (Greene, 1981, p. 107).* Galton wrote and lectured on the necessity of race improvement and suggested governmental regulation of marriage and family size, an approach he called **eugenics**.

Galton's writings attracted a considerable following both in Europe and the United States, and a number of eugenics societies were formed. The eugenics movement had a great deal of snob appeal, for fitness was deemed to be embodied in the upper classes, while the lower classes were associated with criminality, illness, and mental retardation. Moreover, many eugenics societies sought to rid society of crime, as well as such perceived ills as homosexuality, through mandatory sterilization programs.

Although eugenics had its share of critics, its popularity flourished on both sides of the Atlantic until the 1930s. After World War I, the movement was increasingly popular in Europe, but nowhere was it more popular than in Germany, where the movement took a disastrous turn. The idea of a pure race was extolled as a means of reestablishing a strong and prosperous state, and eugenics was seen as scientific justification for purging Germany of her "unfit." Many of Germany's scientists accepted this interpretation (known as *Rassenhygiene* or racial hygiene) and continued to support it during the Nazi period (Proctor, 1988, p. 143), when it served as justification for condemning millions of people to death.

---

*Greene suggests that Darwin also held this belief. Scholars, however, are divided about whether or not Darwin himself held this view.

After World War I, some physical anthropologists turned away from racial classification as the validation of traditional racial concepts, and the goals of the eugenics movement increasingly came into question. Moreover, the synthesis of Mendelian genetics and Darwin's theories of natural selection in the 1930s (see Modern Synthesis, p. 90) influenced all the biological sciences, and physical anthropologists began to apply evolutionary principles to the study of human variation (as illustrated later in this chapter).

Racial classification was not dead, however. Carleton S. Coon (1962) proposed a taxonomy also composed of five groups, based upon a somewhat earlier one developed by R. R. Gates (1948). The nomenclature used in these two systems was the same: Caucasoid, Negroid, Mongoloid, Australoid, and Capoid. Today three large racial groups are recognized by some anthropologists. However, there is hardly concensus on this point.

The Problems of Typological Approaches to Racial Taxonomy

There are numerous problems inherent in racial taxonomies. Classification schemes are *typological* in nature, meaning that categories are discrete and based upon a concept or ideal that comprises a specific set of traits. Typologies may be useful in certain situations. (For example, forensic anthropologists and law enforcement officials frequently use racial criteria to aid in the identification of crime victims.) However, racial typologies are misleading, for there are always individuals in any grouping who do not fit a particular type.

In any so-called racial group there will be individuals who fall into the normal range of variation for another group, with regard to one or even several traits. Although, it is unlikely that anyone is going to mistake a person whose background is Danish for someone whose ancestry is Nigerian, these two individuals could share any number of traits, such as height, body build, or head shape. In fact, they could easily share more similarities with one another than they do with some individuals in their own population—in spite of the fact they differ regarding certain highly noticeable attributes, such as skin color. An important point to remember is that all of these physical characteristics (such as skin color, hair color, head shape) which have been so much a part of the *traditional* concept of race are polygenic in nature. As we discussed in Chapter 3, the precise genetic mechanism for *any* of these traits is not well established. Thus, in their attempts to describe biological/genetic differences among human populations, anthropologists, geneticists, and other contemporary scholars usually prefer more clearly understood (that is, Mendelian) characteristics.

We do not wish to imply that, because traits are polygenic, they have *no* genetic basis. Such is clearly not the case. However, the pattern is more complex; neither the degree of genetic contribution nor the molecular mechanisms involved are known with any precision. In addition, several well-known polygenic traits are thought to have evolved as a result of adaptation. Most especially, variation in skin color among the world's populations is hypothesized to reflect adaptation to such selective factors as solar radiation, skin cancer, and frostbite (see Chapter 6 for a discussion).

Moreover, human biologists today emphasize differences *within* populations as well as *between* them. A good example of this approach is a study by

Harvard population geneticist R. D. Lewontin (1972). Lewontin demonstrated that the vast majority of human variation is explained by differences between individuals in the same groups (or even in the same family), rather than differences between large, geographically distributed populations. These results are understandable in light of the genetic mechanisms we discussed in Chapters 3 and 4. Physical anthropologists focus upon such genetic/evolutionary factors in explaining human diversity (see the remainder of this chapter and Chapter 6).

RACE AND BEHAVIOR

Belief in the relationship between race and specific behavioral attributes is popular even today, but evidence is lacking that personality or any other behavioral trait differs genetically *between* human groups. Most scientists would agree with this last statement, but there is one question that has produced controversy both inside scientific circles and among lay people— whether race (however defined) and intelligence are associated.

Both genetic and environmental factors contribute to intelligence, although it is not yet possible to accurately measure the percentage each contributes. What can be said is that IQ scores and intelligence are not the same thing; IQ scores can change during a person's lifetime, and IQ scores of racial and ethnic groups overlap. Moreover, complex cognitive abilities, however measured, are influenced by multiple loci, and are thus obviously strikingly polygenic.

> The problem in discussing the differences in IQ scores seems to arise when the quantitative differences in scores are converted into qualitative judgments used to rank groups as superior or inferior. Genetics, like all sciences, progresses by the formulation of hypotheses that can be rigorously and objectively tested. When intelligence can be objectively defined and measured (if ever), then genetic methods can be used to quantitatively approach the subject (Cummings, 1991, p. 361).

Innate factors set limits and define potentials for behavior and cognitive ability in any species. In humans, the limits are broad and the potentials are not fully known. Individual abilities result from complex interactions between genetic and environmental factors. One product of this interaction is learning, and the ability to learn has genetic or biological components. Undeniably, individuals vary regarding these biological components. However, elucidating what proportion of the variation in test scores is due to biological factors probably is not possible. Moreover, innate differences in abilities reflect individual variation *within* populations, not inherent differences *between* groups. Comparing populations on the basis of IQ test results is a misuse of testing procedures.

In conclusion, what we really observe when we see biological variations between populations (and individuals) are the traces of our evolutionary past. Different expressions of traits such as skin color, eye color, and shape of face are the results of biological adaptations our ancestors made to local environmental conditions, in a process that began perhaps several hundred thousand years ago. Instead of using these differences as a basis for prejudice and persecution, we should praise them. We should recognize them for what they are, a preserved record of how natural selection shaped our species to meet the varied environmental challenges it faced while expanding to become the dominant form of life on our planet.

Racism

Racism is associated with discriminatory acts and attitudes toward "inferior" races. Racist beliefs are usually based on the alleged inferior mental abilities of a people and are often extended to their moral and ethical character. The belief that a people is genetically inferior may arise as a result of a number of factors, such as conquest, religion, family practices, moral and ethical systems, economic practices, technology, etc. Economic exploitation by an imperialistic power and competition for jobs (as new migrants enter the labor pool as, for example, in the United States and Germany) have been suggested as reasons (or justification) for racist attitudes. In the United States in recent years, riots in urban cities reflect a reaction to what is believed by the rioters to be racist attitudes, racist behavior, and frustrating economic conditions.

Racism is hardly restricted to European and American whites; it is worldwide, found on every continent. Racism is a cultural, not a biological, phenomenon. And, unfortunately, it appears that no matter what we say about the lack of evidence for mental inferiority and raise doubts about the validity of intelligence tests, racism not only flourishes but can lead to terrorism, devastation of populations, local wars, and ultimately, perhaps, nuclear war.

We end our discussion of race and racism with a citation taken from an article, "The Study of Race," written by Sherwood Washburn, a well-known physical anthropologist at the University of California, Berkeley. Although written some years ago, the statement is as fresh and applicable today as it was when it was written:

> . . . Races are products of the past. They are relics of times and conditions which have long ceased to exist.
>
> Racism is equally a relic supported by no phase of modern science. We may not know how to interpret the form of the Mongoloid face, or why Rh is of high incidence in Africa, but we do know the benefits of education and of economic progress. We . . . know that the roots of happiness lie in the biology of the whole species and that the potential of the species can only be realized in a culture, in a social system. It is knowledge and the social system which give life or take it away, and in so doing change the gene frequencies and continue the million-year-old interaction of culture and biology. Human biology finds its realization in a culturally determined way of life, and the infinite variety of genetic combinations can only express themselves efficiently in a free and open society (Washburn, 1963, p. 531).

A Perspective on Race

What can we conclude about the concept of race? Some scholars have argued that the whole subject is so emotionally charged that the term *race* should be avoided altogether. However, while there is no complete consensus on this point, most experts prefer to confront the issues and *relevant* data rather than argue about semantics. As Alice Brues, an eminent scholar, with a lifetime of experience in this field, recently put it:

> A popular political statement now is "There is no such thing as race." I wonder what people are going to think when they hear this. They would have to suppose that the speaker, if he were dropped by parachute into downtown Nairobi, would be unable to tell, by looking around him, whether he was in Nairobi or Stockholm. This could only damage his credibility. . . . the visible differences

between different populations of the world tell everyone that *there is something there*. We had better be prepared to explain what is there and why, before we discuss what it does or does not mean (Brues, 1991).

We have suggested that the nature of cognitive patterning predisposes humans to sort visual cues superficially and to think typologically. Thus, regardless of its biological reality, race has a significance in terms of human perception. In addition, in agreement with the opinion voiced by Brues, other contemporary researchers also see the broader, more traditional, categories as biologically relevant. For example, L. L. Cavalli-Sforza, a leading population geneticist, suggests that the proportion of all human population variation described by geographic and local races together (by some measures, after Lewontin, 1972, estimated at approximately 15%) is biologically significant. Cavalli-Sforza goes on to conclude the most relevant way to sort the large geographic segments of *Homo sapiens*, using both visible phenotypic *and* genetic data, is into three geographic categories: Africans, Europeans, and Easterners (the latter including Asian, Pacific, and New World populations). While certainly representing a minority of the *total* variation exhibited within contemporary *Homo sapiens*, this degree of genetic variation need not necessarily be ignored—or, as some have suggested, deliberately avoided.

Contemporary Approaches to Human Variation

While the traditional view of human variation has emphasized the construction of racial typologies, perspectives in the latter part of the twentieth century (utilizing modern evolutionary theory) have concentrated on more precise aspects of human diversity. In particular, there has developed a focus on *population* biology and the necessity of using precisely determined genetic differences to characterize these populations. Accordingly, Mendelian traits (such as those discussed in Chapter 3) are the primary tools of anthropologists and other biologists who seek to characterize and understand the patterns of human variation. This approach has developed as a subfield called *population genetics*.

THE POPULATION

As implied, population genetics attempts to depict genetic variation within a population framework. Thus, it is first necessary to discuss how population geneticists define the population units they study. A **population** is a group of interbreeding individuals. More precisely, the population is the group within which one is most likely to find a mate. As such, a population is a genetic unit marked by a degree of genetic relatedness and sharing in a common **gene pool**. In theory, this concept is not particularly difficult. Picture a kind of giant blender into which every generation's genes are mixed (by recombination). What comes out in the next generation is a direct produce of the genes going into the pool, which in turn is a direct result of who is mating with whom.

In practice, however, isolating and describing actual human populations is a sticky business. The largest population of *Homo sapiens* that could be described is the entire species, all of whose members are at least potentially capable of interbreeding (but are incapable of interbreeding, fertilely, with

Population A group of individuals from which mates are usually found. A population shares a common gene pool.

Gene pool The total complement of genes shared by the reproductive members in a population.

members of other species). Our species is thus a *genetically closed system* (human/nonhuman hybrids are not known). The problem arises not in describing who potentially can interbreed, but in isolating exactly the patterns of those individuals who are doing so.

Factors that determine mate choice are geographical, ecological, and social. If individuals are isolated into groups in an Alpine village or on an island in the middle of the Pacific, there is not much possibility of finding a mate outside the immediate vicinity. Such **breeding isolates** are fairly easily defined and are a favorite target of microevolutionary studies. Geography plays a dominant role within these isolates through influencing the range of available mates. But even within these limits cultural prescriptions can still play a powerful part in deciding who is most proper among those potentially available.

Breeding isolates Populations geographically (and/or socially) separate and, therefore, easy to define.

Population Genetics

Once the population biologist has isolated a specific human population, the next step is to ascertain what evolutionary forces, if any, are operating on this group. In order to determine whether evolution is taking place, we measure allele frequencies for specific traits and compare the observed frequencies with a set predicted by a mathematical model: the **Hardy-Weinberg equilibrium** equation. This model provides us with a baseline set of evolutionary expectations under *known* conditions.

More precisely, Hardy-Weinberg equilibrium postulates a set of conditions where *no* evolution occurs. In other words, none of the forces of evolution is acting, and all genes have an equal chance of recombining in each generation (that is, random mating of individuals):

Hardy-Weinberg equilibrium The mathematical relationship expressing— under ideal conditions—the predicted distribution of genes in populations; the central theorem of population genetics.

1. The *population* is assumed to be *very large* (therefore, there is no sampling error—*no random genetic drift*)
2. *No mutation* (no new alleles are added by molecular alterations within gametes)
3. *No migration* (no new alleles are being added by influx from outside our target population)
4. *No selection* (specific alleles have no differential advantage over others relative to reproductive success)
5. *Random mating* (panmixia—there exists no bias in who mates with whom; any female is assumed to have an equal chance of mating with any male)

If all these conditions are satisfied, allele frequencies will not change (that is, no evolution will take place) and a permanent equilibrium will be maintained as long as these conditions prevail. An evolutionary "barometer" is thus provided that may be used as a standard against which actual circumstances are compared. Similar to the way a typical barometer is standardized under known temperature and altitude conditions, the Hardy-Weinberg equilibrium is standardized under known evolutionary conditions.

The relationship of the allele frequencies in populations to Mendelian genotypic proportions is a straightforward extension of simple Mendelian genetics. In fact, in 1903, soon after the rediscovery of Mendel's work, the American geneticist and animal breeder W. E. Castle developed a model·

showing the relationship of genes to populations. However, Castle felt the results were so obvious that he did not take the trouble to state unequivocally the conditions for genetic equilibrium nor did he actively push for acceptance of his views.

However, within just five years, the English mathematician G. H. Hardy (1877–1947) and the German physician W. Weinberg (1862–1937) independently reached the same conclusion, and their formulation eventually won wide acceptance. The mathematical relationship of allele and genotype frequencies in populations is therefore usually called the Hardy-Weinberg formula or "law."

Interestingly, we note once again that the science of genetics was advancing intellectually along a broad international front. At the turn of the century, three scientists in three different countries discovered Mendel's initial contribution and realized its implications. Within just another 8 years the application of these principles to populations was again independently reached in three separate countries, and the discipline of population genetics was born.

Under the idealized conditions of Hardy-Weinberg equilibrium no new alleles are added and no alleles removed from the population. Moreover, every allele for a given locus has an equal chance of combining with any other allele at that locus within the gene pool.

The simplest situation applicable to a microevolutionary study is a genetic trait that follows a simple Mendelian pattern and has only two alleles (A, a). As you recall from earlier discussions, there are then only three possible genotypes: AA, Aa, aa. Proportions of these genotypes (AA:Aa:aa) are a function of the **allele frequencies** themselves (percentage of A; percentage of a). In order to provide uniformity for all genetic loci, a standard notation is employed to refer to these frequencies:

Allele frequency The proportion of one allele to all others at a given locus in a population.

Frequency of first allele (A) = p (p = frequency of the dominant allele—if there is dominance)

Frequency of second allele (a) = q (q = frequency of the recessive allele)

Since in this case there are only two alleles, their combined total frequency must represent all possibilities. In other words:

$$p \quad + \quad q \quad = 1 \text{ (unity; that is, 100\% of alleles in the gene pool)}$$
(Proportion (Proportion
of A alleles) of a alleles)

To ascertain the expected proportions of genotypes, we simply compute the chances of the alleles combining with one another into all possible combinations. Remember, they all have an equal chance of combining and no new alleles are being added.

These probabilities are a direct function of the frequency of the two alleles. The chances of all possible combinations occurring randomly can be simply shown as:

$$
\begin{array}{r}
p + q \\
\times \quad p + q \\
\hline
pq + q^2 \\
p^2 + \ pq \\
\hline
p^2 + 2pq + q^2
\end{array}
$$

(mathematically, this is known as a binomial expansion)

What we have just calculated is simply:

ALLELE COMBINATION	GENOTYPE PRODUCED	EXPECTED PROPORTION IN POPULATION
Chances of:		
A combining with A	AA	$p \times p = p^2$
Chances of:		
A combining with a	Aa	
a combining with A	aA	$\begin{array}{l} p \times q \\ p \times q \end{array} = 2pq$
Chances of:		
a combining with a	aa	$q \times q = q^2$

Proportions of genotypes	AA:	Aa:	aa
	p^2	$2pq$	q^2

where p = frequency of dominant allele and q = frequency of recessive allele in a population.

CALCULATING ALLELE FREQUENCIES: AN EXAMPLE

How microevolutionists use the Hardy-Weinberg formula is best demonstrated through an example. Let us return to the classroom "population" we discussed in Chapter 4 (and now assume it consists of 100 individuals). Now that you are aware of the precise definition of a breeding population, you can see that a classroom group does not meet the key prerequisite of social and/or geographic isolation. But once again let us assume that it does and thus represents a good biological population.

In addition, we will use the MN blood group locus as the gene to be measured. This gene produces a blood group antigen*—similar to ABO—located on red blood cells. Since the M and N alleles are codominant, we can ascertain everyone's phenotype by taking blood samples and observing reactions with specially prepared antisera. From the phenotypes we can then directly calculate the allele frequencies. So let us proceed.

All 100 individuals are tested and the results are shown in Box 5-1. Although the match between observed and expected frequencies is not perfect, it is close enough statistically to satisfy equilibrium conditions. Since our population is not a large one, sampling may easily account for the small observed deviations. Our population is therefore probably in equilibrium (that is, it is not evolving). At the minimum, what we can say scientifically is that we cannot reject the *null hypothesis* ("null" meaning nothing, basically a statistical condition of randomness; a statement of equilibrium in this case).

Human Polymorphisms

How do anthropologists study evolution in contemporary populations? The method, as we have outlined, is to apply the techniques of population genetics. The specific tools employed require certain kinds of *simple* genetic traits, ones we have termed *polymorphisms*. We mentioned in Chapter 4 that a **polymorphism** is a trait (the phenotypic expression of a single locus) with two or more alleles in appreciable frequency. How much is "appreciable" is a fairly

Polymorphism *poly*: many; *morph*: form
A genetic locus with two or more alleles in appreciable frequency.

---

*Antigens are large macromolecules, usually proteins, which react specifically with antibodies.

Box 5-1 Calculating Allele Frequencies in a Hypothetical Population

OBSERVED DATA:

Genotype	Number of Individuals*	Percent	Number of Alleles M	N
MM	40	(40%)	80	
MN	40	(40%)	40	40
NN	20	(20%)		40
Totals	100	(100%)	120 + 80 = 200	
		Proportion:	.6 + .4 = 1	

OBSERVED ALLELE FREQUENCIES:

$M = .6(p)$ $p + q$ should $= 1$ (and they do)
$N = .4(q)$

Expected Frequencies What are the predicted genotype proportions if genetic equilibrium (no evolution) applies to our population? We simply apply the Hardy-Weinberg formula: $p^2 + 2pq + q^2$

p^2	=	$(.6) \times (.6)$	= .36
$2pq$	=	$2(.6)(.4) = 2(.24)$	= .48
q^2	=	$(.4) \times (.4)$	= .16
Total			1.00

There are only three possible genotypes (MM:MN:NN) so the total of the relative proportions should equal 1.00; as you can see, they do.

How do these expected frequencies compare with the observed frequencies in our population?

	EXPECTED FREQUENCY	OBSERVED FREQUENCY
MM	.36	.40
MN	.48	.40
NN	.16	.20

*Please note: The whole purpose of using the Hardy-Weinberg equilibrium is to make these kinds of comparisons between observed and expected frequencies. Each individual has two alleles; thus a person who is MM contributes two M alleles to the total gene pool. A person who is MN contributes one M and one N. One hundred individuals, then, have 200 alleles for the MN locus.

arbitrary judgment, but is usually placed at around 1%. In other words, if a population is sampled for a particular genetic trait and frequencies of more than one allele are higher than 1%, the trait is polymorphic.

The limit of 1% is an attempt to control for mutation effects, which should always be adding new alleles much less frequently than our 1% level (mutation rates are probably more like 1/10,000—or lower). So when an allele such as sickle-cell is found in some populations in frequencies approaching 10% (with the normal allele thus approximately 90%), this is clearly polymorphic. The frequencies of the two alleles are higher than can be accounted for by mutation *alone* and thus demands a fuller evolutionary explanation. In this case, the additional mechanism is natural selection.

Clearly, then, the understanding of human genetic polymorphisms demands evolutionary explanations. As students of human evolution, physical anthropologists use these polymorphisms as their principal tool both to measure and understand the dynamics of evolution in modern populations.

In particular, they employ *simple* (that is, Mendelian) genetic polymorphisms whose genetic mechanisms are known. Such *polygenic traits* as stature, IQ, etc. are no doubt partly genetic, but we do not know which or even how many alleles are involved. On the other hand, simple polymorphisms are controlled by one genetic locus, and the different alleles are directly ascertainable at the phenotypic level.

By employing such simple polymorphisms, and by comparing allele frequencies in different human populations, we can reconstruct the evolutionary events that relate these groups with one another.

Polymorphisms Found in Human Blood

In addition to the hemoglobin variants possibly related to malaria, there are a great many other polymorphisms known in human blood. Because samples can be easily obtained and transported, blood has long been the favorite tissue for studying human polymorphisms. Consequently, we know a good deal concerning a wide variety of polymorphisms in red blood cells, white blood cells, and in the blood serum. Other tissues are probably just as variable, but as you will see, most of our current information concerns traits found in human blood.

RED BLOOD CELL ANTIGEN SYSTEMS

ABO   With the first use of transfusions as a medical practice around the turn of the century, serious problems were immediately recognized. Some patients had severe reactions, such as agglutination (clumping) of their blood cells, kidney failure, and even death. Very soon after transfusions became common, the underlying cause of these incompatibilities was shown by Karl Landsteiner, in 1900, to be due to a genetic trait. This trait, called the ABO blood group system, is expressed phenotypically in individuals as antigens located on the surface of their red blood cells. The blood group (that is, what antigens a person has) is directly determined by his/her genotype for the ABO locus. The complications sometimes resulting from transfusions are due to *antigen-antibody* reactions. In a highly sophisticated and specific fashion, the body can recognize foreign antigens (proteins) and combat their invasion by producing specific antibodies that deactivate the foreign substances. Such an *immune response* is normally beneficial, for it is the basis of fighting infections caused by a foreign bacteria or virus. (See pp. 156–160.)

Usually antibodies must be produced when foreign antigens are introduced. However, in the case of ABO, naturally occurring antibodies are already present in the blood serum at birth. Actually, no antibodies are probably "natural," although they may be (as in ABO) stimulated early in fetal life. The genotypes, phenotypes, and antibodies in the ABO system are shown in Table 3-2.

The ABO system is most interesting from an anthropological perspective because the frequencies of the three alleles (A, B, O) vary tremendously among human populations. As the distribution maps indicate (see Fig. 5-1), A or B is only rarely found in frequencies greater than 50%; usually frequencies for these two alleles are considerably below this figure. Most human groups, however, are polymorphic for all three alleles. Occasionally, as in native South American Indians, frequencies of O reach 100%, and this allele is said to be "fixed" in this population. Indeed, in most native New World populations, O is at least 80% and is usually considerably higher. Unusually high frequencies of O are also found in northern Australia, and some islands off the coast show frequencies of 90% and higher. Since these frequencies are considerably greater than for presumably closely related mainland populations, founder effect is probably the evolutionary agent responsible.

In general, the lowest values for O found in the world are in eastern Europe and central Asia. As you might expect, frequencies for A and B can only be relatively higher where O tends to be lower. Generally, B is the rarest of the three alleles and, except for Eskimos, it appears to have been completely absent in the pre-Columbian New World. Moreover, the allele has apparently been introduced into Australia only in recent times.

The B allele reaches its highest peak in Eurasia, where its distribution is the inverse of O. Values up to 20% and occasionally slightly higher are found in a broad area in central Asia, western Siberia, and central Mongolia. The highest reported frequencies for B are found in the Himalaya area, reaching a peak of 25–30%.

Generally, the frequency of B declines gradually in populations the further westward they are in Eurasia. Such a gradual distribution of allele frequencies over space is a good example of what is called a **cline** (see p. 132).

The A allele has two interesting peaks, one among Blackfoot Indians and surrounding groups in North America and the other distributed over almost the entire Australian continent. With frequencies greater than 50%, the Blackfoot display the highest frequencies of A anywhere in the world. Certainly they are divergent from other North American groups, who all have very high frequencies of O (and, therefore, low frequencies of A). How did A increase so much among this one tribe and its close neighbors compared to surrounding populations? Possibly drift (founder effect) is the answer, possibly some unknown selective factor. No one knows.

In Australia, except for the northern part, frequencies of A are generally high—particularly in central Australia, where they are 40% or higher. One tribe has especially high frequencies of A (53%), significantly higher than any surrounding group. Once again, is founder effect responsible? Over the rest of Australia, frequencies of A are fairly even in distribution and are gradually decreasing as populations become further removed from the center of the continent.

We must point out that distributions of alleles for a single genetic trait like ABO do not conclusively demonstrate genetic relationships between populations. For example, the North American Blackfoot and central Australian Mandjiljara have similar frequencies of A, but are obviously not closely related. On the other hand, in South Africa, the San have lower B frequencies than Hottentots with whom they share fairly close genetic ties. In order to understand *patterns* of population relationships, it is absolutely necessary to consider allele frequency distributions for several traits simultaneously (see p. 132).

Why do frequencies of the ABO alleles vary so much in different populations? In some cases, as with the islands off northern Australia and perhaps with the Blackfoot, drift may be the key factor. However, the clinal distribution of alleles (as B in Eurasia; A in Australia) indicates selection may also be playing an important role, for the regularity in the frequency distributions is thought to mirror gradual changes in environments.

If, in fact, selection is operating, what are the specific factors involved? Unfortunately, unlike sickle-cell, there is not as yet any proven association between ABO frequencies and *any* selective agent (such as various diseases,

Cline   A distribution of allele frequencies over space. Actually, the depiction of frequencies by connecting lines of equal frequency (an isopleth), as in temperature indicators on a weather map. See Figures 5-1 and 5-2, for examples.

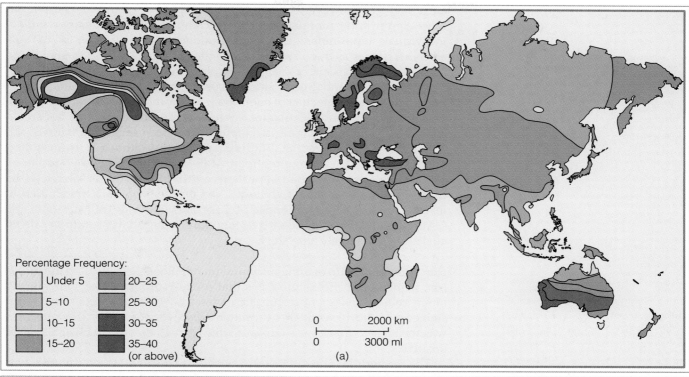

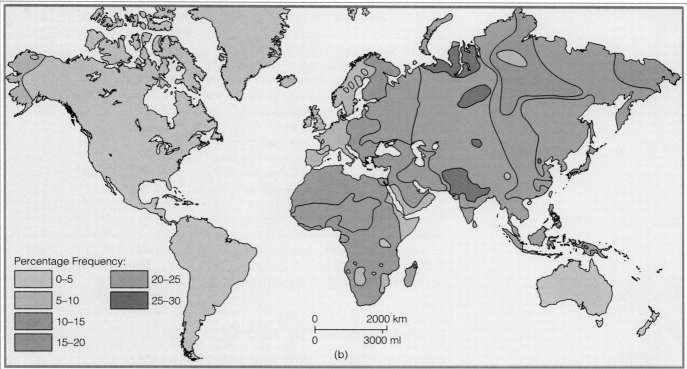

Figure 5-1

(a) *ABO blood group system. Distribution of the A allele in the indigenous populations of the world.* (b) *ABO blood group system. Distribution of the B allele in the indigenous populations of the world. (After Mourant et al., 1976.)*

etc.). There are, however, some suggestive clues. For example, A individuals have significantly more stomach cancer and pernicious anemia, while O individuals have more gastric and duodenal ulcers (Vogel, 1970). Such chronic diseases as these are not that common; indeed, they probably do not affect reproductive success very much, since they occur so late in life.

On the other hand, infectious diseases (as already shown for malaria) are potentially selective factors of enormous significance. Some interesting clinal association between ABO frequencies and incidence of smallpox, tuberculosis, syphilis, bubonic plague, and leprosy have been suggested. Moreover, it has also been suggested that O individuals are more attractive to mosquitoes and are thus bitten more often than A, B, or AB individuals (Wood et al., 1972). Here, too, could be an important contributing factor for infectious disease, since many—malaria, yellow fever, typhus, etc.—are transmitted by insects (Brues, 1977). As yet none of these associations is well substantiated. Consequently, the evolutionary factors influencing the distribution of ABO alleles are still largely a mystery.

Rh Another group of antigens found on red blood cells is called the *Rh system*, named after rhesus monkeys that initially provided the source of red blood cells to make antiserum. Discovered in 1940 by Wiener and Landsteiner (a full forty years after the latter's discovery of ABO!), this antiserum was then tested in a large sample of white Americans, in which 85% reacted positively.

The individuals showing such a positive agglutination reaction are usually called Rh positive (Rh⁺) and those whose blood does not agglutinate with the antiserum are called Rh negative (Rh⁻). These standardized designations refer to an apparently simple two-allele system with DD and Dd as Rh⁺ and the recessive dd as Rh⁻.

Clinically, the Rh factor—like ABO—can lead to serious complications. However, the greatest problem is not so much incompatibilities following transfusions as those between a mother and her developing fetus. For most significant medical applications, Rh⁺ compared to Rh⁻ is accounted for by the three genotypes noted above (DD, Dd, dd). However, the actual genetics of the Rh system are a good deal more complex than explained by just two alleles at one locus. The famous English population geneticist Sir R. A. Fisher suggested that the Rh system is actually three closely linked loci with at least two alleles each (C and c, D and d, E and e).

The distribution of the various allele combinations within the Rh system (which may be pictured as large genes) varies considerably among human populations. Generally Rh⁻ (d) is quite high in European groups, averaging around 40%. African populations also have a fair amount of polymorphism at the D locus, with frequencies of Rh⁻ centering around 25%. Native American and Australians, on the other hand, are almost 100% Rh⁺.

OTHER RED BLOOD CELL ANTIGEN SYSTEMS

MN The pattern of inheritance of the MN blood group that we have referred to previously is very straightforward and is thus a favorite tool in population genetics research. There are three genotypes—MM, MN, NN—all clearly ascertainable at the phenotypic level using antisera obtained from rabbits. Clinically, no observable complications arise due to transfusions or mother-fetus incompatibilities; the MN system is anthropologically important because of its variable distribution among human populations.

Almost all human populations are polymorphic (that is, having both M and N in "appreciable" frequencies), but the relative frequency of the two alleles varies tremendously. In some areas of Australia, M is as low as 2% contrasted with many areas of the New World, where frequencies exceed 90%, even 100% in some areas. The allele M is also found in quite high frequency in Arabia, Siberia, and portions of Southeast Asia.

In addition to ABO, Rh, and MN, there are several other polymorphic red blood cell antigen systems. While not clinically significant like ABO or Rh, many of these are important for anthropological studies of population variation. Table 5-2 lists the currently known major antigen systems of human red blood cells.

POLYMORPHISMS IN WHITE BLOOD CELLS

An important polymorphic trait called the HLA (human lymphocyte antigen) system has been discovered on some white blood cells (lymphocytes). Of great medical importance, HLA loci affect histocompatibility or recognition and rejection of foreign tissues—the reason skin grafts and organ transplants are usually rejected. Genetically, the HLA system is exceedingly complex, and researchers are still discovering further subtleties within it. There are at least seven closely linked loci on chromosome number six, making up the HLA system. Taken together, there are already well over 100 antigens known within the system, with a potential of at least 30,000,000 different genotypes (Williams, 1985). By far, this is the most polymorphic of any known human genetic system.

The component loci of the HLA system function together as a kind of "supergene." In addition to the components of the HLA loci themselves, many other factors affecting immune response are known to exist in the same region of chromosome number six. Altogether, the whole system is called the *major histocompatibility complex* (MHC). (See pp. 156–157.)

The geographic distribution of the various MHC alleles is not yet well known. Some interesting patterns, however, are apparent. For example, Lapps, Sardinians, and Basques show deviations in frequencies of HLA alleles from other European populations, paralleling evidence for ABO, Rh, and MN. In addition, many areas in New Guinea and Australia are quite divergent, possibly suggesting the effects of drift. It is imperative, however, that care be taken in postulating genetic relatedness from restricted polymorphic information. Otherwise, such obviously ridiculous links as some of those proposed from HLA data (for example, Tibetans and Australian aborigines; Eskimos with some New Guineans) would obscure the evolutionary process in human populations (Livingstone, 1980). Since HLA is involved in the superfine detection and deactivation of foreign antigens, selection relative to infectious diseases (particularly those caused by viruses) may also play a significant role in the distribution of HLA alleles.

Evidence is still exceedingly tentative, but some HLA antigens are apparently associated with susceptibility to certain diseases. A disease of the spine called ankylosing spondylitis, multiple sclerosis, and some varieties of hay fever may all result from individuals developing an autoimmune response to their own HLA antigens.

Table 5-2   Other Blood Group Systems Used in Human Microevolutionary Studies

Major Systems	Number of Known Antigens
P	3
Lutheran	2
Kell-Cellano	5
Lewis	2
Duffy	2
Kidd	2
Diego	1
Auberger	1
Xg (sex-linked)	1
Dombrock	1
Stolzfus	1

SOURCE: Lerner and Libby, 1976, p. 354.

Human Polymorphisms: Anthropological Applications

All the patterns of variation in the diverse traits we have discussed may seem somewhat confusing. In fact, without the aid of computer technology it is difficult to gain a clear view of what is going on.

CLINAL DISTRIBUTION OF TRAITS

A relatively recent* approach to the study of human variation is to examine the *clinal distribution* of traits. In using this approach, we consider one trait at a time, examining its geographic distribution or how its frequency changes from one population to another. We have defined cline earlier (p. 128) and shown a well-known example, the distribution of the B allele in Eurasia (Fig. 5-1b).

Human variation is perceived quite differently when approached from a clinal point of view. No attempt is made to construct a typology of traits, but rather to apply the principles of evolution. Is variation in frequency of a trait due to natural selection and adaptation in local areas? Or does it result from migration into or within the clinal area?

Another example of an evolutionary clinal approach may be seen in Dr. Joseph Birdsell's discussion of the distribution of tawny (blond) hair among children in dark-skinned aboriginal populations of Australia. Blond hair has its highest incidence among tribal groups in the Australian western desert, and the frequency then declines on a gradient outward from this center, although not uniformly in all directions. Professor Birdsell writes (1981, pp. 352–353):

> The evolutionary significance of this clinal distribution seems apparent, even though the exact genetic basis for its inheritance has not yet been unraveled. The trait acts as though it was determined by a single codominant gene. It would appear that somewhere in the central region of high frequency, mutations, and probably repeated mutations, occurred from normal dark brown hair to this depigmented variety. The pattern of distribution indicates that it was favored by selection in some totally unknown fashion. Over considerable periods of time, through gene exchange between adjacent tribes, the new mutant gene prospered and spread outward. It seems unlikely that lightly pigmented hair in childhood should in itself have any selective advantage. Rather, it is much more probable that certain effects of this mutant gene have somehow biochemically heightened the fitness of these Aborigines in their generally desert environment.

MULTIVARIATE PATTERNS

More than looking at just one trait at a time, anthropologists seek to understand the *pattern* of several polymorphisms simultaneously. From an analysis of these patterns we hope to reconstruct the evolutionary events and population histories that have shaped the development of human variation observable today. In a sense, we are looking for the family tree of *Homo sapiens*.

With the assistance of computer analysis, we can construct trees, or **dendograms**, such as the one shown in Figure 5-3 based on fifteen different genetic polymorphisms (including ABO, MN, Rh, and HLA). The logic be-

Dendogram (tree diagram) A diagrammatic presentation of population relationships using several genetic traits simultaneously.

---

*J. S. Huxley introduced the clinal concept, as it applied to plants, in 1938.

Figure 5-2

Phenotypic distribution, tawny hair in Australia. Note the concentration of tawny hair in the center of distribution, which can be traced by clines in a decreasing gradient.

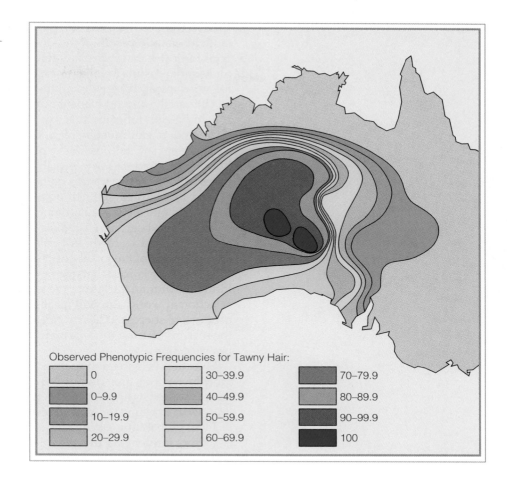

Observed Phenotypic Frequencies for Tawny Hair:

0		30–39.9		70–79.9	
0–9.9		40–49.9		80–89.9	
10–19.9		50–59.9		90–99.9	
20–29.9		60–69.9		100	

hind such a reconstruction is based on the assumption that populations more closely related should be more similar in allele frequencies. Many traits must be used together since drift may cause wide and nonsystematic deviations in the pattern of only a few loci.

Anthropological studies of modern evolution seek to make these kinds of reconstructions, but even abundant allele frequency data do not provide clearcut solutions. The form of the tree varies considerably depending on which loci are employed. A vast variety of possible interpretations can be drawn from the same data. As a population geneticist has stated, "Phylogenetic trees are like flower arrangements: it is enough that they are pretty, without asking that they are meaningful" (N. E. Morton, quoted in Livingstone, 1980, p. 33). Still, such an approach is extremely helpful and provides an alternative to the traditional "racial" studies of the history of human populations.

Understanding Human Polymorphisms: What Makes Evolution Tick?

From the discussion of numerous human polymorphisms in this chapter, you may begin to feel there is a great deal of variability in human populations.

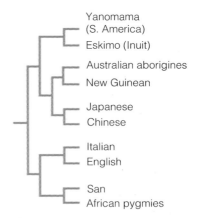

Figure 5-3

Dendrogram "tree" of relationships among human populations derived from statistical analyses of fifteen human polymorphisms. (After Bodmer and Cavalli-Sforza, 1976.)

Indeed there is. Research thus far has but scratched the surface of the vast store of genetic variation in our species. A random sample of various proteins indicates that approximately 28% of all loci in humans are polymorphic, and similar results in other animals suggest such a tremendous store of variation is typical. Where did all this variation come from?

Obviously, any new allele must first be introduced through a mutation. But to be polymorphic this allele *must* somehow spread; in other words, allele frequencies must increase well above low mutation rates.

There are several possible explanations of the ways genes have spread in human populations. One possibility that comes to mind immediately concerns balancing selection, as demonstrated so well by the sickle-cell trait (discussed in Chapter 4). Such a balanced polymorphism fully explains why more than one allele is maintained in relatively high frequency. This mechanism has also been suggested for other human polymorphisms such as ABO, MN, HLA, and so forth, but *none* of these has yet been demonstrated as a clear example of balanced polymorphism.

Whereas it is true that we rarely know how selection pressures directly influence human variation, we certainly can see the gross effects of natural selection at work. You will recall that selection is defined as "differential reproductive success." Clearly, not all humans reproduce equally, and some of the reasons causing these disparities are genetic. Put quite simply, this is natural selection.

Selection pressures may go a long way toward explaining human polymorphisms, but they do not completely account for all the observed variation. Another significant factor, particularly in small populations, is *genetic drift*. Drift explains the spread of alleles due strictly to chance factors.

In all probability, *both* natural selection and genetic drift acted significantly as factors influencing the spread of alleles in human populations. Selection certainly acts on alleles causing severe inherited disorders such as hemophilia, Tay-Sachs, and cystic fibrosis. These are all very deleterious, causing early death. Therefore, the allele causing these diseases should gradually be reduced in frequency (or never have spread initially) in the absence of some special balancing mechanism.

Moreover, selection pressures no doubt also relate to such infectious diseases as malaria, smallpox, typhoid, and plague, which either kill or debilitate much larger numbers of people than the inherited disorders noted in the preceding paragraph. If there are genes that lead to some form of protection (those that build up immunity, for instance) from these infectious diseases, they should spread in human populations. Keep in mind that exposure of human populations to most infectious diseases is greatly influenced by cultural factors, such as settlement patterns, population size, and prevailing standards of sanitation. (See Chapter 6.)

Drift too has been significant, particularly when small human populations become isolated—either socially or geographically. During most of human prehistory, hunting-gathering subsistence groups were probably fairly small, but their available range of mates was expanded considerably due to group outbreeding and mobility. Drift may have played its most decisive role in early agricultural times when human groups were not only small but sedentary as well.

Today, facilitated by mechanized transportation, migration is breaking down genetic isolates throughout the world. As human groups become less and less isolated, we can expect the evolutionary effects of genetic drift to decrease. That does not mean our species has stopped evolving. On the contrary, our ever-increasing disruption of the earth's ecosystem, our over-crowded cities, our synthesized and often inadequate diets, and the manifold psychological stresses of complex society are all producing new kinds of selection pressures. The question is therefore not whether our species is still evolving, but in which direction, how rapidly, and is it evolving rapidly enough to prevent extinction?

Summary

We have discussed how humans have attempted to explain and classify human variation. Classification schemes have usually focused primarily upon skin color, while secondarily relying upon other characters to define racial groupings.

Racial taxonomies are based upon typologies and are not a particularly useful method of either categorizing or explaining phenotypic variation. In any typologically defined human group, there are always individuals who do not conform in all respects to that particular type. Moreover, such groupings tend to overlap with others regarding some traits. Lastly, it has been shown that there exists more genetic/phenotypic variation *within* racial groups than *between* them.

We have also illustrated how *biological determinism* has widely influenced scientific thinking, indeed up to the present day, and has served as a basis for racist views and policies. Numerous studies have amply demonstrated the great complexity in untangling the genetic mechanisms of polygenic inheritance. For behavioral characteristics, such as "intelligence," the difficulties of explanation are enormous, as are the confounding cultural variables. For this reason, contemporary scholars do not accept the premise that *entire* populations ("racial groups") can be sorted using behavioral attributes.

Today, physical anthropologists study evolution in human populations using the perspective of *population genetics*. In order to apply the principles of this perspective, we first must isolate actual human *populations*. As we have seen, in geographically and/or socially isolated situations, this process is relatively straightforward, but, in complex societies, it becomes quite arbitrary.

Once populations are defined, we can apply evolutionary models, such as the Hardy-Weinberg formula, to ascertain whether changes in allele frequency (that is, evolution) are occurring. In human populations, allele frequencies change through one or a combination of the four forces of evolution: mutaton, migration, random genetic drift, and natural selection.

The kinds of genetic traits measured in population genetics studies are called *polymorphisms*, traits with more than one allele in appreciable frequency. Some of these traits, particularly the *sickle-cell trait*, have a direct relation to potent selection pressures.

In addition to hemoglobin, there are many other polymorphisms found in human blood that are of interest to anthropologists. On the red blood cells are several antigen systems, the most important of which are ABO, Rh, and MN. There are also polymorphisms on the white blood cells (HLA, for instance).

All these traits vary considerably among modern human populations and thus demand evolutionary explanations. Such explanations are, however, necessarily complex and must account for interaction of genes and interaction of evolutionary forces. For example, mutation is the usual starting point, but further spread of alleles must involve some combination of natural selection, drift, and migration.

Questions for Review

1. What are typologies? Why are racial typologies inadequate to explain human variation?
2. Why is *race* such a difficult term to define? Give an example of a brief definition and critique it.
3. What is biological determinism? Give an example.
4. What was the eugenics movement, and what was its underlying premise?
5. What are some problems associated with comparing different groups on the basis of IQ test scores?
6. Why is it so important to study human *populations* in order to understand human evolution?
7. Why is it difficult to define actual human populations?
8. Under what conditions does the Hardy-Weinberg equilibrium model hold true? If a deviation from expected frequencies is found, what does that suggest?
9. What is a polymorphism? Why are polymorphisms used in evolutionary studies?
10. Why are so many polymorphisms in human blood known? Give several examples and discuss why they are of evolutionary interest.
11. What is a cline? Discuss how the clinal approach helps explain patterns of human variation.
12. Give a detailed account for a hypothetical human population: (a) how a mutant allele might arise; and (b) how it might spread.

Chapter 6

Contents

Human Adaptability: Meeting the Challenge of the Environment

You can tell from even cursory thumbing through this textbook that the study of human skeletons is a central component of physical anthropology. Indeed, in the United States, the founding of physical anthropology early in this century was largely based upon human skeletal biology. The founders of American physical anthropology included most notably Aleš Hrdlička and Ernest A. Hooton, both of whom were experts in the study of human skeletons.

Still today, human skeletal biology is a primary focus for physical anthropologists. In recent years, 20% of submissions to the *American Journal of Physical Anthropology* have included articles dealing with human skeletal biology, the largest percentage for any subdiscipline of the field (Ubelaker and Grant, 1989).

Physical anthropologists are keenly interested in human biology, both past and present; but for populations no longer living, the most *direct* biological evidence we have is from preserved body parts, most especially those calcified, "hard," tissues—bones and teeth. We thus can learn about changes in body size and proportions and reveal epidemiological patterns and the histories of a variety of significant human diseases. Preserved skeletons also offer direct clues regarding diet and nutritional problems, as well as how past cultures adjusted to the myriad demands of their environments. Additionally, skeletal biologists are interested in sorting out the "biological distance" (that is, population relationships) of past groups. Finally, modern skeletons are crucial in developing techniques for legal identification of recently deceased individuals and for comparing the very ancient remains of early humans (found as mineralized hard tissues; that is, fossils) with physical conditions seen today. Only in this way can we hope to understand how we as a species compare with earlier members of our lineage and ultimately how we came into existence in the first place.

For all these reasons and more, as physical anthropologists we have been and continue to be highly interested in the study of human skeletons. Yet, recently in the United States (as well as in some other countries) strong concerns have been voiced regarding this research, at least as it pertains to certain groups. In North America, especially, deeply felt objections have come from American Indians who regard the permanent curation and ongoing study of remains of their ancestors as a sacrilege and thus incompatible with proper religious respect for these dead individuals. After all, these individuals who make up skeletal collections did not give permission to be removed from their "final" resting places, to say nothing of being placed on shelves in museums or university laboratories.

Many American Indians have understandably been deeply disturbed about such moral issues for some time. In 1989, these concerns received great impetus from congressional action, which was aimed at the Smithsonian Institution. The end result is that large segments of the human skeletal *and* artifactual collections are to be returned to descendants for reburial. Following upon this law, much wider legislation has passed (aimed at *all* institutions receiving federal funding), and in 1993 the Native American Graves Protection and Repatriation Act was implemented. In addition, several states have also enacted similar legislation.

Should *all* American Indian remains be returned for reburial to those descendants who can be identified? Beyond the deep moral convictions of many Native Americans, such a view is now supported by many federal and state legislatures, museum professionals, and academics. It is felt that continued retention of Indian remains is a further manifestation of past racist policies that saw the near obliteration of native Indian culture. And, it is true, the majority of human skeletal remains housed in United States' museums and universities are those of Native Americans. Yet, there are also thousands of other skeletons from many other groups (ancient and modern). Moreover, medical schools throughout the nation maintain teaching collections of thousands more human skeletons. If it is immoral to keep skeletons of one group, why not of all groups?

We might also point out that Native Americans, who insist on the return of bones and artifacts, are removing the sources that are used for reconstructing their culture before the arrival of Europeans. Archeologists and cultural anthropologists have learned a great deal about Indian pre-Columbian history. It seems ironic that in some cases it is the descendants themselves who are responsible for compromising, and ultimately eliminating, research into the life of their ancestors.

Anthropologists are not racists. We study human beings in order to understand the human condition. As scientists, our results belong to all humanity. To return a large proportion of irreplaceable information to the ground—where it will quickly disintegrate—will not only rob current researchers of the opportunity for study, but will also sacrifice all future research for later generations of scientists as well. Furthermore, as a self-perfecting intellectual pursuit, science always attempts to improve results—with new perspectives, new techniques, even entirely new questions. Who is to say what new information can be obtained 50 or 100 years from now, information potentially important to all, including American Indians?

Can some compromise be reached? Justifiable moral concerns regarding religious respect (especially fragile for oppressed minority groups) and scientific ideals are *both* crucially important to our cultural ethic. We therefore *must* find a compromise. Time, however, is running out.

SOURCES

Buikstra, J. E., and C. C. Gordon, "The Study and Restudy of Human Skeletal Series: The Importance of Long-Term Curation," in: A. Cantwell et al., (eds.), *The Research Potential of Anthropological Museum Collection. Annals of the New York Academy of Sciences*, **376**(1981):449–465.

Ubelaker, D. H., and L. G. Grant, "Human Skeletal Remains: Preservation or Reburial?" *Yearbook of Physical Anthropology*, **32**(1989):249–287.

Introduction

In Chapters 4 and 5, we discussed several specific genetic traits that are known to vary among human populations. Some of these, particularly sickle-cell hemoglobin, are probably directly related to selection pressures. Most human variation, however, cannot yet be conclusively tied to any specific selection factor.

In this chapter, we will take up possible adaptive responses in human populations to more general kinds of selection pressures. For example, are there genetic differences in human populations allowing adaptation to heat stress, cold stress, high altitude, ultraviolet radiation, or specific dietary factors? Moreover, have the conditions of modern technological society presented new selection pressures such as crowding, artificial radiation, and noise?

Again, we must emphasize that demonstrating direct effects of natural selection on humans is extremely difficult. So many variables have to be considered simultaneously that clearly proven associations between specific phenotypes and specific environments are not usually possible. Rigorous experimental controls, practical for studies of other organisms, are not feasible for humans. Moreover, adaptations to general kinds of ecological conditions of heat, light, altitude, etc., are made through numerous complex physiological changes. Such adaptations involve several *polygenic* traits, none of which has a clearly understood hereditary basis.

Many different human populations today live under arduous environmental conditions. Some live in scalding temperatures averaging above 100°F in the summer and others survive through frigid winter months averaging −50°F. Still others exist all year long at altitudes above 15,000 feet. In all these cases, the groups living under these severe environmental stresses have made adjustments, both behavioral and physiological. Without the human brain that in turn produces culture (which *is* humankind's ecological niche), none of these demanding environments could ever have been conquered. If culture is the dominant means of human adaptation, are there also biological changes in populations that have been subjected for several generations to severe stresses?

Certainly, general climatic/ecological conditions exert strong selection pressures, and human populations do show differences in their average physiological responses to certain environmental conditions. The question then becomes: *Are these populations more adapted through natural selection (differential success of certain genotypes), or are they just showing a physiological adjustment capacity common to all humans?*

Adaptation and Acclimatization

The way in which humans and other organisms meet the challenges of the environment is through a general process called *adaptation*. This term has a wide variety of meanings, and in its broadest connotation can refer to any changes by which organisms surmount the challenges to life (Lasker, 1969). "This adjustment can be either temporary or permanent, acquired either through short-term or lifetime processes, and may involve physiological, structural, behavioral, or cultural changes aimed at improving the organism's functional performances in the face of environmental stresses" (Frisancho, 1981, p. 2).

Among physical anthropologists and other human biologists, however, a more restricted definition of **genetic adaptation** is usually implied. From this perspective, adaptation is viewed as an *evolutionary* process and, even more precisely, as the result of natural selection. Consequently, biological adaptation applies only to whole populations.

In terms of natural selection, individual organisms cannot adapt; they just produce offspring as well as they can under the circumstances. Biological adaptation occurs only *between* generations as the result of differential reproductive success among all the individuals of the population. Biological adaptations, then, *must* have a genetic basis. As environments change so do selection pressures and so also does the reproductive success of various genotypes. Groups of organisms can respond adaptively to changing environmental conditions only over the span of several generations. In quickly reproducing organisms, demonstrated by the adaptation of mosquito populations to DDT, this process may appear rapid. However, for slowly reproducing organisms, such as *Homo sapiens*, at least a few thousand years are required for significant adaptive shifts. For example, the spread of the sickle-cell allele in the human populations of the western and central portions of Africa took at least 2000 years and perhaps considerably longer (8000–10,000 years?).

On the other hand, all *individual* organisms can respond to environmental changes by physiological adjustments, displaying their phenotypic plasticity. Called **acclimatization**, such responses can occur relatively quickly as in the physiological changes induced by high-altitude stress.

For this reason, some college football teams playing the Air Force Academy in Colorado Springs (elevation 6,008 ft.) like to arrive a day or two early to allow some time for some short-term physiological responses to occur. The same was true of athletes training for the 1968 Olympic Games in Mexico City (elevation 7,347 ft.), who began training months earlier at high-altitude locations to permit a more long-term physiological acclimatization.

Genetic adaptation Genetic changes within populations in response to selection (environmental) pressure; usually takes many generations.

Acclimatization Physiological response within individuals to environmental pressure; usually takes a few weeks to a few months.

Light/Solar Radiation and Skin Color

One kind of environmental stress that varies considerably over the earth (and therefore differentially affects human populations) is the amount of solar radiation.

In response to this kind of environmental stress, the body uses a mechanism that alters the skin pigment. Actually, the color of the skin is influenced by three substances: (1) keratin (yellow) found in the top layer (*stratum corneum*) of the skin and particularly noticeable in individuals having a thick *stratum corneum* (as in many Asians); (2) hemoglobin (red) in the red blood cells; and (3) melanin, a biochemically complex compound produced in the basal layers of the epidermis and secreted by specialized cells called *melanocytes*. Populations differ in skin color as a function of the number of melanocytes, in the manner these cells are bunched, and in the size and number of the melanin granules produced.

Of these pigments, only melanin absorbs ultraviolet light (the end of the spectrum causing radiation), so only melanin can protect against the really harmful effects of solar radiation. One potentially and extremely hazardous result of overexposure to ultraviolet (u-v) solar radiation is skin cancer. An immediate way the body can respond is to increase the production of melanin granules, causing what we call a "tan." All human populations can tan in response to exposure to u-v light, but the effects are obviously more noticeable in those who are more fair-skinned.

Individuals with albinism (Fig. 6-1), a rare (Mendelian) inherited condition found in all human populations, produce no melanin, cannot tan, and in tropical populations often develop skin cancer early in life (see p. 65). For that matter, there is considerable variation in skin cancer incidence in the United States depending on the intensity of u-v light. Among United States whites, rates of skin cancer are five times higher in Texas than in Massachusetts (Damon, 1977, p. 216).

In the United States today, skin cancer (carcinoma) afflicts people mostly late in life—after reproduction is completed; its role as a potent selective agent could thus be questioned.

However, another cancer, malignant melanoma, can affect younger people, and if left untreated, can have fatal consequences. The population incidence of melanoma has increased dramatically in recent years, both in the United States and elsewhere (especially in areas, such as Australia, that experience intense solar radiation). Some of this increase may be influenced by *behavioral* changes, including people spending longer periods sunning themselves and the wearing of less clothing. Furthermore, serious concerns have also been raised in connection with malignant melanoma in regard to the potentially harmful effects of the progressively reduced ozone layer in the earth's atmosphere.

In considering the potentially harmful effects of u-v radiation from an *evolutionary* perspective, three points must be kept in mind: (1) Early on, hominids lived mostly in the tropics, where u-v radiation is more intense than in temperate areas like the United States; (2) unlike modern urban dwellers, most earlier hominids spent the majority of time outside; and (3) they wore little or no clothing. As we will discuss, however, adoption of clothing in temperate climes may have played a role in influencing depigmentation. Thus, it is reasonable to consider protection against skin cancer (including melanoma) and severe sunburn as *potentially* important selective factors influencing the evolution of dark pigmentation.

Another physiological effect caused by sunlight, particularly u-v radiation, is the stimulation in the human body of the production of vitamin D, necessary for normal bone growth and maintenance. Individuals with insufficient vitamin D often develop such growth defects as rickets. Presumably, it would be harmful, particularly to children, to be too dark-skinned in areas where sunlight is low.

Dr. Peter Post has suggested an additional factor that may help explain the distribution of skin color. Epidemiological data from the Korean War (such as more frostbite occurring in black soldiers) as well as experimental evidence led Post to the conclusion that light skin is less susceptible to cold injury. Therefore, in northern latitudes—which not only get less u-v radiation but are also colder than tropical areas—light skin may provide protection against cold injury (Post et al., 1975). There may also be populational differences in subcutaneous blood flow (rather than in skin color) that lead to differing risks of frostbite injury.

So far we have established that: (1) solar radiation exerts potentially harmful environmental stress if too much is absorbed (possibly leading to skin cancer) or if too little is absorbed (leading to insufficient vitamin D production and/or cold injury); and (2) individual human beings can respond by tanning to increased amounts of u-v light.

Figure 6-1

An African albino.

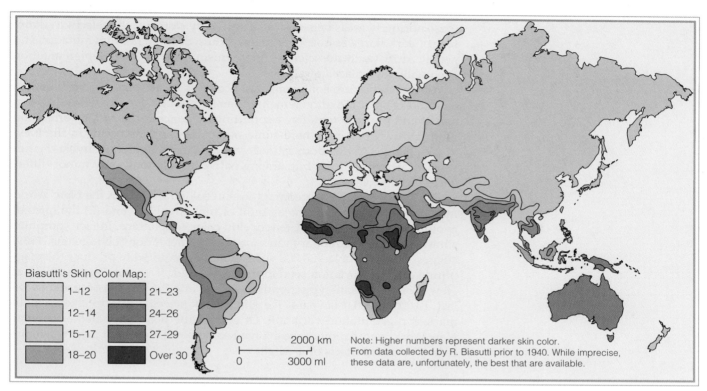

Figure 6-2

Distribution of skin color among the indigenous populations of the world. (After Coon and Hunt, 1965.)

The important question remains: Do populations that have long resided under widely varying u-v conditions show *genetic adaptations* in skin color?

For a long time, data on skin color were inconsistent, but more recent application of reflectance spectrophotometry has removed some of the earlier problems. Such observations of human skin color have shown that average readings vary considerably with latitude and, presumably, amount of u-v light. (See map, Fig. 6-2.) This association is, of course, inconclusive; we still do not know for certain the specific selection factors involved. As we noted, hypothetically, dark skin in areas with high u-v light protects against skin cancer.

Why skin on the average is dark in some areas may therefore be reasonably explained if we *assume* that sunburn, skin cancer, or some other unknown consequence of overexposure to sunlight is an important selection factor. But then why, on the average, are some populations light-skinned? The popular hypothesis here runs as follows: In northern areas, dark skin would be selected against since it would cause underproduction of vitamin D, thereby resulting in growth defects (leading to lower reproductive success).

Another theory explaining why some humans have light skin has been proposed by anthropologists Loring Brace and Ashley Montagu (1977). As with the vitamin D hypothesis, the assumption here is that humans originated in the tropics, where darkly pigmented skin was a selective advantage. According to Brace and Montagu, permanent habitation of extreme northern temperate zones occurred only within the last 100,000 years and was partly made possible by the cultural innovation of warm clothing. Once humans in these northerly areas began to wear full-body clothing, the selective advantage of dark skin was no longer in force; thus, through random mutation and genetic drift (with no selective mechanism opposing it), depigmentation eventually took place.

All this conjecture concerning skin color as an adaptation to differential amounts of solar radiation remains open to question. No proven association exists, and the only tentative supporting evidence is the rough correlation with latitude. But even here some notable exceptions occur. In the New World, there is tremendous latitude variation encompassing almost the full range of u-v conditions; but, among native populations, only minor differences in skin color exist.

The smaller degree of geographic skin color variation in the New World may be explained by (1) the amount of time involved; and (2) the rates of evolutionary change postulated for skin color adaptations. In fact, computer simulations of evolutionary rates for skin pigmentation (Livingstone, 1969) suggest that as many as 30,000 years would be required to produce the magnitude of color variation seen in the Old World. If we further assume that New World population distribution (at least into the tropics) occurred in the last 10,000 to 20,000 years, we should not necessarily *expect* extremely marked pigmentation variation. Of course, the possibility also exists that New World populations have evolved some novel biological mechanism for coping with the effects of u-v light.

The Thermal Environment

Homo sapiens is found in a great variety of habitats, with thermal environments differing from exceedingly hot deserts to the frigid tundra of the Arctic circle. Human groups live through the winter in areas as cold as eastern Siberia, where January temperatures *average* an incredible –63°F. Such extreme environmental conditions place the human body under great stress.

COLD STRESS

The way the human body copes with cold stress is mostly through those physiological adjustments we have termed acclimatization. Perhaps there are some differences between populations in the rate such adjustments occur, but the ability to adjust gradually to cold is a general capacity of all human beings.

The manner of studying human reaction to cold involves either controlled laboratory observations, such as taking skin temperatures of appendages immersed in cold water, or such overall tolerance measurements as the sleeping bag test. This latter method is a testimony to the dedication and foolhardiness of physical anthropologists. Using standardized sleeping bags, experimenters sleep out in the open and contrast the amount of sleep, comfort, and shivering between themselves and natives.

In addition, inferential support for populational adjustment to cold stress has been obtained through the distributional method. In this kind of study, data are gathered from several populations on such physical characteristics as stature and nose shape and are then checked for any correspondence with environmental factors (for example, mean annual temperature, humidity).

From such observations, several mechanisms of physiological acclimatization to cold have been demonstrated in different human populations (after Damon, 1977, p. 222):

1. Redistribution of heat to extremities (shown in the Quechua of South America and Lapps of Scandinavia)
2. Overall metabolic rate increased (shown in Eskimos and in the Alacaluf of Tierra del Fuego—the high protein diet of Eskimos is an important contributing factor among this group)
3. Insulation acclimatization yielding cooler skin surface temperatures, but maintaining internal ones (shown in central Australians and Kalahari San). Such a physiological response may have originated in tropical areas where no real danger of frostbite prevails. However, in northern latitudes, it would be highly maladaptive, and physiological responses have apparently been modified (Steegman, 1975).

It is remarkable how well these physiological changes will eventually buffer the effects of cold. For example, Australian aborigines sleep in the nude with no covering in temperatures close to freezing! In sleeping bag tests in Scandinavia, Norwegian students gradually acclimatized and could sleep although they continued to shiver. An involuntary response, shivering is controlled by the hypothalamus mediated by cold receptors in the skin. By increasing the body's heat production up to three times that of resting temperatures, shivering is an effective response to cold.

Carleton Coon and his associates proposed a cold stress hypothesis to explain facial shape variation among human populations (Coon et al., 1950). Since genetic shifts are seen here to have occurred as the result of evolution, this type of change would be an adaptation (not acclimatization, as in the adjustments just discussed). It is postulated that cold stress selective factors (particularly frostbite) have favored wider (less sharp) noses and larger, more protrusive cheekbones, thus accounting for the evolution of the "Asian face." However, experimental evidence (Steegman, 1970) appears to contradict this hypothesis. In fact, facial temperatures were colder in those individuals with more protrusive cheekbones. Moreover, no consistent correlations exist between temperature and nose shape, although the latter does appear to be influenced by humidity (see the following section).

All the means of tolerating cold stress just discussed are physiological responses seen to some degree in all populations and not merely those most subject to cold conditions. While mechanisms of physiological response to cold may vary somewhat among human groups, as yet we cannot conclusively demonstrate any clear genetic adaptations specific to certain populations.

HEAT AND HUMIDITY

While populations living in extremely cold climates face the problem of conserving heat, those groups living in hot environments face the opposite challenge, how to dissipate excess heat. In fact, the human body can adjust more easily to heat load than it can to extreme cold. Thus, cold is usually considered more of a serious threat to life than heat, unless the latter is accompanied by a lack of water. This greater tolerance of heat as opposed to cold might well reflect the tropical origins of our lineage.

Whereas body build, skin pigmentation (which protects against solar radiation), and the circulation of more blood close to the skin surface are all factors that help the human body adjust to heat stress, the most efficient means for humans is sweating. By cooling the surface of the skin, sweating causes heat to radiate to the surrounding air. In desert climates, individuals can lose up to one quart of water per hour; however, if such rates of water

Axillae Armpits.

loss go unchecked, dangerous tissue dehydration and sodium loss will result. At maximum sweating capacity, the body can lose its entire sodium pool in just three hours—ultimately leading to death (Hanna and Brown, 1979).

The capacity to dissipate heat by sweating is seen in all populations to an almost equal degree. Interestingly, the average number of sweat glands does not vary among human populations. Each of us has approximately 1.6 million sweat (eccrine) glands. In addition, in the **axillae** and groin areas, apocrine glands are found; these, however, are not really involved in heat regulation but are more likely olfactory in nature (scent cues, particularly for sexual attraction?). While humans are not unique for the number or size of their eccrine glands, these are remarkable for their high secretory level. "*Homo sapiens* has the greatest sweating capacity for a given surface area for any known animal" (Newman, 1970).

When introduced into very hot areas, humans acclimatize quite rapidly, the process taking just a few days. Such plasticity seems to characterize all human populations, and no heat adaptations have been found that differentiate one human group from others. "Indeed, the similarity in response of all acclimatized peoples is remarkable" (Hanna and Brown, 1979, p. 179). This physiological adjustment is accomplished through a faster response and increased output of the sweat glands (increasing by as much as four-fold) and a general decrease in the pulse rate and heart output. Again, is it possible that such a rapid and efficient capacity to adjust to heat stress reflects our tropical hominid origins?

More than just temperature, rapid physiological adjustment is also dependent on humidity. All populations seem to be able to adjust quickly to hot, wet climates, but acclimatization to hot, dry areas takes longer. The most consistent data suggesting a connection between physical response and humidity concern nose shape (Weiner, 1954). Populations living in colder areas (where absolute humidity is lower) have narrower noses. Similarly, in deserts (where absolute humidity is also low), narrow noses also are the rule. The physiological explanation is not yet completely understood, but a narrow nose may act as a more efficient humidifier (Steegman, 1975). Such changes in nose shape would obviously be significantly influenced by genetic shifts; that is, this explanation emphasizes adaptation rather than acclimatization.

Another important consideration relates to differential growth rates. During the physiologically *plastic* growth period, young children and adolescents might significantly shift developmental pathways in response to certain environmental stresses. For example, some comparative data suggest that children raised in warmer, wetter climates develop slender trunks and longer extremities than a similar (control) group raised in colder climates (Frisancho, 1981). Through such *developmental* responses the body thus creates more surface area, allowing for more efficient sweat evaporation (see the following section for further discussion of body size and shape).

Clearly, all humans have inherited a genetically based plasticity to deal with heat stress. In this context, it may be said that we have been adapted for adaptability. Even given such a flexible physiological capacity there are limitations (such as the one just cited concerning severe sodium loss). Consequently, humans also adjust to hot climates through a variety of cultural means (Hanna and Brown, 1983). Among the Tuareg people of the Sahara, clothing is worn loosely, thereby allowing sweat to evaporate and additionally protecting the skin from excessive sun exposure. Physical activities are usually performed during the cooler hours, and individuals stay in the shade whenever possible. In the Sahara, the air is hot and dry with solar radiation intense, posing the dual problems of excessive water loss and sunburn. On the other hand, in tropical humid rain forests, such as those occupied by the Semai of Malaya, the reverse is true—sweat evaporation is much slower. Accordingly, these people wear few clothes.

Likewise, human adjustments to cold also are mostly cultural in nature. As we will see later in the text, our ancestors long ago invaded temperate latitudes, and there is little doubt that it was primarily cultural innovation that allowed such a migration in the first place. Evidence of consistent use of fire is at least 500,000 years old. Artificial structures are also exceedingly ancient. Windbreaks may have been constructed in Africa almost 2 million years ago, and by 200,000 years ago more sophisticated structures were being erected in Europe.

There is little direct evidence for the earliest use of clothing. Long before garments were sewn, loose untailored skins, furs, etc., were certainly utilized. Archeological evidence of needles suggests the advent of sewn clothing by at least 35,000 years ago (Chard, 1975). After this, as Brace and Montagu have suggested (see p. 143), *permanent* habitation of really cold areas became possible.

As we see, humans cope with environmental challenges by a *combination* of both biological and cultural strategies, which again underlines the essential biocultural nature of human existence.

Another feature of human physiological response to the thermal environment that has received considerable attention concerns body proportions. Data on heat-related deaths among World War II soldiers in the deserts of North Africa indicate excess quantities of fat or muscle are a hindrance in such an environment. A linear body build is apparently the most advantageous and is reflected in many groups who have been subject to heat stress for a long time: Arabs, Nilotic Africans (Tutsi, Nuer, Dinka, etc.), and central Australians.

BODY SIZE AND SHAPE

Indeed, there seems to be a general relationship between climate and body size/shape within warm-blooded species (that is, both mammals and birds). In general, within a species, body size (weight) increases proportionately as distance from the equator increases. In humans, this relationship holds up fairly well, but there are numerous exceptions. For example, Polynesians basking in the sunny climes of the South Pacific are tall and heavy, whereas Scandinavian Lapps are short and slender.

Presumably, body size and proportion are strongly influenced by genetic mechanisms; thus, shifts in these dimensions should come about primarily as the result of adaptation. Yet, physiological response (that is, acclimatization) may also be playing an important role here. Body weight and limb length are both phenotypically plastic, with significant environmental influence upon them (Hanna and Brown, 1983). Even first-generation migrants to tropical areas (U.S. white children reared in Brazil) show different body proportions (more linear than would be expected). Obviously, this response occurs too quickly to be explained by genetic adaptation. The body during development is being influenced by environmental factors, such as heat, which in turn influences blood flow which, in turn, might well affect the differential growth of bone and other tissues.

Figure 6-3

Different body types.

Nevertheless, some general principles applicable to body size/shape variation seen in other warm-blooded species seem also to apply broadly to *Homo sapiens*:

1. *Bergmann's Rule* involves the relationship of body mass to surface area. As weight (mass) increases, the relative amount of surface area decreases proportionately. Therefore, large size with relatively less surface area for heat loss is an adaptation for more efficient heat maintenance. It is interesting to note that cold-adapted fauna during glacial peaks of the Pleistocene are generally larger than their modern descendants. Moreover, humans are almost certainly less robust than our ancestors during much of the last 1 million years. In humans today, there is also some correspondence of size with climate, since peoples living farther from the equator tend to be larger. Eskimos, who are stocky in physique, are one good example.

2. *Allen's Rule* involves the shape of the body, particularly the appendages. In colder climates, appendages should be short, thereby reducing the amount of surface area. In humans, this is seen as shorter arms and legs, but in other animals, tails, ears, or beaks may be affected.

Considerable data gathered from several human populations generally conform to the above rules. In colder environments, body sizes are larger with broader, longer chests and shorter arms (Roberts, 1973). These relationships pertain most clearly to indigenous New World populations, but they do not apply to the populational distribution of body size and shape found in Africa (Hiernaux, 1968).

Another complication in attempting to apply these rules to humans is that of acclimatization. An individual's body size may reflect much more about short-term physiological adjustment to ecological/dietary conditions than about long-term biological adaptation. For example, an extensive study of more than 15,000 white males in the United States revealed as large a correspondence in body size and temperature (based on the State in which one was born) as that seen for indigenous North American populations (Newman and Munro, 1955). Since this entire group represented recent migrants from generally the same region (Europe), biological adaptation was ruled out (too little time). Acclimatization, therefore, was responsible for the tendency for larger males to predominate in colder parts of the United States. Colder weather may be a direct causative factor, stimulating more physical activity and appetite.

Body size and shape variation among relatively ancient human populations may also be influenced by cultural factors. Alice Brues in an article titled "The Spearman and the Archer" suggested that different body builds are better suited for use of different weapons (Brues, 1959). According to Brues, the most efficient body build for spear use is long and slender, but for using a bow the body should be short with thick muscles. Hypothetically, as bow technology spread several thousand years ago, selection pressures would have shifted favoring a shorter, stockier build. A potential complication here is that most populations that use bows *also* use spears.

A similar scenario to the one above has been proposed by David Frayer (1980). In this theory, body size among our ancestors also changed as a result of cultural variables, but here the key was a shift in size of game animals. From 35,000 to 10,000 years ago, larger, more aggressive game was hunted less and less as our ancestors gradually adopted a more sedentary way of life. Thus, according to this view, the males (who, presumably, were doing most of the big game hunting) gradually became smaller, while female body size remained approximately the same. While biocultural factors have assuredly influenced human body size, these imaginative suggestions still remain unproven.

High-Altitude Stress

Today, perhaps as many as 25 million people live at altitudes above 10,000 ft. In Tibet, permanent settlements exist above 15,000 ft., and in the Andes they can be found at 17,500 ft. (with daily trips to mines at 19,000 ft.)!

At such high altitudes, multiple stresses act on the human body, creating several physiological problems. Most pervasive is the low barometric pressure creating low oxygen pressure in inspired air. Consequently, oxygen diffuses less quickly into the lung membranes and less oxygen eventually reaches the body's tissues (a condition called *hypoxia*). All these problems become particularly critical during any kind of exercise.

High altitude, however, also involves cold stress. In Tibet, winter temperatures plunge to as low as –27°F. In addition, populations living in such environments must also cope with low humidity, high winds, high solar radiation, a limited nutritional base (generally poor agricultural land), and rough terrain.

Initially, human beings respond to high-altitude stress (primarily low oxygen pressure) through short-term compensation, but eventually a more permanent acclimatization develops. When freshly introduced into high-altitude environments, we react by breathing faster and deeper. Gradually, our systems adjust so that respiration rates are permanently increased and the number of red blood cells is also increased. In the Peruvian Andes (from

Figure 6-4

A village in the Andean Highlands.

which our most comprehensive data come), natives have up to 30% more red blood cells than populations at sea level. Such an adjustment allows the blood to carry more oxygen. The right ventricle of the heart may also increase in size, pumping more blood to the lungs. Also, there are probably adjustments in the body tissues to function at lowered oxygen tension.

With the increased physiological demands of pregnancy, hypoxia (oxygen deficiency) could be expected to have negative effects on fertility. However, the data here are somewhat conflicting. A comparative study of Himalayan populations suggests that there is no evidence to support the popular conception that high-altitude stress reduces fertility (Goldstein et al., 1983). In fact, as this study points out, confounding cultural attitudes (such as those affecting the exposure of females to intercourse) must be considered.

On the other hand, high infant mortality has been reported for several groups living at high altitude, most of the problems resulting from respiratory infections. Many of these infant deaths are attributable to the generally poor health care available, but once infants contract bronchitis, tuberculosis, etc., the low oxygen pressure, no doubt, causes further complications. Even in areas with good health care, infant mortality resulting from respiratory problems is greater at high altitudes. For example, in Colorado, infant deaths were nearly twice as common in areas above 8,200 ft. (2,500 m) as at lower elevations (Moore and Regensteiner, 1983).

Other physiological adjustments displayed by highland Andean peoples include lower birth weights, but relatively larger placentas—probably supplying more oxygen to the developing fetus. In addition, slower rates of maturation with delayed sexual maturity may provide more time to grow in an oxygen-poor and nutritionally deprived environment.

Most of the adjustments humans exhibit in response to high-altitude stress can be accounted for by physiological plasticity (acclimatization). However, some effects of natural selection may well cause differential spread of genotypes more adapted to high altitudes.

How do we sort out the possible effects due to adaptation from those due to acclimatization? Once again we are faced with a complex nature/nurture phenomenon and, once again, for humans the answers are far from clear. Laboratory tests may tell us something of the range of variation of human responses, and observations of other animals may tell us something about general physiological plasticity. However, for human populations, so complexly intertwined in a web of environmental/cultural/genetic factors, we require a special methodology. One helpful technique is called the *migrant model*, which compares genetically related populations living under very different environmental conditions. For example, investigations of lung function were done on the Aymara (highland natives) of northern Chile and compared with data from non-Aymara (Spanish) and a group termed "mixed" (Mueller et al., 1979). Upward migrants as well as downward migrants were contrasted with nonmigrants, controlling for age, sex, stature, ethnicity, occupation, and permanence (age at migration and length of stay). Even with all these controls, confounding factors obscure results from such cross-sectional studies. Long-term physiological data collected periodically from the same individuals (longitudinal studies) are therefore also necessary to help untangle the web of genetic, physiological, ecological, and cultural

Figure 6-5

High-altitude factors. (Baker and Little, 1976.)

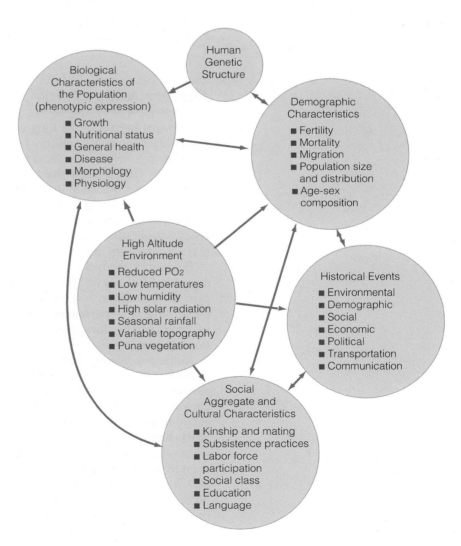

variables. As discussed earlier, for adjustments to heat stress, developmental responses are also apparently quite important for acclimatization to high altitudes. Individuals (migrants) who move to high altitudes as children eventually acquire a physiological capacity equal to that of natives. Individuals who migrate as adults, however, never apparently acclimatize to this degree (Frisancho, 1981).

High-altitude inhabitants may also meet the rigorous demands of their environment through nutritional adaptations. Some evidence points to differences among high-altitude populations in food utilization, particularly fat metabolism. Their typically low fat/low protein/high carbohydrate diet may possibly be a cultural adaptation to living under high-altitude conditions. In addition, alcohol consumption and coca leaf chewing have also been suggested as cultural adjustments to high-altitude stress (particularly, cold). Alcohol facilitates vasodilation, making the skin surface feel warmer. Over the short run, alcohol consumption can thus increase comfort levels. If extended over long periods, however, it can be dangerous, causing greater heat loss and further contributing to possible frostbite.

Coca leaves contain cocaine and may also act to warm surface temperatures. Native chewers claim coca helps alleviate the symptoms of hunger, thirst, fatigue, cold, and pain. Controlled studies show, however, that when consumed in small amounts (as is typical), coca chewing has no observed effect on metabolism or work performance.

Dietary Adaptations

Nutritional behavior has long been a central element in human evolution. For at least the last 1 million years, meat probably has been an important element in human diets. Evidence from modern hunter-gatherers suggests perhaps only about one-third of all calories come from meat, but it still provides a crucial qualitative contribution in the form of essential amino acids. Adult humans can get by on a strictly vegetarian diet, but only with some effort. The increased demands of pregnancy, lactation, or disease make a wholly vegetarian diet even more difficult to sustain. For an infant, the protein sources from mother's milk are essential for normal development.

Beginning around 10,000 years ago, the agricultural revolution wrought a profound ecological impact on human evolution. Domestication of crops provided a larger and more geographically concentrated food resource, permitting both permanent settlements and population expansion, which in turn greatly increased the spread of infectious diseases in human populations.

Moreover, dietary habits shifted profoundly. The varied ecological base characteristic of hunter-gatherers gave way to the generally much more restrictive diets of settled agriculturists. Relying primarily on a few or perhaps just one staple crop, such diets can be exceedingly narrow, giving way easily to malnutrition. Did such massive shifts in human diets bring about any behavioral changes? Perhaps. Some recent evidence has suggested a possible relationship between a low calorie/high carbohydrate diet and increased aggressiveness (Bolton, 1973). When combined with intense physical activity, such diets lead to chronic lowering of blood sugar levels (hypoglycemia), which in turn may be reflected as behavioral alterations.

Such a diet is characteristic of the physically active Qolla Indians of the Andean Highlands. From a limited data base (one village of 1,200 individuals documented over about 15 years), the Qolla have been depicted as unusually aggressive on the basis of an apparently quite high homicide rate (Bolton, 1984). This is a position, however, that has not gone unchallenged (see Lewellen, 1981). In order to determine how characteristically aggressive the entire Qolla cultural group is, as well as the precise degree of their nutritional/metabolic difficulties, further research is required. In any case, many biologists and anthropologists believe there is sufficient data at hand at least to *suspect* a link between diet and behavior.

No Milk, Please!

Probably the best-known genetic adaptation to dietary factors is shown by the population distribution of the ability in adults to digest cow's milk. A main ingredient in milk is the sugar *lactose*, which the body normally breaks down by an enzyme called *lactase*.

In all human populations, infants and young children can digest milk, an obvious necessity to any young mammal. However, in many populations the gene coding for lactase production "switches off" by about 4 years of age. If too much milk is ingested, it ferments in the large intestine leading to diarrhea and severe gastrointestinal upset. Among many African and Asian populations—a majority of humankind today—most individuals are *intolerant* of milk (see Table 6-1). Contrary to contemporary advertising, every body does *not* need milk, at least not as adults. In fact, for millions of human beings, milk consumption leads to severe discomfort.

Quite apparently, lactose intolerance is a hereditary trait, but the pattern of inheritance is not yet clearly established. Some familial data suggest that the trait operates as a simple dominant or, perhaps, is more complicated with three alleles.

The environment also plays a role in expression of the trait (that is, whether a person will show milk intolerance) since intestinal bacteria can somewhat buffer the adverse effects. Because these bacteria will increase with previous exposure to smaller quantities of milk, some acclimatized tolerance can be acquired, even in individuals who are genetically lactase-deficient.

Why do such differences occur in lactose tolerance among human populations? Throughout the Stone Age (that is, prior to 10,000 years ago*), no milk was generally available after weaning in hunting-gathering societies. Perhaps, in such circumstances, continued action of an unnecessary enzyme might get in the way of digesting other foods. Lactose intolerance is widespread among mammals, arguing that some selective advantage does result from halting lactase production in adults (humans *and* other animals). The question then can be asked: Why can some adults (a majority in many populations) tolerate milk? The distribution of lactose-tolerant populations is very interesting, revealing the probable influence of cultural factors on this trait.

European groups, who are generally lactose-tolerant, are partially descended from groups of the Middle East. Often economically dependent on pastoralism, these groups raised cows, goats, etc., and no doubt drank considerable milk. Strong selection pressures would act in such a *cultural* environment to shift allele frequencies in the direction of more lactose tolerance. Modern European descendants of these populations apparently retain this ancient ability.

*Years ago will be abbreviated throughout as y.a.

Table 6-1 Frequencies of Lactose Intolerance

Population Group	Percent
U.S. whites	2–19
Finnish	18
Swiss	12
Swedish	4
African Americans	70–77
Ibos	99
Bantu	90
Fulani	22
Thais	99
Asian Americans	95–100
Native Australians	85

Source: Lerner and Libby, 1976, p. 327.

Undernutrition A diet insufficient in quantity (calories) to support normal health.

Malnutrition A diet insufficient in quality (that is, lacking in some essential component) to support normal health.

Even more informative is the distribution of lactose tolerance in Africa. For example, groups such as the Fulani and Tutsi, who have been pastoralists probably for thousands of years, have much lower rates of lactose intolerance than nonpastoralists. Former hunters and gatherers, such as the Ibo and Yoruba, are as much as 99% lactose-intolerant. (See Table 6-1.) More recently, these groups have abandoned their former subsistence pattern. They do not raise cattle, however, since they have settled in areas infested with tsetse flies.

As we have seen, the geographic distribution of lactose tolerance is related to a history of cultural dependence upon milk products. There are, however, some populations that culturally rely on dairying but are not characterized by high levels of lactose tolerance. It has been suggested that such populations have traditionally consumed their milk produce as cheese and other derivatives in which the lactose has been metabolized through bacterial action (Durham, 1981).

The interaction of human cultural environments and changes in lactose tolerance in human populations is a clear example of biocultural evolution. In the last few thousand years, cultural factors have produced specific evolutionary changes in human groups.

Cultural factors no doubt have influenced the course of human evolution for at least the last 3 million years (probably much longer), and today they are of paramount importance.

MALNUTRITION

While the agricultural revolution brought about a restricted dietary base, most groups were probably able to supplement their diets adequately by hunting small mammals, raising domesticated animals, and so on. However, today the crush of billions of humans almost completely dependent on cereal grains has drastically altered the situation, so that millions face undernutrition, malnutrition, and even starvation.

By **undernutrition** we refer to an inadequate quantity of food. In other words, not enough calories are consumed to support normal health. Exactly what constitutes an "adequate" diet is difficult to ascertain, and estimates of minimum requirements vary widely—body size and activity level are important considerations.

Given these uncertainties there are no precise data on how many human beings are today undernourished, but estimates vary between 16 and 63% of the world's population.

Malnutrition refers to inadequacy of some key element in the diet, such as proteins, minerals, or vitamins. In underdeveloped countries, protein malnutrition is the most common variety, and probably one-fourth to one-third of individuals in the underdeveloped world are protein deficient (M. Newman, 1975). The hallmark of severe protein malnutrition is a generalized disease called *kwashiorkor*, showing typical symptoms of tissue swelling, anemia, loss of hair, and apathy. A related syndrome called *marasmus* is caused by the combined effects of protein *and* calorie deficiency.

More than causing discomfort, malnutrition greatly affects reproduction and infant survival. Malnourished mothers have more difficult labor, more premature births, more children born with birth defects, higher prenatal mortality, and generally lower birth weights of newborns. Given all these potential physiological difficulties, it is surprising that overall *fertility* among malnourished mothers is not disrupted more than it is. Moderate chronic malnutrition (unless it becomes exceedingly severe, approaching starvation) has only a small effect on the number of live births (Bongaarts, 1980).

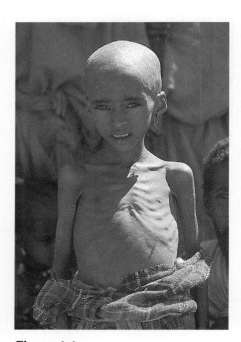

Figure 6-6

Kwashiorkor. Ethiopia.

MALNUTRITION AND DEVELOPMENT

Children born to malnourished mothers are already at a disadvantage. They are smaller and behind in most aspects of physical development. After birth, if malnourished conditions persist, such children fall further behind due to their mothers' generally poor lactation (the milk quantity may be cut by as much as one-half).

Growth processes often slow down greatly when environmental insults are severe (malnutrition and/or disease). Later on, a period of accelerated growth (called the *catch-up period*) can make up some of the deficit. However, there are some critical periods in which growth in certain tissues is normally very rapid. If a severe interruption occurs during one of these periods, the individual may never catch up completely. For example, severe malnutrition during the last trimester of fetal life or during the first year of infancy can have marked effects on brain development. Children who had died from complications accompanying severe malnutrition and were subsequently autopsied showed reduced brain size and weight, as well as fewer numbers of brain cells (Frisancho, 1978).

Researchers estimate that in some countries one-half of all newborns die before the age of 5. Of the estimated 60 million deaths per year worldwide, perhaps as many as 20 million are due to dietary deprivation (Dumont and Rosier, 1969). Not all of these people "starve to death," but most die as a result of weakened resistance to a whole set of infectious and gastrointestinal diseases.

Infectious disease, in particular, seems to act in a feedback relationship with malnutrition. Inadequate nutrition can interrupt the normal functioning of the immune response by reducing the number of active cells or antibodies available (see the following section). "In summary, a vicious cycle between malnutrition, infection, and immunodeficiencies is established, further intensifying malnutrition, facilitating new infection or permitting existing infection to become more severe" (Frisancho, 1978, p. 181).

Disease and Human Adaptation

Without question, one of the primary challenges to survival faced by all humans is that of disease. Diseases vary tremendously in their causes and their consequent effects on human health. For example, diseases may originate from any one, or a combination of, the following factors: hereditary (for example, cystic fibrosis, sickle-cell anemia); metabolic (vitamin deficiencies, such as rickets); degenerative (for example, heart disease); cell malignancy (many varieties of cancer, for instance); or infections (for example, malaria).

Human disease does not only result from a complex set of physiological causes—cultural factors are also a crucial element. Settlement patterns and architectural style greatly influence the spread of disease-carrying pathogens (as viruses and bacteria). In New Hebrides, the typical Melanesian house is not only designed to be "ghost-tight" but also air-tight, thereby greatly facilitating the spread of respiratory diseases among the occupants (Weiner, 1977). Settlement patterns and population density are also most important. Before urbanization (with its large permanent settlements) became characteristic (10,000–5000 y.a.), airborne infections (influenza, common cold, measles, smallpox) were of less significance; in moderately small communities, there is insufficient quantity and variety of contacts among individuals to perpetuate these diseases (Weiner, 1977).

Domestication of animals also brought the risk of disease. Of course, the development of domesticated animal varieties initially was itself a culturally directed process. Mediating cultural factors further influencing disease are: which animals are kept; in how close proximity; and what (if any) sanitary practices are followed. In the Arctic, for example, pathogens (tapeworm, rabies) carried by domestic dogs can be significant factors affecting human health.

Ritual, too, can be a contributing factor to the spread of disease. In Yemen, schistosomiasis (a fluke worm infection) is sometimes spread through communal use of ceremonial pools, and the kuru viral infection was spread in some New Guinea highland groups by ritual cannibalism of the brains of one's dead relatives.

Finally, major ecological modifications usually have marked impacts on disease. As we discussed in Chapter 4, the spread of slash-and-burn agriculture cleared previously forested areas, created more stagnant pools, and consequently greatly stimulated mosquito breeding—a crucial vector in the spread of malaria. Likewise, unsanitary crowded urban conditions contribute to an increase in the rat population size, and these animals also act as a vector in exposing humans to a host of infectious diseases. The best known of these diseases is bubonic plague, which in the thirteenth-century "Black Death" epidemic is estimated to have killed one-third the population of Europe.

For thousands of years, the interaction of biology and culture has produced fertile conditions for some diseases while limiting the spread of others. The great twentieth-century advances in controlling many infectious diseases have not, of course, eliminated human disease, but have simply shifted the focus. As average life span increased, degenerative syndromes, such as coronary artery disease, have become much more prevalent. Such crucial cultural factors as diet and psychological stress also have contributed to this increase.

INFECTIOUS DISEASE

Those diseases, however, which have had the most dramatic and long-lasting impact on human populations are infectious in nature. We have seen the potent effect of malaria and the consequent spread of the sickle-cell allele (see pp. 101–103). Several other hereditary traits have also been suggested as possible biological mechanisms providing resistance against malarial infection.

Infection refers to the introduction into the body of foreign organic matter; these may include microbes (viruses, bacteria, protozoa), fungi, or even entire multicellular organisms (such as worms). Each of us is equipped with a genetically programmed defense apparatus—called the *immune response*—which discriminates such foreign invaders from our own cells and attempts to isolate and deactivate them.

Major histocompatibility complex (MHC)   The large genetic complex (located in humans on chromosome #6) that plays a central part in immune response—recognition of foreign antigens and production of specialized cells to deactivate them.

The Immune Response   The immune response is made up of several components, the primary one of which includes several linked loci on chromosome number 6. In addition to the seven HLA loci (see p. 131), there are nearby a large number of additional loci. These code for specific proteins (antigens) characteristic of various cell populations that are integral parts of the immune response. The entire genetic region as a whole (HLA and associated regions) is called the **major histocompatibility complex**.

What stimulates the immune response are antigens—the introduction into the body of proteins perceived as different from self. Actually, our bodies can recognize *any* foreign molecule, even nourishing ones that originate in other organisms. The only way to incorporate these vital nutritive materials is to have them first pass through the digestive tract where they are broken down by enzymes and then absorbed through the intestinal walls as amino acids.

Other foreign antigens that enter the body via the respiratory tract or through breaks in the skin surface elicit an immune response. It is this ability to recognize any foreign cell that causes a reaction in blood transfusions of unmatched type. Since red blood cells lack nuclei, blood matches are relatively easy to make. Most other tissues, however, contain nucleated cells, and proper matches are much more difficult to obtain, as in kidney or liver transplants.

Occasionally, the immune response fails to distinguish truly foreign materials from self, and one's own cells are attacked. Such a reaction is termed an *autoimmune response*. Medical research has recently implicated such a process as an important contributory agent in several human diseases: a severe form of spinal arthritis (ankylosing spondylitis); rheumatoid arthritis; multiple sclerosis; and juvenile onset diabetes.

The cells that control the immune response are a variety of white blood cells called *lymphocytes*, which are small, spherical cells, usually found in the blood, spleen, and lymph system. Lymphocytes can arise either directly from bone marrow (called B-cells), or may mature within the thymus gland (called T-cells). Both these B-cells and T-cells are essential for an efficient immune response. B-cells have receptor areas on their surface that, when stimulated by a foreign antigen, cause the cells to differentiate into plasma cells. These plasma cells can in turn produce antibodies (immunoglobulins), complex protein arrangements that can deactivate a foreign antigen (by physically attaching to it). Humans possess several different loci that contribute to assembling these antibodies. It is estimated that, at birth, each of us potentially can recognize up to one million different foreign antigens and can quickly assemble appropriate antibodies (without question, a marvelously flexible system).

Once antibodies have been produced, the system has a capacity to "remember." If later exposure should occur, the antibodies can then be produced much faster. It is this mechanism that provides for **immunity** and explains why mild early exposure environmentally or through a vaccine provides later resistance.

In addition to the antibody production of B-cells, T-cells contribute to immune response in a complex fashion. Since the action of T-cells can (though not always) be a direct cell process, their role is usually referred to as the *cell-mediated response*. There are several populations of T-cells, each characterized by different antigenic properties. Some directly attack and destroy foreign cells (T-effectors, or T-killer cells); others send molecular messages to B-cells, stimulating antibody production (T-helpers); still others act to switch off the helper activity and terminate the immune response (T-suppressors).

Immune response can thus be seen as a complex system with the capacity to make specific antibodies against foreign antigens and to recognize and deactivate cells containing such foreign materials. Moreover, considerable flexibility is provided in that once the response is begun, it can be halted.

Another related function of the immune system is its ability to recognize and destroy our own cells that have gone awry. In this way, early cancerous cells are normally contained. Since cell mutations or viruses can often cause highly irregular cell development, we would be overwhelmed with cancerous tissues if we had no regulatory mechanism. In fact, some forms of cancer probably develop due to a failure of the immune response.

Immunity An organism's ability to recognize and deactivate foreign antigens very quickly as a consequence of earlier (mild) exposure (for example, through vaccination).

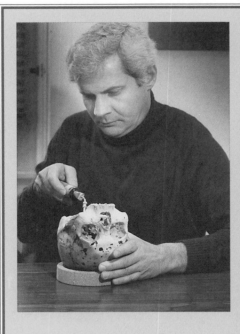

Dr. Donald J. Ortner has been with the Department of Anthropology, National Museum of Natural History, Smithsonian Institution for his entire professional career. He has served in various curatorial and administrative roles including departmental chair. He also holds a visiting professorship at the University of Bradford in England where he collaborates with colleagues in a major study of human skeletal biology during the Medieval period.

My interest in anthropology was kindled during my undergraduate career in the late 1950s. At the time, I was a zoology major at a small liberal arts college. Courses in anthropology were not offered, but a major in sociology was available. The professor of sociology had the reputation among the students of being one of the most creative and stimulating on campus, so I took one of the introductory courses. The professor's reputation was well deserved and I took many more of the classes in sociology; among these offerings was a readings course in which I read several books on anthropology including Clyde Kluckhohn's classic *Mirror for Man*, Ruth Benedict's *Patterns of Culture*, and many of Margaret Mead's semi-popular books on her field of work in the Pacific. I also read Ashley Montague's *Man: His First Million Years* and William Howell's account of human evolution, *Mankind in the Making*.

Anthropology was becoming chic and my discovery of the subject was very heady stuff for me. In my senior year I decided to work on a master's degree in general anthropology. One of the courses I took during the master's program was an introduction to physical anthropology taught by Professor Gordon T. Bowles, a student of the legendary Harvard physical anthropologist, Ernest A. Hooton. During the course I learned anthropometry and osteology using archaeological human remains in the laboratory sessions. Because of my zoology background, this work came fairly easily and I was fascinated with a subject area that combined my interest in zoology and anthropology.

I completed the master's course work and began my thesis research, which was an exercise in the dynamics of acculturation, a specialized form of cultural change stimulated by the contact between two or more societies. This was a subject being discussed and debated with great vigor at that time.

Despite my interest in the biological sciences, I still had not decided on a career as a physical anthropologist. That shift began when, in 1963, I accepted an appointment as a research assistant for Dr. J. Lawrence Angel, who had just taken a position as curator of physical anthropology at the Smithsonian Institution. Professor Bowles had been a graduate teaching assistant during Dr. Angel's undergraduate and early graduate student days at Harvard (that link was undoubtedly a significant factor in my success in obtaining the position).

It is hard to imagine anyone working under Dr. Angel not being affected by his infectious enthusiasm for physical anthropology. He was an extraordinary teacher and particularly so in one-on-one learning situations, and there were many of those during the years I worked with him. By the late 1960s, I had decided to complete my doctorate in physical anthropology and received an advanced research fellowship from the Smithsonian Institution to do so. I completed all course requirements in a year and returned to the Smithsonian. Shortly thereafter, I was appointed to the position of assistant curator of physical anthropology. That was the start of my career as a curator/scientist in one of the great research institutions of the world.

My early scientific interests had developed in the areas of calcified tissue biology and, specifically, what bone histology and chemistry might tell us about the biology of past human populations. During my doctoral program I studied with Dr. Ellis Kerley who had done some of the pioneering work using features of bone histology for estimating age at death. Because bone tissue serves both biomechanical and physiological functions, the potential exists for learning much more about archaeological human populations if we can manage to unlock and interpret the information.

Since that time, of course, there has been an explosion of research, particularly on the chemistry of bone. Stable isotopes have revealed and continue to provide important information about diet and other aspects of our ancestors' lives. Analysis of bone histology is now a fairly standard method in forensic anthropology, and many researchers have enlarged our knowledge of how to interpret the histological features

seen in bone tissue. DNA and the other ancient biomolecules in archaeological bone samples, such as immunoglobulins, are beginning to reveal information that was almost unimaginable during my graduate student days.

While I have retained a research interest in both bone histology and biochemistry, my research focus for the past 20 years has been on skeletal paleopathology. The basic research interest in human adaptation has remained unchanged, but I became fascinated with the impact of disease on human evolution. This interest was certainly influenced by an unforgettable afternoon I spent with the late Professor Adolf Schultz. We were in his office at the University of Zurich and were discussing his research on the presence of skeletal abnormalities in wildshot primates. I had read his paper on the subject and was amazed that such serious problems could exist in animals that were apparently living quite successfully at the time they were shot. Professor Schultz had a wonderful sense of humor and remarked that I should not be overly influenced by the anthropologists at the University of California at Berkeley and their emphasis on predation as a major factor influencing human evolution. He expressed the opinion that disease was almost certainly far more important, and that I would do well to explore that line of research. I am very glad that I did, although the more I learn, the greater there seem to be more questions than answers.

I wish I were better able to pass on useful career advice to young students today. Circumstances are very different today than when I was a graduate student. Jobs were plentiful then and most new Ph.D.s had several offers from which to choose. I often wonder how I would fare if I were completing my degree today and how much difficulty I would have doing the research that I so much enjoy and value. One important trend in physical anthropology is a research methodology increasingly dependent on biochemistry. I struggle to keep even a general working knowledge of this subject and encourage young students to take as much chemistry and mathematics as time permits.

While I wish opportunities for careers in anthropology were greater, I still encourage a student who really wants to become a physical anthropologist to do so. Intelligence, creativity, and hard work are as essential today as they always have been; and there is still room for fine young scholars to make a major contribution to science. You may have to be more flexible in the jobs you take and in the direction of your research. Nevertheless, opportunities persist and important research problems remain to be solved by coming generations of scientists. Good luck!

The immune response has been adapted in a wide variety of vertebrates; an apparatus similar to that of humans has been discovered in the mouse, pig, rabbit, rhesus monkey, and chimpanzee (Amos and Kostyu, 1980). We and other organisms are constantly exposed to possible danger by a variety of foreign antigens (insect or snake venom, for example). Most especially, however, the immune response has evolved to protect against infection by microbes. Natural selection has thus endowed the entire human species with a finely tuned defense mechanism.

Although every individual has a unique tissue type and consequently varies in some genetic components of the immune system, it remains to be determined whether *populations* differ in their immune response to specific diseases. The history of plague, measles, smallpox, influenza, and other diseases suggests that natural selection could well have acted differentially on human populations. The questions remain: What diseases are linked to populational differences in immune response? What ecological/evolutionary factors brought them into being? How might individuals be evaluated for risk to specific diseases? What kinds of therapeutic intervention may mitigate or even prevent the development of a variety of human diseases? One of the great frontiers of medical and evolutionary research concerns the attempt to answer these questions.

AIDS   In the last few years, the general public has come to hear a good deal about the immune system as a result of the catastrophic AIDS epidemic. As most of you know, AIDS is an abbreviation for Acquired Immune Deficiency Syndrome. This name indicates that the major problem (a severely compromised immune system) is *acquired*; that is, individuals become infected during their lifetime. We have known for a while now of inherited problems that disturb immune function, and many of you have seen pictures of children so-affected living within sterile bubbles. While tragic in their ramifications, these genetically caused syndromes are exceedingly rare, affecting only a handful of individuals. AIDS, however, is acquired as a viral infection that can devastate one's natural immunity. It thus has the potential to spread widely in human populations—obviously a major concern to us all (and, undoubtedly, a terrifying prospect for some).

The magnitude of the problem is truly catastrophic in its dimensions. As a result, a tremendous amount of research energy is being devoted to AIDS— in the laboratory, the clinic, and in the field, where epidemiological data are gathered. It is virtually impossible to give a completely up-to-date account of this disease, as our data change constantly. At this writing, we are able to make some reasonably firm statements concerning cause and some general predictions of future trends.

First of all, AIDS is known to be caused by a virus, one called a *retrovirus*. Differing nomenclature has been used (HTLV-III, LAV, ARV), but a recent consensus of an international committee has agreed to designate the AIDS virus as HIV (Human Immunodeficiency Virus). Viruses may store their genetic information as DNA (like the herpes family) or as RNA (like polio, smallpox, influenza, measles). As a type of RNA virus, HIV functions as a *retrovirus*, and it is able to convert its genetic structure into DNA, which can then be permanently incorporated into our own DNA. The viral genes thus become part of the genetic structure of host cells, take over the machinery of certain of these cells, and produce more viral particles, even to the point of killing some of these cells. A chronic infection results—potentially for the lifetime of the individual (even if it does not kill).

The virus—with its genetic material neatly inserted directly into the host cell's DNA—may there lie dormant for years. The time period from first infection to the onset of life-threatening symptoms is termed the *latency period*, which in the United States now averages close to 11 years (but with dramatic individual variation, ranging from less than 2 years to perhaps two decades). The whole sequence, from initial infection to diagnostic (severe) symptoms and ultimately to death, is oftentimes referred to as *HIV disease*. AIDS itself (sometimes called *frank AIDS* or *full-blown AIDS*) is the stage at which life-threatening symptoms appear.

Another terribly complicated aspect of retroviruses is that they are exceedingly variable and subject to rapid mutation. In other words, it may not be possible to develop a *single* vaccine effective against all strains of the AIDS-causing virus.

Individuals are exposed to the virus through exchange of bodily fluids—most notably blood and/or semen. While in the United States AIDS has predominantly affected homosexual men and intravenous drug users, it is anticipated that, in the next few years, it will spread among the heterosexual community as well. Indeed, AIDS is already widespread in central and eastern Africa, where it is primarily a heterosexual disease (Quinn et al., 1986).

The virus thus enters a human through direct and intimate contact with bodily fluids from someone carrying the virus. Once infected, individuals make antibodies to the HIV virus. Currently used screening tests check for seropositivity, that is, presence of these antibodies in the blood (antibodies are usually detectable six months after infection).

Not everyone exposed to the virus will necessarily develop full-blown AIDS. Current estimates, which vary widely, suggest that a majority (up to 75% or more) of those exposed eventually develop the disease. Indeed, some experts believe that given enough time, *everyone* exposed will in time develop AIDS. What, then, exactly is AIDS? First of all, AIDS is characterized by an immune system that is severely compromised. The virus appears to attack certain white blood cells critical in immune response (T-helper cells), and its multiplication leads to the death of such cells but not necessarily other types of host cells (such as macrophages and neurons). Also, with AIDS, the regulation of the production of antibodies that normally would protect a person against other infections runs amok, leading to the synthesis of nonfunctional antibodies. Basically, the entire immune system becomes dysfunctional. As a result, an individual is unable to ward off ubiquitous infectious agents that are innocuous to a normal person. These *opportunistic infections* (a variety of viral, bacterial, protozoan, and fungal agents) are what then kill the individual. At present, treatment has proven sadly ineffective, and, once the immune system fails, the disease is always lethal.

We reiterate, however, that certainly not everyone who has been exposed to the virus will become infected; and of those infected, not everyone necessarily will progress to full-blown AIDS. That is not to downplay its significance. Through August, 1993, more than 315,000 Americans were diagnosed as having AIDS—with more than 242,000 recorded deaths.

There are no precise estimates of how many Americans *already* have been infected. Given the likely rate of progression to full-blown AIDS, it can be conservatively estimated that the number of AIDS cases and number of deaths will more than double before the end of the decade. Just considering the direct medical costs in the United States, the financial burden will be staggering (estimated at 8 to 16 billion dollars per year in 1991) (Barnes, 1986).

Until breakthroughs emerge, little help will be available for the potential one-half million affected Americans in the next few years. Worldwide, during this same period, hundreds of thousands (perhaps millions) more could get AIDS with most, if not all, dying from the disease.

Some hope does exist: An effective vaccine (useful for those not yet exposed) does seem a reasonable expectation. Especially with breakthroughs in recombinant DNA technology, it has been possible to sequence most of the envelope proteins of the HIV virus—probably the best avenue to realizing an effective vaccine. Yet, the problems are enormous, and most experts do not foresee a safe and effective product generally available for at least five years (and probably much longer).

A further moral problem exists regarding the *testing* of any new vaccine. Human volunteer subjects could be used, but the ethics of doing so are most debatable. Many researchers believe the best animal model on which to test is the chimpanzee. Nowhere near a sufficient number of chimpanzees now in captivity is available for such testing. It thus might mean decimating most (if not all) of the still free-ranging populations to solve the human problem of AIDS. Will such a circumstance prove necessary? And, if so, is it worth such a price?

The Hazards of Modern Life

The specter of tens of millions dying annually because of dietary deprivation or hundreds of thousands dying from AIDS are but two of the many hazards humanity has created for itself. The cultural pace set by technological, urbanized humankind is radically altering our environments and presumably selection pressures as well. As yet, however, the specific adaptive responses are unknown.

ARTIFICIAL RADIATION

One of the potential perils receiving wide public attention is the danger of humanmade radiation. We are all constantly subjected to natural forms of radiation (called background sources) as we are bombarded by cosmic rays from above and from below by radiation-emitting elements in the earth's crust (radium and thorium, for instance).

Worldwide, there is considerable variation in the amount of such background radiation (particularly correlated with altitude), but a typical natural dose for an individual (that is, a "whole body") over a 30-year period is on the order of 3,000 to 5,000 mrems.*

We are concerned with radiation hazards because of their potentially harmful biological effects. In particular, radiation is a known cause of mutation (changes in DNA sequence). Agents like radiation that cause mutations are called **mutagens**.

Mutagen An agent that mutates (alters) the DNA of a cell.

Estimating possible genetic damages of increased radiation involves considerable guesswork, but the dangers are alarming. If there were an approximate 10-fold increase in annual background radiation (from 500 to 5000 mrems, say) by artificial sources (nuclear weapons, medical sources, nuclear

*Radiation is measured in absorption units. A rem (radiation equivalent for man) is a unit expressing the biological effects of a standard dose (one roentgen) of radiation; 1,000 mrems = 1 rem.

Box 6-1   Artificial Radiation

Dosage effects of radiation tend to accumulate through time, so that several small doses can eventually have biologically harmful ramifications. However, a single large dose will probably do more damage than several small ones, where cells at least have some opportunity for repair.

Accidental exposure to very large doses of radiation at one time will cause severe radiation sickness that especially affects areas of rapidly forming cells, such as the gastrointestinal tract, skin, and blood-forming marrow. A very large single dose of radiation usually causes irreparable damage and can be lethal. The long-term effects of smaller radiation exposure are not well known, but experimental evidence suggests increased incidence of cataracts (scarring of the cornea of the eye), increased frequency of several varieties of cancer, and accelerated aging (Gerson, 1977).

RADIATION EXPOSURE LEVELS*

Lethal dose (would kill 50% of population)	400,000 mrems/ single dose**
Maximum permissible to an individual without clearly harmful effects	500 mrems/year
Exposure from background sources	120 mrems/year
Exposure from medical sources	70 mrems/year

*Extrapolated from experimental evidence and observation on humans who have been exposed.

**Note: A lethal dose is extremely large compared to dosages normally incurred.

power plants/waste), an estimated 50,000 new cases of inherited disease would appear worldwide in the first generation alone. Eventually the effects would translate into as many as 500,000 additional cases every generation. (See Box 6-1.)

SOURCES OF ARTIFICIAL RADIATION

Nuclear Weapons   Most of the evidence concerning the effects of nuclear explosions on humans comes from long-term studies of the survivors of Hiroshima and Nagasaki and their descendants.

Comparative studies conducted initially by the Atomic Bomb Casualty Commission and later by the Radiation Effects Research Foundation surprisingly have not demonstrated any proven association among survivors' offspring for congenital defects, stillbirth rate, newborn mortality, or childhood mortality. Among those who were themselves directly exposed to the explosion (including *in utero*), there is an increase in chromosomal abnormalities. Since these usually cause death or sterility, they are not generally passed on to the next generation. For those who were severely exposed, there is also a sharp increase in overall mortality rates. It would seem that the effects of radiation exposure of the magnitude of Hiroshima and Nagasaki cause severe biological effects in the first generation, but surprisingly few in future generations (Schull et al., 1981). However, long-term effects may initially appear "masked" as recessive mutations that will express themselves as lethals somewhere down the road. We may well see some of these biological costs as the studies of the Japanese descendants continue. Much concern also

Figure 6-7

Hiroshima, several months after the atomic bomb was dropped in August, 1945.

surrounds the possible dangers of atmospheric nuclear testing. Prior to 1963, the United States and the former Soviet Union exploded several large devices in the atmosphere. The total radiation produced, however, was not an important mutagenic factor, for a dosage less than 1% of background radiation was generated.

Medical Sources   From medical practice, the major source of biologically harmful radiation exposure is X-rays, particularly if the gonads are exposed. As a diagnostic tool, X-rays are extremely helpful, but great caution must be used—particularly in individuals who have not completed reproduction. Even more hazardous is the X-ray exposure of a developing fetus, for an early somatic mutation may be ramified into major abnormalities.

Radiation is also used for therapeutic purposes in the treatment of some cancers. Such exposure, however, applies only to a tiny fraction of the population, and these few individuals are usually critically ill before exposure. Given the dire circumstance there is often little choice, but harmful side effects are significant. While the treatment is designed to slow down the progress of a lethal tumor, it can stimulate the onset of other cancers (in skin, thyroid, and bone, for example).

Nuclear Power Plants   Hazards from conventional nuclear power plants can potentially come from either release of radioactive elements in the fission process or release from waste material. Barring a major accident, the kinds of materials *likely* to escape from a nuclear power plant are not exceedingly radioactive. On the other hand, a major failure (that is, a "meltdown") of the plant's radioactive core could be catastrophic.

The most serious accident yet to occur at a nuclear power plant took place at Chernobyl in the Ukraine on April 26, 1986. As a result of human error and a test procedure gone terribly wrong, the reactor building exploded, releasing large amounts of radioactive isotopes into the atmosphere (*Nature*, 1986). The resulting fire further damaged the reactor core (leading to at least a partial meltdown), burned for several days, and released substantially more radioactivity.

Spreading from the Ukraine, the radioactive cloud passed over eastern Europe, Scandanavia, and eventually reached England on May 2 (ApSimon and Wilson, 1986). The fallout came down on Europe mostly as a result of rainfall carrying the radioactive material. By the time the "cloud" had reached the Western Hemisphere, it had dissipated to such an extent as to prove of no significant danger.

How much harm was done, however, in Europe? Most immediately, at least 31 deaths have been reported by authorities—primarily due to severe radiation suffered by plant workers and firemen in the immediate vicinity. The long-term impacts are not yet fully understood. On the basis of estimates of radioactive release, some experts place the eventual cost at approximately 4,000 additional cancer deaths over the next 30 years (that is, above and beyond what would have occurred without the accident) (*Nature*, 1986).

In the United States, the most serious nuclear plant accident occurred at the Three Mile Island facility near Harrisburg, Pennsylvania, on March 28, 1979. Due to mechanical failure and human error, the plant's cooling system failed to operate correctly, causing the nuclear reactor's fuel core to overheat, and bringing the plant dangerously close to a meltdown. In addition, a large (1,000 cubic foot) bubble of explosive hydrogen gas formed within the reac-

Figure 6-8

Chernobyl.

tor building, and this potentially dangerous situation was only brought under control after five days.

Waste material (as a direct product of uranium fission) from nuclear power plants can be highly radioactive and must be disposed of with extreme caution. Usually, such material is buried in special underground facilities hopefully far from dense population centers and active geological faults.

Careful monitoring around nuclear power plants has thus far shown little radiation pollution—well within minimum safety limits; potential dangers persist, however. The possibility of a major leak at a plant or waste site due to carelessness, sabotage, or earthquake continues to cause much apprehension.

CHEMICALS AND MUTATIONS

Today, more significant than radiation as a mutagenic agent is the wide variety of synthesized chemicals we eat, breathe, and with which we come into physical contact. We might be startled to learn that few of these exotic chemicals so widely used in business, agriculture, food processing, and the drug industry have received adequate enough systematic testing to measure their mutagenic danger accurately.

A clarification of terms is required. Researchers use three different but somewhat overlapping terms for agents that negatively affect health/cell function. *Mutagen* (or mutagenic) refers to an agent that actually alters the genetic material (DNA) of a cell. A mutagen can affect somatic cells or gametic cells. A **carcinogen** (carcinogenic) simply means any agent that promotes cancer (many carcinogens will also be mutagens of somatic cells). Finally, a **teratogen** (teratogenic) is an agent that in any way disrupts *in utero* development, potentially leading to a birth defect. Alcohol can be a powerful teratogen, and, if consumed in high enough amounts in the months during pregnancy, can lead to a host of problems for the neonate (and is termed *fetal alcohol syndrome*). Some agents that act as teratogens can also be mutagenic.

Not only those chemicals produced by human innovation have mutagenic effects; some of those formed naturally also have striking mutagenic properties. For example, aflatoxin—a substance formed from mold on peanuts and other organic substances—is one of the strongest mutagens known. In addition, in laboratory animals, numerous other chemicals found in common foods have been shown to be mutagenic and/or carcinogenic. Among those foods containing such possibly harmful substances are black pepper, mushrooms, celery, parsley, figs, and cocoa powder (that is, chocolate) (Ames, 1983). You should note that "harmful" here relates to experimental evidence using other organisms (mostly bacteria) as models. There are no current estimates regarding possible risks for humans.

We often read of experimental evidence (on lab animals) pointing to possibly harmful effects of cyclamates, saccharin, Alar, and so forth. After some public furor and industry protests, these substances are usually removed from the market—not so much because we understand their effects on humans, but because we fear their possibilities.

Cyclamate is apparently not a mutagen itself, but it can be converted into a substance that is. Caffeine may also increase the likelihood of mutation by interfering with DNA repair. In all these cases, however, the direct evidence obtained from laboratory organisms is still unclear when extrapolated to human beings.

Carcinogen An agent that promotes cancer (often a mutagen as well).

Teratogen An agent that disrupts development.

CROWDING

Another human problem realized only since the advent of agricultural settlements is crowding. Today, the stresses of humanity pressing against humanity are becoming ever more apparent throughout most of the inhabited world.

Crowding is defined as a problem primarily in terms of population density—in other words, the number of people per unit area. Population densities alone, however, do not measure the human stress involved. More relevant here is the *quality* of life possible, which in turn is dependent on technological sophistication, architectural design, and prevailing cultural values.

What is most significant in determining whether an individual feels crowded is his/her microenvironment, or what is sometimes called "personal space." In some urban areas of the United States and many parts of the underdeveloped world, several families crowd into housing units designed for single families. The amount of personal space per individual is thus reduced to just a few dozen square feet. Experimental data support this aspect of immediate space, since the strongest density-dependent correlations with social pathologies concern the number of people per room (Altman, 1978).

How much space is required for individuals to feel comfortable and function normally depends on the individual and the situation. In addition to actual physical space, other important aspects include: cleanliness, heat, odor, ventilation, whether individuals can be mobile within the space provided, whether they are in the crowded conditions voluntarily or not, and most importantly, how long they are required to stay in such conditions (ranging from a few minutes to a lifetime). Individual tolerance of crowded conditions and ability to adjust to altered quantity and quality of social interactions also show marked variation.

While there are no *absolute* measures of minimum space requirements, a general standard of 38 sq. ft. per person has been recommended for United States penal institutions. If this is taken as a rough standard, the following extremely crowded conditions come into sharper focus:

Figure 6-9

Hong Kong. A side alley packed with humanity.

	SQ. FT./PERSON
Crowded disco	10
Nineteenth-century London slum	9
Nazi concentration camp at Belsen	3
New York subway at rush hour	2
Black Hole of Calcutta (a notorious prison)	2

As humans pack themselves in ever larger numbers into smaller areas, what effects can we expect? Numerous experimental studies have shown serious behavioral disturbances among overcrowded animals. Moreover, there are also physiological alterations, such as increased production of steroids. The exact functions of these substances are still unclear, but they seem to be secreted in generally stressful situations.

Observations of overcrowding in animals either in the laboratory (rats, mice) or in natural populations (among deer and lemmings, for example) indicate three major kinds of behavioral and reproductive abnormalities (Damon, 1977):

1. disruption of reproduction, ovulation, sperm function, mating, nest building, lactation

2. increase in incidence of abortions, stillbirths, infant mortality
3. increase in aggression, particularly by males

The direct pathological associations of overcrowding in animals, however, are still far from clear. If growth is slow in mice populations, they generally will adjust, showing no more mortality than a control group. Moreover, definite associations of disease incidence and overcrowding are also not clearly established. Sometimes animals (normally social) have higher incidences of disease when they are isolated; other animals show more disease symptoms when crowded.

What does all this experimental evidence from animals mean for humans? Very few studies have been done on crowding using human data, but as yet no clearly harmful associations of overcrowding have been demonstrated.

We must reemphasize that the concept of crowding is not strictly a biological one but has important cultural connotations as well. In fact, most researchers consider "crowding" as primarily a psychological subjective state. Typically, some sort of stress is implied. This is believed to be derived from individual perceptions of too little physical and/or psychological space (social overload theory) or from feelings of loss of personal control over interpersonal interactions ("thwarting" theory).

In many cultures, close physical contact with other humans is seen as highly desirable, whereas in others it is avoided. For example, the !Kung San* of the Kalahari Desert live in an environment with vast open space. In fact, their overall population density (approximately one person per ten square miles) is among the lowest in the world (Draper, 1973). However, San deliberately arrange their living space—huts in tight circles with few physical barriers—in order to provide maximum interpersonal contact. A possible explanation of this kind of behavior is that it is a cultural means of coping with the cold during the long, chilly Kalahari nights. Indeed, this arrangement creates the equivalent effect of thirty people living in a single room! The !Kung do not have to live closely together but clearly prefer to do so. How we then perceive their personal environment (as overcrowded or not) depends largely on what cultural definition we apply.

NOISE

One by-product of crowding in urban, heavily industrialized areas is noise. The largest contributor to noise pollution is made by mechanical devices. We are all constantly bombarded by the sounds of planes, buses, cars, construction equipment, and even music.

An obvious physical effect of excessive noise (high amplitude) is a deterioration of hearing ability. Urban dwellers on the average perform less well on hearing tests than rural folk. Such loss of hearing is seen particularly in airline workers, construction personnel, and rock band members. Just 2 hours in a disco can adversely affect one's hearing—even permanently. Noise-induced hearing loss may be quite common. Two different studies estimate the number of individuals in the United States suffering from such hearing loss at between 4.5 and 5 million people (Bugliarello et al., 1976).

Clearly, extremely high levels of noise produce harmful effects, but what about moderate noise levels? Some evidence suggests such pollution can lead to a loss of sleep and reduced concentration (Damon, 1977). We all have

*The mark ! indicates a clicking sound in the pronunciation of Kung San.

experienced such noise levels (for example, with traffic or construction equipment) and obviously considerable adaptability is possible. Particularly if the noise is steady and predictable, we can learn to "phase it out." But are we really able to ignore it completely? Some extremely tentative data suggest that continuous noise pollution may produce harmful consequences in humans. For example, in the area around a London airport, admissions to mental hospitals are significantly higher than in less noisy areas (Damon, 1977).

In recognition of the harmful effects of noise pollution around airports, a California Superior Court decision in 1970 awarded $740,000 to 549 property owners around Los Angeles International Airport for "loss of full enjoyment of their property" (Anthrop, 1973). Debate concerning noise pollution from jet aircraft peaked in the early 1970s over the proposed development of a commercial supersonic transport (SST). Eventually, the U.S. Senate withdrew federal support for an American SST; the English/French-built supersonic *Concorde* began operation in the mid-1970s, but has been allowed only restricted access to a few United States airports.

Summary

In this chapter, we have investigated human responses to a variety of environmental stresses: solar radiation, heat, cold, high altitude, malnutrition, disease, artificial radiation, crowding, and noise. We have seen that in most cases individual humans make physiological adjustments to such environmental stress—what we have termed *acclimatization*.

We have also posed the question of adaptation: Do human populations vary in the proportions of genotypes in response to general ecological stress? The answer to this last query is still open, since it necessitates a demonstration of specific selection pressures affecting differential reproductive success—a most tricky task for human data!

While still unproven, we may reasonably postulate that variable conditions of solar radiation, the thermal environment, nutrition, disease, and altitude have led to differential success of genotypes influencing body size/ shape, skin pigmentation, the immune response, and so forth.

We may also, with some reason, postulate that cultural environments of the technological, urban, overcrowded twentieth century are also acting to shift selection pressures. The real question is: How?

Questions for Review

1. What are the differences between adaptation and acclimatization? Illustrate through the example of high altitude adjustments.
2. Under what conditions might light skin color be adaptive? Under what conditions might dark skin color be adaptive?
3. What physiological adjustments do humans show in coping with cold stress?
4. What physiological adjustments do humans show in coping with heat stress?
5. What does body size and shape have to do with climate adaptation?

6. How do humans cope with high altitude stress (both physiologically and culturally)?

7. Give an explanation for the distribution of lactose intolerance among the world's populations.

8. How might malnutrition cause changes in selection pressures? Describe what kinds of data would *test* for such changes.

9. Discuss how human disease is influenced by an interaction of biocultural factors.

10. A foreign antigen has just entered your body. Discuss how your body recognizes it as foreign and deals with it.

11. What causes AIDS? What is the difference between "HIV disease" and full-blown AIDS?

12. What are the various possible sources of artificial radiation? Why is there so much concern over radiation pollution?

13. Discuss how crowding and noise *might* affect selection pressures.

Contents

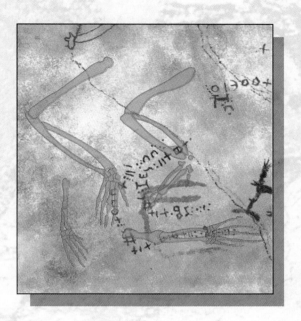

Evolutionary History

Issue 4 A Cosmic Calendar

How can we possibly conceive of the awesome stretch of time that has been flowing since, scientists inform us, our universe was first formed by the cosmic explosion called the Big Bang 15 billion years ago? In *Drag-* *ons of Eden*, Carl Sagan (1977) has condensed this prodigious period into one year he calls "The Cosmic Calendar." There are three parts to the calendar.

1. A pre-December calendar. A list of a few of the significant events in the history of the universe and earth in the first 14 billion years, represented by the 334 days from January 1 through November 30

2. A month of December calendar. Events of the last 1.25 billion years represented by the month of December

---

PRE-DECEMBER DATES

Big Bang	January 1
Origin of the Milky Way Galaxy	May 1
Origin of the solar system	September 9
Formation of the Earth	September 14
Origin of life on Earth	≈September 25
Formation of the oldest rocks known on Earth	October 2
Date of oldest fossils (bacteria and blue-green algae)	October 9
Invention of sex (by microorganisms)	≈November 1
Oldest fossil photosynthetic plants	November 12
Eukaryotes (first cells with nuclei) flourish	November 15

DECEMBER 31

Appearance of early hominoids, ancestors of apes and humans	1:30 P.M.
First hominids	10:30 P.M.
Widespread use of stone tools	11:00 P.M.
Domestication of fire by *Homo erectus**	11:46 P.M.
Beginning of most recent glacial period	11:56 P.M.
Seafarers settle Australia	11:58 P.M.
Extensive cave painting in Europe	11:59 P.M.
Invention of agriculture	11:59:20 P.M.
Neolithic civilization; first cities	11:59:35 P.M.
First dynasties in Sumer, Ebla, and Egypt; development of astronomy	11:59:50 P.M.
Invention of the alphabet: Akkadian Empire	11:59:51 P.M.
Hammurabic legal codes in Babylon; Middle Kingdom in Egypt	11:59:52 P.M.
Bronze metallurgy; Mycenaean culture; Trojan War; Olmec culture; invention of the compass	11:59:53 P.M.
Iron metallurgy; first Assyrian Empire; Kingdom of Israel; founding of Carthage by Phoenicia	11:59:54 P.M.
Asokan India; Ch'in Dynasty China; Periclean Athens; birth of Buddha	11:59:55 P.M.
Euclidean geometry; Archimedean physics; Ptolemaic astronomy; Roman Empire; birth of Jesus	11:59:56 P.M.
Zero and decimals invented in Indian arithmetic; Rome falls; Moslem conquests	11:59:57 P.M.
Mayan civilization; Sung Dynasty China; Byzantine Empire; Mongol invasion; Crusades	11:59:58 P.M.
Renaissance in Europe; voyages of discovery from Europe and from Ming Dynasty China; emergence of the experimental method in science	11:59:59 P.M.
Widespread development of science and technology; emergence of a global culture; acquisition of the means for self-destruction of the human species; first steps in spacecraft planetary exploration and the search for extraterrestrial intelligence	Now: The first second of New Year's Day

---

*See p. 406 for Issue on *Homo erectus*' association with fire.

3. A December 31 calendar. From 10:30 P.M. (the first humans) until midnight (now), this interval represents the last 2.5 million years

Examine the calendar and the place of *Homo sapiens* in a time perspective. Modern humans appeared a bit more than a minute before 12:00 midnight. You may feel humble before the immensity of time of our universe, or you may feel proud of the human achievements accomplished in such a brief speck of time.

SOURCE

Sagan, Carl, *Dragons of Eden*. New York: Random House, Inc., 1977.

Calendar reprinted by permission of the author and the author's agents, Scott Meredith Literary Agency, Inc., 845 Third Avenue, New York, New York 10022

1 year	=	15,000,000,000 years
1 month	=	1,250,000,000 years
1 day	=	41,000,000 years
1 minute	=	29,000 years
1 second	=	475 years
1 billion years	=	24 days

DECEMBER   COSMIC CALENDAR

SUNDAY	MONDAY	TUESDAY	WEDNESDAY	THURSDAY	FRIDAY	SATURDAY
	1 Significant oxygen atmosphere begins to develop on Earth	2	3	4	5 Extensive vulcanism and channel formation on Mars	6
7	8	9	10	11	12	13
14	15	16	17 Precambrian ends. Paleozoic Era and Cambrian Period begin. Invertebrates flourish	18 First Oceanic plankton Trilobites flourish	19 Ordovician Period First fish, first vertebrates	20 Silurian Period First vascular plants. Plants begin colonization of land
21 Devonian Period begins. First insects. Animals begin colonization of land	22 First amphibians First winged insects	23 Carboniferous Period First trees First reptiles	24 Permian Period begins. First dinosaurs	25 Paleozoic Era ends Mesozoic Era begins	26 Triassic Period First mammals	27 Jurassic Period First birds
28 Cretaceous Period First flowers Dinosaurs become extinct	29 Mesozoic Era ends Cenozoic Era and Tertiary Period begin First cetaceans First primates	30 Early evolution of frontal lobes in the brains of primates First hominids. Giant mammals flourish	31 End of the Pliocene epoch. Quaternary (Pleistocene and Holocene Period) First humans			

Introduction

In the preceding chapters, we surveyed the genetic mechanisms that are the foundation of the evolutionary process. Moreover, Chapters 5 and 6 show in detail how *microevolutionary* changes are investigated in contemporary human populations. In this chapter, we turn to the *macroevolutionary* process. We thus will review aspects of vertebrate (and specifically mammalian) evolution over the great time depth of these major groups. The fundamental perspectives reviewed here concerning geological history, principles of classification, and modes of evolutionary change will serve as a basis for topics covered throughout the remainder of this text.

The Human Place in the Organic World

There are millions of different species of life forms living today. If we were to include microorganisms, the total would surely exceed tens of millions. When you further add all the vast multitudes of species that are now *extinct*, the total is staggering—perhaps hundreds of millions!

How do biologists cope with all this diversity? As is typical for *Homo sapiens*, scientists approach complexity through simplification. Thus, biologists group life forms together or, in other words, they construct a **classification** system. For example, today there are probably more than 15 million species of animals, including primarily insects. No one knows exactly how many species there are, as more than 90% have yet to be scientifically described or named.

Nevertheless, even with the tens of thousands of species that biologists do know something about, there is still too much diversity to handle conveniently. The solution is to organize the diversity into groupings to (1) reduce the complexity and (2) indicate evolutionary relationships.

All life on earth is part of an organic continuum. From the beginnings of life, more than 4 billion years ago, all life forms have shared in a common ancestry. Our contemporary attempts to organize the bewildering array of organisms that have evolved make relative interpretations of relationships. Since all organisms fall *somewhere* on the biological continuum, our conclusions simply place humans, for example, within this continuous framework and then judge as to which other organisms are evolutionarily closer to our lineage and which are more distant.

Organisms that move about and ingest food (but do not photosynthesize, as in plants) we call *animals*. More precisely, the multicelled animals are placed within the group called the **Metazoa**. Within the Metazoa there are more than 20 major groups termed *phyla* (sing., *phylum*). One of these phyla is the **Chordata**, animals with a nerve cord, gill slits (at some stage of development), and a stiff supporting cord along the back called a *notochord*. Most chordates today are **vertebrates**, in which the notochord has become a vertebral column (which gives its name to the group); in addition, vertebrates also have a developed brain and paired sensory structures for sight, smell, and balance.

The vertebrates themselves are subdivided into six classes: bony fishes, cartilaginous fishes, amphibians, reptiles, birds, and mammals. We will discuss mammalian classification in the following section.

Classification The ordering of organisms into categories, such as phyla, orders, families, to show evolutionary relationship.

Metazoa Multicellular animals. A major division of the Animal Kingdom.

Chordata (Chordates) The phylum of the Animal Kingdom that includes vertebrates.

Vertebrates Animals with bony backbones. Includes fishes, amphibians, reptiles, birds, and mammals.

Taxonomy

Before we go further, however, it is useful to discuss the bases of animal classification. The field that specializes in delineating the rules of classification is called *taxonomy*. Organisms are classified firstly, and most traditionally, on the basis of physical similarities. Such was the basis of the first systematic classification devised by Linnaeus in the eighteenth century (see Chapter 4). Still today, basic physical similarities are considered a good starting point in postulating schemes of organic relationships. In order for similarities to be useful, however, they *must* reflect evolutionary descent. For example, the bones of the forelimb of all terrestrial air-breathing vertebrates (tetrapods) are so similar in number and form (Fig. 7-1) that the obvious explanation for the striking resemblances is that all four kinds of air-breathing vertebrates ultimately derived their forelimb structure from a common ancestor.

Such structures that are shared by descendants on the basis of descent from a common ancestor are called **homologies**. Homologies alone are the reliable indicators of evolutionary relationship. But we must be careful not to draw hasty conclusions from superficial similarities. For example, both bats and birds have wings, but should not be grouped together on this basis alone. In many other respects (for example, only birds have feathers; only mammals have fur), bats and birds clearly are *not* closely related. Such structural features as the wing of a bird and the wing of a bat that superficially appear to be similar and have evolved through common function are called **analogies**. The separate development of analogous structures comes about in evolution through a process called *parallelism*. In making consistent evolutionary interpretations and devising classifications that reflect these interpretations, evolutionary biologists must concentrate on the homologies and treat the analogies as extraneous "noise."

Nor is it sufficient simply to isolate the homologies. For certain purposes, some structural homologies are much more informative than others. To return to our example, the forelimbs of air-breathing vertebrates are all similar in overall structure. Some may be adapted into wings, others into legs. If we were to group birds and bats on the basis of a functional (derived) modification into a wing, we would be assuming the common ancestor of both already possessed wings. From fossil evidence, this clearly was *not* the case.

Homologies Similarities between organisms based on descent from a common ancestor.

Analogies Similarities between organisms based strictly on common function with no assumed common evolutionary descent.

Figure 7-1

Homologies. The similarities in the bones of these animals can be most easily explained by descent from a common ancestor.

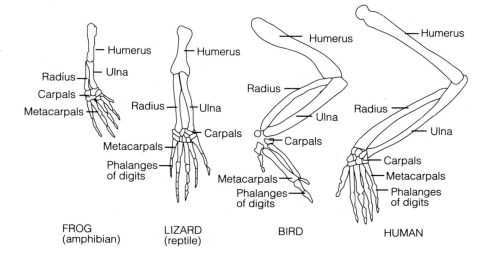

FROG (amphibian) LIZARD (reptile) BIRD HUMAN

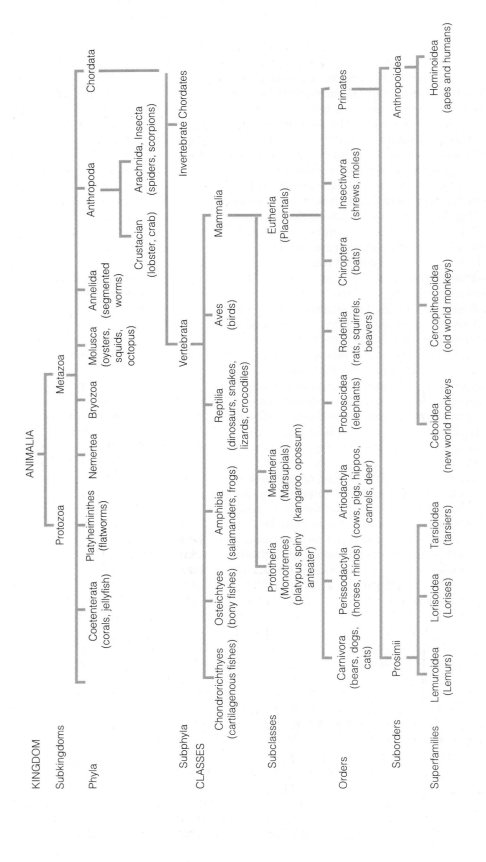

Figure 7-2

Classification chart. Modified from Linnaeus. All animals are placed in certain categories based on structural similarities. Not all members of categories are shown. For example, there are up to 20 orders of placental mammals (8 are depicted). A comprehensive classification of the Primate Order is presented in Chapter 8.

Nor can we sort birds from bats or frogs from lizards on the basis of the number of bones in the forelimb. They all possess *generally* similar structures (presumably which they all *did* inherit from a common vertebrate ancestor). We would say, therefore, that the basic forelimb structure for all tetrapods is **primitive**.

On the other hand, as we noted, *only* birds have feathers and *only* mammals have fur. In comparing mammals with other vertebrates, presence of fur is a **derived** characteristic. Similarly, in describing birds, feathers are derived only in this group.

So, how does one know which kinds of characteristics to use? The answer is determined by which group one is describing and with what it is being compared. For the most part, it is usually best to use those character states that reflect more specific evolutionary adaptations; in other words, derived character states usually are the more informative. Moreover, when grouping two forms together (say, a bat with a mouse, both as mammals), this should be done *only* when they show **shared derived** characteristics (here, both possessing fur).

Primitive Relating to a character state that reflects an ancestral condition, and thus not diagnostic of those derived lineages usually branching later.

Derived Relating to a character state that reflects a more specific evolutionary line, and thus more informative of precise evolutionary relationships.

Shared derived Relating to specific character states shared in common between two forms and considered the *most* useful for making evolutionary interpretations.

Time Scale

In addition to the staggering array of living and extinct life forms, biologists must also contend with the vast amount of time that life has been evolving on earth. Scientists have also devised simplified schemes—but in this case to organize *time*, not organic diversity.

Geologists, in particular, have formulated the **Geological Time Scale** (Fig. 7-3). Very large time spans are organized into eras and periods. Periods, in turn, can be broken down into epochs (as we will do later in the text for the most recent part of geological history to organize the discussion of primate evolution).

Geological Time Scale The organization of earth history into eras, epochs, and periods. Commonly used by geologists and paleoanthropologists.

Vertebrate Evolutionary History—A Brief Summary

In broad outline, there are three eras: the Paleozoic, the Mesozoic, and the Cenozoic. The first vertebrates appeared early in the Paleozoic (during the Cambrian Period) 500 million years ago (m.y.a.) and probably go back considerably further. It is the vertebrate capacity to form bone that accounts for their more complete fossil record *after* 500 m.y.a.

During the Paleozoic, several varieties of fishes (including the ancestors of modern sharks and bony fishes), amphibians, and reptiles all appeared. In addition, at the end of the Paleozoic, close to 250 m.y.a., several varieties of mammal-like reptiles were also diversifying. It is widely thought that some of these forms gave rise to the mammals.

The evolutionary history of vertebrates and other organisms during the Paleozoic and Mesozoic was profoundly influenced by geographic events. We know that the positions of the earth's continents have dramatically shifted during the last several hundred million years. This process, called **continental drift**, is explained by the geological theory of *plate tectonics*, which views the earth's crust as a series of gigantic moving and colliding plates. Such massive geological movements can induce volcanic activity

Continental drift The movement of continents on sliding plates of the earth's surface. As a result, the position of large land masses has shifted dramatically in the last 250 million years.

Box 7-1   Evolutionary Processes

ADAPTIVE RADIATION

The potential capacity of an organism to multiply is practically unlimited; its ability to increase its numbers, however, is regulated largely by the available resources of food, shelter, and space. As the size of a population increases, its food, shelter, and space decrease, and the environment will ultimately prove inadequate. Depleted resources engender pressures that will very likely induce some members of the population to seek an environment where competition is considerably reduced and the opportunity for survival and reproductive success increased. This evolutionary tendency to exploit unoccupied habitats may eventually produce an abundance of diverse species.

An instructive example of the evolutionary process known as *adaptive radiation* may be seen in the divergence of the stem reptiles to the profusion of different forms of the late Paleozoic, and especially the Mesozoic. It is a process that has taken place many times in evolutionary history when a life form rapidly takes advantage, so to speak, of the many now available ecological niches.

The principle of evolution illustrated by adaptive radiation is fairly simple, but important. It may be stated thus: *A species, or group of species, will diverge into as many variations as two factors allow—(1) its adaptive potential and (2) the adaptive opportunities of the available zones.*

In the case of reptiles, there was little divergence in the very early stages of evolution, when the ancestral form was little more than one among a variety of amphibian water-dwellers. A more efficient kind of egg had already developed and, although it had great adaptive potential, there were few zones to invade. However, once reptiles became fully terrestrial, there was a sudden opening of available zones—ecological niches—accessible to the adaptive potential of the reptilian evolutionary grade.

This new kind of egg provided the primary adaptive ingredient of the reptilian form that freed reptiles from attachment to water; strengthened limbs and skeleton for locomotion on land followed. The adaptive zones for reptiles were not limitless; nevertheless, continents were now open to them with no serious competition from any other animal. The reptiles moved into the many different econiches on land (and to some extent in the air and sea), and as they adapted to these areas, they diversified into a large number of species. This spectacular radiation burst with such evolutionary rapidity, it may well be termed an adaptive explosion.

GENERALIZED AND SPECIALIZED CHARACTERISTICS

Another aspect of evolution closely related to that of adaptive radiation involves the transition from *generalized* to *specialized characteristics*. These two terms refer to the adaptive potential of a particular trait: one that is adapted for many functions is termed generalized whereas a trait that is limited to a narrow set of ecological functions is called specialized.

For example, a generalized mammalian limb has five fairly flexible digits adapted for many possible functions (grasping, weight support, digging). In this respect, our hands are still quite generalized. On the other hand (or foot), there have been many structural modifications in our feet suited for the ecologically specialized function of stable weight support.

These terms are also sometimes used when speaking of the adaptive potential of whole organisms. For example, the aye-aye (a curious primate living in Madagascar) is a highly specialized animal structurally adapted in its dentition for an ecologically narrow rodent/woodpecker-like niche—digging out insect larvae with prominent incisors.

The notion of adaptive potential is a relative judgment and can estimate only crudely the likelihood of one form evolving into another form or forms. Adaptive radiation is a related concept, for only a generalized ancestor can provide the flexible evolutionary basis for such rapid diversification. Only a generalized organism with potential for adaptation into varied ecological niches can lead to all the later diversification and specialization of forms into particular ecological niches.

ERA	PERIOD	(Began m.y.a.)	EPOCH	(Began m.y.a.)
CENOZOIC	Quaternary	1.8	Holocene Pleistocene	.01 1.8
CENOZOIC	Tertiary	65	Pliocene Miocene Oligocene Eocene Paleocene	5 22.5 37 53 65
MESOZOIC	Cretaceous	136		
MESOZOIC	Jurassic	190		
MESOZOIC	Triassic	225		
PALEOZOIC	Permian	280		
PALEOZOIC	Carboniferous	345		
PALEOZOIC	Devonian	395		
PALEOZOIC	Silurian	430		
PALEOZOIC	Ordovician	500		
PALEOZOIC	Cambrian	570		
PRE-CAMBRIAN				

Figure 7-3

Geological Time Scale.

(as, for example, all around the Pacific rim), mountain building (for example, the Himalayas), and earthquakes. Living on the edge of the Pacific and North American plates, residents of the Pacific coast of the United States are acutely aware of some of these consequences, as illustrated by the explosive volcanic eruption of Mt. St. Helens or the frequent earthquakes in Alaska and California.

Geologists, in reconstructing earth's physical history, have established the prior (significantly altered) positioning of major continental land masses. During the Paleozoic, the southern continents (South America, Africa, Antarctica, Australia, and India) were closely joined into one land mass known as *Gondwanaland* (Fig. 7-4). Similarly, the northern continents (North America, Europe, and Asia) were brought closely together, forming another supercontinent, called *Laurasia*. By the end of the Paleozoic, both these land areas were further joined into one colossal continent called *Pangea*. However, during the Mesozoic, Pangea soon (geologically speaking) began to break up. When the Mesozoic ended (*circa* 65 m.y.a.), the positions of the continents had approached their present locations.

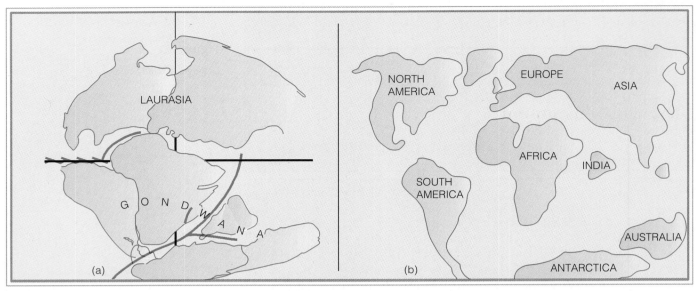

Figure 7-4

Continental drift. Changes in position of the continental plates from Late Paleozoic to Late Eocene. (a) The position of the continents during the Mesozoic (circa 125 m.y.a.). Pangea is breaking up into a northern land mass (Laurasia) and a southern land mass (Gondwana-land). (b) The position of the continents during the Late Eocene (after 40 m.y.a.).

Ecological niche Specific environmental setting to which an organism is adapted.

Adaptive radiation The relatively rapid expansion and diversification of an evolving group of organisms as they adapt to new niches.

Epochs A category of the geological time scale; a subdivision of period. In the Cenozoic, epochs include: Paleocene, Eocene, Oligocene, Miocene, Pliocene (from the Tertiary), and the Pleistocene and Recent (from the Quaternary).

Cerebrum The outer portions of the brain; in vertebrates, divided into right and left hemispheres.

Neocortex The outer (cellular) portion of the cerebrum, which has expanded through evolution, particularly in primates, and most especially in humans. The neocortex is associated with higher mental function.

The evolutionary ramifications of this long-term continental drift were profound. Groups of land animals became effectively isolated from each other by large water boundaries; the distribution of reptiles and mammals was significantly influenced by continental movements. Although not producing such dramatic continental realignments, the process continued through the Mesozoic and into the Cenozoic. The more specific consequences of continental drift on early primate evolution are discussed in Chapter 11.

During most of the Mesozoic, reptiles were the dominant land vertebrates and exhibited a broad expansion into a variety of **ecological niches**, which included flying and swimming forms. Such a fairly rapid expansion marked by diversification of many new species is called an **adaptive radiation**. No doubt, the most famous of these highly successful Mesozoic reptiles are the dinosaurs, which themselves evolved into a wide array of sizes and lifestyles. Dinosaur paleontology, never a boring field, has advanced several startling notions in recent years: that many dinosaurs were warm-blooded; that some varieties were quite social and probably also showed considerable parental care; that many forms went extinct as the result of major climatic changes to the earth's atmosphere from collisions with comets or asteroids; and, finally, that not all dinosaurs went entirely extinct, with many descendants still living and doing remarkably well (that is, all modern birds).

The first mammals are known from fossil traces fairly early in the Mesozoic, but the first *placental* mammals cannot be positively identified until quite late in the Mesozoic, *circa* 70 m.y.a. This highly successful mammalian adaptive radiation is thus almost entirely within the most recent era of geological history, the Cenozoic.

The Cenozoic is divided into two periods, the Tertiary (about 63 million years duration) and the Quaternary, from about 1.8 m.y.a. up to and including the present. Because the above division is rather imprecise, paleontologists more frequently refer to the next level of subdivision within the Cenozoic, the **epochs**. There are seven epochs within the Cenozoic, the Paleocene, Eocene, Oligocene, Miocene, Pliocene, Pleistocene, and Holocene (the last often referred to as "the Recent"). (See Fig. 7-3.)

Mammalian Evolution

Following the extinction of dinosaurs and many other Mesozoic forms (at the beginning of the Cenozoic), there was a wide array of ecological niches open for rapid expansion and diversification of mammals. Indeed, the Cenozoic was an opportunistic time for mammals and it is known as the Age of Mammals. Mesozoic mammals were small animals, about the size of mice, which they resembled superficially. The mammalian adaptive radiation of the Cenozoic saw the rise of the major lineages of all modern mammals. Mammals, along with birds, replaced reptiles as the dominant terrestrial vertebrate.

How do we account for the rapid success of mammals? Several characteristics relating to learning and general flexibility of behavior are of prime importance. In order to process more information, mammals were selected for larger brains than those typically found in reptiles. In particular, the **cerebrum** became generally enlarged, especially the outer covering, the **neocortex**, which controls higher brain functions. In mammals, the cerebrum has expanded so much that it came to comprise the majority of brain volume; moreover, greater surface convolutions evolved, creating more surface area, and thus providing space for even more nerve cells (neurons).

For an animal to develop such a large and complex organ as the mammalian brain, a longer, more intense period of growth is required. This slower development can occur internally (*in utero*) as well as after birth. While internal fertilization, and especially internal development, are not unique to mammals, the latter is a major innovation among terrestrial vertebrates. Other forms (birds, most fish, and reptiles) incubate their young externally by laying eggs (oviparous), while mammals, with very few exceptions, give

Table 7-1 Mammalian Innovations (Distinguishing Mammals from Reptiles)*

Major Complex	Associated Features
Homoiothermy	Hair/fur; sweat glands; increased metabolism
Heterodontism	Strengthened jaw; increased dietary diversity
Reproductive efficiency	Viviparity; suckling (increased parental investment)

*There is some evidence that homoiothermy, fur, and viviparity are more common among animals than once believed.

Figure 7-5

Mesozoic mammal. A speculative reconstruction of what a Mesozoic mammal might have looked like. Probably no bigger than a kitten, and with mammalian teeth, these animals were capable of attacking small lizards.

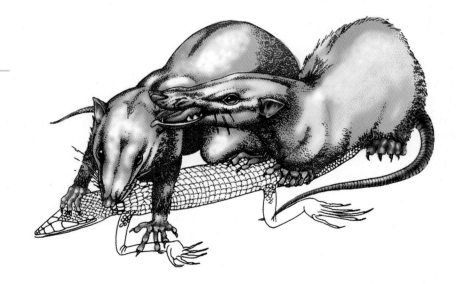

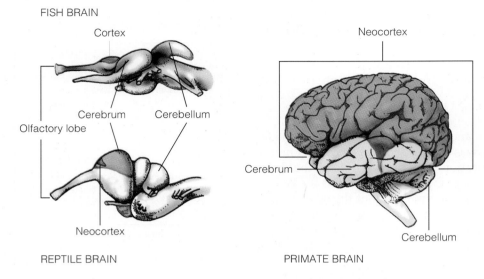

Figure 7-6

Lateral view of brain. The illustration shows the increase in the cerebral cortex of the brain. The cerebral cortex integrates sensory information and selects responses.

REPTILIAN (alligator)
Homodont: no differentiation of teeth

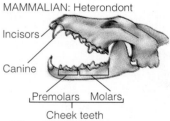

MAMMALIAN: Heterondont

Figure 7-7

Reptilian and mammalian teeth.

birth to live young and are thus called **viviparous**. Even among mammals, however, there is considerable variation among the major groups in how mature the young are at birth. As we will see below, it is in mammals like ourselves, the *placental* forms, where development *in utero* goes the furthest.

Another distinctive feature of mammals is seen in dentition. While living reptiles consistently have similarly shaped teeth (called a *homodont* dentition), mammals have differently shaped teeth. This varied pattern, termed a **heterodont** dentition, is reflected in the primitive mammalian array of dental elements, which includes: 3 incisors, 1 canine, 4 premolars, and 3 molars for each quarter of the mouth. Since the upper and lower jaws are usually the same and are symmetrical for both sides, this "dental formula" is conventionally illustrated by dental quarter (see Box 8-3, p. 223, for a more complete discussion of dental patterns as they apply to primates). Thus, with 11 teeth per quarter segment, the primitive mammalian dental complement includes a total of 44 teeth. Such a heterodont arrangement allows mammals to process a potentially wide variety of foods. Incisors can be used for cutting, canines for grasping and piercing, and premolars and molars for crushing and grinding.

A final point regarding teeth relates to their disproportionate representation in the fossil record. As the hardest, most durable portion of a vertebrate skeleton, teeth have the greatest likelihood of becoming fossilized (that is, mineralized). As a result, the vast majority of the available fossil data for most vertebrates, including primates, consists of teeth.

Another major adadaptive complex which distinguishes contemporary mammals from reptiles is **homoiothermy**, the maintenance of a constant internal body temperature. Also colloquially (and incorrectly) called warm-bloodedness, this central physiological adaptation is also seen in contemporary birds (and also probably in many dinosaurs as well).

Major Mammalian Groups

There are three major subgroups of living mammals: the egg-laying mammals (monotremes); the pouched mammals (marsupials); and the placental mammals. The monotremes are extremely primitive and are considered more distinct from marsupials or placentals than these latter are from each other.

The most notable distinction differentiating the marsupials from the placentals is the form and intensity of fetal development. In marsupials, the young are born extremely immature and must complete development in an external pouch. It has been suggested (Carrol, 1988) that such a reproductive strategy is more energetically costly than retaining the young for a longer period *in utero*. In fact, this is exactly what placental mammals have done, through a more advanced placental connection (from which the group gets its popular name). But perhaps even more basic than fetal nourishment, was the means to allow the mother to *tolerate* her young internally over an extended period. Marsupial young are born so quickly after conception that there is little chance for the mother's system to recognize and have an immune rejection of the fetal "foreign" tissue. But in placental mammals, such an immune response would occur were it not for the development of a specialized tissue that isolates fetal tissue from the mother's immune detection, and thus prevents tissue rejection. Quite possibly, this innovation is the central factor in the origin and initial rapid success of placental mammals (Carrol, 1988).

In any case, with a longer gestation period, the central nervous system especially of placental mammals could develop more completely in the fetus. Moreover, after birth, the "bond of milk" between mother and young also would allow more time for complex neural structures to form. It should also be emphasized from a *biosocial* perspective that this dependency period not only allows for adequate physiological development, but also provides for a wider range of learning stimuli. That is, the young mammal brain, exposed

Viviparous   Giving birth to live young.

Heterodontism   Having different teeth. Characteristic of mammals whose teeth consist of incisors, canines, premolars, and molars.

Homoiothermic (Homoiothermy)   The ability to maintain a constant, internal body temperature through physiological means, independent of environmental factors. Whereas reptiles today rely upon exposure to the sun to raise energy levels and body temperature, birds and mammals do not. Some dinosaurs also appear to have been homoiothermic.

Figure 7-8

Spiny anteater, a monotreme.

Figure 7-9

Wallaby with infant in pouch, marsupials.

Box 7-2   Convergent and Parallel Evolution

CONVERGENT EVOLUTION

The discussion of marsupials offers an opportunity to present another evolutionary process, *convergent evolution*. We pointed out (in Box 7-1, Evolutionary Processes) that in the early stages of development, there is a tendency for newly evolved forms to become highly diversified when they invade varied environments. The diversification results from the modification of the ancestral form in adapting to new ecological niches.

Convergent evolution is the process in which two *unrelated* groups of organisms, living in similar but separate environmental conditions, develop a similar appearance and lifestyle. That is, similar environmental demands make for similar phenotypic responses (Mayr, 1970, p. 365). This should not be surprising since the requirements of adapting to a particular environment would require modifications of physical traits. Two similar environments could, therefore, result in similar adaptive characters.

Striking examples of convergence are the pouched mammals of Australia and placental mammals. Australia was isolated from South America before the great placental mammalian radiation of the Cenozoic, and marsupials survived because they were free from the competition of the more efficient placentals. When placental mammals became prominent in the Cenozoic, only a few were able to invade Australia (via island-hopping from Southeast Asia).

Without competition, the pouched mammals spread into the varied environments of the isolated continent. There were marsupials that resembled, to a lesser or greater degree, a wolf, cat, flying squirrel, groundhog, anteater, mole, and mouse. And they occupied ecological niches similar to the placental mammals they resembled (Simpson et al., 1957, p. 470).

The variety of marsupials illustrates adaptive radiation; the resemblance in form due to similarity of econiches illustrates convergent evolution.

PARALLEL EVOLUTION

A process similar to convergent evolution is *parallel evolution*. However, in parallel evolution the ancestral form is less remote and, thus, descendant lines share a greater degree of homology than in convergent evolution. For example, the muriqui (a New World monkey) and the gibbon (an Old World small-bodied ape) both possess elongated upper appendages. These two forms are members of independent primate lineages that diverged from each other more than 30 m.y.a. Dating to this time, the last common ancestor of these lines did *not* possess this trait. Thus, it was acquired (as a derived feature) separately in both lineages, presumably as a result of similar adaptive pressures in a tree-living setting. The fact that these lines retain significant shared homology, setting common limits on evolutionary direction, defines this process as parallel evolution (rather than convergence).

through observation of the mother's behavior as well as perhaps other adults, and through play with age mates, is a receptacle for a vast amount of information. It is not sufficient to have evolved a brain capable of learning. Collateral evolution of mammalian social systems has ensured that young mammal brains are provided with ample learning opportunities and are thus put to good use.

Modes of Evolutionary Change

Speciation The process by which new species are produced from earlier ones. The most important mechanism of macroevolutionary change.

We have discussed evolution from both a *microevolutionary* perspective in Chapters 5 and 6 and from a *macroevolutionary* one in this chapter. The major evolutionary factor underlying macroevolutionary change is **speciation**, the

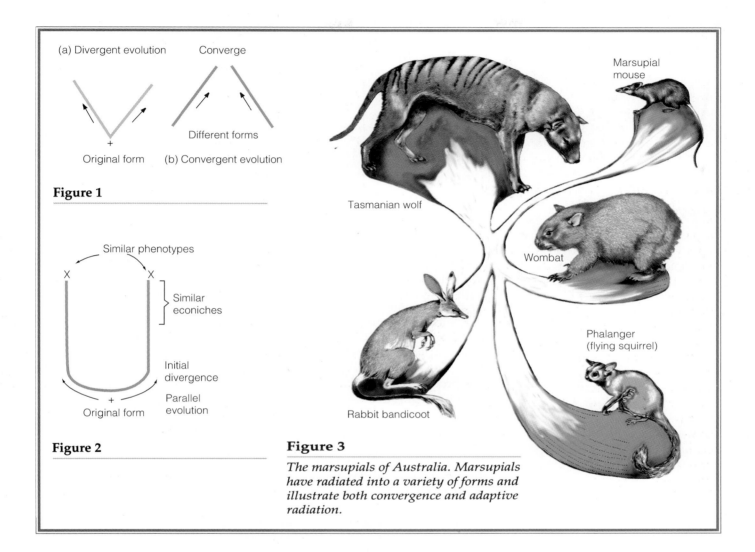

(a) Divergent evolution   Converge

Different forms

Original form   (b) Convergent evolution

Figure 1

Similar phenotypes

X   X

Similar
econiches

Initial
divergence

Original form   Parallel
evolution

Figure 2

Marsupial
mouse

Tasmanian wolf

Wombat

Phalanger
(flying squirrel)

Rabbit bandicoot

Figure 3

*The marsupials of Australia. Marsupials
have radiated into a variety of forms and
illustrate both convergence and adaptive
radiation.*

process whereby new species first arise. As you will recall, we have defined
a species as a group of *reproductively isolated* organisms, a characterization
that follows the biological species concept (Mayr, 1970). According to this
same view, the way new species are first produced involves some form of isolation. Picture a single species of some organisms (baboons, for example)
composed of several populations distributed over a wide geographic area.
Gene exchange (migration) will be limited if a geographic barrier such as an
ocean, mountain range, or sufficient distance effectively separates these populations. This extremely important form of isolating mechanism is termed
geographic isolation.

Now if one population (A) is separated from another population (B) (Fig.
7-10) by a mountain range, individual baboons of population A will not be
able to mate with individuals from B. As time passes (several generations),

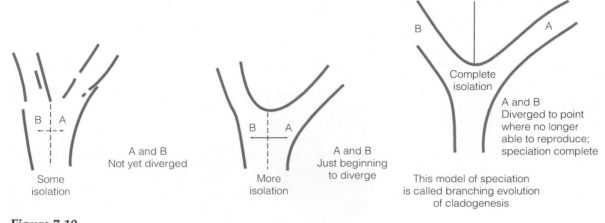

Figure 7-10

A speciation model.

genetic differences will accumulate in both populations. If population size is small, we can predict that genetic drift will cause allele frequencies to change in both populations. Moreover, since drift is *random* in nature, we would not expect the effects to be the same. Consequently, the two populations will begin to diverge.

As long as gene exchange is limited, the populations can only become more genetically different with time. Moreover, further difference would be expected if the baboon groups are occupying slightly different habitats. These additional genetic differences would be incorporated through the process of natural selection. Certain individuals in population A may be most reproductively fit in their own environment, but would show less reproductive success in the environment occupied by population B. Thus, allele frequencies will shift further, and the results will be divergent in the two groups.

With the cumulative effects of genetic drift and natural selection acting over many generations, the result will be two populations that—even if they were to come back into geographic contact—could no longer interbreed fertilely.

More than just geographic isolation might now apply. There may, for instance, be behavioral differences interfering with courtship—what we call *behavioral isolation*. Using our *biological* definition of species, we now would recognize two distinct species, where initially only one existed.

Until recently, the general consensus among evolutionary biologists was that microevolutionary mechanisms could be translated directly into the larger-scale macroevolutionary changes, most especially, speciation (also called *transspecific evolution*). A smooth gradation of change was assumed to run directly from microevolution into macroevolution. A representative view was expressed by a leading synthesist, Ernst Mayr:

> The proponents of the synthetic theory maintain that all evolution is due to accumulation of small genetic changes, guided by natural selection, and that transspecific evolution is nothing but an extrapolation and magnification of events that take place within populations and species (Mayr, 1970, p. 351).

In the last decade, this view has been seriously challenged. Many theorists now believe that macroevolution cannot be explained *solely* in terms of accumulated microevolutionary changes. Many current researchers are convinced that macroevolution is only partly understandable through microevolutionary models.

GRADUALISM VS. PUNCTUATIONALISM

The traditional view of evolution has emphasized that change accumulates gradually in evolving lineages—the idea of "phyletic gradualism." Accordingly, the complete fossil record of an evolving group (if it could be recovered) would display a series of forms with finely graded transitional differences between each ancestor and its descendant. The fact that such transitional forms are only rarely found is attributed to the incompleteness of the fossil record, or, as Darwin called it, "a history of the world, imperfectly kept, and written in changing dialect."

For more than a century, this perspective dominated evolutionary biology, but in the last 15 years some biologists have called this notion into serious question. The evolutionary mechanisms operating on species over the long run are often not continuously gradual. In some cases, species persist for thousands of generations basically unchanged. Then, rather suddenly, at least in evolutionary terms, a "spurt" of speciation occurs. This uneven, nongradual process of long stasis and quick spurts has been termed **punctuated equilibrium** (Gould and Eldredge, 1977).

What the punctuationalists are disputing concerns the "tempo" and "mode" of evolutionary change commonly understood since Darwin's time. Rather than a slow, steady tempo, this alternate view postulates long periods of no change punctuated only occasionally by sudden bursts. From this observation, punctuationalists concluded that the mode of evolution, too, must be different from that suggested by classical Darwinists. Rather than gradual accumulation of small changes in a single lineage, advocates of punctuated equilibrium believe an *additional* evolutionary mechanism is required to push the process along. They thus postulate *speciation* as the major influence in bringing about rapid evolutionary change. Speciation can result from *microevolutionary* factors, most especially genetic drift and natural selection. However, once speciation occurs, particularly when accelerated rapidly, punctuationalists argue that it then directs *macroevolution* in a way quite distinct from what microevolutionists *alone* would predict.

How well does the paleontological record agree with the predictions of punctuated equilibrium? Indeed, considerable fossil data show long periods of stasis punctuated by occasional quite rapid changes (on the order of 10,000 to 50,000 years). Intermediate forms are rare, not so much because the fossil record is poor, but because the speciation events and longevity of these transitional species were so short we should not expect to find them very often.

The best supporting evidence for punctuated equilibrium has come from the fossilized remains of marine invertebrates. How well, then, does the vertebrate and especially the primate fossil record fit the punctuationalist model? In studies of Eocene primates, rates of evolutionary change were shown to be quite gradual (Gingerich, 1985; Brown and Rose, 1987; Rose, 1991). In another study, here of Paleocene plesiadapiforms, evolutionary changes were also quite gradual. Although no longer considered primates, these forms show a gradual rate of change in another, closely related, group of mammals. The predictions postulated by punctuationalists have thus far not been substantiated in those evolving lineages of primates for which we have adequate data to test the theory.

Punctuated equilibrium   The concept that evolutionary change proceeds through long periods of stasis, punctuated by rapid periods of change.

It would, however, be a fallacy to assume that evolutionary change in primates or in any other group must therefore be of a completely gradual tempo. Such is clearly not the case. In all lineages, the pace assuredly speeds up and slows down due to factors that influence the size and relative isolation of populations. In addition, environmental changes as they influence the rapidity and long-term direction of natural selection must obviously also be considered. In conclusion, then, as postulated by the modern synthesis, microevolution and macroevolution need not be "decoupled" as some evolutionary biologists have recently suggested.

Summary

This chapter surveyed background information concerning vertebrate and, more specifically, mammalian evolution. Perspectives on organic diversity and geological time scale were discussed. Early vertebrate evolution was briefly reviewed, with emphasis palced on the origin and diversification of mammals, especially placental mammals. Two fundamental features shared by all mammals are herterodontism and homoiothermy. In addition, the crucial role of continental drift as it influenced mammalian evolution was highlighted. Finally, the contemporary debate concerning the tempo and mode of evolutionary change (that is, the gradualist versus punctuationalist models) was also discussed.

Questions for Review

1. What are the two primary goals of organic classification?
2. What are the major groups of vertebrates?
3. What are the major eras of geological time over which vertebrates have evolved?
4. What primary features distinguish mammals—especially placental mammals—from other vertebrates?
5. What is meant by homology? Contrast with analogy, using examples.
6. Why do biologists, in making interpretations of evolutionary relationships, concentrate on derived features as opposed to primitive ones? Give an example of each.
7. What is meant by continental drift? How might have continental drift influenced the evolution and diversification of mammals during the Mesozoic?
8. What is heterodontism? What is one major functional ramification of this feature?
9. What is homoiothermy? How do modern placental mammals differ from contemporary reptiles in this feature?
10. Contrast the gradualist view of evolutionary change with a punctuationalist view. Give an example from mammalian (primate) evolution that supports one view or the other.

Chapter 8

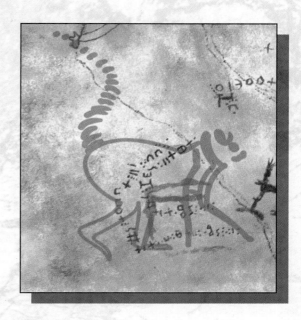

Contents

Living Primates

In the past 20 years or so, there has been an increased awareness that gorillas, far from being the savage beasts of King Kong fame, are actually intelligent, gentle animals that typically resort to violence only when threatened. This awareness has developed in part through the popularization of field studies of wild mountain gorillas, particularly by Dr. George Schaller and the late Dr. Dian Fossey. In addition, the publicity accorded Dr. Francine Patterson's language study with the well-known lowland gorilla, Koko, has generated something of a love affair between many Americans and the gorilla.

Because these kinds of research tend to capture the imagination of the general public, and also owing to the popularity of the movie *Gorillas in the Mist*, the mountain gorilla has been accorded a place very much in the spotlight of popular culture. But, unfortunately, serious problems confront the remaining few mountain gorillas, and the tragic reality is that the continued survival of this magnificent primate is far from certain.

The habitat of the mountain gorilla (*Gorilla gorilla beringei*) is largely restricted to a series of mostly extinct volcanoes known as the Virungas. These tropical, densely forested mountains, some of which soar to over 14,000 feet, straddle the shared borders of Rwanda, Zaire, and Uganda in central Africa (Fig. 1).

Probably never as numerous as the two subspecies of lowland gorilla, the mountain gorilla today numbers only about 620 in the wild.

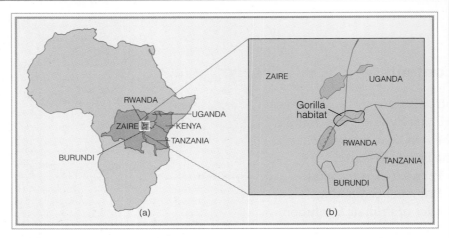

Figure 1

Map of central Africa showing Rwanda, Zaire, and Uganda with location of mountain gorilla habitat.

There are no captive mountain gorillas. The single most serious threat to their continued existence is habitat loss resulting from forest clearing by a rapidly expanding human population. Illegal hunting of other species, which indirectly affects gorillas, also continues to be a factor; however, protection has been tenuously afforded by governmental jurisdiction of remaining gorilla habitat.

Earlier in this century, almost all the Virunga chain was fortunately set aside for preservation, but as human encroachment was not strictly prohibited, protected areas are smaller today than in the past. The 96-square-mile portion in Zaire is called the Parc National des Virungas. The Rwandan section is the Parc National des Volcans (Volcanoes National Park), currently comprising about 54 square miles, or about one-half of 1 percent of Rwanda's total land area. Approximately 320 gorillas currently live in these two national parks. In Uganda, the Kigezi Gorilla Sanctuary is home to a few animals, and an additional

300 are found in the Impenetrable Forest, the only known mountain gorilla habitat outside the Virungas. Being appropriately named, this forest is off limits to all but the most intrepid of backpackers.

The mountain gorilla was first recognized and described as a distinct subspecies in 1902, but no behavioral studies were conducted until George Schaller's pioneering work in Zaire in 1959–1960. Following in Schaller's footsteps, Dian Fossey in 1967 established Kariosoke, a research station located in the forest between Mt. Karisimbi and Mt. Visoke. In time, she was to become world-famous, not only for field studies, detailed in her popular book, *Gorillas in the Mist*, but also for her efforts to eliminate poaching and restrict human access to park areas.

Figure 2

Cultivated fields and grazing land encroach upon national park boundaries. Forested slopes are part of the Parc National des Volcans.

Indeed, her unceasing dedication to preserving the mountain gorilla led to much conflict and probably contributed to her still unsolved murder on December 26, 1985.

Today, Rwanda, a small country of approximately 10,000 square miles (a bit smaller than the state of Maryland), faces the same problems seen in most of the world's developing nations (unchecked population growth, poverty, and lack of access to goods and services, to name a few). With a population density of over 700 people per square mile, Rwanda is the most densely inhabited country in Africa. The current population numbers almost 8 million and grows at an annual rate of 3.4 percent. On average, a Rwandan woman gives birth to 8.6 children and, given the traditional impor-

tance placed upon children and the considerable influence of the Catholic Church, governmental efforts to control population increase have not met with notable success.

With its exploding human population, the Rwandan countryside is among the most intensively cultivated regions in the world; indeed, terraced fields and grazing lands extend right up to national park boundaries. Prior to the efforts of Dian Fossey and others, the few park rangers who existed were largely ineffective in preventing illegal cattle grazing and tree cutting in protected areas. Furthermore, poachers constituted an extremely serious threat to wildlife, a threat that, although reduced, has still not been eliminated.

Today the target species of poachers' snares are primarily small antelopes (bushbuck and duiker). But, as is always the case with traps, snares do not exclusively take targeted animals, and they have caught more than a few gorillas. Although gorillas are usually able to break free,

they may not be able to rid themselves of the wire or rope noose that continues to cut into a wrist or ankle. All too often this results in the loss of a limb, if not death from infection. Moreover, in the past, the hunting of gorillas for meat or for skulls and hands to be sold to tourists took a heavy toll on mountain gorilla groups. It was these deadly practices with their tragic consequences that Dian Fossey fought to end.

As devastating as continued forest clearing, cattle grazing, and poaching are for wildlife in Rwanda, it is important to remember the very real problems faced by an increasingly hard-pressed human population. In 1991, Rwanda's annual gross national product per capita was a mere $310.00, compared to a figure

Figure 3

Tour guides dismantle a poacher's snare encountered while leading tourists through the forest.

of $21,000.00 for the United States. Only 48 percent of Rwandans living in rural areas had access to safe drinking water, and just 55 percent had sanitation facilities.

These few statistics (and these are but a few) represent the serious and, in some cases, desperate conditions faced by real people. Translated to the local level, where people are attempting simply to "get by," the needs of wildlife (including gorillas) are of no practical concern. The resulting dilemma, seen throughout the Third World today, is that the needs of ever-growing numbers of humans must always be weighed against those of ever-dwindling numbers of wildlife populations.

The traditional perspective of most cultures is that wildlife and forests represent resources to exploit or obstacles to overcome. This view

is frequently shared, not only by the governments of developing countries, but also the governments of industrialized nations seeking to invest in them. It is therefore fortunate indeed that, through education efforts, an increasing number of Rwandans now see the continued existence of the gorillas and natural areas as beneficial.

One way to protect an endangered species, at least for a while, is to turn it into an economic asset. This approach has met with considerable success in Rwanda and Zaire. In 1979 the Rwandan government, in conjunction with a group of conservation organizations, formed the Mountain Gorilla Project to increase tourism, reduce poaching, and educate local villagers as to the importance of gorilla conservation. Today, after coffee and tea, tourism is the third largest source of foreign revenue for Rwanda. Although the lush tropical beauty of Rwanda's terraced hills and forested mountains are cer-

tainly appealing, most of this small country's allure for foreign tourists is embodied in the mountain gorilla.

Currently in Rwanda there are four habituated gorilla groups available for tourist viewing. Visitors must be accompanied by trained guides and their access is strictly limited to 8 per group per day. Prior to late 1990, an estimated 8000 tourists traveled annually to Rwanda to make the arduous trek up the densely covered slopes and experience the magic of time spent among these magnificent animals.

Unfortunately, since October, 1990, Rwanda has suffered from a devastating civil war that has all but destroyed tourism, in spite of an agreement between government and rebel forces not to interfere with tourists or gorillas. In February, 1993, the cease-fire that had held for several months ended in ferocious fighting. Tragically, over one million Rwandans were displaced and sent to refugee camps, where many died. Many others were killed during fighting in and around the villages at the base of the mountains. For the first time since the beginning of the war, the research station at Kariosoke had to be evacuated and all scientific staff were sent home.

The courage of the Rwandan field staff at Karisoke cannot be overstated. At great personal risk, they continued to track the gorilla study groups almost daily to ascertain their safety and well-being. Perhaps as evidence of the commitment many Rwandans feel to the gorillas, only one animal, a well-known silverback named Mrithi, sadly fell victim to the conflict. Mrithi, who was featured in the movie *Gorillas in the Mist*, was shot and killed, probably accidentally, in May, 1992. His

Figure 4

The body of adult male gorilla Digit after poachers had decapitated him and cut off his hands. (This graphic photograph, which has appeared in prior editions of this book, has elicited strong responses both positive and negative from students and instructors. We continue to include it at the specific request of the late Dr. Dian Fossey, who provided it.)

salaries are largely derived from the tourist trade.) But scientific staff have returned to Karisoke and the damage the station incurred is being repaired. Moreover, tourists are beginning to trickle back, and the trackers who take them into the forests dismantle traps and snares as they encounter them (Fig. 3). Additionally, the Dian Fossey Gorilla Fund (DFGF), founded in memory of the much-loved silverback killed by poachers on New Year's Eve, 1977 (Fig. 4), finances some antipoaching efforts. However, these measures are hardly sufficient to the task in the face of widespread hunger and devastation.

Certainly the only hope of preserving the mountain gorilla in Rwanda is continued peace, surely a tenuous expectation. Unfortunately, the situation in Zaire is little better, for civil war in that country has practically made travel there impossible. Furthermore, sporadic

group has now broken up to some extent, and all but one member are accounted for.

On August 3, 1993, a peace treaty was signed and as of this writing, it is holding. However, the effects of the conflict are devastating. Hundreds of thousands of displaced people have now returned to destroyed villages and ruined crops. Many have resorted to cutting trees in the forest, and poaching has increased by at least twentyfold.

The resultant loss of tourist-generated revenue has meant that park guards cannot be paid and the government cannot afford armed antipoaching patrols. (Park guard

Figure 5

Female mountain gorilla forages in the safety of her protected forest habitat.

fighting in eastern Zaire could potentially pose a threat to gorilla groups in that country as well.

In addition to maintaining peace, it is essential that other nations help the Rwandan people. If their population growth is allowed to continue at its current pace, and if their current patterns of subsistence and land use continue, they will have little option but to clear what forest remnants they possess. Such practices would produce short-term gain for a mere handful of people, and the long-term consequences would be disastrous.

Eco-tourism is one approach that appears to offer solutions beneficial to everyone, humans and gorillas alike. But eco-tourism also has its critics. There are justifiable fears that close contact with humans will have severe consequences for wild animals, particularly primates. Gorillas are susceptible to the same illnesses that afflict humans, particularly respiratory ailments. Infectious diseases, such as tuberculosis and pneumonia, could literally wipe out an entire gorilla group. Additionally, opening the forest to tourism, even on a limited scale, could eventually result in the construction of new roads, and even perhaps small airstrips, all destructive of the very forests that need protection.

Admirably, before the war, the Rwandan government acted responsibly and has taken much advice from the DFGF and other organizations to ensure that threats to the gorillas were minimized. In addition, the government, in collaboration with the DFGF, continues to promote scientific research in the Virungas.

The problems facing the Rwandans and the mountain gorilla are staggering, and the best solutions are far from perfect. But if mountain gorillas are to be saved, it must be done by means that also help the Rwandan people. The salvation of the gorillas, if indeed it occurs, is likely to be won through their exploitation as economic assets to those countries fortunate enough to have them as residents. We can only hope the humans who share their world with these extraordinary animals find their association mutually beneficial. Otherwise, it is all too likely that, in the not too distant future, the mists that shroud the Virunga volcanoes will conceal neither the breathtakingly beautiful forests, nor the magnificent mountain gorilla (Fig. 5).

SOURCES

Fossey, Dian. *Gorillas in the Mist*. Boston: Houghton Mifflin, 1983.

Schaller, George B. *The Mountain Gorilla*. Chicago: University of Chicago Press, 1963.

Vedder, Amy. "In the hall of the mountain gorilla," *Animal Kingdom*, 92(3):30–43, 1989.

World Resources Institute. *The 1992 Information Please Environmental Almanac*. Boston: Houghton Mifflin, 1992.

Special appreciation goes to Dieter Steklis and Pat McGrath, President, The Dian Fossey Gorilla Fund, for providing valuable historical details and up-to-date information for this issue.

Introduction

We have seen that humans are a certain kind of placental mammal, a primate. This order of rather diverse animals is characterized by a set of evolutionary trends that sets it apart from other mammals. In this chapter, we will discuss what characteristics link us to our primate cousins, and we will explore some of the fascinating and unique adaptations that the nonhuman primates display. (Numerous physical characteristics, especially those relating to the skeleton, are discussed in this chapter. For a detailed comparison of human and nonhuman skeletons, see Appendix A.)

This chapter describes the *physical* characteristics that define the Primate order, gives a brief overview of the major groups of living primates and introduces another means of comparing living primates through genetic data. The following two chapters concentrate on the *behavioral* features that characterize nonhuman primates. Evolution has produced a continuum of life forms, as demonstrated physically, genetically, or behaviorally. If we are to understand the major components that have shaped hominid evolution, the starting point must be systematic comparison of ourselves with other closely related organisms; that is, other primates.

Primate Evolutionary Trends

Structurally, primates are not easily distinguished as a group chiefly because of the fact that, as an order, we and our close relatives have remained quite *generalized*. Unlike the specialized dentition of rodents or the specialized limbs with great reduction of digits found in artiodactyls (cows, deer, camels, pigs), primates are characterized by their *lack* of extreme structural specializations.

For this reason, it is difficult to point to a single anatomical feature that can be applied exclusively and universally to the primates. Some primate anatomists, however, do suggest derived characteristics of the primate cranium, especially the region around the auditory canal (Szalay and Delson, 1979). (See Box 8-1.) At a more general level, there is a group of **evolutionary trends** (Clark, 1971) which, to a greater or lesser degree, characterize the entire order. Keep in mind, these are a set of *general* tendencies and are not equally expressed in all primates. Indeed, this situation is one that we would expect in such a diverse group of generalized animals. In addition, trends are not synonymous with *progress*. In evolutionary terms, we are using "trend" only to reflect a series of shared common characteristics (that is, general homologies).

Evolutionary trends General structural and behavioral traits that are commonly shared by a related group of organisms.

Following is a list of those evolutionary trends that taken together tend to set the primates apart from other mammals. Together, these define what Clark and others have called "the primate pattern." A common evolutionary history with similar adaptations to common environmental challenges is reflected in the limbs and locomotion; teeth and diet; and in the senses, brain, and behavior of the animals that make up the order.

A. *Limbs and Locomotion*

  1. *Retention of five digits* in the hands and feet—*pentadactyly.* As in primitive mammals, this characteristic is found in all primates, though some show marked reduction of the thumb (for example,

Box 8-1   Primate Cranial Anatomy

Several significant anatomical features of primate crania help us distinguish primates from other mammals. Continuing the mammalian trend of increasing brain development, primates go even further as shown by their well-expanded brain cases. In addition, the primate trend of increased dependence on vision is shown by the generally large eye sockets; less emphasis on smell is shown in the reduced snout; the shift to using hands for grasping (instead of using the front teeth for this purpose) is revealed in the dentition; and the tendency toward more upright posture is indicated by the relationship of the head to the spinal column.

Some of the specific anatomic details seen in all modern and most fossil primate crania are:

1. Eye sockets are enclosed circumferentially by a complete ring of bone, compared to other placental mammals where the ring is incomplete (no **postorbital bar**). This bony arrangement provides protection for the eyes.

2. The entrance into the skull for the spinal column, the *foramen magnum* (Latin: "big hole") on the base of the skull, faces more downwards instead of backwards as it does in other completely quadrupedal mammals. The position of the foramen magnum indicates the direction of the spinal column and is related to the posturing and balancing of the head on the trunk.

3. The face of primates is reduced (snout shortened) with the axis at the base of the skull bending, thus pulling the face more underneath the brain case. This arrangement now provides a greater vertical distance in the movable lower jaw from the point of pivot (*P*) to the plane of the teeth (*T*), allowing more biomechanical action for up-and-down crushing, grinding, etc., instead of just simple back-and-forth tearing and gnashing.

4. The ear region containing the middle ear ossicles is completely encircled by a bony encasement (bulla) whose floor is derived from a particular segment of the temporal bone. Most primate paleontologists consider this feature and the formation of a postorbital bar as the structurally best diagnostic characteristics of the Primate order.

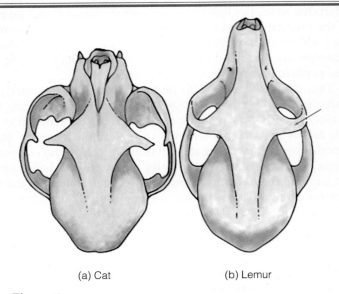

(a) Cat   (b) Lemur

Figure 1

Postorbital bar. A characteristic of primates.

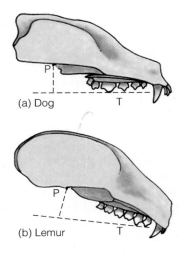

(a) Dog   T

(b) Lemur   T

Figure 2

Basi-cranial flexion relative to tooth row. In primates, the skull base is more flexed, elevating the point of pivot (P) further above the tooth row and thereby increasing the force of chewing. (© 1959 by W. E. Le Gros Clark.)

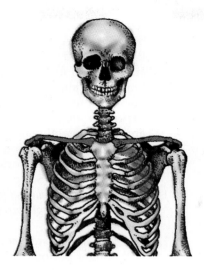

Figure 8-1

Primate (macaque) hand.

Figure 8-2

Position of the clavicle in the human skeleton.

spider monkeys, langurs) or the second digit (for example, lorises). In no case is reduction as extreme as that seen in such animals as cows or horses.

2. *Nails instead of claws.* A consistent characteristic on at least some digits of all contemporary primates. Unlike rodents or cats, most primates must climb by wrapping their hands and feet around branches and holding on by grasping. This grasping function is further aided by the presence of tactile pads at the ends of digits.

3. *Flexible hands and feet* with a good deal of **prehensility** (grasping ability). This feature is associated directly with the lack of claws and retention of five digits.

4. *A tendency toward erectness* (particularly in the upper body). Shown to some degree in all primates, this tendency is variously associated with sitting, leaping, standing, and, occasionally, walking.

5. *Retention of the clavicle* (collarbone). Seen in all primates. The clavicle has been lost in many other quadrupedal mammals. In primates, the clavicle allows for more flexibility of the shoulder joint.

B. *Teeth and Diet*

6. *A generalized dental pattern*, particularly in the back teeth (molars). Characteristic of primates, such a pattern contrasts with the highly specialized molars seen in herbivores.

7. *A lack of specialization in diet.* This attribute is usually correlated with a lack of specialization in teeth. In other words, primates can generally be described as *omnivorous*.

C. *Senses, Brain, and Behavior*

8. *A reduction of the snout* and the proportionate reduction of the smell (olfactory) areas of the brain. Seen in all contemporary primates, but baboons show a secondary (coming later) increase of a *dental* muzzle (that is, the face projects because the jaws and front teeth are large and forward-placed).

Postorbital bar   The bony element that closes in the outside of the eye orbit—a characteristic of primates.

Prehensility   Adapted for grasping.

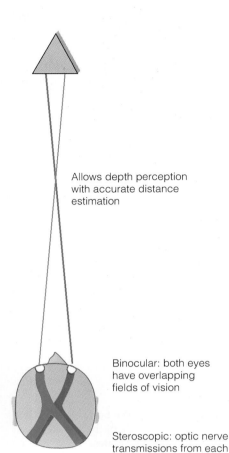

Allows depth perception with accurate distance estimation

Binocular: both eyes have overlapping fields of vision

Steroscopic: optic nerve transmissions from each eye are relayed to *both* sides of the brain

Figure 8-3

Binocular, stereoscopic vision. Fields of vision overlap and sensory information from each eye is relayed to both sides of the brain.

Nocturnal   Active at night.

Arboreal   Adapted to life in the trees.

Adaptive niche   The whole way of life of an organism: where it lives, what it eats, how it gets food, and so forth.

Substrate   The surface on which an animal moves or rests.

9. *An increased emphasis on vision* with elaboration of visual areas of the brain. A trend related to the decreased dependence on smell: Binocular and stereoscopic vision is a further elaboration where visual fields of the two eyes overlap, transmitting both images to the brain, thus allowing depth perception. Except for some specialized **nocturnal** forms, color vision is most likely present in all primates.

10. *Expansion and increasing complexity of the brain.* A general trend among placental mammals and one especially true of primates. In primates this expansion is most evident in the visual and association areas of the neocortex and to some degree in the motor cortex and cerebellum. (See p. 182.)

11. *A more efficient means of fetal nourishment*, as well as *longer periods of gestation (with single births the norm), infancy,* and extension of the whole life span.

12. *A greater dependency on highly flexible learned behavior* is correlated with longer periods of infant and child dependency. As a result of both these trends, parental investment in each offspring is increased so that although fewer young are born, they receive more efficient rearing.

13. *Adult males often associate permanently with the group.* A behavioral trait rarely seen in other mammals, but widespread among the primates.

The Arboreal Adaptation

The single most important factor influencing the evolutionary divergence of primates (with elaboration of all the trends just noted) was the adaptation to **arboreal** living. While other placental mammals were adapting to grasslands, subterranean or even marine environments, primates found their **adaptive niche** in the trees. Indeed, some other mammals also were adapting to arboreal living, but primates found their home (and food) mainly in the treetops and at the ends of terminal branches. This environment—with its myriad challenges and opportunities—was the one in which our ancestors established themselves as a unique kind of animal.

Primates became primates *because* of their adaptation to arboreal living. We can see this process at work in their reliance upon vision for primary sensory input (as opposed to their depending chiefly on a sense of smell). In a complex environment with uncertain footholds, acute vision with depth perception is a necessity. Climbing can be accomplished by either digging in with claws or grasping around branches with prehensile hands and feet. Primates adopted the latter strategy, which allowed a means of progressing on the narrowest and most tenuous of **substrates**. Thus, we also see in primates pentadactyly, prehensility, and flattened nails. In addition, the varied foods found in an arboreal environment (such as fruits, leaves, berries, gums, flowers, insects, small mammals) led to the primate omnivorous adaptation and, hence, to retention of a generalized dentition.

Finally, the long life span, increased intelligence, and more elaborated social system are primate solutions to coping with the manifold complexities of their arboreal habitat (that is, such factors as varied and seasonal food resources; and potential predators from above, below, and in the trees). This crucial development of increased behavioral flexibility may have been further stimulated by a shift from noctural (nighttime) to **diurnal** (daytime) activity patterns (Jerison, 1973).

A recent critique of the traditional arboreal explanation for the origin of primate structure has been proposed by Matt Cartmill (1972, 1992) of Duke University. Cartmill points out that the most significant primate trends—close-set eyes, grasping extremities, and reduced claws—may *not* have arisen from adaptive advantages in an arboreal environment.

According to this alternative theory, ancient primates may have first adapted to living in bushy forest undergrowth and only the lowest branches of the forest canopy. All these traits would have been well suited for an animal that foraged for fruits and insects. Particularly in searching for insects, early primates are thought to have relied heavily on vision, and this reconstruction is hence called the *visual predation hypothesis.*

The close-set eyes, by permitting binocular vision and thus depth perception, would have allowed these primates to judge accurately the distance from their prey without moving their heads, similar to the hunting manner of cats and owls. The regression of the olfactory sense is then viewed as a necessary result of the eye orbits coming closer together. Grasping extremities may have initially been an adaptation for pursuing insects along very narrow supports (like twigs) in the forest undergrowth. Feet, as well as hands, would be prehensile to allow the animal to maintain support while snaring its prey with both hands.

The visual predation hypothesis is as internally consistent and as likely an explanation for the early evolution of primates as the arboreal theory. In fact—given the fossil record and the morphology typical of many contemporary prosimians—it may be a better explanation for the functional developments among the *earliest* primates. In particular, the small body size and insectivorous diet seen in several living prosimians and a similar adaptation inferred from the fossilized remains of many very early primates are consistent with the visual predation hypothesis.

The visual predation ("bug snatching") hypothesis and the arboreal theory are not mutually exclusive explanations. The complex of primate characteristics could have begun in nonarboreal settings, but would have become even more adaptive once the bug snatching was done *in the trees.*

At some point, in fact, the primates did take to the trees in earnest, and that is where the vast majority still live today. Whereas the basic primate structural complexes may have been initially adapted for visual predation, they became ideally suited for the arboreal adaptation that followed. We would say then that primates were "preadapted" for arboreal living.

Diurnal   Active during daylight hours.

The Living Primates

When we apply the set of evolutionary trends discussed in the preceding section, we are able to classify a remarkable array of living forms as members of the same mammalian order, the Primates. We and our primate cousins, you will recall, share these characteristics due to **homology**. In other words, primates are part of a single evolutionary radiation, and the traits we all share derive from a common evolutionary descent. Please note, however, that "homologies" can be indicators of *primitive* relationships rather than more *derived* features (see p. 177). In this sense, characteristics such as pentadactyly and retention of the clavicle serve to provide only general evolutionary evidence.

Homology   Similarities between organisms based on common evolutionary descent.

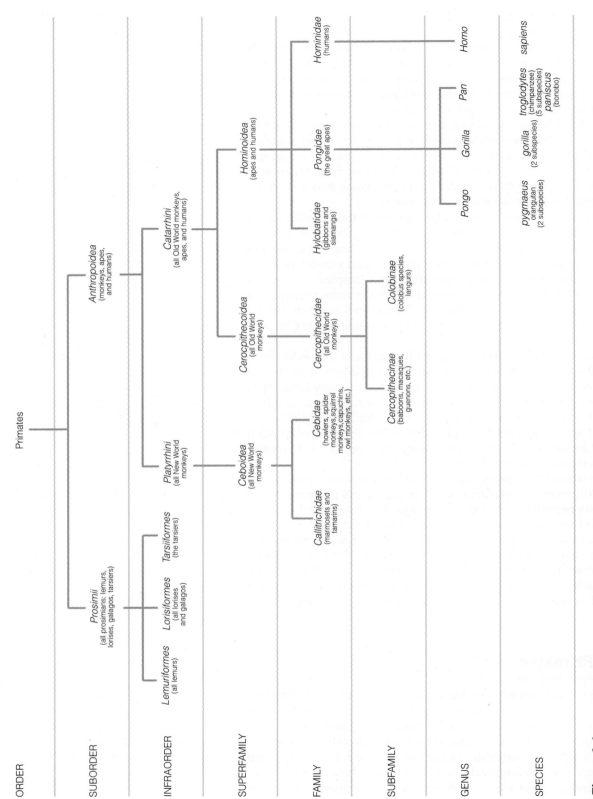

| ORDER | SUBORDER | INFRAORDER | SUPERFAMILY | FAMILY | SUBFAMILY | GENUS | SPECIES |

Primates

Prosimii
(all prosimians: lemurs, lorises, galagos, tarsiers)

Anthropoidea
(monkeys, apes, and humans)

Lemuriformes
(all lemurs)

Lorisiformes
(all lorises and galagos)

Tarsiiformes
(the tarsiers)

Platyrrhini
(all New World monkeys)

Catarrhini
(all Old World monkeys, apes, and humans)

Ceboidea
(all New World monkeys)

Cercopithecoidea
(all Old World monkeys)

Hominoidea
(apes and humans)

Callitrichidae
(marmosets and tamarins)

Cebidae
(howlers, spider monkeys, squirrel monkeys, capuchins, owl monkeys, etc.)

Cercopithecidae
(all Old World monkeys)

Hylobatidae
(gibbons and siamangs)

Pongidae
(the great apes)

Hominidae
(humans)

Cercopithecinae
(baboons, macaques, guenons, etc.)

Colobinae
(colobus species, langurs)

Pongo

Gorilla

Pan

Homo

pygmaeus
orangutan
(2 subspecies)

gorilla
(2 subspecies)

troglodytes
(chimpanzee)
(5 subspecies)

paniscus
(bonobo)

sapiens

Figure 8-4

Traditional primate taxonomic classification. This abbreviated taxonomy illustrates how primates are grouped into increasingly specific categories. Only the more general categories are shown, except for the great apes and humans.

Table 8-1   Traditional Classification of the Primates

	Latin Name	Common Name
SUBORDER	PROSIMII	PROSIMIANS
Superfamily	Lemuroidea	lemurs
Superfamily	Lorisoidea	lorises
Superfamily	Tarsioidea	tarsier
SUBORDER	ANTHROPOIDEA	ANTHROPOIDS
Superfamily	Ceboidea	New World monkeys
Superfamily	Cercopithecoidea	Old World monkeys
Superfamily	Hominoidea	hominoids (apes and humans)

PRIMATE CLASSIFICATION

We reviewed several principles of classification in Chapter 7 in our discussion of mammalian evolution. Here we become much more precise, narrowing our emphasis specifically to the Primate order. The living primates have been traditionally categorized into their respective subgroupings as shown in Fig. 8-4. This classification is based upon many of the categories originally constructed by Linnaeus in the eighteenth century and is modified by more contemporary biologists, especially George Gaylord Simpson's influential classification of mammals (Simpson, 1945).

As more detailed data relating to primate classification have been collected (especially including biochemical/genetic data—see p. 223), some conclusions have changed. Of course, a major objective of any classification is to show *relationships*, specifically evolutionary relationships. With consistent data provided by more clearly genetically based evidence (as opposed to traditional comparisons of **morphology**), some revisions to traditional classifications have proved necessary. It must be pointed out that not all anthropologists or other scholars have completely accepted the revised terminology suggested in Tables 8-2 and 8-4. The vast majority of experts, however, do accept the evolutionary implications. Nevertheless, the situation remains dynamic, with no full consensus regarding which is the most appropriate terminology.

Morphology   The physical structure of an organism; its size and shape.

Table 8-2   Revised Classification of the Primates

	Latin Name	Common Name
SUBORDER	Strepsirhini	strepsirhines
Superfamily	Lemuroidea	
Superfamily	Lorisoidea	
SUBORDER	Haplorhini	haplorhines
Superfamily	Tarsioidea	
Superfamily	Ceboidea	
Superfamily	Cercopithecoidea	
Superfamily	Hominoidea	

Table 8-3 Traditional Classification of the Hominoidea

	Latin Name	Common Name
SUPERFAMILY	Hominoidea	hominoids
FAMILY	Hylobatidae	hylobatids (gibbons and siamangs)
FAMILY	Pongidae (Genera: *Pongo*; *Pan*; *Gorilla*)	pongids ("great apes") orangutan, chimpanzee, bonobo, gorilla
FAMILY	Hominidae (Genus: *Homo*)	humans

The two areas of primate classification that have stimulated the greatest discussion and suggestions for major revisions are:

1. the evolutionary relationship of the tarsier
2. the evolutionary relationships of the great apes—relative to each other and to humans.

The tarsier, as we will see (p. 211), is a highly derived animal, displaying several unique physical characteristics. Traditionally, it has been classified as a **prosimian** (with lemurs and lorises) and thus contrasted with **anthropoids** (monkeys, apes, and humans). (See Table 8-1.)

However, data from protein comparisons and directly from the DNA (as well as from some morphological features—see p. 212) are now interpreted as relating the tarsier closer to anthropoids (monkeys, apes, and humans) than to lemurs and lorises. Thus, a revised classification is necessary. Moreover, given the strict rules of classification, new formal names for the groups are also mandated.

Another important point to make is that various classifications may display these relationships somewhat differently. For example, rather than two suborders (as listed in Table 8-2), the contrast can instead be made at the semiorder level. Then, for the Haplorhini, two suborders (one for the tarsier, the other collectively for monkeys, apes, and humans) can be employed. Again, the point is to show relationships. Classifications may vary simply because they make more or fewer distinctions. The number of levels in a formal classification (for example, whether we use semiorder or not) depends on the number of *meaningful* evolutionary contrasts we choose to make. Thus, some classifications will differ, but may not, in fact, be contradictory.

The second area of primate classification where significant modifications have been suggested involves the **hominoids**. Traditionally, the classification was quite simple, proposing three families within the Hominoidea.

However, once again modification is required, as the biochemical and molecular data are even more unambiguous than for the tarsier. The traditional classification misrepresents the *actual* genetic and evolutionary relationships. The problem lies with how to classify the great apes. Traditionally, chimpanzees, bonobos, gorillas, and orangutans were included together in the same family (Pongidae), separate from the hominids. Now we know this alignment is inaccurate. The closest links are among the *African* forms (chimpanzees, bonobos, gorillas, *and* humans) in contrast to the one Asian form, the orangutan.

Thus, we see the traditional term *pongid* now has limited evolutionary meaning. The pongids (or great apes), as traditionally defined, are not a single (**monophyletic**) group, but, in fact, represent two evolutionary distinct

Prosimian A member of the suborder of Primates, the Prosimii, traditionally including lemurs, lorises, and tarsiers.

Anthropoid A member of the suborder of Primates, the Anthropoidea, including monkeys, apes, and humans.

Hominoid A member of the superfamily, Hominoidea. The group includes apes and humans.

Monophyletic A grouping of organisms (a taxon) that share a common ancestor.

Table 8-4   Revised Classification of the Hominoidea

	Latin Name	Common Name
SUPERFAMILY	Hominoidea	
FAMILY	Hylobatidae*	Small-bodied hominoids
		Large-bodied hominoids**
		Asian form (orangutan)
		African forms (chimpanzee, bonobo, gorilla, human)

*Gibbons and siamangs are still classified similarly to the above.

**There is no general consensus yet on which formal terms to use; here we employ the common terms currently in widest usage.

albeit morphologically similar groups (African and Asian). Even more to the point, the African apes (chimpanzee, bonobo, gorilla) are more closely related to humans (*Homo*) than they are to the orangutan.

PRIMATE LOCOMOTION

A basic way to understand the variety of living primates is through comparison of their locomotory behavior. Since so much of the body, including especially the musculoskeletal system, is involved in locomotion, we can get a good handle on comparative primate anatomy through a structural-functional approach that emphasizes locomotory behavior.

Almost all primates are, at least to some degree, quadrupedal, meaning they use all four limbs to support the body during locomotion. However, to describe most primate species in terms of only one or even two forms of locomotion would be to overlook the wide variety of methods many may use to get about. Many primates employ more than one form of locomotion, and they owe this ability to their generalized structure.

By retaining basic mammalian limb morphology, which includes five digits on hands and feet, primates do not show the specializations seen in many mammals. For example, through the course of evolution, horses and cattle have undergone a reduction of the number of digits from the primitive pattern of five, to one and two, respectively. Moreover, they have developed hard, protective coverings in the form of hooves. While these structures are adaptive in prey species whose survival depends upon speed and stability, they restrict the animal to only one type of locomotor pattern. Moreover, limb function is limited entirely to support and locomotion, while the ability to manipulate objects is completely lost.

Although the majority of quadrupedal primates are arboreal, terrestrial quadrupedalism is fairly common (as in some lemurs, baboons, and **macaques**). Typically, the limbs of terrestrial quadrupeds are approximately of equal length, with forelimbs being 90% (or more) as long as hindlimbs (Fig. 8-5). In arboreal quadrupeds, forelimbs are shorter and may be only 70 to 80% as long as hindlimbs (Fig. 8-6).

Quadrupeds are also characterized by a relatively long and flexible *lumbar spine* (the portion of the spine between the ribs and the pelvis; that is, the lower back). This lumbar flexibility permits the animal to bend the body during running, thus positioning the hindlimbs and feet well forward under the body and enhancing the ability to propel the animal forward. (Watch for this

Macaque   (muh-kak')

Figure 8-5

Skeleton of a terrestrial quadruped (savanna baboon). (Redrawn from original art by Stephen Nash. In: Fleagle, John, Primate Adaptation and Evolution, 1988. New York: Academic Press.)

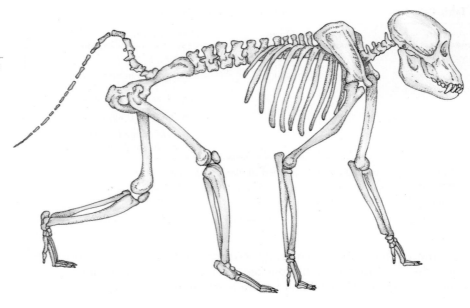

the next time you see slow motion footage of cheetahs or lions on television.)

Another form of locomotion is *vertical clinging and leaping*, seen in many prosimians. As the term implies, vertical clingers and leapers support themselves vertically by grasping onto trunks of trees while their knees and ankles are tightly flexed (Fig. 8-7). Forceful extension of their long hindlimbs allows them to spring powerfully away in either a forward or backward direction. Once in midair, the body rotates so the animal lands feet first on the next vertical support.

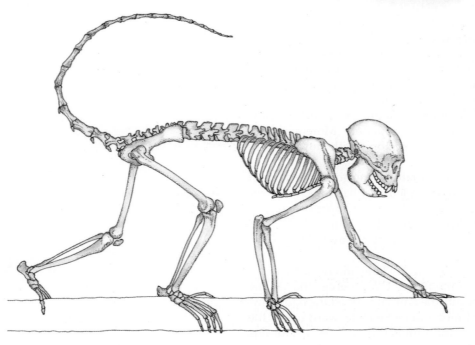

Figure 8-6

Skeleton of an arboreal New World monkey, the bearded saki. (Redrawn from original art by Stephen Nash. In: Fleagle, John, Primate Adaptation and Evolution, 1988. New York: Academic Press.)

Figure 8-7

Skeleton of a vertical clinger and leaper (indri). (Redrawn from original art by Stephen Nash. In: Fleagle, John, Primate Adaptation and Evolution, 1988. New York: Academic Press.)

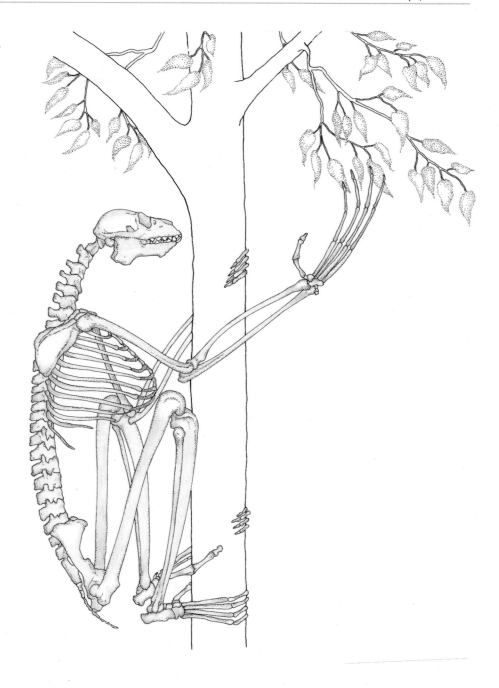

A third type of primate locomotion is *brachiation* or arm-swinging, where the body is alternatively supported under either forelimb. Because of anatomical modifications at the shoulder joint, all the apes (and humans) are capable of true brachiation. However, only the small gibbons and siamangs of Southeast Asia use this form of locomotion almost exclusively.

Brachiation is seen in species characterized by arms longer than legs, a short stable lumbar spine, long curved fingers, and reduced thumbs (Fig. 8-8). Because these are traits seen in all the apes, it is believed that, although none of the "great apes" (orangutan, gorilla, and chimpanzee) habitually

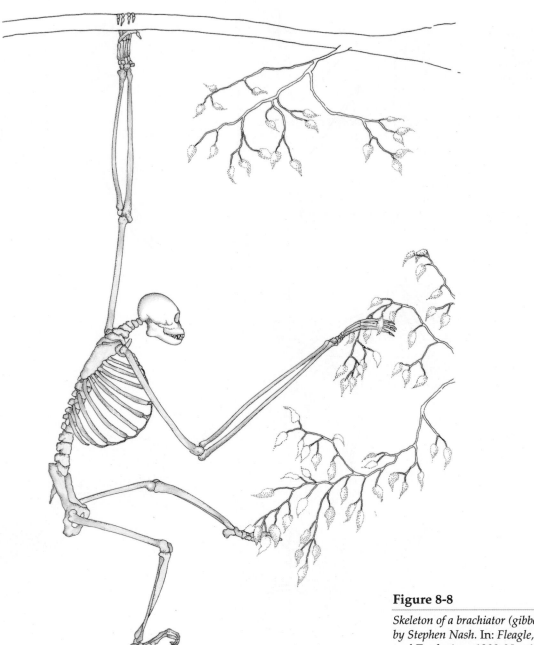

Figure 8-8

Skeleton of a brachiator (gibbon). (Redrawn from original art by Stephen Nash. In: *Fleagle, John,* Primate Adaptation and Evolution, *1988. New York: Academic Press.)*

brachiates today, they most likely inherited these characteristics from brachiating or perhaps climbing ancestors.

Some monkeys, particularly New World monkeys, are termed *semibrachiators*, as they practice a combination of leaping, with some arm-swinging. In some New World species, arm-swinging and other suspensory behaviors are enhanced by use of a *prehensile tail* which, in effect, serves as a marvelously effective grasping fifth "hand." It should be noted that prehensile tails are strictly a New World phenomenon and are not seen in any Old World primate species (see Box 8-2).

Grades of Primate Evolution

In terms of size, structure, and behavior, contemporary primates certainly represent a varied group of animals. What is even more remarkable about the living primates is that they still display in some form all the major grades of evolution that primates have passed through over the last 60 million years.

An evolutionary grade is, in Mayr's terms, "A group of animals similar in level of organization" (Mayr, 1970). We do not use the term, as some evolutionary biologists have done, to imply a strict commonality of evolutionary descent and/or an equivalent adaptive response (suggesting selection above the species level). In fact, such processes are not now believed to be accurate depictions of macroevolution (Eldredge and Cracraft, 1980). (See p. 187.)

You should also note that the concept of grade does not imply any inferiority or superiority. Grades only reflect different stages of organizational levels seen during primate evolution—from more primitive to more derived. (See p. 177.)

PROSIMIANS

The most primitive, or least derived, of the primates are the true prosimians, the lemurs and lorises. By "least derived" we mean that these prosimians, taken as a group, are more similar anatomically to their earlier mammalian ancestors than are the other primates (monkeys and apes). Therefore, they tend to exhibit certain more primitive characteristics, such as a more pronounced reliance on *olfaction* (sense of smell). Their increased olfactory capa-

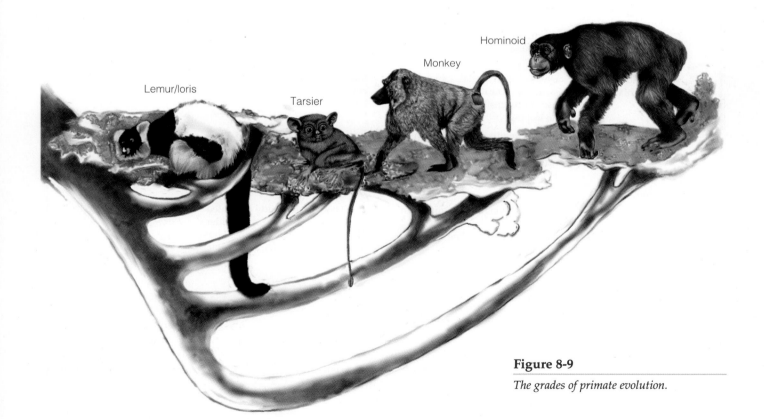

Figure 8-9

The grades of primate evolution.

Box 8-2   Tale of the Limbs

Besides teeth (and diet), the other major functional complex most useful in describing both extant (living) and extinct primates relates to the structure of the limbs and the form of locomotion.

A meaningful functional description of locomotion among contemporary primates should include position of the body, which limbs are used, the manner and frequency they are employed, and the nature of the substrate (such as wide tree branch, narrow branch,

flat ground). By understanding the locomotory behavior of contemporary primates we can analyze their respective limb structures and form meaningful *structural-functional correlations*. With such a perspective, we can then interpret fossil primates and reconstruct their probable locomotory behavior. A common locomotory classification of contemporary primates with their typical structural correlates is shown below (after Napier and Napier, 1967):

Category	Description of Behavior	Structural Correlates	Examples
A. Vertical clinging and leaping	leaping in trees with propulsion from hindlimbs, clinging with forelimbs for vertical support	elongated hindlimbs, particularly ankle area, upper body held semi-erect	tarsier, galago
B. Quadrupedalism	using all limbs relatively equally; body horizontal	front- and hindlimbs relatively equal length; spine flexible	
1. Slow climbing	slow, cautious climbing; often associated with capturing insects	widely abducted (spread) thumb, reduction of 2nd digit	potto, slow loris
2. Branch running and walking	walking or running on tops of branches, also leaping	generalized quadruped; limbs equal sized; spine flexible	ring-tailed lemur, all marmosets, squirrel monkey, guenons
3. Ground running and walking	quadrupedal walking and running on ground, also tree climbing	all limbs elongated, body size usually larger than strictly arboreal species	baboons, most macaques, patas monkey
4. New World "semibrachiation"	usually quadrupedal, some arm-swinging beneath branches with use of prehensile tail; little or no leaping	forelimbs elongated; fingers often curved, thumb reduced	howler monkey, spider monkey
5. Old World "semibrachiation"	usually quadrupedal with arm-swinging and often considerable acrobatic leaping from branch to branch	forelimbs elongated; fingers often curved, thumb reduced	colobines (colobus, langurs)
C. Ape locomotion			
1. True brachiation	acrobatic swinging arm-over-arm along (under) same branch, associated with feeding on small terminal branches	small body size, greatly elongated forelimb, curved fingers, shoulder joint oriented upward, upper body held fairly erect; spine not flexible	gibbon, siamang

Category	Description of Behavior	Structural Correlates	Examples
2. Quadrumanous climbing	slow deliberate climbing using all four limbs for grasping	large body size, hip joint flexible like shoulder, upper body held erect, spine not flexible	orang
3. Knuckle walking	on ground semiquadrupedal, but hands supported on knuckles; while in trees considerable arm-swinging	large body size, elongated forelimbs; stable wrist joint; upper body held erect; spine shortened and inflexible	chimp, gorilla
D. Bipedalism*	strictly terrestrial, standing, striding, running upright; weight alternately on single hindlimb	medium-large body size, hindlimb elongated; pelvis altered for support and muscular leverage; feet altered for stable support with little flexibility, toes shortened; upper body completely erect; head balanced on spine; spine shortened and inflexible	human

*True bipedalism among the primates is an adaptation only of modern humans and our hominid ancestors. Thus, the structural correlates associated with this functional complex are crucial in determining the status of our possible ancestors.

It is important to remember that the above classification is a *simple* one, intended to give a sense of the range of locomotory behaviors among the primates. However, if not viewed carefully, it can obscure the diversity of locomotory behavior within a species; indeed, that displayed by a single animal.

Some species are, of course, less varied than others in terms of their typical locomotory repertoire. For example, baboons are easily classified as "quadru-peds," as this is mostly what they do. Likewise, humans are "bipeds," since this is pretty much exclusively what we do. Nevertheless, many primate species are quite diverse in how (and where) they move about. David Pilbeam (1986, p. 298) has summarized some of the most salient features of the locomotory behavior of several species, three examples of which are listed below.

	Terrestrial				Arboreal				
	TERRESTRIAL/ ARBOREAL	BIPED	QUADRUPED WALK/RUN	KNUCKLE WALK	KNUCKLE WALK	QUADRUPED WALK/RUN	LEAP SWAY	QUADRUPED CLIMB	ARM-SWING BRACHIATE	BIPED
Baboon	50/50	2	48	—	—	25	20	5	—	—
Orang	—/100	—	—	—	—	13	15	51	21	—
Chimp	50/50	2	—	48	3	11	6	15	10	5

(Figures are relative percent of behavior. Note especially the marked behavioral diversity of the chimp.)

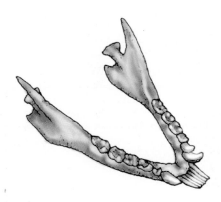

Figure 8-10

Prosimian dental comb, formed by forward projecting incisors and canines. The first lower premolar has become modified to be more canine-like in shape, size, and function.

Rhinarium (rine-air'-ee-um) The moist, hairless pad at the end of the nose seen in most mammalian species. The rhinarium enhances an animal's ability to smell.

bilities (compared to other primates) are reflected in the presence of a moist, fleshy pad (**rhinarium**) at the end of the nose and in the relatively long snout, which gives prosimians a somewhat doglike appearance. Moreover, prosimians mark territories with scent in a manner not seen in many other primates.

There are numerous other distinctions that set prosimians apart from the anthropoids, including somewhat more laterally placed eyes, differences in reproductive physiology, and shorter gestation and maturation periods. Prosimians also possess a dental specialization known as the "dental comb." The dental comb is formed by forward-projecting lower incisors and canines, and together these modified teeth are used in grooming and feeding (Fig. 8-10).

Primate Grade I: Lemurs and Lorises There are two groupings of prosimians: lemurs and lorises. Lemurs are found only on the island of Madagascar and adjacent islands off the east coast of Africa. As the only primates on Madagascar, which comprises some 227,000 square miles, lemurs diversified into numerous and varied ecological niches without competition from the higher primates (that is, monkeys and apes). Thus, while lemurs became extinct elsewhere, the 22 surviving species on Madagascar represent a kind of "living fossil," preserving an evolutionary grade that has long since vanished elsewhere.

Lemurs range in size from the small mouse lemur, with a body length (head and trunk) of only 5 inches, to the indri, with a body length of a little over 2 feet (Napier and Napier, 1985). While the larger lemurs are diurnal and exploit a wide variety of dietary food items such as leaves, fruit, buds, bark, and shoots, the smaller forms (mouse and dwarf lemurs) are nocturnal and are insectivorous.

Lemurs display considerable variation regarding numerous other aspects of behavior. While many are primarily arboreal, others, such as the ring-tailed lemur (Fig. 8-11), are more terrestrial. Some arboreal species are quadrupeds, and others (sifaka and indri) are vertical clingers and leapers (Fig.

Figure 8-11

Ring-tailed lemur.

Figure 8-12

Sifakas in native habitat in Madagascar.

8-12). Socially, several species are gregarious and live in groups of 10 to 25 animals composed of males and females of all ages (ring-tailed lemur and sifaka). Others (the indri) live in monogamous family units, and several nocturnal forms are mostly solitary.

Lorises, which are very similar in appearance to lemurs (Fig. 8-13), were able to survive in continental areas by adopting a nocturnal activity pattern at a time when most other prosimians became extinct. In this way, they were (and are) able to avoid competition with more recently evolved primates (the diurnal monkeys).

The five loris species (loris, in the strict sense) are found in tropical forest and woodland habitats of India, Sri Lanka, Southeast Asia, and Africa. Also included in the same general category are 6 to 9 species (Bearder, 1987) of galago, which are widely distributed throughout most of the forested and woodland savanna areas of sub-Saharan Africa (Fig. 8-15).

Locomotion in lorises is a slow, cautious climbing form of quadrupedalism, and flexible hip joints permit suspension by hindlimbs while the hands are used in feeding. All galagos, however, are highly agile and active vertical clingers and leapers. Some lorises and galagos are almost entirely insectivorous; others supplement their diet with various combinations of fruit, leaves, gums, and slugs. Lorises and galagos frequently forage for food alone (females leave infants behind in nests until they are older). However, ranges overlap and two or more females occasionally forage together or share the same sleeping nest.

Both lemurs and lorises represent the same general adaptive level. They both have good grasping and climbing abilities and a fairly well developed visual apparatus, although vision is not completely stereoscopic, and color vision may not be as well developed as in higher primates. Most retain a claw, commonly called a "grooming claw," only on the second toe. Lemurs and lorises also have prolonged life spans as compared to most other small-bodied mammals, averaging about 14 years for lorises and 19 years for lemurs.

Primate Grade II: The Tarsier Today there are three recognized species of tarsier, all restricted to island areas in Southeast Asia where they inhabit a wide range of forest types, from tropical forest to backyard gardens (Fig. 8-17). Tarsiers are nocturnal insectivores, leaping onto prey (which may also include small vertebrates) from lower branches and shrubs. They appear to form stable pair bonds, and the basic tarsier social unit is a mated pair and their young offspring (MacKinnon and MacKinnon, 1980).

Anatomically, the tarsier presents a rare and puzzling blend of characteristics not seen in other primates. It is unique in that its enormous eyes, which dominate much of the face, are immobile within their sockets. To compensate for its inability to move the eyes, the tarsier is able to rotate its head 180 degrees in a decidedly owl-like manner.

Like lemurs and lorises, tarsiers are traditionally classified as prosimians because of their small body size, large ears, unfused mandible (lower jaw), and grooming claws. However, they also share several derived physical characteristics with anthropoids, such as lack of a rhinarium. Moreover, biochemically, tarsiers are more closely related to anthropoids than to lemurs or lorises (Dene et al., 1976). However, with regard to chromosomes, tarsiers are set apart from either group.

Today, many primatologists classify tarsiers closer to anthropoids than to prosimians. One alternate scheme places lemurs and lorises in a relatively

Figure 8-13

Slow loris.

Figure 8-14

Distribution of modern lemurs.

Figure 8-15

Galago or "bush baby."

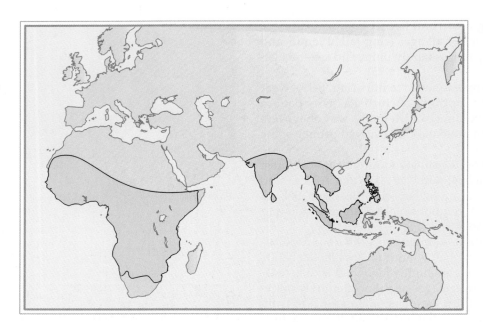

Figure 8-16

Distribution of modern lorises and galagos.

Figure 8-17

Tarsier.

Callitrichidae (kal-eh-trick'-eh-dee)

Cebidae (see'-bid-ee)

new suborder, *Strepsirhini* (moist nosed); and tarsiers are included along with monkeys, apes, and humans in another suborder, the *Haplorhini* (dry nosed) (Szalay and Delson, 1979). Other systems have also been proposed but, at this point, none has been agreed upon, and the tarsier remains a taxonomic problem. (See pp. 201–202 for further discussion.)

THE ANTHROPOIDS

Several features distinguish the anthropoids from the prosimians. These include:

1. generally larger body size
2. larger brain (in absolute terms and relative to body weight)
3. more rounded skull
4. complete rotation of eyes to front of face to permit full binocular vision
5. back wall of eye orbit completed
6. no rhinarium (implying reduced reliance upon the sense of smell)
7. more complex social systems
8. more parental care
9. increased gestation and maturation periods
10. more mutual grooming

Primate Grade III: Monkeys The monkey grade of evolution is today the most varied group of primates. Approximately 70 percent of all primates (about 130 species) are monkeys. (It is frequently impossible to give precise numbers of species, as the taxonomic status of some primates remains in doubt. Also, primatologists are still making new discoveries.) Monkeys are divided into two groups separated by geographical area (New World and

Old World), as well as by several million years of separate evolutionary history.

New World Monkeys The New World monkeys exhibit a wide range of size, diet, and ecological adaptation. In size, they vary from the tiny marmosets (about 12 ounces) to the 20-pound howler monkey (Figs. 8-19 and 8-20). New World monkeys are almost exclusively arboreal, and some never come to the ground. Like Old World monkeys, all except one species (the douroucouli or owl monkey) are diurnal. Although confined to the trees, New World monkeys can be found in a wide range of arboreal environments throughout most forested areas in southern Mexico and Central and South America.

One of the characteristics distinguishing New World monkeys from those found in the Old World is the shape of the nose. New World forms have broad, widely flaring noses with outward facing nostrils. Conversely, Old World monkeys have narrower noses with downward facing nostrils. This difference in nose form has given rise to the terms *platyrrhine* (flat-nosed) and *catarrhine* (downward-facing nose) to refer to New and Old World anthropoids, respectively.

New World monkeys are divided into two families, **Callitrichidae** and **Cebidae**. The callitrichids (marmosets and tamarins) are the most primitive of monkeys, retaining claws instead of nails and usually giving birth to twins instead of one infant.

Marmosets and tamarins are mostly insectivorous, although marmoset diet includes gums from trees, and tamarins also rely heavily upon fruits. Locomotion is quadrupedal, and their claws aid in climbing vertical tree trunks, much in the manner of squirrels. Moreover, some tamarins employ vertical clinging and leaping as a form of travel.

Socially, callitrichids live in extended family groupings composed usually of a mated pair, or a female and two adult males, and their offspring. Marmosets and tamarins are among the few primate species in which males are heavily involved in infant care.

There are at least 30 cebid species ranging in size from the squirrel monkey (body length: 12 inches) to the howler (body length: 24 inches). Diet varies, with most relying on a combination of fruit and leaves supplemented to varying degrees by insects.

Most cebids are quadrupedal but some—for example, the spider mon-

Figure 8-18

Distribution of modern tarsiers.

Figure 8-19

A pair of golden marmosets.

Figure 8-20

Howler monkey.

Figure 8-21

Distribution of modern New World monkeys.

Figure 8-22

A New World monkey prehensile tail. Shown here in a spider monkey.

key—are semibrachiators (see Box 8-2). Some cebids, including the spider and howler, also possess powerful prehensile tails that are used not only in locomotion but also for suspension under branches while feeding on leaves and fruit. Socially, most cebids are found in either groupings of both sexes and all age categories, or in monogamous pairs with subadult offspring.

Old World Monkeys   The monkeys of the Old World display much more morphological and behavioral diversity than is seen in New World monkeys. After humans, Old World monkeys are the most widely distributed of all living primates. They are found throughout sub-Saharan Africa and southern Asia, ranging from tropical jungle habitats to semiarid desert and even to seasonally snow-covered areas in northern Japan.

Most Old World monkeys are quadrupedal and mostly arboreal, but some (baboons, for example) are also adapted to life on the ground. Whether in trees or on the ground, these monkeys spend a good deal of time sleeping, feeding, and grooming while sitting with their upper bodies held erect. Usually associated with this universal sitting posture are areas of hardened skin on the rear end (**ischial callosities**) that serve as sitting pads. Old World monkeys also have a good deal of manual dexterity, and most have well-developed tails that serve in communication and balance.

Within the entire group of Old World monkeys there is only one taxonomically recognized family: **Cercopithecidae**. This family, in turn, is divided into two subfamilies: the **cercopithecines** and **colobines**.

The cercopithecines are the more generalized of the two groups, showing a more omnivorous dietary adaptation and distinctive cheek pouches for storing food. As a group, the cercopithecines eat almost anything, including fruits, seeds, leaves, grasses, tubers, roots, nuts, insects, birds' eggs, amphibians, small reptiles, and small mammals (the last seen in baboons).

The majority of cercopithecine species, such as many arboreal and colorful guenons (Fig. 8-23), but also including the largely terrestrial savanna baboons (Fig. 8-25), as well as the hamadryas baboons (Fig. 8-26), are all

Ischial callosities   Patches of tough, hard skin on the rear ends of Old World monkeys and chimpanzees.

Cercopithecidae   (serk-oh-pith'-eh-sid-ee)

Cercopithecines   (serk-oh-pith'-eh-seens)

Colobines   (kole'-uh'-beans)

Figure 8-23

Adult male sykes monkey, one of several species of guenon.

found in Africa. However, the several species of macaque, which include the well-known rhesus monkey, are widely distributed in southern Asia and India.

Colobine species are more limited dietarily, specializing more on mature leaves, a behavior that has led to their designation as "leaf-eating monkeys." The colobines are found mainly in Asia, but both the red colobus and black-

Figure 8-24

Distribution of modern Old World monkeys.

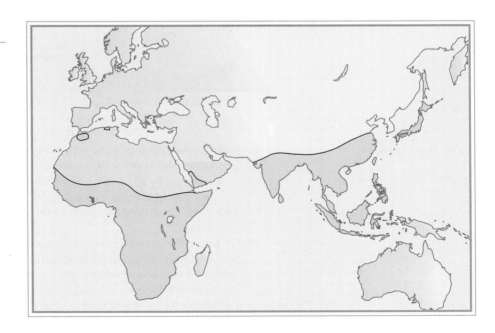

(a)

(b)

Figure 8-25

Savanna baboons.
(a) *male;* (b) *female.*

Figure 8-26

Hamadryas one-male groups. Note difference in size between large-bodied males and smaller females. Note also presence of infants.

Estrus (ess'-truss)

and-white colobus are exclusively African (Fig. 8-27). Other colobines include several species of Asian langur and the proboscis monkey of Borneo.

Locomotory behavior among Old World monkeys includes arboreal quadrupedalism (guenons, macaques, and langurs); terrestrial quadrupedalism in baboons, patas, and macaques; and semibrachiation and acrobatic leaping in colobus.

Marked differences in body size or shape between the sexes, referred to as *sexual dimorphism*, is typical of some terrestrial species and is particularly pronounced in baboons and patas. In these species, male body weight (up to 80 pounds in baboons) may be twice that of females.

Females of several species (especially baboons and some macaques) exhibit pronounced cyclical changes of the external genitalia. These changes,

Figure 8-27

Free-ranging black-and-white colobus monkey.

including swelling and redness, are associated with **estrus**, a hormonally initiated period of sexual receptivity in female mammals correlated with ovulation.

Several types of social organization characterize Old World monkeys, and there are uncertainties among primatologists regarding some species. In general, colobines tend to live in small groups, with only one or two adult males. Savanna baboons and most macaque species are found in large social units comprising several adults of both sexes and offspring of all ages. Monogamous pairing is not common in Old World monkeys, but is seen in a few langurs and possibly one or two guenon species.

Monkeys, Old and New World: A Striking Case of Parallel Evolution   We have mentioned several differences between monkeys in the Old World compared to those in the New World. However, the striking fact remains that they are *all* monkeys. By this statement, we mean that they all are adapted to a similar (primarily arboreal) way of life. With the exception of the South American night monkey (*Aotus*), they are diurnal, and all are social, usually fairly omnivorous, and quadrupedal, though with variations of this general locomotory pattern (see Box 8-2).

These similarities are all the more striking when we consider that Old and New World monkeys have gone their separate evolutionary paths for tens of millions of years. In fact, a noted primatologist, E. L. Simons (1969), suggests the split may have occurred more than 50 m.y.a. Both forms of monkey would then have evolved independently from separate prosimian ancestors. The current consensus among researchers, however, disputes this claim (Hoffstetter, 1972; Ciochon and Chiarelli, 1980) and postulates both Old and New World monkeys arose in Africa from a common monkey ancestor and later reached South America by "rafting" over on logs or pieces of drifting vegetation. (It should be noted that South America and Africa were consid-

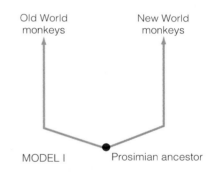

Figure 8-28

Monkey origins. Model I.

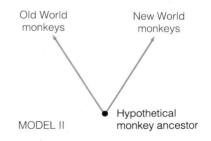

Figure 8-29

Monkey origins. Model II.

Figure 8-30

Distribution of modern Asian apes.

Hylobatidae (high-lo-baht'-id-ee)

Pongidae (ponj'-id-ee)

Hominidae (hom-in'-id-ee)

erably closer together earlier in the Cenozoic. In addition, migration over water barriers may have been facilitated by "island hopping" over a chain of volcanic islands.)

In either case, what is most remarkable is that the two forms of monkey have not diverged more than they have—given the time depth of separate evolutionary history in the two hemispheres. What we see today in the diverse arboreal adaptations of monkeys is then a result of **parallel evolution** (see p. 184). Similar ecological selective forces, mainly in tropical arboreal environments, led to structural evolution in different but parallel directions. The result is that the same grade of primate we today recognize as "monkey" evolved in both New and Old Worlds.

PRIMATE GRADE IV: HOMINOIDS

The Apes The superfamily Hominoidea includes the "lesser" apes placed in the family **Hylobatidae** (gibbons and siamangs); the great apes in the family **Pongidae** (orangutans, gorillas, bonobos, and chimpanzees); and humans (family: **Hominidae**).

Apes differ from monkeys in numerous ways, including:

1. generally larger body size, except for the lesser apes
2. absence of a tail
3. shortened trunk (lumbar area relatively shorter and more stable)
4. differences in position and musculature of the shoulder joint (adapted for suspensory locomotion)
5. more complex behavior
6. more complex brain and enhanced cognitive abilities
7. increased period of infant development and dependency

Gibbons and Siamangs The eight gibbon species and the closely related siamang are today found in the southeastern tropical areas of Asia. These an-

Figure 8-31

White-handed gibbon, Oakland Zoo.

Figure 8-32

Female orangutan, San Francisco Zoo.

imals are the smallest of the apes, with a long, slender body weighing 13 pounds in the gibbon (Fig. 8-31) and 25 pounds in the larger siamang.

The most distinctive structural feature of gibbons and siamangs is related to their functional adaptation for brachiation. Consequently, they have extremely long arms, long, permanently curved fingers and short thumbs, and powerful shoulder muscles. These highly specialized locomotory adaptations may be related to feeding behavior while hanging beneath branches.

The diet of both gibbons and siamangs is largely composed of fruit. Both (especially the siamang) also eat a variety of leaves, flowers, and insects.

The basic social unit is the monogamous pair with dependent offspring. As in marmosets and tamarins, male gibbons and siamangs are very much involved in rearing their young. Both males and females are highly territorial and protect their territories with very elaborate and ear-splitting whoops and sirenlike "songs."

The Orangutan   The orangutan (*Pongo pyqmaeus*) (Fig. 8-32) is represented by two subspecies found today only in heavily forested areas on the Indonesian islands of Borneo and Sumatra. Due to poaching by humans and continuing habitat loss on both islands, the orangutan faces imminent extinction in the wild.

Orangutans are slow, cautious climbers whose locomotory behavior can best be described as "four-handed," referring to the tendency to use all four limbs for grasping and support. Although they are almost completely arboreal, orangutans do sometimes travel quadrupedally on the ground. Orangutans are also very large animals with pronounced sexual dimorphism (males may weigh 200 pounds or more and females less than half that amount).

In the wild, orangutans lead largely solitary lives, although adult females are usually accompanied by one or two dependent offspring. Diet is primarily **frugivorous**, but bark, leaves, insects, and meat (on rare occasions) may also be eaten.

Frugivorous   (fru-give'-or-us)
Having a diet composed primarily of fruit.

(a)

(b)

Figure 8-33

Mountain gorilla, Rwanda. (a) Male; (b) female.

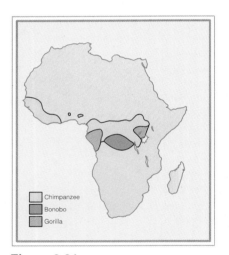

Figure 8-34

Distribution of modern African apes.

The Gorilla The largest of all living primates, the gorilla (*Gorilla gorilla*) is today confined to forested areas in West Africa (the lowland gorilla) and the mountainous areas of East and Central Africa (the mountain gorilla) (Fig. 8-33). Gorillas exhibit marked sexual dimorphism, with males weighing up to 400 pounds and females around 200 pounds. Due to their weight, adult gorillas are largely terrestrial, adopting a semiquadrupedal (knuckle-walking) posture on the ground.

Gorillas live in family groups consisting of one or more large *silverback males*, a few adult females, and subadult offspring. The term *silverback* refers to the saddle of white hair across the back of fully adult (at least 12 or 13 years of age) male gorillas. The dominant silverback may tolerate the presence of younger adult males, presumably one of his sons.

Although gorillas have long been considered ferocious wild beasts, in reality they are shy and gentle vegetarians (Schaller, 1963; Fossey, 1983). When threatened, males can be provoked to attack and certainly they will defend their group, but the reputation gorillas have among humans is little more than myth. Sadly, because of their fierce reputation, the clearing of habitat for farms, and big game hunting, gorillas have been hunted to extinction in many areas. Moreover, although there are perhaps 40,000 lowland gorillas remaining in parts of West Africa today, they are endangered, and the mountain gorilla (probably never very numerous) numbers only about 600 (see Issue, p. 190, this chapter).

The Chimpanzee Probably the best known of all nonhuman primates is the chimpanzee (Fig. 8-35). Often misunderstood because of their displays in zoos, circus acts, and sideshows, the chimpanzee's true nature did not become known until long hours of fieldwork in their natural environments provided a reliable picture. Today, chimpanzees are found in equatorial Africa, stretching in a broad belt from the Atlantic Ocean in the west to Lake Tanganyika in the east. Their range, however, is patchy within this large geographic area, and with further habitat destruction, it is becoming even more so.

Actually there are two species of chimpanzee: the "common" chimpanzee (*Pan troglodytes*) and the bonobo (*Pan paniscus*). Because the bonobo is smaller than some (but not all) chimpanzees, it has often been called the "pygmy chimpanzee." However, the differences in body size are not great enough to warrant such a distinction. Bonobos do, however, exhibit several intriguing anatomical and behavioral differences from chimpanzees. These differences include a more linear body build, dark face from birth, and tufts of hair at the side of the face (Fig. 8-36). Behaviorally, bonobos appear to be somewhat less aggressive and excitable, and male-female bonding is more important than in *troglodytes*.

Unfortunately, bonobos have not been well studied in the wild, although several research projects are currently in progress. This is indeed fortunate, as the bonobo's range is limited to a portion of central Zaire where, due to continuing habitat loss, this still largely unknown species is in grave danger of extinction.

Chimpanzees (*troglodytes* more so than *paniscus*) are in many ways structurally similar to gorillas, with corresponding limb proportions and upper-body shape. This similarity is due to commonalities in locomotion when on the ground (quadrupedal knuckle walking). Indeed, many authorities (for example, Tuttle, 1990) consider chimps and gorillas as members of a single genus. However, the ecological adaptations of the chimp and gorilla differ, with chimps spending more time in the trees. Moreover, whereas gorillas are typically placid and quiet, chimpanzees are highly excitable, active, and noisy.

Chimpanzees and bonobos are smaller than the other great apes and, while they are sexually dimorphic, sex differences are not as pronounced as in orangutans and gorillas. While male chimpanzees may weigh over 100 pounds, females may weigh at least 80.

(a)

(b)

Figure 8-35

Chimpanzees. (a) Male; (b) female.

Figure 8-36

Female bonobos with young in native habitat in Zaire.

Figure 8-37

A male lowland gorilla.

In addition to quadrupedal knuckle walking, chimpanzees (particularly youngsters) may brachiate while in the trees. When on the ground, they frequently walk bipedally for short distances when carrying food or other objects. One adult male at Jane Goodall's study area in Tanzania frequently walked bipedally due to an arm paralyzed by polio (Goodall, 1986). Chimpanzee social behavior has been studied in the wild at numerous field sites in Africa, the best known of which is Gombe National Park in Tanzania. Details of chimpanzee social behavior are discussed in Chapter 10.

Chimpanzees live in large, fluid communities of as many as 50 individuals or more. At the core of a chimpanzee community is a group of bonded males. Although relationships between these males are not always peaceful or stable, nevertheless they act as a group to defend territory and are highly intolerant of unfamiliar chimpanzees, especially nongroup males.

Although chimpanzees are said to live in communities, there are few times, if any, when all members are together. Indeed, it is the nature of chimpanzees to come and go so that the individuals they encounter vary from day to day. Moreover, adult females tend to forage either alone or in the company of their offspring. Such a foraging group could comprise several chimps, as females with infants often accompany their own mothers and their younger siblings. A female may also leave her community either to join another group permanently, or temporarily while she is in estrus. This behavioral pattern may serve to reduce the risk of mating with close male relatives, for males apparently never leave the group in which they were born.

Chimpanzee social behavior is very complex, and individuals form lifelong attachments with friends and relatives. Indeed, the bond between mothers and infants often remains strong until one or the other dies. This may be a considerable period, as it is not unusual for some chimpanzees to live into their midthirties, and some continue into their forties.

Humans Humans (family: Hominidae; genus: *Homo*) belong to the one remaining genus of the superfamily Hominoidea, a genus that today consists of only one species, *Homo sapiens*. Our primate heritage is shown again and again in the structure of our body: our dependence on vision; our lack of

Box 8-3   Tale of the Teeth

Extremely important for interpreting the relationships of *both* living and fossil forms are the number and kinds of teeth present. There are four different kinds of teeth found in a generalized placental mammal and primates have almost universally retained all four types: incisors, canines, premolars, and molars. A shorthand device for showing the number of each kind of tooth is called a **dental formula**. This formula indicates the teeth in one-quarter of the mouth (since the arrangement of teeth is symmetrical and usually the same in upper and lower jaws). For example, the dental formula in New World monkeys for cebids is 2-1-3-3 (2 incisors, 1 canine, 3 premolars, and 3 molars in each quarter of the mouth—a total of 36 teeth); and 2-1-3-2 in marmosets. The formula in *all* Old World monkeys, apes, and humans is normally 2-1-2-3—a total of 32 teeth. Most lemur and loris dental formulae are 2-1-3-3 (total of 36), but the highly specialized aye-aye shows (for a primate) remarkable reduction in numbers of teeth

$$\frac{1\text{-}0\text{-}1\text{-}3^*}{1\text{-}0\text{-}0\text{-}3}$$

for a total of only 18 teeth.

Relative dental formulae are extremely useful indicators of evolutionary relationships because they are normally under tight genotypic control. In other words, environmental influence will usually not alter the tooth formula. In making studies of primate dental phenotypes, we are quite certain, therefore, that our comparisons are based on structural homologies. Thus,

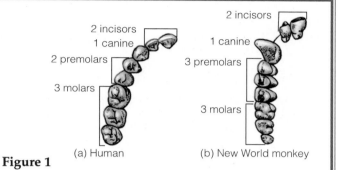

2 incisors
1 canine
2 premolars
3 molars

(a) Human

2 incisors
1 canine
3 premolars
3 molars

(b) New World monkey

Figure 1

Dental formulae. The number of each kind of tooth is given for one-quarter of the mouth.

similarities in structure (relative numbers of teeth) can be used as indicators of evolutionary similarity.

Dental evidence is extremely important in the interpretation of fossils, since teeth—the hardest component of the body—are the most commonly fossilized part and comprise the vast majority of fossil primate discoveries. In addition, cusp pattern and functional wear can be used to help reconstruct dietary behavior in fossil animals. The identification of diet is of central importance in any attempt to reconstruct the nature of the ecological niche, and ultimately the whole way of life of a fossil form.

---

*When the formula differs in the lower jaw from that of the upper jaw, both are shown. For example, the tarsier has one less incisor in each half of its lower jaw than it does in its upper jaw:

$$\frac{2\text{-}1\text{-}3\text{-}3}{1\text{-}1\text{-}3\text{-}3.}$$

---

reliance on olfactory (smell) cues; and our flexible limbs and grasping hands are all long rooted in our primate, arboreal past. Indeed, among the primates, we show in many ways the most developed set of primate characteristics. For example, the development of our cerebral cortex and reliance on learned behavior with resulting complexity in social behavior are but elaborations of long-established primate trends.

As we will discuss in the next chapter, there are several features of humans and our most immediate ancestors that distinguish us from other primates. However, probably the most distinctive, and certainly that most clearly observable in our earliest (hominid) ancestors is our unique manner of locomotion. The striding, bipedal gait with alternating support placed on a single hindlimb has required significant structural modifications in the pelvis and leg. By isolating similar structural modifications in the remains of fossil animals, we are able to distinguish our closely related or direct ancestors.

Dental formula The arrangement of teeth showing the number of each type (incisors, canines, premolars, and molars).

PHOTOGRAPH BY DEDE HATCH

Meredith F. Small is associate professor of anthropology at Cornell University where she teaches biological anthropology and primatology. She received a Ph.D. in anthropology from the University of California at Davis in 1980. She has studied four species of macaques in captivity and in the field, concentrating on female mating behavior. This work is summarized in her recent book Female Choices: Sexual Behavior of Female Primates *(Cornell University Press, 1993). She writes academic articles based on her research, and popular science for magazines and newspapers.*

In an introductory anthropology course during my junior year in college, we viewed the movie *Dead Birds*, a film about the aboriginal Dani of New Guinea. Some images were shockingly alien. I sat stunned as the elders chopped off the fingers of a little girl as a sign of mourning for a tribe member. And some images were intimately familiar—the way men and women occupied their days with work and play. Watching that film, I was overwhelmed by the knowledge that I could spend the rest of my life comparing wildly different groups such as the Dani and my fellow college juniors; I could actually *study* the human species. So I became an anthropology major and filled all my electives with every anthropology course that was offered.

My most dynamic teacher at that time was an archaeologist, and, in his footsteps, I signed on for a dig the following summer. I quickly learned to hate dust, and every night I would scream for a hot shower and clean hair—I knew that archaeology was not for me. Even so, I still remember clearly one afternoon when the sharp point of a pink arrowhead peeked through a mound of my dirt, the first artifact found that year. After graduation, I decided to sample another subdiscipline and moved to the University of Colorado for graduate work in paleontology. It was my job to figure out where a population of Nubians, represented by 10,000-year-old cranial bones, came from and why they had disap-

peared. I thought the analysis of those bones would lead me some day to study other, even older, fossil humans, but again, I was derailed into yet another subdiscipline.

In the fall of 1975, just after finishing my master's thesis, I enrolled in a course in primatology. Until then, I hadn't thought much about our primate relatives, although like my fellow graduate students I knew the taxonomy and skeletal biology of prosimians, monkeys, and apes, but I knew nothing about their diet, behavior, or social systems. And I never thought much about what their behavior might mean to the evolution of the human species. In our readings for that class, I was immediately struck by the simple descriptions of female monkeys and apes—females were portrayed as mothers and nothing else. Walking home after school one day, I found myself mumbling to no one in particular: "This can't be true. Human females do many things besides bring up babies. What else are these female monkeys doing? I don't have children and I have a life, what about female monkeys and apes?" This thought developed into a compelling question that I asked any anthropologist within earshot: "What else do female primates do besides have babies?" I ran into Peter Rodman from the University of California at Davis during the annual meeting of the American Association of Physical Anthropologists the following spring. He had an answer—Rodman suggested I work on a Ph.D. in primatology and start addressing that question myself.

In 1978 I began watching two species of macaques, rhesus and bonnets, at the Davis Primate Center, concentrating on the behavior of mothers and nonmothers during the breeding season and the following birth season. As I learned more evolutionary theory and explored the writings of other men and women who were trying to figure out the complexities of female primate behavior, I became fascinated by the many issues involved in individual reproductive success. What is the usual reproductive life course of a female primate? What is a "best" mate? Do females prefer some males over others? Why do some babies make it and others don't? How do these questions relate to the evolution of human female reproductive strategies?

My seemingly scattered training in the various branches of anthropology turned out to be a help rather than a handicap. I knew from experience that there were many ways to approach any question. I applied this reasoning to my work on female reproductive success by incorporating both behavior and biology. I've looked at the chromosomes of stillborn macaques, evaluated the birth and growth rates of infants, watched estrous females move from male to male in search of a mating partner, and compared the social behavior of females based on their reproductive status. I've stayed up late into the night processing blood, slipped down muddy cliffs while following an estrous female as she went after a particular male, and stood still as a friendly monkey sat on my shoulder and groomed my hair. I've discovered that females, like males, are strategizing creatures with personal agendas that attempt to improve their reproductive success.

I've stayed with macaques as a study species because I see them as the generic monkey, a basic primate stock from which we all evolved. Recently I, like all my primatological colleagues, have become concerned with the future welfare of my subjects. Although I continue to have a special interest in female behavior, I'm also drawn to issues of conservation. I recently began a study on the effect of tourism on temple monkeys, the longtail macaque, in Bali, Indonesia. Primates are always tourist attractions, and as tourism increases worldwide, populations of lemurs in Madagascar, apes in Africa, and monkeys worldwide are increasingly threatened by well-meaning tourists who just want to have a look. It's time, I think, for primatologists to come to the aid of the very animals they study. Tourism might be one route to keep the chain saws out of monkey habitats, but what happens to normal monkey life when their territory is invaded every day by bus loads of bipedal cousins?

We anthropologists are comfortable investigating and thinking about both biology and culture, and every subject on earth potentially has an anthropological bent. As a result, anthropologists are master generalists, and we end up in all sorts of professions from academics to corporate life. After all, once you recognize that humans are just primates with clothes on, mainly concerned with food, sex, and status just like their nonhuman primate cousins, human behavior in any arena makes complete sense.

Figure 8-38

Fusion of two small chromosomes. This fusion produces one large chromosome (human chromosome number 2?).

Primate Chromosomes, Proteins, and DNA

The classification of primates used thus far in this chapter has employed the traditional approach of looking for homologies in morphological traits. However, another relatively new perspective with enormous potential for helping to clarify taxonomic problems compares karyotypes (chromosome numbers, shapes, banding patterns, see p. 24), proteins, and even roughly correlates the DNA code itself.

The usefulness of this approach is immediately obvious. When we compare outward morphology, such as limb proportions and dental formulae, we are comparing phenotypes, usually far removed from their underlying genetic basis. However, what we are really after in the construction of classification schemes are homologies, traits based on common evolutionary descent. In other words, we want to compare traits that are inherited—those coded directly in the genotype.

Direct protein products of DNA, such as hemoglobin and serum proteins (found in the blood), are excellent indicators of homologies. If two species of primates are systematically similar in their protein structure, we can infer their DNA sequences are also similar. When two species share similar DNA, that means both inherited the same blueprint (with minor revisions) from a common ancestor. Thus, we have *direct* indicators of real homologies. Two primates that superficially resemble one another (some New World and Old World monkeys, for example) may in fact not be closely related at all. Using outward morphology alone may be confusing due to unknown effects from parallel evolution. But such evidence as biochemical data and karyotype comparisons avoids some of these pitfalls, and shows Old and New World monkeys as genetically (and evolutionarily) quite distinct.

Primatologists utilizing these techniques have, in conjunction with biochemists, in the last few years added considerable insight into our classifications of the primate order. A point worthy of mention: In most cases, biochemical evidence has reaffirmed the taxonomies constructed from comparative morphological studies (thereby supplying an extremely important independent source of data). When contradictions with traditional taxonomies have cropped up, much needed new knowledge has been gained. For example, classifying the orang with the African great apes superficially makes good sense since their outward body structures appear similar. Biochemical evidence, however, shows that both Asian apes (orangs and gibbons) are quite distinct from chimps and gorillas. Since our classifications are designed to reflect evolutionary relationships, they will have to be revised in the future to accord with this new information. (See discussion, p. 201.)

The way the various chromosomal and biochemical techniques are performed requires considerable technological sophistication, but their applications are straightforward. For example, two species can be compared for karyotype. The more closely two species are related, the closer their karyotypes should be. When one looks at the chromosomes of the hominoids, it is readily apparent that humans and the great apes are all quite similar, with gibbons and siamangs having the most distinctive (that is, derived) pattern (Stanyon and Chiarelli, 1982; Mai, 1983).

Among the large-bodied hominoids, the orang karyotype is the most conservative, with humans and the African apes displaying more derived features. It is interesting to note that the fossil data (which we'll take up in Chapter 12) also now suggest that orangs are probably the most conservative (that is, primitive) of the large hominoids.

Within the human/gorilla/chimp group there are a tremendous number of similarities of the structural arrangement and banding patterns of almost all the chromosomes. A relatively small number of alterations are required to transform all three living species from a theoretical ancestor (Yunis and Prakash, 1982).

The exact sequence of evolutionary relationships among humans and the African great apes is still in some dispute. Some tentative chromosomal data have suggested that humans and chimps share a more recent ancestry after separating from gorillas (Yunis and Prakash, 1982). A more controlled study, however, with consideration of within-species variation of karyotype (Stanyon and Chiarelli, 1982), has supported the more traditional branching order, where humans and *both* African apes diverge first—followed later by a separation of chimps and gorillas.

Detailed protein structures can be compared, as between chimp and human hemoglobin, by isolating the amino acid sequences. Comparisons between humans and the African great apes for the approximately half dozen proteins analyzed in this manner show striking similarities; they are either identical or show a difference of only one or two amino acids in the entire sequence (as you will recall, the hemoglobin beta chain is 146 amino acids long).

Another method used to contrast proteins in different species is not as precise as a detailed protein analysis but is less time-consuming and less costly. By measuring the strength of reaction to specially prepared antisera, similarities in proteins are calibrated on a relative scale, indicating *antigenic distance*. This approach, developed by Vincent Sarich and Allan Wilson at the University of California, Berkeley, has enabled many more proteins to be compared among a wide variety of different primate species. The results again generally tally favorably with traditional classifications.

Moreover, differences in DNA strands themselves can be compared using an elaborate technique called DNA hybridization. Scientists have performed some remarkable experiments in which double strands of DNA from two different species are artificially *separated* and then recombined into a new molecule, a hybrid DNA unlike anything nature ever concocted. The genetic (and evolutionary) similarity of the two species is then calculated by measuring the number of mismatched base pairs along the hybrid sequence (in other words, places where the two sides of the molecule are not complementary: A with T, G with C, etc.).

As in the other techniques discussed above, DNA hybridization has reaffirmed the basic tenets of primate classification. Indeed, better than any of the other approaches, DNA hybridization has shown how close genetically we and the African great apes are. A recent systematic application of this relatively new and fascinating technique (Sibley and Ahiquist, 1984) has shown that humans and chimps are closer genetically than *either* is to the gorilla and, in fact, even closer than two similar species of gibbons. Or, for that matter, humans and chimps are more similar than zebra and horse or goat and sheep. On the basis of these results, it would be entirely consistent to classify human and chimps (perhaps, gorillas as well) within the *same* genus. In other words, we would continue to be called *Homo sapiens*, while the chimp would be classed as *Homo troglodytes*. Certainly, not everyone is prepared to accept this terminology; nevertheless, it underlines the basic genetic/evolutionary facts.

Finally, the revolution in molecular biology brought about by recombinant DNA research has now made it possible to sequence directly the nucleotides of humans and other organisms (Goodman et al., 1983). As a result—when this new technique has been more widely applied—we should be able to ascertain even more unambiguously the precise genetic/evolutionary relationships among the primates.

Summary

Primates are an order of placental mammals characterized by their generalized limb structure, dependence on vision, lack of reliance on smell, developed brain (particularly cerebral cortex), and complex social organizations. All these evolutionary trends have developed, or at least have been elaborated, as a direct result of adaptation to an arboreal environment.

Living primates today represent four major grades of evolution that correspond to various stages of primate evolution over the last several million years. These grades are:

    I. Lemurs and lorises
   II. Tarsiers
  III. Monkeys (New World and Old World)
  IV. Hominoids (apes and humans)

Traditionally, primatologists made comparisons of anatomy and behavior. In recent years, considerable additional understanding of evolutionary relationships has been contributed by studies of DNA, chromosomes, and gene products.

We are a primate and our ancestors have been primates for at least 65 million years. Only by looking at humans *as primates* can we hope to understand the kind of animal we are and how we came to be this way.

Questions for Review

1. How are primates similar to other placental mammals?
2. Discuss how binocular vision, prehensility, and an expanded cerebral cortex are adaptations for an arboreal niche.
3. What are the various superfamilies of the primate order? To which one do humans belong?
4. Discuss the geographic distribution and ecological adaptations of contemporary prosimians.
5. What are the most important differences between prosimians and anthropoids?
6. How do monkeys in the Old and New Worlds exhibit parallel evolution?
7. What are some important relationships between limb structure and locomotion in contemporary primates?
8. In what ways are humans typical primates?
9. How does biochemical evidence indicate homologies? Why are effects due to parallel evolution more likely to cloud the picture for morphological traits than for biochemical traits?

Chapter 9

Contents

Fundamentals
of
Primate Behavior

The use of nonhuman animals for experimentation is an established practice, long recognized for its benefits to human beings, as well as to nonhuman animals. Currently, an estimated 17 to 22 million animals are used annually in the United States for the testing of new vaccines and other methods of treating or preventing disease, as well as for the development of innovative surgical procedures. Nonhuman animals are also used in psychological experimentation and in the testing of consumer products.

The prevalence of animal testing stems, in part, from the traditional Judeo-Christian view that humans are separate from the rest of the Animal Kingdom and that they are to have dominion over other life forms. Tragically, the dominion theory is frequently used to justify exploitation, and it is all too commonly seen as free of obligation or responsibility.

Because of biological and behavioral similarities shared with humans, nonhuman primates are among those species most desired for biomedical research. According to figures from the United States Department of Agriculture (USDA), 42,620 primates were used in laboratory studies in 1991. On average about 50,000 are used annually, with approximately 3000 being involved in more than one study. The most commonly used primates are baboons, vervets, various macaque species, squirrel monkeys, marmosets, and tamarins. Because they are more costly than other species (such as mice, rats, rabbits, cats, and dogs), primates are usually reserved

for medical and behavioral studies and not for the testing of such consumer goods as, for example, cosmetics or household cleaners. (It should be noted that many cosmetic companies *claim* they no longer perform tests on animals.)

Although work with primates has certainly benefited humankind, these benefits are expensive, not only monetarily but in terms of suffering and animal lives lost. The development of polio vaccine in the 1950s serves as one example of the costs involved. Prior to the 1950s, polio had killed and crippled millions of people worldwide. Now the disease is almost unheard of, at least in developed nations. But included in the price tag for polio vaccine were the lives of 1.5 *million* rhesus macaques, mostly imported from India.

Unquestionably, the elimination of polio and other diseases is a boon to humanity, and such achievements are seen as part of the obligation of medical research to promote the health and well-being of humans. But at the same time, serious questions have justifiably been raised about such medical advances made at the expense of literally millions of nonhuman animals, many of whom are primates. Indeed, one well-known primatologist, speaking at a conference a few years ago, questioned whether we can morally justify depleting populations of threatened species solely for the benefit of a single, highly overpopulated one.

This question will seem extreme, if not absurd, to many readers, especially in view of the fact that the overwhelming majority of people would argue that *whatever* is necessary to promote human health and longevity is justified. Many would also argue that nonhuman animals

have no rights, insofar as "rights" customarily refer to legal or moral relationships among humans. Nevertheless, the question raises several issues and does deserve some consideration.

One area of controversy regarding laboratory primates is housing. Traditionally, lab animals have been kept in small metal cages, usually one or two per cage. Cages are usually bare, except for food and water, and are frequently stacked one on top of another, so their inhabitants find themselves in the unnatural situation of having animals above and below them, as well as on each side.

The primary reason for small cage size is simple. Small cages are less expensive than large ones and they require less space (space is also costly). Moreover, sterile, unenriched cages (that is, cages that lack objects for manipulation or play) are easier, and therefore cheaper, to clean. But for such curious, intelligent animals as primates, these easy-to-maintain facilities result in a deprivation that leads to depression, neurosis, and psychosis. (The application of these terms to a nonhuman context is criticized as being anthropomorphic by many who believe that nonhuman animals, including primates, cannot be said to have psychological needs.)

Chimpanzees, reserved primarily for AIDS and hepatitis B research, probably suffer more than any other species from inadequate facilities. Dr. Jane Goodall (1990) has published a description of the conditions she encountered in one lab she visited in Maryland. In this lab, she saw two- and three-year-old chimpanzees housed, two together, in cages measuring 22 inches square and 24 inches high. Obviously, movement for these youngsters was virtually impossible, and they had been housed in this manner for over three months. At this same lab and others, adult chimps, infected with HIV or hepatitis, were confined alone for several years, in small isolation chambers where they rocked back and forth, seeing little and hearing nothing of their surroundings.

Fortunately, conditions are improving. There has been increased public awareness of existing conditions and the need for change; and there is, among some members of the biomedical community, a growing sensitivity toward the special requirements of primates.

In 1991, amendments to the Animal Welfare Act were enacted to require all labs to provide minimum standards for the humane care of all "warm-blooded" animals. (For some reason, this category does not include birds, mice, and rats.) These minimum standards provide specific requirements for cage size based upon weight of the animal. For example, primates weighing less than 2.2 pounds must have 1.6 square feet of floor space per animal and the cage must be at least 20 inches high. Those weighing more than 55 pounds are allotted at least 25.1 square feet of floor space per animal and at least 84 inches (7 feet) of vertical space.

Clearly, the enclosures described above are not sufficiently large for normal locomotor activities, and this could certainly contribute to psychological stress. One method of reducing such stress is to provide cages with objects and climbing structures (even part of a dead branch is a considerable improvement and costs nothing). Several facilities are now implementing such procedures. Also, many laboratory staff are now trained to provide enrichment for the animals in their care. Moreover, the Maryland lab that Dr. Goodall observed no longer maintains chimpanzees in isolation chambers. Rather, they are now housed with other animals in areas measuring 80 cubic feet, and are provided with enrichment devices.

Aside from the treatment of captive primates, there continues to be concern over the depletion of wild populations in order to provide research animals. Actually, the number of wild-caught animals used in research today is small compared to the numbers lost to habitat destruction and hunting for food (see p. 259). However, in the past, particularly in the 1950s and 1960s, the numbers of animals captured for research were staggering. In 1968, for example, 113,714 primates were received in the United States alone!

Most fortunately, the number of animals imported into the United States has declined dramatically since the Convention on Trade in Endangered Species (CITES) was ratified in 1973 (see p. 261). In 1984, for example, the United States imported 13,148 primates (Mittermeir and Cheney, 1987). On average, the United States annually imports some 20,000 (some from breeding colonies in the country of origin). Although it would be best if no free-ranging primates were involved, at least these figures represent a substantial improvement over the situation seen in the 1960s.

However, not all countries are members of CITES, and even some member nations either illegally continue to receive primates for use, or they act as conduits for the transport of captured animals to non-CITES countries. Moreover, many countries, such as Brazil and India, that possess indigenous primate populations, have developed a local trade for their own research.

It is important to note that biomedical research accounts for only a small part of the demand for primates captured live in the wild. Actually, the exotic pet trade provides a much greater share of the market, both locally and internationally. Probably even more important is the hunting or live capture of primates for human consumption. This is especially true in parts of West Africa and Asia. Moreover, in several Asian countries there is growing demand for animal products (including primate) for medicinal purposes.

In response to concerns for diminishing wild populations and regulations to protect them, a number of breeding colonies have been established in the United States and other countries to help meet demands for laboratory animals. In the United States, there are seven federal primate centers and a number of smaller colonies, some of which are maintained by universities and others by private institutions and even animal dealers. Additionally, in 1986, the National Institutes of Health established a National Chimpanzee Breeding Program to provide chimpanzees primarily for AIDS and hepatitis B research.

There is growing recognition that captive born and reared primates, as opposed to wild-caught animals, are more amenable to handling and use. Chimpanzees and monkeys have been taught, for example, to extend an arm through their cages for purposes of blood drawing or other procedures. Not only does this eliminate the need for sedation and/or restraint, but anxiety and suffering are greatly reduced.

Furthermore, in late 1989, the United States Fish and Wildlife Service upgraded the status of wild chimpanzees from "threatened" to "endangered." The endangered status was not applied to animals born in captivity, but the upgrade was intended to provide additional protection for free-ranging populations. Unfortunately, even with all the policies now in place, there is no guarantee that some wild-born chimps will not find their way into research labs.

The animal rights movement has been described by many in the scientific community as "anti-science," or "anti-intellectual." Certainly, there are extremists in the an-imal rights movement for whom these labels are appropriate. But, to categorize in this manner all who have concern for animals and, in this case, primates, is unjustified. There are many concerned members of the biomedical and scientific communities, including the authors of this text, to whom these labels do not apply.

It is neither anti-science nor anti-intellectual to recognize that humans who derive benefits from the use of nonhuman species have an obligation to reduce suffering and provide adequate facilities for highly intelligent, complex animals. This obligation does not necessitate laboratory break-ins. But improvement does mean that individual members of the biomedical community must become yet more aware of the requirements of captive primates. Moreover, those involved in primate testing, and the granting agencies that fund them, should be kept well informed as to the status of wild primate populations. Lastly, and perhaps most importantly, existing laws that regulate the capture, treatment, and trade of wild-caught animals *must* be more strictly enforced.

Undoubtedly, humankind has much to gain by using nonhuman primates for experimentation. But we clearly have a moral obligation to ensure their survival in the wild, as well as to provide them with hu-mane treatment and enriched captive environments. But most of all, we owe them respect as complex, intelligent, and sensitive animals, who are not that different from ourselves. If we grant them this, the rest should follow.

SOURCES:

Goodall, Jane. *Through a Window*. Boston: Houghton-Mifflin, 1990.

Holden, Constance. "Academy Explores Use of Laboratory Animals," *Science*, 242:185, October, 1988.

Mittermeir, R. A., and D. Cheney, "Conservation of Primates in their Habitats," in: Smuts, B., et al., eds. *Primate Societies*, Chicago: University of Chicago Press, pp. 477–496, 1987.

United States Department of Agriculture. Subchapter A—Animal Welfare. Washington, D.C.: U.S. Government Printing Office, Publication Number 311-364/60638, 1992.

Note: We would like to express special appreciation to Dr. Shirley MacGreal, President, International Primate Protection League, and to Dr. Thomas L. Wolfle, Director, Institute of Laboratory Animal Resources, for providing information for this issue.

Introduction

How can we better understand human behavior? Solely observing an urbanized industrialized society such as ours will not tell us very much of our hominid heritage. After all, we have been urbanized for only a few thousand years, and the industrial revolution is merely a few centuries old, barely a flicker in evolutionary time. Consequently, to understand what behavioral components may have shaped our evolution, we need a perspective broader than that which our own culture supplies. Since little is known about early hominid behavior, we study the behavior of contemporary animals adapted to environments similar to those of early hominids in the hope of gaining insight into early hominid evolution.

In this chapter, we place nonhuman primate behavior in the context of its possible relationship to human behavior; that is, we address the question: Does the study of nonhuman primates serve as a window on (or model for) human behavior? Or are nonhuman primates so different in behavior from hominids that the uniqueness of the latter derives little from the former?

Behavior and Human Origins

What does it mean to be human? There are several *physical* characteristics, such as adaptations for bipedal locomotion and enlarged brain, that characterize humans and—to varying extents—our hominid ancestors. But from a strictly structural point of view, we are not really that unique compared to other primates, especially when compared with the great apes. In patterns of dentition, bone development, muscle structure, and so forth, we and the other hominoids are very similar, reflecting a fairly recent shared ancestry. (Probably no more than 7 or 8 million years [m.y.] at most separate us from the African great apes.) Indeed, in the nonrepeated portions of DNA, humans and chimpanzees are 98% identical. So what, precisely, is it that distinguishes the human animal?

Quite clearly, it is behavioral attributes that most dramatically set humans apart. Human culture is our strategy for coping with some of life's challenges. No other primate even comes close to the human ability to modify environments. Communication through symbolic language is yet another uniquely human characteristic (see pp. 272–279 for a discussion of cognitive abilities in nonhuman primates). In addition, several other features differentiate humans from the majority of other primates. These are summarized in the following list, but keep in mind that any one of these attributes may be found in one or another primate species. While *all* of these are part of human behavior, there is no other primate species of which this may be said. For example, humans are bipedal; however, some apes occasionally walk bipedally, but not regularly. All primates learn, as do all mammals, but none learns nearly as much as humans, and so forth.

Humans are bipedal.

Humans live in permanent bisexual social groups with males often bonded to females.

Humans have large brains relative to body weight and are capable of *complex* learning.

Partly as a consequence of neurological reorganization, humans make *highly advanced* use of symbolic language.

Also related to neurological developments and bipedality, *cultural* response has become the *central* hominid adaptive strategy.

Humans obtain food through some male/female division of labor; moreover, food is actively transported back to a base camp (home) for purposes of sharing.

There is a relaxation of the estrous cycle and concealed ovulation in humans, so that females can be sexually receptive throughout the year.

These traits are fairly characteristic of all modern humans. Moreover, much of this behavioral complex is thought to be a good *baseline* for the early stages of hominid emergence. In fact, behavioral reconstructions are often central to theories explaining how hominids came to be hominids in the first place.

Nonhuman Primates

Modern African apes and humans last shared an ancestor in common somewhere between 8–5 m.y.a. according to most experts. Researchers believe that ape behavior has changed since then, but not nearly as much as the behavior of hominids, who developed culture as their strategy of adaptation. Therefore, if we are interested in what hominid behavior might have been like before culture became a significant factor, and if we wish to know what behaviors may have led hominids to become dependent on culture, we may find clues in the behavior of our closest relatives, the nonhuman primates. (See Chapter 10 for further discussion.)

Studies of nonhuman primates also assist with present human behavioral problems. Humans are *not* monkeys or apes, of course, but similarities do

Figure 9-1

These baboons have adapted quadrupedally to a terrestrial savanna life.

exist. For example, the way human infants learn to love and bond to mother and then family is reflected in the infant behavior patterns of monkeys and apes. It is, after all, possible that "The more we can learn about the evolutionary history and adaptations of other primate forms, the more we will know about the processes which shaped our own species" (Lancaster, 1975, p. 5).

Of course, another important rationale for studying nonhuman primates is to better understand them in their own right. As we will discuss later in this chapter, many contemporary primate species are in imminent danger of extinction. To provide adequate protection for these remnant populations, considerable knowledge regarding a wide array of subjects is necessary, including ranging behavior, diet, reproductive physiology, parental care, and group structure. Without such knowledge, even the present slim hopes for survival of numerous species in the wild will vanish.

Species of primates are numerous, and their behavior varies a good deal. Nevertheless, there are characteristics common to most, if not all, primates. Most primates live in tropical or semitropical regions, but a few, such as the Japanese macaque and some langurs, have adapted to cold weather. Although they vary, primates are mainly **diurnal**, a few are **crepuscular**, and others, especially among prosimians, are **nocturnal**. Relatively few nonhuman primates are terrestrial—savanna baboons and gorillas are the best known; most others are arboreal. Intelligence, a difficult concept to define, is another characteristic common to primates, and it is generally conceded that all primates are more intelligent than most, if not all, other mammals (see Chapter 10 for further discussion).

Living in social groups (see Box 9-1) is one of the major characteristics of primates, who solve their major adaptive problems within this social context. For other animals, "mating, feeding, sleeping, growth of the individual, and protection from pedators are usually matters for the solitary individual to solve, but for . . . primates they are most often performed in a social context" (Lancaster, 1975, p. 12).

Diurnal   Active during the day.

Crepuscular   (kre-pus´-kew-ler)
creper: dark, dusty
Active at twilight or dawn.

Nocturnal   Active at night.

Figure 9-2

Chimpanzee family, a long-term cohesive unit. These individuals associate often throughout their lives.

Box 9-1 Types of Nonhuman Primate Social Groups*

1. *One-male.* A single adult male, several adult females, and their offspring. This is the commonest primate mating structure, in which only one male actively breeds (Jolly, 1985). Usually formed by a male or males joining a kin group of females. Females usually form the permanent nucleus of the group. Examples: guenons, orangs, gorillas, some pottos, some spider monkeys, patas.

2. *Multimale/Multifemale.* Several adult males, several adult females, and their young. Several of the males reproduce. The presence of several males in the group may lead to tension and to a dominance hierarchy. Examples: some lemurs, macaques, mangabeys, savanna baboons, vervets, squirrel monkeys, spider monkeys, chimpanzees.

3. *Family, or monogamous.* A mated pair and their young. Usually arboreal, minimal sexual dimorphism, frequently territorial. Adults usually do not tolerate other adults of the same sex. Not found among great apes, and least common of the breeding structures among nonhuman primates. Examples: gibbons, indris, titis, sakis, owl monkeys, pottos.

SOURCES

Jolly, 1985; Napier and Napier, 1985.

---

*These are called breeding groups by Jolly and permanent groupings by Napier and Napier. There are also other groupings, such as foraging groups, hunting groups, all female or male groups, and so on. Like humans, nonhuman primates do not always maintain one kind of group; single male groups may sometimes form multimale groups and vice versa. The gelada and hamadryas baboons, for example, are listed here as one-male groups but "form herds of 100 or more at night when they move towards the safety of the steep cliffs where they sleep" (Napier and Napier, 1985, p. 61). Also, variability is seen in other forms, for example, red colobus monkeys (see p. 242).

Many different patterns of social groupings exist among the primates. Typically, the primate social group includes members of all ages and of both sexes, a composition that does not vary significantly during the annual cycle. This situation differs from that of most mammals, whose adult males and females associate only during the breeding season, and whose young of either sex do not usually remain with the adults after reaching puberty.

Because they remain together over a long period of time, members of the specific primate group learn to know each other. They learn—as they must—how to respond to a variety of actions that may be threatening, cooperative, or indifferent. In such social groups, individuals must be able to evaluate a situation before acting. Evolutionarily speaking, this would have placed selective pressure on social intelligence which, in turn, would select for brains that could assess such situations and store the information. One of the results of such selection would be the evolution of proportionately larger and more complex brains, especially among the higher primates (that is, anthropoids).

Primate Field Studies

While other disciplines, such as psychology and zoology, have long been concerned with nonhuman primates, the study of these animals in their *natural habitats* has primarily become a focus of anthropology. Early work—that done before World War II—was especially stimulated through the influence of the American psychologist Robert Yerkes, who in the late 1920s and 1930s sent students out to the field to study gorillas, chimpanzees, and howler monkeys. It was the last of these studies by Clarence Ray Carpenter (along with his work on gibbons) that stands out particularly as a hallmark of early primate field investigations.

American anthropologists became vitally involved somewhat later—the 1950s—following the lead established by Sherwood Washburn who, with his colleague, Irven DeVore, carried out a pioneering study of savanna baboons in the late 1950s. At about the same time, Phyllis Dolhinow was researching langurs in India and George Schaller was collecting data on mountain gorillas in Africa. And, of course, there is the famous research that Jane Goodall began with chimpanzees in 1960. In addition, primate studies were also being pursued in the 1950s by Japanese anthropologists, who actively began their long-term study of Japanese macaques in 1952 (see p. 284). They have since extended their fieldwork to include numerous other species elsewhere in Asia and in Africa.

The key aspect of these field studies is that they attempt to collect and synthesize information on **free-ranging** animals. That is, the animals are in their "natural" settings in which they travel, feed, mate, and so forth without severe constraints imposed by humans.

Free-ranging Applied to animals living in their natural habitat.

Several points, however, must be kept in mind. Free-ranging does not necessarily imply that these animals remain uninfluenced by human activities. With the exception of an exceedingly impenetrable forest just recently explored in Zaire, it is highly unlikely that there is a single group of nonhuman primates elsewhere in the world that has not experienced some human interference. Indeed, the incredibly rapid destruction of tropical rainforests (see pp. 259–263) now threatens the very existence of most nonhuman primates. Moreover, while "free-ranging" implies that animals move about on their own volition to find food, in several cases (Japanese macaque studies, Jane Goodall's early work at Gombe Stream) the animals have been **artificially provisioned** by the observers. This means, of course, that some of their food comes from other than normal or natural sources. We would also expect that

Artificially provisioned Food made available to primates by humans.

Figure 9-3

Black-and-white colobus monkeys high up in the forest canopy. Can you spot the animals? Imagine trying to recognize them as individuals!

the different levels of provisioning employed would affect the free-ranging behavior of the animals in foraging and other activities.

Why, then, is artificial provisioning practiced? The answer relates to the difficulties involved in following free-ranging primates. As discussed in Chapter 8, most species of nonhuman primates live in the tropical rainforests of the Americas, Africa, and Asia. Dense foliage and ground cover severely inhibit the movement of observers as they attempt to follow their study animals. Perhaps even worse, these animals are usually high up in the forest canopy, obscured from vision, and are often moving rapidly. Then there are almost invariably numerous individuals in a social group who can be expected to exhibit highly individualistic behaviors. The problem: How does one recognize individuals under such field conditions? In fact, individuals frequently cannot be recognized accurately, so that the best that can be accomplished is to record the sex and approximate age of the animals. Some provisioning of the study animals draws them into the open, where they can be observed and recognized.

Because of these problems, the most systematic information thus far collected on free-ranging animals comes from species that spend considerable time on the ground (including langurs, gorillas, chimps) and most especially those species that travel and feed frequently in open (that is, mostly treeless) country (for example, macaques, baboons, vervet monkeys, patas monkeys). Note that the selection and emphasis on certain species in this and the next chapter reflect this research bias.

Another research tack pursued by some anthropologists involves studying primates, not in their natural habitats, but rather in large provisioned colonies, where at least some movement, group dynamics, etc., are possible. Probably the best example of this type of research is the long-term study of rhesus macaques conducted on Cayo Santiago Island off the coast of Puerto Rico. First established in 1938, the island population now totals close to 1,000 individuals (Richard, 1985).

Despite significant gaps in our knowledge about many aspects of primate behavior, we nevertheless presently have field data on more than 100 nonhuman primate species. The information from this fascinating and rapidly advancing discipline of primatology forms the remainder of this chapter.

The Ecology of Nonhuman Primates

For those anthropologists who study free-ranging primates, the key considerations have always been (1) to characterize the nature of the animals' environments and (2) to hypothesize how these environments shape primate social behavior.

Early on, researchers routinely recorded the types of food eaten, the distances traveled to get to food/water/sleeping sites, the size of groups, the composition of groups, and so on. In the 1970s, an emerging perspective called **socioecology** grew out of this approach and looked at such factors as the following regarding the possible effects on primate social groups:

1. quantity and quality of different kinds of food (caloric value, digestive energy required, net value to the animals)
2. activity patterns—are the animals nocturnal or diurnal?
3. distribution of food resources (widely spread or tightly packed?)

Socioecology The study of primates and their habitats; specifically, attempts to find patterns of relationship between the environment and primate social behavior.

4. distribution of water
5. distribution of predators
6. distribution of sleeping sites

A great deal of enthusiasm resulted from this approach and led to new research directions as well as attempts to synthesize the information in order to discern broad patterns for the entire order. Initially, schemes were relatively simple and attempted to show very broad aspects of ecological/behavioral correlations (Crook and Gartlan, 1966; Crook, 1970; Eisenberg et al., 1972). Rather quickly, as more data accumulated, it became obvious that primates in the wild displayed considerably more variability of social behavior than these simple schemes could accommodate.

As a result, more sophisticated approaches have evolved (Clutton-Brock and Harvey, 1977; Richard, 1985). Primatologists now view ecology, behavior, and biology as complexly interdependent. In addition to the general ecological factors listed above, primatologists must also consider an animal's body size, relative brain size, metabolism, reproductive physiology, the distribution of food resources into "food patches," and the nutritional value of foods and how they are selected and processed. (See Fleagle, 1988, for a good discussion of these factors.) Moreover, the variability exhibited between closely related species (and even *within* the same species) in ecological adaptations must be understood. Also, the way primates relate to their overall surrounding biological communities, especially to other species of primates, must be described. Indeed, it is a common phenomenon for many prosimian and monkey species to travel, and to socially relate over long periods with other primate species. Do they eat different foods? How do they efficiently subdivide their habitat? These questions, too, must be addressed. Lastly, it is of interest to study why primates select certain foods and avoid others. What is the nutritional value of insects, fruits, leaves, nuts, gums, small mammals, etc., that are available to them? What toxins exist in certain plant foods that could do harm? Thus, as a central focus of ecology, let us turn to the diets of nonhuman primates.

Figure 9-4

Rhesus macaques. Part of the large colony on Cayo Santiago Island.

What Do Primates Eat?

Certainly a basic way any animal relates to its environment concerns the foods it finds and eats. We mentioned in Chapter 8 that primates are omnivorous, implying they eat many plant and animal foods. But as Alison Richard has pointed out (1985, p. 167), omnivory is rarely carefully defined—and, as such, does not constitute a particularly useful concept.

It is more productive, then, to describe in some detail what primates actually eat. Of course, most primate species do in fact have quite diversified diets. For example, macaques, like most primates, are primarily vegetarians. Yet, when we consider ground cover accumulation of snow (which is an important seasonal factor for Japanese macaques), we can see that very different foods may be exploited. Consequently, in the winter, rhesus macaques in highland Pakistan eat tough plant leaves (oak), pine needles, pine gum, and herb roots. At other times of the year, they eat flower blossoms, fruits, grasses, and seeds (Richard, 1985). This is perhaps an extreme case (for most primates do not live in such seasonal environments, and foods are thus more consistently available). And, in fact, most species do concentrate on a particular combination of food sources. Special terminology has been devised to describe the type of diet as characterized by the most predominant type of food:

1. insectivore—primarily eats insects
2. folivore—primarily eats leaves
3. frugivore—primarily eats fruits
4. gramnivore—primarily eats seeds
5. gumnivore—primarily eats gums

Even at this general level, characterizing particular primate species according to this scheme is frequently difficult; still, some species are easier to classify than others. Chimps in all parts of their range where they have been observed eat primarily fruits (i.e., they are primarily frugivorous). On the other hand, olive baboons (one variety of savanna baboons) show dietary diversity in different areas of their range. In one area of Kenya, they eat primarily grass blades and seeds, but little fruit. In Ethiopia, however, they spend almost half their time eating fruit. Although there are certainly differences in the environment between the two regions, it has been suggested that the dietary differences may also relate to differences in food-harvesting techniques (Richard, 1985). Indeed, such differences in local *traditions* can dramatically influence primate behavior, a point to which we will return in Chapter 10.

ENVIRONMENT AND SOCIAL BEHAVIOR

In the remainder of this chapter and Chapter 10, we will discuss various aspects of nonhuman primate social behavior. An ecological focus can, in many ways, be utilized to illuminate much of primate behavior (see Jolly, 1985, and Richard, 1985, for excellent discussions of this perspective). Here, we cannot adequately discuss all the ways primatologists use ecological, behavioral, and biological data. Nor can we completely summarize the huge amount of information that has accumulated in recent years. What is important, however, is to get a sense of how this approach is used currently by primatologists; hence, we will discuss a comprehensive example of such primate ecological research.

Five Monkey Species in the Kibale Forest, Uganda   One of the most detailed and controlled studies of primate socioecology has been undertaken in the Kibale Forest of western Uganda (Struhsaker and Leyland, 1979). The five species thus far studied in detail are all varieties of Old World monkeys and include black-and-white colobus (*Colobus guereza*), red colobus (*Colobus badius*), mangabey (*Cercocebus albigena*), blue monkey (*Cercopithecus mitus*), and the redtail monkey (*Cercopithecus ascanius*). In addition to these five Old World monkey species, there are also in the Kibale Forest two other monkey species (*Cercopithecus* and the "savanna baboon"), as well as the potto, two species of galago, and the chimpanzee (for a discussion of the latter, see Ghiglieri, 1984). Indeed, there are eleven different species of nonhuman primates at Kibale and together they display the greatest number of total individuals and highest primate biomass for any site yet described (Waser, 1987). In the study under discussion (Struhsaker and Leyland, 1979), comparisons are facilitated as all species were sampled using similar methodologies. This avoids the pitfall of making comparisons between highly variable research strategies, a problem usually unavoidable in making cross-species comparisons. Moreover, the research at Kibale is important because this region is

Figure 9-5

Kibale Forest habitat, Uganda.

probably the least disturbed habitat where primates have been studied long-term.

While **sympatric**, numerous fascinating differences exist among the five species. Body weights vary considerably (3–4 kg for redtails and up to 7–10 kg for the mangabey and colobus species). Diet also differs at a gross level, with the two colobus species eating primarily leaves (that is, they are folivorous) and the other three species showing more dietary diversity: concentration on fruits supplemented by insects.

At the same time, several aspects of social organization varied among the five species. For example, the red colobus and mangabey had several adult males in the group, while only one fully adult male was typically present in the other species. Furthermore, all five species occasionally had solitary males moving independently of the bisexual groups, but bachelor groups (consisting solely of adult and subadult males) did not typically form (as has been observed in other primates, such as langurs and gelada baboons). Even among the mostly multimale bisexual species there is a marked difference. In mangabeys, the females are the permanent core of the group (with males transferring out), while in red colobus, it is the females who transfer (with the males remaining the long-term residents) (Struhsaker and Leyland, 1987). Indeed, there is so much variability that Struhsaker and Leyland could find little correlation between social organization and gross feeding ecology.

More detailed analysis of feeding patterns showed even further differences. For instance, while both colobus species eat mostly leaves, they still exploit different resources. (Black-and-white colobus eat considerably more mature leaf blades, some high in protein; red colobus, on the other hand, eat a wider variety of leaves, but usually not mature ones, as well as fruits and shoots.) Perhaps correlated with these dietary differences are the observations that black-and-white colobus spend less time feeding but more time resting and, in contrast, red colobus range further and live in higher density

Sympatric Animals living in the same area. Two or more species whose habitats partly or largely overlap.

(that is, higher biomass). In addition, some species show dramatic variability from month to month. Among redtail monkeys, the proportion of fruit in the monthly diet varies from as low as 13% to as much as 81% (Richard, 1985).

Ecological patterns and social ramifications are unquestionably most complicated. In the same forest at Kibale, the closely related species black-and-white colobus and red colobus show marked differences in social organization. (Black-and-white colobus are found in one-male groups, red colobus in multimale/multifemale groups. See Box 10-1.) Yet in another area (the Tana River Forest of Kenya), red colobus have only one-male groups (like black-and-white at Kibale) and *both* males and females transfer (unlike either colobus species at Kibale) (Richard, 1985). The distinct impression one gathers from attempts to find correlations is that many primate species are exceedingly flexible regarding group composition, a fact that makes generalizing an extremely tentative undertaking at best.

Still, the highly controlled nature of the Kibale study makes some comparisons and provisional generalizations such as the following possible:

1. The omnivores (mangabeys, redtails, blues) locomoted more than the folivores (the two colobus). That is, they spent a greater proportion of the time they were observed either moving in the trees or on the ground.
2. Among the omnivores there is an inverse relationship of body size and group size (that is, the smaller the body size, the larger the group tends to be); also among the omnivores, there is a direct relationship of body size with **home range**.
3. Omnivores were spatially more dispersed than folivores.
4. Female sexual swelling (see p. 217) was obvious only in those species (red colobus and mangabeys) that lived in multimale groups.
5. Feeding, spacing, group residency, dispersal, and reproductive strategies may be very different for males and females of the same species. These considerations have become a central focus of ecological and sociobiological research (see p. 249).

Because of the complexity of the social relationships among primates, long-term studies are absolutely necessary. As Struhsaker and Leyland conclude from their studies at Kibale, "Meaningful data on group dynamics and probable degree of genetic relatedness among the members can only be collected by observing groups for at least half the adult life span, which for most Old World monkeys means a period of five to six years" (1979, p. 222). Alison Richard (1985) is even more conservative in generalizing about long-term ecological patterns. She suggests such patterns should be observed at least as long as the periodicity of cycles of critical resources. For Old World monkeys, then, as much as ten generations might be required—a total of up to eighty years of study!

Clearly, the kinds of data now emerging from primate ecological research (and its manifold social and biological connections) pose tremendous interest and opportunities for primatologists. However, the challenges involved in collecting such data are equally great.

Home range The area exploited by an animal or social group. Usually given for one year—or for the entire lifetime—of an animal.

Social Behavior

Since primates solve their major adaptive problems in a social context, we might expect that they participate in a number of activities to reinforce the integrity of the group for purposes of holding it together. The better known of these activities are described in the sections that follow.

(a) savanna baboons

(b) patas monkeys

(c) black-and-white colobus monkeys

(d) chimpanzees

ASPECTS OF SOCIAL BEHAVIOR

Grooming   Almost all primates groom one another. **Grooming** occurs in other animal species, but social grooming is a unique primate activity and plays an important role in the life of most primates. It serves hygienic functions since it removes ectoparasites, dead skin, and debris from the skin and fur, but has other important functions as well. It has been called a social lubricant because it eases the interaction between male/female and higher/lower rank, where there is a possibility of friction. It has also been called "the social cement of primates from lemur to chimpanzee" (Jolly, 1984, p. 207) since it helps in maintaining the organization of the group. Grooming is often reciprocal with roles interchanged—the groomer may become the groomee, a process resulting in the establishment of friendly social relations among the animals in the group.

Figure 9-6

Grooming primates.

Grooming   Cleaning through the hair and fur.

(a)

(b)

Figure 9-7

Great ape displays. (a) a gorilla chest-beating display; (b) chimpanzee with hair erect (piloerection).

Dominance Also referred to as *dominance hierarchy* and *status* rank. The domination of some members of a group by other members. A hierarchy of ranked statuses sustained by hostile, or threat of hostile, behavior, which may result in greater access to resources, such as sleeping sites, food, and mates.

Dominance* Dominance rank, or status rank, may be measured by priority access to a desired object, such as food or mates, and also by the result of threat situations. A dominant individual is given priority, and in a confrontation is the one that usually does not give way. It is believed, although not all primatologists agree, that because dominant males compete more successfully for fertile females than do subordinate males, they have greater reproductive success. Also, dominant females, because they compete for food more successfully than subordinate females, are thus provided with more energy for offspring production and have greater reproductive success than subordinate females (Fedigan, 1983).

In many primate societies males are generally dominant over females of the same age; older or stronger individuals supplant weaker ones; and each group member must learn its rank in the hierarchy, at least within its own sex and age class. "Further, the length of time spent in the group, called 'residence' or male 'tenure,' also correlates significantly with rank, positively in the case of macaques . . . and negatively with the case of baboons" (Fedigan, 1983, pp. 111–112). Dominant males are sometimes responsible for protecting the troop from predators as well as for defense against other troops if that situation should arise. They may also, as in savanna baboons, act as "policemen" to break up fights among juveniles, females, and other adult males within their troop.

Dominance hierarchies are adaptive because they operate to avoid conflict, obviously essential for animals living in permanent social groups. When two individuals compete for the same scarce item, the dominant one assumes priority by threat behavior. Thus, dominance serves to organize social inter-

*See Fedigan, 1983, for a review of dominance theory.

actions; individuals know where they belong within the social hierarchy and act accordingly, avoiding chaotic, unorganized social relations. The result is a more or less smoothly functioning order of priority, which reduces endless quarrels and potentially dangerous conflicts for scarce resources.

From the individual's perspective, dominance also has advantages. As noted, the dominant (higher-ranking) animal gains priority access to scarce resources, such as desired food items, sleeping sites, or mates. The direct influence of dominance in gaining priority access to mates is a subject of some debate—especially as the necessary long-term data for most species are lacking. (We will refer to this topic in the section on "sociobiology.")

Mother-Infant Relationship   The basic social unit among primates is the female and her infants. Adult males **consort** with females for mating purposes, but they may or may not participate as members of the social unit. Observations both in the field and in captivity suggest that this mother-offspring core provides the group with its stability.

The **mother-infant attachment**, one of the most basic themes running throughout primate social relations, begins at birth. A primate infant's first bond (in the anthropoids especially) is to its mother. After birth, the infant clings to its mother while she performs her daily activities, often without seeming regard for her offspring's success in holding on. Quite often, however, as she leaves for some activity, a mother will gather her infant protectively to her body. Unlike other social animals, in which the newborn are left in a nest or den, the clinging primate infant develops a closeness with the mother that does not end with weaning. This closeness is often maintained throughout life in some species and is reflected in grooming behavior that continues between mother and offspring even after the children reach adulthood.

The crucial role played by primate mothers was clearly demonstrated by the Harlows (1959), who raised some infant monkeys with surrogate mothers fashioned from cloth and metal, respectively, and other monkeys with no mothers at all.

In what is probably the most famous experiment, young monkeys were given access to two different surrogates—one made of bare wire, the other

Consortship   Exclusive relationship of one adult male and one adult female (usually, but not always, in estrus).

Mother-infant attachment   The attachment between mother and her offspring. One of the most basic themes running through primate social relations.

Figure 9-8

Primate mothers and their infants.

(a)

(b)

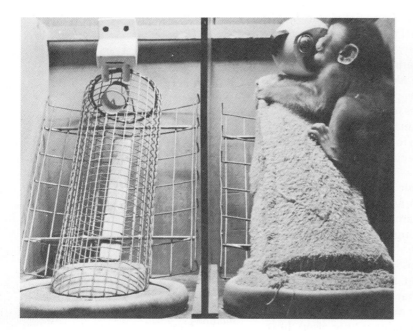

Figure 9-9

Wire mother and cloth mother.

covered with soft cloth (see Fig. 9-9). Without exception, the young animals preferred close contact with the cloth surrogate, even when the wire one provided the nourishment (through a bottle with nipple). The infants would transfer to the (nourishing) wire surrogate solely to feed and would still spend up to 20 hours per day clinging to the cloth "mother."

These results have been generalized to demonstrate the requirement for early attachment for primates in general, including humans. Moreover, the attachment apparently is reinforced especially through tactile stimulation.

In another experiment (Harlow and Harlow, 1961), monkeys raised without a mother sat passively in their cages and stared vacantly into space. Some punished themselves by chewing their arms until blood flowed. Those raised with a surrogate mother acted similarly, but somewhat less dramatically. None of the males or females raised without real or surrogate mothers ever achieved any semblance of normal sexual behavior. No motherless male ever successfully copulated, and such males often violently assaulted the female with whom they were paired. Females (those raised without mothers as well as those raised with cloth mothers) that were successfully impregnated and bore young, paid very little attention to their infants. A mother often brushed away her baby "as if she were brushing off flies" or crushed her infant to the floor, and these mothers rarely held their infants or protected them as normal mothers do.

The Harlows conclude: "We only know that these monkeys without normal mothering and without peer affectional relationships have behaved toward their infants in a manner completely outside the range of even the least adequate of normal mothers" (1961, p. 55).

In more recent studies, Professor Suomi of the University of Wisconsin Primate Laboratory and a student of Harlow, has confirmed the importance of the mother-infant relationship. Even brief separations from the mother have lasting effects. He further points out that peer relationships suffer if the individual does not have a good relationship with its mother (Greenberg, 1977).

His review of isolation studies has led Suomi to emphasize that social isolation initiated early in life can have devastating effects on subsequent development and behavior for many species of primates. The primate deprivation syndrome that results from early isolation is characterized by displays of abnormal self-directed and stereotypic behavior and by gross deficits in all aspects of social behavior (Suomi et al., 1983, p. 190).

Infants are mainly cared for by the mother, of course, but adult males are also known to take more than a casual interest. This phenomenon has frequently been noted among male hamadryas baboons, who sometimes "adopt" an infant. "He then carries it en route, allows it to sleep huddled against his belly at night, and prevents it from moving too far away" (Kummer, 1971, pp. 81–82). Even more dramatically in the New World, among marmosets and tamarins the males provide most of the direct infant care, carrying the infants everywhere, while only transferring them back to their mother for nursing.

What may be an extension of the mother-infant relationship has been called **alloparent**, or "aunt" behavior. This type of behavior occurs among many animal species but is most richly expressed in primates, and some researchers believe it is found among all social primates. Usually, the alloparents crowd around the infant and attempt to carry, cuddle, groom, hold, or just touch it. Some species, like the common langur, are well known for their aunts, and as many as eight females may hold the infant during its first day of life. Among patas monkeys, the mother may threaten a female that touches her baby, so the interested female resorts to a subtle maneuver. "A patas female may begin to groom a mother's arm and then slowly and cautiously transfer her grooming to the infant within it" (Kummer, 1971, p. 80).

Several functions are suggested for alloparenting. If the mother dies, the infant stands a chance of being adopted by an alloparent or other individual of the group. The practice may bind together the adults of the group, since it may be more convenient for the mother to leave her infant occasionally with another female. It may also assist the training of **nulliparous** females for motherhood.

Male-Female Relationship   A close sexual bond between adult males and females is not common among the higher primates, although it does occur. In one-male groups, the adult males keep females close by and maintain a very alert eye for any wandering adult male. Some researchers suggest that the one-male group is adaptive in arid regions where food is scarce and widely scattered, and attack by predators a constant peril. An adult male is protection for the females and offspring, and the structure of only one male to a group diminishes the consumption of reduced food resources.

Forest monkey groups, such as the black-and-white colobus and guenons, are also often composed of one-male groups. Here, scarcity of food is not a problem and predators, such as leopards, hunt by stealth. The best defense is constant vigilance by all concerned. The adult male's role, therefore, is minimal, and one male is adequate for protective and reproductive functions. And, as we shall see shortly, with only one male present, there is less competition for food, leaving more for females with dependent young.

The one-male/one-female "monogamous" or family group is characteristic of gibbons and siamangs (but not great apes), some monkeys, as well as the indri. This particular group composition can be understood in terms of adaptation to the environment. A gibbon family of one adult male, one adult female, and their offspring controls a small patch of tropical forest, which

Alloparent   An individual other than a parent who exhibits parental behavior.

Nulliparous   null: none, not any
parous: birth
Never having given birth.

Figure 9-10

Baboon male carrying an infant, an example of alloparenting.

provides enough food for a small group. Gibbons jealously protect this territory from neighbors. When a young gibbon reaches maturity, it is driven out by the adult of the same sex, thus maintaining the small size of the group and its limited food supply.

Special male-female bonds are also apparent in multimale/multifemale groups, although they may be less permanent than those just noted for one-male groups. In baboons, "friendships" may develop between adult males and adult females. Smuts (1985) has suggested that this arrangement provides protection for the female (against other males) and presumably increases sexual access for the male. Moreover, short-term consortships are seen both in baboons and especially in chimpanzees. Finally, close male-female bonding, reinforced by frequent sexual activity, has been observed among bonobos.

Role Separation between Adults and Young   Among primates, especially the anthropoids, there is a relatively long growth period spent in the protected environment of the social group. It is during this learning stage, when the young play and learn the skills needed in adulthood, that the intelligence characteristic of primates develops. Once the young begin to spend increasing amounts of time away from their mothers, they join with peers to form play groups. They play for many hours every day, learning many of the skills required by adults, free from anxiety because alert adults are always present. Dependent young stay very close to their mothers in almost constant physical contact. In most anthropoids, the young may ride on their mother's back for a period of several months and up to 3–4 years in gorillas and chimpanzees. The separation of roles between adults and young enable the young to learn and practice the social, intellectual, and physical skills they will need as adults.

Role Separation by Sex   Perhaps one of the most interesting points to be made about the separation of sex roles is that there is often very little separation. Except for the protective role played by males and the childbearing

Figure 9-11

Male baboon courting estrous female. Sexual dimorphism is readily apparent.

and nursing role of the mother, in many primate species both sexes perform similar functions. Females are expected to obtain their own food, as are juveniles after they are weaned, and there is little sharing of food.

Among terrestrial primates, there is very often a sexual dimorphism in body size, weight, muscularity, distribution of hair on the body, and size of canines. Usually associated with separate roles, the larger size (as in baboons and gorillas) enables the male to play a protective role relative to predators (in baboons) or other males of the species (in gorillas). The large size of males in some species is most likely the result of competition among males for reproductive access (called "sexual selection" by Darwin. In those species without sexual dimorphism, the females may be highly aggressive, as in gibbons, and join the males in defense of their territory.

Sociobiology

The sociobiological perspective has recently become widely used in biology. In the last 15 years, this approach has been applied to a wide variety of animals, including nonhuman primates (see Barash, 1982, for a good general review of sociobiology). Indeed, for primatological interpretations, **sociobiology** holds a central position as a theoretical framework for a majority of current researchers (for example, Richard, 1985; Richard and Schulman, 1982; Smuts et al., 1987; Small, 1984; Hausfater and Hrdy, 1984; Ghiglieri, 1984; Pusey and Packer, 1987; Smuts, 1987; Harvey et al., 1987). Beyond the suppositions concerning nonhuman primates, some contemporary scholars even go so far as to extend this field to the interpretation of *human* primates as well.* Naturally, not all primatologists, and certainly not all anthropologists, are sociobiologists. Indeed, sociobiology has created and continues to generate a great deal of controversy.

Sociobiology An evolutionary approach to the explanation of behavior, emphasizing the role of natural selection.

First brought to popular attention in 1975 by Harvard zoologist E. O. Wilson, this approach can be traced to the pioneering works of R. A. Fisher (1930), J. B. S. Haldane (1932), W. D. Hamilton (1964), G. C. Williams (1966), and Robert Trivers (1971, 1972). Following publication of Wilson's monumental synthesis, vehement arguments exploded both inside and outside academia. What has caused all this furor, and what relevance does sociobiology have to understanding primates, particularly human primates?

Sociobiologists are basically classical Darwinists, postulating the evolution of behavior through the operation of natural selection. Sociobiologists assume that, if any behavior has a genetic basis, its evolutionary impact will be directly measured by its effect on reproductive success. In other words, with behavioral phenotypes (just as with physical morphology), the success of genes underlying the phenotypes will be determined by their influence on reproduction. Individuals with genotypes coding for behaviors leading to higher reproductive success than other individuals will, by definition, be more fit. Consequently, they should pass on their genes at a higher rate. Sociobiologists believe genotypes have evolved in this way, producing such phenomena as sterile worker castes in bees, courtship dances in birds, and scent-marking in dogs. As a speculative model, this reasoning is all well and good. In fact, much of the theoretical way natural selection is discussed

*Some publications reflect this trend. See *Child Abuse and Neglect*, Gelles and Lancaster, 1987; *Parenting Across the Life Span*, Lancaster et al., 1987; *The Biology of Moral Systems*, Alexander, 1987; *Homicide*, Daly and Wilson, 1987; *Despotism and Differential Reproduction*, Betzig, 1987.

in Chapter 4 of this text utilizes terminology and concepts developed by sociobiologists.

When applied to relatively simple organisms—social insects, for example—sociobiological theory has proven of tremendous explanatory value. In fact, sophisticated molecular biological research with the DNA of marine snails has identified a family of genes that produces specific proteins whose combined action in turn governs the animal's egg-laying behavior (Scheller and Axel, 1984). This is of note because, for the first time, something that could be termed "complex" behavior has been traced to a specific genetic mechanism (that is, DNA sequences that have been decoded).

Of course, neither insects nor snails are mammals (to say nothing of primates). The major dispute arises, then, when trying to postulate the actual mechanics of behavioral evolution in complex social animals with flexible neurological responses like primates. Which behaviors among primates have a genetic basis, and how do these behaviors influence reproductive success?

In order to answer the first question, we will have to learn considerably more about genotype/phenotype interactions in complex traits. Such an understanding is probably decades away. To answer the second question, we will need accurate data on reproductive success in primate groups similar to that shown for birds in Chapter 4 (p. 100). As of yet, such data are almost completely lacking, but it is hoped this situation will be remedied in the near future. Thus, sociobiology as an *explanation* of primate behavior remains mostly a matter of open speculation. Application of evolutionary models specifically to explain human behavior are presently even more speculative.

Obtaining conclusive data for primates and other mammals, we will see, is no easy matter. A good starting point, however, is framing hypotheses concerning behavioral evolution on the basis of the evidence that does exist. A good example of such a perspective is Sarah Blaffer Hrdy's (1977) explanation of infanticide among langur monkeys of India.

Langurs typically live in social groups composed of one adult male, several females, and their offspring. Other males without mates associate in bachelor groups. These peripheral males occasionally attack, violently overthrow the previous reproductive male, and take over the group. Frequently following this oftentimes bloody contest, even more aggressive behavior ensues. The infants, fathered by the previous male, are attacked and killed. The adult females in the group usually try to interfere with the males' infanticidal intentions, but to little avail. In the end, most or all the infants are killed.

Why should langurs behave so? Are they not dooming their species to ultimate extinction by such destructive actions? The answer, according to sociobiologists, is *not* in terms of the species. Male langurs do not know they are members of so-and-so species, nor, if they did, would they care what its future would be. Natural selection theory, as clarified by sociobiology, teaches us that individuals act to maximize their *own* reproductive success, no matter what its ultimate effect may be on the species.

Ostensibly, that is exactly what the male langur is doing. By killing the infants, he avoids a two to three year wait before the females come back into estrus. Once the infants are dead, the females stop lactating and become reproductively accessible to the newly arrived male. He can then inseminate them much earlier than would have been the case had he waited while the young (in which he had no genetic interest) were reared.

We might reasonably ask why the females should allow their infants to be slaughtered. Actually, females do attempt to resist infanticide, but their

Figure 9-12

Langur monkeys.

efforts in the face of large, aggressive, and determined males usually fail. Interestingly, it is not the infant's mother who assaults the attacking male, but other females in the group. Some writers suggest that these females are closely related (sisters of the mother, for example) and, if so, sociobiological theory provides an explanation for such seemingly **altruistic** behavior. Since individuals share genes with close relatives, they can contribute to their *own* reproductive success by aiding their relatives' offspring.

In diploid species (like langurs, humans, and all vertebrates), individuals share, on the average, $\frac{1}{2}$ their genes with parents and, likewise, $\frac{1}{2}$ with full siblings. For example, when a langur defends her sister's offspring, she is helping contribute genes to the next generation; genes she shares in common with her nieces and nephews (on the average she shares $\frac{1}{4}$ her genes in common with them). In this way, genes that underlie such cooperative behavior may spread in populations.

Of course, there are many possible strategies. Aiding a relative does not always completely inhibit one's own reproduction. The success of an individual's genes (that is, one's fitness in natural selection terms) is then measured as the sum of one's own offspring *plus* those of close relatives ("discounted" according to how closely they are related: $\frac{1}{4}$ for her nieces and nephews, half-siblings, or grandchildren, $\frac{1}{8}$ for first cousins, etc.).

Langurs are, of course, not doing this consciously. As is true of the cooperative female defense efforts noted above, females are not making conscious choices as if they *knew* the alternatives. What occurs is simply that individuals who behave one way will have higher reproductive success than those individuals behaving in another way. Consequently, their genes (including any that underlie this behavior) are differentially passed onto the next generation, theoretically just another example of natural selection acting on phenotypic variation. In this case, behavior is the phenotype.

The social pattern among common (hanuman) langurs is not extremely clear-cut, and controversy thus exists regarding the observations and interpretations of infanticide in this species. Geographically, infanticide has been

Altruism   Helping others without direct benefit to oneself.

seen (or logically deduced) at three field sites, but has not been seen at two others. As a result, some experts (most notably, Boggess, 1984) have argued that infanticide is *not* that common, is not adaptive, and could better be described as a "social pathology." Nevertheless, it has been observed by other researchers (Struhsaker and Leyland, 1987) that female counter strategies (such as post-conception estrus) have developed among langurs, thus arguing against the social pathology hypothesis. As we will see shortly in our discussion of the limitations of sociobiological research (p. 256), controversies such as this are not easy to resolve.

Beyond langurs, however, it must be considered that infanticide is, after all, not that uncommon among primates. Infanticidal episodes have been observed (or surmised) in redtail monkeys, red colobus, blue monkeys (these three from studies at Kibale, see p. 240), savanna baboons, howler monkeys, gorillas, and chimpanzees (Struhsaker and Leyland, 1987), and have been documented in at least 84 human societies. Infanticide is not uncommon among nonprimate species as well (for example, cats and rodents). Interestingly, in the majority of these cases (chimps and humans are exceptions), infanticide occurred in conjunction with a male transfer into a group or a change in the status (and reproductive access?) of an adult male. Moreover, only exceedingly rarely has it been thought that a male was attacking one of his own offspring. (An instance, however, has been reported among chimpanzees.) In both these patterns, the circumstances under which infanticide is seen conform to the expectations of the Hrdy model (what could be termed "sexual selection").

Sociobiological interpretations have also been applied to a wide range of other behaviors seen in primates. For example, the extremely large testes of male chimpanzees have been explained as an adaptation to a fairly promiscuous mating pattern—where several males successively copulate with an estrous female (a kind of "sperm competition") (Popp and DeVore, 1979). Also, the differential ranging patterns of male and female orangutans have been viewed as the result of differing reproductive strategies between sexes and maximization of food resources (Galdikas, 1979).

MALE AND FEMALE REPRODUCTIVE STRATEGIES

The reproductive strategies of primates, especially how they differ between the sexes, has been a primary focus of sociobiological research. When we consider the tremendous degree of care required by young, growing primate offspring, it is clear that tremendous investment by at least one parent is necessary. Indeed, primates are among the most *K-selected* (that is, high parental investment in but a few young) of all mammals (see Box 9-2). And, most especially, it is usually the mother who carries most of the burden (before, of course, as well as after birth). Primate offspring are **altricial**; that is, they are helpless at birth and totally dependent upon their mothers. Not only does the mother provide nourishment, but the infant must be carried everywhere. The young develop slowly (particularly constrained by brain growth), and in so doing, are exposed to expanded learning opportunities within a *social* environment.

Such an interplay between behavior and biology has promoted a feedback relationship that has led to larger brains, even slower development, and yet more chances for learning. Particularly in the large-bodied hominoids (great apes and humans) and most dramatically of all in the hominid line, this trend has been further emphasized, eventually producing the distinctively human primate. Thus, what we see in ourselves and our closest primate kin (and

Altricial Dependent at birth. A relative measure. At the other end of the spectrum, we say young are "precocial." Among mammals, primates are relatively altricial.

Box 9-2   r- and K-Selection*

Differing reproductive strategies are found in various organisms and can influence numerous aspects of biology and behavior.

r-SELECTION   A strategy in which numerous offspring are born (or hatched) and usually mature rapidly. There is little parental investment in each. Moderate to high mortality is shown. Such strategies are seen in insects and most fish.

K-SELECTION   A strategy in which only a few young are born (or hatched) and take longer to mature (*in utero*, incubation, and afterward), thus considerable parental investment is involved in each. Consequently, mortality is fairly low. Such strategies are common to birds and mammals.

Note: Neither strategy is necessarily advantageous over the other. r-selection may work well in diverse and fairly rapidly changing environments, in which young disperse widely. K-selection, conversely, may work better in fairly stable environments.

You should realize, however, that insects are by far the fastest reproducers (r-selectionists *par excellence*) among animals and are probably the most successful animal form, if number of species, number of individuals, or biomass are taken as criteria. Even among the primarily K-selected mammals, the rodents (the most r-selected of the group) are probably the most successful.

_____

*The "r" and "K" are simply used as mathematical terms (that is, coefficients) and do not stand for anything themselves.

presumably in our more recent ancestors as well) is a strategy wherein a few "high quality," slowly maturing offspring are produced through extraordinary investment by the parent(s), usually the mother. Taken to an extreme, birth spacing (the time between live births following successful rearing or death of the previous offspring) is pushed to the limits in the great apes, with gorillas giving birth approximately every four years, chimps only every five to six years, and orangs even more slowly than this. Consequently, a female chimp may only have opportunities for about five live births in her entire reproductive life span, and certainly not all of these are likely to survive into adulthood (a female chimp with three grown children is doing very well indeed). Finding food, avoiding predators, finding mates, and especially, caring for and protecting the extremely dependent young are all difficult challenges for nonhuman primates. Moreover, among most contemporary species, males and females face and resolve these challenges by means of different strategies.

As a result of the heavy cost of carrying and caring for offspring, females especially are put under physiological stress. For the majority of nonhuman primates, females spend most of their adult lives either pregnant or lactating. Accordingly, the metabolic demands are quite high. A pregnant or lactating female primate, although perhaps only half the size of her male counterpart, may require about the same amount of calories per day. Even then, her physical resources may be drained over the long run. For example, analysis of chimpanzee skeletons from Jane Goodall's population at Gombe shows significant loss of bone and bone mineral in older females (Sumner et al., 1989).

It is not surprising, then, that considerable attention in current primatological research has been directed to the biological and social role of females. Sociobiological perspectives (with concentration on reproductive issues) have contributed to this trend (see Small, 1984). Early in the development of modern primate field studies, notably in discussions of savanna baboons, a definite male bias emerged. Workers seemed especially fascinated by the dominance interactions of the adult males, and consequently paid little attention to what the females were doing. Since 1970, however, the situation has been corrected, not the least reason being that much of the crucial research was done by female primatologists.

Male-male relationships are thus now only one aspect of what is considered important in defining nonhuman primate social behavior. As Alison Richard (1985, pp. 206–207) has suggested in describing primate reproductive behavior, "The following discussion focuses upon the reproductive life of female primates, therefore, and we shall simply assume that males provide willing and able partners when called upon."

Further, as mentioned in our discussion of primate ecology (see p. 242), there may be real differences in the ways male and female primates exploit their environments. Perhaps due to the higher energy/metabolic needs of females, it has been argued (Wrangham, 1980) that they must concentrate their efforts around high-yielding food patches (for example, particular fruiting trees). Since there is a limited number of such resources, females would tend to defend these areas against other females. However, in order to mount an effective defense, it may take more than one adult female. With whom, however, should an adult female associate? Here, too, sociobiology predicts a likely answer. In sharing resources, it would be most advantageous for an individual to bond with a close relative (for example, a sister). In so doing, not only her own offspring, but other young in the group (potentially her nieces, nephews, etc.) are related to her and share genes. As a result, a female's inclusive fitness (see Box 9-3) is increased.

Carrying this model further, the pattern of female-female kin-based social bonding may also help explain dispersal patterns among many primates (Pusey and Packer, 1987). In most species of Old World monkeys, it is the male who transfers (usually as a young adult). The long-term social core of the group is thus composed of females, who likely share some degree of genetic relatedness. Conversely, males who transfer *into* new groups are unlikely to share much genetic relatedness with other adults.

As we noted in Box 9-1, in several primate groups only one adult male is found socially bonded to a group of females. In these cases (for example, hamadryas baboons, patas monkeys, most groups of red colobus) at least one breeding male is required, of course, for reproductive purposes and possibly to aid in defense against predators. But why should females tolerate more than one adult male in their group? Again, sociobiological/socioecological perspectives can possibly explain the evolution of multimale societies among primates. Some resources are harder to defend, so females may, in a sense, "use" males to help aid in defense of food patches. In addition, for some animals, like savanna baboons, concerted action by numerous adult males apparently is crucial in predator defense.

We do not wish to convey an opposite bias to the early period of modern primatology by suggesting that *males* are doing next to nothing. In all primate societies, the interplay of behavior is extremely complex for *all* individuals. We, in fact, see a marked degree of variability among different species in male parental care, male dispersal, and ecological constraints.

We have observed that, in langurs, male and female reproductive interests may be quite different. Indeed, it has been argued that, in the long run, neither the reproduction of females *nor* males is really helped by infanticide. But in the short run, the presence of one infanticidal male in a group, potentially acting to serve his own reproductive interest, sets a whole chain of events in

Box 9-3   Sociobiological Concepts and Terminology

ALTRUISM   Self-sacrificing behavior (technically costly in Darwinian fitness). On the surface, it may appear harmful to the individual as, for example, in the case of sterile worker castes in social insects, such as bees. However, through behaviors that contribute to *inclusive fitness* (see below), genotypes might actually spread (through relatives), even though some individuals may have no offspring themselves.

COST/BENEFIT ANALYSIS   Borrowed from economic theory, this approach attempts to measure potential costs and benefits to individual reproductive success (or inclusive fitness) of certain behaviors. Though theoretically intriguing, in practice this is most difficult to apply.

DARWINIAN FITNESS   The proportional contribution of genes (compared to other individuals) as a measure of one's *individual* reproductive success (i.e., number of successful offspring). (See p. 100.)

FITNESS   Generally, a measure of reproductive success, relative to others in the group, taken as the lifetime contribution of genes to successive generations.

INCLUSIVE FITNESS   The *total* contribution of genes through offspring *and* other relatives. Relatives are devalued on the basis of closeness of genetic relatedness, which prompted the British biologist J. B. S. Haldane's famous quip, "I would gladly lay down my life for two sibs or eight cousins." This phenomenon, first clearly elucidated in social insects, may provide a clue to some forms of altruism.

KIN SELECTION   The process in which genes are contributed to successive generations through relatives other than offspring. In this way, *inclusive fitness* is improved.

NATURAL SELECTION   The process in which some genotypes (individuals) contribute genes disproportionately to successive generations as a result of differential net reproductive success (see p. 100).

PARENTAL INVESTMENT   Any behavior or contribution of a parent (gametes, energy, time, risk) to an offspring at the cost of investing in other offspring.

PROXIMATE EXPLANATION   A way to explain a behavior on the basis of immediate social/ecological/physiological factors. For example, an individual baboon may leave his natal group following a dominance encounter to avoid future encounters with particular older, larger, and more dominant males (see ultimate explanation).

REPRODUCTIVE VALUE   The *potential* remaining reproductive output of an individual. This can be assessed at different stages of the life cycle, so that a 15-year-old baboon female has less reproductive value than an 8-year-old baboon female.

SEXUAL SELECTION   The process by which certain physical traits or behavior evolve to facilitate success in competition among one sex for access to matings with the other sex. This notion was championed by Darwin. The large horns of the male mule deer or the large size and aggressive behavior in the male walrus are examples.

ULTIMATE EXPLANATION   The explanation of a behavior as coming about through natural selection (that is, differential reproductive success). As such, the behavior would become established only over a long period of time.

motion, so that other males are induced to behave similarly. Here, it is apparently the case that immediate, individual reproductive success can act to shape social determinants—even at the cost of the whole group, and perhaps even to the detriment of the *individuals* within the group as well. Glenn Hausfater, one of the leading researchers concerned with ascertaining reproductive success in primates, especially as related to infanticide, has put this relationship nicely:

> Thus, infanticide is an excellent example of a behavioral strategy that produces a short-term increase in reproductive success for some individuals of one sex but that thereby also locks adults of both sexes into patterns of behavior that ulti-

(a)

(b)

Figure 9-13

Primate mothers with nursing infants.

mately result in a decreased rate of reproduction for themselves and for their population as a whole. As with so many other examples in modern behavioral ecology, the present analysis of langur infanticide supports the prevailing notion that evolution does not favor behavior that is "good for the species," but rather behavior that is good for the individual and, moreover, "good" only in the short-run (Hausfater, 1984, p. 281).

Numerous other examples of variability of male/female strategies are known among primates. For example, in gibbons and some cebids (titis and owl monkeys) the typical social group is monogamous. Perhaps even more distinctive, in most callitrichids (marmosets and tamarins), two adult males regularly mate with one adult female (that is, they are **polyandrous**) (Goldizen, 1987). In all of these examples, typically it is the adult male(s) who is most responsible for parental care. In chimps yet another pattern is seen. Males are the ones who are tightly bonded (presumably for organized defense against other potentially aggressive males—see p. 281), and it is the females who disperse by transferring to a new group, usually when they are young adults.

Polyandrous poly: many
androus: males
Two or more males mating with one female.

Thus, as we have said before, there is no simple relationship of biology, ecology, and behavior among primates. Nor, obviously, can simplistic evolutionary scenarios adequately account for the diversity of behavior among primates. What makes sociobiology (and its ecological correlates) so important, however, is that it provides a framework to ask *relevant* questions, thus helping shape future research. Nevertheless, sociobiological interpretation has been subject to considerable criticism by other biologists and social scientists.

Primate Sociobiology—Limitations and Critiques

As we have seen, sociobiological interpretation has had dramatic impact on directions of current research—on reproductive strategies, male/female behavioral differences, ecological patterning, and much more.

However, sociobiologists have not been without their critics. Indeed, most primatologists who use theoretical models from sociobiology readily admit some of the current methodological shortcomings. For example, Richard and Schulman (1982, pp. 243–244), in a review of primate sociobiological research, list the following central problems for those attempting to apply this approach:

1. The lack of long-term data on the demography and social behavior of large groups of individually known animals
2. The lack of long-term, fine-grained data on the distribution of resources in time and space
3. The nearly complete absence of information on genetic relatedness through the male line
4. The difficulty in assigning reproductive and other costs and benefits to particular behaviors
5. Our almost total ignorance of the genetics of primate social behavior
6. The untestable nature, even under the best of conditions, of many sociobiological models

Some critics have gone even further to question the basic validity of sociobiology as a perspective. Eminent Harvard biologists Stephen Jay Gould and Richard Lewontin (1979) have portrayed sociobiology as a teological (circular-reasoned) pursuit. In making this point, Gould and Lewontin compare sociobiological adaptive "stories" to the wistful, naive renderings of Candide's sidekick, Dr. Pangloss (from Voltaire's classic satire *Candide*). Even in the most humiliating of circumstances, Pangloss would philosophize that, "All is for the best in the best of all possible worlds." In similar fashion, Gould and Lewontin see sociobiologists devising their scenarios to create perfectly adaptive situations.

Is natural selection indeed such a clearly self-perfecting process? Of course, no one can say for certain, since we see only a small slice of possible evolutionary strategies among living animals; but evidence does suggest that natural selection often works simply "to get by." In this way, a whole host of marginal traits and behaviors could endure for substantial periods of time. The recent lemurs of Madagascar (see p. 210) are a case in point.

Just a few hundred years ago, the island was inhabited by a host of different lemur species, but human intervention caused rapid extinction of many forms. Consequently, the survivors (like the indri) have probably moved into a variety of habitats from which competitors had once excluded them. Without such competition they now make do, but probably could not be described as particularly well adapted.

> The lemurs alive today inhabit forests from which many species, some of them probably competitors, have vanished. It is not difficult to imagine that the surviving lemurs have expanded their life-style to include foods and perhaps whole habitats from which they were once excluded by competitors. It does not matter that they do not make very good use of these new resources, so long as they do not have to compete with more efficient animals. In short, there is no reason to suppose that the distribution, feeding habits, and social organization of lemurs today are the results of long, slow evolutionary process, each species finely tuned to make the best of its environment. More likely, what we see are animals getting by and making ecological experiments after two thousand years of rapid evolutionary change (Richard, 1985, pp. 356–358).

Of course, this is not an evolutionary situation that has had much time to reach equilibrium. But when we look at *any* modern primate, can we be assured that they are not changing (perhaps rapidly)? Are they then showing particularly functional adaptations, and if so, to which circumstances? Are they in equilibrium? Have they ever been in equilibrium? Beyond these thorny theoretical difficulties, sociobiologists must address the type of information needed to test at least limited hypotheses. Presently, however, it is the lack of long-term precise data that most bedevils attempts to make sociobiology more scientific. As Sarah Blaffer Hrdy has noted:

> In order to evolve, strategies must on average increase the reproductive fitness of those animals who enact them. Nevertheless, small sample sizes and the near-total absence of lifetime reproductive output means that at this stage it is rarely possible either to confirm or exclude most of the hypothetical strategies being proposed. Furthermore, limited funds, limited hours, and most especially the rapid destruction of tropical forests together with their primate inhabitants make it unlikely that we will ever have such data for more than a few selected groups belonging to a handful of wild species. Hence a few long term studies, such as those carried out among the Amboseli baboons will loom large in interpretation of primate evolution (1984a, p. 106).

Indeed, among wild primates, the longest-term studies concern Old World monkeys (baboons at Amboseli or Gilgil in Kenya) or chimpanzees in Tanzania (Gombe and Mahale), but still encompass barely two complete generations. Data from captive (for example, Cayo Santiago) or heavily provisioned populations (for example, Japanese macaques) are more complete, but are difficult to interpret, given the potentially large disruption of behavior these animals have experienced.

Since primates (especially anthropoids) are so long-lived, as Hrdy notes, it may be difficult *ever* to get the kinds of data we really need to test sociobiological models adequately. For other animals (who reproduce faster) the situation is considerably better. Most notable is a population of red deer on an island off the coast of Scotland for which detailed records were kept on reproductive success of all individuals (over 200) for 12 years (Clutton-Brock et al., 1982).

Behavioral Data and Objectivity in Science Perhaps an even more nagging problem than lack of long-term data is the very nature of the information itself. Primates are highly complex animals. Their behavior does not reduce down to simple discrete categories that can readily be described. Indeed, for behavioral studies it is often the case that the kinds of data collected and conclusions reached are often the product of the kinds of questions asked, the methodologies employed, and perhaps most importantly (and underlying everything else), the particular training and orientation of the observer.

We do want to make it clear that most scientists attempt to be objective and, in fact, often recognize that they have biases that must be controlled. Moreover, the great majority of scientists are honest in the presentation of research findings. In those few cases where human failings have overwhelmed scientific objectivity, the perpetrators are usually culled out by other researchers, who constantly challenge ideas and in so doing try to advance the field.

Nevertheless, when dealing with mostly subjective data—such as that on primate behavior—it is often exceedingly difficult to resolve differences of opinion without years of data accumulation and at least some agreement on basic methodologies.

As Hrdy has courageously acknowledged concerning challenges to her interpretation of langur infanticide:

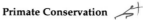

It has struck me more than once that critics of the sexual selection model some-times apply a double standard: The criteria for accepting negative evidence appear to be far less stringent than the criteria applied to support the sexual selection model. . . . My own writing errs in the opposite direction, a conse-quence of the evolutionary bias of my own world view (1984b, p. 317).

When researchers noted for integrity differ so profoundly not only over inter-pretation of the evidence but even on the point of what is admissible as evidence, we must look for underlying causes. Inevitably, what researchers see is affected by expectations about their natural world and the way that biological and social systems "ought" to work; the resulting disagreement will not be easily resolved. Often frustrating, invariably time-consuming and inefficient, such debates remain, nevertheless, the best antidote we possess against the biases implicit in every researcher's world view (1984b, p. 319).

Primate Conservation

Probably the greatest challenge facing primatologists of the next generation is the urgent need to find ways to preserve in the wild what is left of primate species. It cannot be overstated how imminent the danger is. Without massive changes in public opinion and in the economics of countries with surviving rainforests, it will not be long before there are few primates left in the wild.

Indeed, the problem ranges far beyond primates. Habitat destruction in rainforests rushes ahead at a startling rate, swallowing huge tracts of forests and annihilating *all* those populations within them. Tragically, these very areas are among the richest biological communities known, and include more than one-half of all mammalian and bird species. When one also in-cludes the vast number of insects found in these habitats, literally millions of different life-forms are threatened.

Perhaps it would be best to outline the dimensions of the crisis. Tropical rainforests once spanned vast areas of Central and South America, Central Africa (and Madagascar), and Southeast Asia (see Fig. 9-14). More than 90% of living primates live in what is left of these tropical forests, and they are vanishing rapidly. No precise estimates exist, as so many countries are involved, and national governments are, understandably, reluctant to reveal such details. In any case, researchers place the current rate of destruction at 25 to 50 million acres per year (or an area the size of New York State devas-tated every year!) (Mittermeier, 1982). Another way to look at it is to consider that anywhere between 12.5 and 100 acres are lost every minute (Lovejoy, 1982).

Much of the motivation behind the devastation of the rainforests is, of course, economic—the short-term gains from clearing forest to create imme-diately available (but poor) farmland or ranchland; from use of trees for lum-ber and paper products; or from large-scale mining operations (with their necessary roads, digging, etc., all of which cause habitat destruction). Regionally, the loss of rainforest ranks as a national disaster for some coun-tries. For example, the West African nation Sierra Leone had an estimated 15,000 square miles of rainforest earlier in this century. Today, only 535 square miles remain. At least 70% of this destruction has occurred since World War II (Teleki, 1986). People in the Third World are also short of fuel and most frequently use whatever firewood is obtainable. It is estimated that 1.5 billion people in the Third World are short of fuelwood (Mittermeier and Cheney, 1987).

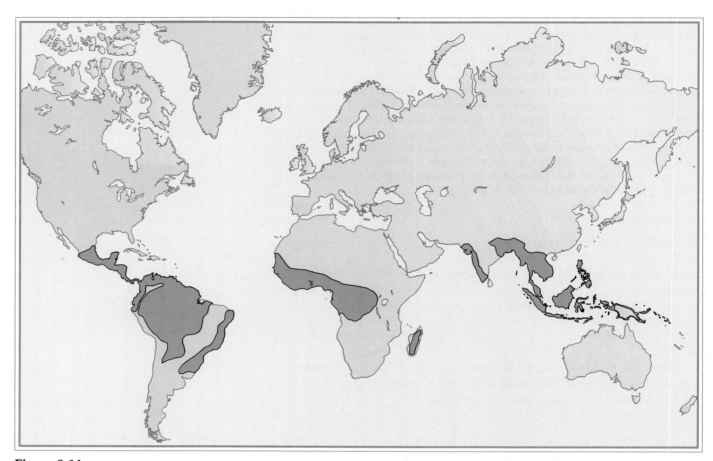

Figure 9-14

Tropical rainforests of the world (modern distribution before recent, massive destruction).

While habitat destruction is far and away the leading danger to contemporary nonhuman primates, assaults against them from other directions are happening as well. Primates in many areas are hunted for food, particularly in the Americas and western and central Africa. "Thousands are killed every year for the pot" (Mittermeier, 1982). Primates are also hunted for their pelts as, for example, the skins of black-and-white colobus monkeys. It is estimated that 2 million skins of this species alone were taken by hunters, primarily for sale in the United States and Europe, just in the last decade of the nineteenth century (Mittermeier, 1982).

Insofar as the food question is concerned, the choices for local human inhabitants are far from easy. Most tropical rainforests are located in Third World countries that face current massive overpopulation and continued high growth rates. Malnutrition and undernutrition are thus major problems, and are worsening. It is sobering to consider that the horrible starvation so well publicized in Ethiopia and Somalia in the last few years is probably just the tip of the iceberg. Starvation on a massive scale will almost certainly become commonplace in Africa (and elsewhere) before the end of this century.

Primates have also been captured live for zoos, biomedical research, and the exotic pet trade (see Issue, p. 230). The practice peaked in the mid-twentieth century and much of it involved the rhesus macaque for use in

Biography   Dian Fossey—A Hero for the Twentieth Century

Despite her articles, a well-received book, and her eighteen years of dedicated work with the wild mountain gorillas, Dian Fossey, ironically, came into the full glare of media attention only after her death on December 26, 1985. She was brutally murdered in her cabin at the Karisoke Research Center, Rwanda, Africa, which she established and directed.

Dian was born in San Francisco in 1932. As a child, she loved animals, but was only allowed to keep goldfish. She later said that the first trauma of her life was the death of her pet goldfish, a trauma that foreshadowed the later tragic and brutal death of her favorite gorilla (named Digit), in 1977.

Interrupting her career as an occupational therapist, Dian borrowed $8,000 in 1963 to go on a seven-week African safari. Her purpose was to observe animals, especially gorillas. There, she met renowned anthropologist Dr. Louis Leakey, who later sponsored her long-term study of mountain gorillas in the Virunga Volcanos, first in Zaire and then in the Parc National des Volcans in Rwanda.

Beginning in 1967, Dian achieved great success, and she came to understand gorilla behavior better than anyone else in the world. Living alone in her cabin, mostly isolated from her staff and occasional students, she became disillusioned with people who failed to share her concern for gorillas. Shortly before her death she told a reporter, "I have no friends. The more you learn about the dignity of the gorilla, the more you want to avoid people."

Increasingly over the years, Dian's concerns turned to what she termed "active conservation." She vigorously led and directed antipoaching patrols against native poachers who, with their snares for other game, posed the most severe threat to gorilla survival in the Virunga Volcanos.

While teaching briefly at Cornell University, Dian completed the book *Gorillas in the Mist*, which ap-

Dian Fossey.

peared in 1983. With this work, and *National Geographic* articles, public lectures, and television appearances, Dian tirelessly and effectively campaigned to educate the public to a better understanding of gorillas and their endangered plight in Africa.

For eighteen years Dian lived and worked heroically with mountain gorillas. Hopefully, she did not die in vain. The Rwandan government has indicated that not only will the research center she established be maintained, but it will be strengthened and enlarged. Perhaps in death Dian Fossey will achieve what eluded her in life: absolute protection for the mountain gorillas. In her devotion to these animals, Dian will be remembered for generations as one of the heroes of the twentieth century. Without her work, it is doubtful that mountain gorillas would have survived to the twenty-first.

Biruté M. F. Galdikas

medical research. Live capture has declined dramatically since the implementation of the Convention on Trade in Endangered Species of Wild Flora and Fauna (CITES) in 1973. Currently, 87 countries have signed the treaty, agreeing not to allow trade in species listed by CITES as being endangered. However, even some countries that are CITES members are still occasionally involved in illegal primate trade (Japan and Belgium, among others).

Box 9-4   Primates in Danger*

About one-fourth of all living primate species live on the African continent; that is, 50 to 60 of the world total of 180 to 200 species. Although Africa is a large continent, primates inhabit a relatively small area of it, and much of it is greatly threatened from expanding agriculture and commercial lumbering.

The basic problem in Africa can easily be seen from the following:

1. Forest land is diminishing; for example, of the 49,900 km² of forests in southern Ivory Coast in 1966, only 33,000 km² remained in 1974, a loss of 31% in only 8 years
2. The human population rate increased over 3% for the 1980–1990 decade
3. The food supply is decreasing because of environmental factors, inefficient agricultural techniques, and lack of capital resources. From 1970 to 1980, the annual increase in food production was –1.1% per capita

As a result of the increase in population and lack of a similar increase in the rate of food production, there is agricultural pressure on forests. Where pressures on forest land are not great, monkeys and apes are often hunted for food. It is possible that by the end of the century, 13 species of very distinct local populations could be extinct if significant action is not taken to reverse the forces currently acting against them.

In 25 years another 10 species will be in danger if current trends continue. An informed guess is that in 50 years time, in the absence of major conservation action, about *half the African primate fauna* could be extinct or verging on extinction.

What can be done? Some suggestions: identify the most urgent conservation priorities; educate all involved as to the meaning, value, and practice of primate (and other resource) conservation; establish more effective wildlife reserves in forest areas; work in close collaboration with African countries; demonstrate to Africans, especially residents of rural Africa, that conservation *can* provide them with tangible benefits.

*Adapted from John Oates.

African Primates in Danger of Extinction

Species/ Subspecies Common Name	Location	Estimated Size of Remaining Population	Species/ Subspecies Common Name	Location	Estimated Size of Remaining Population
Barbary macaque	North Africa	23,000	Preuss's red colobus	Cameroon	8000
Tana River mangabey	Tana R., Kenya	800–1100	Bouvier's red colobus	Congo Republic	?
Sanje mangabey	Uzungwa Mts., Tanzania	1800–3000	Tana River red colobus	Tana R., Kenya	200–300
Drill	Cameroon, Bioko	?	Uhehe red colobus	Uzungwa Mts., Tanzania	10,000
Preuss's guenon	Cameroon, Bioko	?	Zanzibar red colobus	Zanzibar	1500
White-throated guenon	Southwest Nigeria	?	Mountain gorilla	Virungavolcanoes (Rwanda, Uganda, and Zaire) and impenetrable forest (Uganda)	550–650
Pennant's red colobus	Bioko	?			

Faced with overwhelming economic hardship, cash-poor nations seek foreign investment and an influx of capital. But what do they have to offer that will produce ready cash? Their natural resources are their most immediately available commodity, so in reality their very landscapes are being chopped, packaged, and exported. This—as Sierra Leone illustrates—is only a stopgap, for in barely an instant resources will all be gone. In the face of such an onslaught, nonhuman primates are merely pawns in a worldwide catastrophe-in-the-making.

What, then, is the status of free-ranging primates today? Of the approximately 180–250 species, 67 (one out of three) are already considered endangered, and another 26 (one out of seven) are listed as *highly* endangered. These latter could be extinct by the end of the century (Mittermeier, 1982). "And, I must emphasize that these are minimum estimates . . . Almost every time a researcher goes out to study a poorly known species, we find that it is necessary to add yet another primate to the endangered list" (Mittermeier, 1982, p. 14).

There are no simple solutions. The world's booming human population, the uneven distribution of wealth among the world's peoples, and the understandable, but short-sighted, attempts by nations to maximize income all would seem to offer little hope for turning the situation around. It is obviously already too late for many species. What will the next few decades bring, and what will our descendants say of us?

Summary

We have seen in Chapter 8 that, structurally, the primate order is a most diverse group. In this chapter, we have seen that *socially* as well, primates are both complex and diverse. Indeed, the myriad demands of primate existence have produced these living forms through an integrated process of *biosocial* evolution.

While the scope of this book does not allow us to touch upon all the fascinating aspects of primatological research, we have introduced some of the more dynamic areas. In particular, we have showed that ecological challenges and how they act to influence primate social relationships are a central concern of current primatology. Another main focus of many contemporary researchers involves evolutionary explanations (through natural selection) of primate behavior. This approach, called sociobiology, is not without its drawbacks and its detractors, both within and outside primatology. Nevertheless, along with ecological considerations, such a perspective has allowed researchers to frame a whole array of new questions concerning primate behavior. We may never have complete answers to these questions, but we can gain useful information only by *attempting* to answer what we consider relevant questions. Such is the nature of science, particularly the science of behavior.

Beyond these methodological considerations, there are specific avenues of research that have been used to provide information on the evolution of human behavior. It is to this information that we turn in the next chapter.

Questions for Review

1. Discuss several reasons for studying nonhuman primates.
2. What features are unique to humans (or at least tend to distinguish humans from other primates)?
3. Why should primates be studied in free-ranging circumstances?
4. What are the primary methodological obstacles to studying free-ranging primates?
5. Given the methodological constraints, which primates are known best in free-ranging circumstances?
6. What major aspects of the environment are thought to influence social behavior of nonhuman primates?
7. Discuss how the study of the five species of primates in the Kibale Forest contributes to our understanding of primate socioecology.
8. What behavioral traits are common to all nonhuman primates?
9. What are the functions of grooming? Displays? Dominance?
10. Why is the mother-infant bond so crucial for primates?
11. What experimental evidence is there to argue for this strong mother-infant attachment?
12. What is the basis of sociobiology?
13. Discuss the sociobiological explanation for infanticide in langurs.
14. Give examples of how male and female nonhuman primates differ in their adaptive strategies.
15. Discuss some of the major limitations of sociobiological research.
16. What problems does artificial provisioning create?
17. Why have primatologists placed so much emphasis on socioecology in recent years?
18. Three types of nonhuman primate groups are given in Box 9-1. Can you give reasons for this variation in social organization in nonhuman primates?

Chapter 10

Contents

Primate Models for Human Evolution

Disease and Injury among the Gombe Chimpanzees:
Evidence from the Skeleton

Chapters 9 and 10 focus on primate behavior as ascertained through *behavioral* studies of free-ranging animals. In this primatological approach, generalizations regarding behavior, ecology, social structure, status hierarchies, and so forth are gleaned from field observations of living animals.

Another approach, one that uses the skills of skeletal biology, can also be utilized. We discussed in the Issue for Chapter 6 some of the techniques and concerns of skeletal biologists who study *human* remains. Similar methodologies can be used to study patterns of disease and injury in nonhuman primates as well. In this way, information not normally available to the field observer can be used to complement behavioral data.

Jane Goodall's chimpanzee research project at Gombe National Park (the longest-term study of any free-ranging nonhuman primate) has also been the source of a remarkable collection of chimpanzee skeletons. In those instances where chimpanzee bodies were recovered soon after death, the remains were placed in special containers and allowed to decompose. Later, the bodies were cleaned of remaining soft tissue and sent to the United States for curation (and now the collection comprises more than 20 skeletons). What makes these bones so important is that for many individuals their histories (including age at death, disease episodes, traumatic incidents, reproductive status) are known in great detail. Accordingly, the skeletal data can be used to illu-

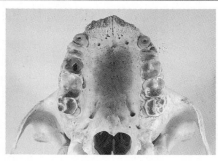

Figure 1

Upper dentition in the chimpanzee Flo, an old female, showing severe wear and other complications.

minate and supplement the behavioral information regarding many aspects of chimpanzee "life history."

At Gombe (as well as in many free-ranging animals *and* preindustrial human populations), the most common type of skeletal problems are found in the dentition. In all the older individuals at Gombe (those estimated at over 39 years of age), severe dental wear, abscesses, and loss of teeth are widely manifested in the dentition (Kilgore, 1989). One female named Flo, probably the oldest individual in the sample (and the

most famous), is estimated to have been at least 43 years old at death (Goodall, 1986); however, she may have been even older, perhaps close to 50 (Goodall, personal communication). At the time of her death this aged female showed severe dental wear, had lost several teeth, and displayed a total of nine dental abscesses (Fig. 1). Such severe dental problems could easily have compromised Flo's ability to process food, and thus may well have been a contributory cause to her death.

Other studies of the Gombe skeletons have shown that older chimpanzees, especially females, suffer considerable loss of bone mass—perhaps as a result of the demands of pregnancy and lactation (Sumner et al., 1989). In addition, detailed study of two Gombe adult females who suffered from polio also has provided insights into comparative disease mechanisms among apes and humans (Morbeck et al., 1991).

Another common health problem at Gombe is trauma (serious injury due to accidents or interpersonal aggression). Of the 12 fairly complete adult skeletons available for analysis, 10 show some indication of trauma (Jurmain, 1989; Jurmain, n.d.). Some of these injuries are clearly due to severe falls. For example, the old male Hugo (estimated at 39 years at death) has a crushed right ankle (calcaneus; see Fig. 2), probably resulting from landing on his right leg after a considerable fall. Goodall (personal communication) observed that Hugo limped into camp one day and continued to limp for several weeks. Another probable

Figure 2

Left and right calcanei (ankle bones) in Hugo, an adult male. The right ankle is crushed, probably from a fall.

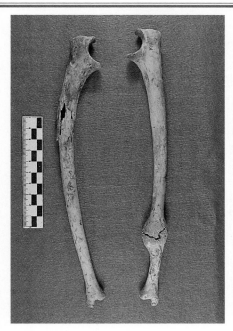

Figure 3

Right and left ulnae in Madam Bee, an adult female, showing a partially healed fracture of the right side (on the right). The bone may have been broken in the attack that resulted in her death.

victim of a severe fall was Flo, who shows a well-healed fracture of her right clavicle (collarbone). Serious falls are probably not particularly uncommon among arboreal primates (as has been suggested previously from a study of gibbon skeletons). Indeed, Goodall (1986) presents data from a two-year period in which 51 falls were observed. Of 36 falls where distance was noted, 13 were over 33 feet (10 meters). Moreover, two individuals (one infant, one adult) are known

to have died from falls. During early human evolution, when hominids were still at least partially exploiting arboreal habitats, the risks of serious falls must have also been a factor.

One partially healed injury bears testimony to the violent interpersonal nature of some social interactions at Gombe. As discussed in this chapter (pp. 281–282), in the early 1970s the Gombe community split into two groups. In the next few years numerous violent attacks (on the smaller southern community) were witnessed, some of which proved lethal. In the end (by 1977), all but one of the 10 members of the splinter group had either been killed or had disappeared (and were presumed dead). One of the victims was a female, Madam Bee (aged 28 at death). The ferocity and duration of many of these attacks startled the researchers and their reports are among the most poignant accounts in primatological literature.

Between September, 1974, and September, 1975, Madam Bee was *seen* to be attacked four separate times. Additionally, the observers believed she was attacked other times as well. The final assault proved fatal. During this incident she was violently beaten by several males who struck her, stamped repeatedly on her, and dragged her along the ground.

The scars of Madam Bee's violent death are clearly seen in her skeleton. Her right forearm (ulna) has a partially healed fracture, which was completely separated at the time it was first inspected in the laboratory (Fig. 3).

Apparently, the forearm had been fractured a few weeks prior to her death (probably in one of the unwitnessed attacks) and appears to have been broken again during the final, fatal attack. It is revealing to note that the field reports record that dur-

ing the last attack Madam Bee was dragged for some distance by one arm (a trauma that could easily have separated her partially healed ulna). Thus, the skeletal data further supports and supplements the behavioral observations. The incident that led to the initial fracture was not seen, but it had important consequences for this unfortunate female chimp. That Madam Bee would have spent her last weeks trying to move about with one forelimb fractured and the other partially paralyzed (from a bout with polio in 1966) would explain her extremely emaciated appearance prior to the fatal attack in September, 1975.

Further telltale clues are also seen in the skeletons of other Gombe chimpanzees. In two individuals apparent bite wounds are found; one injury is unhealed (another fatality of the intergroup attacks), while the other shows evidence of considerable healing (Fig. 4)—at a

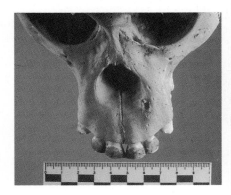

Figure 4

Healed bite wound in McDee, an adolescent male.

time *prior* to field documentation of any of the types of interpersonal aggression noted above. Thus, again, the skeletons tell us stories of the lives and deaths of primates in the wild. When such skeletal evidence is correlated with comprehensive behavioral data (so extraordinarily well documented at Gombe), the picture becomes more complete and more compelling. Nevertheless, even for nonhuman primate populations for which little or no behavioral data exist, similar approaches by skeletal biologists can yield fascinating and otherwise unobtainable information (Lovell, 1990).

SOURCES

Goodall, Jane, *The Chimpanzees of Gombe. Patterns of Behavior*. Cambridge, Mass.: The Belknap Press of Harvard University, 1986.

Jurmain, R., "Trauma, Degenerative Disease, and Other Pathologies among the Gombe Chimpanzees," *American Journal of Physical Anthropology*, 80: 229–237, 1989.

Jurmain, R., "Patheopathology: Approaches to the Study of Disease in Nonhuman Primates and Humans," *Evolutionary Anthropology*, n.d.

Kilgore, L., "Dental Pathologies in Ten Free-Ranging Chimpanzees from Gombe National Park, Tanzania," *American Journal of Physical Anthropology*, 80: 219–227, 1989.

Lovell, N., *Patterns of Injury and Illness in Great Apes. A Skeletal Analysis*. Washington, D.C.: Smithsonian Institution Press, 1990.

Morbeck, M. E., A. Zihlman, D. Sumner, and A. Galloway, "Poliomyelitis and Skeletal Asymmetry in Gombe Chimpanzees," *Primates*, 32: 77–91, 1991.

Sumner, D. R., M. E. Morbeck, and J. Lobick, "Apparent Age-related Bone Loss Among Adult Female Gombe Chimpanzees," *American Journal of Physical Anthropology*, 79: 225–234, 1989.

Introduction

One characteristic that distinguishes primates, as a group, from other mammals is increased neurological complexity. Such physiological development is directly reflected in behavioral complexity or, to put it simply, intelligence. The predilection to live in social groups was one of several factors that provided selective pressures favoring intelligence, especially *social* intelligence, as an adaptive strategy for primates.

Primates exhibit a propensity for forming long-term social bonds that frequently include complex alliances and friendships. This predisposition for complex social life provided a foundation for the evolution of the earliest hominids. One of the hallmarks of later hominid evolution is increased relative brain size, but the foundations of neurological complexity were laid long before bipedal hominids made stone tools. Those foundations are still evident today in behavioral patterns shared by human and nonhuman primates.

Within the social sciences, human behavior has traditionally been considered separately from that of all other organisms, even other primates. This perspective has consistently avoided biological explanations for human behavior, emphasizing that most (if not all) of human behavior is *learned*.

Certainly, human behavior *is* predominantly learned. But the *ability to learn* and behave in complex ways is ultimately rooted in biological (genetic) factors, and natural selection has favored increased learning capacities and behavioral modification in the human lineage.

In the last two decades there has been a growing consensus, particularly among primatologists, that certain human predispositions reflect patterns also seen in other primates. Moreover, because we do share an evolutionary history with oher primates, a useful approach in developing a better understanding of the evolution of human behavior is to identify in other species those factors that also produced specific patterns in humans. This approach places human behavior, although unarguably unique, within a biological and evolutionary context. (Note: see the discussion of sociobiology in Chapter 9, pp. 249–259.

A biological perspective does not assume that all human abilities and behavioral patterns are genetically determined or unalterable. Rather, such an approach aids in explaining *how* certain patterns may have come about, and what their adaptive significance might be. Within this framework, the plasticity of human behavior is clearly recognized and emphasized.

As Hinde (1987, p. 413) warns, "Attempting to draw parallels in behavior between human and nonhuman species is a dangerous pastime." Hinde proceeds to caution that, owing to the number and diversity of both primate species and human cultures, it is not difficult to find comparable behaviors in nonhuman and human primates. Once shared behavioral patterns have been identified, it is easy to support almost any hypothesis one develops, regardless of its validity. However, as Hinde further emphasizes, if one recognizes the risks and limitations of drawing comparisons between species, investigations of shared behavioral *patterns* and principles can be a fruitful endeavor.

All the considerations discussed in this chapter regarding the evolution of social behavior in *all* primates (including humans) are ultimately grounded physiologically in the central nervous system. Moreover, the physiological organization of primate neurology is, in turn, directly correlated with growth development, body size, and metabolism, all components of what primatologists have termed "life history."

What follows in this chapter are a few of the many examples of nonhuman primate development and social behavior believed by researchers to have implications for human behavior. Some topics are controversial, and all interpretations are somewhat theoretical. Nevertheless, all the perspectives are significant for achieving the central goal of this book, namely, understanding human evolution.

Aspects of Life History and Body Size

Life history Basic components of an animal's development and physiology, viewed from an evolutionary perspective. Such key components include body size, proportional brain size, metabolism, and reproduction.

In the last decade, primatologists have become increasingly interested in broad generalizations regarding primate life styles, maturation, and reproduction, topics that are all subsumed under the category **life history**. A crucial factor that crosscuts all these aspects of life history is body size. By *body size*, we mean some overall measure of body mass, sometimes given as a linear measure, such as stature, but (more critically) some estimate of weight. In modeling significant features of human evolution, a broad comparative perspective using data from other primates can be useful. We can obtain rough estimates of the body size of ancient hominids from preserved skeletal evidence, especially through extrapolation from joint size. In those rare instances where partial (or even mostly complete) skeletons are preserved, details concerning limb proportions, relative brain size, and so forth can also be tentatively determined. As we will see in succeeding chapters, there are two quite famous partial skeletons (both from East Africa) now available for such reconstruction.

Among living primates body size is extraordinarily diverse, ranging from the tiny mouse lemur (66 grams; 2.4 ounces) to the massive gorilla (117 kilograms; 258 pounds). And, of course, there is an array of species falling all along the spectrum between these extremes. Several critical features of primate life history are correlated with variation in adult body size. For example, small-bodied species tend to specialize in insectivorous diets, while only larger-bodied species are leaf eaters (that is, folivorous). It should be noted that almost *all* species eat some fruit, but how this component is *supplemented* varies considerably and is correlated with body size. Supplementing a diet made up largely of fruits is necessary, for while they are high in calories, fruits lack protein. Primates thus acquire protein from other sources—insects, young buds, leaves, and shoots. In addition, some highly specialized species exploit exudates; that is, tree gums.

Small animals have very high energy needs (per unit of body mass), and for them, insects are an extremely efficient source of calories and protein. However, an animal can capture only so many insects per day, thus placing an upper limit on body size for species that rely heavily on insects to supplement their diet.

On the other hand, to process leaves (especially mature leaves containing cellulose), an animal needs a specialized gut—with unusually long intestines and/or fermentation chambers. This physiological adaptation is necessary to digest large amounts of low-energy food, giving microorganisms (bacteria) the opportunity to break down cellulose and neutralize plant toxins. Clearly, it takes a relatively large animal to house a large gut. As a general rule, primarily insectivorous primates weigh less than 1.1 pounds (500 grams), while most folivores are 10 times larger, exceeding 11 pounds (5 kilograms) (Aiello, 1992).

Tied closely to these dietary factors, body size is also correlated with metabolic rate. The larger an animal, the more efficient its thermal control (see Bergmann's rule, Chapter 6), and thus proportionally the lower its metabolic rate. "Thus large animals expend less energy and consequently need less food than small animals. Put more simply, two 5-kg (11-pound) monkeys require more food than a single 10-kg (22-pound) monkey" (Fleagle, 1988, p. 233). The content of the diet also frequently correlates with metabolism (usually measured as basal metabolic rate). On average, folivores have a lower metabolism than other primates—an especially relevant factor when controlling comparisons for animals of roughly equal body size.

Locomotion and habitat (substrate) preference, too, are partly correlated with overall body size. Most arboreal primates are small and practice some leaping. Those that are somewhat larger but still arboreal tend to exhibit more suspensory behavior, and the largest primates of all tend to be at least partly terrestrial. Primates that weigh over 22 pounds (10 kilograms) are almost always *primarily* terrestrial in their habitat preference. These relationships, however, are not quite this simple. Adaptive solutions such as locomotory behavior are always compromises among competing requirements. While large size might help a primate be more efficient in metabolism, it hinders arboreal locomotion—and might even preclude access to some of the most nutritious food items, located at the ends of small terminal branches. On the ground, larger size might, in some cases, discourage predators, but it will also, at the same time, make the animal more conspicuous.

BODY SIZE AND BRAIN SIZE

Body size is closely correlated with brain size. Clearly, an animal the size of a chimpanzee (100 pounds) has a larger brain than a squirrel monkey (adult weight, 2 pounds). However, in making such a superficial comparison of *absolute* brain size, one is ignoring the more important consideration of *proportional brain size.*

Moreover, it has been known for some time that, in mammals in general, not only is brain size tied directly to body size, but the relationship is not completely linear. In other words, in cross-species comparisons, as body weight increases, brain size does not necessarily increase at the same rate.

The predictable relationship between body and brain size has been called the index of **encephalization** (Jerison, 1973). The degree of encephalization can be a very powerful analytical tool, as it provides a gauge of the expected amount of brain for any given body size. Most primates fall close to the predicted curve, but there is one notable exception: *Homo sapiens.* Modern humans have a brain size well beyond that expected for a primate of our body weight. It is this *residual* degree of encephalization that must be explained as a unique and central component of recent human evolution. Using these same analytical perspectives as applied to the fossil materials in the next several chapters, you will see that earlier members of genus *Homo* as well as more primitive hominids (*Australopithecus*) are not nearly as encephalized as modern *H. sapiens.*

Timing of growth also provides an interesting contrast. In nonhuman primates, the most rapid period of brain development occurs either before or immediately after birth. In humans, rapid growth occurs at *both* developmental stages—so that already large-brained neonates continue to show considerable brain expansion for at least the first year after birth. The metabolic

Encephalization The proportional size of the brain relative to some other measure, usually some estimate of overall body size.

Allometry   Also called "scaling," allometry is the differential proportion among various anatomical structures. For example, the relative size of the brain changes during the development of an individual. Moreover, scaling effects must also be considered when comparing species.

Figure 10-1

Rhesus macaque male open mouth threatens another male.

Communication   Any act that conveys information, in the form of a message, to another. Frequently, the result of communication is a change in the behavior of the recipient. Communication may not be deliberate in that it may be the result of involuntary processes or a secondary consequence of an intentional action.

Autonomic   Autonomic responses are physiological manifestations not under voluntary control. An example in chimpanzees would be the erection of body hair during excitement. An example in humans is blushing. Both convey information regarding emotional states but neither is a deliberate behavior and communication is not intended.

costs of such rapid and sustained neurological growth are enormous, sapping more than 50% of the infant's metabolic output (Aiello, 1992).

Carefully controlled comparisons are essential in making cross-species generalizations regarding animals of differing body sizes (a point to keep well in mind when we discuss early hominids, most of which varied notably from *Homo sapiens* in body size). Such controls relate to considerations of what is called *scaling*, or (more technically) **allometry**. These allometric comparisons have now become increasingly important in understanding contemporary primate life history variables and adaptations. Moreover, similar approaches, as directly borrowed from these primate models, are now also routinely applied to interpretation of the primate/hominid fossil record.

Communication

Communication is universal among animals and is accomplished by means of an array of scents, behaviors, and **autonomic** responses. Any act that communicates, by definition *conveys meaning and influences the behavior of others;* however, communication may or may not be deliberate on the part of the performer.

Largely unintentional behaviors, such as body posture, convey information about an animal's emotional state. For example, a crouched position indicates a certain degree of insecurity or fear, while a purposeful striding gait implies confidence. Likewise, autonomic responses to threatening or novel stimuli, such as raised body hair (in most species) or enhanced body odor (in gorillas), indicate fear or excitement.

Over evolutionary time, those behaviors and motor patterns that originated in specific contexts assumed increasing importance as communicatory signals. For example, crouching initially aided in avoiding physical attack. In addition, this behavior conveyed that the individual was fearful, submissive, and nonaggressive. Thus, crouching became valuable not only for its primary function, but for its communicatory role as well, and natural selection increasingly favored it for this secondary role. In such a manner, over time, the expression of specific behaviors may thus become elaborated or exaggerated because of their value in enhancing communication.

Among the more deliberate primate behaviors that serve as communication are a wide variety of gestures, facial expressions, and vocalizations, some of which we humans share. Among many species, a mild threat is indicated by an intense stare. (For this reason, people should avoid eye contact with captive primates.) Humans, too, glare to show disapproval, and certainly we find prolonged eye contact, particularly with strangers, very discomforting. Some other primate threat gestures (not typical of humans) include: a quick yawn to expose canine teeth (baboons, macaques) (Fig. 10-1); bobbing back and forth in a crouched position (patas monkeys); and branch shaking (many monkey species, chimpanzees).

There are also behaviors to indicate submission, reassurance, or amicable intentions. In addition to crouching, baboons indicate submission by turning their hindquarters toward another. Chimpanzees may bend at the waist and bob the upper body.

In many species, reassurance takes the form of touching, patting, hugging, or holding hands (Fig. 10-2). As already mentioned in Chapter 9, grooming also serves in a number of situations to indicate submission or reassurance.

A wide variety of chimpanzee and bonobo facial expressions indicate emotional states (Fig. 10-3). These include the well-known play face (also

(a)   (b)

seen in several other species, including a modified form in humans) associated with play behavior; and the fear grin (seen in many primates) to indicate fear and submission.

By describing a few communicative behaviors shared by many primates (including humans), we do not intend to convey that these gestures are dictated solely by genetic factors. Indeed, if primates are not reared within a relatively normal social context, such behaviors may not be performed appropriately, for their contextual manifestations are *learned*. But, the underlying *predisposition* to learn and use them, and the motor patterns involved in their execution, are genetically influenced, and these factors do have adaptive significance. Therefore, theories about how such expressive patterns evolved focus upon motor patterns and the original context in which they occurred.

Primates (and other animals) also use **displays**; that is, repetitively elaborated combinations of gestures and movements in communication. Moreover, many complex displays incorporate various combinations of **ritualized** behaviors.

Common gorilla displays are chest slapping and the tearing of vegetation to indicate excitement or threat. Likewise, a chimpanzee may threaten an opponent by screaming and waving its arms, sometimes while brandishing

Figure 10-2

(a) Adolescent male savanna baboons holding hands; (b) male chimpanzee (at left) touches outstretched hand of crouching, submissive female in a gesture of reassurance.

Displays   Sequences of stereotyped behaviors that serve to communicate emotional states. Nonhuman primate displays are most frequently associated with reproductive or agonistic behavior.

Ritualized behavior   Ritualized behaviors are exaggerated and removed from their original context to convey information.

Relaxed   Relaxed with dropped lip   Horizontal pout face (distress)   Fear grin (fear/excitement)   Full play face

Figure 10-3

Chimpanzee facial expressions. (Redrawn from Goodall, 1986)

sticks and branches (Fig. 10-4). These actions may all be seen as *intention movements* that originated as sequences of motor patterns involved in actual fighting or attack.

Mounting, as seen in baboons, is a good example of a *ritualized* behavior (Fig. 10-5). Higher-ranking individuals mount the hindquarters of more subordinant animals in the manner of copulation, not to mate, but to express dominance. (It should be noted that when mounting serves a communicatory function, mounters and mountees may be members of the same sex.) In most anthropoid species characterized by one-male or multi-male, multi-female groups, males (the mounters in the mating context) are socially dominant to females. Thus, in the context of communication, the mounter assumes the male reproductive role. Likewise, presentation of the hindquarters in solicitation of mounting indicates submission or subordination by the mountee. As communication, these behavior patterns are entirely removed from their original (reproductive) context, and they function rather to reinforce and clarify the respective social roles of individuals in specific interactions.

As already emphasized, group living is crucial to survival for most primates. Living in groups provides better protection from predators and facilitates protection of resources. But social living also has drawbacks, for in groups there is competition for resources and position within dominance hierarchies (Walters and Seyfarth, 1987). Therefore, the group must maintain a balance between competitive and cooperative behaviors, and these goals are achieved through communication.

Efficient communication facilitates social life and, indeed, it makes social life possible. Therefore, natural selection has favored not only the elaboration and ritualization of many gestures and displays, but also the complexity of the neurological structures that underlie them.

The traditional view has been that nonhuman communication consists of mostly involuntary vocalizations and actions that convey information solely about the emotional state of the animal (anger, fear, and so on). Nonhuman

Figure 10-4

Male chimpanzee displays at public at San Francisco Zoo.

Figure 10-5

One young male savanna baboon mounts another as an expression of dominance.

Figure 10-6

Group of free-ranging vervets.

animals were not considered capable of communicating about external events, objects, or other animals, either in close proximity or removed in space or time. For example, it was assumed that when a startled baboon barks, its fellow baboons know only that is startled. What they do not know is what elicited the bark, and this they can only ascertain by looking around. In general, then, it has often been stated that nonhuman animals, including primates, use a *closed system* of communication, where the use of vocalizations and other modalities does not include references to specific external phenomena.

In recent years, these views have been challenged. For example, it is now known that vervet monkeys (Fig. 10-6) use specific vocalizations to refer to particular categories of predators, such as snakes, birds of prey, and leopards (Struhsaker, 1967; Seyfarth, Cheney, and Marler, 1980a, 1980b). When researchers made tape recordings of various vervet alarm calls and played them back within hearing distance of free-ranging vervets, they observed differing responses to various calls. In response to leopard-alarm calls, the monkeys climbed trees; eagle-alarm calls caused them to look upward and run into bushes; and snake-alarm calls elicited visual searching of nearby grass.

These results demonstrate that vervets use distinct vocalizations to refer to specific components of the external environment. These calls are not involuntary, and they do not refer solely to the emotional state (alarm) of the individual (although this information is also conveyed). While these significant findings dispel certain long-held misconceptions about nonhuman communication (at least for some species), they also indicate certain limitations. Vervet communication is restricted to the present—so far as currently established, no vervet can communicate about a predator it saw yesterday or one it might see in the future.

Other studies have demonstrated that numerous nonhuman primates, including, among others, cottontop tamarins (Cleveland and Snowdon, 1982), red colobus (Struhsaker, 1975), and gibbons (Tenaza and Tilson, 1977), produce distinct calls that have specific references. There is also growing evidence that many birds and some nonprimate mammals use specific predator alarm calls (Seyfarth, 1987; Hensen, 1992).

In contrast to that of other species, human communication or *language* employs a set of either written or spoken symbols that refer to concepts, other people, objects, and so on. This set of symbols is said to be *arbitrary*, in that it has no inherent relationship to whatever it stands for. For example, the English word *flower* when written or spoken, neither looks, smells, nor feels like the thing it represents.

Humans can recombine their linguistic symbols in an infinite variety of ways to create new meanings and can use language to refer to events, places, objects, and people far removed in both space and time. For these reasons, language is described as an *open* system of communication, based upon the human ability to think symbolically.

Language, as distinct from other forms of communication, has been considered a uniquely human achievement, setting humans apart from all other species. But, work with captive apes has raised doubts about certain aspects of this supposition. While many people remain skeptical about the capacity of nonhuman primates to use language, reports from psychologists (especially those who work with chimpanzees) leave little doubt that apes can learn to interpret visual signs and use them in communication.

No mammal, other than humans, has the ability to speak. However, the fact that apes cannot speak has less to do with lack of intelligence than to differences in the anatomy of the vocal tract and *language-related structures in the brain*.

Because of failed attempts by others to teach young chimpanzees to speak, psychologists Beatrice and Allen Gardner designed a study to test language capabilities in chimpanzees by teaching an infant female named Washoe to use ASL (American Sign Language for the deaf). Beginning in 1966, the Gardners began teaching Washoe signs in the same way parents would instruct a deaf human infant (Fig. 10-7). In just over three years, Washoe acquired at least 132 signs. "She asked for goods and services, and she also

Figure 10-7

Washoe signing "hat" when questioned about a woolen hat.

asked questions about the world of objects and events around her" (Gardner et al., 1989, p. 6).

Years later, an infant chimpanzee named Loulis was placed in Washoe's care. Researchers wanted to determine if Loulis would acquire signing skills from Washoe and other chimpanzees in the study group. Within just eight days Loulis began to imitate the signs of others. Moreover, Washoe also deliberately *taught* Loulis some signs. For example, instructing him to sit ". . . Washoe placed a small plastic chair in front of Loulis, and then signed CHAIR/SIT to him several times in succession, watching him closely throughout" (Fouts et al., 1989, p. 290).

There have been other chimpanzee training experiments. The chimp Sara, for instance, was taught by Professor David Premack to recognize plastic chips as symbols for various objects. The chips did not resemble the objects they represented. For example, the chip that represented an apple was neither round nor red. Sara's ability to associate chips with concepts and objects to which they bore no visual similarity implies some degree of symbolic thought.

Another chimp, Lana, worked with a specially designed computer keyboard. After six months, Lana recognized symbols for 30 words and was able to request food and answer questions through the computer (Rumbaugh, 1977).

Dr. Francine Patterson, who taught ASL to Koko, a female lowland gorilla, claims that Koko uses more than 500 signs. Furthermore, Michael, an adult male also involved in the gorilla study, has a considerable sign vocabulary, and the two gorillas communicate with each other via signs.

Questions have been raised about these types of experimental work. Do gorillas and chimpanzees really understand the signs they learn, or are they merely imitating their trainers? Do they learn that a symbol is a name for an object or, simply, that executing that symbol will produce that object?

The researchers who directed these projects are convinced that apes demonstrate at least a limited capacity to use signs to communicate. From an evolutionary perspective, these experiments may suggest clues to the origins of human language. Humans are the only species in which individuals *spontaneously* develop language simply through exposure and without being deliberately taught. However, there is now abundant evidence to argue that humans are not the only species capable of at least some degree of symbolic or representational thought, and it seems clear that the distinctions between humans and other species are not as absolute as most people have previously thought.

As communication became increasingly important during the course of human evolution, natural selection favored anatomical and neurological changes that enhanced our ancestors' ability to use spoken language. However, this trend would not have been possible if early hominids had not already been predisposed to language development. Many of the survival skills we see in modern primates were present in our prehominid ancestors. In other words, the common ancestor we share with the African great apes was a highly intelligent animal, capable of complex and efficient forms of communication (as are all its modern descendents).

In nonhuman primates, vocalizations are not completely controlled by the **motor cortex**. However, some of the regions of the brain involved in human speech production *are* located in the motor cortex, and they direct movement of the mouth, larynx, and the tongue, but *only as those movements pertain to language*. Damage to these neural tracts does not cause paralysis (as damage

Motor cortex   The *cortex* of the brain, the outer layer, is composed of nerve cells or neurons. The *motor cortex* is that portion pertaining to outgoing signals involved in muscle use.

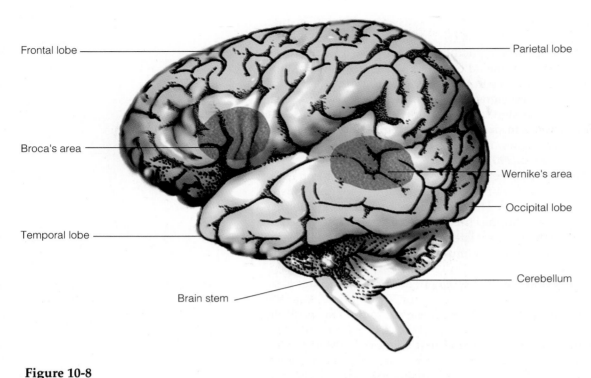

Frontal lobe

Broca's area

Temporal lobe

Brain stem

Parietal lobe

Wernike's area

Occipital lobe

Cerebellum

Figure 10-8

Left lateral view of human brain showing major regions and areas involved in speech.

to other areas will do), but it will disturb speech, demonstrating that these structures are adapted to movements related specifically to speech production. However, human speech involves much more than simply the motor control of specific muscle groups.

In most humans, language function is located primarily in the left hemisphere, including the left temporal lobe (see Fig. 10-8). In particular, two regions—*Wernicke's* and *Broca's* areas—are directly involved in the perception and production (respectively) of spoken language. But the perception and production of speech involves much more than these two areas, and use of written language requires still other systems.

Association areas, composed of thousands of neural connections, integrate information sent from other parts of the cerebral cortex. Information relating to visual, olfactory, tactile, and auditory stimuli can first be combined and then relayed to Broca's area, where it is translated for speech production. This remarkable human ability depends upon interconnections between receiving areas for all sensory stimuli. While the brains of other species have such association areas, they do not have the ability to transform this information and create language.

In discussions of human evolution, much emphasis is placed upon increased brain size, both in relative and absolute terms (see pp. 271–272). While increased brain size is certainly important, it was the *reorganization* of neurological structures that permitted the development of language. Although the study of comparative brain structure is still in its infancy, much current evidence suggests that *new* structures and novel connections have not been the basis for neurological differences among species. Rather, systematic reorganization, elaboration, and/or reduction of existing structures, or shifts in the proportions of existing connections, have been far more important (Deacon, 1992). Language is a function of interrelationships among many cortical areas, each of which corresponds to an area in nonhuman primates.

Some researchers argue that language capabilities appeared late in human evolution (that is, with the wide dispersal of modern *Homo sapiens* some 30,000 years ago). Others postulate a much earlier origin, possibly with the appearance of the genus *Homo* 2 m.y.a. Whichever scenario is true, language came about as complex and efficient forms of communication gained selective value in our lineage. But, again, this result would not have been possible if early hominids had not been preadapted to acquire language skills.

Affiliative Behaviors

Within primate societies, there is a constant interplay between aggression, which can lead to group disruption, and **affiliative** behaviors that promote group cohesion.

Conflict within a group frequently develops out of competition for resources, including mating partners as well as food items. Instead of actual attacks or fighting, most intragroup aggression occurs as various signals and displays, frequently within the context of a dominance hierarchy. Likewise, the majority of such situations are resolved through various submissive and appeasement behaviors.

Although some level of aggression is useful in maintaining order within the group and protecting either individual or group resources, aggression can also be destructive and even result in death. Affiliative or friendly behaviors reduce levels of aggression by defusing potentially dangerous situations, reinforcing bonds between individuals, and promoting group cohesion.

Common affiliative behaviors include reconciliation, consolation, and simple amicable interactions between friends and relatives. Most such behaviors involve physical contact which, as we have already discussed, is one of the most important factors in primate development and is crucial in promoting peaceful relationships in primate social groupings.

Following a conflict, chimpanzee opponents frequently move, within minutes, to reconcile (de Waal, 1982). Reconciliation takes many forms, including hugging, kissing, and grooming. Even uninvolved individuals may take part, either grooming one or both participants or forming their own grooming parties. In addition to grooming, bonobos are unique in their use of sex to promote group cohesion, restore peace after conflicts, and relieve tension within the group (de Waal, 1987, 1989).

Because interpersonal relationships are as crucial to nonhuman primates as they are to humans, the bonds between individuals can last a lifetime. These relationships serve a variety of functions. Individuals of many species form alliances in which one supports another against a third. Alliances or coalitions, as they are also called, can be used to enhance the status of members. At Gombe, the male chimpanzee Figan achieved alpha status because of support from his brother (Goodall, 1986, p. 424). In fact, chimpanzees so heavily rely upon coalitions and are so skillfull politically that an entire book, appropriately entitled *Chimpanzee Politics* (de Waal, 1982), is devoted to the topic.

Affiliative Pertaining to amicable associations between individuals. Affiliative behaviors, such as grooming, reinforce social bonds and promote group cohesion.

Altruism is seen in many primate species. One laboratory study provides an example. Rhesus macaques were taught to pull chains for food rewards. Subsequently, other monkeys were placed in nearby cages, within sight and hearing of the trained monkeys. The experimental design was then changed so that chain-pulling not only provided food, but it also administered an electric shock to the neighboring monkeys. In most cases, once the chain-pulling monkeys had seen and heard the responses of their fellows, they ceased pulling their chains, even though this meant they were deprived of food rewards (Masserman et al., 1964).

Numerous examples of altruism have been reported in chimpanzees. Offspring, even as adults, protect their mothers; siblings protect siblings; and mothers, their young. Adoption of orphans is seen as an altruistic act and is known to exist at least in chimpanzees, macaques, and baboons.

Jane Goodall speculates that altruism (in humans as well as nonhuman primates) arose out of the caretaking behaviors of parents, usually mothers. Many stories tell of self-sacrificing behavior of primate mothers. Chimpanzees who engage in cooperative hunts of red colobus monkeys exploit this facet of maternal behavior. By choosing as prey those females accompanied by offspring, the chimpanzees increase their chances of catching not one meal but two; for they know that colobus mothers frequently either defend their babies or remain close by while the latter are being eaten, and thus the mothers, too, become victims (Goodall, 1986).

Aggressive Interactions

Conspecifics Members of the same species.

Interactions *between* groups of **conspecifics** can be just as revealing as those that take place *within* groups. For many primate species, especially those whose ranges are small, contact with one or more other groups of the same species is a daily occurrence, and the form of these encounters can vary from species to species.

Territories The territory is that portion of an individual's or a group's home range actively defended against intrusion, particularly by conspecifics.

Between groups, aggression can be used to protect resources through defense of **territories**. Primate groups are associated with a *home range*. Within the home range is a portion called the **core area**. This area contains the highest concentration of predictable resources and it is where the group most frequently may be found. Although portions of the home range may overlap with the home range of one or more other groups, core areas of adjacent groups do not overlap. The core area can also be said to be a group's territory, and it is defined as that portion of the home range defended against intrusion by other groups. However, in some species, other areas of the home range may also be defended. Whatever area is defended, that portion is termed the *territory*.

Core area The portion of a home range containing the highest concentration and most reliable supplies of food and water. The core area is frequently the area that will be defended.

Not all primates are territorial. In general, territoriality is associated with species whose ranges are sufficiently small to permit patrolling and protection (for example, gibbons and vervets). Among many species (for example, squirrel monkeys, rhesus macaques, and baboons), group encounters are usually nonaggressive. Nonterritorial tree dwellers use vocalizations to avoid other groups—they space themselves throughout the forest canopy with minimal contact.

Chimpanzees do not exhibit all the traits typical of true territorial behavior (Goodall, 1986), but males in particular are highly intolerant of unfamiliar chimpanzees, especially other males. Therefore, intergroup interactions are almost always characterized by aggressive displays, chasing, and actual fighting.

Members of chimpanzee communities frequently travel to areas where their range borders or overlaps that of another community. These peripheral areas are not entirely safe, and before entering them chimps usually hoot and display to determine if other animals are present. They then remain silent, listening for a response. If members of another community should appear, some form of aggression will ensue until one group retreats.

Male chimpanzees (sometimes accompanied by one or two estrous females) commonly patrol borders. During patrols, party members travel silently in compact groupings. They stop frequently to sniff, look around, or climb tall trees, where they may sit for an hour or more surveying the region. During such times individuals are tense, and a sudden sound, such as a snapping twig, causes them to touch or embrace in reassurance (Goodall, 1986). It is most apparent from their tension and very uncharacteristic silence that the chimpanzees are quite aware they have ventured into a potentially dangerous situation.

If a border patrol happens upon one or two strangers, the patrollers most surely will attack. However, if they encounter a group larger than their own, they themselves may be attacked, or at least chased.

Recent discussion among primatologists has focused upon aggression between groups of the same species and whether the primary motivation is solely territoriality (that is, protection of resources in a given area) or whether other factors are also involved (Cheney, 1987; Manson and Wrangham, 1991; Nishida, 1991). Much of this discussion has centered upon intergroup aggression and lethal raiding in chimpanzees, and has emphasized implications for human evolution and behavior as well.

Beginning in 1974, Jane Goodall and her colleagues witnessed at least five unprovoked and extremely brutal attacks by groups of chimpanzees (usually, but not always, males) upon lone individuals. To explain these attacks, it is necessary to point out that by 1973 the original Gombe community (Kasakela) had divided into two distinct groups, one located in the north and the other in the south of what had once been a single original group's home range. In effect, the southern splinter group (Kahama community) had denied the others access to part of their former home range.

By 1977 all seven males and an older female of the Kahama group were either known or suspected to have been killed. Observed attacks, some of twenty minutes duration, were joint efforts involving several Kasakela animals, usually adult males, using their teeth, hands, and feet, and, on one occasion, rocks. In some cases, one animal would hold the victim down while others bit, pounded, and jumped upon him or her.

The ferocity of these attacks cannot be overstated, and they very much altered previously held views of chimpanzees as peaceful, less violent versions of ourselves. While it is not possible to identify, with certainty, the motivation of the aggressors, it is abundantly clear that they intended to incapacitate their victims (Goodall, 1986).

Goodall (1986) has suggested that the attacks strongly imply that, although chimpanzees do not possess language and do not wage war as we know it, they do exhibit behaviors which, if present in early hominids, could have been precursors to war:

> The chimpanzee, as a result of a unique combination of strong affiliative bonds between adult males on the one hand and an unusually hostile and violently aggressive attitude toward nongroup individuals on the other, has clearly

reached a stage where he stands at the very threshold of human achievement in destruction, cruelty, and planned intergroup conflict. If ever he develops the power of language—and, as we have seen, he stands close to that threshold, too—might he not push open the door and wage war with the best of us? (Goodall, 1986, p. 534).

A situation similar to that at Gombe has also been reported for a group of chimpanzees located in the Mahale Mountains south of Gombe. Between 1966 and 1983, all the males of a small chimpanzee community (K-group) disappeared. When the number of adult males decreased to one, those cycling females who had remained in K-group's home range migrated permanently to another community (M-group). Although no attacks were actually observed, there is circumstantial evidence that, over the course of several years, most of the K-group males met the same fate as the Kahama group at Gombe (Nishida et al., 1985; Nishida et al., 1990).

Lethal, unprovoked aggression between groups of conspecifics is *known* to occur in only two mammalian species: humans and chimpanzees. Prior to its discovery in chimpanzees, such lethal aggression was thought to be an exclusively human endeavor, motivated by territoriality. In the past few years, a number of researchers have posed various questions within the theoretical framework that specific aggressive patterns may be explained by similar factors operating in both species. Manson and Wrangham (1991, p. 370) state:

> These similarities between chimpanzees and humans suggest a common evolutionary background. Thus, they indicate that lethal male raiding could have had precultural origins and might be elicited by the same set of conditions among humans as among chimpanzees.

Philopatric *Philopatry*. Refers to remaining in one's natal group or home range as an adult. In most species, members of one sex disperse from their natal group as young adults, and members of the philopatric sex remain. In the majority of nonhuman primates, the philopatric sex is female.

In both species, males are **philopatric** and form lifelong bonds within their social group. Indeed, the core of a chimpanzee community is a group of closely bonded males who, because of their long-term association, act cooperatively in various endeavors, including hunting and attack. In most other primate species, females are the philopatric sex, and in some species (notably macaques and baboons), females may cooperate in aggressive encounters against females from other groups. (Usually these conflicts develop as contests for resources and they do not result in fatalities.) Generally, then, conflicts between groups of conspecifics involve members of the philopatric sex.

Efforts to identify the social and ecological factors that predispose human and chimpanzee males to engage in lethal attacks have led to hypotheses that attempt to explain the function and adaptive value of these activities. In this context, the benefits and costs of extreme aggression must be identified. The principal benefit to aggressors is acquisition of reproductive and material resources (that is, mating partners and food). Costs include risk of injury or death and loss of energy expended in performing aggressive acts.

Exogamous *Exogamy* is a mating system whereby individuals find mating partners from outside their natal group. When applied to humans, the term may refer to marriage rules that dictate marriage with partners from another social grouping (for example, village, kinship group, or clan).

Manson and Wrangham (1991) suggest that, in chimpanzees, lethal intergroup aggression is a male activity *because* males are the philopatric sex. In most traditional human cultures, residence is *patrilocal*, meaning that males reside in the village or area in which they were born and raised. Therefore, males maintain lifelong associations with other males, many of whom are genetically related to them, and they form the bonded social core of the village. Since most human groups are **exogamous**, these men marry women from other villages. Therefore, women, who transfer into their husbands' villages, must live apart from their close relatives and are not able to maintain the same tightly bonded social networks typical of men.

Second, Manson and Wrangham propose that chimpanzees attack because costs are low due to the numerical superiority of the aggressors. Third, these authors maintain the primary benefit to aggressors is the acquisition of reproductive females, through acquisition of either the females themselves or the territory the females occupy.

Goodall (1986) and Nishida (Nishida et al., 1985; Nishida et al., 1990; Nishida, 1991) deemphasize the importance of female acquisition. They propose that protection of home range and expansion of territory (that is, obtaining material resources) are the primary motivations for intergroup aggression.

Although the precise motivation of chimpanzee intergroup aggression may never be fully elucidated, it is clear that a number of interrelated factors are involved. Moreover, although chimpanzees do not meet all the criteria developed for true territorial behavior (Goodall, 1986), it appears that various aspects of resource acquisition and protection are involved. Through careful examination of shared aspects of human and chimpanzee social life, we can develop hypotheses regarding how intergroup conflict arose in our own lineage.

Cultural anthropologist Napoleon Chagnon (1979, 1988) has argued that among the Yanomamo Indians of Brazil, competition for mates between males is the motivation behind warfare between groups. The Yanomamo are a warlike people with over 30 percent of male deaths attributed to violence. Chagnon believes that the majority of hostilities either *within* or *between* villages (with raids leading to deaths, then revenge raids leading to more fatalities, and so on) is caused initially by competition for females. These phenomena are explained as functions of the same sociobiological principles that operate in chimpanzees, in full recognition of the obvious differences between the two species regarding weaponry, language, and mating systems (Manson and Wrangham, 1991). Chagnon (1988, p. 986), using the terminology of sociobiology states, "Men who demonstrate their willingness to act violently and exact revenge for the deaths of kin may have higher marital and reproductive success."

Early hominids and chimpanzees may well have inherited from a common ancestor the predispositions that have resulted in shared patterns of strife between populations. It is not possible to draw direct comparisons between chimpanzee conflict and human warfare owing to later human elaborations of culture, use of symbols (for example, national flags), and language. But it is important and intriguing to speculate upon the fundamental issues that may have led to the development of similar patterns in both species.

Primate Cultural Behavior

One important trait of nonhuman primates, especially chimpanzees, that makes them attractive models for our hominid ancestors may be called *cultural behavior*. Although many cultural anthropologists and others prefer to reserve the term *culture* exclusively for human behavior, most biological anthropologists feel it is appropriate to use the term in discussions of nonhuman primates as well. Undeniably, there are many aspects of culture that are uniquely human and, again, one must be cautious in interpreting nonhuman animal behavior. But we would argue that the human *aptitude for culture,* as a means of adapting to the environment, is an elaboration of behaviors typical of other primate species.

Cultural behavior is learned behavior, and it is passed from generation to generation not biologically, but through learning. While humans *teach* their young, free-ranging nonhuman primates do not appear to do so. However, all mammals are capable of learning, and primates, as a group, possess this capacity to greater degree than other mammals. We have already mentioned (in Chapter 9) that primate infants, through observing their mothers and others, learn about appropriate behaviors as well as food items and so on. In the same way, they learn to use and modify objects to achieve certain ends. In turn, their own offspring will observe their activities. What emerges is a *cultural tradition* that may eventually come to typify an entire group or even a species.

Two famous examples of cultural behavior were seen in a study group of Japanese macaques on Koshima Island (Fig. 10-9). In 1952, Japanese researchers began provisioning the 22-member troop with sweet potatoes. The following year, a young female named Imo began washing her potatoes in a freshwater stream prior to eating them. Within three years, several monkeys had imitated her and adopted the practice; however, they had switched from using the stream to taking their potatoes to the ocean nearby. (Perhaps they liked the salt seasoning.)

In 1956, the Koshima primatologists began scattering wheat grains onto the sandy beach, and again, Imo introduced a novel behavior. Instead of picking out wheat grains one at a time (as the researchers had expected), Imo picked up handfuls of grain and sand and dropped them together into the water. The sand sank, the wheat kernels floated, and the inventive Imo simply scooped them off the water and ate them. Just as with potato washing, others imitated Imo's technique until the new behavior eventually became common throughout the troop.

The Japanese researchers proposed that dietary habits and food preferences are learned, and that potato washing and wheat floating were examples of nonhuman culture. Because these practices arose as innovative solutions to problems (how to clean potatoes and how to separate wheat from sand) and were imitated by others until they became traditions within

Figure 10-9

Japanese macaque washing potatoes.

(a)

(b)

the group, they were seen as containing elements of human culture (and were therefore in some ways seen as analogous to it).

Among chimpanzees we see more elaborate examples of cultural behavior in the form of *tool use*. This point is a very important one, for traditionally, tool use (along with language) was said to set humans apart from other animals.

Chimpanzees insert twigs and grass blades into termite mounds in a practice called "termite fishing" (see Fig. 10-10). When termites seize the twig, the chimpanzee withdraws it and eats the attached insects. Chimpanzees modify some of their stems and twigs by stripping the leaves—in effect, manufacturing a tool from the natural material. Chimps can, to some extent, alter objects to a "regular and set pattern" and have been observed preparing objects for later use at an out-of-sight location (Goodall, 1986). For example, a chimp will very carefully select a piece of vine, bark, twig, or palm frond and modify it by removing leaves or other extraneous material, then break off portions until it is the proper length. Chimps have also been seen making these tools even before the termite mound is in sight.

Such tool preparation has several implications. First, the chimpanzees are engaged in an activity that prepares them for a future (not immediate) task at a spatially removed location. Such behavior implies considerable planning and forethought. Second, the careful selection of just the right shape and size of raw material indicates a preconceived idea of what the tool will look like, to suit the purpose for which it is intended. These are extremely complex behaviors, previously believed by scientists to be the exclusive domain of humans.

Chimps also crumple and chew handfuls of leaves, which they dip into the hollow of a tree where water has accumulated. Then they suck the water from their newly made "leaf sponges," water that otherwise would have been inaccessible to them. Leaves are also used to wipe substances from fur;

Figure 10-10

(a) Female chimpanzee using a tool to "fish" for termites at Gombe National Park, Tanzania. (b) A chimpanzee at the Sacramento, California Zoo also uses a tool in the same manner as free-ranging animals.

twigs are sometimes used as toothpicks; stones may be used as weapons; and various objects, such as branches and stones, may be dragged or rolled to enhance displays. Lastly, sticks or leaves are used as aids in processing mammalian prey, but with one exception these practices appear to be incidental. The one exception, observed in chimpanzees in the Tai forest (Ivory Coast), is the frequent use of sticks to extract marrow from long bones (Boesch and Boesch, 1989).

Chimpanzees in numerous West African study groups use hammerstones with platform stones to crack nuts and hard-shelled fruits. Several bird and mammalian species use stones in some manner to obtain food (for example, Egyptian vultures and sea otters). Wild capuchin monkeys smash objects against stones (Izawa and Mizuno, 1977) and their use of stones in captivity (both as hammers and *anvils*) has been reported (Visalberghi, 1990). (Stones serve as anvils when fruit or other objects are bashed against the rock surface.) In nature, chimpanzees are the only nonhuman animal to use stones both as hammers and anvils to obtain food. They are the only nonhuman primate that consistently and habitually makes and uses tools (McGrew, 1992).

Chimpanzees exhibit regional variation regarding both the types and methods of tool use. Use of stone hammers and platforms is confined to West African groups. Likewise, at central and eastern African sites, termites are obtained by means of stems and sticks, while at some West African locations, it appears no tools are used in this context (McGrew, 1992).

Regional dietary preferences are also noted for chimpanzees (Nishida et al., 1983; McGrew, 1992). For example, oil palms are exploited for their fruits and nuts at many locations, including Gombe, but even though they are present in the Mahale Mountains, they are not utilized by chimpanzees. Such regional patterns in tool use and food preferences are reminiscent of the cultural variations characteristic of humans.

McGrew (1992) presents eight criteria for the recognition of cultural behaviors in nonhuman species (Table 10-1). Of these, the first six were established by the pioneering cultural anthropologist Alfred Kroeber (1928); the last two were added by McGrew and Tutin (1978). McGrew (1992) demonstrates that Japanese macaques meet the first six criteria. However, all the macaque examples have developed, in some way, from human interference (which is not to say they all resulted directly from human intervention). To avoid this difficulty, the last two criteria were added (see Table 10-1).

Chimpanzees unambiguously meet the first six criteria, although not all groups meet the last two because most study groups have had to be at least

Table 10-1   Criteria for Cultural Acts in Other Species

Innovation	New pattern is invented or modified
Dissemination	Pattern acquired (through imitation) by another from innovator
Standardization	Form of pattern is consistent and stylized
Durability	Pattern performed without presence of demonstrator
Diffusion	Pattern spreads from one group to another
Tradition	Pattern persists from innovator's generation to the next
Nonsubsistence	Pattern transcends subsistence
Naturalness	Pattern shown in absence of direct human influence
Adapted from Kroeber, 1928, and McGrew and Tutin, 1978. In: McGrew, 1992.	

minimally provisioned. However, all criteria are met by at least some chimpanzees in some instances (McGrew, 1992). While it is obvious that chimpanzees do not possess human culture, we cannot overlook the implications that tool use and local traditions of learned behavior have for early hominid evolution.

Utilizing sticks, twigs, and stones enhances chimpanzees' ability to exploit resources. Learning of these behaviors occurs during infancy and childhood, partly as a function of prolonged contact with the mother. Also important in this regard is the continued exposure to others provided by living in social groupings. These statements also apply to early hominids. While sticks and unmodified stones do not remain to tell tales, surely our early ancestors used these same objects as tools in much the same manner as do chimpanzees.

Human culture has become the environment in which modern *Homo sapiens* lives. Quite clearly, use of sticks in termite fishing and hammerstones to crack nuts is hardly comparable to modern human technology. However, modern human technology had its beginnings in the kinds of cultural behaviors we observe in other primates. To state such does not mean that nonhuman primates are "on their way" to becoming human, as some would interpret these observations. Remember, evolution is not a goal-directed enterprise, and if it were, nothing dictates that modern humans necessarily constitute an evolutionary goal. Such a conclusion is purely a "species-centric" view and has no validity in discussions of evolutionary processes.

Moreover, nonhuman primates have probably been capable of certain cultural behaviors for millions of years. Presumably, as we have stated, the common ancestor humans share with chimpanzees undoubtedly used sticks and stones to exploit resources, and perhaps, as weapons. These behaviors are not newly developed in our close relatives; rather, they have only been recently documented by humans. Further analysis of these capabilities in nonhuman primates in their social and ecological context may elucidate more definitely how cultural traditions emerged in our lineage.

Summary

Various aspects of nonhuman primate behavior and adaptation have been discussed as they pertain to modern humans and to human evolution. Such capacities as efficient communication (including language), affiliation, intergroup aggression, and cultural behavior are explained within an evolutionary framework. Moreover, these capabilities, and the similarity of their expression in many primate species, argue for their adaptive significance in complex social settings.

Language and tool use, like most human capacities, can be seen as elaborations of patterns observed in many nonhuman primates. Humans reflect their evolutionary heritage as primates and stand as one component of a biological continuum.

Questions for Review

1. How can aspects of human behavior be explained in terms of biological evolution without necessarily postulating that complex behaviors are under *strict* genetic control?
2. How is body size in primates related to diet and metabolism?

3. What is meant by encephalization? Give an example of how this concept would be useful in comparing different primate species.
4. What are ritualized behaviors? Give an example.
5. Explain how natural selection acts to enhance the communicatory role of some behaviors. Give an example.
6. How does human language differ from most nonhuman communication? What is the evidence to suggest that some nonhuman primates share certain language abilities seen in humans?
7. Briefly discuss neurological changes occurring in human evolution that relate to language function.
8. What is the role of *affiliative* behaviors in primate societies? Discuss three examples.
9. What is the nature of encounters between different groups of chimpanzees? Describe documented examples and discuss theories that have been proposed to explain them.
10. What are some examples of cultural behavior in nonhuman primates? Why do physical anthropologists consider it valid to refer to these activities as *culture*? How are these examples relevant to understanding human evolution?

Chapter 11

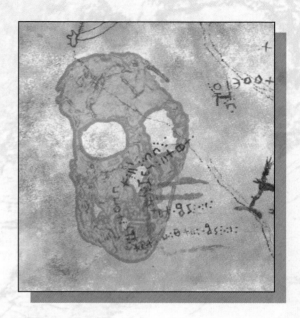

Contents

Primate Evolution

Issue ⤴ Is There a Bigfoot?

Ancient legends tell of Sasquatch, a strange, hairy, bipedal creature prowling the wilds of North America. In fact, Sasquatches, abominable snowmen, and other such creatures have been reported from at least 100 separate areas of the world. In North America, they have been reported most often from British Columbia, Washington, Oregon, and northern California. Various unexplained beasts, however, have also been "seen" from Alaska to Mexico and from the Pacific Coast to northern Michigan. Tales of these creatures, which are usually called *Bigfoot*, are today even further embellished as sightings, footprints, hair fragments, feces, and even photographs have been collected. Are we dealing with fact or fiction?

If Bigfoot lives, what could it be? Reports are consistent, detailing a very large (eight to twelve foot), upright animal. Its size, hair, and location (in the cold Northwest) all imply a mammal. Its body shape and locomotion further limit the possibilities. Possibly it is a bear, but the gait and footprints are not right. What is left then? A hominoid of some sort?

Is this possible? In any objective pursuit of knowledge we must admit that *anything* is possible, but some things are highly improbable. What kinds of hominoids are native to the New World? The only definite remains of indigenous hominoids in North, Central, or South America are those of *Homo sapiens* (and these are relatively recent—in the last 20,000 years or so).

If Bigfoot is a hominoid, where did it come from? The closest fossil primate matching the dimensions of the fleeting Sasquatches is *Gigantopithecus*. Remains of this extinct hominoid are well known from the Old World during the Pleistocene, but none has ever been found in the New World. Such a big animal has exceedingly large teeth, which generally have a fairly good chance of being preserved. From China alone there are more than 1,000 *Gigantopithecus* teeth, and this giant hominoid has not roamed the forests of China for half a million years. It seems very strange indeed. If *Gigantopithecus* (or one of its supposed descendants) is still living, why have we not found any bones or teeth of this form? If such a large animal has existed for tens of thousands of years, where is the hard evidence?

What about the hundreds of sightings? Could they all have been faked? Probably not. Many of these people, no doubt, saw *something*. Perhaps often they saw bears; the imagination can greatly influence our objectivity when primed with romantic tales of mythical beasts. What about footprints, photos, hairs, and fecal material? The prints (at least many of them) could have been faked, and so too with the photos (the primary evidence—a 16-mm film taken in northern California in 1967). Such a circumstance would suggest an elaborate, deliberate hoax, not a happy conclusion, but entirely possible (as you will see with Piltdown). The hairs and fecal material are from some animal, perhaps one already known, perhaps one yet to be discovered. The possibility exists that there are large terrestrial mammals in remote areas of North America unknown to science. Bigfoot may be such an animal. However, of all the possibilities, the suggestion that this creature is a hominoid is about the least likely imaginable.

The conclusion that Bigfoot is an archaic hominoid is therefore both unlikely and far from conclusively established. But it is not *completely* impossible. However, descendant populations of gigantopithecines would have had to migrate from China (through thousands of miles of environments exceedingly inhospitable to such a forest-adapted form), ending up in the American Northwest. In so doing, perhaps they left nary a trace all along the way. Furthering our improbable conjectures, perhaps they have existed in North America for at least 500,000 years, without leaving a single fossil remnant. Finally, perhaps they still exist today, but deliberately conceal themselves and meticulously dispose of their dead.

All of this, of course, assumes these are intelligent animals deliberately avoiding contact with humans. Evolution has endowed humans with a marvelous brain and also a wonderful imagination. Science gives us the *tool* to use that imagination in a constructive and useful way. The more outrageous or exotic the claim, the more incontrovertible must be the evidence to support it!

SOURCES

Napier, John. *Bigfoot; The Yeti and Sasquatch in Myth and Reality*. London: Jonathan Cape, 1972.

Sanderson, Ivan T. *Abominable Snowmen: Legend Come to Life*, New York: Chilton Co., 1961.

Shuman, James B. "Is There an American Abominable Snowman?" *Reader's Digest*, January 1969, pp. 179–186.

Introduction

In Chapters 7, 8, 9, and 10, you were introduced to the time scale of evolution, placental mammals, and particularly the primate order. We now turn to the fossil history of primates over the last 60 million years. With what you now know of primate anatomy (teeth, limbs, etc.) and social behavior, you will be able to "flesh out" the bones and teeth that comprise the evolutionary record of primate origins. In this way, the ecological adaptations and evolutionary relationships of these fossil forms to each other (and to contemporary primates) will become more meaningful. Please note that when we look at primate evolution, we are looking at our own evolution as well.

Time Scale

A brief review of the geological time scale will be helpful in understanding primate evolution during the Cenozoic.

Before discussing the fossil primates, we should caution that the formal taxonomic names for the various families and genera are horrendous to pronounce and even harder to remember. Unfortunately, there is no other adequate way to discuss the material. We must make reference to the standard nomenclature. As an aid, we suggest you refer to the margin notes, pronunciation guide, and glossary for those names considered most significant.

ERA	EPOCH	APPROXIMATE BEGINNING (M.Y.A.)
Cenozoic	Pleistocene	1.8
	Pliocene	5
	Miocene	22.5
	Oligocene	37
	Eocene	53
	Paleocene	65
Mesozoic	Cretaceous	135

Early Primate Evolution

The roots of the Primate Order go back to the beginning of the placental mammal radiation, circa 65 m.y.a. At this time, the earliest primates were diverging from quite early, primitive placental mammals. As discussed in Chapter 8, strictly classifying even the living primates on the basis of clearly defined, shared derived characteristics is not an easy task. The further back we go in the fossil record, the more primitive, and, in many cases, the more generalized the fossil primates become. Such a situation makes classifying very early members of the Primate Order all the more difficult.

As a case in point, the earliest identifiable primates were long thought to be a Paleocene group known as the plesiadapiforms. Among the best known of this widespread extinct lineage was the genus *Plesiadapis*. However, even for the better known of these fossil forms, the evidence was generally quite fragmentary, based mostly on jaws and teeth. In just the last

5 years much more complete remains of plesiadapiforms have been discovered in Wyoming, including a nearly complete cranium and several elements from the hand and wrist.

As a result of new analyses of this more complete evidence, the plesiadapiforms have been removed from the Primate Order altogether. From distinctive features (shared derived characteristics) of the cranium and hands, these Paleocene mammals are now thought to be closely related to the colugo. (The colugo is sometimes called a "flying lemur," a name that is an unfortunate misnomer, as this animal is not a lemur and does not fly, but glides.) This group of unusual mammals is probably closely linked to the early roots of primates, but had apparently already diverged by Paleocene times.

Given these new and major reinterpretations, which basically throw out everything that had been *assumed* about early primates, we are left with extremely scarce traces of the beginnings of primate radiation. Some paleontologists have suggested that other recently discovered bits and pieces from the Paleocene of North Africa *may* be that of a primitive, very small primate. Until more evidence is found, and remembering the lesson of the plesiadapiforms, it is best, at present, to withhold judgment.

Ancient Landscapes and Early Primate Evolution

The distribution and the eventual fate of early primate forms is understandable only within the context of the environments in which these animals lived. First and foremost, we must remember that 60 m.y.a. land masses were not arranged as they are today. As we discussed on p. 177, the continents have "drifted" to their present position, carried along on the shifting plates of the earth's surface.

During the late Mesozoic, the huge conglomerate land mass called Pangea began to break up into northern and southern continents. To the north, North America, Europe, and Asia were joined into Laurasia; to the south, Africa, South America, Australia, India, and Antarctica formed Gondwanaland (see Fig. 7-4a). Throughout the Mesozoic, the two basic land masses continued to move, with Gondwanaland breaking up into the southern continents. In the north, the continents also were separating, but North America and Europe continued to be connected through Greenland and would remain close to each other for several millions of years. As we will see, this "northern connection" had a very significant influence on the geographic distribution of early primates. In fact, North America and Europe remained in close proximity until mid-Eocene times (circa 45 m.y.a.) (see Fig. 7-4b).

What makes all this geologic activity relevant to primate (and other paleontological) studies is that land-living animals could cross over land bridges, but were effectively cut off by water barriers. Thus, we see species of *Plesiadapis* in *both* North America and Europe. As far as primates go, then, from their earliest beginnings (65+ m.y.a.) up until 40 m.y.a., they were mostly limited to North America and Europe (between which some migration was still possible). With further continental movements, the "New World" and "Old World" became completely separated and thereby influenced the evolutionary histories of primates still living today (see p. 217).

As the continents moved, climatic conditions changed dramatically. In the Mesozoic and into the Paleocene, the continental masses were clustered closer to the equator, and as Laurasia in particular moved north, its climate

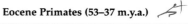

cooled. Moreover, the fragmenting of the land masses and the consequent altering of marine flow patterns (less exchange between northern and southern seas) caused the climate to cool even further.

Finally, these climatic shifts also heavily affected plant communities. Rather than the primitive, mostly tropical flora characteristic of the Mesozoic (ferns, cycads, etc.), what we see emerging in the Cenozoic is the rapid radiation of new varieties of plants, including flowering plants, deciduous trees, and grasses. Many of these plants are frequently pollinated by insects. As insects thus became more abundant, so did the animals who fed on them—including early primates. The world was never to be the same again.

Clearly, then, it is extremely important to interpret primate evolution within the context of the earth's changing environments.

Eocene Primates (53–37 m.y.a.)

The first fossil forms that are clearly identifiable as primates appear during the Eocene. These can now be called prosimians and closely resemble the loris/lemur evolutionary grade. Primate diversification accelerates during this epoch, with 4 new families and more than 60 genera represented during the 16-million-year span of the Eocene.

The Eocene may be characterized as the heyday of prosimians, who attained their widest geographic distribution and broadest adaptive radiation during this period. Indeed, almost four times as many genera are found in the Eocene than are known for the whole world today (16 living genera, with 10 of these confined to Madagascar).

The most diversified and best-known Eocene primates are members of the lemurlike Adapidae, which includes some 10 genera. The four best known of these are:

Cantius	North America and Europe
Adapis (Ad´-a-pis)	Europe
Notharctus (Noth-ark´-tus)	North America
Smilodectes (Smi-lo-dek´-teese)	North America

Some of these animals have been known from fossil evidence for a remarkably long time. In fact, the initial discovery of *Adapis* was made in France in 1821 and first described by Cuvier.

As mentioned, all these animals are fairly lemurlike in general adaptive level and show distinctive primate tendencies. For example, they all now have a complete postorbital bar, larger, rounder braincases, nails instead of claws, and the eyes are rotated forward, allowing overlapping fields of perception and thus binocular vision. In the limb skeleton, further developments in prehensility are suggested, and some evidence points to the presence of an opposable large toe. In all these respects, we see the typical primate adaptive strategies allowing exploitation of an arboreal environment. Whereas these forms resemble lemurs in overall anatomical plan, they do not show the same specializations seen in contemporary lorises and lemurs, such as development of the dental comb (see p. 210).

The separate evolution of the Madagascar (Malagasy) lemurs may date to late Eocene times, but since this island was already isolated by a deep channel from mainland Africa, they apparently reached their island sanctuary by unintentionally floating over on drifting debris.

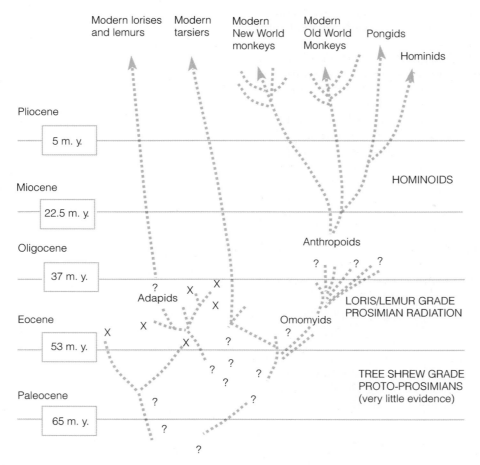

Figure 11-1

Summary, early primate evolution.

Omomyidae (oh´-moh-my´-eh-dee)

The other major group of Eocene prosimians is the family **Omomyidae**, known from numerous specimens of jaws and teeth. Omomyids are the most widely distributed of known Eocene prosimians, with discoveries in North Africa and Europe, and a few specimens from Asia as well.

The earlier members of the family are somewhat more generalized than the later ones and may form an ancestral basis for all later anthropoids; that is, New World monkeys, Old World monkeys, apes, and hominids. Additionally, some of the omomyids from the late Eocene of Europe have been suggested as closely related to the tarsier. However, many of the similarities noted are apparently superficial ones, not necessarily indicating any unique (that is, shared-derived) relationship (Fleagle, 1988). Nevertheless, at least one feature, the position of the olfactory portion of the brain, links these Eocene forms with later haplorhines (see p. 202). Also of interest is the fact that, in later epochs, there are forms quite clearly sharing tarsierlike affinities, from the Oligocene in Egypt and from the Miocene in Thailand.

New World Monkeys

The center of action for primate evolution after the close of the Eocene is confined largely to the Old World, for only on the continents of Africa and Eurasia can we trace the evolutionary development of apes and hominids.

However, the New World, while geographically separated from the Old World, was not completely devoid of anthropoid stock, for here the ceboids evolved in their own right.

Any discussion of ceboid evolution and its relation to Old World anthropoid developments must consider crucial geological events, particularly continental drift. In the late Eocene and early Oligocene, South America was an island continent separate from North America and Africa.

In such a geological context, the introduction of monkeys into South America poses a certain problem. As already mentioned, some authorities have postulated that, because the open water distance between South America and Africa was still not very great, monkeys, originating in Africa, could then have rafted to the New World (Gavan, 1977; Ciochon and Chiarelli, 1980).

In any case, that Old and New World primates share any evolutionary history since at least the Early Oligocene (37–35 m.y.a.) is unlikely. There is no trace of the Old World lineage anywhere in the New World following this time until fully modern *Homo sapiens* walked into the New World during the late Pleistocene.

While primate fossils abound in the Western Hemisphere (particularly North America) during the Early Cenozoic, the record is extremely sparse later on. For the entire span of Oligocene to late Pleistocene, we have only a few bits and pieces, a jaw fragment from Bolivia, a nearly complete skull from Texas, several specimens from southern Argentina, and a few other small fragments from Colombia and Jamaica. Together, all the evidence comprises barely a dozen individuals. Thus, tracing the evolutionary heritage of New World monkeys with any degree of certainty is a difficult task.

Old World Anthropoids

The focus of our attention will henceforth exclusively be the Old World (Europe, Asia, Africa), for this area is where our ancestors have lived for the past 35 million years. This evolutionary and geographic fact is reflected in the grouping of Old World anthropoids (Old World monkeys, apes, and humans) into a common infraorder (Catarrhini) as opposed to the infraorder for New World monkeys (Platyrrhini).

Oligocene (37–22.5 m.y.a.)

It is apparent that during this epoch a great deal of evolutionary action was taking place; by the end of the Oligocene, Old World monkeys and hominoids were probably evolving along their separate evolutionary pathways. No doubt, diverse species of anthropoids were adapting to varied ecological niches in Africa and probably Asia and Europe as well. Unfortunately, the fossil record for the entire period is limited to only one locality in Egypt, 60 miles southwest of Cairo. This site, called the *Fayum*, is today an extremely arid region 100 miles inland, but, in Oligocene times, it was located close to the Mediterranean shore and was traversed by meandering streams crisscrossing through areas of tropical rain forest. The extremely rich fossil-bearing beds were laid down during the early Oligocene, between 37 and 31 million years ago. (Some dating suggests dates as early as 40 m.y.a.; that is, back to the late Eocene.)

Figure 11-2

Location of the Fayum, an Oligocene primate site in Egypt.

Apidium   (A-pid'-ee-um)

Much of the Fayum fossil material is quite fragmentary. Consequently, evolutionary interpretations are not as unambiguous as we would like. Given the nature of the material, the classification of the fossils into recognized genera and species (always a difficult task) is somewhat disputed. The leading researcher of the Fayum fossil primates, E. L. Simons of Duke University, has recognized seven different genera from the Fayum, six anthropoids and one prosimian (Simons, 1985). In addition, the new tarsier-like fossil previously mentioned would add yet another form to this impressive tally (Fleagle, 1988). Altogether, an estimated 1,000 specimens have been recovered from the remarkably productive Fayum area. The three best known of these genera are discussed below.

Apidium **(Two Species)**   A well-known 30-million-year-old fossil species from the Fayum is **Apidium**, represented by about 80 jaws or partial dentitions and over 100 postcranial elements. This animal, about the size of a squirrel, had several anthropoidlike features, but also shows quite unusual aspects in its teeth. *Apidium*'s dental formula (see p. 223) is 2-1-3-3, which indicates a retained third premolar not found in any contemporary Old World anthropoid. For that matter, extremely few fossil anthropoids in the Old World have a third premolar. Some researchers suggest, therefore, that this genus and its close relatives (together called the parapithecids) may lie near or even *before* the divergence of Old and New World anthropoids. As noted, *Apidium* is represented by a large array of specimens, both dental and from the limb skeleton. The teeth suggest a diet composed of fruits and perhaps some seeds. In addition, preserved remains of the limbs indicate that this creature was a small arboreal quadruped, adept at leaping and springing.

Propliopithecus **(Two Species)***   Among the first fossils found at the Fayum was an incomplete *Propliopithecus* mandible recovered in 1907. Unfortunately, since detailed geological and paleontological methods were not yet developed, the precise geological position of this form is not known.

Morphologically, this fossil is a quite generalized Old World anthropoid, displaying a 2-1-2-3 dental formula. In almost every relevant respect, this early *Propliopithecus* form is quite primitive, not showing particular derived tendencies in any direction. Both species appear small to medium in size (8 to 13 pounds) and were most likely fruit-eaters. To date, only this one specimen represents this *Propliopithecus* (*haeckeli*) species.

The second *Propliopithecus* species is considerably better known, with several new specimens discovered at the Fayum between 1977 and 1979. Geologically, this species (*P. chirobates*) comes from the upper beds and is, therefore, probably later in time than the isolated *haeckeli* specimen. Consequently, it is not surprising that *chirobates* is more derived in several anatomical features. Still, this form is a remarkably primitive Old World anthropoid. Considerably more evolutionary change would be required to transform this animal into anything distinctively recognizable as either an ape or a monkey.

Earlier interpretations of fragmentary remains of this fossil suggested affinities with gibbons (Simons initially proposed a separate genus rank, "Aeolopithecus"). However, more complete discoveries have shown that such an evolutionary relationship is not likely (Kay et al., 1981).

---

*Some primatologists have suggested a third species of *Propliopithecus* (*P. markrafi*) at the Fayum (Fleagle and Kay, 1983). This species, however, is also known from only a single specimen.

Aegyptopithecus   The most complete and probably evolutionarily most significant fossil from the Fayum is *Aegyptopithecus*, which is known from several well-preserved crania of different-aged individuals as well as numerous
jaw fragments and several limb bones (most of which have been found quite
recently). The largest of the Fayum anthropoids, *Aegyptopithecus* is roughly
the size of a modern howler monkey, 13 to 18 pounds (Fleagle, 1983). *Aegyptopithecus* is important because, better than any other fossil, it bridges the gap
between the Eocene prosimians on the one hand and the Miocene hominoids
on the other.

With a dental formula of 2-1-2-3, *Aegyptopithecus* shows the familiar Old
World anthropoid pattern. More detailed aspects of the dentition possibly
align this Oligocene form with the Miocene hominoids (which we shall
discuss shortly), but the evolutionary affinities are not presently well established. In most respects, the dentition is primitive for an Old World anthropoid, without specifically derived features in either the hominoid or Old
World monkey direction. Recently, there has been a change in interpreting
Old World monkey dental evolution. It was previously believed that the dental patterns (particularly, the molar cusp pattern) seen in Old World monkeys
were the more **primitive** and, conversely, the Y-5 seen in hominoids (see Fig.
11-3) were more **derived** from the ancestral **catarrhine** condition. Reevaluation of the fossil materials now suggests that, if anything, the Old World
monkey pattern is more derived, and the hominoid cusp arrangement is the
more primitive. (See Fig. 11-4.)

The establishment of the "polarities" of primitive/derived characteristics
is crucial to making sound evolutionary interpretations. However, the trajec-
tories of evolutionary change are not always easy to ascertain. The determination of the ancestral catarrhine molar cusp pattern is only one example. In
the subsequent section on Miocene hominoids, we will encounter several further dilemmas in sorting out such issues.

Even more primitive than the teeth of *Aegyptopithecus* is the skull, which is
small and resembles the skull of a monkey in some details. Brain size and relative proportions can be reconstructed from internal casts of the crania thus
far discovered. It appears that the brain was somewhat intermediate between
that of prosimians and anthropoids. The visual cortex was large compared to

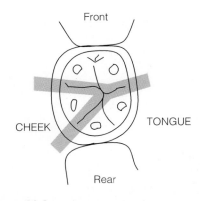

Figure 11-3

*The dryopith Y-5 pattern. A characteristic
feature of hominoid molars.*

Primitive   A character state of an organism that is inherited from an ancestor
(before a divergence) when comparing
with another lineage.

Derived   Character state found only in
particular lineages—and thus indicative
of forms *after* a divergence.

Catarrhine   The group (infraorder)
comprising all Old World anthropoids,
living and extinct.

Figure 11-4

*Establishing polarities in character
states among Old World anthropoids,
an example.*

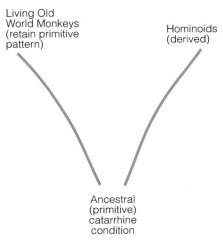

(a) Previous view — polarities of molar
cusp pattern

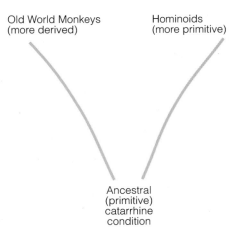

(b) Revised view

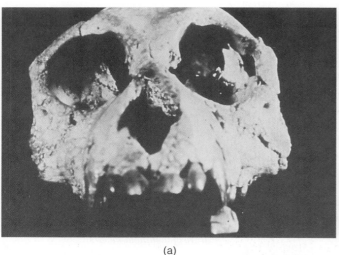

(a)

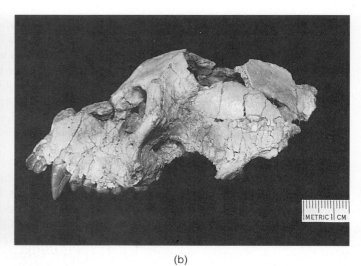

(b)

Figure 11-5

Aegyptopithecus *skull from the Fayum, Egypt. Oligocene, circa 33 m.y.a. Discovered in 1966. (a) Front view; (b) side view.*

prosimians, with concomitant reduction of the olfactory bulbs, but the frontal lobes were not especially expanded. Even considering the relative small size of this animal, the brain—estimated at only 30 to 40 cm^3 (Radinsky, 1973)—was by no means large.

Evidence from the limb skeleton also reveals nothing particularly distinctive. From analysis of limb proportions and muscle insertions, primatologist John Fleagle (1983) has concluded that *Aegyptopithecus* was a short-limbed, heavily muscled, slow-moving, arboreal quadruped.

Further detailed study of *Aegyptopithecus'* anatomy has even allowed primatologists to speculate about the social behavior of this ancient primate. For instance, dental remains from different individuals vary greatly in canine size. This fact implies that male/female differences (sexual dimorphism) were quite marked. Such sexual dimorphism in modern primates is frequently associated with polygynous mating patterns and competition among males for mates. Thus, we may infer these behaviors were typical of *Aegyptopithecus*.

All in all, *Aegyptopithecus* presents somewhat of a paleontological enigma. In most respects, it is quite primitive as an Old World anthropoid, and could thus be potentially an ancestor for *both* Old World monkeys and hominoids. There are some slight yet suggestive clues in the teeth that have led some researchers (most notably, E. L. Simons) to place *Aegyptopithecus* on the hominoid line. Primarily because of the primitive aspects of this creature, other researchers (for example, Fleagle and Kay, 1983) are not as convinced.

Table 11-1   Inferred General Paleobiological Aspects of Oligocene Primates

	Weight Range	Substratum	Locomotion	Diet
Apidium	850–1,600 gm (2–3 lb)	arboreal	quadruped	fruit seeds
Propliopithecus	4,000–5,700 gm (8½–9 lb)	arboreal	quadruped	fruit
Aegyptopithecus	6,700 gm (15 lb)	arboreal	quadruped	fruit some leaves?
*(After Fleagle, 1988)				

There remains, then, the problem of how to classify *Aegyptopithecus*. Even though they recognize that this fossil may well have lived before the major evolutionary split between Old World monkeys and hominoids (see Fig. 11-1), John Fleagle and Richard Kay still opt to call *Aegyptopithecus* a hominoid. Accordingly, they recognize that the superfamily Hominoidea then becomes what they term a "wastebasket" category (that is, it is used for convenience, but does not reflect phylogenetic reality). This is one solution, although it will not satisfy all researchers. Perhaps, for the moment, it would be best to regard *Aegyptopithecus* (as well as the other Fayum anthropoids) as "primitive catarrhines," without referring them to particular superfamilies.

Early Fossil Anthropoids: Summary

The spectacular array of fossils from the Fayum in the period between 35 m.y.a. and 33 m.y.a. demonstrates that anthropoids were radiating along several evolutionary lines. As with the earlier primate fossil material from the Eocene, the fragmentary nature of the Oligocene fossil assemblage makes precise reconstruction of these evolutionary lines risky.

Given the primitive nature of these fossil forms, it is wise, for the present, not to conclude specifically how these animals relate to later primates. In earlier primatological studies (as well as earlier editions of this book), such conclusions were made, but reanalysis of the fossil material from the perspective of primitive/derived evolutionary modifications has cast serious doubt on many of these interpretations. The new interpretations, however, are still far from certain. As we have mentioned, untangling the polarity of primitive versus derived evolutionary states is a most difficult task. Many paleontologists would like to establish a clear link between these Oligocene fossils (particularly *Propliopithecus* and *Aegyptopithecus*) and the unambiguously hominoid forms of the Miocene. Unfortunately, on the basis of current data, this kind of clarity is not yet possible:

As you may recall from the Oligocene fossil anthropoid forms just discussed, *Apidium* (and its parapithecid relatives) may be placed near or even before the split of Old and New World anthropoids. Such a circumstance actually accords quite well with an *African* origin for New World anthropoids and their reaching South America presumably early in the Oligocene (see p. 295). *Aegyptopithecus* (and its relatives, including *Propliopithecus*) are seen by most as preceding the major split in catarrhine (Old World anthropoid) evolution; that is, prior to the divergence of Old World monkeys from the ancestral stock of all hominoids. It would appear, then, based upon this circumstantial evidence, that this most major of Old World anthropoid evolutionary splits occurred late in the Oligocene or very early in the Miocene.

Hominoids: Large/Small; African/Asian; Fossil/Modern

Before we discuss the complex history of hominoid evolution, a brief review of their basic evolutionary relationships is in order. While not very diverse at all, the living hominoids (which comprise only 6 genera and 14 species) do serve as a model for most of the major radiations that existed in the past.

Figure 11-6

Major branches in anthropoid evolution.

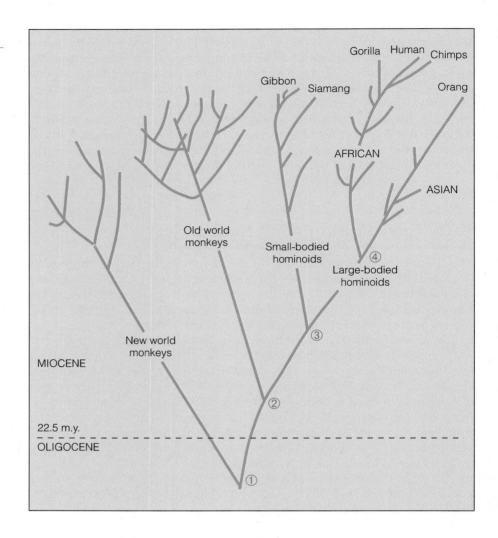

Based on size, the two major subgroupings are termed *small-bodied* and *large-bodied*; small-bodied varieties comprise the gibbon and siamang, and would also include all their ancestors and related sidebranches back to the time they split from the other major hominoid branch, the large-bodied forms. (See Fig. 11-1.)

As we discussed in Chapter 8, there are four genera of large-bodied hominoids living today: *Pongo* (the orang), *Gorilla*, *Pan* (chimps and bonobos), and *Homo*. In turn, these four forms can be subdivided into two major subgroups: Asian large-bodied (the orang) and African large-bodied (gorillas, chimps, and humans). Again, these subgroup designations can be used to denote their respective lineages back to the time when they split from one another.

We can attempt to understand the diversity (and, admittedly, confusing complexity) of the fossil record by reconstructing the fragments and by projecting our conclusions forward to later forms, most especially those species living today. Or, on the other hand, we can use the living forms and infer referentially (backward); in so doing, we attempt to highlight the major adaptive radiations that occurred in the past. For example, the increasing refinement of biochemical data obtained from contemporary primates discussed in Chapter 8 is a major advance in the use of such referential models.

One serious drawback exists, however, if we limit ourselves *strictly* to these referential models. Of all the primates that have ever existed, only a small proportion are still living today. As we saw for the Eocene, there were many more varieties of prosimians than survive today. Moreover, during the Miocene (discussed subsequently), there were many more hominoid species than the few that currently exist. We thus must be very careful not to limit our interpretations to simple models derived from living forms only. Finally, we should not expect all fossil forms to be directly or even particularly closely related to extant varieties. Indeed, we should expect the opposite; that is, most extinct varieties vanish without leaving descendants.

Nevertheless, in combining fossil interpretations (from functional anatomy and ecology) and referential models (especially biochemical data), most primate evolutionists would agree that there have been four major "events" (or evolutionary splits) in prehominid anthropoid evolution: (1) between Old World and New World anthropoids; (2) between Old World monkeys and hominoids; (3) between small-bodied and large-bodied forms of hominoids; and (4) between the Asian and African lines of large-bodied hominoids. (See Fig. 11-6.)

Miocene (22.5–5 m.y.a.)—Hominoids Aplenty

If the Eocene was the age of prosimians and the Oligocene the time of great diversity for early anthropoids, the Miocene was certainly the epoch of hominoids.

A great abundance of hominoid fossil material has been found in the Old World from the time period 22–7 m.y.a. The remarkable evolutionary success represented by this adaptive radiation is shown in the geographic range already established for hominoids during this period. Miocene hominoid fossils have been discovered in France, Austria, Spain, former Czechoslovakia, Greece, Hungary, China, India, Pakistan, Turkey, Saudi Arabia, Egypt, Uganda, Kenya, and Namibia. While several intriguing discoveries potentially relating to gibbon evolution have been discovered at Miocene sites, the vast majority of this hominoid material relates to large-bodied forms. Unless we state otherwise, all further discussion of Miocene hominoids refers only to large-bodied varieties.

Interpretations of this vast array of fossil material (now including more than 500 individuals, and perhaps as many as 1,000) were greatly complicated for several decades due to inadequate appreciation of the range of biological variation that a single genus or species could represent. As a result, the taxonomic naming of the various fossil finds became a terrible muddle, with close to 30 genera and over 100 species proposed. The biological implications of such taxonomic enthusiasm were unfortunately not seriously considered. In such an atmosphere, it was possible for two genera to be named—one with only upper jaws represented, the other with only lower jaws, each matching the other!

It is not difficult to understand why such confusion arose if we consider that discoveries of these fossils spanned more than 100 years (the earliest find came from France in 1856) and took place on three continents. Not until the early 1960s did scientists systematically study *all* the material, the result being a considerable simplification of the earlier confusion. As a result of this research, E. L. Simons and David Pilbeam "lumped" the vast majority of

Miocene forms into only two genera: one presumably quite "pongidlike" and the other "hominidlike." In just the last few years, however, a tremendous amount of new data has come to light from both new field discoveries and finds in museum collections of previously unrecognized material. Consequently, it is now apparent that the Simons-Pilbeam simplification went too far. Hominoid evolutionary radiation during the Miocene produced a whole array of diverse organisms, many of which have no living descendants (and thus no clear analog among living higher primates).

As these new discoveries are analyzed, many of the perplexing problems concerning Miocene hominoids should be solved. For the moment, it is possible to make only general interpretive statements regarding Miocene hominoid adaptive patterns.

PALEOGEOGRAPHY AND MIOCENE HOMINOID EVOLUTION

As they were to early primate evolution (see p. 292), the factors of changing geography and climates (at work as well in the Miocene) are also crucial to interpretations of the later stages of primate evolution. The Oligocene reveals a proliferation of early Old World anthropoid forms from one area in North Africa. In the Early Miocene, the evidence is also restricted to Africa, with fossils coming from rich sites in the eastern part of the continent (Kenya and Uganda). It would thus appear, on the basis of current evidence, that hominoids originated in Africa and experienced a successful adaptive radiation there before dispersing to other parts of the Old World.

The hominoids would maintain this exclusive African foothold for some time. The earliest of these East African hominoid fossils is more than 20 m.y. old, and later fossil finds extend the time range up to at least 13 m.y.a. For most of this period, East Africa is thought to have been more heavily forested, with much less woodlands and grasslands (savannas) than exist today (Pickford, 1983).

As in the earlier Cenozoic, the shifting of the earth's plates during the Miocene played a vital role in primate evolution. Before about 16 m.y.a., Africa was cut off from Eurasia; consequently, once hominoids had origi-

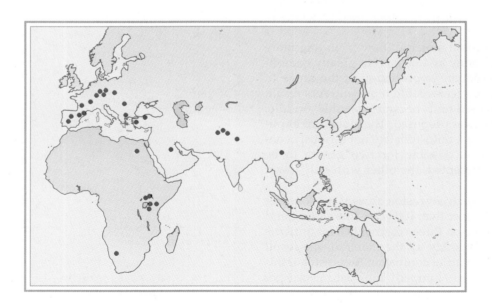

Figure 11-7

Miocene hominoid distribution—fossil sites thus far discovered.

nated there in the Early Miocene, they were isolated. However, around 16 m.y.a., the African plate "docked" with Eurasia (Bernor, 1983) through the Arabian Peninsula, a contact that was to revolutionize mammalian faunas of the later Miocene. Many forms, such as proboscideans, giraffoids, and pigs, which originated in Africa now migrated into Eurasia (van Couvering and van Couvering, 1976). Apparently, among these mid-Miocene intercontinental pioneers were some hominoids. Since they had evolved in the mainly tropical setting of equatorial Africa, most of the earlier hominoids probably remained primarily arboreal. Accordingly, it has been suggested that a relatively continuous forest would have been necessary across the Afro-Arabian-Eurasian land bridge.

Ecological changes were, however, already afoot in Africa. By 16 m.y.a., the environment was becoming drier, with less tropical rainforest and, conversely, more open woodland/bushland and savanna areas emerging (Bernor, 1983; Pickford, 1983). In other words, the environments in East Africa were being transformed more into their contemporary form. With the opportunities thus presented, some African hominoids were almost certainly radiating into these more open niches about 16 to 17 m.y.a. Part of this adaptation probably involved exploitation of different foods and more ground-living than practiced by the arboreal ancestors of these hominoids. Some partly terrestrial, more woodland or mosaic environment-adapted hominoids were probably thus on the scene and fully capable of migrating into Eurasia, even through areas that were not continuously forested.

The environments throughout the Old World were, of course, to alter even more. Later in the Miocene, some of these environmental shifts would further influence hominoid evolution and may have played a part in the origin of our own particular evolutionary lineage, the hominids. More on this later.

MIOCENE HOMINOIDS—CHANGING VIEWS AND TERMINOLOGY

So, throughout the Miocene, environmental and geographic factors imposed constraints on hominoids as well as opened new opportunities to them. Over a time span of close to 15 million years, hominoids in the middle two-thirds of the Miocene were successful indeed. Once they migrated into Eurasia, they dispersed rapidly and diversified into a variety of species. After 14 million years ago, we have evidence of widely distributed hominoids from Pakistan, India, Turkey, Greece, Hungary, China, and western Europe. Much of this material has only recently been uncovered and is incredibly abundant. For example, from Lufeng in southern China alone, 5 partial skulls and more than 1,000 teeth have been found in the past 15 years (Wu and Oxnard, 1983). The other areas have also yielded many paleontological treasures in recent years. Moreover, recent searches of museum collections in East Africa, as well as resurveys of fossil sites, have uncovered yet more fossils (Walker and Teaford, 1989).

Given this quantity of new information, it is not surprising that heretofore existing theories of early hominoid evolution have been reevaluated. In fact, it would not be unfair to describe the last decade as a "revolution" in paleontological views of Miocene hominoid evolution. With a great deal of this recent fossil material still unanalyzed, all the answers are not presently at hand. In fact, the more fossils found, the more complicated the situation seems to become. In order to simplify matters, we will organize the fossil material primarily on the basis of geography and secondarily on the basis of chronology. Moreover, we will suggest only tentative evolutionary relationships in most cases, as this is the best that can be currently concluded.

Figure 11-8

Proconsul africanus *skull. Discovered by Mary Leakey in 1948. (From early Miocene deposits on Rusinga Island, Kenya.)*

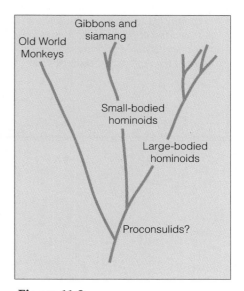

Figure 11-9

The probable evolutionary placement of the East African proconsulids before the split of small- and large-bodied hominoids.

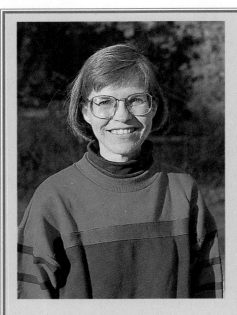

Mary Ellen (M.E.) Morbeck studies primate anatomy, behavior, ecology, and evolution. Professor of anthropology and anatomy at the University of Arizona, she earned her undergraduate degree from the University of Colorado (B.A. 1967) and graduate degrees from the University of California, Berkeley (M.A. 1970, Ph.D. 1972). In addition to university teaching and research, Morbeck is committed to promoting public understanding of science. She also enjoys world travel and exploring the natural areas of the American Southwest.

I expected to become an elementary school teacher—a traditional career choice for women—when I began college in the early 1960s. My advisor told me to take psychology or physical anthropology instead of the "freshman flunk-out" biology course. I didn't know about anthropology. I had never thought about what it means to be human or how we got to be the way we are. But Margaret Mead always seemed to be in the news. So, I chose physical anthropology (and soon discovered that it was human biology, and not Dr. Mead's area of expertise!).

That first anthropology class showed me how to think about humans in terms of natural history and evolution. Bones and casts of fossil hominids captivated me. I switched my major to anthropology but continued with teacher-training courses. I looked for opportunities to learn about archaeological excavation and to develop skills in skeletal analyses. My friends made me think about graduate school and my professors encouraged me to apply. As always, my parents were supportive. But I had to assure them that, when rejected (or, if really lucky, after earning a M.A. degree), I would follow their practical advice and finish my teaching credential.

I couldn't not "do" anthropology. At the same time, I never strayed from a commitment to teaching.

Sharing ideas about anthropology through university courses and teaching in museums and schools soon became intertwined with research. Today, I see both activities at the core of my professional life.

I went to graduate school at the University of California, Berkeley. Sherry Washburn showed me how to connect the many "anthro-bytes" I had learned as an undergraduate: first, how to link bones and anatomy with behavior as expressed in particular environments; and, second, how to use comparative and functional approaches to explain past and present variation among primates. Paleoanthropology was my initial focus and I went to Africa and Europe to study Miocene fossil hominoids. Later, I looked more closely at the relationships of anatomy, behavior, and ecology.

Paleoanthropology was the initial focus of my graduate research project. Only a few years after my first physical anthropology course, I went to Africa and Europe to excavate fossil sites and to study bones and teeth of *Proconsul* and other Miocene fossil hominoids.

Fossils document when, where, and under what circumstances we evolved. Bones and teeth are the

AFRICAN FORMS (23–14 M.Y.A.)

A wealth of early hominoid fossils has come from the deep and rich stratigraphic layers of Kenya and Uganda. These diverse forms are presently classified within at least 2 separate families, including perhaps 9 different genera (Fleagle, 1988). Indeed, important and mostly new finds (from the 1980s) have been uncovered, suggesting as many as 3 further hominoid genera in an as-yet-undetermined (and possibly a third) family. In other words, over the 9-million-year period for which we have evidence, as many as 12 differ-

now-mineralized, left-over hard parts of once-living individuals. They provide a glimpse at the lifeways and life cycles of our ancestors and close relatives. I use a form-function approach to understand skeletal features and behavior correlates. For example, limb proportions, joint size and shape, and muscle attachment sites relate to biomechanics of movement and weight-bearing abilities. These in turn allow feeding and locomotion behavior oftentimes directly related to survival and reproduction. But fossils (fragmentary bones-turned-to-stone) provide only limited information about *individuals*, their lives, their populations and ecological communities, and, in addition, their species and evolutionary history.

I wanted to find out more about *all* of the factors that contribute to the bone size, shape, and structure that we study at one point in an individual's life—the time of death as recorded in fossils. And I wanted to find out more about how bones and teeth function as part of survival throughout the life stages. Using comparative and functional approaches, I looked more closely at relationships of anatomy, behavior, and ecology and, later, at patterns of

growth, development, and aging in contemporary primates. My laboratory work over the years continues to emphasize both behavior and anatomy via skeletal analyses and cadaver dissections as well as field observations of locomotion and laboratory studies of growth in living primates.

Although I originally focused on anatomy and behavior, I also wanted to connect individuals with populations and assess their genetic legacies. This interest led me to the expanding literature on life history and population biology. My current research on the skeletal biology and lifelong behaviors of the Gombe chimpanzees continues to bring many of my earlier studies to fruition.

During the past several years, Jane Goodall has provided skeletons of free-ranging chimpanzees for analyses by our research team, including myself, Adrienne Zihlman, and two of the contributors to this text, Robert Jurmain and Lynn Kilgore. The skeletons of Flo, her son Flint and others, combined with recorded experiences of the same individuals during life and, for females, their reproductive profiles, give us a rare opportunity to test hypotheses about what we can (and cannot) read in the bones and teeth about the role of the individual in evolution. The Gombe chimpanzee

skeletons and the individuals who "owned" them reveal what bones and teeth (and fossils) tell us about evolutionary processes related to life histories of individuals, the sexes, populations, and species.

Now, using comparative, functional, and evolutionary approaches, I look forward to once again studying fossils of apes and humans with a stronger "real animal, real lives" perspective. The more we understand the factors that shape anatomy and behavior during life and how these factors, in turn, relate to survival and reproduction, the more reliable will be our interpretations of fossilized anatomy. And, finally, from this understanding also will come greater reliability in reconstructing the behaviors suggested in the fossil record of our own evolution.

ent hominoid genera have been sampled from East Africa, with the potential for yet more as the fossil sample accumulates.

Most of the newer material has yet to be described completely, and relationships among specimens are uncertain. The best samples and thus best-known forms are those of the genus *Proconsul* (belonging to the proconsulid family). From the full array of proconsulid remains (mostly dental pieces), considerable variation is apparent. Body size estimates range from that of a small monkey (about 10 pounds) to as large as a female gorilla (about 150 pounds). Environmental niches were probably also quite varied, for some species were apparently confined to dense rainforests, while others potentially exploited more open woodlands. Some researchers have also suggested considerable diversity of locomotory behaviors, including perhaps some forms that were at least partly terrestrial (Fleagle, 1988). Indeed, when on the ground, some of these proconsulids may even have occasionally adopted a bipedal stance (Pilbeam, 1988).

The dentition of all the proconsulid forms is, however, quite uniform, showing the typical Old World anthropoid pattern of 2-1-2-3. Moreover, these forms all display broad upper central incisors and large sexually dimorphic canines. In the molars, the enamel is fairly thick, but the softer dentin below penetrates well into these cusps, so that the enamel wore through fairly quickly with use (Kelly and Pilbeam, 1986). There is also the characteristic hominoid Y-5 pattern of cusps, seen in the lower molars (see Fig. 11-3). We can get some idea of diet from these teeth, which suggest that most forms were probably fruit-eaters.

From those well-preserved pieces of crania (representing currently only one species), brain size estimates are at least as large or larger than contemporary Old World monkeys (although probably not as large as contemporary hominoids; note, however, that *relative* brain size compared to body size is the crucial feature—a tricky estimate indeed for incomplete fossilized fragments). The surface features of the brain, as inferred from interior surfaces of cranial bones, do not apparently show the derived characteristics of living large-bodied hominoids (Falk, 1983). In fact, they show many primitive hominoid features similar to that seen in gibbon brains (Pilbeam, 1988).

A full understanding of the evolutionary relationships of the East African hominoids has not yet been attained. Indeed, in many cases, the classification still remains a muddle. For example, one fossil (discovered in the 1950s) from Rusinga Island in Kenya has been renamed and reassigned to different evolutionary groups at least six times. Just as paleoanthropologists begin to think that the situation is becoming better defined, new fossil discoveries muddy the waters still further. Some of this new material may date as early as 18–17 m.y.a., but most of it is in the range 16–14 m.y.a. Thus, for the most part, these finds are *later* than the proconsulids just discussed. It is not so surprising, then, to find that *Proconsul* is a more primitive hominoid (i.e., less derived). In fact, many primate evolutionists (Andrews, 1985; Pilbeam, 1988) would place *Proconsul* before the split of small- and large-bodied hominoids (as shown in Fig. 11-6). Therefore, while *Proconsul* may *not* actually have been the last common ancestor of gibbons as well as all large-bodied hominoids (including us), something resembling it may well have been.

In 1992, a new find was announced—that of a fossil hominoid from an unexpected locale, Namibia in southwestern Africa. Dated from approximately 13 m.y.a., this new specimen (a half-portion of a mandible) is just slightly younger than the East African hominoids discussed above.

From initial analysis, this specimen clearly appears to be a large-bodied hominoid, perhaps from an animal weighing about 35 pounds. However, more precise conclusions must await more complete analysis and, perhaps, more complete discoveries.

EUROPEAN FORMS (13–11 M.Y.A.)

Although they are the first of the Miocene hominoids to have been discovered, the European varieties still remain enigmatic. Very few fossils have been discovered, and what has been found consists almost entirely of jaws and lower dentitions. Among the only features that distinguish this varied lot of specimens from France, Spain, Austria (and maybe Hungary, too) is that the molar teeth are thin-enameled (that is, the dentin penetrates far into the cusps). Most researchers would place all these forms into the genus *Dryopithecus*.

Discovery of similar forms from the Rudabanya Mountains in Hungary during the 1970s have complicated matters further. Initially thought to be similar to the thick-enameled varieties from southern and southwestern Asia (see below), the Hungarian fossils are now placed closer to *Dryopithecus* from western Europe. Nevertheless, many researchers still believe the Rudabanya fossils are probably a distinct genus (*Rudapithecus*) (Kelly and Pilbeam, 1986). It seems unlikely that any of these *Dryopithecus*-group fossils are related closely to any living hominoid.

SOUTH/SOUTHWEST ASIAN FORMS (?16–7 M.Y.A.)

Three sites from Turkey have yielded fragmentary fossil hominoid remains dating to the early Middle Miocene (16–14 m.y.a.). As we noted on page 303, following "docking" of the Arabian plate with East Africa about 16 m.y.a., land routes became available for expansion from Africa into Eurasia. It would thus seem, from these Turkish remains, that hominoids quickly took advantage of this route and reached Eurasia by 16 m.y.a. Most researchers would assign these remains to the genus *Sivapithecus*.

Far more complete samples of *Sivapithecus* have been recovered from southern Asia, in the Siwalik Hills of India and Pakistan. Most dramatically, over the last 15 years, paleoanthropologists led by David Pilbeam of Harvard University have recovered numerous excellent specimens from the Potwar Plateau of Pakistan. Included in this superb Pakistani collection is a multitude of mandibles (15 in all, some of which are nearly intact), many postcranial remains, and a partial cranium, including most of the face (Pilbeam, 1982).

Sivapithecus from Turkey and Pakistan was probably a good-sized hominoid, ranging in size from 70–150 pounds. It probably inhabited a mostly arboreal niche, and its locomotion was "apelike," at least in the sense that *Sivapithecus* most likely displayed some suspensory abilities (Pilbeam, 1988).

Sivapithecus differs morphologically from *Proconsul* or *Dryopithecus* in its dentition and facial anatomy. The front teeth, especially the upper central incisors, are often quite large, while the canines are fairly good-sized (low-crowned and robust). There are, however, large discrepancies in canine size among *Sivapithecus* individuals, partly because some species were larger overall, but also because there was considerable variation (sexual dimorphism) within the same species. In diet, like most other hominoids, *Sivapithecus* was probably a fruit-eater.

The first lower premolar is also quite variable in shape. Usually it is fairly sectorial in shape; that is, it shows the shearing surface typical of most catarrhines (consequently, this is probably the primitive condition). The most distinctive aspect of *Sivapithecus* dentition is seen in the posterior (back) teeth, where molars are large, flat-wearing, and thick-enameled (with dentin not penetrating far into the cusps).

The thickness of the enamel cap has played a significant role in recent interpretations of Miocene hominoid evolution. Among living hominoids, relative to body size, humans have by far the thickest enamel caps. Gorillas and chimps have thin enamel, but orangs could be described as moderately

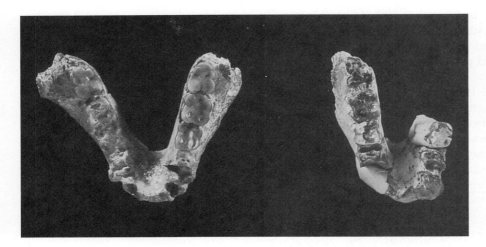

Figure 11-10

Two Sivapithecus *mandibles from the Potwar Plateau, Pakistan. Discovered in 1976 and 1977. Approximate age, 9 million years.*

thick (Ward and Pilbeam, 1983). Thick, in fact very thick, enamel is also seen in early hominids (in the time period 4–1 m.y.a.). As we have seen in *Proconsul* and *Dryopithecus*, enamel thickness itself varies, but dentin usually penetrates into the cusps, so that the enamel wears through during use—in a manner similar to living African apes.

Probably, the most characteristic anatomical aspects of *Sivapithecus* are seen in the face, especially the area immediately below the nose (Ward and Kimbel, 1983). Facial remains of *Sivapithecus* from Pakistan and Turkey have concave profiles and projecting incisors (and, overall, remarkably resemble the modern orangutan). In particular, the partial cranium discovered in 1980 at the Potwar Plateau (Pakistan, circa 8 m.y.a.) and published two years later (Pilbeam, 1982) bears striking similarities to the orangutan. (See Fig. 11-11.) The published description of this specimen, with illustrations similar to those shown here, had a tremendous impact on paleoanthropology. As we have seen (p. 202), biochemical evidence demonstrates the distinctiveness of the orang from the African apes and humans; here, then, was fossil evidence suggesting some ancient Asian traces of the orang lineage. As a result, the views of biochemists and paleoanthropologists agree more closely (pp. 310–311).

It must be noted, however, that, except for the face and jaw, *Sivapithecus* is *not* like an orangutan. In fact, especially in the postcranium (that is, all skeletal parts except the head), *Sivapithecus* is distinctively *unlike* an orang, or any other known hominoid, for that matter. For example, the forelimb suggests a unique mixture of traits, indicating probably some mode of arboreal quadrupedalism but with no suspensory component. In most respects, then, *Sivapithecus* could be described as *highly derived* (Pilbeam, 1986).

Many earlier fossil-based interpretations of Miocene evolutionary affinities had, of course, to be reevaluated. As we hinted at the beginning of our discussion of Miocene hominoids (p. 301), in the 1960s E. L. Simons and David Pilbeam suggested a Middle Miocene hominoid as the first hominid (that is, clearly diverged on our particular line and separate from that leading to any extant ape). According to this view, this early hominid was *"Ramapithecus"**—known at that time mostly from India, with some bits from East Africa.

---

*"*Ramapithecus*" is shown in quotes, as the genus is no longer recognized as a legitimate separate entity (that is, it is not a valid taxon).

We have already illustrated some of the dramatic new discoveries of the 1970s and early 1980s. As a consequence of these later discoveries, the earlier suggestion that *"Ramapithecus"* was a definite hominid was seriously questioned and has now been rejected altogether. One primary advocate of this revised view is Pilbeam (1977, 1982, 1986), an initial architect of the earlier widely accepted theory. Pilbeam, who has led the highly successful paleoanthropological project at the Potwar Plateau, has been swayed by the new fossils recovered there and elsewhere. These more complete specimens (like that shown in Fig. 11-11) are dentally very similar to what had been called *"Ramapithecus."* Researchers now simply lump *"Ramapithecus"* with *Sivapithecus.*

In summary, then, the fossil remains of *Sivapithecus* from Turkey and India/Pakistan are the most clearly derived large-bodied hominoids we have from the whole Miocene. While some forms (e.g., *Proconsul*) are seemingly quite primitive and others (*Dryopithecus*) are derived in directions quite unlike any living form, *Sivapithecus* has several derived features of the face, linking it evolutionarily with the orangutan. The separation of the Asian large-bodied hominoid line from the African stock (leading ultimately to gorillas, chimps, and humans) thus occurred at least 12 m.y.a. (Pilbeam, 1988). (See Fig. 11-12.)

Other Miocene Hominoids

Pliopithecus   Another interesting but still not well-understood hominoid is *Pliopithecus*, from the middle and late Miocene of Europe. Since this is a fairly

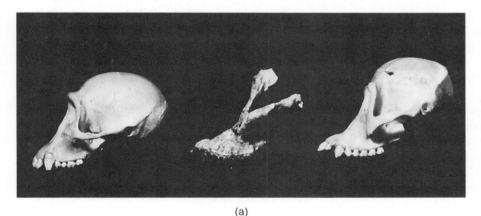

(a)

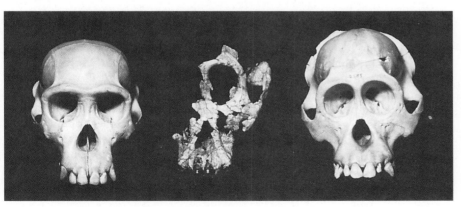

(b)

Figure 11-11

Comparison of Sivapithecus *cranium (center) with modern chimpanzee (left) and orangutan (right). The* Sivapithecus *fossil is specimen GSP 15000 from the Potwar Plateau, Pakistan, circa 8 m.y.a. (a) Lateral view; (b) frontal view.*

Box 11-1　　Timing the Hominid-Pongid Split

One of the most fundamental of all questions in human evolution is: When did the hominid line originate? Or, to put it another way: When did we last share a common ancestry with our closest living relatives, the African great apes?

Scientists have taken different perspectives in attempting to answer this question. The traditional approach of paleontology is still the most common. Recent years have produced considerably more paleontological sophistication through a vast new array of fossil material, more precise chronometric dating, and more rigorous interpretation of primitive-derived characteristics. Still, the fossil record remains incomplete, and significant gaps exist for some of the most crucial intervals. So the question still persists: How old is the hominid line?

Data drawn from a completely different perspective have also been applied to this problem. As advocated by Vincent Sarich and the late Allan Wilson of the University of California, Berkeley (1967), this perspective utilizes comparisons of living animals. By calibrating the overall immunological reactions of proteins from different species, by sequencing the amino acids within proteins, or by doing DNA hybridization or DNA sequencing (see pp. 226–227), living species can be compared to each other.

Certainly, such data are immensely valuable in demonstrating *relative* genetic distances among contemporary organisms (as we discussed in Chapter 8). However, proponents of this view go considerably further and postulate that biochemical distance can be used directly to calculate evolutionary distance. In other words, a "molecular clock" is thought to provide unambiguous divergence dates for a host of evolutionary lineages, including hominids/pongids (Sarich, 1971).

Several hotly disputed assumptions are required, however, to perform this feat. Most importantly, the rate of molecular evolution must be constant over time. Such regularity could be accomplished if rates of change were constant within a class of proteins or if selection pressures remained constant. Since environmental changes are decidedly not constant through time, the latter assumption is not valid. As for the first point, while neutral mutations certainly do occur (and perhaps do so quite frequently), many researchers are not convinced that most mutations are neutral (for example, see Livingstone, 1980). Moreover, even if mutation were mostly neutral, major evolutionary shifts may still be quite nongradual in tempo—given the suggested punctuated mode of change (see p. 187).

Another possible complicating factor concerns generation length. Those species that reproduce in shorter periods of time should (according to strict application of the molecular clock) show, for the same period of time, greater amounts of molecular evolution than more slowly reproducing forms (Vogel et al., 1976). Given the variation in generation lengths, it is not justifiable to make strict linear reconstruction for divergence times among prosimians, monkeys, and hominoids.

In fact, recently collected molecular data (in which DNA sequences are *directly* compared) indicate that the molecular clock does not run constantly with time. Rather, there is a marked *slowdown* in molecular divergence rate among primates, and most especially

small hominoid (estimated at 11–16 pounds; Fleagle, 1988), for several years primatologists suggested *Pliopithecus* was a gibbon ancestor. Moreover, dental features were also thought to mirror gibbon morphology. However, these similarities are superficial at best. In those respects in which *Pliopithecus* resembles contemporary small-bodied hominoids, the features are all primitive for hominoids in general. In fact, for most relevant anatomical details, *Pliopithecus* is a remarkably primitive hominoid (in fact, at least as primitive as *Proconsul*). This is surprising, given its relatively late date and Eurasian distribution (where hominoids are generally more derived than their African cousins). It may be that *Pliopithecus* is a long-surviving descendant of an

among the hominoids. Such a phenomenon is thought to be a function of greater generation length among higher primates when compared to other mammals (Li and Tanimura, 1987).

Another problem is that there is no certain indicator of molecular evolutionary rates; different proteins yield significantly different rates of evolution and thus greatly influence inferences about divergence times (Corruccini et al., 1980). In fact, the *greatest* margin of error would occur in attempting to calculate relatively recent evolutionary events—for example, the hominid-pongid split.

Analysis of amino acid sequences of proteins by another group of biochemists (at Wayne State University in Detroit) has confirmed that, indeed, rates of molecular evolution are not constant, but are rather characterized by periods of acceleration and *deacceleration* (the latter being particularly true in the last few million years). Thus, these researchers conclude: "For proteins demonstrating striking shifts in rates of amino acid substitutions over time, it is not possible to calculate accurate divergence dates within Anthropoidea using the molecular clock approach. Our analysis of amino acid sequence data of several proteins by the clock model yields divergence dates, particularly within the Hominoidea, that are far too recent in view of well-established fossil evidence" (Goodman et al., 1983, p. 68).

As a result of such criticisms of the "clock," some paleontologists have been skeptical of its claimed applications. For example, Milford Wolpoff (of the University of Michigan) argues that, "Probably the best way to summarize the very disparate points raised is that the 'clock' simply *should not* work" (Wolpoff, 1983a, p. 661).

Naturally, not everyone takes so negative a view of the clock approach. Vincent Sarich continues to believe firmly in its basic accuracy (when applied correctly) and, justifiably, feels vindicated by recent recalibrations of theories derived from fossil evidence, which bring them closer to the biochemically derived hypotheses.

The fossils themselves are not going to provide the whole answer. The paleontological record is usually too incomplete to provide clearcut ancestor-descendant associations. More fossils will always help, of course, but the way we think about them (i.e., the questions we raise about them) is also crucial in framing workable theories.

The biochemical perspective has been important in that it has articulated key issues for evolutionary consideration (for example, the place of the orang in relation to other large-bodied hominoids). The interplay between the paleontological and biochemical perspectives has thus been most productive. In fact, these viewpoints agree more now on several aspects of hominoid evolution than they did just a few years ago. The greatest furor has been raised from overly strong claims for the unique validity of either approach. We have shown in this chapter that more fossil evidence *and* more controlled analyses have forced previous views to be reconsidered. Moreover, it is equally unfair to portray the clock approach as a complete answer. As one of the leading advocates of this method has stated, "The clock is one of an approximate, not metronomically perfect nature" (Cronin, 1983, p. 116).

Early Miocene, very primitive ancestor, one that antedated the radiation of major hominoid lineages. (See Fig. 11-12.)

Greece ("Ouranopithecus," 12–11 m.y.a.)　　From the Ravin de la Pluie near Salonika, Greece, have come several hominoid specimens (mostly mandibles, but also a partial face) discovered in the 1970s. Because the molar teeth have thick enamel, researchers initially grouped these finds with *Sivapithecus*. However, recent analysis of the critical facial anatomy (Kelly and Pilbeam, 1986) has shown that the Greek finds are not similar to *Sivapithecus* (or the orang), but their molar morphology also makes them unlike *Dryopithecus*.

Figure 11-12

Evolutionary relationships of hominoids.

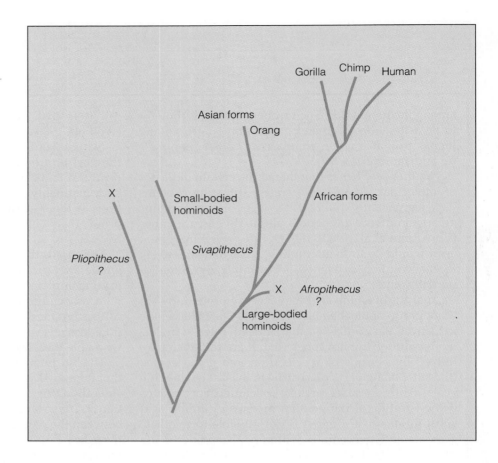

The evolutionary relationships of this Greek hominoid thus still remain a mystery.

Lufeng, Yunnan Province, Southern China (8–7 m.y.a.)   As we mentioned earlier, the recent discoveries from the Lufeng site in southern China have been remarkable, now totaling over 1,000 specimens (including several crania, mostly crushed mandibles, and hundreds of isolated teeth). Since the fossil collection is so large, and since the crania are in need of much restoration, most of the material has yet to be fully described. Therefore, conclusions regarding this most important fossil collection must remain highly tentative. Indeed, there is still argument concerning how many genera are represented among the Lufeng hominoids, with some experts favoring two, while others see only one genus. Ongoing interpretation of the vast dental remains has led some researchers (Kelly and Pilbeam, 1986) to suggest that *only* one species may be represented. If so, this would be an extremely variable species, most likely reflecting extreme sexual dimorphism. In fact, such a degree of sexual dimorphism (at least dentally) would exceed that seen even in the modern orang (where males are more than twice the size of females). We have discussed in Chapter 9 (see pp. 252–256) the differing reproductive strategies displayed by contemporary male and female primates. It thus becomes interesting to speculate about the social structure of these apparently highly dimorphic Miocene forms. (Note: *Most* Miocene hominoids from East Africa, Europe, and Asia seem to display marked sexual dimorphism.)

Like the Greek fossils discussed in the preceding section, the evolutionary relationships of the Chinese specimens are unclear. They also do not show the shared derived features of the *Sivapithecus*-orangutan lineage. Determining exactly where they fit thus remains a major challenge for primate evolutionists.

Other East African Hominoids (18–14 m.y.a.)   As we discussed on page 306, some fossil material (much of it quite recently discovered) is dated generally later than the proconsulids and does not comfortably fit within the same evolutionary grouping. Most notable have been new finds from northern Kenya at Kalodirr and Buluk. One form, called *Afropithecus*, from Kalodirr is a very large hominoid with hints from the dentition of a possible link specifically with African large-bodied hominoids (Fig. 11-12). Buluk is more tantalizing yet. With a quite early provisional date of 17–18 m.y.a., a thick-enameled hominoid shows some resemblances to *Sivapithecus* from Asia (Leakey and Leakey, 1986). It is possible, then, that this lineage had diverged early in the Miocene of Africa and only later migrated to Eurasia, where some descendants apparently formed the ancestral basis for the orangutan line.

In order to combine all the suggested branching points discussed over the last several pages, we summarize together these suggested evolutionary relationships in Fig. 11-13. The placement and number of question marks

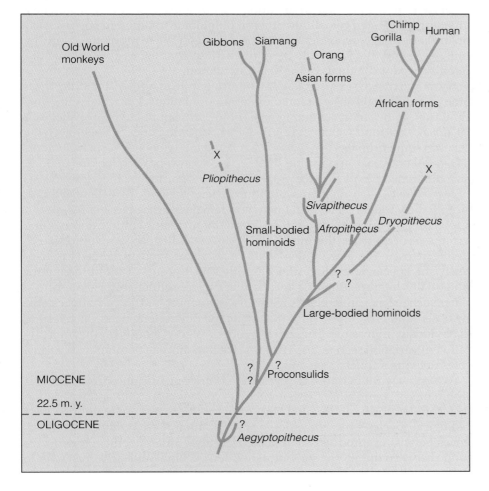

Figure 11-13

Summary of evolutionary relationships, Miocene hominoids.

indicate continued uncertainty. In other words, treat most of the suggested relationships (all those other than *Sivapithecus*-orangutan) as highly tentative.

The Meaning of Genus and Species

Our discussion of fossil primates has introduced a multitude of cumbersome taxonomic names. We should pause at this point and reasonably ask: Why use so many names like *Proconsul*, *Dryopithecus*, and *Sivapithecus*? What does such naming mean in evolutionary terms?

Our goal when applying genus, species, or other taxonomic labels to groups of organisms is to make meaningful biological statements about the variation that is present. When looking at populations of living or long extinct animals, we are assuredly going to see variation. This situation is true of *any* sexually reproducing organism due to the factors of recombination (see Chapter 2). As a result of recombination, each individual organism is a unique combination of genetic material, and this uniqueness is usually reflected to some extent in the phenotype. In addition to such *individual variation*, we see other kinds of systematic variation in all biological populations. *Age changes* certainly act to alter overall body size, as well as shape, in many animals. One pertinent example for fossil hominoid studies is the great change in number, size, and shape of teeth from deciduous (milk) teeth (only 20 present) to the permanent dentition (32 present). It obviously would be a great error to assign two different fossil hominoids to different species *solely* on the basis of age-dependent dental criteria. If one were represented only by milk teeth and the other only by permanent teeth, they easily could be differently aged individuals of the *same* population.

Variation due to sex also plays an important role in influencing differences among individuals observed in biological populations. Differences in structural traits between males and females of the same population are called *sexual dimorphism*, and we have seen that great variation does exist between the sexes in some primates (for example, gorillas and baboons) in such elements as overall body size and canine size. As we have seen when looking at body size differences, as well as differences in tooth size, among the same species of *Sivapithecus*, a reasonable assumption is that what we are really viewing is simply the variations between males and females of the *same* species.

Keeping in mind all the types of variation present within interbreeding groups of organisms, the minimum biological category we would like to define in fossil primate samples is the *species*. As previously defined in Chapter 5, the species is biologically described as a group of interbreeding or potentially interbreeding organisms that are reproductively isolated from other such groups. In modern organisms, this concept is theoretically testable by observations of reproductive behavior. In animals long dead, such testing is obviously impossible. Therefore, in order to get a handle on the interpretation of variation seen in fossil groups like the Miocene hominoids, we must refer to living animals.

We know without doubt that variation is present. The question is: What is its biological significance? Two immediate choices occur: Either the variation is accounted for by individual, age, and sex differences seen within every biological species—**intraspecific**—or the variation present represents differences between reproductively isolated groups—**interspecific**. How do we judge between the alternatives intra- or interspecific? We clearly must refer to

Intraspecific   Within one species.

Interspecific   Between two or more species.

already defined groups where we can observe reproductive behavior—in other words, contemporary species.

If the amount of morphological variation observed in fossil samples is comparable with that seen today *within species of closely related forms*, then we should not "split" our sample into more than one species. We must, however, be careful in choosing our modern analogs, for rates of morphological evolution vary widely among different groups of mammals. In interpreting past primates, we do best when comparing them with well-known species of modern primates.

Our evolutionary interpretations of the vast array of variable Miocene hominoids is greatly simplified by adhering to relevant biological criteria:

1. First we must look at *all* relevant material. We are not justified in splitting fossil groups into several species on the basis of only presumed differences in the sample (Simons and Pilbeam's contribution was a major step in rectifying this situation for Miocene hominoids).
2. We must statistically reconstruct the variation observed in our often very small fossil *samples* to realistic dimensions of actual biological *populations*. Every piece of every bone found is part of an individual, who in turn was part of a variable interbreeding population of organisms.
3. We then refer to known dimensions of variation in closely related groups of living primates, keeping in mind expected effects of age, sexual dimorphism, and individual variation.
4. Our next step is to extrapolate the results to the fossil sample and make the judgment: How many species are represented?
5. Since fossil forms are widely scattered in time, we also must place the different species within a firm chronology.
6. Finally, we would like to make interpretations (at least, educated guesses) concerning which forms are evolutionarily related to other forms. To do this, we must pay strict attention to primitive as opposed to derived characteristics.

Following the above steps will greatly reduce the kind of useless confusion that has characterized hominoid studies for so long. We do not, however, wish to convey the impression that the biological interpretation of fossils into taxonomic categories is simple and unambiguous. Far from it! Many complexities must be recognized. Even in living groups, sharp lines between populations representing only one species and populations representing two or more species are difficult to draw. For example, a chain of interbreeding subspecies in gulls exchanges genes at overlapping boundaries. However, at the terminal ends of the chain, two subspecies (species?) live side-by-side along the coasts of Europe with little or no hybridization (Fig. 11-14). In practice, isolating exactly where species boundaries begin and end is exceptionally difficult, especially in a dynamic situation like that represented by gulls.

In contexts dealing with extinct species, the uncertainties are even greater. In addition to the overlapping patterns of variation *over space*, variation also occurs *through time*. In other words, even more variation will be seen in such **paleospecies**, since individuals may be separated by thousands or even millions of years. Applying strict Linnaean taxonomy to such a situation presents an unavoidable dilemma. Standard Linnaean classification, designed to take account of the variation present at any given time, describes a static situation. However, when dealing with paleospecies we are often involved in great spans of time and thus with much additional variation.

Paleospecies A group of organisms from different periods classified within the same species.

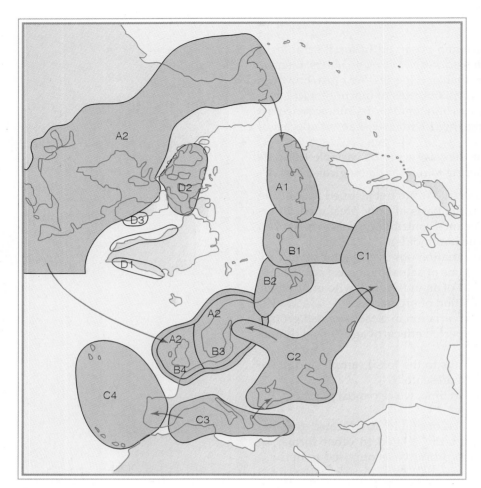

Figure 11-14

Circular overlap in gulls. A, B, C are subspecies of Larus argentatus. *D (L. glaucoides) is a separate species. All along the chain, subspecies interbreed (C1 with C2; C3 with C4, etc.) but at the terminal ends, A2 lives side-by-side with B3 and B4 and does* not *interbreed. Where does one then draw species designations?*

Where do we establish meaningful species boundaries in such a dynamic situation? Often, our task is made easier because of the incompleteness of the fossil record. Quite frequently, fossil samples are separated by great gaps of time (as between A and C in Fig. 11-15) and the morphological differences may therefore also be clearcut. In such a case, we feel quite comfortable calling these different species. But what about fossil populations (B, for example) that are intermediate in both time and morphology? This question has no easy answer. Any taxonomic designation in such a continuously evolving lineage is by necessity going to be arbitrary.

Such a line, which has no speciation events, is referred to as anagenetic. For such a lineage, many evolutionary biologists see no point in making separate species designations—that is, the entire line is seen as a single paleospecies (Eldredge and Cracraft, 1980). Many biologists believe, in fact, that long, gradual transformations of this type are not the rule, but that branching (i.e., speciation) is much more typical of evolutionary change. (Once again, the view of the punctuationalists—see p. 187.)

Moreover, it is imperative in evolutionary interpretation to understand ancestor-descendant relationships. Most paleontologists have traditionally made anatomical comparisons and then immediately constructed evolutionary trees (also called *phylogenies*). Recently, another perspective has been advanced. In this approach, a detailed interpretation of primitive versus derived states must first be explicitly stated. Only then can patterns of relationships be shown.

These are best interpreted in the form of a *cladogram* (a set of relationships shown as a hypothesis). In fact, usually several cladograms can be constructed from the same set of data. Those that are seen as most economically explaining the patterns of derived characteristics are then provisionally accepted, while less adequate ones are rejected. Such a perspective has been termed **cladistics**, and has injected a good deal more objectivity into paleontology (Eldredge and Cracraft, 1980). It must be pointed out, however, that not all paleontologists have accepted this approach. A basic assumption of cladistic analysis is that trait *patterns* are developed as the result of ancestor-descendant relationships and, conversely, that parallelism (an anagenetic line) (see p. 184) has little import. In primate evolution, this assumption may not hold true; an analysis of morphological features in lemurs and lorises showed that 80% of the traits studied displayed some parallelism (Walker et al., 1981).

The next level of formal taxonomic classification, the *genus*, presents another problem. In order to have more than one genus, we obviously must have at least two species (reproductively isolated groups), and, in addition, the species must differ in a basic way. A genus is therefore defined as a group of species composed of members more closely related to each other than they are to species from another genus.

Grouping contemporary species together into genera is largely a subjective procedure wherein degree of relatedness becomes a mostly relative judgment. One possible test for contemporary animals is to check for results of hybridization between individuals of different species—rare in nature but quite common in captivity. If two normally separate species interbreed and produce live, though not necessarily fertile, offspring, this process shows genetically that they are not too distant and that they probably should be classified into a single genus. Well-known examples of such interspecific crosses within one genus are horses with donkeys (*Equus caballus* × *Equus asinus*) or lions with tigers (*Panthera leo* × *Panthera tigris*). In both these cases, the close morphological and evolutionary similarities (as well as similar chromosomal arrangements) between these species are confirmed by their occasional ability to produce live hybrids.

As mentioned, we cannot perform breeding experiments with animals that are extinct, but another definition of genus becomes highly relevant. Species that are members of one genus share the same broad adaptive zone or, in Sewall Wright's terminology (Mayr, 1962), a similar "adaptive plateau." What this represents is a general ecological life style more basic than the particular ecological niches characteristic of species. This ecological definition of genus can be an immense aid in interpreting fossil primates. Teeth are the most often preserved parts, and they are usually excellent general ecological indicators. Therefore, if among the Miocene hominoids some animals appear to inhabit different adaptive/ecological zones (for example *Proconsul* vs. *Sivapithecus*), we are justified in postulating more than one genus present.

Operationally, then, categorization at the genus level becomes the most practical biological interpretation of fragmentary extinct forms. While species differences necessarily were also present (probably in great complexity), these are usually too intricate to recognize in incomplete material.

As a final comment, we should point out that classification by genus is also not always a clearcut business. Indeed, the argument among primate

Cladistics The school of evolutionary biology that seeks to make hypotheses through interpreting patterns of primitive/derived characteristics.

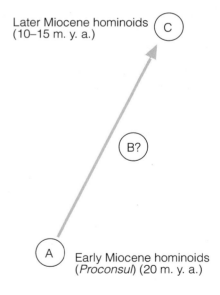

Figure 11-15

Evolution in a continuing evolving lineage (an anagenetic line). Where does one designate the different species?

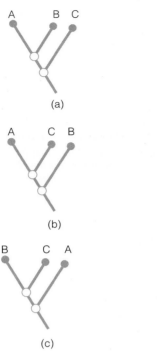

Figure 11-16

Cladograms. Three alternative statements representing evolutionary relationships among three taxa. (a) C diverges earliest, with A and B sharing a more recent common ancestor; (b) B diverges earliest, with A and C sharing a more recent common ancestor; (c) A diverges earliest, with B and C sharing a more recent common ancestor.

biologists over whether the chimp and gorilla represent one genus (*Pan troglodytes, Pan gorilla*) or two different genera (*Pan troglodytes, Gorilla gorilla*) demonstrates that even with living animals the choices are not always clear. Or, for that matter, some researchers—pointing to the very close *genetic* similarities between humans and chimps—would place these in the same genus (*Homo sapiens, Homo troglodytes*). When it gets this close to home, it gets even more difficult to be objective!

Summary

In this chapter, we have traced the evolutionary history of our primate origins between 60 and 10 m.y.a. Beginning in the late Cretaceous, the earliest primate ancestors were probably little more than arboreally adapted insectivores. In the Paleocene, there are, as yet, still no clearly derived primate forms apparent (despite prior claims to the contrary). In the following epoch, the Eocene, we begin to see an abundant diversification of primates that are readily identifiable. During this epoch, the lemurlike adapids begin their evolutionary radiation. Early anthropoid origins may also date to sometime in the late Eocene. In addition, Old and New World primates apparently shared their last common ancestry in the Eocene or early Oligocene and have gone their separate ways ever since.

In the Old World, the Oligocene reveals a large number of possible early anthropoid ancestors at the Fayum. By and large, all these are primitive Old World anthropoids, and none of the modern lineages (Old World monkeys, gibbons, large-bodied hominoids) can definitely be traced into the Oligocene.

The Miocene reveals an incredibly abundant and highly complex array of hominoid forms, mostly those of large-bodied varieties. More than 10 different genera and probably dozens of species are represented in those remains discovered in Africa, Asia, and Europe. Some early forms from Kenya and Uganda (the proconsulids) are more primitive than the majority of hominoids from Eurasia. While again there is little firm evidence tying these fossil forms to extant apes or ourselves, some tentative evidence suggests that *Sivapithecus* is closely related to the ancestors of the orang. Where, then, are the ancestors of the African apes or, even more relevantly, of ourselves? In the next six chapters, we will seek to answer this question.

Questions for Review

1. Why is it difficult to distinguish the earliest members of the primate order from other placental mammals? If you found a nearly complete skeleton of an early Paleocene mammal, what structural traits might lead you to believe it was a primate?
2. Compare the fossil primates of the Eocene with living members of the primate order.
3. If you (as an expert physical anthropologist) were brought remains of a fossil hominoid from South America purported to be 30 million years old, why might you be skeptical?
4. What kinds of primates were evolving at the Fayum in Oligocene times? What is meant by saying they are primitive catarrhines?

5. Compare and contrast the anatomical features of proconsulids with *Sivapithecus*.

6. How did the shifting of the earth's plates, as well as climatic changes, affect hominoid evolution in the Miocene?

7. What is meant by "small-bodied" hominoid compared to "large-bodied" hominoid?

8. If two fossil groups are classified as *Sivapithecus indicus* and *Sivapithecus sivalensis*, at what taxonomic level is the distinction being made? What are the biological implications of such a classification?

9. If two fossil groups are classified as *Dryopithecus* and *Sivapithecus*, at what taxonomic level is this distinction? What are the biological implications?

Chapter 12

Contents

Paleoanthropology

Has our evolution, both cultural and biological, been systematically and deliberately tampered with by beings from other worlds? Popularized by Erich von Däniken in a series of fantastically successful books (1968, 1970, 1973), this bizarre theory has been further promulgated in movies and television. Is it possible?

Scientific inquiry cannot "prove" *anything* impossible, but it can attempt to demonstrate what is probable. Von Däniken is correct in asserting that, given the vast number of stars (and planets) in the universe, there is a high probability of intelligent life out there *somewhere*. Of all these life forms, however, how many are capable of efficient interstellar travel (necessitating speeds approaching that of light)? Furthermore, even if some life forms possessed this technology, where would they look for other intelligent life? If they randomly sampled all "inhabitable" planets in the universe, their probability of finding us would be low indeed. Perhaps, however, they are watching or listening for signs. They might assume, as we have, that an intelligent life form with even a modest degree of technological sophistication could produce radio waves. In the hope of hearing such an intergalactic message, we have turned our own ears to the heavens. (Funding for this project, however, was discontinued by the United States Congress late in 1993.)

If creatures "out there" have done likewise, they may *eventually* hear our radio signals. However, we have been producing such communications for only the last sixty years or so (and these radio waves have only traveled about sixty light years). Special frequency signals aimed specifically at distant worlds have only been initiated in the last few years. Consequently, on the basis of simple logical deduction, it would seem unlikely that we have even been detected, to say nothing of actually playing host to extraterrestrial travelers.

Remember, however, that whereas such a postulation is exceedingly improbable, it is not completely impossible. What, then, of evidence?

Von Däniken has audaciously postulated that extraterrestrial beings have visited earth dozens of times. Nor did they just visit; they helped construct huge monuments. They even assisted with the writing of tablets and making of maps, and let themselves become deified by the masses of humble *H. sapiens* in the bargain.

Surely mysteries abound in the archeological record, which is incomplete and, thus, far from perfect. However, that fact does not justify postulating the unlikely, the bizarre, or the ridiculous when a much more probable (but admittedly, less exciting) explanation is easily found. Indeed, much of von Däniken's primary "hard" evidence has been debunked. The huge pyramids of Egypt and Mesoamerica, the mysterious geometric designs of Nazca, Peru, and the formidable stone monuments of Easter Island have all been demonstrated as *human* achievements using relatively simple technological principles and good old-fashioned human labor. It should also be noted that some scholars have detected a certain racist tinge to von Däniken's postulation. He does not suggest any European civilization required extraterrestrial assistance, but only those from other geographic areas— mostly in what we now call the Third World.

If, in 100,000 years, future generations of archeologists were to excavate some of the "wonders" of our world, they would (in the absence of written records) be struck by the seeming incongruities and mysteries. The incredible Gothic cathedrals of Europe, built during a period of economic and political disorganization, would appear a giant paradox. Did space beings build them? Or, even closer to home, the massive vaults excavated into the Rockies housing the genealogical records of the Mormon Church might also confuse and befuddle our descendants. Yet, the architects and engineers in Utah clearly did not require or receive extraterrestrial assistance in constructing this marvel.

Human beings routinely achieve the incredible, the fantastic, the inexplicable, and they do it on their own. After all, the New York Mets did win the World Series back in 1969!

SOURCES

Von Däniken, Erich. *Chariots of the Gods?* New York: G. P. Putnam's Sons, 1968.

———. *Gods from Outer Space.* New York: G. P. Putnam's Sons, 1970.

———. *Gold of the Gods.* New York: G. P. Putnam's Sons, 1973.

Introduction

In previous chapters, we have seen how humans are classed as primates, both structurally and behaviorally, and how our evolutionary history coincides with that of other primates. However, we are a unique kind of primate, and our ancestors have been adapted to a particular kind of life-style for several million years. Some kind of large-bodied hominoid may have begun this process more than 10 m.y.a., but, beginning about 4 m.y.a., evidence from Africa reveals much more definite hominid relationships. Moreover, the hominid nature of remains preserved in East Africa 2.5 m.y.a. is revealed by more than the morphological structure of teeth and bones; we know these animals are hominids also because of the way they behaved—emphasizing once again the *biocultural* nature of human evolution. In this chapter, we will discuss the methods scientists use to explore the secrets of early hominid behavior. We will then demonstrate these through the example of the best-known early hominid site in the world: Olduvai Gorge in East Africa.

Definition of Hominid

If any Miocene hominoid fossils represent the earliest stages of hominid diversification, our definition of them as hominid must then primarily be a *dental* one. Teeth and jaws are most of what we have of these Miocene forms. However, dentition is not the only way to describe the special attributes of our particular evolutionary radiation and is certainly not the most distinctive of its later stages. Modern humans and our hominid ancestors are distinguished from our closest living relatives (the great apes) by more obvious features than proportionate tooth and jaw size. For example, various scientists have pointed to other hominid characteristics, such as large brain size, bipedal locomotion, and toolmaking behavior, as being most significant in defining what makes a hominid a hominid (as opposed to a pongid, a cercopithecoid, or anything else for that matter). This last definition—humans as toolmakers—is the one that we wish to discuss in this chapter. The important structural attributes of the hominid brain, teeth, and locomotory apparatus will be discussed in the next chapter, where we investigate early hominid anatomical adaptations in greater detail.

BIOCULTURAL EVOLUTION: HUMANS AS TOOLMAKERS

Although other primates do occasionally make tools (see Chapter 10), only hominids depend on culture for their survival. We and our close hominid ancestors alone have the ability to "impose arbitrary form on the environment" (Holloway, 1969). For example, chimps who use termite sticks have a direct and immediate relationship with the raw material and purpose of the tool. Such is not the case in most human cultural behavior, which usually involves several steps often quite arbitrarily removed from a direct environmental context.

We are defining culture primarily as a mental process. The human mind—presumably the minds of our hominid ancestors as well—has the unique capacity to *create* symbols. When a chimp sees water, it probably sees only the immediate environmental setting plus any learned experiences that are directly associated. Humans, however, can introduce all kinds of additional meanings, such as "holy water," physically identical to all other water but with symbolic value. A chimp can see water and know from experience it is wet, drinkable, etc. However, the chimp is almost certainly not capable of grasping the superimposed, arbitrary ideas invented and understood only by humans. (We are being somewhat cautious here in noting claims of what a chimpanzee can and cannot do. The history of anthropology is littered with the wreakage of overly dogmatic assertions of just this kind!)

Obviously, we cannot "get inside the head" of a nonhuman primate to know exactly what it is or is not thinking. The assumptions we have made are derived from behavioral observations in natural habitats, as well as results of learning experiments. However, as discussed in Chapter 10, among scientists there is still considerable dispute concerning the behavioral capacities of other primates; the assumptions expressed here reflect the views of the authors. Humans, of course, also have the capacity to manipulate their environments in infinitely more complex ways than other animals. The simple human invention of a watertight container, such as a hollowed-out gourd or an ostrich egg, its persistent use communicated through generations, and its transport over considerable distance is more complex than cultural behaviors attributed to nonhuman primates. However, the difference is more one of degree than kind when we recall quite sophisticated behaviors, such as the rock carrying and nut smashing conducted by chimpanzees in West Africa.

Culture as a complex adaptive strategy has become central to human evolution and has acted as a potent selective force to mold our anatomical form over the last several million years. In the archeological record, early cultural behavior is seen in the preserved remains of stone implements, traces of a uniquely human activity. "The shaping of stone according to even the simplest plan is beyond the behavior of any ape or monkey" (Washburn, 1971, p. 105).

Thus, when we find stone tools made to a standardized pattern, we know we have found a behavior indicator of a hominid, and *only* hominid, adaptation. We are justified, then, in defining hominids as habitual toolmakers, *culturally dependent* animals, distinct in this respect in at least degree, if not

Figure 12-1

Early stone tools. Traces of hominid behavior, from Olduvai Gorge, East Africa, about 1.6 m.y.a.

Table 12-1 Contributing Specialties to Paleoanthropology

Physical Sciences	Biological Sciences	Social Sciences
Geology	Physical Anthropology	Archeology
Stratigraphy	Paleoecology	Cultural Anthropology
Petrology	Paleontology	Ethnography
(rocks, minerals)	(fossil animals)	Psychology
Pedology	Palynology	Ethnoarcheology
(soils)	(fossil pollen)	
Geophysics	Primatology	
Chemistry		
Geomorphology		
Taphonomy		

kind, from all other primates. Of course, there is much more to culture than just systematic tool use. However, for the archeological record of early hominids, all we have preserved is the *material* cultural remains of portions of their tool kits. Whatever the remainder of their culture might have been like, we are unable to say. That is why we say, "behavior does not fossilize."

The Strategy of Paleoanthropology

In order to understand human evolution adequately, we obviously need a broad base of information. The task of recovering and interpreting all the clues left by early hominids is the work of the paleoanthropologist. Paleoanthropology is defined as "the science of the study of ancient humans." As such, it is a diverse *multidisciplinary* pursuit seeking to reconstruct every possible bit of information concerning the dating, structure, behavior, and ecology of our hominid ancestors. In just the last few years, the study of early humans has marshalled the specialized skills of many diverse kinds of scientists. Included primarily in this growing and exciting adventure are the geologist, archeologist, physical anthropologist, and paleoecologist (see Table 12-1).

The geologist, usually working with an anthropologist (often an archeologist), does the initial survey work in order to locate potential early hominid sites. Many sophisticated techniques can aid in this search, including aerial and satellite photography. Paleontologists may also be involved in this early search, for they can help find fossil beds containing faunal remains; where conditions are favorable for the bone preservation of such specimens as ancient pigs and elephants, conditions may also be favorable for the preservation of hominid remains. In addition, paleontologists can (through comparison with known faunal areas) give quick estimates of the approximate age of fossil sites without having to wait for the more expensive and time-consuming chronometric analyses. In this way, fossil beds of the "right" geologic ages (that is, where hominid finds are most likely) can be isolated.

Once potential areas of early hominid sites have been located, much more extensive surveying begins. At this point, the archeologist takes over in the search for hominid "traces." We do not necessarily have to find remains of early hominids themselves to know they consistently occupied a particular area. Behavioral clues, or **artifacts**, also inform us directly and unambiguously about early hominid occupation. Modifying rocks according to a consistent plan, or simply carrying them around from one place to another (over

Artifacts Traces of hominid behavior; very old ones are usually of stone. The objects either must be consistently modified or transported and collected in some consistent fashion.

fairly long distances), are behaviors characteristic of no other animal but a hominid. Of course, *just* the fact that a rock has been moved is not sufficient evidence to draw such a conclusion. Depositional forces, such as stream action, will certainly move objects. Even other animals, for example, vultures or sea otters, will occasionally do so (in a real sense they also use rocks as tools). It is the consistent use and collection (caching) of such objects at a central place that intimates a uniquely hominid pattern. Therefore, when we see such behavioral evidence at a site, we know absolutely that hominids were present.

More than likely, early hominids sometimes utilized implements of wood or bone, and probably began doing so several million years ago (6–4 m.y.a.?). It is not altogether clear, however, just how many of these potential tools were available without *first* processing them with stone. Naturally pointed pieces of wood could probably have been utilized as digging sticks or perhaps for puncturing an ostrich egg (to make a watertight container). Beyond this, it probably would have been quite difficult to make much use of wood resources without some modification; yet, how could this have been done without something harder with which to cut, scrape, or sharpen (that is, stone tools)? Bone is even more intractable and would seem also to have been "off-limits" to hominids without some stone implement to crush, cut, etc. Probably the only bone sources available were splinters left behind at kills by large carnivores. This all remains, of course, speculative, since *direct* evidence is not available. Unfortunately, these organic materials usually are not preserved, and we thus know little about such early tool-using behavior.

On the other hand, our ancestors at some point showed a veritable fascination with stones, for these provided not only easily accessible and transportable weights (to hold down objects, such as skins and windbreaks) but also the most durable and sharpest cutting edges available at that time. Luckily for us, stone is almost indestructible, and early hominid sites are virtually strewn with thousands of stone artifacts. The earliest artifact site now documented is from the Omo region of Ethiopia, dating from at least 2.4 m.y.a. Another contender for the "earliest" stone assemblage is from the Hadar area, farther to the north in Ethiopia—dated 2.0–2.5 m.y.a.

Once an area is clearly demonstrated as a hominid site, much more concentrated research will then begin. We should point out that a more mundane but very significant aspect of paleoanthropology not shown in Table 12-1 is the financial one. Just the initial survey work in usually remote areas takes many thousands of dollars, and mounting a concentrated research project takes several hundred thousand dollars. Therefore, for such work to go on, massive financial support is required from governmental agencies and/or private donations. A significant amount of the paleoanthropologist's efforts and time are necessarily devoted to writing grant proposals or to speaking on the lecture circuit to raise the required funds for this work.

Once the financial hurdle has been cleared, a coordinated research project can commence. Usually headed by an archeologist or physical anthropologist, the field crew will continue to survey and map the target area in great detail. In addition, they will begin to search carefully for bones and artifacts eroding out of the soil, take pollen and soil samples for ecological analysis, and carefully recover rock samples for chronometric dating. If, in this early stage of exploration, the field crew finds a fossil hominid, they will feel very lucky indeed. The international press usually considers human fossils the most exciting kind of discovery, a situation that produces wide publicity, often working to assure future financial support. More likely, the crew will accumulate much information on geological setting, ecological data, particularly faunal remains, and, with some luck, archeological traces (hominid artifacts).

After long and arduous research in the field, even more time-consuming and detailed analysis is required back in the laboratory. The archeologist must clean, sort, label, and identify all the artifacts, and the paleontologist must do the same for all faunal remains. The kinds of animals present, whether forest browsers, woodland species, or open-country forms, will greatly help in reconstructing the local **paleoecological** settings in which early hominids lived. In addition, analysis of pollen remains by a palynologist will further aid in a detailed environmental reconstruction. All of these paleoecological analyses can assist in reconstructing the diet of early humans (see p. 346). Many complex kinds of contributions go into assembling and interpreting the relevant data in such analyses.

More information will be provided by analysis of soil samples by a **pedologist**, and rock and mineral samples by a **petrologist**. A geomorphologist may also be asked to reconstruct the sequence of past geologic events, including volcanics, mountain building, earth movements, such as faulting, and changes in the orientation of the earth's magnetic pole. Also, the **taphonomy** of the site must be established in order to understand its depositional history—that is, whether the site is of a *primary* or *secondary* context.

As work progresses in later field seasons with more laboratory analyses, even more experts from other scientific specialties may be consulted. If a hominid bone or tooth is eventually recovered, a physical anthropologist will clean it, reconstruct it if necessary, describe it in minute anatomical detail, and attempt to relate it to other fossil hominid finds. The archeologist may decide that a particularly well-preserved location or the site of a hominid discovery calls for precise archeological excavation. In order to recover and record all relevant information in such an undertaking, thousands of work-hours are required to excavate even a relatively small area (a few dozen square feet). An extensively detailed *microstratigraphic analysis* may also be useful in re-creating the precise conditions of sedimentation, thus calling for the specialized skills of a taphonomist.

In the concluding stages of interpretation, the paleoanthropologist will draw together the following essentials:

1. *Dating*
   geological
   paleontological
   geophysical
2. *Paleoecology*
   paleontology
   palynology
   geomorphology
3. *Archeological traces of behavior*
4. *Anatomical evidence from hominid remains*

From all this information, the paleoanthropologist will try to "flesh out" the kind of animal that may have been our direct ancestor, or at least a very close relative. In this final analysis, still further comparative scientific information may be needed. Primatologists may assist here by showing the detailed relationships between the structure and behavior of humans and that of contemporary nonhuman primates (see Chapters 8 through 10). Cultural anthropologists may contribute ethnographic information concerning

Paleoecological paleo: old
ecological: environmental setting
The study of ancient environments.

Pedologist pedon: ground, soil
An expert in the study of soil.

Petrologist petr: rock
An expert in the study of rocks and minerals.

Taphonomy *taphos*: dead
The study of how bones and other materials come to be buried in the earth and preserved as fossils. A taphonomist studies such phenomena as the processes of sedimentation, action of streams, preservation/chemical properties of bone, and carnivore disturbance factors.

Russell L. Ciochon is associate professor of anthropology at the University of Iowa where he teaches courses on human origins and primate evolution, ecology, and behavior. He received his Ph.D. from the University of California, Berkeley. Ciochon's current research interests are the paleoanthropology of Southeast Asia, China, and India and the archaeology of Southeast Asia from the Paleolithic to the rise of state-society.

From my earliest memories, I was always interested in science. When other kids in the neighborhood were playing baseball, I wanted to go butterfly-collecting or launch model rockets. I clearly fit the stereotype of a "science nerd." I can't say when I first became aware of physical anthropology and archaeology, but I do have early memories of keeping a scrapbook of newspaper articles about the discoveries of Louis Leakey in Africa and reading about the mysterious temples of Angkor Wat in *National Geographic*. I grew up in San Jose, California, where as an elementary school student, I first learned about the California Indians who had lived in the Santa Clara Valley only a few hundred years before. During hiking trips to the surrounding hills it was easy to turn up arrowheads left by these first Californians, which I did with relish.

In junior high and in high school I took every science class I could. I distinctly remembered learning about DNA and the theory of evolution for the first time in my eighth grade biology class. In this experimental biology class, there was even a chapter on human evolution, where I was introduced to "Peking Man" and "Neanderthal Man."

I entered college in 1966 at the height of the "space race." I began taking courses in engineering and math but I found this curriculum lacked an essential natural sciences focus. In the spring of 1968, I read *The Naked Ape* by Desmond Morris, which forever changed my career goals. All at once everything seemed to fall into place. Physical anthropology seemed to be the ideal career choice. In this field, I could combine my interest and background in the natural sciences with fieldwork in faraway locales. In one year, I took every anthropology course offered at San Jose State. I settled on the subfield of paleoanthropology and primate evolution as my specialty. I then decided to transfer to the University of California, Berkeley, where I could take more advanced anthropology courses that would better prepare me for graduate school. This turned out to be a very opportune decision because the year I had arrived at U. C., Berkeley, it was nationally ranked as the top-rated program in anthropology. There, I took courses from such well-known physical anthropologists as Sherwood Washburn, Vincent Sarich, and F. Clark Howell. I began to focus more on the fields of primate evolution and primate anatomy. I was especially influenced by the writings of Elwyn Simons, a paleoprimatologist then at Yale University who had mounted major expeditions in search of fossil primates on three continents.

Berkeley followed the mentor system of graduate studies, whereby a student works very closely with a single faculty member. I applied to work with paleoanthropologist F. Clark Howell, one of the best decisions I ever made. Clark Howell was an active field researcher who had spent virtually every summer overseas doing fieldwork. He thought that students should also have the same opportunity. In the summer of 1971, before I attended my first graduate class, Clark Howell asked me to join the Omo Research Expedition, a paleoanthropological project in search of Plio-Pleistocene hominids in southern Ethiopia that Howell directed. At 23 years of age, I was the youngest member of an international research team of 20 scientists. It was the golden opportunity that solidified my career choice as a physical anthropologist. That summer, I gained valuable field experience in Africa and met many of the leading paleoanthropologists of the day, such as Louis and Mary Leakey, John Robinson, and Phillip Tobias, as well as a host of younger researchers, such as Richard Leakey,

Frank Brown, Kay Behrensmeyer, Elisabeth Vrba, and Donald Johanson, who are today some of the leading figures in our field.

As a graduate student working with Clark Howell, I was able to design my own customized graduate curriculum. I took seminars from all the physical anthropology faculty and spent all of the rest of my time taking courses outside of anthropology in the fields of geology, paleontology, zoology, human anatomy, statistics, and evolutionary biology. This broad-based background especially prepared me for a career in primate evolution and paleoanthropology. In this area of research, fieldwork is essential for new discoveries and you cannot accomplish this fieldwork without such a broad-based background. It is possible to become a paleoanthropologist only by studying fossil specimens in museums, but you cannot make new fossil discoveries without fieldwork. By 1974, I had completed my formal graduate training and had settled on a dissertation topic concerning the Plio-Pleistocene evolution of the Old World monkeys of Africa. This decision was prompted by the many discoveries of fossil monkeys made by the Omo Expedition on which I had worked.

As part of my dissertation research I journeyed to museums in Europe, Africa, and Asia. In March of 1975, I arrived in Burma and Southeast Asia for the first time. I traveled to Mandalay and met with geologists at the local university who were eager to begin a collaborative project. My timing was very

good. The Union of the Socialist Republic of Burma, as it was then called, had just been opened for tourist visits, and Americans were being welcomed because the involvement of the United States in the Vietnam War was drawing to a close. I returned to Berkeley to complete my dissertation research and began writing grants for my new project in Burma. I teamed up with Berkeley paleontologist Donald Savage and in 1977 began a three month expedition to Burma. On our next expedition to Burma in 1978, we discovered new remains of the earliest known anthropoid, *Amphipithecus*, the common ancestor of monkeys, apes, and humans.

In 1983 on another expedition in search of early anthropoids, I traveled to southern China where I first saw the beautiful limestone tower karsts of Guangxi whose caves had yielded the giant extinct ape, *Gigantopithecus*. After the China project, I decided to again go to Burma to visit my colleagues there. My first stop on this journey was Bangkok, Thailand, where I looked up a friend I had first met at the American Embassy in Burma. Serving as a foreign service officer, my friend had since been transferred to the American Embassy in Bangkok. When I told him about the magnificent tower karst, in southern China, he mentioned he had seen similar limestone towers in northern Vietnam during the war. He suggested I contact the Vietnamese to see if they were interested in research on *Gigantopithecus*. This was another turning point in my career. The next day I visited the Vietnamese embassy in Bangkok to meet with the science attaché. After a two-hour discussion, I discovered that Vietnamese scientists at the Institute of Archaeology in Hanoi were indeed working on collaborative field projects. Though no American anthropologists had yet visited

Hanoi, the attaché offered his assistance in contacting the Institute to set a research visit.

Since there were no diplomatic contacts between the United States and Vietnam, it took more than three years of negotiations and grant writing to obtain the necessary entry visas and funding to undertake the project. In January, 1987, accompanied by archaeologist John Olson, I made my first visit to Hanoi. Six years later, I am the veteran of eight research visits to Vietnam. I have organized two major expeditions there involving numerous scientists—the most recent expedition was in the spring of 1993. My research in Vietnam on Giganto has also been the subject of films for National Geographic Explorer and BBC television. After my first visit there in 1987, I discovered that Vietnamese scientists had been the first to document the coexistence of *Homo erectus* and *Gigantopithecus* at a cave site in Lang Son Province near the Chinese border. For the past six years, I have focused my research efforts on the paleobiology and adaptations of *Gigantopithecus*. With new discoveries being made in China and Southeast Asia all of the time, I plan to make this region the focus of my research efforts for many years to come.

the varied nature of human behavior, particularly ecological adaptation of those groups exploiting roughly similar environmental settings as those found at our hominid site (for example, the San of South Africa). Ethnoarcheologists can assist further by demonstrating how observed behavioral patterns (as implement manufacture and meat eating) actually end up in the ground as artifacts. Finally, neuroanatomists, psychologists, and linguists may aid physical anthropologists in the reconstruction of physiological/behavioral information suggested by the fossil hominid remains, such as brain dimensions and their relationship to language capacities.

The end result of years of research by dozens of scientists will (we hope) produce a more complete and accurate understanding of human evolution—how we came to be the way we are. Both biological and cultural aspects of our ancestors pertain to this investigation, each process developing in relation to the other.

Paleoanthropology in Action—Olduvai Gorge

Figure 12-2

Major paleoanthropological projects.

Several paleoanthropological projects of the scope discussed above are now or have recently been in progress in diverse places around the globe. The most important of these include: David Pilbeam's work in the Miocene beds of the Potwar Plateau of western Pakistan (circa 13–7 m.y.a.); Don Johanson's project in the Hadar area of Ethiopia (circa 3.7–1.6 m.y.a.); a now completed research project along the Omo River of southern Ethiopia (circa 4–1.5 m.y.a.) directed by F. Clark Howell (both the Howell and Johanson projects have sometimes been forced to cease work due to warfare in Ethiopia); Richard Leakey's fantastically successful research near Lake Turkana (formerly Rudolf) in northern Kenya (circa 2.5–1.5 m.y.a.); and Mary Leakey's famous investigations at Olduvai Gorge in northern Tanzania (circa 1.85 m.y.a.–present). Mary Leakey retired from active fieldwork in the mid-1980s. Current research at Olduvai is being coordinated by the Institute of Human Origins in Berkeley, California, in cooperation with Tanzanian scholars. Finally, under the direction of Phillip Tobias, several hominid localities have been systematically explored in South Africa over the last several years. The most productive of these sites is Swartkrans (discussed in Chapter 13).

Of all these early hominid localities, the one that has yielded the finest quality and greatest abundance of paleoanthropological information concerning the behavior of early hominids has been Olduvai Gorge.

First "discovered" in the early twentieth century by a German butterfly collector, Olduvai was soon thereafter scientifically surveyed and its wealth of paleontological evidence recognized. In 1931, Louis Leakey made his first trip to Olduvai Gorge and almost immediately realized its significance for studying early humans. Since 1935, when she first worked there, up to her retirement, Mary Leakey directed the archeological excavations at Olduvai.

Located in the Serengeti plain of northern Tanzania, Olduvai is a steep-sided valley resembling a miniature version of the Grand Canyon. In fact, the geological processes that formed the gorge are similar to what happened in the formation of the Grand Canyon. Following millions of years of steady accumulation of several hundred feet of geological strata (including volcanic, lake, and river deposits), faulting occurred 70,000 years ago to the east of Olduvai. As a result, a gradient was established, causing a rapidly flowing river to cut through the previously laid strata, eventually forming a gorge 300 feet deep—similar to the way the Colorado River cut the Grand Canyon.

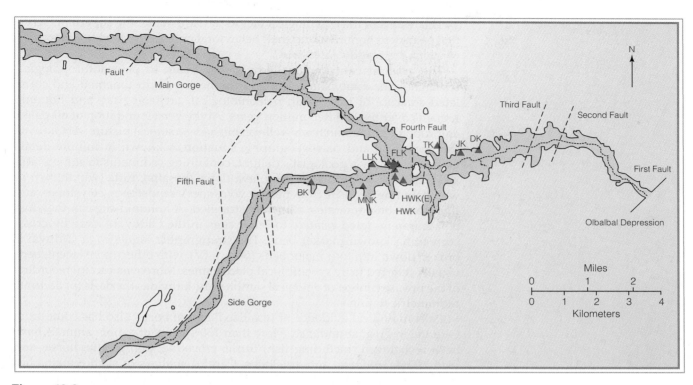

Figure 12-3

Olduvai Gorge. A sketch map showing positions of the major sites and geologic localities.

Olduvai today is a deep ravine cut into an almost mile-high grassland plateau of East Africa, and extends more than 25 miles in total length. In fact, if one were to include all the side gulleys and ravines, the area of exposures would total more than seventy miles with potentially hundreds of early hominid sites. Climatically, the semiarid pattern of present-day Olduvai is believed to be similar to most of the past environments preserved there over the last 2 million years. The surrounding countryside is a grassland savanna broken occasionally by scrub bushes and acacia trees. It is a noteworthy fact that this environment presently (as well as in the past) supports a vast number of large mammals (such as zebra, wildebeest, and gazelle), representing an enormous supply of "meat on the hoof."

Geographically, Olduvai is located on the western edge of the eastern branch of the Great Rift Valley of Africa. The geological processes associated with the formation of the Rift Valley makes Olduvai (and the other East African sites) extremely important to paleoanthropological investigation. Three results of geological rifting are most significant:

1. Faulting, or earth movement, exposes geological beds near the surface that are normally hidden by hundreds of feet of accumulated overburden
2. Active volcanic processes cause rapid sedimentation and thus often yield excellent preservation of bone and artifacts that normally would be scattered by carnivore activity and erosion forces
3. Volcanic activity provides a wealth of radiometrically datable material

The results of these geological factors at Olduvai are the superb preservation of ancient hominids and their behavioral patterns in datable contexts, all of which are readily accessible.

The greatest contribution Olduvai has made to paleoanthropological research is the establishment of an extremely well-documented and correlated *sequence* of geological, paleontological, archeological, and hominid remains over the last two million years. At the very foundation of all paleoanthropological research is a well-established geological picture. At Olduvai, the geological and paleogeographic situation is known in minute detail. Olduvai is today a geologist's delight, containing sediments in some places 350 feet thick accumulated from lava flows (basalts), tuffs (windblown or waterlain fine deposits from nearby volcanoes), sandstones, claystones, and limestone conglomerates, all neatly stratified. A hominid site can therefore be accurately dated relative to other sites in the Olduvai Gorge by cross-correlating known marker beds. The stratigraphic sequence at Olduvai is broken down into four major beds (Beds I–IV), with other, more recent, beds usually referred to by specific local place names. Moreover, careful recording of the precise context of gelological samples also provides the basis for accurate radiometric dating.

Paleontological evidence of fossilized animal bones also has come from Olduvai in great abundance. More than 150 species of extinct animals have been recognized, including fish, turtle, crocodile, pig, giraffe, horse, and many birds, rodents, and antelopes. Careful analysis of such remains has yielded voluminous information concerning the ecological conditions of early human habitats. In addition, precise analysis of bones directly associated with artifacts can sometimes tell us about the diets and hunting capabilities of early hominids. (There are some reservations, however—see Box 12-1, p. 342.)

The archeological sequence is also well documented over the last 2 million years. Beginning at the earliest hominid site in Bed I (1.85 m.y.a.), there is already a well-developed stone tool kit, including chopping tools as well as some small flake tools (Leakey, 1971). Such a tool industry is called *Oldowan* (after Olduvai) and continues into Bed II with some small modifications, after which it is called *Developed Oldowan*. In addition, around 1.6 m.y.a., the first appearance of a new tool kit, the *Acheulian*, occurs in the Olduvai arche-

Figure 12-4

Aerial view of Olduvai Gorge. Volcanic highlands are visible to the south.

Biography   Louis S. B. Leakey 1903–1972

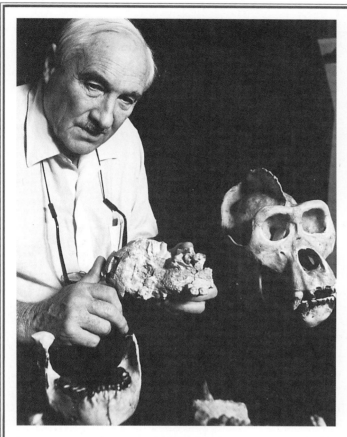

Louis Leakey displaying casts of fossil hominid discoveries from East Africa. To the right is the skull of a male gorilla.

Called the "Charles Darwin of prehistory," Louis Leakey was truly a man for all seasons. Blessed with a superior intellect and an almost insatiable curiosity, Leakey untiringly quested after knowledge, which to him included everything there was to know about everything. His interests encompassed not just prehistory, archeology, and paleontology but modern African wildlife, African peoples, languages, and customs. He once stalked, killed, and butchered a gazelle with just his bare hands and stone tools he had fashioned himself. He had previously attempted to use only his teeth and hands to dismember dead animals, but found it impossible, leading him to the conclusion that early hominids also *must* have used stone tools for butchering. Leakey also was a leading authority on handwriting, a skill he put to good use as the chief of British military intelligence for Africa during World War II.

The child of British missionary parents, Louis was born in a Kikuyu village in 1903—probably one of the first white children born in East Africa. His upbringing was to be as much African as European, and he was actually initiated into the Kikuyu tribe. Sworn to a sacred oath of silence, Louis never revealed the secret rites of initiation, even to his wife Mary.

Following his early training in the African bush, Louis was dispatched to England for a more formal education, eventually receiving his degree from Cambridge. His consuming interest, however, was focused on Africa, where he returned to begin exploration of prehistoric sites—leading his first expedition in 1926 at the age of 23! In 1931, Leakey made his first trip to Olduvai Gorge with the German paleontologist Hans Reck. Louis liked to relate years later how he found the first stone tool in context at Olduvai within an hour of his arrival there!

In the next forty years, the fantastic discoveries at Olduvai by Louis and his archeologist wife, Mary, as well as their extensive work at other sites all around the Rift Valley, were to make them famous to professional and layperson alike.

However, perhaps Louis's greatest contribution was not the many discoveries he made himself, but his ability to stimulate and involve others. The definitive research on all the great apes was initiated by Louis Leakey, who personally recruited Jane Goodall to work with chimpanzees, Dian Fossey to investigate the mountain gorilla, and Biruté Galdikas to learn the secrets of the orang. Louis's greatest legacy is probably that all these projects continue today.*

---

*The research goes forward on the mountain gorillas despite the tragic death of Dian Fossey in 1985.

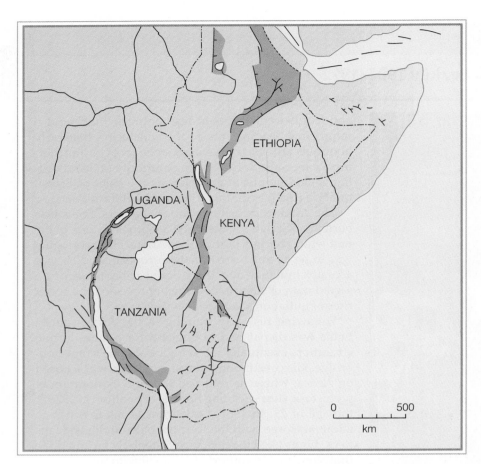

Figure 12-5

The East African Rift Valley system.

ological record. This industry is characterized by large bifacial (that is, flaked on both sides) tools commonly known as hand-axes and cleavers. For several hundred thousand years, Acheulian and Developed Oldowan are *both* found side-by-side at Olduvai, and the relationship between these parallel tool kits remains to be determined.

Finally, remains of several fossilized hominids have been found at Olduvai, ranging in time from the earliest occupation levels (circa 1.85 m.y.a.) to fairly recent *Homo sapiens*. Of the more than forty individuals represented, many are quite fragmentary, but a few (including four crania and a nearly complete foot) are excellently preserved. While the center of hominid discoveries has now shifted to other areas of East Africa, it was the initial discovery by Mary Leakey of the *"Zinjanthropus"* cranium at Olduvai in July, 1959, that focused the world's attention on this remarkably rich area. "Zinj" provides an excellent example of how financial ramifications directly result from hominid bone discoveries. Prior to 1959, the Leakeys had worked sporadically at Olduvai on a financial shoestring, making marvelous paleontological and archeological discoveries. Yet, there was little support available for much needed large-scale excavations. However, following the discovery of "Zinj," the National Geographic Society funded the Leakeys' research, and within the next year, more than twice as much dirt was excavated than during the previous thirty! Ongoing work at Olduvai has yielded yet further hominid discoveries. In 1987, a partial skeleton of a small hominid was found by researchers from the Institute of Human Origins.

Dating Methods

As we have discussed, one of the key essentials of paleoanthropology is putting sites and fossils into a chronological framework. In other words, we want to know how old they are. How, then, do we date sites—or, more precisely, the geological strata in which sites are found? The question is both reasonable and important, so let us examine the dating techniques used by paleontologists, geologists, and archeologists.

Scientists use two kinds of dating for this purpose—relative and **chronometric** (also known as *absolute dating*). Relative dating methods tell you that something is older, or younger, than something else, but not how much. If, for example, a cranium were found at a depth of fifty feet, and another cranium at seventy feet at the same site, we usually assume the cranium discovered at seventy feet is older. We may not know the date (in years) of either one, but we would know that one is older (or younger) than the other. Whereas this may not satisfy our curiosity about the actual number of years involved, it would give some idea of the evolutionary changes in cranial morphology (structure), especially if a number of crania at different levels were found and compared.

This method of relative dating is called **stratigraphy** and was one of the first techniques to be used by scholars working with the vast period of geologic time. Stratigraphy is based upon the law of superposition, which states that a lower stratum (layer) is older than a higher stratum. Given the fact that much of the earth's crust has been laid down by layer after layer of sedimentary rock, like the layers of a cake, stratigraphy has been a valuable aid in reconstructing the history of earth and life on it.

Stratigraphic dating does, however, have a number of problems connected with it. Earth disturbances, such as volcanic activity, river activity, and faulting (earthquakes), among others, may shift about strata of rock or the objects in them, and the chronology of the material may be difficult or even impossible to reconstruct. Furthermore, the elapsed time period represented by a particular stratum is not possible to determine with much accuracy.

Another method of relative dating is *fluorine analysis*, which applies only to bones (Oakley, 1963). Bones in the earth are exposed to the seepage of

Chronometric   chrono: time
metric: measure
A dating technique that gives an estimate in actual numbers of years.

Stratigraphy   Sequential layering of deposits.

Figure 12-6

View of the Main Gorge at Olduvai. Note the clear sequence of geological beds. The discontinuity to the right is a major fault line.

Biography   Mary Leakey 1913–

Mary Leakey, one of the leading prehistorians of this century, spent most of her professional life living in the shadow of her famous husband. But to a considerable degree, Louis's fame is directly attributable to Mary. Justly known for his extensive fieldwork in Miocene sites along the shores of Lake Victoria in Kenya, Louis is quite often associated with important hominoid discoveries. However, it was Mary who, in 1948, found the best-preserved *Proconsul* skull ever discovered.

The names Louis Leakey and Olduvai Gorge are almost synonymous, but here, too, it was Mary who made the most significant single discovery—the "Zinj" skull in 1959. Mary had always been the supervisor of archeological work at Olduvai while Louis was busily engaged in traveling, lecturing, or tending to the National Museum in Nairobi.

Mary Leakey did not come upon her archeological career by chance. A direct descendant of John Frere (who because of his discoveries in 1797, is called the father of Paleolithic archeology), Mary always had a compelling interest in prehistory. Her talent for illustrating stone tools provided her entry into African prehistory, and was the reason for her introduction to Louis in 1933. Throughout her career, she has done all the tool illustrations for her publications, and has set an extremely high standard of excellence for all would-be illustrators of Paleolithic implements.

A committed, hard-driving woman of almost inexhaustible energy, Mary conducted work at Olduvai, where she spent most of the year. Busily engaged

Mary Leakey at the site of the "Zinj" find on the thirteenth anniversary of its discovery.

seven days a week, she supervised ongoing excavations, as well as working on the monumental publications detailing the fieldwork already done.

Since Louis's death in 1972, Mary, to some degree, has had to assume the role of traveling lecturer and fund raiser. Today, she lives outside Nairobi, where she energetically continues her research and writing.

groundwater, usually containing fluorine. The longer bones lie in the earth, the more fluorine they incorporate during the fossilization process. Therefore, bones deposited at the same time in the same location should contain the same amount of fluorine. The use of this technique by Professor Oakley of the British Museum in the early 1950s exposed the Piltdown (England) hoax by demonstrating that the human cranium was considerably older than the jaw found with it (Weiner, 1955). Lying in the same location, the jaw and cranium should have absorbed approximately the same quantity of fluorine. But the cranium contained significantly more than the jaw, which meant that it (the cranium) had lain in the ground a good deal longer than the jaw. It was unlikely that the cranium had met an untimely demise while the jaw lingered on for thousands of years. The discrepancy of fluorine content led Oakley and others to a closer examination of the bones, and they found that the jaw was not that of a hominid at all but of a young adult orangutan! (See p. 350.)

Unfortunately, fluorine is useful only with bones found at the same location. Because the amount of fluorine in groundwater is based upon the local river system and local conditions, it varies from place to place. Also, some groundwater may not contain any fluorine. For these reasons, comparing bones from different localities by fluorine analysis is impossible.

In both these methods—stratigraphy and fluorine analysis—the age of the rock stratum and the objects in it are difficult to calculate. To determine the absolute number of years of age, scientists have developed a variety of chronometric techniques called radiometric dating methods because they are based on the phenomenon of radioactive decay. The theory is quite simple: Certain radioactive isotopes of elements are unstable, disintegrate, and form an isotopic variation of another element. Since the rate of disintegration follows a definite mathematical pattern, the radioactive material forms an accurate geological time clock. By measuring the amount of disintegration in a particular sample, the number of years it took for the amount of decay is then known. Chronometric techniques have been used for dating the immense age of the earth as well as artifacts less than a thousand years old. Several techniques have been employed for a number of years and are now quite well known.

Uranium 238 (^{238}U) decays to form lead and the process has a **half-life** of 4.5 billion years. That is, one-half of the original amount of ^{238}U is lost in 4.5 billion years and through various processes becomes lead. Therefore, if a chunk of rock is measured and one-half of the uranium has been converted to lead, the age of that piece of rock is 4.5 billion years. In another 4.5 billion years, half the remaining ^{238}U would have decayed. The isotope ^{238}U has proven a useful tool in dating the age of the formation of the earth.

Another radiometric technique involves potassium 40 (^{40}K)—which produces argon 40 (^{40}Ar)—with a half-life of 1.3 billion years. Known as the K/Ar, or potassium-argon method, this procedure has been extensively used by paleoanthropologists in dating materials in the 1 to 5 million year range, especially in East Africa. Organic material, such as bone, cannot be measured, but the rock matrix in which the bone is found can be. K/Ar was used to date the deposit containing the *Zinjanthropus* skull (it actually dated a volcanic layer above the fossil).

Rocks that provide the best samples for K/Ar are those heated to an extremely high temperature, such as that generated by volcanic activity. When the rock is in a molten state, argon 40, a gas, is driven off. As the rock cools and solidifies, potassium (^{40}K) continues to break down to ^{40}Ar, but now the gas is physically trapped in the cooled rock. In order to obtain the date of the rock, it is reheated and the escaping gas measured. Potassium-argon has been used for dating very old events, such as the age of the earth, as well as those up to 10,000 years old.

A well-known radiometric method popular with archeologists is carbon 14 (^{14}C), with a half-life of 5,730 years. It has been used to date material from less than 1,000 years to as much as 75,000 years, although the probability of error rises rapidly after 40,000 years. The ^{14}C technique is based upon the following natural processes: Cosmic radiation enters the earth's atmosphere, producing neutrons, which react with nitrogen to produce a radioactive isotope of carbon, ^{14}C. As the ^{14}C is diffused around the earth with the earth's rotation, it mixes with carbon 12 (^{12}C) and is absorbed by plants in their life processes. It is then transferred to herbivorous animals that feed on plants and to carnivores that feed on herbivores. Thus, ^{14}C and ^{12}C are found in all living forms at a fixed ratio. When an organism dies, it no longer absorbs ^{14}C,

Half-life The amount of time it takes a radioactive isotope to change half its initial (or remaining) amount to a byproduct. If ^{238}U changes to lead with a half-life of 4.5 billion years, that means it takes this amount of time to convert half the ^{238}U to lead.

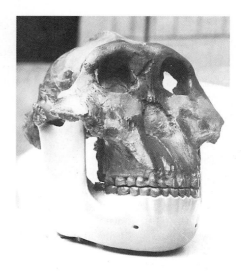

Figure 12-7

Zinjanthropus *cranium. Discovered by Mary Leakey at Olduvai Gorge in 1959. The skull and reconstructed jaw depicted here are casts at the National Museums of Kenya, Nairobi.*

Great Moments in Prehistory   Discovery of Zinjanthropus July 17, 1959

That morning I woke with a headache and a slight fever. Reluctantly I agreed to spend the day in camp.

With one of us out of commission, it was even more vital for the other to continue the work, for our precious seven-week season was running out. So Mary departed for the diggings with Sally and Toots [two of their dalmatians] in the Land-Rover, and I settled back to a restless day off.

Some time later—perhaps I dozed off—I heard the Land-Rover coming up fast to camp. I had a momentary vision of Mary stung by one of our hundreds of resident scorpions or bitten by a snake that had slipped past the dogs.

The Land-Rover rattled to a stop, and I heard Mary's voice calling over and over: "I've got him! I've got him! I've got him!"

Still groggy from the headache, I couldn't make her out.

"Got what? Are you hurt?" I asked.

"Him, the man! *Our* man," Mary said. "The one we've been looking for [for 23 years]. Come quick, I've found his teeth!"

Magically, the headache departed. I somehow fumbled into my work clothes while Mary waited.

As we bounced down the trail in the car, she described the dramatic moment of discovery. She had been searching the slope where I had found the first Oldowan tools in 1931, when suddenly her eye caught a piece of bone lodged in a rock slide. Instantly, she recognized it as part of a skull—almost certainly not that of an animal.

Her glance wandered higher, and there in the rock were two immense teeth, side by side. This time there was no question: They were undeniably human. Carefully, she marked the spot with a cairn of stones, rushed to the Land-Rover, and sped back to camp with the news.

The gorge trail ended half a mile from the site, and we left the car at a dead run. Mary led the way to the cairn, and we knelt to examine the treasure.

I saw at once that she was right. The teeth were premolars, and they had belonged to a human. I was sure they were larger than anything similar ever found, nearly twice the width of modern man's.

I turned to look at Mary, and we almost cried with sheer joy, each seized by that terrific emotion that comes rarely in life. After all our hoping and hardship and sacrifice, at last we had reached our goal—we had discovered the world's earliest known human.

From: "Finding the World's Earliest Man," by L.S.B. Leakey, *National Geographic Magazine*, 118(September 1960):431. Reprinted with permission of the publisher.

---

which then decays at a constant rate to nitrogen 14 (^{14}N) and a beta particle. It takes 5,730 years for half the amount of ^{14}C to become ^{14}N.

Let us say that charcoal, the remains of a campfire, is found at an archeological site and measured for the ^{14}C:^{12}C ratio. Suppose the findings show only 25% of the original ^{14}C remains as indicated by the ^{14}C:^{12}C ratio. Since it takes 5,730 years for half the ^{14}C atoms to become ^{14}N, and another 5,730 years for half the remaining ^{14}C to become ^{14}N, the sample must be about 11,460 years old. Half the remaining ^{14}C will become ^{14}N in the next 5,730 years, leaving 12.5% of the original amount. This process continues, and as you can see, there would be very little ^{14}C left after 40,000 years, when measuring becomes difficult.

Other chronometric techniques that do not involve radioactive elements are *dendrochronology*, or dating by tree rings, especially developed for the American Southwest, and *varve chronology* (annual glacial deposit), particularly useful for the late Pleistocene and the post-Pleistocene in northern Europe. Although neither of the techniques has a direct bearing on dating early human fossils, they are both ingenious dating methods with important regional applications.

We should stress that none of these methods is precise, and that each method is beset with problems that must be carefully considered during laboratory measurement and in the collection of material to be measured. Because the methods are imprecise, approximate dates are given as probability statements with a plus or minus factor. For example, a date given as 1.75 ± .2 m.y.a. should be read as a 67% chance that the actual date lies somewhere between 1.55 and 1.95 m.y.a.

There are, then, two ways in which the question of age may be answered. We can say that a particular fossil is x number of years old, a date determined usually either by K/Ar or ^{14}C chronometric dating techniques. Or, we can say that fossil X lived before or after fossil Y, a relative dating technique.

DATING METHODS AT OLDUVAI

Olduvai has proven a rich and varied source for numerous dating techniques, and as a result it has some of the best-documented chronology for any hominid site in the Lower or Middle Pleistocene.

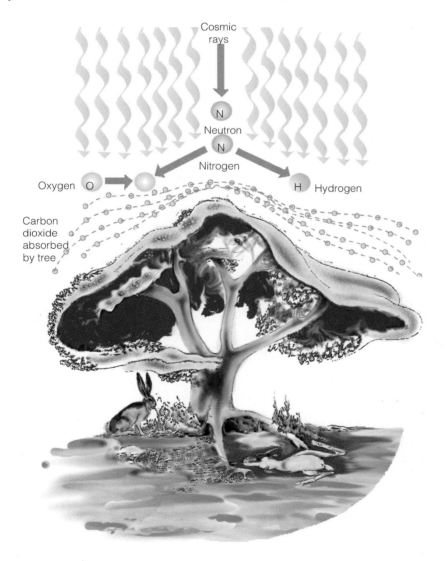

Figure 12-8

Carbon-14 dating. Cosmic rays bombard the upper atmosphere, producing neutrons. When these collide with nitrogen, small amounts of ^{14}C are produced. The ^{14}C combines with oxygen to form carbon dioxide. The carbon dioxide containing ^{14}C is absorbed by plants, and eventually animals feeding on the plants add ^{14}C to their bodies. When the plant or animal dies, it ceases to absorb ^{14}C and the ^{14}C changes back to nitrogen at a regular rate.

Potassium-argon dating had its birth as a paleoanthropological tool in the early 1960s with its application to the dating of the "Zinj" site at Olduvai. To everyone's amazement, including Louis Leakey's, the chronometric age was determined at more than 1.75 m.y.a.—more than twice the age depth previously assumed for the *whole* Pleistocene. As a result of this one monumental date (Leakey et al., 1961), the entire history of the Pleistocene and our corresponding interpretations of hominid evolution had to be rewritten.

Potassium-argon (K/Ar) is an extremely valuable tool for dating early hominid sites and has been widely used in areas containing suitable volcanic deposits (mainly in East Africa). At Olduvai, K/Ar has given several reliable dates of the underlying basalt and several tuffs in Bed I, including the one associated with the "Zinj" find (now dated at 1.79 ± .03 m.y.a.). When dating relatively recent samples (from the perspective of a half-life of 1.3 billion years for K/Ar, *all* paleoanthropological material is relatively recent), the amount of radiogenic argon is going to be exceedingly small. Experimental errors in measurement can therefore occur as well as the thorny problem of distinguishing the atmospheric argon normally clinging to the outside of the sample from the radiogenic argon. In addition, the initial sample may have been contaminated or argon leakage may have occurred while it lay buried.

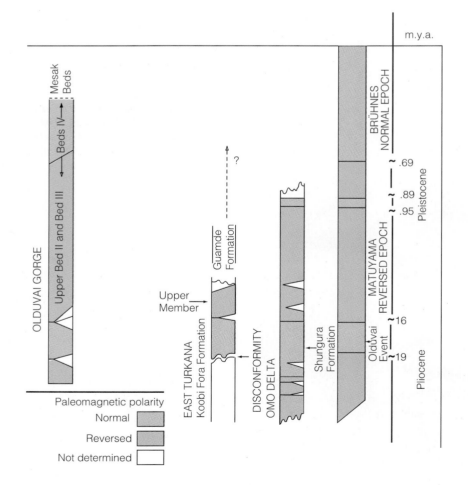

Figure 12-9

Paleomagnetic sequences correlated for major East African sites—Olduvai, East Turkana, Omo. (After Isaac, 1975.)

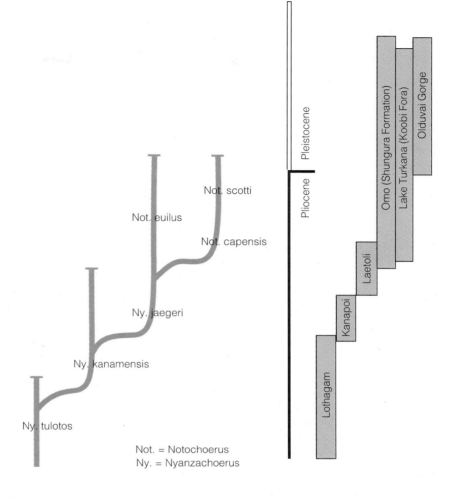

Figure 12-10

Partial biostratigraphic sequence of pigs. Used to correlate East African sites. (After White and Harris, 1977.)

Not. = Notochoerus
Ny. = Nyanzachoerus

Due to the potential sources of error, K/Ar dating must be cross-checked using other independent methods. Once again, the sediments at Olduvai (particularly in Bed I) provide some of the best examples of the use of many of these other dating techniques.

Fission-track dating is one of the most important techniques for cross-checking K/Ar determinations. The key to fission-track dating is that uranium 238 (^{238}U) decays regularly by spontaneous fission so that, by counting the fraction of uranium atoms that have fissioned (shown as microscopic tracks caused by explosive fission of ^{238}U nuclei), we can ascertain the age of a mineral or natural glass sample (Fleischer and Hart, 1972). One of the earliest applications of this technique was on volcanic pumice from Bed I at Olduvai, giving a date of 2.30 (± .28) m.y.a.—in good accord with K/Ar dates.

Another important means of cross-checking dates is called **paleomagnetism**. This technique is based on the constantly shifting nature of the earth's magnetic pole. Of course, as anyone knows, the earth's magnetic pole is now oriented in a northerly direction, but this situation has not always been so. In fact, the orientation and intensity of the geomagnetic field have undergone numerous documented changes in the last few million years. From our pres-

Paleomagnetism Dating method based on shifting magnetic poles.

Box 12-1   Are the Sites at Olduvai Really "Sites"?

The generally agreed-upon interpretation of the bone refuse and stone tools discovered at Olduvai has been that most, if not all, of these materials are the result of hominid activities. Recently, however, a comprehensive reanalysis of the bone remains from Olduvai localities has challenged this view (Binford, 1981, 1983). Archeologist Lewis Binford criticizes those drawn too quickly to the conclusion that these bone scatters are the remnants of hominid behavior patterns while simultaneously ignoring the possibility of other explanations. For example, he forcefully states:

> All the facts gleaned from the deposits interpreted as living sites have served as the basis for making up "just-so stories" about our hominid past. No attention has been given to the possibility that many of the facts may well be referable to the behavior of nonhominids (Binford, 1981, p. 251).

From specifics concerning the kinds of animals present, which body parts were found, and the differences in preservation among these skeletal elements, Binford concluded that much of what is preserved could be explained by carnivore activity. This conclusion was reinforced by certain details observed by Binford himself in Alaska—details on animal kills, scavenging, the transportation of elements, and preservation as the result of wolf and dog behaviors. Binford describes his approach thus:

I took as 'known,' then, the structure of bone assemblages produced in various settings by animal predators and scavengers; and as 'unknown' the bone deposits excavated by the Leakeys at Olduvai Gorge. Using mathematical and statistical techniques I considered to what degree the finds from Olduvai Gorge could be accounted for in terms of the results of predator behavior and how much was 'left over' (Binford, 1983, pp. 56–57).

In using this uniquely explicit approach, Binford arrived at quite different conclusions from those previously suggested by other archeologists:

> For instance, the very idea of a site or living floor assumes conditions in the past for which there is no demonstration. In fact, it assumes the very "knowledge" we would like to obtain from the archeological remains. Site and living floor identifications presuppose that concentrations and aggregations of archeological and other materials are only produced by man. Are there not other conditions of deposition that could result in aggregations of considerable density found on old land surfaces? The answer must be a resounding yes.

And, later, he concludes:

> It seems to me that one major conclusion is justified from the foregoing analysis: The large, highly publicized sites as currently analyzed carry little specific information about hominid behavior . . . arguments about base camps, hominid hunting, sharing of food, and so forth

ent ethnocentric point of view, we call a northern orientation "normal" and a southern one "reversed." Major epochs of geomagnetic time are:

Normal
0.7 m.y.a.
Reversed
2.5 m.y.a.
Normal
3.4 m.y.a.
Reversed
,
,
,
,
?

Paleomagnetic dating is accomplished by carefully taking samples of sediments that contain magnetically charged particles. Since these particles

are certainly premature and most likely wildly inaccurate (Binford, 1981, pp. 281–282).

Binford is not arguing that *all* of the remains found at Olduvai have resulted from nonhominid activity. In fact, he recognized that "residual material" was consistently found on surfaces with high tool concentrations "which could *not* be explained by what we know about African animals" (Binford, 1983).

Support for the idea that at least some of the bone refuse was utilized by early hominids has come from a totally different perspective. Recently, researchers have analyzed (both macroscopically and microscopically) the cutmarks left on fossilized bones. By experimenting with modern materials, they have further been able to delineate clearly the differences between marks left by stone tools as opposed to those left by animal teeth (or other factors) (Bunn, 1981; Potts and Shipman, 1981). Analysis of bones from several early localities at Olduvai showed unambiguously that these specimens were utilized by hominids, who left telltale cutmarks from stone tool usage. The sites thus far investigated reveal a somewhat haphazard cutting and chopping, apparently unrelated to deliberate disarticulation. It has thus been concluded (Shipman, 1983) that hominids scavenged carcasses (probably of carnivore kills) and did *not* hunt large animals themselves. Materials found at later sites (postdating 1 m.y.a.), on the other hand, do show deliberate disarticulation, indicating a more systematic hunting pattern, with presumably meat transport and food sharing as well (Shipman, 1983).

If early hominids (close to 2 m.y.a.) were not hunting consistently, what did they obtain from scavenging the kills of other animals? One obvious answer is, whatever meat was left behind. However, the positioning of the cutmarks suggests that early hominids were often hacking at nonmeat-bearing portions of the skeletons. Perhaps they were simply after bone marrow, a substance not really being exploited by other predators (Binford, 1981).

The picture that emerges, then, of what hominids were doing at Olduvai around 1.8 m.y.a. hardly suggests consistent big game hunting. In Binford's words:

> . . . this is evidence of man eating a little bit of bone marrow, a food source that must have represented an infinitesimally small component of his total diet. The signs seem clear. Earliest man, far from appearing as a mighty hunter of beasts, seems to have been the most marginal of scavengers (Binford, 1983, p. 59).

maintain the magnetic orientation they had when they were consolidated into rock (many thousands or millions of years ago), we have a kind of "fossil compass." Then the paleomagnetic *sequence* is compared against the K/Ar dates to check if they agree. Some complications can arise, for during an epoch a relatively long period of time can occur where the geomagnetic orientation is the opposite of what is expected. For example, during the reversed epoch between 2.5–0.7 m.y.a. (Matuyama epoch) there was a time period called an *event*, lasting about 160,000 years, where orientations were normal. As this phenomenon was first conclusively demonstrated at Olduvai, it is appropriately called the *Olduvai Event*.

However, once these oscillations in the geomagnetic pole are well worked out, the sequence of paleomagnetic orientations can provide a valuable cross-check (concordant dating) for K/Ar and fission-track age determinations.

A final dating technique employed in the Lower Pleistocene beds at Olduvai and other East African sites is based on the regular evolutionary changes in well-known groups of mammals. This technique, called *faunal correlation* or **biostratigraphy**, provides yet another means of cross-checking the other

Biostratigraphy Dating method based on evolutionary changes within an evolving lineage.

methods. Animals that have been widely used in biostratigraphical analysis in East Africa and South Africa are fossil pigs (suids), elephants (proboscids), antelope (bovids), rodents, and carnivores. From areas where dates are known (by K/Ar, for instance), approximate ages can be extrapolated to other, less well-known areas by noting which genera and species are present.

All these methods, potassium-argon, fission-track, paleomagnetism, and biostratigraphy have been used in dating Beds I and II at Olduvai. So many different dating techniques are necessary because no single one is perfectly reliable by itself. Sampling error, contamination, and experimental errors can all introduce ambiguities into our so-called "absolute" dates. However, the sources of error are different for each technique, and therefore cross-checking among several independent methods is the most certain way of authenticating the chronology for early hominid sites.

Excavations at Olduvai

Because the vertical cut of the Olduvai Gorge provides a ready cross section of 2 million years of earth history, sites can be excavated by digging "straight-in" rather than finding them by having first to remove tons of overlying dirt. In fact, sites are usually discovered by merely walking the exposures and observing what bones, stones, etc., are eroding out.

Several dozen hominid sites (at a minimum, they are bone and tool scatters) have been surveyed at Olduvai, and Mary Leakey has extensively excavated close to twenty of these. An incredible amount of paleoanthropological information has come from these excavated areas, data which can be generally grouped into three broad categories depending on implied function:

1. *"Butchering" localities.* Areas containing one or only a few individuals of a single species of large mammal associated with a scatter of archeological traces. An elephant "butchering" site and another containing a *Deinotherium* (a large extinct relative of the elephant) have been found at levels approximately 1.7 m.y.a. Both sites contain only a single animal, and it is impossible to ascertain whether the hominids actually killed these animals or exploited them (either for meat or, perhaps, simply to extract marrow) after they were already dead. A third butchering locality dated at approximately 1.2 m.y.a. shows much more consistent and efficient exploitation of large mammals by this time. Remains of 24 *Pelorovis* (a giant extinct relative of the buffalo, with horn spans more than ten feet across!) have been found here, and Louis Leakey suggested they were driven into a swamp by a band of hominids and then systematically slaughtered (Leakey, 1971).

2. *Quarry localities.* Areas where early hominids extracted their stone resources and initially fashioned their tools. At such sites, thousands of small stone fragments are found of only one type of rock usually associated with no or very little bone refuse. At Olduvai, a 1.6–1.7 million-year-old area was apparently a chert (a rock resembling flint) factory site, where hominids came repeatedly to quarry this material.

3. *Multipurpose localities.* Also called campsites. General purpose areas where hominids possibly ate, slept, and put the finishing touches on their tools. The accumulation of living debris, including broken bones of many animals of several different species and many broken stones (some complete tools, some waste flakes) is a basic human pattern. As the late Glynn Isaac noted:

Figure 12-11

Excavations in progress at Olduvai. This site is more than one million years old. It was located when a hominid ulna (arm bone) was found eroding out of the side of the gorge.

The fact that discarded artifacts tend to be concentrated in restricted areas is itself highly suggestive. It seems likely that such patches of material reflect the organization of movement around a camp or home base, with recurrent dispersal and reuniting of the group at the chosen locality. Among living primates this pattern in its full expression is distinctive of man. The coincidence of bone and food refuse with the artifacts strongly implies that meat was carried back—presumably for sharing (Isaac, 1976, pp. 27–28). (See Box 12-1 for a different interpretation.)

Several such multipurpose areas have been excavated at Olduvai, including one that is over 1.8 million years old (DK I—see Box 13-2). This site has a circle of large stones forming what at one time was thought to be a base for a windbreak; however, this interpretation is now thought to be unlikely. Whatever its function, without the meticulous excavation and recording of modern archeological techniques, the presence of such an archeological feature would never have been recognized. This point requires further emphasis. Many people assume archeologists derive their information simply from analysis of objects (stone tools, gold statues, or whatever). However, it is the **context** and **association** of objects (that is, precisely where the objects are found and what is found associated with them) that give archeologists the data they require to understand the behavioral patterns of ancient human populations. Once pot hunters or looters pilfer a site, proper archeological interpretation is never again possible.

The types of activities carried on at these multipurpose sites remains open to speculation. Archeologists had thought, as the quote by the late Glynn Isaac above indicates (and as also argued by Mary Leakey), that they functioned as "campsites." Lewis Binford has forcefully critiqued this view, and has alternatively suggested much of the refuse accumulated is the result of nonhominid (that is, predator) activities (see Box 12-1). Another possibility, suggested by Richard Potts (1984), postulates that these areas served as collecting points (caches) for stone tools. This last interpretation has received considerable support from other archeologists in recent years.

Context The environmental setting where an archeological trace is found.

Association What an archeological trace is found with.

Box 12-2   Olduvai Site Names

The naming of sites at Olduvai is a marvelous wonder concocted from fascinating combinations of the English alphabet. Sites are designated with such shorthand abbreviations as FLK, MNK, LLK, etc. The "K" stands for Korongo, Swahili for gully (Olduvai is made up of dozens of side gullies). The first initial(s) is usually, though not always, that of the individual who made an important discovery at that locality. For example, FLK stands for Frida Leakey Korongo (Louis's first wife), MNK is Mary Nicol Korongo (Mary Leakey's maiden name), and LLK is Louis Leakey Korongo (where

Louis found a hominid cranium in 1961). When more than one site is found in the same gully, those discovered later are given directional orientations relative to the initial site. For example, FLK is the main site name where "Zinj" was found in 1959. FLK N (that is, "FLK North," where the elephant and *Deinotherium* butchering sites occur at slightly different levels) is just north of the main site, and FLK NN ("FLK North North," the location of yet another important hominid discovery) is just a bit farther north up the gully.

Diet of Early Hominids

Paleoanthropological research is concerned with more than the recovery and recording of bones and artifacts. We are trying to reconstruct what kind of animal our ancestor was. Paleoanthropology must therefore be centrally concerned with interpretation of the behavioral patterns of early hominid populations.

One of the most important questions we would like to answer about early hominid behavior is: What did they eat? Scattered broken bone debris associated with artifacts *may* provide direct evidence concerning one important aspect of early human dietary behavior. However, we must not forget that modern analogs like the San of South Africa clearly show us that vegetable

Figure 12-12

A dense scatter of stone and some fossilized animal bone from a site at Olduvai, dated at approximately 1.6 m.y.a. Some of these remains are the result of hominid activities.

foods, which usually leave little trace in the archeological record, probably made up a large part (even a majority) of the caloric intake of early hominids. As Glynn Isaac noted, reconstructing dietary behavior is like navigating around an iceberg—four-fifths of what is of interest is not visible (Isaac, 1971, p. 280).

Postulated diets available to hominids 1–2 m.y.a. with use of only a simple digging stick as a tool include: berries, fruits, nuts, buds, shoots, shallow-growing roots and tubers, most terrestrial and smaller aquatic reptiles, eggs and nesting birds, some fish, molluscs, insects, and all smaller mammals (Bartholomew and Birdsell, 1953).

Olduvai has shown that the range of postulated meat resources was possibly exploited in Beds I and II (1.85–1.0 m.y.a.). Fossils of turtles, rodents, fish, birds, pigs, horses, and small antelopes are all fairly common at many Olduvai sites. Of course, exactly how much of these remains was eaten—as opposed to having just "dropped dead" there or having been preyed upon by other animals—is still undetermined (see Box 12-1). Evidence for fish eating has also come from a comparably aged site in southern Ethiopia (the Omo), where fish bones have been found in hominid coprolites (fossilized feces).

Thanks to the extraordinary dedication of Louis and Mary Leakey, just one relatively small area of northern Tanzania has provided a continuous record of the development of hominids and their behavior for almost 2 million years. Without Olduvai we would know much less than we do about the emergence of human culture prior to 1 m.y.a.

Summary

The biocultural nature of human evolution requires that any meaningful study of human origins examine both biological and cultural information. The multidisciplinary approach of paleoanthropology is designed to bring together varied scientific specializations in order to reconstruct the anatomy, behavior, and environments of early hominids. Such a task is centered around the skills of the geologist, paleontologist, paleoecologist, archeologist, and physical anthropologist.

Much of what we know about the origins of human culture between 1 and 2 m.y.a. comes from archeological excavations by Mary Leakey at Olduvai Gorge in East Africa. Olduvai's well-documented stratigraphic sequence, its superior preservation of remains, and the varied dating techniques possible there have made it an information bonanza for paleoanthropologists. Excavated sites have yielded a wealth of bones of fossil animals, as well as artifact traces of hominid behavior. Ecological reconstructions of habitat and dietary preferences are thereby possible and inform us in great detail concerning crucial evolutionary processes affecting early hominid populations.

In the next two chapters, we will survey the fossil hominid evidence in South and East Africa that inform us directly about human origins during the Plio-Pleistocene.

Questions for Review

1. Why are cultural remains so important in interpretating human evolution?
2. How are early hominid sites found, and what kind of specialist is involved in the excavation and analysis of paleoanthropological data?
3. What kinds of paleoanthropological information have been found at Olduvai Gorge? Why is this particular locality so rich in material?
4. What kinds of dating techniques have been used to date early hominid sites at Olduvai? Why is more than one technique necessary for accurate dating?
5. Why are context and association so important in the interpretation of archeological remains?
6. What different activities can be inferred from the different kinds of sites at Olduvai? Discuss alternative views in the interpretation of these "sites."
7. How do we infer what early hominids were eating? Give a brief list of the kinds of food that were probably exploited.

Chapter 13

Contents

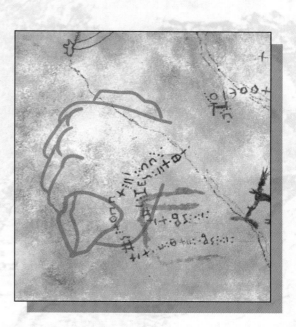

Plio-Pleistocene Hominids

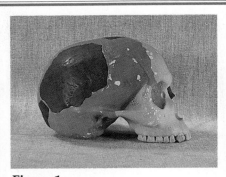

Figure 1

The Piltdown skull.

When first announced to the world in 1912, *Eoanthropus dawsoni* ("Dawson's Dawn Man") created an anthropological sensation. Found during 1911 in Sussex in the south of England by Charles Dawson, a lawyer and amateur geologist/antiquarian, this "fossil" was to confuse, bewilder, and befuddle two generations of anthropologists. "Piltdown man," as he popularly came to be called, was comprised of a fragmented skull and parts of a lower jaw. The enigma of the fossil from the very beginning was the combination of a large *sapiens*-like calvarium (initially estimated at 1,070 cm³, but later shown to be more like 1,400 cm³) with an apelike lower jaw.

Most tantalizing of all, Piltdown was apparently extremely ancient, associated with long extinct fauna, such as mastodon, hippo, and rhino, all suggesting a date of early Pleistocene. A puzzling feature was the presence of these early fossils mixed in with clearly late Pleistocene fauna. The prevailing consensus, however, was that Piltdown was indeed ancient, "the earliest known representative of man in Western Europe."

Despite its seeming incongruities, Piltdown was eagerly accepted by British scientists, including A. Keith, Elliot Smith, and Smith Woodward (all later knighted). What made the fossil such a delectable treat was that it confirmed just what had been expected, a combination of *modern* ape and *modern* human characteristics—a true "missing link." We, of course, now know that no ancestral fossil form is a fifty-fifty compromise between modern ones, but represents its own unique adaptation. In addition to mistaken enthusiasm for a missing link, the fossil also represented a "true" man as opposed to the obviously primitive beasts (Java man, Neandertals) found elsewhere. Such a fervently biased desire to find an "ancient modern" in the human lineage has obscured evolutionary studies for decades and still causes confusion in some circles.

While generally accepted in England, experts in France, Germany, and the United States felt uneasy about Piltdown. Many critics, however, were silenced when a second fragmentary find was announced in 1917 (actually found in 1915) in an area two miles away from the original site. The matter stood in limbo for years, with some scientists as enthusiastic supporters of the Piltdown man and others remaining uneasy doubters. The uneasiness continued to fester as more hominid material accumulated in Java, China, and particularly the australopithecines in South Africa. None of these hominids showed the peculiar combination of a human cranium with an apelike jaw seen in Piltdown, but actually indicated the reverse pattern.

The final proof of the true nature of the Dawn Man came in the early 1950s, when British scientists began an intensive reexamination of the Piltdown material. In particular, fluorine analysis (see Chapter 12) performed by Kenneth Oakley showed both the skull and jaw to be relatively recent. Later, more extensive tests showed the jaw to be younger than the skull and *very* recent in date. Now a much more critical eye was turned to all the material. The teeth, looking initially as though they had been worn down flat in the typical hominid fashion, were apparently ape teeth filed down deliberately to give that impression. The mixed bag of fauna was apparently acquired from all manner of places (a fossil elephant came from Tunisia in North Africa!), and the jaw was deliberately stained with chromate to match the older fossils in color. Finally, some "tools" found at Piltdown also met the hand of a forger, for the bone implements showed modifications that apparently could only have been made by a metal knife.

The "fossil" itself was probably purchased from local dealers. The skull probably came from a moderately ancient grave (a few thousand years old), and the jaw was a specially broken, filed, and stained mandible of a fairly recently deceased adolescent orang! The evidence was indisputable: a deliberate hoax. But who did it?

Just about everyone connected with the "crime" has, at one time or another, been implicated—beginning with Piltdown's discoverer: Charles Dawson. Yet, Dawson was an amateur, and, thus, may have lacked the expertise to carry out the admittedly crafty job of anatomical modification.

In addition, at various times, suspicions have been cast toward neuroanatomist Sir Grafton Elliot Smith, geologist W. J. Sollas, and, French philosopher and archeologist, Father Pierre Teilhard de Chardin.

One individual who had largely escaped suspicion was Sir Arthur Keith. At the time of the Piltdown discovery, he was a "rising star" in the field of anatomy in England. Later, and throughout much of the first half of this century, he would be the preeminent English scholar of human evolution. Recently, grave suspicions have even been leveled at Sir Arthur. Frank Spencer in his *Piltdown: A Scientific Forgery*, notes that Keith probably had the most to gain from the whole affair. Perhaps so, but he probably also had the most to lose. One seemingly damning new piece of evidence is presented by Spencer: In 1912, in the *British Medical Journal* Keith anonymously authored a contribution containing details that at that time were still "secret." Spencer concludes that Keith was the likely mastermind behind the whole forgery and probably used Dawson as a willing accomplice.

Still, there is not an ironclad case against Keith, Dawson, or any of the other "principals." In this kind of uncertain (and suspicious) atmosphere, yet another intriguing possibility has been raised:

. . . there was another interested figure who haunted the Piltdown site during excavation, a doctor who knew human anatomy and chemistry, someone inter-

Figure 2

The Piltdown committee: The individuals central to the "discovery" and interpretation of the Piltdown "fossil." Back row, standing, left to right: Mr. F. O. Barlow (maker of the casts), Prof. G. Elliot Smith (anatomist), Mr. C. Dawson ("discoverer"), Dr. A. Smith Woodward (zoologist). Front row, seated: Dr. A. S. Underwood (dental expert), Prof. A. Keith (anatomist), Mr. W. P. Pycraft (zoologist), Sir Ray Lankester (zoologist). From the painting by John Cook.

ested in geology and archeology, and an avid collector of fossils. He was a man who loved hoaxes, adventure and danger; a writer gifted at manipulating complex plots; and perhaps most important of all, one who bore a grudge against the British science establishment. He was none other than the creator of Sherlock Holmes, Sir Arthur Conan Doyle (Winslow and Meyer, 1983, p. 34).

Doyle, as a medical doctor, certainly possessed the anatomical knowhow to craft the forgery. His other avocations—chemistry, geology, and especially, anthropology—also would have been useful to him *if* he were the forger.

In a remarkable piece of detective work (worthy of the master sleuth Sherlock Holmes himself), John

Winslow has assembled a convincing array of *circumstantial* evidence against Doyle who, first of all, is the only suspect that can be shown to have had ready access to all the elements of the forgery. He was friendly with collectors or dealers who easily could have provided him with the cranium, the orang jaw, and the stone tools. As far as the animal fossils are concerned, Doyle also could have acquired many of the local (English) fossils from collector friends, but some of the odd bits obviously are from elsewhere (most likely, Malta and Tunisia). And, interestingly enough, Doyle had traveled to Malta a few years before Piltdown came to light, and may have been in Tunisia as well. At the very least, he was closely acquainted with people who had been to this part of North Africa.

But what of motive? As rich and as successful a figure as Doyle would seem an unlikely candidate for such a ruse. Winslow, however, has also found some clues that suggest Sir Arthur *may* indeed have had a motive.

Doyle was a longtime spiritualist who believed firmly in the occult and in extrasensory powers. He bore little patience with scientific critics of such views, whom he regarded as closed-minded. In particular, he had a special rival, Edward Ray Lankester, one of the most renowned evolutionists of the early twentieth century. Perhaps, as Winslow speculates, Doyle invented the whole scheme as a farce to embarrass the scientific establishment and, most especially, Lankester.

"So the case against Doyle is made. Besides the necessary skill, contacts, knowledge, and opportunity to qualify as the hoaxer, Doyle also had sufficient motive and an inviting target, Lankester" (Winslow and Meyer, 1983, p. 42).

Fascinating as it all is, we may never know whether the creator of Sherlock Holmes was also the Piltdown forger. Eighty years after the crime, the trail has grown stone cold—the forger covered his tracks very well indeed!

SOURCES

Spencer, Frank. *Piltdown: A Scientific Forgery*. New York: Oxford University Press, 1990.

Weiner, J. W. *The Piltdown Forgery*. London: Oxford University Press, 1955.

Winslow, John Hathaway, and Alfred Meyer. "The Perpetrator at Piltdown," *Science '83*, September, 1983, pp. 33–43.

Introduction

In the last two chapters, we have seen that various researchers have attempted to define hominids (both living *and* extinct) primarily on the basis either of dental traits or through interpretation of presumed toolmaking behavior. As it turns out, neither of these criteria have proven very useful when applied to the *earliest* evidence of the hominid lineage.

In this chapter, we will review the discoveries of what is now a very large collection of early hominids from East and South Africa. Dating to the time period between four and one million years ago, this remarkable group of fossil hominids now consists of several thousand specimens representing several hundred individuals.

Through analysis of these materials paleoanthropologists have concluded that the primary functional adaptation that best distinguishes the hominid lineage is the development of bipedal locomotion. This chapter reviews firstly the history, context, and basic morphology of these discoveries and then (in Chapter 14) we take up the varied, and often confusing, interpretations of these finds.

Characteristics of Hominids:
The Central Role of Bipedal Locomotion

As we discussed in Chapter 8, there is a general tendency in all primates for erect body posture and some bipedalism. However, of all living primates, efficient bipedalism as the primary form of locomotion is seen *only* in hominids. Functionally, the human mode of locomotion is most clearly shown in our striding gait, where weight is alternately placed on a single fully extended hindlimb. This specialized form of locomotion has developed to a point where energy levels are used to near peak efficiency. Such is not the case in nonhuman primates, who move bipedally with hips and knees bent and maintain balance in a clumsy and inefficient manner.

From a survey of our close primate relatives, it is apparent that, while still in the trees, our ancestors were adapted to a fair amount of upper body erectness. Prosimians, monkeys, and apes all spend considerable time sitting erect while feeding, grooming, or sleeping. Presumably, our early ancestors also displayed similar behavior. What caused these forms to come to the ground and embark on the unique way of life that would eventually lead to humans is still a mystery. Perhaps natural selection favored some Miocene hominoid coming occasionally to the ground to forage for food on the forest floor and forest fringe. In any case, once it was on the ground and away from the immediate safety offered by trees, bipedal locomotion became a tremendous advantage.

First of all, bipedal locomotion freed the hands for carrying objects and for making and using tools. Such early cultural developments then had an even more positive effect on speeding the development of yet more efficient bipedalism—once again emphasizing the dual role of biocultural evolution. In addition, in the bipedal stance, animals have a wider view of the surrounding countryside, and, in open terrain, early spotting of predators (particularly the large cats, such as lions, leopards, and saber-tooths) would be of critical importance. We know that modern ground-living primates, such as the savanna baboon and chimpanzee, will occasionally adopt this posture to

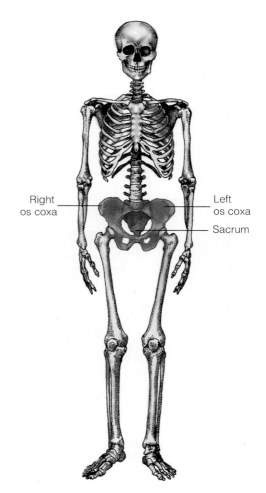

Figure 13-1

The human pelvis. Various elements shown on a modern skeleton.

Right os coxa

Left os coxa

Sacrum

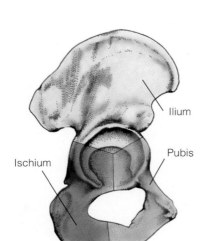

Figure 13-2

The human os coxa. Composed of three bones (right side shown).

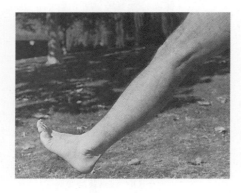

Figure 13-3

The knee in full extension.

"look around" when out in open country. Certainly, bipedal walking is an efficient means of covering long distances, and when large game hunting came into play (several million years after the initial adaptation to ground-living), further refinements in the locomotory complex may have been favored. Exactly what initiated the process is difficult to say, but all these factors probably played a role in the adaptation of hominids to their special niche through a special form of locomotion.

Our mode of locomotion is indeed extraordinary, involving as it does a unique kind of activity in which "the body, step by step, teeters on the edge of catastrophe" (Napier, 1967, p. 56). The problem is to maintain balance on the "stance" leg while the "swing" leg is off the ground. In fact, during normal walking, both feet are simultaneously on the ground only about 25% of the time, and, as speed of locomotion increases, this figure becomes even smaller.

In order to maintain a stable center of balance in this complex form of locomotion, many drastic structural/functional alterations are demanded in the basic primate quadrupedal pattern. Functionally, the foot must be altered to act as a stable support instead of a grasping limb. When we walk, our foot is used like a prop, landing on the heel and pushing off on the toes, particularly the big toe. In addition, the leg must be elongated to increase the length of the stride. The lower limb must also be remodeled to allow full extension of the knee and to allow the legs to be kept close together during walking, thereby maintaining the center of support directly under the body. Finally, significant changes must occur in the pelvis to permit stable weight transmission from the upper body to the legs and to maintain balance through pelvic rotation and altered proportions and orientations of several key muscles.

The major structural changes that are required for bipedalism are all seen in the earliest hominids from East and South Africa. In the pelvis, the blade (ilium—upper bone of the pelvis) is shortened top to bottom, which permits more stable weight support in the erect position by lowering the center of gravity. In addition, the pelvis is bent backward and downward, thus altering the position of the muscles that attach along the bone. Most importantly, the gluteus medius (glue-tee´-us meed´-ee-us) now becomes a very large muscle acting to stabilize the trunk and keep it from slumping to the unsupported side while the body is supported on one leg. The gluteus maximus (glue-tee´-us max´-a-mus) also becomes important as an extensor—to pull the thigh back—during running, jumping, and climbing. (See Appendix A.)

Other structural changes shown by even the earliest definitively hominid postcranial evidence further confirm the morphological pattern seen in the pelvis. In addition, the vertebral column, known from beautifully preserved specimens from South and East Africa, shows the same forward curvature as in modern hominids, bringing the center of support forward and allowing rotation of the bottom of the vertebral column (sacrum) below, thereby getting it out of the way of the birth canal. In addition, the lower limb is elongated and is apparently proportionately about as long as in modern humans. Fossil evidence of a knee fragment from South Africa and pieces from East Africa also shows that full extension of this joint was possible, thus allowing the leg to be completely straightened, as when a field goal kicker follows through.

Structural evidence for the foot is not abundant in South Africa, but there is one ankle bone from Kromdraai and a few other recently discovered pieces. These foot bones show mixed patterns and probably belonged to an animal that was a well-adapted biped but still retained considerable climbing

Figure 13-4

Os coxae. (a) Homo sapiens; *(b) early hominid (Australopithecus) from South Africa; (c) chimpanzee. Note especially the length and breadth of the iliac blade.*

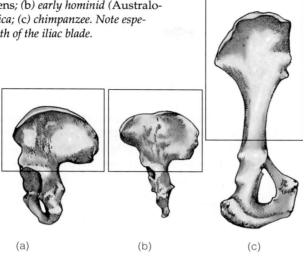

(a)   (b)   (c)

ability. More complete evidence for evolutionary changes in the foot skeleton comes from Olduvai Gorge in East Africa, where a nearly complete hominid foot is preserved, and from the Hadar in Ethiopia, where numerous foot elements have been recovered. As in the ankle bone from South Africa, the East African fossils suggest a well-adapted bipedal gait. The arches are developed and the big toe is pulled in next to the other toes, but some differences in the ankle also imply that considerable flexibility was possible (for climbing?). As we will see below, some researchers have recently concluded that many early forms of hominids probably spent considerable time in the trees. Moreover, they may not have been quite as efficient bipeds as has previously been suggested (see p. 364).

Early Hominids in the Plio-Pleistocene

The beginnings of hominid differentiation almost certainly have their roots in the late Miocene (circa 5–10 m.y.a.). Sometime during the period between 8 and 4 m.y.a., hominids began to adapt more fully to their peculiar ground-living niche, and fossil evidence from this period would be most illuminating, particularly any remains indicating a bipedal adaptation. However, scant information is presently available concerning the course of hominid evolution during this significant 4-million-year gap. But beginning around 4 m.y.a., the fossil record picks up considerably. We now have a wealth of fossil hominid material from the Pliocene and the earliest stages of the Pleistocene (5–1 m.y.a.), and this whole span is usually referred to as the Plio-Pleistocene.

The East African Rift Valley

Stretching along a more than 1,200-mile trough extending through Ethiopia, Kenya, and Tanzania from the Red Sea in the north to the Serengeti plain in the south is the eastern branch of the Great Rift Valley of Africa. This massive

Figure 13-5

A nearly complete hominid foot (OH 8). From Olduvai Gorge, East Africa.

geological feature has been associated with active mountain building, faulting, and vulcanism over the last several million years.

Because of these gigantic earth movements, earlier sediments (normally buried under hundreds of feet of earth and rock) are literally thrown to the surface, where they become exposed to the trained eye of the paleoanthropologist. Such earth movements have exposed Miocene beds at sites in Kenya, along the shores of Lake Victoria, where abundant remains of early fossil hominoids have been found. In addition, Plio-Pleistocene sediments are also exposed all along the Rift Valley, and paleoanthropologists in recent years have made the most of this unique opportunity.

More than just exposing normally hidden deposits, rifting has stimulated volcanic activity, which in turn has provided a valuable means of chronometrically dating many sites in East Africa. Unlike the sites in South Africa (see pp. 373–379), those along the Rift Valley are *datable* and have thus yielded much crucial information concerning the precise chronology of early hominid evolution.

The Earliest East African Hominid Sites

The site that focused attention on East Africa as a potential paleoanthropological gold mine was Olduvai Gorge in northern Tanzania. As discussed in great detail in Chapter 12, this site has offered unique opportunities because of the remarkable preservation of geological, paleontological, and archeological records. Following Mary Leakey's discovery of "Zinj," in 1959 (and the subsequent dating of its find site at 1.75 m.y.a. by the K/Ar method), numerous other areas in East Africa have been surveyed and several intensively explored. We will briefly review the geological and chronological background of these important sites beginning with the earliest.

EARLIEST TRACES

For the period preceding 4 m.y.a. only very fragmentary remains possibly attributable to the Hominidae have been found. The earliest of these fossils comes from the Lake Baringo region of central Kenya and the Lake Turkana basin of northernmost Kenya. (A brief summary of the fossil discoveries from these regions is listed in Box 13-1.)

LAETOLI (LYE´-TOLL-EE)

Thirty miles south of Olduvai Gorge in northern Tanzania lie beds considerably older than those exposed at the gorge. With numerous volcanic sediments in the vicinity, accurate K/Ar testing is possible and provides a date of 3.50–3.60 m.y.a. for this site.

Since systematic fossil recovery began at Laetoli in 1974, twenty-three fossil hominid individuals have been found, consisting almost exclusively of jaws and teeth with fragmentary postcranial remains of one immature individual (Johanson and White, 1979; White, 1980).

In February, 1978, Mary Leakey announced a remarkable discovery at Laetoli: fossilized footprints embossed into an ancient volcanic tuff approximately 3.5 m.y.a.! Literally thousands of footprints have been found at this

Box 13-1   Earliest Fossil Material Possibly Referable to the Hominidae

In central Kenya in the Lake Baringo area, fragmentary fossils have been discovered at three different geological formations and two sites.

FORMATIONS:

1. Ngorora Formation (age approximately 9 m.y.–13 m.y.)—one partial upper molar. Not much can be said about this tooth, except that it is "hominoidlike."
2. Lukeino Formation (age approximately 5.1 m.y.–6.3 m.y.)—one lower molar. While some authorities believe this tooth has "distinct hominid resemblances" (Howell, 1978), detailed metrical analysis indicates this tooth is clearly primitive as a hominoid and not derived as a hominid (Corruccini and McHenry, 1980).
3. Chemeron Formation (age approximately 1.5–4 m.y.)—one isolated temporal bone from the side of a skull (see Appendix A). This fossil has recently been reevaluated (Hill et al., 1992) and has attracted considerable new interest. Indeed, with an estimated age of 2.4 million years, the assignment by Andrew Hill and his colleagues of this fossil as a member of genus *Homo* would make this specimen the *earliest yet discovered representative of our genus.*

LOCALITIES:

1. Tabarin (4–5 m.y.)—a site west of Lake Baringo, where a partial hominid lower jaw was found in February, 1984. The find—a small fragment containing two molar teeth—has been suggested as a very early hominid, the earliest species of *Australopithecus* (Hill and Ward, 1988).
2. Samburu Hills—to the north and west of Lake Baringo, some other early and potentially highly productive fossil-bearing beds have recently been explored. In the Samburu Hills of north-central

Kenya, a team led by Hidemi Ishida of Osaka University discovered a partial hominoid jaw in August, 1982. Consisting of the left half of an upper jaw with five teeth in place, this find has been *very* provisionally estimated at 8 million years old. Detailed descriptions are not yet available, but are eagerly awaited by paleoanthropologists.

From the Lake Turkana region of northern Kenya, two other localities have yielded Late Miocene/Early Pliocene fossils that some scholars suggest belong to the hominid family.

1. Lothagam—located on the southwest side of Lake Turkana, no radiometric dates exist for this site (faunal correlation suggests a date of around 5.5 m.y.a.). Only one fossil has been found, the back portion of a mandible with one molar in place. Although this specimen is too fragmentary for any firm decision to be based on it, it is certainly a hominoid and *may* be an early primitive hominid (Kramer, 1986) and possibly, as with the Tabarin jaw fragment, is an early *Australopithecus* (Hill et al., 1992). Caution must be used in making phylogenetic judgments for any of these fragmentary late Miocene discoveries. As we go back ever closer to the hominid-African pongid divergence, the distinguishing characteristics become more difficult to nail down—especially when dental remains are all that we have.
2. Kanapoi—located close to Lothagam on the southwest side of Lake Turkana, Kanapoi yielded just one potentially hominid specimen, the lower end of an upper arm bone, or humerus.

    Dating of Kanapoi, also by means of faunal correlation, gives a date of approximately 4 m.y.a. Like Lothagam, the hominid material is too fragmentary to allow much elaboration, except to note that it appears hominid. Also like Lothagam, surface surveys at Kanapoi revealed no archeological traces.

Figure 13-6

Hominid footprint from Laetoli, Tanzania. Note the deep impression of the heel and the large toe (arrow) in line (adducted) with the other toes.

remarkable site, representing more than twenty different kinds of animals (Pliocene elephants, horses, pigs, giraffes, antelopes, hyenas, and an abundance of hares). Several hominid footprints have also been found, including a trail more than 75 feet long, made by at least two—and perhaps three—individuals (Leakey and Hay, 1979). (See Fig. 13-6.)

Such discoveries of well-preserved hominid footprints are extremely important in furthering our understanding of human evolution. For the first time we can make *definite* statements regarding locomotory pattern and stature of early hominids. Initial analysis of these Pliocene footprints compared to modern humans suggests a stature of about 4 feet, 9 inches for the larger individual and 4 feet, 1 inch for the smaller individual.

Studies of these impression patterns clearly show that the mode of locomotion of these hominids was fully bipedal (Day and Wickens, 1980). As we have discussed, the development of bipedal locomotion is *the* most important defining characteristic of early hominid evolution. Some researchers, however, have concluded that these early hominids were not bipedal in quite the same way that modern humans are. From detailed comparisons with modern humans, estimates of step length, cadence, and speed of walking have been ascertained, indicating that the Laetoli hominids moved in a "strolling" fashion with a rather short stride (Chateris et al., 1981).

HADAR (HA-DAR´) (AFAR TRIANGLE)

Potentially one of the most exciting areas for future research in East Africa is the Afar Triangle of northeastern Ethiopia, where the Red Sea, Rift Valley, and Gulf of Aden all intersect. Initial K/Ar dating has suggested an age of up to 3.6 m.y.a. for the older hominid fossils and 2.5 m.y.a. for the upper artifactual-bearing beds (Johanson and Edey, 1981). These dates must be considered provisional until systematically corroborated by other laboratories and other dating techniques (Curtis, 1981).

Some of the chronology at the Hadar appears clearcut. For example, there is general agreement that the Lucy skeleton (see Fig. 13-8) is about 3 million

Figure 13-7

Hadar deposits, northeastern Ethiopia.

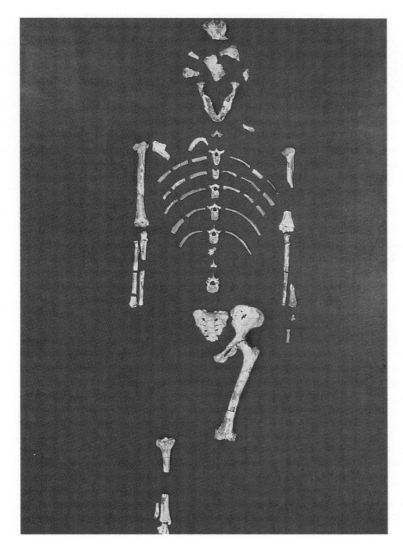

Figure 13-8

"Lucy," a partial hominid skeleton. Discovered at the Hadar in 1974.

years old. Analysis of the older beds, however, has led to some ambiguity regarding their precise dating. Study of one of the volcanic tuffs at Hadar has suggested a correlation (that is, the result of the same volcanic eruption) with well-defined tuffs at Omo in southern Ethiopia and East Lake Turkana in northern Kenya (see below). On the basis of this chemical fingerprinting of tuffs (Brown, 1982), the paleomagnetic data, and biostratigraphic interpretations (Boaz et al., 1982), some researchers have concluded the 3.6 million year date for the earlier beds at Hadar is too old; accordingly, they suggest a basal date for the hominid-bearing levels of around 3.2–3.4 m.y.a.

However, opinion still varies. The proposed correlation of the volcanic tuffs across northeastern Africa is not accepted by all researchers (e.g., Aronson et al., 1983). Moreover, the biostratigraphy is also subject to differing interpretations (White, 1983).

A 300,000 to 400,000 year discrepancy may not seem all that important, but it is a most significant time period (10% of the total *known* time range of hominids). To form a consistent theory of exactly what was going on in the Plio-Pleistocene, we need precise chronological controls.

The chronologies, however, often take years of study to sort out. Most crucially, cross-correlations among different dating techniques (K/Ar, biostratigraphy, paleomagnetism, fission-track) must be determined. The most recent calibrations with improved methods of K/Ar dating suggest a basal date close to 3.4 m.y.a.

Due to the excellent preservation conditions in the once-lakeside environment at Hadar, an extraordinary collection of fossilized bones has been discovered—6,000 specimens in the first two field seasons alone! Among the fossil remains, at least 36 hominid individuals (up to a maximum of as many as 65) have been discovered (Johanson and Taieb, 1980).

Two extraordinary discoveries at Hadar are most noteworthy. In 1974, a partial skeleton called "Lucy" was found eroding out of a hillside. This fossil is scientifically designated as Afar Locality (AL) 288-1, but is usually just called Lucy (after a popular Beatles' song, "Lucy in the Sky with Diamonds"). Representing almost 40% of a skeleton, this is one of the two most complete individuals from anywhere in the world for the entire period before about 100,000 years ago.*

The second find, a phenomenal discovery, came to light in 1975 at AL 333. Don Johanson and his amazed crew found dozens of hominid bones scattered along a hillside. These bones represented at least 13 individuals including 4 infants. Possibly members of one social unit, this group has been argued to have all died at about the same time, thus representing a "catastrophic" assemblage (White and Johanson, 1989). However, the precise deposition of the site has not been completely explained, so this assertion must be viewed as quite tentative. (In geological time, an "instant" could represent many decades or centuries.) Considerable cultural material has been found in the Hadar area—mostly washed into stream channels, but some stone tools have been reported in context at a site dated at 2.5 m.y.a., potentially making the findings the oldest cultural evidence yet discovered.

Unfortunately, over the last decade, political instability in Ethiopia has caused frequent interruptions of field research at the Hadar. However, in the last three years considerable further surveying has been done in the Afar Triangle (and elsewhere in Ethiopia). Aided by satellite photography (from the

---

*The other is a recently discovered *H. erectus* skeleton from west of Lake Turkana, Kenya (see p. 424).

GREAT MOMENTS IN PREHISTORY

Discovery of the Hadar "Family," November to December, 1975

On November 1, I set out for the new area with photographer David Brill and a visiting scientist, Dr. Becky Sigmon.

Climbing into my Land Rover, David asked, "When do we find our next hominid?"

"Today," I replied.

In less than an hour, anthropology student John Kolar spotted an arm-bone fragment. From some distance away, Mike Bush, a medical student, shouted that he had found something just breaking the ground surface. It was the very first day on survey for Mike.

"Hominid teeth?" he asked, when we ran to him. There was no doubt.

We called that spot Afar Locality 333 and scheduled full excavation for the next day.

Morning found me at 333, lying on my side so that I could wield a dental pick to excavate the upper-jaw fragment Mike had found. Michèle Cavillon of our motion-picture crew called to me to look at some bones higher up the hill.

Two bone fragments lay side by side—one a partial femur and the other a fragmentary heel bone. Both were hominid.

Carefully, we started scouring the hillside. Two more leg bones—fibulae—showed up, but each from the same side. The same side? That could only indicate two individuals.

Then from high on the slope came a cry, "Look at the proximal femur—it's complete!" Turning I saw, outlined against the blue sky, the top end of a thigh bone. Even from a distance I could tell that it was not Lucy-size; it was much larger. Slowly I groped up the hillside and held the femur.

Mike wanted to come look but was distracted by finding two fragments composing a nearly complete lower jaw. The entire hillside was dotted with the bones of what were evidently at least two individuals.

We held a strategy meeting. Maurice [geologist Maurice Taieb] established that the bones we found on the surface had originally been buried several yards up the slope. Mike chose a crew of seven workers to survey carefully every inch of the area and collect all bone material, sifting even the loose soil.

Time was of the essence. Rainstorms during the months of our absence could wash away fragments that would be lost forever down the ravines. I felt I was moving through a dream: Each day produced more remains.

The picture became tangled. Another upper jaw of an adult came to light. The wear pattern on the lower jaw we'd found did not match either of the uppers. At least three individuals had to be represented. More mandible fragments appeared that could not be definitely fitted to either upper jaw. Extraordinary! We had evidence of perhaps as many as five adults of the genus *Homo*.*

Apart from teeth and jaws, we recovered scores of hand and foot bones, leg bones, vertebrae, ribs, even a partial adult skull. A baby tooth turned up, suggesting the presence of a sixth hominid at the site. Then a nearly complete lower jaw of a baby appeared, as well as an almost intact palate with baby teeth. Not heavily worn, the teeth suggested that their possessor was only about 3 years old.

So we had evidence of young adults, old adults, and children—an entire assemblage of early hominids. All of them at one place. Nothing like this had ever been found!

SOURCE:

"Ethiopia Yields First 'Family' of Early Man," by Donald C. Johanson, *National Geographic Magazine*, Vol. 150, pp. 790–811, December 1976. Reprinted with permission of the publisher.

---

*Johanson and his colleagues later assigned all this material to *Australopithecus afarensis* (see p. 362).

United States space shuttle) that identified those geological exposures most likely to yield fossil discoveries, ground teams have recovered numerous new specimens from the Hadar, including cranial fragments, mandibles, and some post-cranial elements (Asfaw, 1992; Wood, 1992a).

Hominids from Laetoli and Hadar

The fossil finds from Laetoli and Hadar *may* well be from the earliest hominids. The discoveries from these two sites certainly represent the earliest *collection* of hominid remains that have yet been found. From these two areas several hundred hominid specimens have been recovered, representing a minimum of 60 individuals and perhaps as many as 100. In addition, it has been suggested that fragmentary specimens from other (possibly even earlier) locales in East Africa are remains of the same species as that found at Laetoli and Hadar. Most scholars refer to this species as *Australopithecus afarensis*, and the fossils from Tabarin and Lothagam (see Table 13-1) may also be members of this **taxon**. In addition, some finds from northernmost Kenya and southern Ethiopia (at sites where later quite numerous hominids have also been recovered—see below) have also been suggested as possible members of *Australopithecus afarensis*.

What exactly is *A. afarensis*? Without question, it is more primitive than any of the **australopithecine** material from South Africa or East Africa (discussed subsequently). In fact, *A. afarensis* is the most primitive of any definitely hominid group thus far found anywhere. By "primitive," we mean that *A. afarensis* is less evolved in any particular direction than is seen in later species of *Australopithecus* or *Homo*. That is to say, *A. afarensis* shares more primitive features with other early homin*oids* (such as *Dryopithecus, Sivapithecus*, etc.) and with living pongids than is true of later hominids, who display more derived characteristics.

For example, the teeth are quite primitive. The canines are often large, pointed teeth that slightly overlap; the first lower premolar is semisectorial, and the tooth rows are parallel or even posteriorly convergent (see Fig. 13-9).

Taxon (pl. Taxa)   A population (or group of populations) that is judged to be sufficiently distinct and is assigned to a separate category (such as genus or species).

Australopithecine   (os-tral-oh-pith´-e-seen)
The colloquial name for members of the genus *Australopithecus*.

Table 13-1   Summary of East African Hominid Discoveries

Site Name	Location	Age (m.y.a.)	Hominids
Olduvai	N. Tanzania	1.85–1	48 specimens; australopithecines; early *Homo*
Turkana	N. Kenya (eastern side of Lake Turkana)	1.9–1.3	More than 150 specimens; many australopithecines; several early *Homo*
	West side of Lake Turkana	2.5–1.6	1 cranium (australopithecine) 1 nearly complete skeleton (*Homo erectus*)
Hadar	N.E. Ethiopia	3.5–3.0	Minimum of 36 individuals (maximum of 65); early australopithecine (*A. afarensis*)
Laetoli	N. Tanzania	3.6–3.5	24 hominids; early australopithecine (*A. afarensis*)

The pieces of crania that are preserved also display several primitive hominoid characteristics, including a compound sagittal/nuchal crest in the back (see Fig. 13-10), as well as several primitive features of the cranial base. Cranial capacity estimates for *A. afarensis* show a mixed pattern when compared to later hominids. A provisional estimate for the one partially complete cranium (see Fig. 13-10b)—apparently a large individual—gives a figure of 500 cm³, but another, even more fragmentary, cranium is apparently quite a bit smaller and has been estimated at about 375 cm³ (Holloway, 1983). Thus, for some individuals (males?), *A. afarensis* is well within the range of other australopithecine species, but others (females?) may be significantly smaller. However, a detailed depiction of cranial size for *A. afarensis* as a species is not possible at this time—this part of the skeleton is unfortunately too poorly represented. One thing is clear: *A afarensis* had a small brain, probably averaging for the whole species not much over 420 cm³.

A host of postcranial pieces have been found at Hadar (mostly from the partial skeleton "Lucy," and from individuals at AL 333). Initial impressions suggest that the upper limbs are long relative to the lower ones (also a primitive hominoid condition). In addition, the wrist, hand, and foot bones show several differences from modern humans (Susman et al., 1985). Stature can now be confidently estimated: *A. afarensis* was a short hominid. From her partial skeleton, Lucy is figured to be only 3.5–4 feet tall. However, Lucy—as demonstrated by her pelvis—was a female, and at Hadar and Laetoli, there is evidence of larger individuals as well. The most economical hypothesis explaining this variation is that *A. afarensis* was quite sexually dimorphic—the larger individuals are male and the smaller ones such as Lucy are female. Estimates of male stature can be approximated from the larger footprints at Laetoli, inferring a height of about 5 feet. If we accept this interpretation, *A. afarensis* was a very sexually dimorphic form. In fact, for overall body size, this species may have been as dimorphic as *any* living primate (that is, as much as gorillas, orangs, or baboons).

In a majority of dental and cranial features, *A. afarensis* is clearly more primitive than are later hominids. This should not come as too great a surprise, since *A. afarensis* is 1 million years older than most other East African finds and perhaps .5–.7 million years older than the oldest South African hominid. In fact, from the neck up, *A. afarensis* is so primitive, that without

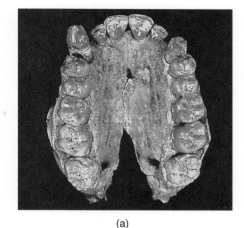

(a)

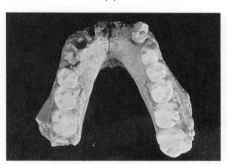

(b)

Figure 13-9

Jaws of Australopithecus afarensis. *(a) Maxilla, AL-200-1a, from Hadar, Ethiopia. (Note the parallel tooth rows and large canines.); (b) mandible, LH 4, from Laetoli, Tanzania. This fossil is the type specimen for the species,* Australopithecus afarensis.

Figure 13-10

Comparison of hominoid crania. (a) Human; (b) Australopithecus afarensis *composite cranium assembled from three individuals—AL 333-45, 200-1a, and 400-1a; (c) chimpanzee.*

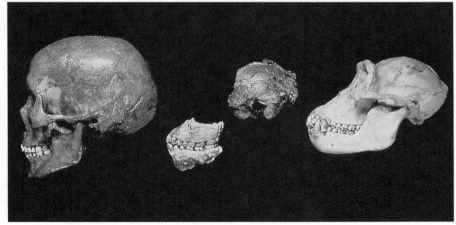

(a)   (b)   (c)

any evidence from the limb skeleton, one would be hard-pressed to call it a hominid at all (although the back teeth are large and heavily enameled, unlike pongids, and the position of the foramen magnum indicates an upright posture). In the teeth particularly, *A. afarensis* is in some ways reminiscent of Miocene hominoids (for example, *Sivapithecus*) (Greenfield, 1979).

What then makes *A. afarensis* a hominid? The answer is revealed by its manner of locomotion. From the abundant limb bones recovered from Hadar and those beautiful footprints from Laetoli we know unequivocally that *A. afarensis* walked bipedally when progressing on the ground. Whether Lucy and her contemporaries still spent considerable time in the trees, and just how efficiently they walked, have become topics of major dispute.

LOCOMOTION OF *AUSTRALOPITHECUS AFARENSIS*

A comprehensive analysis of the postcranial anatomy of *A. afarensis* by Jack Stern and Randall Susman of the State University of New York at Stony Brook has challenged the view that this early hominid walked bipedally, much as you or me (Stern and Susman, 1983). Their interpretation is based upon many parts of the skeleton (limbs, hands, feet, pelvis, etc.), which they have compared with other hominids (fossil and modern), as well as with great apes.

Such features as long, curved fingers and toes, long upper limbs but short lower limbs (Jungers, 1982; Susman et al., 1985), the positioning of the hip and knee joints, and pelvic orientation, have led these researchers to two conclusions: (1) *A. afarensis* was capable of efficient climbing and probably spent considerable time in the trees (sleeping, feeding, escaping from predators, etc.); and (2) while on the ground, *A. afarensis* was a biped, but walked with a much less efficient bent-hip, bent-knee gait than that seen in modern humans.

As might be expected, these conclusions themselves have also been challenged. While pointing out some slight differences from modern humans in postcranial anatomy, Owen Lovejoy (1988) and his associates (for example, Latimer, 1984) see nothing that suggests these hominids were arboreal or, conversely, that precluded them from being *very* efficient bipeds. Moreover, Lucy's "little legs" may not really be that small, considering her small body size (although her arms were apparently quite long) (Wolpoff, 1983b).

Other researchers have also noted differences between the postcranium of *A. afarensis* and later hominids. Interestingly, however, in many respects the hand and pelvis of *A. afarensis* are extremely similar to some later australopithecines from South Africa (Suzman, 1982; McHenry, 1983).

From all this debate, little has yet emerged in the way of consensus, except that all agree the *A. afarensis* did exhibit some kind of bipedal locomotion while on the ground. In searching for some middle ground between the opposing viewpoints, several researchers have suggested that *A. afarensis* could have been quite at home in the trees *as well as* being an efficient terrestrial biped (Wolpoff, 1983b; McHenry, 1983). As one physical anthropologist has surmised:

> One could imagine these diminutive early hominids making maximum use of *both* terrestrial and arboreal resources in spite of their commitment to exclusive bipedalism when on the ground. The contention of a mixed arboreal and terrestrial behavioural repertoire would make adaptive sense of the Hadar australopithecine forelimb, hand, and foot morphology without contradicting the evidence of the pelvis (Wolpoff, 1983b, p. 451).

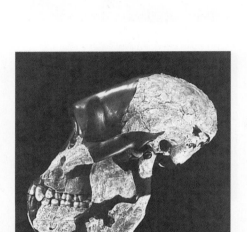

Figure 13-11

Australopithecus afarensis *reconstructed cranium—using evidence from several individuals and filling in portions for which no fossil data exist.*

Later East African Hominid Sites

An assortment of fossil hominids have been recovered from geological contexts with dates after 3 m.y.a. at several localities in East Africa. Up to 10 different such sites are now known (in the time range of 1–3 m.y.a.), but here we will concentrate on the three most significant ones: East Lake Turkana, West Lake Turkana (both of these in northern Kenya), and Olduvai Gorge (in northern Tanzania).

EAST LAKE TURKANA (TUR-CAN´-AH)

Geologically, the situation at East Lake Turkana is exceedingly complex, with deep sections of lake and river deposits crisscrossed by the effects of **tectonic movements**, stream action, and volcanic activity. While the latter is useful in providing material for radiometric dating, the geological complexities have made the precise chronology of the area a matter of dispute.

The later sediments have been securely dated at 1.3–1.6 m.y.a., and consensus on this part of the chronology has existed for several years. However, there has been considerable dispute regarding the earlier levels, particularly a key volcanic bed called the KBS **tuff**. This geological bed (and the associated hominids) are now dated to about 1.8 m.y.a.

As noted, numerous hominids have been discovered at East Lake Turkana in the last decade. The current total exceeds 150 hominid specimens, probably representing at least 100 individuals, and this fine sample includes several complete crania, many jaws, and an assortment of post-cranial bones.

Next to Olduvai, Turkana has yielded the most information concerning the behavior of early hominids. More than 20 archeological sites have been discovered, and excavation or testing has been done at 10 localities. Two sites are of particular interest and are both directly associated with the KBS tuff (age, therefore, 1.8 m.y.a.). One is a combination of stone artifacts with the broken bones of several species, whereas the other is the "butchering" site of an extinct form of hippopotamus. The stone tools from these earlier sedi-

Tectonic movements Movements of the earth's plates that produce mountain building, earthquakes, volcanoes, and rifting.

Tuff A geological deposit resulting from volcanic ash (either windblown or waterlaid).

Figure 13-12

Excavations in progress. East Lake Turkana, northern Kenya.

ments at Turkana are in many ways reminiscent of the Oldowan industry in Bed I at Olduvai (with which they are contemporaneous).

WEST LAKE TURKANA

Across the lake from the fossil beds discussed above are other deposits that recently have yielded new and very exciting discoveries. In 1984, on the west side of Lake Turkana, a nearly complete skeleton of a 1.6-million-year-old *Homo erectus* child was found (see p. 423), and the following year a well-preserved cranium, 2.5 million years old, was also found. This latter discovery, the black skull, is a most important discovery and has caused a major reevaluation of Plio-Pleistocene hominid evolution (see below).

OLDUVAI GORGE

The reader should by now be well acquainted with this remarkable site in northern Tanzania, particularly with its clear geological and chronological contributions. Hominid discoveries from Olduvai now total about 50 individuals, ranging in time from 1.85 m.y.a. to Upper Pleistocene times less than 50,000 years ago.

Hominids from Olduvai and Lake Turkana

Most fossil hominids from Olduvai, West Lake Turkana, and especially East Lake Turkana are later in time than the *A. afarensis* remains from Laetoli and Hadar (by at least 500,000 years). It is thus not surprising that they are more derived, in some cases dramatically so. Also, these later hominids are considerably more diverse. Most researchers accept the interpretation that all the hominids from Laetoli and Hadar are members of a single taxon, *A. afarensis*. However, it is clear that the remains from the Turkana area and Olduvai collectively represent multiple taxa—two different genera and perhaps up to five or six different species. Current discussion on how best to sort this complex material is among the most vehement in paleoanthropology. Here we summarize the broad patterns of physical morphology. In Chapter 14 we will take up the various schemes that attempt to interpret the fossil remains in a broader evolutionary context.

Following 2.5 m.y.a., later (and more derived) representatives of *Australopithecus* are found in East Africa. This is a most distinctive group that has popularly been known for some time as "robust" australopithecines. By "robust" it had generally been meant that these forms—when compared to other australopithecines—were larger in body size. However, recent, more controlled studies (Jungers, 1988; McHenry, 1988; McHenry, 1992) have shown that all the species of *Australopithecus* overlapped considerably in body size. As we will see below, "robust" australopithecines have also been found in South Africa.

As a result of these new weight estimates, many researchers have either dropped the use of the term "robust" (along with its opposite, "gracile") or present it in quotation marks to emphasize its conditional application. We believe the term "robust" can be used in this latter sense, as it still emphasizes important differences in the scaling of craniodental traits. In other words, even if they are not larger overall, robust forms are clearly robust in the skull and dentition.

Dating to approximately 2.5 m.y.a., the earliest representative of this robust group (that is, clade) comes from northern Kenya on the west side of Lake Turkana. A complete cranium (WT-17,000—"the black skull") was unearthed there in 1985 and has proven to be a most important discovery. This skull, with a cranial capacity of only 410 cm^3, has the smallest definitely ascertained brain volume of any hominid yet found. In addition, the form has other primitive traits, quite reminiscent of *A. afarensis*. For example, there is a compound crest in the back of the skull, the upper face projects considerably, the upper dental row converges in back, and the cranial base is extensively pneumatized—that is, it possesses air pockets (Kimbel et al., 1988).

What makes the black skull so fascinating, however, is that mixed with this array of distinctively primitive traits are a host of derived ones linking it to other members of the robust group (including a broad face, a very large palate, and a large area for the back teeth). This mosaic of features neatly places skull 17,000 between earlier *A. afarensis* on the one hand and the later robust species on the other. Because of its unique position in hominid evolution, WT-17,000 (and the population it represents) has been placed in a new species—*Australopithecus aethiopicus*.

Around 2 m.y.a. different varieties of even more derived members of the robust lineage are on the scene in East Africa. As well documented by finds at Olduvai and East Turkana, robust australopithecines have relatively small cranial capacities (ranging from 510–530 cm^3) and very large, broad faces with massive back teeth and lower jaws. The larger (probably male) individuals also show a raised ridge, called a **sagittal crest**, along the midline of the cranium. The first find of a recognized Plio-Pleistocene hominid in East Africa, in fact, was of a nearly complete robust australopithecine cranium, discovered in 1959 by Mary Leakey at Olduvai Gorge (see p. 338). As a result of Louis Leakey's original naming of the fossil (as "*Zinjanthropus*"), this find is still popularly referred to as "Zinj." However, it and its other conspecifics in East Africa are now usually placed in the species, *A. boisei*.

EARLY *HOMO*

In addition to the robust australopithecine remains in East Africa, there is another Plio-Pleistocene hominid that is quite distinctive. In fact, as best documented by fossil discoveries from Olduvai and East Turkana, these materials have been assigned to the genus *Homo*—and thus are different from all species assigned to *Australopithecus*.

The earliest appearance of genus *Homo* in East Africa may be as ancient as that of the robust australopithecines. As we have discussed, a robust australopithecine (the black skull from West Turkana) has been dated to approximately 2.5 m.y.a. New reinterpretations of the Chemeron temporal fragment from the Lake Baringo region of central Kenya (see Box 13-1) have suggested that early *Homo* may also be close to this same antiquity (estimated age of 2.4 m.y.a.) (Hill et al., 1992). Given that the robust australopithecine lineage was already diverging at this time, it is not surprising to find the earliest representatives of the genus *Homo* also beginning to diversify. Nevertheless, one temporal bone does not provide indisputable proof. Further early remains in well-dated contexts will help provide confirmation.

The presence of a Plio-Pleistocene hominid with a significantly larger brain than seen in *Australopithecus* was first suggested by Louis Leakey in the early 1960s on the basis of fragmentary remains found at Olduvai Gorge.

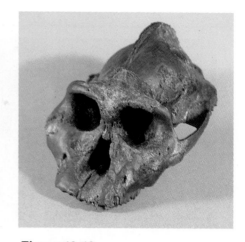

Figure 13-13

The "black skull" WT-17,000, discovered at West Lake Turkana in 1985. This specimen is provisionally assigned to Australopithecus aethiopicus.

Sagittal crest Raised ridge along the midline of the cranium where the temporal muscle (used to move the jaw) is attached.

UNIVERSITY OF ALBERTA PHOTO SERVICES

Nancy Lovell graduated from Simon Fraser University with a BA (Honors) in Archaeology and earned a PhD from Cornell University. She taught at Hobart and William Smith Colleges and spent a year at the University of California (Berkeley) as a Social Sciences and Humanities Research Council of Canada postdoctoral fellow before joining the faculty at the University of Alberta. Her specialties are human osteoarchaeology, paleopathology, and comparative primate skeletal pathology.

It was 10 years after I graduated from high school that I discovered anthropology, when I was taking university night classes just out of interest. I'd always loved to travel, so anthropology was a natural field of study for me. I found, however, that prehistoric cultures caught my interest more than did contemporary cultures, probably because I felt a sense of mystery about the past. When I was faced with the fact that I'd have to attend classes during the day if I wanted to continue, I quit my job as a travel agent and went back to school full-time to study for a B.A. in archaeology. Although most archaeology emphasizes material cultural remains, such as pottery or stone tools, to me the most interesting raw material was human skeletal remains. I was intrigued by the challenge of puzzling out the different characteristics of each individual, such as how old they were when they died and what kinds of injuries and illnesses they'd experienced in their lifetime. Each person exhibits their own unique "persona" in their bones, which reflects, among other things, their occupation, social position, and health. But in spite of this uniqueness I am always humbled by the fact that all humans share certain life experiences, even over a separation in time of thousands of years. Death is, after all, the great leveler.

When I began graduate school I decided to focus on paleopathology, the study of health in antiquity. Because my undergraduate degree was in archaeology, most of my research has involved the assessment of injury and illness in archaeological contexts, and my area of specialization is the study of associations of health and nutrition with socioeconomic status. In particular, I'm interested in how social class systems affected the kind of physical labor people engaged in, their living conditions, the quantity and quality of food that they could obtain, and the availability of health care. I've examined these associations during the formative periods of the Indus Valley and ancient Egyptian civilizations, and have conducted archaeological field work in India, Pakistan, and Egypt. In addition to excavation, much of my research is done on human skeletal remains that were excavated as long as a century ago and which are currently housed in museums. Travel thus continues to be an important part of my life. Due to my teaching commitments, however, my research can be conducted only during the summer, which means absences from home of several months as well as sometimes unpleasant working conditions—it can be unbearably hot in Egypt in July!

Although most of my research involves archaeological human remains, as a graduate student I realized that much of our paleopathological interpretation was necessarily subjective and informed by our cultural biases. We had little "base line" data on illness and injury in nonhuman animals and so were inadequately prepared to investigate human injury and illness in adaptive and selective contexts. Since injury and illness may have been much more important selective factors in the evolution of animals that do not possess culture as a buffer to environmental stressors, I've conducted research also on the skeletal pathology of the alloprimates, who are our closest relatives—the chimpanzees, gorillas, and orangutans.

The pursuit of a career in physical anthropology can be a difficult one, especially in today's employment market. What influenced me most as an undergraduate, and what led me to pursue graduate work and an eventual academic career, was the encouragement I received from a couple of my professors. I volunteered to help with their research, and was eventually rewarded with part-time work and the opportunity to collaborate on research projects. Paying positions in physical anthropological research are few for students who can't offer previous experience or special skills, but by volunteering a few hours a week in the research lab, many students obtain both a sense of whether they enjoy the daily routine of research, as well as the hands-on experience that can translate later into paid work, letters of recommendation for jobs or graduate school, or even publication. Students who think of graduate school as simply an extension of their undergraduate program are in for an unpleasant surprise. There is a real qualitative difference, and the demands are great. Students are expected to work independently to a large degree, and those who have difficulties with goal-setting and meeting deadlines often find themselves in trouble. Further, students are too often seduced by the "glamor" of research, particularly archaeological excavation in foreign countries, and fail to consider whether their personal goals and priorities are compatible with such a lifestyle.

Leakey and his colleagues gave a new species designation to these fossil remains, naming them *Homo habilis.*

The *Homo habilis* material at Olduvai ranges in time from 1.85 m.y.a. for the earliest to about 1.6 m.y.a. for the latest. Due to the fragmentary nature of the fossil remains, interpretations have been difficult and much disputed. The most immediately obvious feature distinguishing the *H. habilis* material from the australopithecines is cranial size. For all the measurable *H. habilis* skulls, the estimated average cranial capacity is 631 cm³ compared to 520 cm³ for all measurable robust australopithecines and 442 cm³ for the less robust species (McHenry, 1988). *Homo habilis,* therefore, shows an increase in cranial size of about 20% over the larger of the australopithecines and an even greater increase over some of the smaller-brained forms (from South Africa, discussed below).

In their initial description of *H. habilis,* Leakey and his associates also pointed to differences from australopithecines in cranial shape and in tooth proportions (larger front teeth relative to back teeth and narrower premolars).

The naming of this fossil material as *Homo habilis* (handy man) was meaningful from two perspectives. First of all, Leakey inferred that members of this group were the early Olduvai toolmakers. If true, how do we account for a robust australopithecine like "Zinj" lying in the middle of the largest excavated area known at Olduvai? What was he doing there? Leakey has suggested he was the remains of a *habilis* meal! Excepting those instances where cutmarks are left behind (see pp. 342–343), we must point out again that there is no clear way archeologically to establish the validity of such a claim. However, the debate over this assertion serves to demonstrate that cultural factors as well as physical morphology must be considered in the interpretation of hominids as biocultural organisms. Secondly, and most significantly, by calling this group *Homo,* Leakey was arguing for at least *two separate branches* of hominid evolution in the Plio-Pleistocene. Clearly only one could be on the main branch eventually leading to *Homo sapiens.* By labeling this new group *Homo* in opposition to *Australopithecus,* Leakey was guessing he had found our ancestors.

Since the initial evidence was so fragmentary, most paleoanthropologists were reluctant to accept *H. habilis* as a valid taxon distinct from *all* australopithecines. Differences from the hyperrobust East African variety (*A. boisei*) were certainly apparent; the difficulties arose in trying to distinguish *H. habilis* from the more gracile australopithecines from South Africa, particularly for dental traits that considerably overlap.

Later discoveries, especially from Lake Turkana, of better-preserved fossil material have shed further light on early *Homo* in the Plio-Pleistocene. The most important of this additional material is a nearly complete cranium (ER-1470) discovered at East Lake Turkana in 1972. With a cranial capacity of 775 cm³, this individual is well outside the known range for australopithecines and actually overlaps the lower boundary for *Homo erectus.* In addition, the shape of the skull vault and face are in many respects unlike that of australopithecines. However, the face is still quite robust (Walker, 1976), and the fragments of tooth crowns that are preserved indicate the back teeth in this individual were quite large.

Additional discoveries at Turkana also strongly suggest the presence of a hominid lineage contemporaneous with and separate from australopithecines. Another skull discovered in 1972 (ER 1590) is similar to 1470 and may even be larger! Moreover, several mandibles, including two nearly complete specimens (ER 820 and 992), have tooth proportions (relatively larger front

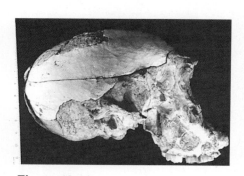

Figure 13-14

A nearly complete skull (OH-24, "Twiggy") from Olduvai Gorge. Initially assigned to "H. habilis."

Figure 13-15

The Kenyan team at East Lake Turkana. Kamoya Kimeu (driving) is the most successful fossil hunter in East Africa. He is responsible for dozens of important discoveries.

teeth) characteristic of our genus. Finally, several postcranial remains discovered at Turkana show a taller, more gracile group than that inferred for robust australopithecines. The dating of all this crucial early *Homo* material from Turkana is tied to the dating of the KBS tuff. As we discussed on page 360, the dating of this key bed has recently been established at around 1.8 m.y.a. Thus, the earliest *Homo* materials at Turkana *and* Olduvai are contemporaneous (that is, 1.8–2.0 m.y.a.).

Other Plio-Pleistocene sites also have revealed possible early members of the genus *Homo*. From the Omo in southern Ethiopia, scattered remains of a few teeth and small cranial fragments are similar in pattern to other comparable early *Homo* material. In addition, a newly discovered very partial skeleton from Olduvai Gorge (OH-62) is extremely small-statured (less than 4 feet, probably) and has several primitive aspects in its limb proportions (Johanson et al., 1987). (See p. 397.)

Figure 13-16

A nearly complete "early Homo" cranium from East Lake Turkana (KNM-ER 1470). One of the most important single fossil hominid discoveries from East Africa.

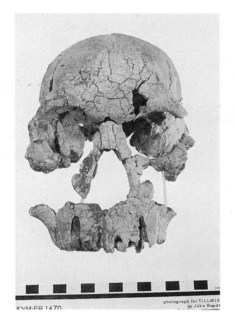 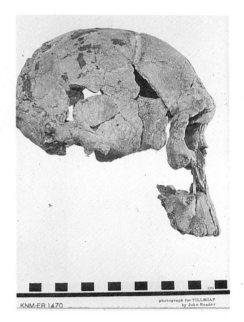

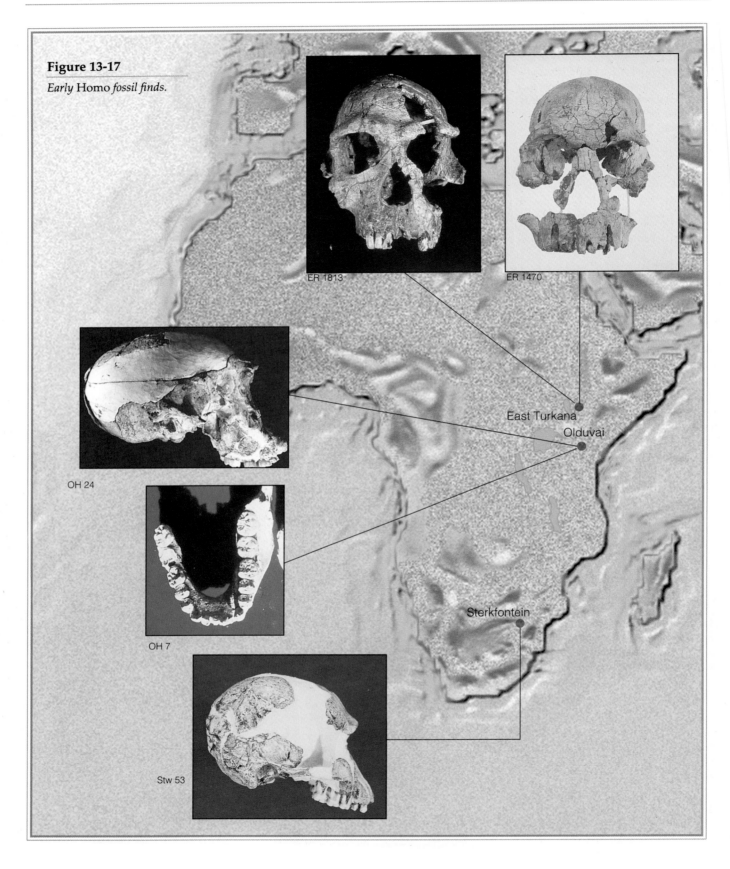

Figure 13-17

Early Homo *fossil finds.*

Box 13-2   Hominid Origins

"In each great region of the world the living mammals are closely related to the extinct species of the same region. It is, therefore, probable that Africa was formerly inhabited by extinct apes closely allied to the gorilla and chimpanzee, and as these two species are now man's nearest allies, it is somewhat more probable that our early progenitors lived on the African continent than elsewhere."

SOURCE:

Charles Darwin. *The Descent of Man*, 1871.

Even more troublesome are two crania from East Turkana (ER-1805 and ER-1813), which do not fit very neatly into the same species with individuals such as ER-1470. Some experts contend that *all* of these individuals can be included within a broad intraspecific umbrella, including most especially a presumed high degree of sexual dimorphism. Others (Lieberman et al., 1988; Wood, 1992b) are not as convinced (see p. 397), and would thus argue for at least two species of early *Homo*. We will return to this important point in more detail in Chapter 14.

On the basis of evidence from Olduvai and particularly from Lake Turkana we can reasonably postulate that one or more species of early *Homo* was present in East Africa probably by 2.4 m.y.a., developing in parallel with at least one line (*A. boisei*) of australopithecines. These two hominid lines lived contemporaneously for a minimum of 1 million years, after which the australopithecine lineage apparently disappears forever. At the same time, most probably the early *Homo* line was emerging into a later form, *Homo erectus*, which, in turn, developed into *H. sapiens*.

South Africa: Earliest Discoveries

The first quarter of this century saw the discipline of paleoanthropology in its scientific infancy. Informed opinion considered the likely origins of the human family to be in Asia, where fossil forms of a primitive kind of *Homo* had been found in Indonesia in the 1890s. Europe was also considered a center of hominid evolutionary action, for spectacular discoveries there of early populations of *Homo sapiens* (including the famous Neandertals) and millions of stone tools had come to light, particularly in the early decades of this century.

Few knowledgeable scholars would have given much credence to Darwin's prediction (see Box 13-2) that the most likely place to find early relatives of humans would be on the continent of Africa. It was in such an atmosphere of preconceived biases that the discoveries of a young Australian-born anatomist were to jolt the foundations of the scientific community in the 1920s. Raymond Dart arrived in South Africa in 1923 at the age of 30 to take up a teaching position in anatomy at the University of Witwatersrand in Johannesburg. Fresh from his evolution-oriented training in England under some of the leading scholars of the day (especially, Sir Grafton Elliot Smith), Dart had developed a keen interest in human evolution. Conse-

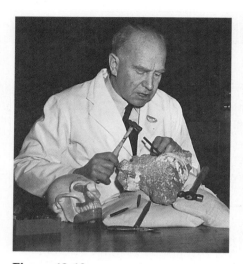

Figure 13-18

Dr. Raymond Dart, shown working in his laboratory.

Endocast   An endocast is a solid (in this case, rock) impression of the inside of the skull showing the size, shape, and some details of the surface of the brain.

quently, he was well prepared when startling new evidence began to appear at his very doorstep.

The first clue came in 1924 when one of Dart's students saw an interesting baboon skull on the mantelpiece while having dinner at the home of the director of the Northern Lime Company, a commercial quarrying firm. The skull, that of a large baboon, had come from a place called Taung about 200 miles southwest of Johannesburg. When Dart saw the skull, he quickly recognized it as an extinct form and asked that any other interesting fossil material found be sent to him for his inspection.

Soon thereafter he received two boxloads of fossils and immediately recognized something that was quite unusual, a natural **endocast** of the inside of the braincase of a higher primate, but certainly no baboon. The endocast fit into another limestone block containing the fossilized front portion of skull, face, and lower jaw. However, these were difficult to see clearly, for the bone was hardened into a cemented limestone matrix called *breccia*. Dart patiently chiseled away for weeks, later describing the task: "No diamond cutter ever worked more lovingly or with such care on a priceless jewel—nor, I am sure, with such inadequate tools. But on the seventy-third day, December 23, the rock parted. I could view the face from the front, although the right side was still imbedded. . . . What emerged was a baby's face, an infant with a full set of milk teeth and its permanent molars just in the process of erupting. I doubt if there was any parent prouder of his offspring than I was of my Taung baby on that Christmas" (Dart, 1959, p. 10).

As indicated by the formation and eruption of teeth, the Taung child was probably about 3–4 years of age at death. Interestingly, the rate of development of this and many other Plio-Pleistocene hominids was more like that of apes than modern *Homo* (Shipman, 1987; Bromage and Dean, 1985). Dart's initial impression that this form was a hominoid was confirmed when he could observe the face and teeth more clearly. However, as it turned out, it took considerably more effort before the teeth could be seen completely, since Dart worked four years just to separate the upper and lower jaws.

But Dart was convinced long before he had an unimpeded view of the dentition that this discovery was a remarkable one, an early hominoid from South Africa. The question was, what kind of hominoid? Dart realized it was

Figure 13-19

(a) *The Taung child discovered in 1924. The endocast is in back with the fossilized bone mandible and face in front;* (b) *Taung. Location of the initial australopithecine discovery.*

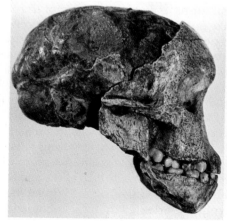

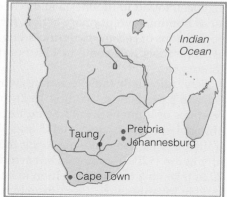

(a)   (b)

GREAT MOMENTS IN PREHISTORY

Raymond Dart and the Discovery of the Taung Child, November, 1924

On his return Young told me that at Taung he had met an old miner, Mr. M. de Bruyn, who for many years had taken a keen interest in preserving fossils. Only the previous week he had brought quite a number of stone blocks containing bone fragments to Mr. Spiers' office. When Young mentioned my interest to Mr. Spiers, Spiers gave instructions for them to be boxed and railed to me.

I waited anxiously for their arrival, reasoning that if fossilized baboon skulls were such a common feature at Taungs many other, more interesting specimens might be found there. Of course, the packages turned up at the most inappropriate time.

I was standing by the window of my dressing room cursing softly while struggling into an unaccustomed stiff-winged collar when I noticed two men wearing the uniform of the South African Railways staggering along the driveway of our home in Johannesburg with two large wooden boxes.

My Virginia-born wife Dora, who was also donning her most formal outfit, had noticed the men with the boxes and rushed in to me in something of a panic.

"I suppose those are the fossils you've been expecting," she said. "Why on earth did they have to arrive today of all days?" She fixed me with a business-like eye. "Now Raymond," she pleaded, "the guests will start arriving shortly and you can't go delving in all that rubble until the wedding's over and everybody has left. I know how important the fossils are to you, but please leave them until tomorrow."

At the time, however, this seemed of little importance when I considered the exciting anthropological bits and pieces that the boxes from Taungs might contain. As soon as my wife had left to complete her dressing I tore the hated collar off and dashed out to take delivery of the boxes which meanwhile obstructed the entrance to the *stoep*. I was too excited to wait until my African servants carried them to the garage, and or-

dered them to leave the crates under the pergola while I went in search of some tools to open them.

(Later on that momentous day, my wife told me that she had twice remonstrated with me but had been ignored. I had no recollection of any interruptions.)

I wrenched the lid off the first box and my reaction was one of extreme disappointment. In the rocks I could make out traces of fossilized eggshells and turtle shells and a few fragmentary pieces of isolated bone, none of which looked to be of much interest.

Impatiently I wrestled with the lid of the second box, still hopeful but half-expecting it to be a replica of its mate. At most I anticipated baboon skulls, little guessing that from this crate was to emerge a face that would look out on the world after an age-long sleep of nearly a million years.

As soon as I removed the lid a thrill of excitement shot through me. On the very top of the rock heap was what was undoubtedly an endocranial cast or mold of the interior of the skull. Had it been only the fossilized brain cast of any species of ape it would have ranked as a great discovery, for such a thing had never before been reported. But I knew at a glance that what lay in my hands was no ordinary anthropoidal brain. Here in lime-consolidated sand was the replica of a brain three times as large as that of a baboon and considerably bigger than that of any adult chimpanzee. The startling image of the convolutions and furrows of the brain and the blood vessels of the skull was plainly visible.

I stood in the shade holding the brain as greedily as any miser hugs his gold, my mind racing ahead. Here, I was certain, was one of the most significant finds ever made in the history of anthropology.

SOURCE:

Adventures with the Missing Link by Raymond Dart, 1959. Reprinted with permission of the author.

extremely improbable that this specimen could have been a forest ape, for South Africa has had a relatively dry climate for many millions of years. Even though the climate at Taung was not as arid as was previously believed (Butzer, 1974), it was an unlikely place to find an ape!

If not an ape, then, what was it? Features of the skull and teeth of this small child held clues that Dart seized upon almost immediately. The entrance of the spinal column into the brain (the foramen magnum at the base of the skull) was further forward in the Taung child than in modern great apes, though not as much as in modern humans. From this fact Dart concluded that the head was balanced *above* the spine, indicating erect posture. In addition, the slant of the forehead was not as receding as in apes, the milk canines were exceedingly small, and the newly erupted first molars were large, broad teeth. In all these respects, the Taung fossil looked more like a hominid than a pongid. There was, however, a disturbing feature that was to confuse and befuddle many scientists for several years: the brain was quite small. Recent studies have estimated the Taung child's brain size at approximately 405 cm^3, which translates to a fully adult size of only 440 cm^3, not very large when compared to modern great apes, as the following tabulation (Tobias, 1971, 1983b) shows:

	RANGE (cm^3)	MEAN (cm^3)
Chimpanzee	282–500	394
Gorilla	340–752	506
Orang	276–540	411

As the tabulation indicates, the estimated cranial capacity for the Taung fossil falls within the range of all the modern great apes, and gorillas actually *average* about 10% greater. It must, however, be remembered that gorillas are very large animals, whereas the Taung child represents a population whose average adult size may have been less than sixty pounds. Since brain size is partially correlated with body size, comparing such differently sized animals cannot be justified (see Chapter 10). A more meaningful contrast would be with the bonobo (*Pan paniscus*), whose body weight is comparable. Bonobos have adult cranial capacities averaging 356 cm^3 for males and 329 cm^3 for females, and thus the Taung child versus a *comparably sized* pongid displays a 25% increase in cranial capacity.

Despite the relatively small size of the brain, Dart saw that it was no pongid. Details preserved on the endocast seemed to indicate that the association areas of the parietal lobes were relatively larger than in any known pongid. However, recent reexamination of the Taung specimen has shown that the sulcal (folding) pattern is actually quite pongidlike (Falk, 1980, 1983).

We must emphasize that attempts to discern the precise position of the "bumps and folds" in ancient endocasts is no easy feat. The science of "paleoneurology" is thus often marked by sharp differences of opinion. Consequently, it is not surprising that the other leading researcher in this field, Ralph Halloway (1981), disagrees with the conclusion by Falk (just cited) and suggests, alternatively, that the Taung endocast has a more hominidlike sulcal pattern.

Realizing the immense importance of his findings, Dart promptly reported them in the British scientific weekly *Nature* on February 7, 1925. A bold venture, since Dart, only 32, was presumptuously proposing a whole new view of human evolution! The small-brained Taung child was christened by Dart *Australopithecus africanus* (southern ape of Africa), which he saw as a kind of halfway "missing link" between modern apes and humans. The concept of a

Figure 13-20

A bonobo. A modern pongid probably similar in body size to many of the australopithecines.

single "missing link" between modern apes and humans was a fallacious one, but Dart correctly emphasized the hominidlike features of the fossil.

A storm of both popular and scholarly protest greeted Dart's article, for it ran directly counter to prevailing opinion. Despite the numerous hominid fossils already discovered, widespread popular skepticism of evolution still prevailed. The year 1925 was, after all, the year of the Scopes "monkey trial" in Tennessee. The biggest fly in the ointment to the leading human evolutionists of the day—Arthur Keith and Grafton Elliot Smith—was the small size of the brain compared to the relatively large proportions of the face and jaws. At that time, anthropologists generally assumed that the primary functional adaptation distinguishing the human family was an immense increase in brain size, and that dental and locomotory modifications came later. This view was seemingly confirmed by the Piltdown discovery in 1911, which displayed the combination of a large brain (estimated at 1,400 cm^3, well within the range of modern humans) with an apelike jaw (see pp. 350–352). Keith even went so far as to postulate a "Cerebral Rubicon" of 750 cm^3 below which—by definition—no hominid could fall. Most scientists in the 1920s thus regarded this little Taung child as an interesting aberrant form of ape.

Hence, Dart's theories were received with indifference, disbelief, and scorn, often extremely caustic. Dart realized more complete remains were needed. The skeptical world would not accept the evidence of one fragmentary, immature individual no matter how highly suggestive the clues. Clearly, more fossil evidence was required, particularly more complete crania of adults. Not an experienced fossil hunter himself, Dart sought further assistance in the search for more australopithecines.

South African Hominids Aplenty

Soon after publication of his controversial theories, Dart found a strong ally in Dr. Robert Broom. A Scottish physician and part-time paleontologist, Broom's credentials as a fossil hunter had been established earlier with his

Figure 13-21

Dr. Robert Broom.

Figure 13-22

Australopithecine sites in South Africa.

Sterkfontein (Sterk´-fon-tane)

Kromdraai (Kromm´-dry)

Swartkrans (Swart-kranz)

Makapansgat (Mak-ah-pans´-gat)

highly successful paleontological work on early mammal-like reptiles in South Africa.

Although interested, Broom was unable to participate actively in the search for additional australopithecines because of prior commitments and did not seriously undertake explorations until 1936. However, soon thereafter he met with incredible success. From two of Dart's students, Broom learned of another commercial limeworks site, called **Sterkfontein**, not far from Johannesburg. Here, as at Taung, the quarrying involved blasting out large sections with dynamite, leaving piles of debris that often contained fossilized remains. Accordingly, Broom asked the quarry manager to keep his eyes open for fossils, and when Broom returned to the site in August, 1936, the manager asked, "Is this what you are looking for?" Indeed, it was, for Broom held in his hand the endocast of an adult australopithecine—exactly what he had set out to find! Looking further over the scattered debris, Broom was able to find most of the rest of the skull of the same individual.

Such remarkable success, just a few months after beginning his search, was not the end of Broom's luck, for his magical touch was to continue unabated for several more years. In 1938, he learned from a young schoolboy of another australopithecine site at **Kromdraai** about one mile from Sterkfontein, and, following World War II (1948), he found yet another australopithecine site, **Swartkrans**, in the same vicinity. A final australopithecine site, **Makapansgat**, was excavated in 1947 by Raymond Dart, who returned to the fossil-discovering bandwagon after an absence of over twenty years.

Numerous extremely important discoveries came from these additional sites, discoveries that would eventually swing the tide of intellectual thought to the views Dart expressed back in 1925. Particularly important was a nearly perfect cranium and a nearly complete pelvis, both found at Sterkfontein in 1947. As the number of discoveries accumulated, it became increasingly difficult to simply write the australopithecines off as aberrant apes.

Although Robert Broom was an absolute wizard at finding fossils, his interpretations of them were clouded by an irresistible urge to give each new discovery a different taxonomic label. Consequently, in addition to Dart's *A. africanus* from Taung, a disconcertingly large number of other names have been used at various times for the South African australopithecines. The problem with all this taxonomic splitting was a lack of appreciation for the relevant biological principles underlying such elaborate interpretations (see Chapter 11 for a discussion of the meaning of taxonomic statements).

By 1949, at least thirty individuals were represented from the five South African sites. That year represents an important turning point, since it marks the visit to South Africa and the resulting "conversion" of W. E. Le Gros Clark. As one of the leading human evolutionists of the day, Sir Wilfrid Le Gros Clark's unequivocal support of the australopithecines as small-brained early hominids was to have wide impact. But the tides of wisdom had begun to turn even before this. Writing in 1947, Sir Arthur Keith courageously admitted his earlier mistake:

> When Professor Dart of the University of Witwatersrand, Johannesburg, announced in *Nature* the discovery of a juvenile *Australopithecus* and claimed for it human kinship, I was one of those who took the point of view that when the adult was discovered, it would prove to be nearer akin to the living African anthropoids—the gorilla and chimpanzee. . . . I am now convinced of the evidence submitted by Dr. Robert Broom that Professor Dart was right and I was wrong. The Australopithecinae [formal designation of the australopithecines

GREAT MOMENTS IN PREHISTORY   **Dr. Broom and the Discovery of the Kromdraai Ape-Man**

On the forenoon of Wednesday, June 8, 1938, when I met Barlow, he said, "I've something nice for you this morning"; and he held out part of a fine palate with the first molar-tooth in position. I said, "Yes, it's quite nice. I'll give you a couple of pounds for it." He was delighted; so I wrote out a cheque, and put the specimen in my pocket. He did not seem quite willing to say where or how he had obtained it; and I did not press the matter. The specimen clearly belonged to a large ape-man, and was apparently different from the Sterkfontein being.

I was again at Sterkfontein on Saturday, when I knew Barlow would be away. I showed the specimen to the native boys in the quarry; but none of them had ever seen it before. I felt sure it had not come from the quarry, as the matrix was different. On Tuesday forenoon I was again at Sterkfontein, when I insisted on Barlow telling me how he had got the specimen. I pointed out that two teeth had been freshly broken off, and that they might be lying where the specimen had been obtained. He apologized for having misled me; and told me it was a school-boy, Gert Terblanche, who acted as a guide in the caves on Sundays, who had picked it up and given it to him. I found where Gert lived, about two miles away; but Barlow said he was sure to be away at school. Still, I set out for his home. There I met Gert's mother and sister. They told me that the place where the specimen was picked up was near the top of a hill about half a mile away, and the sister agreed to take me up to the place. She and her mother also told me that Gert had four beautiful teeth at school with him.

The sister took us up the hill, and I picked up some fragments of the skull, and a couple of teeth; but she said she was sure Gert had some other nice pieces hidden away. Of course, I had to go to school to hunt up Gert.

The road to the school was a very bad one, and we had to leave the car, and walk about a mile over rough ground. When we got there, it was about half-past twelve, and it was play time. I found the headmaster, and told him that I wanted to see Gert Terblanche in connection with some teeth he had picked up. Gert was soon found, and drew from the pocket of his trousers four of the most wonderful teeth ever seen in the world's history. These I promptly purchased from Gert, and transferred to my pocket. I had the palate with me, and I found that two of the teeth were the second pre-molar and second molar, and that they fitted on to the palate. The two others were teeth of the other side. Gert told me about the piece he had hidden away. As the school did not break up till two o'clock, I suggested to the principal that I should give a lecture to the teachers and children about caves, how they were formed, and how bones got into them. He was delighted. So it was arranged; and I lectured to four teachers and about 120 children for over an hour, with blackboard illustrations, till it was nearly two o'clock. When I finished, the principal broke up the school, and Gert came home with me. He took us up to the hill, and brought out from his hiding place a beautiful lower jaw with two teeth in position. All the fragments that I could find at the spot I picked up.

SOURCE:

Finding the Missing Link by Robert Broom (2nd Ed.), 1951. By permission of C. A. Watts/Pitman Publishing Ltd., London.

as a subfamily of the hominids] are in or near the line which culminated in the human form (Keith in Le Gros Clark, 1967, p. 38).

With the exposé of the Piltdown forgery in the early 1950s, the path was completely cleared for the nearly unanimous recognition of the australopithecines as early hominids. With this acceptance also came the necessary recognition that hominid brains had their greatest expansion *after* earlier changes in teeth and locomotory systems. In other words, the rates of evolution in one functional system of the body vary from other systems, thus displaying the **mosaic** nature of human **evolution**.

Mosaic evolution Rate of evolution in one functional system varies from other systems.

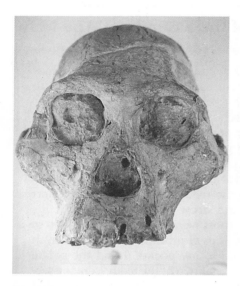

Figure 13-23

A gracile australopithecine cranium from Sterkfontein (Sts. 5). This specimen is the best preserved gracile skull yet found in South Africa. Discovered in 1947.

Figure 13-24

Sir Arthur Keith.

Hominids from South Africa

The Plio-Pleistocene hominid discoveries from South Africa are most significant. First, they were the earliest to be discovered in Africa and helped point the way to later discoveries in East Africa. Second, the morphology of the South African hominids shows broad similarities to the forms in East Africa, but with several distinctive features, which argues for separation at least at the species level. Finally, there is a large assemblage of hominid fossils from South Africa, and exciting discoveries are still being made.

Even today, the evidence from South Africa continues to accumulate. The search in recent years has continued at Sterkfontein, Kromdraai, Swartkrans, and Makapansgat. An important portion of pelvis was found at Swartkrans in 1970, and a partial cranium was found at Sterkfontein (west pit) in 1976. Indeed, discoveries are now coming faster than ever. In the last few years alone more than 150 *new* specimens have come to light at Sterkfontein. In addition, several important new discoveries have been made at Swartkrans. A truly remarkable feast of early hominids, the total number of remains from South Africa exceeds 1,500 (counting all teeth as separate items), and the number of individuals is now more than 200.

From an evolutionary point of view, the most meaningful remains are those from the australopithecine pelvis, which now includes portions of nine os coxae (see p. 354). Remains of the pelvis are so important because, better than any other area of the body, this structure displays the unique requirements of a bipedal animal, such as modern humans *and* our hominid forebears. (For anatomical comparisons, see Appendix A.)

"ROBUST" AUSTRALOPITHECINES

In addition to the discoveries of *A. aethiopicus* and *A. boisei* in East Africa, there are also numerous finds of robust australopithecines in South Africa from sites at Kromdraai and most especially at Swartkrans. Like their East African cousins, the South African robust forms also have small cranial capacities (the only measurable specimen equals 530 cm^3), large broad faces, and very large premolars and molars (although not as massive as in East Africa). Owing to the differences in dental proportions, as well as important differences in facial architecture (Rak, 1983), most researchers now agree there is a species-level difference between the later East African robust variety (*A. boisei*) on the one hand and the South African group (*A. robustus*) on the other.

Despite these differences, all members of the robust lineage appear to be specialized for a diet made up of hard food items, such as seeds and nuts. For many years, paleoanthropologists (for example, Robinson, 1972) had speculated that robust australopithecines concentrated their diet on more heavy vegetable foods than is seen in the diet of other early hominids. Recent research that included the examining of microscopic polishes and scratches on the teeth (Kay and Grine, 1988) has confirmed this view.

Another assumption that has persisted for many years concerns the toolmaking capabilities of robust forms. Put bluntly, most anthropologists did not think robust forms had much of a capacity here—at least not insofar as stone tools go. However, new evidence of hand bones from Swartkrans in South Africa has led Randall Susman (1988) to conclude otherwise. He suggests that robust australopithecines (*A. robustus*) found at this site had fine manipulative abilities, and thus could well have been the maker of the

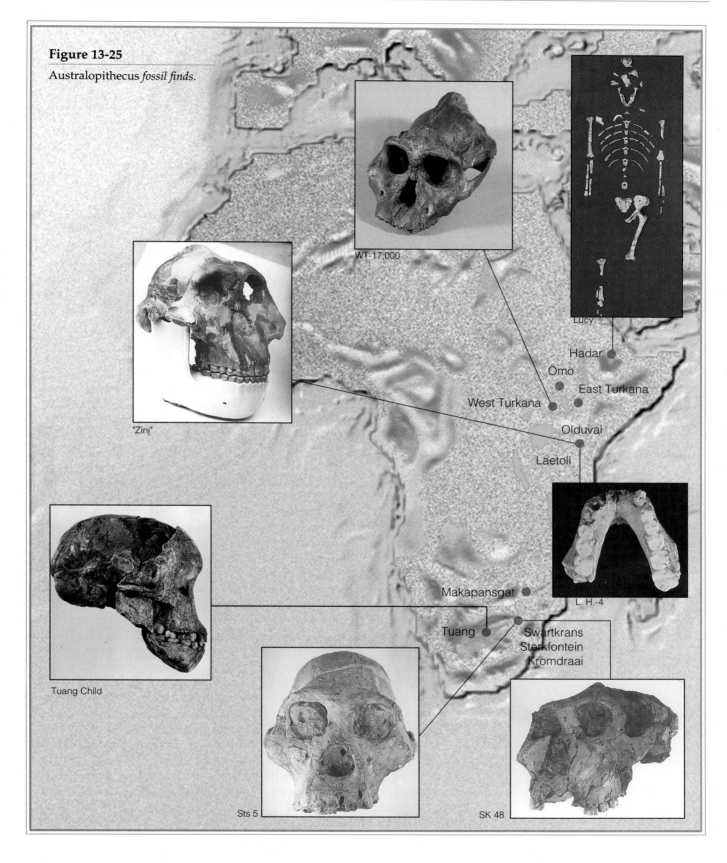

Figure 13-25

Australopithecus *fossil finds.*

WT-17,000

Lucy

Hadar

Omo

East Turkana

West Turkana

Olduvai

Laetoli

"Zinj"

L. H.-4

Makapansgat

Tuang

Swartkrans
Sterkfontein
Kromdraai

Tuang Child

Sts 5

SK 48

Table 13-2   Estimated Body Weights for *Australopithecus* Species

	Average Weight[1]		Average Weight[2]		Range[2]	
	LB	KG	LB	KG	LB	KG
A. afarensis	111.6	50.6	112.4	51.0	67.0–149.2	30.4–67.7
A. africanus	100.3	45.5	101.4	46.0	72.8–127.0	33.0–57.6
A. robustus	105.2	47.7	108.0	49.0	81.8–126.8	37.1–57.5
A. boisei	101.6	46.1	108.5	49.2	72.8–152.8	33.0–69.3

[1]After McHenry, 1988.
[2]After Jungers, 1988.

Oldowan tools also discovered at Swartkrans. However, in addition to robust australopithecines at Swartkrans, another hominid (*Homo*) is also represented (albeit in small numbers). So precisely *who* was responsible for the stone tools we find at Swartkrans (or in East Africa at Olduvai, East Turkana, etc.) is still largely a matter of conjecture (Klein, 1989).

"GRACILE" AUSTRALOPITHECINES

Another variety of australopithecine (also small-brained, but not as large-toothed as the robust varieties) is known from Africa. However, while the robust lineage is represented in both East and South Africa, the other australopithecine (gracile) form is known only from the southern part of the continent. First named *A. africanus* by Dart for the single individual at Taung, this australopithecine is also found at Makapansgat and, especially, at Sterkfontein.

Traditionally, it has been thought that there was a significant variation in body size between "gracile" and "robust" forms. As we mentioned earlier and as shown in Table 13-2, there is not much difference in body size between "robust" and "gracile" australopithecines. In fact, most of the differences between the two forms are found in the face and dentition.

The face structure of the gracile australopithecines is more lightly built and somewhat dish-shaped compared to the more vertical configuration seen in robust specimens. As we noted above, in robust individuals, a raised ridge along the midline of the skull is occasionally observed. Indeed, at Sterkfontein among the larger individuals (males?) a hint of such a sagittal crest is also seen. This structure provides additional attachment area for the large temporal muscle, which is the primary muscle operating the massive jaw below. Such a structure is also seen in some modern apes, especially male gorillas and orangs; however, in most australopithecines, the temporal muscle acts most efficiently on the back of the mouth and is therefore not functionally equivalent to the front tooth emphasis seen in great apes (see Fig. 13-26).

The most distinctive difference observed between gracile and robust australopithecines is in the dentition. Compared to modern humans, they both have relatively large teeth, which are, however, definitely hominid in pattern. In fact, more emphasis is on the typical back-tooth grinding complex among these early forms than the forms of today; therefore, if anything, australopithecines are "hyperhominid." Robust forms emphasize this trend to an extreme degree, showing deep jaws and much-enlarged back teeth, particularly the molars, severely crowding the front teeth (incisors and canines) together. Conversely, the gracile australopithecines have proportionately larger front teeth compared to the size of their back teeth. This contrast is seen most clearly in the relative sizes of the canine compared to the first premolar: in robust individuals, the first premolar is clearly a much larger tooth than the small canine (about twice as large) whereas, in gracile specimens, it only averages about 20% larger than the fairly good-sized canine (Howells, 1973).

These differences in the relative proportions of the teeth and jaws best define a gracile, as compared to a robust, form. In fact, most of the differences in skull shape we have discussed can be directly attributed to contrasting jaw function in the two forms. Both the sagittal crest and broad vertical face of the robust form are related to the muscles and biomechanical requirements of the extremely large-tooth-chewing adaptation of this animal.

EARLY *HOMO* IN SOUTH AFRICA

As in East Africa, early members of the genus *Homo* have also been found in South Africa, apparently living contemporaneously with australopithecines. At both Sterkfontein (Member 5) and Swartkrans, fragmentary remains have been recognized as most likely belonging to *Homo*. In fact, Ron Clarke (1985) has shown that the key fossil of early *Homo* from Sterkfontein (Stw-53) is nearly identical to the OH-24 *Homo habilis* cranium from Olduvai.

However, a problem with both OH-24 and Stw-53 is that, while most experts agree that they belong to the genus *Homo*, there is considerable disagreement as to whether they should be included in the species *habilis*. The relationships of the Plio-Pleistocene fossil hominids to one another and the difficulties of such genus and species interpretation will be the major topic of Chapter 14.

(a) Hominid (robust australopithecine)

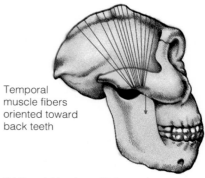

Temporal muscle fibers oriented toward back teeth

(b) Pongid (male gorilla)

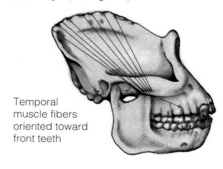

Temporal muscle fibers oriented toward front teeth

Figure 13-26

Sagittal crests and temporal muscle orientations. Hominid compared to pongid.

Summary

In East and South Africa during the better part of this century, a vast collection of early hominids has been gathered, a collection totaling more than 500 individuals (and thousands of fossil specimens). While considerable evolution occurs during the Plio-Pleistocene (approximately 3 million years are covered in this chapter), all forms are clearly hominid, as shown by their bipedal adaptation. The time range for this hominid material extends back to nearly 4 million years in East Africa, with the earliest and most primitive hominid now recognized—*Australopithecus afarensis*.

Later hominids of a robust lineage are known in East Africa (*A. aethiopicus*; *A. boisei*) and South Africa (*A. robustus*). These groups seem to come on the scene about 2.5 m.y.a. and disappear around 1 m.y.a.

In addition, a smaller-toothed (but not necessarily smaller-bodied) "gracile" form is known exclusively from South Africa, beginning at a time range estimated at around 2.5 m.y.a. However, owing to the geologic complexity, dating control in South Africa is *much* more tenuous than in East Africa. Thus we cannot be certain of any of these dates for South African hominids.

Finally, best known again in East Africa (but also found in South Africa), a larger-brained and smaller-toothed variety is also present perhaps as early as 2.4 m.y.a. This species, called *Homo habilis*, is thought by most paleoanthropologists to lie closer to our ancestry than the later varieties of australopithecines.

Questions for Review

1. In East Africa all the early hominid sites are found along the Rift Valley. Why is this significant?
2. Compare the various East African Plio-Pleistocene sites for the kinds of cultural information uncovered.
3. How do the dating problems of the lower beds at Hadar illustrate the necessity for cross-correlation of several dating techniques?
4. Why was Raymond Dart's announcement of a small-brained bipedal hominoid greeted with such skepticism in 1925?
5. What led Dart to suggest the Taung child was *not* an ape?
6. What was Robert Broom's contribution to revealing the hominid nature of the South African australopithecines?
7. (a) Why is postcranial evidence (particularly the lower limb) so crucial in showing the australopithecines as definite hominids? (b) What particular aspects of the australopithecine pelvis and lower limb are hominidlike?
8. What hominid sites have yielded remains of *A. afarensis*? In what ways is the fossil material more primitive than that for other hominids from South and East Africa?
9. What kinds of robust australopithecines have been found in East Africa? How do they compare with South African australopithecines?
10. Why are some Plio-Pleistocene hominids from East Africa called "early *Homo*" (or *H. habilis*)? What does this imply for the evolutionary relationships of the australopithecines?
11. What did Louis Leakey mean by using the specific name *habilis* for a fossil hominid from Olduvai?

Chapter 14

Contents

Plio-Pleistocene Hominids: Organization and Interpretation

Anthropologists have long been concerned with the behavioral evolution of our species. Accompanying changes in anatomy (locomotion, dentition, brain size and shape) were changes in mating patterns, social structure, cultural innovations, and, eventually, language. In fact, changes in these behavioral complexes are what mostly *explain* the concomitant adaptations in human biological structure.

We are, then, vitally interested in the behavioral adaptations of our early hominid ancestors. In seeking to reconstruct the behavioral patterns of these early hominids, anthropologists use inferences drawn from modern primates, social carnivores, and hunting-gathering people (see Chapter 10). In addition, they derive information directly from the paleoanthropological record (see Chapter 12).

Despite numerous detailed and serious attempts at such behavioral reconstructions, the conclusions must largely remain speculative. In point of fact, behavior does not fossilize. Accordingly, researchers must rely considerably upon their imaginations in creating scenarios of early hominid behavioral evolution. In such an atmosphere, biases often emerge; these biased renditions, in turn, stimulate heated debates and alternative scenarios—often as narrow as those being attacked.

Among the most controversial topics in anthropology, and one that has displayed some of the most glaring biases, is the debate concerning origins of hominid gender-role differences. Did early hominid males have characteristically different behavioral adaptations than their female counterparts? Did one sex dominate the frontier of early hominid cultural innovation? And if one sex did lead the way, which one?

A now well-known rendition of early hominid behavioral development was popularized in the 1960s and 1970s. According to this "man, the hunter" theory, the hunting of large animals by males was the central stimulus of hominid behavioral evolution. According to such widely read works as Desmond Morris' *The Naked Ape* (1967) and several books by Robert Ardrey (including *The Hunting Hypothesis*, 1976), early apish-looking forms *became* hominids as a result of a hunting way of life. As Ardrey states, "Man is man, and not a chimpanzee, because for millions upon millions of evolving years we killed for a living" (1976, p. 10).

In this reconstruction, the hunting of large, dangerous mammals by co-operating groups of males fostered the development of intelligence, language, tools, and bipedalism. Increased intelligence accompanied by the development of weapons is also blamed in this scenario for the roots of human aggressiveness, murder, and warfare.

This "man, the hunter" scenario further suggests that while the males are leading the vanguard in

hominid evolution, females remain mostly sedentary, tied to the home base by the burden of dependent young. Females may have contributed some wild plant foods to the group's subsistence, but this is not seen as a particularly challenging (and certainly not a very noble) endeavor. In this situation of marked division of labor, sexual relationships quickly changed. Males, constantly away from the home base (and thus away from the females too), could not keep a watchful eye over their mates. In order to better ensure fidelity, monogamy came into being. In this way, a male would be assured that the young in which he invested were his own. This important factor of male-female bonding as a product of differential foraging patterns has more recently been restated by Owen Lovejoy (1981).

From the female's point of view, it would be beneficial to maintain a close bond with a provisioning male. Consequently, she would want to appear "attractive," and thus, through time, the female breasts and buttocks would become more conspicuous. Besides rearing their young and being attractive sex objects, females were useful to males in another way. Groups of male hunters living in the same area might occasionally come into potentially dangerous competition for the same resources. As a means of solidifying political ties between groups, the males would thus routinely exchange females (by giving or "selling" their daughters to neighboring bands).

Thus, in a single stroke, this complex of features accounts for human intelligence, sexual practices, and political organization.

As might be expected, such a male-centered scenario did not go unchallenged. Ignoring females or relegating them to a definitely inferior role in human behavioral evolution drew sharp criticism from several quarters. As Sally Slocum notes:

So, while the males were out hunting, developing all their skills, learning to cooperate, inventing language, inventing art, creating tools and weapons, the poor dependent females were sitting back at the home base having one child after another and waiting for the males to bring home the bacon. While this reconstruction is certainly ingenious, it gives one the decided impression that only half the species—the male half—did any evolving. In addition to containing a number of logical gaps, the argument becomes somewhat doubtful in the light of modern knowledge of genetics and primate behavior (Slocum, 1975, p. 42).

In fact, such a rigid rendering of our ancestors' behavior does not stand up to critical examination. Hunting is never defined rigorously. Does it include only large, terrestrial mammals? What of smaller mammals, sea mammals, fish, and birds? In numerous documented human societies, females actively participate in exploiting these latter resources.

Moreover, nonhuman primates do not conform to predictions derived from the "man, the hunter" model. For example, among chimpanzees, females do most of the toolmaking, not the males. Finally, in most nonhuman primates (most mammals, for that matter), it is the females—not the males—who choose with whom to mate.

Granting that the hunting hypothesis does not work, what alternatives have been proposed? As a reaction to male-centered views, Elaine Morgan (1972) advanced the "aquatic hypothesis." In this rendition, females are seen as the pioneers of hominid evolution. But rather than having the dramatic changes of hominid evolution occur on the savanna, Morgan has them take place on the seashore. As females lead the way to bipedal locomotion, cultural innovation, and intellectual development, the poor males are seen as splashing pitifully behind.

Unfortunately, this scenario has less to back it up than the hunting hypothesis. Not a shred (even a watery one) of evidence has ever been discovered in the contexts predicted by the aquatic theory. Little is accomplished by such unsubstantiated overzealous speculation. Chauvinism—whether male or female—does not elucidate our origins and only obscures the evolutionary processes that operated on the *whole* species.

Another interesting aspect of these different behavioral "theories" has been pointed out by cultural anthropologist Misia Landau. She notes that these theories are like mythic stories with a hero emerging (from the forest) and ultimately conquering the challenges of existence (by boldly going bipedally onto the savanna). It could also be noted that in most of these myths, traditionally the hero is a male who acts to defend, provide for, and inseminate the females (who, otherwise, are not given much consideration). While the pattern is not as rigid as the hunting hypothesis advocates would have us believe, in the vast majority of human societies, hunting of large, terrestrial mammals is almost always a male activity. In fact, a comprehensive cross-cultural survey shows that of 179 societies, males do the hunting exclusively in 166, both sexes participate in 13, and in *no* group is hunting done exclusively by females (Murdock, 1965).

In addition, as we noted in Chapter 10, there is some incipient division of labor in foraging patterns among chimpanzees. Females tend to concentrate more on termiting, while hunting is done mostly by males. Early hominids, expanding upon such a subsistence base, eventually adapted a greater sexual division of labor than found in any other primate. Two points, however, must be kept in mind. First, both the gathering of wild plant foods and the hunting of animals would have been indispensable components of the diet. Consequently, *both* males and females always played a significant role. Secondly, the strategies must always have been somewhat flexible. With a shifting, usually unpredictable resource base, nothing else would have worked. As a result, males probably always did a considerable amount of gathering and in most foraging societies still do. Moreover, females—while not usually engaged in the stalking and killing of large prey—nonetheless contribute significantly to meat acquisition. Once large animals have been killed, there still remain the arduous tasks of butchering and transport back to the home base. In many societies, women and men participate equally in these activities.

A balanced view of human behavioral evolution must avoid simplistic and overly rigid scenarios.

As stated by Adrienne Zihlman, a researcher concerned with reconstructing early hominid behavior:

Both sexes must have been able to care for young, protect themselves from predators, make and use tools, and freely move about the environment in order to exploit available resources widely distributed through space and time. It is this range of behaviors—the overall behavioral flexibility of both sexes—that may have been the primary ingredient of early hominids' success in the savanna environment (Zihlman, 1981, p. 97).

Following the notion developed by Landau that much of the literature on the evolution of human behavior resembles story telling, anthropologist Linda Fedigan concluded her own comprehensive review of the topic (1986):

People will not stop wanting to hear origin stories and scientists will not cease to write scholarly tales. But we can become aware of the symbolic content of our stories, for much as our theories are not independent of our beliefs, so our behavior is not independent of our theories of human society. In these origin tales, we try to coax the material evidence into telling us about the past, but the narrative we weave about the past also tells us about the present.

SOURCES

Ardrey, Robert. *The Hunting Hypothesis.* New York: Atheneum, 1976.

Dahlberg, Frances (ed.). *Woman the Gatherer.* New Haven, CT: Yale University Press, 1981.

Fedigan, Linda. "The Changing Role of Woman in Models of Human Evolution," *Annual Review of Anthropology,* 15(1986): 25–66.

Landau, Misia. "Human Evolution as Narrative," *American Scientist,* 72(1986): 262–268.

Lovejoy, C. Owen. "The Origin of Man," *Science,* 211(1981):341–350.

Morgan, Elaine. *The Descent of Woman.* New York: Stein and Day, 1972.

Morris, Desmond. *The Naked Ape.* New York: McGraw-Hill, 1967.

Murdock, G. P. *Culture and Society.* Pittsburgh: University of Pittsburgh Press, 1965.

Slocum, Sally. "Woman the Gatherer: Male Bias in Anthropology," in *Toward an Anthropology of Women,* R. R. Reiter, ed. New York: Monthly Review Press, pp. 36–50, 1975.

Zihlman, Adrienne L. "Women as Shapers of the Human Adaptation," in *Woman the Gatherer,* op. cit., pp. 75–120, 1981.

Introduction

We have seen in the last chapter that a vast and complex array of early hominid material has been discovered in South and East Africa. In just the past few years, particularly in the eastern part of the continent, a great number of new discoveries have been made. We now have Plio-Pleistocene hominid collections totaling close to 200 individuals from South Africa and probably more than 300 from East Africa. Given the size and often fragmentary nature of the sample, along with the fact that a good deal of it is so recently discovered, we should not be surprised that many complications arise when it comes to interpretation. In addition, both popular enthusiasm and the strong personalities often connected with fossil hominid discoveries have generated even more confusion.

In this chapter, we will look at several hypothetical reconstructions that attempt to organize the huge amount of Plio-Pleistocene hominid material. We ask you to remember that these are hypotheses and must remain so, given the incomplete nature of the fossil record. Even considering the seemingly very large number of fossils there is a *great* deal of time over which they were distributed. If we estimate about 500 total individuals from all African sites recovered thus far for the period 4–1 m.y.a., we still are sampling just one individual for every 6,000 years! Until much of the new material from East Africa has been properly analyzed and detailed reports published, we cannot form even reasonably secure hypotheses without extreme difficulty. At the present time, only a few East African hominids have been thoroughly studied; all the rest are thus far described in preliminary reports.

It will no doubt appear that many opposing and conflicting hypotheses attempt to describe exactly what is going on in human evolution during the crucial period between 4 and 1 m.y.a. And, indeed, there are many hypotheses. Hominid fossils are intriguing to both scientists and nonscientists, for some of these ancient bones and teeth are probably those of our direct ancestors. Equally intriguing, some of these fossils are representatives of populations of our close relatives that apparently met with extinction. We would like to know how these animals lived, what kinds of adaptations (physical and cultural) they displayed, and why some continued to evolve while others died out.

Geology and Dating Problems in South Africa

While, as we saw in the last two chapters, the geological and archeological context in East Africa is oftentimes straightforward, the five South African early hominid sites are much more complex geologically. All were discovered by commercial quarrying activity, which greatly disrupted the geological picture and, in the case of Taung, completely destroyed the site.

The hominid remains are found with thousands of other fossilized bones embedded in limestone cliffs, caves, fissures, and sinkholes. The limestone was built by millions of generations of shells of marine organisms during the Pre-Cambrian—more than 2 billion years ago—when South Africa was submerged under a shallow sea. Once deposited, the limestones were cut through by percolating groundwater from below and rain water from above, forming a maze of caves and fissures often connected to the surface by narrow shafts. Through these vertical shafts and horizontal cave openings,

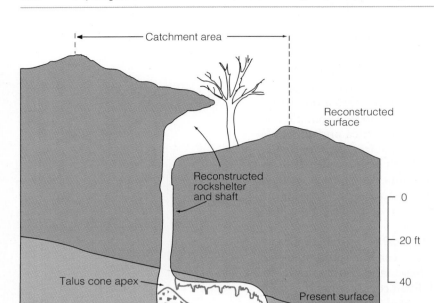

Figure 14-1

Swartkrans, geological section. The upper (reconstructed) part has been removed by erosion since the accumulation of the fossil-bearing deposit. (After Brain, 1970.)

Osteodontokeratic osteo: bone
dento: tooth
keratic: horn

bones either féll or were carried in, where they conglomerated with sand, pebbles, and soil into a cementlike matrix called *breccia*.

As the cave fissures filled in, they were constantly subjected to further erosion forces from above and below, so that caves would be partially filled, then closed to the surface for a considerable time, and reopened again to commence accumulation thousands of years later. All this activity yields an incredibly complex geological situation that can only be worked out after the most detailed kind of paleoecological analysis.

Since bones accumulated in these caves and fissures largely by accidental processes, it seems likely that none of the South African australopithecine sites are *primary* hominid localities. In other words, unlike East Africa, these are not areas where hominids organized activities, scavenged food, etc.

Just how did all the fossilized bone accumulate and, most particularly, what were the ancient hominids doing there? In the case of Swartkrans, Sterkfontein, and Kromdraai, the bones probably accumulated through the combined activities of carnivorous leopards, saber-toothed cats, and hyenas. However, the unexpectedly high proportion of primate (baboon and hominid) remains suggests that these localities were the location (or very near the location) of primate sleeping sites, thus providing ready prey for the predators (Brain, 1981).

Raymond Dart argued enthusiastically for an alternative explanation, suggesting the hominids camping at Makapansgat regularly used bone, tooth, and horn remains as tools, which he has grandly called the **osteodontokeratic** culture complex. Analogies with modern Hottentot food habits indicate the bone accumulation at Makapansgat may be accounted for simply by hominid and carnivore eating practices. Recent paleoecological work at Makapansgat has thrown Dart's assertions into even greater doubt. Apparently, remains accumulated here primarily in a similar fashion to Sterkfontein and Swartkrans—through a narrow shaft entrance. Therefore, large animals could have entered but not departed the deep subterranean cavern. Makapansgat, like Sterkfontein and Swartkrans, probably also represents the accumulated debris of carnivore activity (perhaps hyenas) outside the cave entrance.

So little is left of the final site, Taung, that accurate paleoanthropological reconstructions are not feasible.

Due to the complex geological picture, as well as lack of appropriate material such as volcanics for chronometric techniques, dating the South African early hominid sites has posed tremendous problems. Without chronometric dating, the best that can be done is to correlate the faunal sequences in South Africa with areas such as East Africa where dates are better known (this approach is called "biostratigraphy"—see p. 343). Faunal sequencing of this sort on pigs, bovids such as antelopes, and Old World monkeys has provided the following tenuous chronology:

LOCATION	AGE
	1 m.y.
Swartkrans	
Kromdraai	
	2 m.y.
Sterkfontein/Taung	
Makapansgat	3 m.y.

Attempts at paleomagnetic dating (see p. 341) suggest an age of 3.3–2.8 m.y.a. for Makapansgat (Brock et al., 1977), thus pushing the estimates to the extreme limits of those provided by biostratigraphy. In fact, some researchers believe the paleomagnetic results are ambiguous and continue to "put their money" on the biostratigraphic data, especially those dates determined by analysis of pig and monkey fossils. From such considerations, they place the South African early hominid sites as much as one-half million years later (that is, for Makapansgat, around 2.5 m.y.a.) (White et al., 1981). This is crucial, since it places *all* the South African hominids after *Australopithecus afarensis* in East Africa.

Interpretations: What Does It All Mean?

By this time, it may seem anthropologists have an almost perverse fascination in finding small scraps buried in the ground and then assigning them confusing numbers and taxonomic labels impossible to remember. We must realize that the collection of all the basic fossil data is the foundation of human evolutionary research. Without fossils, our speculations would be completely hollow. Several large, ongoing paleoanthropological projects discussed in Chapter 12 are now collecting additional data in an attempt to answer some of the more perplexing questions about our evolutionary history.

The numbering of specimens, which may at times seem somewhat confusing, is an attempt to keep the designations neutral and to make reference to each individual fossil as clear as possible. The formal naming of finds as *Australopithecus, Homo habilis, Homo erectus,* etc., should come much later, since it involves a lengthy series of complex interpretations. The assigning of generic and specific names to fossil finds is more than just a game, although some paleoanthropologists have acted as if it were just that. When we attach a particular label, such as *A. boisei,* to a particular fossil, we should be fully aware of the biological implications of such an interpretation (see p. 314).

Box 14-1
A Visit to the Plio-Pleistocene: East Lake Turkana, Late One Afternoon

If an observer could be transported back through time and climb a tree in the area where the Koobi Fora Formation was accumulating, what would he see?

As the upper branches are reached, the climber would find himself in a ribbon of woodland winding out through open areas. A kilometer or so away to the west would be seen the swampy shores of the lake, teeming with birds, basking crocodiles, and *Euthecodons*. Here and there are schools of hippos. Looking east, in the distance some ten or twelve kilometers away lie low, rolling hills covered with savanna vegetation. From the hills, fingers of trees and bush extend fanwise out into the deltaic plains. These would include groves of large *Acacia*, *Celtis*, and *Ficus* trees along the watercourses, fringed by shrubs and bushes. Troops of colobus move in the tree tops, while lower down are some mangabey. Scattered through the bush, the observer might see small groups of waterbuck, impala, and kudu, while out in the open areas beyond, would be herds of alcelaphine antelope and some gazelle (*Megalotragus* and *Antidorcas*). Among the undergrowth little groups of *Mesochoerus* pigs rootle, munching herbage.

Peering down through the branches of the tree, the climber would see below the clean sandy bed of a watercourse, dry here, but with a tidemark of grass and twigs caught in the fringing bushes and showing the passage of seasonal floods. Some distance away down the channel is a small residual pool.

Out beyond the bushes can be seen large open floodplains, covered with grasses and rushes, partly dry at those seasons of the year when the lake is low and when the river is not in spate. Far across the plains, a group of four or five men approach; although they are too far off for the perception of detail, the observer feels confident that they are men because they are striding along, fully upright, and in their hands they carry staves.

To continue the reconstruction in a more purely imaginative vein: as the men approach, the observer becomes aware of other primates below him. A group of creatures has been reclining on the sand in the shade of a tree while some youngsters play around them. As the men approach, these creatures rise and it becomes apparent that they too are bipedal. They seem to be female, and they whoop excitedly as some of the young run out to meet the arriving party, which can now be seen to consist mainly of males. The two groups come together in the shade of the tree, and there is excited calling, gesturing, and greeting con-

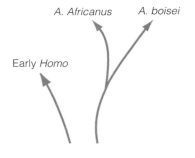

Figure 14-2

Phylogenetic interpretation. Early Homo *generically distinct from australopithecines.*

Even more basic to our understanding of human evolution, the use of taxonomic nomenclature involves interpretations of fossil relationships. For example, two fossils such as "Zinj" and ER 406 are both usually called *A. boisei*. What we are saying here is they are both members of one *interbreeding* species. These two fossils can now be compared with others, like Sts. 5 from Sterkfontein, which are usually called *A. africanus*. What we are implying now is that "Zinj" and ER 406 are more closely related to each other than *either* is to Sts. 5. Furthermore, that Sts. 5 (*A. africanus*) populations were incapable of successfully interbreeding with *A. boisei* populations is a direct biological inference of this nomenclature.

We can carry the level of interpretation even further. For example, fossils such as ER-1470 are called early *Homo* (*Homo habilis*). We are now making a genus-level distinction, and two basic biological implications are involved:

1. *A. africanus* (Sts. 5) and *A. boisei* ("Zinj" and ER 406) are more closely related to each other than either is to ER-1470.
2. The distinction between the groups reflects a basic difference in adaptive level (see Chapter 11).

tacts. Now the observer can see them better, perhaps he begins to wonder about calling them men; they are upright and formed like men, but they are rather small, and when in groups they do not seem to engage in articulate speech. There are a wealth of vocal and gestural signals in their interaction, but no sustained sequential sound patterns.

The object being carried is the carcass of an impala, and the group congregates around this in high excitement; there is some pushing and shoving and flashes of temper and threat. Then one of the largest males takes two objects from a heap at the foot of the tree. There are sharp clacking sounds as he squats down and bangs these together repeatedly. The other creatures scramble around picking up the small sharp chips that have been detached from the stones. When there is a small scatter of flakes on the ground at his feet, the stone worker drops the two chunks, sorts through the fragments and selects two or three pieces. Turning back to the carcass, this leading male starts to make incisions. First the belly is slit open and the entrails pulled out; the guts are set on one side, but there is excited squabbling over the liver, lungs, and kidneys; these are torn apart, some individuals grab pieces and run to the periphery of the group. Then the

creatures return to the carcass; one male severs skin, muscle, and sinew so as to disengage them from the trunk, while some others pull at limbs. Each adult male finishes up with a segment of the carcass and withdraws to a corner of the clearing, with one or two females and juveniles congregating around him. They sit chewing and cutting at the meat, with morsels changing hands at intervals. Two adolescent males sit at the periphery with a part of the intestines. They squeeze out the dung and chew at the entrails. One of the males gets up, stretches his arms, scratches under his armpits and then sits down. He leans against the tree, gives a loud belch and pats his belly. . . . *End of scenario.*

SOURCE:

"The Activities of Early Hominids" by Glynn Ll. Isaac. In *Human Origins. Louis Leakey and the East African Evidence*, G. Isaac and E. R. McCown, eds. The Benjamin/Cummings Publishing Company, Inc. © 1976.

From the time that fossil sites are first located to the eventual interpretation of hominid evolutionary events, several steps are necessary. Ideally, they should follow a logical order, for if interpretations are made too hastily, they confuse important issues for many years. A reasonable sequence is:

1. Selection and surveying of sites
2. Excavation of sites; recovery of fossil hominids
3. Designating individual finds with specimen numbers for clear reference
4. Cleaning, preparation, and detailed study and description of fossils
5. Comparison with other fossil material—in chronological framework if possible
6. Comparison of fossil variation with known ranges of variation in closely related groups of living primates
7. Assigning taxonomic names to fossil material

The task of interpretation is still not complete, for what we really want to know in the long run is what happened to the populations represented by the fossil remains. Indeed, in looking at the fossil hominid record, we are looking for our ancestors. In the process of eventually determining those populations that are our most likely antecedents, we may conclude some hominids are on evolutionary side branches. If this conclusion is accurate, they necessarily must have eventually become extinct. It is both interesting and relevant to us as hominids to try to find out what caused some earlier members of our family to continue evolving while others died out.

Continuing Uncertainties—Taxonomic Issues

As previously discussed, paleoanthropologists are crucially concerned with making biological interpretations of variation found in the hominid fossil record. Most especially, researchers endeavor to assign extinct forms to particular genera and species. We saw that, for the diverse array of Miocene hominoids, the evolutionary picture is exceptionally complex. As new finds accumulate, there persists continued uncertainty even as to family assignment, to say nothing of genus and species!

For the Plio-Pleistocene, the situation is considerably clearer. First of all, there is a larger fossil sample from a more restricted geographic area (South and East Africa) and from a more concentrated time period (spanning 3 million years, from 4–1 m.y.a.). Secondly, more complete specimens exist (for example, "Lucy"), and we thus have good evidence for most parts of the body. Accordingly, there is considerable consensus on several basic aspects of evolutionary development during the Plio-Pleistocene. First of all, researchers agree unanimously that these forms are hominids (members of the family Hominidae). Secondly, and as support for the first point, all these forms are seen as well-adapted bipeds, committed at least in part to a terrestrial niche. Moreover, researchers agree as to genus-level assignments for most of the forms (although some disagreement exists regarding how to group the robust australopithecines).

As for species-level designations, little consensus can be found. Indeed, as new fossils have been discovered (for example, WT 17,000 and OH 62), the picture seems to muddy further. Once again, we are faced with a complex evolutionary process. In attempts to deal with it, we impose varying degrees of simplicity. In so doing, we hope to understand evolutionary developments more clearly—not just for introductory students, but also for professional paleoanthropologists and textbook authors! Nevertheless, evolution is not necessarily a simple process, and thus disputes and disagreements are bound to arise, especially in making such fine-tuned interpretations as species-level designations.

We discuss below some ongoing topics of interest and occasional disagreement among paleoanthropologists dealing with Plio-Pleistocene hominids. You should realize, however, that such continued debate is at the heart of scientific endeavor; indeed, it provides a major stimulus for further research.

Here, we raise questions regarding four areas of taxonomic interpretation. In general, there is still reasonably strong agreement on these points, and we follow the current consensus as reflected in recent publications (Fleagle, 1988; Grine, 1988a; Klein, 1989).

(1) How many species are there at Hadar and Laetoli (i.e., is *Australopithecus afarensis* one species)?
Some paleoanthropologists argue that what has been described as a single species (especially regarding the large Hadar sample) actually represents at

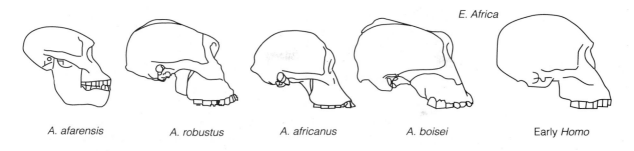

E. Africa

A. afarensis   A. robustus   A. africanus   A. boisei   Early Homo

Figure 14-3

Plio-Pleistocene hominids.

least two separate species (taxa). However, it is clear that all australopithecines were highly variable, and thus the pattern seen at Hadar might well represent a single, highly dimorphic species. Most scholars accept this interpretation, and it is best, for the moment, to follow this more conservative view. As a matter of good paleontological practice, it is desirable not to overly "split" fossil samples until compelling evidence is presented.

(2) How many genera of australopithecines are there?
Several years ago a plethora of generic terms was suggested by Robert Broom and others. However, in the 1960s and 1970s, most researchers agreed to "lump" all these forms into *Australopithecus*. With the discovery of early members of genus *Homo* in the 1960s (and its general recognition in the 1970s), most researchers also recognized the presence of our genus in the Plio-Pleistocene as well.

In the last five years an increasing tendency has arisen to resplit some of the australopithecines. With the recognition that the robust group (*aethiopicus*, *boisei*, and *robustus*) forms a distinct evolutionary lineage (a clade), many researchers (Howell, 1988; Grine, 1988a) have argued that the generic term, "Paranthropus" should be used to set these robust forms apart from *Australopithecus* (now used in the strict sense). We thus would have *Paranthropus aethiopicus*, *Paranthropus boisei*, and *Paranthropus robustus* as contrasted to *Australopithecus afarensis* and *Australopithecus africanus*.

We agree that there are adequate grounds to make a genus-level distinction, given the evolutionary distinctiveness of the robust clade as well as its apparent adaptive uniqueness (as recently further confirmed by microwear studies of teeth). However, for *closely related taxa*, such as we are dealing with here, making this type of interpretation is largely arbitrary. (See discussion, pp. 314–318.) As the single genus *Australopithecus* has been used for three decades in the wider sense (to include all robust forms), and as it simplifies terminology, we follow the current consensus and continue the traditional usage—*Australopithecus* for all small-brained, large-toothed Plio-Pleistocene hominids (including all five recognized species: *A. afarensis*, *A. aethiopicus*, *A. africanus*, *A. robustus*, and *A. boisei*).

(3) For the South African robust australopithecines, how many species existed?
As we have discussed in the last chapter, there are robust australopithecines from two sites in South Africa, Kromdraai and Swartkrans. Owing to subtle differences in morphology, some researchers (Howell, 1988; Grine, 1988b) make a species distinction between Kromdraai [*A. (Paranthropus) robustus*]

Figure 14-4

Morphology and variation of robust australopithecines (note both the typical features and range of variation as shown in different specimens).

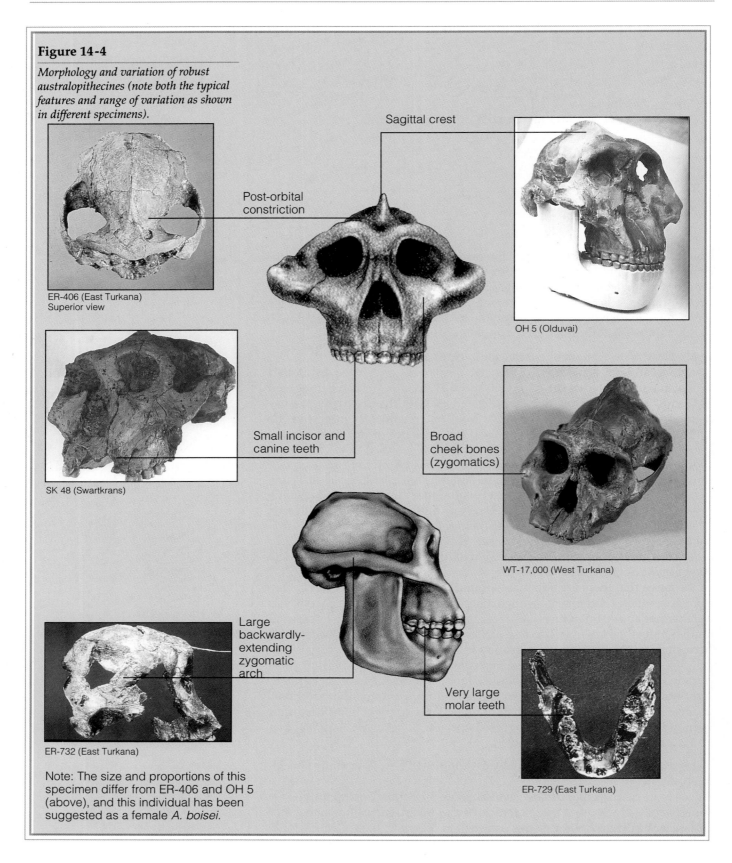

ER-406 (East Turkana)
Superior view

Sagittal crest

Post-orbital constriction

OH 5 (Olduvai)

SK 48 (Swartkrans)

Small incisor and canine teeth

Broad cheek bones (zygomatics)

WT-17,000 (West Turkana)

Large backwardly-extending zygomatic arch

Very large molar teeth

ER-732 (East Turkana)

ER-729 (East Turkana)

Note: The size and proportions of this specimen differ from ER-406 and OH 5 (above), and this individual has been suggested as a female *A. boisei.*

on the one hand and Swartkrans [*A.* (Paranthropus) *crassidens*] on the other. Moreover, even though the dating of these sites is equivocal (see above), it appears Kromdraai is slightly older than Swartkrans. Thus, these researchers also speculate that *robustus* may have evolved into *crassidens*.

It must be admitted, however, that the differences among these forms are small, and making such subtle interpretations is bound to generate disagreements. For the present, most scholars remain comfortable in treating all the South African robust forms as one species.

(4) How many species of early *Homo* existed?

Here is another species-level type of interpretation that is unlikely soon to be resolved. Yet, as it strikes closer to home (that is, our own genus) than the issue above for robust australopithecines, the current debate is generating more heat.

Whether we find resolution or not, the *form* of the conflicting views is instructive. Of course, the key issue·is evaluating variation as *intra-* or *inter*specific. Those who would view all the nonaustralopithecine African hominids (circa 2.5–1.6 m.y.a.) as one species point out that all Plio-Pleistocene hominid species show extreme intraspecific variation. Much of this variation is assumed to reflect dramatic sexual dimorphism. These scholars are thus reasonably comfortable in referring to all this material as *Homo habilis* (Tobias, 1991). Other researchers, however, see too much variation to accept just one species, even a very dimorphic one. Comparisons with living primates show that what is called *H. habilis* differ amongst themselves more than do male and female gorillas (Lieberman et al., 1987) or that the *pattern* of variation does not fit that seen intraspecifically in any extant species (Wood, 1992). Consequently, we have an added complication: Must we now construct *yet another species of early Homo in addition to habilis*? Several researchers believe there is no other alternative, but do not as yet agree on a new name. The recent discovery of the fragmentary partial skeleton at Olduvai Gorge does not help resolve the issue, but actually may cloud it further. This specimen is a very small individual, and thus presumably a female. How much sexual dimorphism did *H. habilis* display? Were males (on average) two to three times as large as females? We do not know the answers to these questions; but their framing in biological terms as intra- versus interspecific variation and the use of contemporary primate models demonstrates the basis for ongoing discussion.

For the moment, it is best not to assign formal names to the possible subsets (that is, "new" species of early *Homo*). There is a growing consensus among paleoanthropologists that more than one species has been subsumed in the grouping called *Homo habilis*. The authors also think the current evidence argues (at least slightly) in favor of a multiple taxa interpretation. However, it is sufficient, certainly in the context of this textbook, to refer to all these fossils as "early *Homo*" (and thus not worry about subtle, complex species-level interpretations).

Another problem with the so-called "early *Homo*" fossil sample is that it overlaps in time with the earliest appearance of *Homo erectus* (discussed in Chapter 15). As a result, several specimens of what has been labeled "early *Homo*" (or *H. habilis*) may actually belong to *H. erectus*. At about 1.6 m.y.a., *H. erectus* apparently replaced earlier members of genus *Homo* quite rapidly. At sites (especially East Turkana and Swartkrans) where fragmentary traces of this process are evident, it poses a major challenge to distinguish exactly what is early *Homo* and what is *H. erectus*.

Putting It All Together

The interpretation of our paleontologic past in terms of which fossils are related to other fossils and how they are all related to us is usually shown diagrammatically in the form of a **phylogeny**. Such a diagram is a family tree of fossil evolution. This kind of interpretation is the eventual goal of evolutionary studies, but it is the final goal, only after adequate data are available to understand what is going on.

Another, more basic, way to handle these data is to divide the fossil material into subsets. This avoids (for the moment) what are still problematic phylogenetic relationships. Accordingly, for the Plio-Pleistocene hominid material from Africa, we can divide the data into three broad groupings:

Set I. Early, primitive, *Australopithecus* (3–4 m.y.a.).
This grouping comprises a single species, *A. afarensis*—the best known from Laetoli and Hadar. This species is characterized by a small brain, large teeth (front and back), and a bipedal gait (probably still allowing for considerable climbing).

Set II. Later, more derived, *Australopithecus* (1–2.5 m.y.a.; possibly as early as 3.0 m.y.a.).
This group is composed of numerous species (most experts recognize at least three; some researchers subdivide this material into five or more species). Remains have come from several sites in both South and East Africa. All of these forms have very large back teeth and do not show appreciable brain enlargement (that is, encephalization) compared to *A. afarensis*.

Set III. Early *Homo* (1.8–2.4 m.y.a.).
The best known are from East Africa (East Turkana and Olduvai), but early remains of *Homo* have also been found in South Africa (Sterkfontein, also possibly at Swartkrans). Composed of possibly just one, but probably more than one, species. Early *Homo* is characterized (compared to *Australopithecus*) by greater encephalization, altered cranial shape, as well as smaller (especially molars) and narrower (especially premolars) teeth.

Whereas hominid fossil evidence has accumulated in great abundance, the fact that so much of the material has been discovered so recently makes any firm judgments concerning the route of human evolution premature. However, paleoanthropologists are certainly not deterred from making their "best guesses," and thus diverse speculative hypotheses have abounded in recent years. The vast majority of more than 300 fossils from East Africa is still in the descriptive and early analytical stages. At this time, the construction of phylogenies of human evolution is analogous to building a house with only a partial blueprint. We are not even sure how many rooms there are! Until the existing fossil evidence has been adequately studied, to say nothing about possible new finds, speculative hypotheses must be viewed with a critical eye.

In the following pages, we will present several phylogenies representing different and opposing views of hominid evolution. We suggest you do not attempt to memorize them, for they *all* could be out of date by the time you read this book. It will prove more profitable to look at each one and assess the biological implications involved. Also, note which groups are on the main line of human evolution leading to *Homo sapiens* and which are placed on extinct side branches.

Phylogeny A schematic representation showing ancestor-descendant relationships usually in a chronological framework.

PHYLOGENY A.
Afarensis Comon Ancestor Theory
(after Johanson and White, 1979)

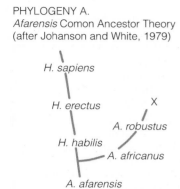

Note: *Afarensis* postulated as common ancestor to all Plio-Pleistocene hominids

PHYLOGENY B
Multiple Lineage Early Divergence
(after Senut and Tardieu, 1985)

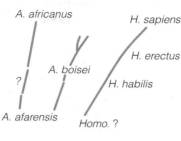

Note: Major split occurs before *A. afarensis*. Possible multiple lineages in Plio-Pleistocene.

PHYLOGENY C
Africanus Comon Ancestor Theory
(after Skelton, et al. 1986)

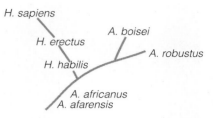

Note: Major split occurs after *A. africanus*. Therefore, *A. africanus* is seen as still in our lineage as well as that of more derived australopithecines.

PHYLOGENY D
Early Robust Lineage
(after Delson, 1986; 1987)

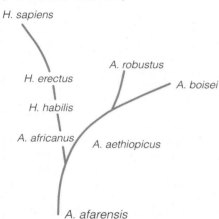

PHYLOGENY E
Distinct *africanus/robustus* Lineage
(after Vrba, 1988)

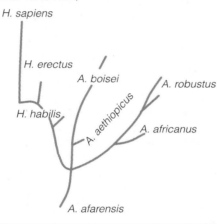

PHYLOGENY F
Africanus Ancestor of *robustus* and *Homo*; East African Robust Distinct (after Kimbel, et al., 1988)

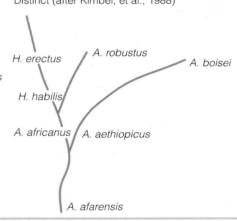

PHYLOGENY G
Africanus on unique lineage
(after Kimbel, et al.,1988)

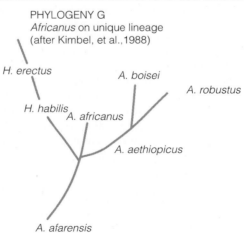

Figure 14-5

Phylogenies of hominid evolution.

Judy Myers Suchey is a professor of Anthropology at California State University, Fullerton. She is Diplomate of the American Board of Forensic Anthropology and serves as a consultant to the Coroner of Los Angeles County, Orange County, San Bernardino County, and Riverside County.

As a teenager I lived in Brookings, South Dakota, where the topic of fossils and human evolution was not part of the school curriculum. During my first semester at the University of Kansas (1961), I enrolled in an introductory physical anthropology course, a large lecture class taught by Dr. William M. Bass. Like many others in that class, I became fasci-

nated with the world of bones and fossils and I devoted much time to learning the many terms in the textbook. The following semester, Dr. Bass encouraged me to pursue a project in my Honors Biology class, in the area of physical anthropology. He and I worked together on the examination of a prehistoric skull from South Dakota, the end result being my first publication at the young age of 19. This modest article, published in a local museum bulletin, gave me my first taste of cooperative work on a skeletal project. Although entranced with this field, it never occurred to me that I could embark on a career involving a Ph.D. program, so I continued in my pursuit of becoming a nurse, an acceptable goal for a small-town girl of limited vision. While at the Medical Center I discovered that my personality type did not fit nursing. Taking orders on a daily basis grated on my nerves and I was not the most supportive person for many of my patients. Clearly, the career was a mismatch and following the urging of both my Honors Biology professor and Dr. Bass, I returned to college to pursue a career in physical anthropology. I was far more comfortable in a laboratory piecing together fragmented bones than in the hospital wards, and I knew that I had made the right choice. I began to spend my free time pursuing skeletal tasks.

Twice I was hired on summer archaeological excavations and these turned out to be valuable learning experiences. Being fair-skinned and intolerant to heat, I could not endure the physical labor of excavation in either Kansas or South Dakota, so I was hired as the cook! Not only did I learn how to prepare meals for hungry crew members (among whom were Richard Jantz, Douglas

Ubelaker, Ted Rathbun, and P. Willey), I also learned a lot about anthropology, human nature, and teamwork. While at the University of Kansas, Dr. Bass shared his forensic experiences with us. I remember the examination of a large male body burned inside a boxcar and a small skeletonized child encased in lime and found inside a suitcase. I took several advanced courses in physical anthropology, which included one seminar on forensic anthropology. I left the University of Kansas after receiving an M.A. degree so I could determine if a teaching career would be possible for me. To this day, the introductory class in biological anthropology is my favorite course, even though I have taught it well over 100 times.

For personal reasons, I ended up establishing myself in southern California at California State University, Fullerton. It was here that I was assigned my first forensic case in 1969 when human bones were found inside a car submerged in a lake. My services were instantly needed on a variety of cases, some going back to 1937! I found that I was located in a forensic anthropologists' dream location. Murder victims from the populated Los Angeles and Orange County areas were often tossed or buried in shallow graves in the surrounding desert or wilderness terrain. There was a great need for skills in skeletal identification and I offered my services free of charge, provided that I could bring my students with me to the coroner facility.

These same students also provided valuable assistance in skeletal searches in remote areas.

Realizing that the Ph.D. degree was essential to establishing myself in both the academic and forensic worlds, I enrolled at the University of California, Riverside. Here, I studied methods of anthropological inquiry, statistics, and computer programming. Eventually, my consulting practice became somewhat restricted due to legal complications concerning AIDS in the autopsy setting. Consequently, the coroner's office discouraged me from bringing students into the autopsy facilities for research and/or participation in cases.

It is now nearly 25 years since that first case and I can reflect on a variety of experiences in some 2,000 forensic cases on which I have worked during this period. My consulting practice is nonprofit and research oriented. I believe the key to my success in the forensic setting resides in my willingness to work any case, skeletonized or fleshed, to the best of my ability. If I didn't know how to accomplish a certain task, I either learned or referred the case to a colleague. I felt responsible to the agencies I worked for and I disrupted my personal life on practically any occasion to come to the autopsy room or go to the scene to assist.

The press has painted forensics as a glamorous career, with financial profits implied, and that's the general idea of the field held by outsiders. Forensics *is* fascinating and exciting, but not particularly glamorous, and few practicing it earn much money. There are very few full-time positions as a forensic anthropologist. Students considering a forensic career should first test whether they can stomach autopsies. If possible, attend an autopsy on a badly decomposed body and help deflesh the skeletal segments needed for analysis of the case (basic identification and/or cause of death). If this experience can't be arranged, find a road-kill (animal) and prepare the skeleton for the start of a comparative mammalian collection. Either experience will tell you if you can survive the fundamental experiences you are sure to encounter in the forensic arena. With this step conquered, there are many more to take. A solid grounding in skeletal biology is important in the assessment of skeletal cases from a legal standpoint. In this regard, I conducted research in the autopsy facility at the Department of Coroner, Los Angeles. I removed some 1,500 pubic bone pairs and a lesser number of other elements for an age/sex determination project. This research has been ongoing for some 15 years with some 50 to 100 scientists involved in some aspect of it. I learned a lot about skeletal variability as well as forensic techniques in general. While at the autopsy facility, the pathologists shared professional information with me and I began to cooperate with them when the cause of death was being sought on fragmented, mutilated, or skeletonized cases. Cooperation is the key in forensic work. Scientists must know the limits of their knowledge and how to interface with other specialists on the case. Narrowing one's field of specialty and learning it well is important. Respecting the boundaries of one's own knowledge and the boundaries of one's profession is a necessity in the legal world. This philosophy must be adhered to as one analyzes, writes reports, and testifies in court. Teamwork is essential and the other specialists involved may include law enforcement personnel, coroner's investigators, pathologists, dentists, and criminalists.

Becoming a forensic anthropologist consultant to an agency requires accepting responsibility. One's personal life must be disrupted when crises occur. Immediate situations in forensics demand quick response; for example, disaster identification, at-scene recovery, and settling disputes when construction workers uncover bone (human or nonhuman; prehistoric or forensic). I find myself at the mercy of my pager, cellular phone, and vehicle, always equipped with excavation and processing equipment in the trunk. Rarely am I in a physical anthropology laboratory. Usually, I work at the scene (applying anthropological techniques to skeletal recovery in the wilderness or desert) or in the autopsy room. The key to becoming a forensic anthropologist is hard work and integrity coupled with responsibility and service to agencies that need help.

Interpreting the Interpretations

In Fig. 14-5 we present several alternative phylogenies explaining early hominid evolution. All these schemes postdate 1979, with the first inclusion of *A. afarensis* as the most likely common ancestor of all later hominids (Johanson and White, 1979). Since the early 1980s, most paleoanthropologists have accepted this view. One exception is shown in Phylogeny B (after Senut and Tardieu, 1985), but this position—based upon the premise that *afarensis* is actually more than one species—has not been generally supported.

We have not included evolutionary schemes prior to 1979, as they do not account for the crucial discoveries at Hadar and Laetoli of *Australopithecus afarensis*. These now-outdated models frequently postulated *A. africanus* as the common ancestor of later *Australopithecus* (robust varieties) and early *Homo*. In modified form this view is still continued in some respects. (See Phylogeny C.)

Indeed, probably the most intractable problem for interpretation of early hominid evolution involves what to do with *A. africanus*. Carefully look at the different evolutionary reconstructions to see how various researchers deal with this still complicated issue.

Conclusions/Summary

After two chapters detailing hominid evolution in the Plio-Pleistocene, many students probably feel frustrated by what must seem to be endlessly changing and conflicting interpretations. However, after 70 years of discoveries of early hominids in Africa, there are several general points upon which most researchers agree:

1. *A. afarensis* is the earliest definite hominid.
2. *A. afarensis* as defined probably represents only one species.
3. *A. afarensis* is probably ancestral to all later hominids (or is very closely related to the species that is).
4. *A. aethiopicus* is ancestral solely to the "robust" group (clade), linking it with earlier *afarensis* as well as with one (or both) later robust species.
5. *A. africanus* is not related uniquely to *A. robustus* (a view depicted in Fig. 15-4, Phylogeny A, but now rejected by its original proposers; also shown in Phylogeny E).
6. All robust australopithecines are extinct by 1 m.y.a. (or shortly thereafter).
7. All australopithecine species (presumably early *Homo* as well) were highly variable, showing extreme sexual dimorphism.
8. Since there is so much intraspecific variation, on average there was not much difference in body size among australopithecine species.
9. *A. africanus* was probably not the last common ancestor of the robust lineage *and* genus *Homo* (i.e., Phylogeny C is probably not entirely correct).
10. All forms (*Australopithecus* and early *Homo*) were relatively large-brained compared to comparably sized apes, but *afarensis* and *africanus* not especially so (most marked in *Homo*).
11. All forms (including some members of early *Homo*) had large back teeth.
12. There was substantial parallelism in physical traits among early hominid lineages.

13. Given the current state of knowledge, there are several equally support-able phylogenies. In fact, in a recent publication, three leading re-searchers (Bill Kimbel, Tim White, and Don Johanson, 1988) make this point; moreover, they note that of four possible phylogenetic reconstruc-tions (resembling, in Fig. 14-5, Phylogenies D, E, F, and G), they have not reached agreement among themselves as to which is the most likely.

Thus, as points 1 through 12 make clear, we have come a long way in reaching an understanding of Plio-Pleistocene hominid evolution. Never-theless, a truly complete understanding is not at hand. Such is the stuff of science!

Questions for Review

1. What kinds of dating techniques have been used in South Africa?
2. Why is the dating control better in East Africa than in South Africa?
3. Discuss the first thing you would do if you found an early hominid and were responsible for its formal description and publication. What would you include in your publication?
4. Discuss two current disputes regarding taxonomic issues concerning early hominids. Try to give support for alternative positions.
5. Why would one use the taxonomic term *Paranthropus* in contrast to *Australopithecus*?
6. What is a phylogeny? Construct one of early hominids 1–4 m.y.a. Make sure you can describe what conclusions your scheme makes. Also, it would be good if you could defend it!
7. Discuss at least two alternative ways that *A. africanus* is currently incor-porated into phylogenetic schemes.

Chapter 15

Contents

Homo erectus

After a brush fire, there are animals that take advantage of the available food, such as carcasses of burnt animals, fallen bees' nests, roasted plants, etc. "Bush fires in Africa and probably elsewhere," writes Professor Gowlett, University of Liverpool, "are used by intelligent predators as a means of trapping prey. Animals such as the cheetah will position themselves so as to pounce on animals fleeing from the flames, and hawks will do the same" (1984, p. 56). Gowlett repeats a traveler's story that apes, probably gorillas, would warm themselves around an abandoned fire until the fire burned out. It follows that if nonhuman animals are intelligent enough to make use of fire, it is quite likely that early hominids did so as well. As Professor Henry Lewis, of the University of Alberta, puts it:

It is difficult to accept that an animal with the mental capacity and physical dexterity to make even the simplest stone tools would not have recognized the advantages of using fire—to heat and illuminate caves or open sites, not to mention cooking food or affecting plants and animals—and been able to maintain it and move it from place to place (1989, p. 14).

An important distinction exists between the *making* of fire and the *use* of fire captured from natural sources. Some very ancient methods that could have been used deliberately to make fire could have included striking sharp rocks together or rubbing wood together to create sparks through friction. Without such technological innovations, earlier hominids would have been limited to obtaining and transporting fire from natural sources, such as lightning strikes and geothermal localities.

The archeological evidence may, however, never be sufficiently complete to allow this distinction to be made with much precision. Nevertheless, *at minimum*, the consistent use of fire would have been a major technological breakthrough and could have had potentially marked influence on hominid biological evolution as well. For example, as a result of cooking, food items would have been more tender, thus chewing stresses would have been reduced, perhaps leading also to selection for reduced size of the dentition.

It is logically possible that australopithecines took advantage of, and used, naturally occurring fire, but the evidence relating to the use of fire is not always easy to interpret. At open-air sites, for example, remains suggesting an association between hominids and burning may be found. However, ashes may already have been blown away, and stones and bones blackened by fire could be the result of a natural brush fire, as could charcoal and baked earth. Furthermore, remains found on the surface of a site might be the result of a natural fire that occurred long after the hominids had left. Another problem is that at many sites, the burned material is too scanty to serve as causal evidence of fire. (Indeed, this should remind you of the critical thinking dictum that "correlation does not necessarily equal causation.")

The difficulties of working with evidence at "use" sites (where fire was probably not deliberately made) also apply to sites where hominids ignited the fires. These are often referred to as controlled fires, and it is the earliest makers (or at best *systematic* users) of fire that interest us in this Issue. Some sort of regular *control* of this important resource is the real key here. We cite Gowlett once again:

The control of fire is of critical importance to humanity; it provides warmth, protection and a means of cooking. For early man it was also a technological catalyst—with the aid of fire numerous processes became easier—wooden objects could be shaped and flint could be heated so that it flaked more easily. . . . [it] is so rooted in culture that it has a symbolic significance; religion has its fire-gods and innumerable habits and rites connected with fire have been recorded, revealing its deep spiritual importance. The ability to control and use fire sets man apart from the rest of the natural world (1984, p. 56).

The above quotes have suggested several possible advantages controlled use of fire may have provided to earlier hominids, including:

1. warmth
2. cooking meat and/or plant foods, thus breaking down fibers and, in

the case of many plants, neutralizing toxins
3. fire-hardening wood, such as the end of a spear
4. facilitating the predictable flaking of certain stone materials, thus aiding in the production of stone tools
5. chasing competing predators (such as bears) from caves and keeping dangerous animals at bay
6. providing illumination in caves and, more fundamentally, extending usable light into the night

This last implication of human control of fire may have had a profound effect on human sleep cycles, and with it alterations in activity patterns, neurological functioning, and hormonal balance. In fact, recent experiments have suggested that humans still today can readily (and comfortably) adjust to "natural" light/dark cycles with periods of inactivity of up to 14 hours (thus simulating winter conditions *prior* to the systematic control of fire).

Since controlling fire is so important to humans, it would be useful to know who tamed the wild flames and when, where, and how they did it. With that knowledge we could learn much more about the culture of our ancient ancestors and their evolution. Archeologists are not certain who the first firemakers were. Some believe *Homo erectus* may have been first, but the evidence has been questioned; others believe it was archaic *H. sapiens* (discussed in Chapter 16) who invented the earliest method of making fire.

Caves may be a more probable source for finding humanmade fire since caves, except at the entrance, are damp, very dark, and impossible for habitation without light. Also, by the time humans began to occupy caves, they may have invented a method of making fire. It is possible, of course, to carry a natural fire into a cave, which is another snag in determining whether the fire was made or natural.

Probably the cave best known to paleoanthropologists is Zhoukoudian (discussed in this chapter), not far from Beijing, China, where both Chinese and Western archeologists have been working for more than 60 years. Evidence of fire is abundant, but the evidence (such as charred animal bones, layers of ash, charcoal, and burned stone artifacts) has led to differing interpretations by archeologists. The Chinese scholars and many of their colleagues who have worked at Zhoukoudian are convinced that *H. erectus*, who inhabited the cave, made and controlled fire, perhaps as much as half a million years ago. Other archeologists, led by Lewis Binford of Southern Methodist University, doubt this and believe the layers of ash are not really ash and that other remains of burning in the cave were most likely due to natural causes.

There are also open *H. erectus* sites in China where there appears to be evidence for deliberately made fires, and several caves in Europe, provisionally dated to about 300,000 years ago, have yielded evidence of fire possibly made by archaic *H. sapiens*. But, again, not all archeologists are persuaded that humans were responsible.

Other prehistorians are sure that Neandertals (discussed in Chapter 16) who built hearths were the first to make fire—toward the end of the Middle Pleistocene (circa 125,000 years ago). A deliberately built hearth is probably the best evidence for human-controlled fire. Ancient hearths are usually built with stone pebbles, arranged in a circular or oval shape to constrain the fire within the stone boundaries. The presence of numerous hearths at a site (like finding a box of matches near a fire) tends to serve as proof that the fires were probably started by humans. It is the absence of hearths that is so troublesome at the older sites, and which immediately signals a doubt that the fire was made (or even systematically used) by hominids. It will take the development of carefully constructed interpretive techniques to overcome the difficulties of solving the case of the first significant controllers of fire.

SOURCE:

Binford, Lewis P. and Chuan Kuntto, "Taphonomy at a Distance: Zhoukoudian, the Cave Home of Beijing Man," *Current Anthropology*, **26**:413–442, 1985.

Introduction

We have traced the earliest evidence of hominid evolution in the prior two chapters, which reviewed the abundant fossil material from Africa documenting the origins of *Australopithecus* and genus *Homo* during the Pliocene and early Pleistocene. In this chapter, we take up what might be called the next stage of hominid evolution, the appearance and dispersal of *Homo erectus* (see Fig. 15-1).

Homo erectus is a widely distributed species of hominid that also has a long temporal record spanning over one million years. Our discussion will focus on the defining physical characteristics of *Homo erectus* compared to what came immediately before (early *Homo*) and what came immediately after (*Homo sapiens*). Of course, as we have emphasized, hominid evolution has long been characterized by a biocultural interaction. In the context of tracing the origins and expansion of *Homo erectus*, it is *only* through explaining the behavioral capacities (in concert with morphological change) that we can understand the success of this hominid species. Thus, we also will highlight some of the abundant archeological evidence and concomitant biocultural reconstructions that have so long occupied and fascinated paleoanthropologists.

Homo erectus—Names and Geographic Distribution

The discoveries of fossils now referred to as *H. erectus* go back to the last century. Later on in this chapter we will discuss in some detail the historical background of these earliest discoveries in Java and those somewhat later in China. From this work, as well as presumably related finds in Europe and North Africa, a variety of taxonomic names were suggested. The most significant of these earlier terms were *Pithecanthropus* (for the Javanese remains) and *Sinanthropus* (for the fossils from northern China). In fact, you may still see these terms in older sources or occasionally used colloquially and thus placed in quotation marks (for example, "Pithecanthropus").

It is important to realize that taxonomic *splitting* (which this terminology reflects) was quite common in the early years of paleoanthropology. Only after World War II and with the incorporation of the Modern Synthesis (see p. 90) into paleontology (from the work of George Gaylord Simpson and others) did more systematic biological thinking come to the fore. Following this trend, in the early 1950s Harvard biologist Ernst Mayr (a student of Simpson's) proposed that all of the material previously referred to as "Pithecanthropus," "Sinanthropus," and so forth be included in a single species of genus *Homo*—*H. erectus*. This reclassification proved to be a most significant development on two counts:

1. It reflected the incorporation of modern evolutionary thinking into hominid paleontology
2. The simplification in terminology, based as it was on sound biological principles, refocused research away from endless arguments regarding classification to broader population, behavioral, and ecological considerations

We have mentioned the significant *H. erectus* discoveries from Java and China. With *H. erectus*, hominids *for the first time* expanded out of Africa. Discoveries in the last few decades have established the oldest *well-dated* finds of *H. erectus* in East Africa. In fact, some of these discoveries are from geological contexts radiometrically dated as old as 1.6 m.y.a. (see below). However, after one million years ago *Homo erectus* migrated out of eastern Africa, eventually to occupy South and North Africa, south and northeastern Asia, and perhaps Europe as well. A recent, as not yet fully described, hominid mandible has been suggested as indicating the arrival of *H. erectus* in eastern Europe (at a site in the Republic of Georgia) as early as 1.5 m.y.a.*

The dispersal of *Homo erectus* from Africa was influenced by climate, topography, water boundaries, and access to food and other resources. Paleoenvironmental reconstructions are thus of crucial importance in understanding the expansion of *H. erectus* to so many parts of the Old World. The long temporal span of *H. erectus* begins very early in the **Pleistocene** and extends to fairly late in this geologic epoch. To comprehend the world of *Homo erectus*, we must understand how environments shifted during the Pleistocene.

Pleistocene   The epoch of the Cenozoic from 1.8 m.y.a. until 10,000 y.a. Literally, meaning "ice age." This epoch is associated with continental glaciations in northern latitudes.

The Pleistocene (1.8 m.y.a.–10,000 y.a.)

During much of the Pleistocene (also known as the Age of Glaciers), large areas of the Northern Hemisphere were covered with enormous masses of ice, which advanced and retreated as the temperature fell and rose. An early classification of glacial (and interglacial) Europe divided the Pleistocene into four major glacial periods: Günz, Mindel, Riss, and Würm. However, climatic conditions varied in different areas of Europe, and glacial periods are also now known from the North Sea, England, and Eastern Europe. New dating techniques (see pp. 335–339) have revealed a much more complex account of glacial advance and retreat. There were many oscillations of cold and warm temperatures during the Pleistocene that affected both plants and animals. "The Pleistocene record shows that there were about 15 major cold periods and 50 minor advances during its 1.5-m.y. duration, or one major cold period every 100,000 years" (Tattersal, et al., 1988, p. 230).

At one time (and still used by some scholars), the Plio-Pleistocene boundary was defined by the appearance of certain mammals at the beginning of the Pleistocene. Since the appearance of these mammals—modern horse, Indian elephant—occurs at different times on different continents, this criterion could not be used on a worldwide basis. What was needed was an event that occurred everywhere on earth at the same time, and just such an event was found in the reversal of the earth's magnetic field (Dalrymple, 1972). This marker was a reversal in the geomagnetic pole, called the Oldowan Event and dated to 1.8 m.y.a. (see p. 343). This date is now generally agreed to be the beginning of the Pleistocene.

The Pleistocene, which lasted more than 1.75 m.y., was a significant period in hominid evolutionary history and encompassed the appearance and disappearance of *Homo erectus.* By the end of the Pleistocene, modern humans had already appeared, dependence on culture as the human way of life had dramatically increased, and domestication of plants and animals—one of the

---

*If this date should hold up, this find (from Dmanisi, Republic of Georgia) would be the earliest documented appearance of a hominid *anywhere* outside of Africa.

Figure 15-1

Major Homo erectus *sites.*

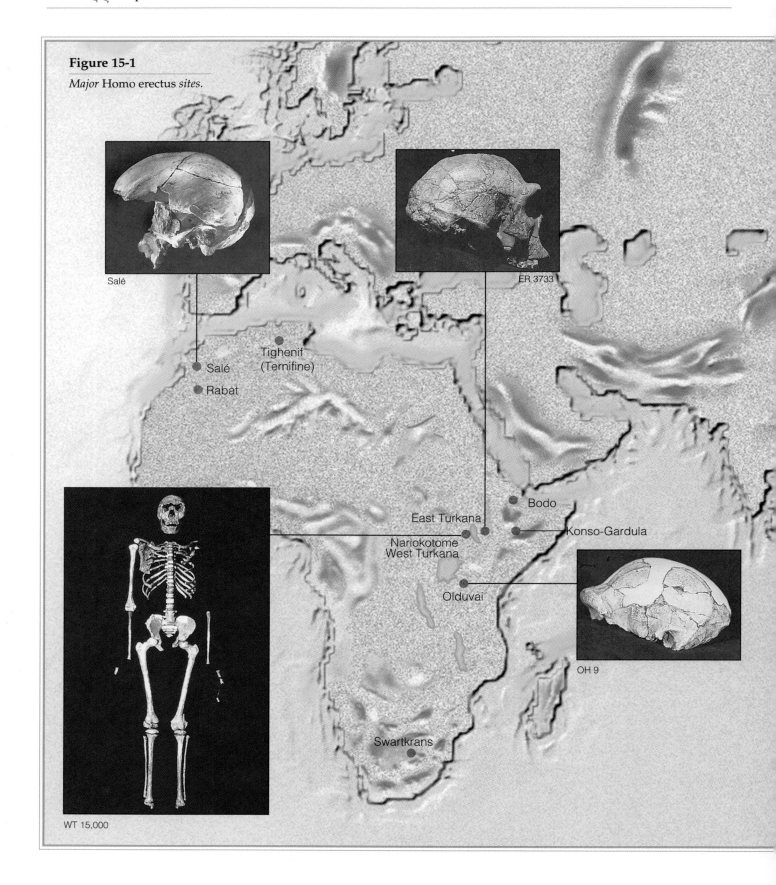

Salé

ER 3733

Tighenif
(Ternifine)

Salé

Rabat

Bodo

East Turkana

Konso-Gardula

Nariokotome
West Turkana

Olduvai

OH 9

Swartkrans

WT 15,000

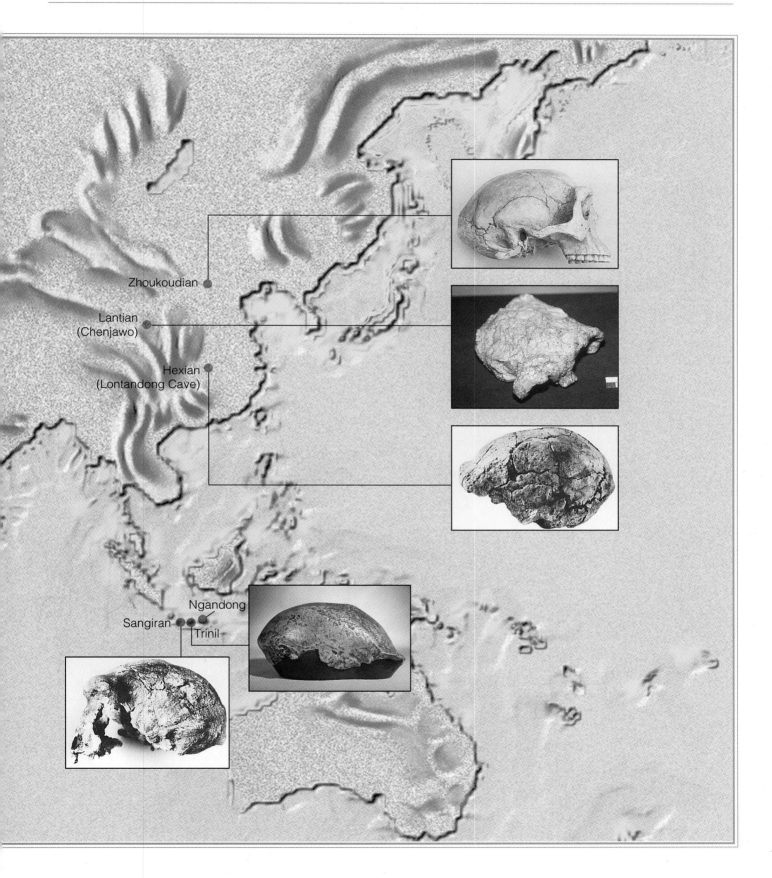

Zhoukoudian

Lantian
(Chenjawo)

Hexian
(Lontandong Cave)

Ngandong

Sangiran

Trinil

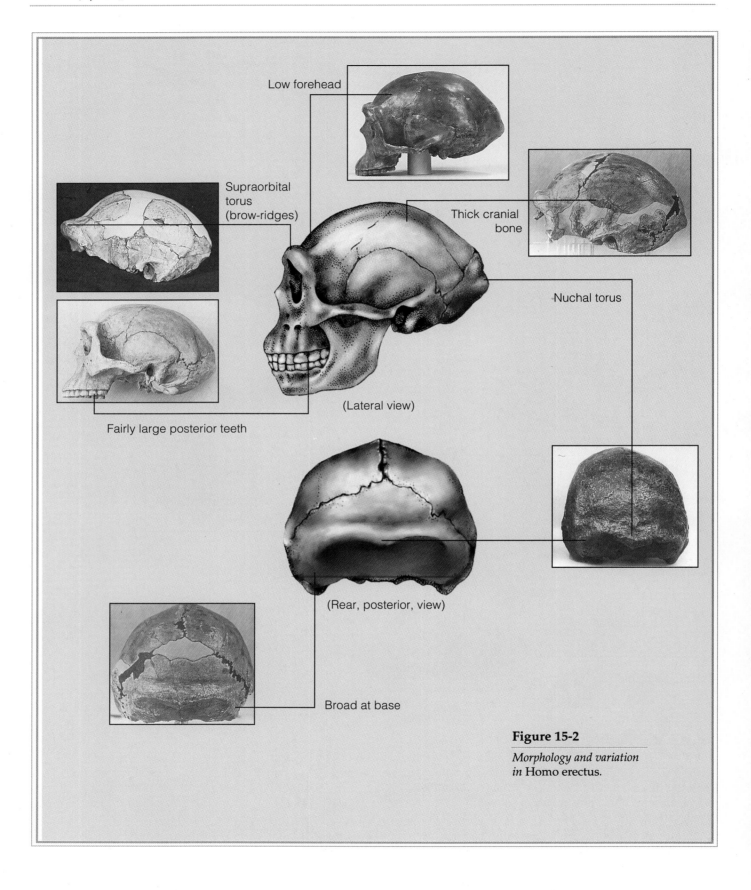

Low forehead

Supraorbital torus (brow-ridges)

Thick cranial bone

Nuchal torus

Fairly large posterior teeth

(Lateral view)

(Rear, posterior, view)

Broad at base

Figure 15-2

Morphology and variation in Homo erectus.

great cultural revolutions of human history—was either about to commence or had already begun.

Given this background on the time span in which *H. erectus* evolved and lived, let us examine more closely this predecessor of *H. sapiens*.

The Morphology of *Homo erectus*

BRAIN SIZE

Homo erectus differs in several respects, both from early *Homo* and from *Homo sapiens*. The most obvious feature is cranial size (which, of course, is closely related to brain size). Early *Homo* has cranial capacities ranging from as small as 500 cm^3 to as large as 800 cm^3. *H. erectus*, on the other hand, shows considerable brain enlargement and has a cranial capacity range of 750–1,250 cm^3 (with a mean slightly greater than 1,000 cm^3). However, in making such comparisons, two key questions must be borne in mind: (1) What is the comparative sample? (2) What were the overall body sizes of the species being compared?

In relation to the first question, you should recall that many scholars are now convinced that there was more than one species of early *Homo* in East Africa around 2 m.y.a. If so, only one of these could have been ancestral to *H. erectus*. (Indeed, it is possible that neither species gave rise to *H. erectus* and that perhaps we have yet to find direct evidence of the ancestral species.) Taking a more optimistic view, that at least one of the data subsets in the fossil record is a likely ancestor of later hominids, the question still remains—"Which one?" If we choose the smaller-bodied sample of early *Homo* as our presumably ancestral group, then *H. erectus* shows as much as a 40% increase in cranial capacity. However, if the comparative sample is the larger-bodied group of early *Homo* (as exemplified by ER-1470), then with *H. erectus* we see a 25% increase in cranial capacity.

As we previously discussed in Chapter 10, brain size is closely tied to overall body size (a relationship termed *encephalization*). We have also made a point of the *increase* in *H. erectus* brain size; however, it must be realized that *H. erectus* was also considerably larger overall than earlier members of the genus *Homo*. In fact, when *H. erectus* is compared to the larger-bodied early *Homo* sample, *relative* brain size is about the same (Walker, 1991). But, *absolute* brain size in *Homo erectus* is approximately 30% less than the average for *H. sapiens*. Moreover, when one considers relative brain/body proportions, *H. erectus* was notably less encephalized than modern *H. sapiens* (although the difference would not be as dramatic in comparison with archaic forms of *sapiens*—see Chapter 16).

BODY SIZE

As we have just mentioned, another feature displayed by *H. erectus*, compared to earlier hominids, is a dramatic increase in body size. For several decades little was known of the postcranial skeleton of *H. erectus*. However, with the discovery of a nearly complete skeleton in 1984 from Nariokotome on the west side of Lake Turkana and its recent detailed analysis (Walker and Leakey, 1993), the data base is now much improved. From this specimen (and from less complete individuals at other sites), *Homo erectus* adults are estimated to have weighed over 100 pounds with a mean adult stature of about

5 feet 6 inches (Ruff and Walker, 1993). Another point to keep in mind is that there was apparently considerable sexual dimorphism in *Homo erectus*—at least as reflected by the East African specimens. Thus, for male adult body size, the weights and stature in some individuals may have been considerably greater than the *average* figures just mentioned. In fact, it is estimated that if the Nariokotome boy had survived, he would have attained an adult-stature of over 6 feet (Walker, 1993). Females were probably considerably smaller, but may still have been as large, on average, as the presumptive males of even the large early *Homo* sample (Walker, 1993).

Associated with the large stature (and explaining the significant increase in body weight) is also a dramatic increase in body robusticity. Muscle insertion areas are more emphasized in *H. erectus* (compared to either early *Homo* or modern *H. sapiens*) and bone thickness also increased. In fact, this characteristic of very heavy body build was to dominate hominid evolution not just during *H. erectus* times, but through the long transitional era of archaic *sapiens* as well. Only with the appearance of anatomically modern *H. sapiens* do we see the more gracile skeletal structure, which is still characteristic of most modern populations.

CRANIAL SHAPE

The cranium of *Homo erectus* displays a highly distinctive shape, partly as the result of brain size increase, but probably more correlated with significant body size (robusticity). The ramifications of this heavily built cranium are reflected in thick cranial bone (most notably in Asian specimens) and large brow ridges (supra-orbital tori) in the front of the skull and a projecting nuchal torus in the back of the skull.

The vault is long and low, receding back from the large brow ridges with little forehead development. Moreover, the cranium is wider at the base compared to earlier *or* later species of genus *Homo*. The maximum breadth is below the ear opening, giving a pentagonal contour to the cranium (when viewed from behind). In contrast, crania of early *Homo*, and especially *H. sapiens*, have more vertical sides and the maximum width is *above* the ear openings.

DENTITION

The dentition of *Homo erectus* is much like that of *Homo sapiens*, but the earlier species exhibits somewhat larger teeth. However, compared to early *Homo*, *H. erectus* does show some dental reduction. This trend is especially evident when the comparison is with the larger early *Homo* subset (as exemplified by ER 1470, who had very large tooth sockets, especially for the back teeth).

Another interesting feature of the dentition of some *H. erectus* is seen in the incisor teeth. On the back (distal) surfaces, the teeth are scooped out, forming a surface reminiscent of a shovel. Accordingly, such teeth are referred to as "shovel-shaped" incisors (Fig. 15-3). It has been suggested that teeth shaped in this manner are an adaptation in hunter-gatherers for processing foods, a contention not yet proven (or really even framed in a testable manner). One thing does seem likely: shovel-shaped incisors are probably a primitive feature of the species *H. erectus*—as the phenomenon has been found not just in the Chinese specimens but also in the early individual from Nariokotome (Kenya).

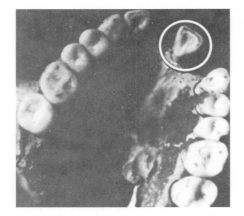

Figure 15-3

Shovel-shaped incisors.

Historical Overview of *Homo erectus* Discoveries

In our discussion of Plio-Pleistocene hominids, we traced the evolutionary developments in *chronological* order; that is, discussing the oldest specimens first. Here, we take a different approach and will discuss the finds in the historical order in which they were discovered. We believe this approach is useful, as the discoveries cover a broad range of time—indeed, almost the entire history of paleoanthropology. Given this relatively long history of scientific discovery, the later finds were assessed in the light of earlier ones (and thus can still be best understood within an historical context).

JAVA

Scientific discoveries are normally the result of careful planning, hard work, and thorough knowledge of the subject. In addition, they are frequently tales of luck, adventure, and heartbreak, which brings us to the story of Eugene Dubois, a Dutch anatomist (Fig. 15-4).

Dubois was the first scientist to deliberately design a research plan that would take him from the lab to where the fossil bones were buried, or might be buried. Up until this time, embryology and comparative anatomy were considered the proper method of studying humans and their ancestry, and the research was done in the laboratory. Dubois changed all this.

The latter half of the nineteenth century was a period of intellectual excitement. In Europe, Darwin's *Origin of Species* (published in 1859) provoked scientists as well as educated laymen to take opposing sides, often with heated emotion. In Germany, for example, the well-known zoologist Ernst Haeckel eagerly supported Darwin's statement that humans descended from apes and even suggested the name for the missing transitional link between the two: *Pithecanthropus alalus* (the ape man without speech). He was criticized by Rudolf Virchow, a famous pathologist and one of Europe's most famous scientists (also, Haeckel's one-time zoology professor), who publicly and scornfully disagreed with these speculations.

In 1856, a strange skull had been recovered near Düsseldorf, Germany. This specimen is now known as Neandertal, but when a description of it was published, scientific opinion was again divided and feelings ran high. Opinions about the Neandertal specimen and other fossil bones that turned up in Europe kept science and the keenly interested lay public in a constant tumult for many years.

This stimulating intellectual climate surrounded the youthful Eugene Dubois, born in Holland in 1858, a year before Darwin's *Origin* and two years after the discovery of the Neandertal skull. Trained as an anatomist, Dubois left Holland for Sumatra in 1887 to search for, as he phrased it, "the missing link." Dubois went to work immediately and soon unearthed a variety of animal bones, including orang, gibbon, and several other mammalian species. However, his successes soon diminished and Dubois switched his fieldwork to the neighboring Indonesian island of Java. Dubois started working in Java in 1890, and he found the banks of the Solo River to be the most productive area; he thus concentrated his efforts there, near the town of Trinil.

In October, 1891, the hired field crew unearthed a skullcap that was to become internationally famous. The following year, a femur was recovered about fifteen yards upstream in what Dubois claimed was the same level as the skullcap. When he examined it, Dubois discerned at once that it resem-

Figure 15-4

Eugene Dubois, who found the first H. erectus.

bled a human femur. He assumed the skullcap (with a cranial capacity of over 900 cm³) and the femur belonged to the same individual.

After studying these discoveries for a few years, Dubois startled the world in 1894 with a paper provocatively entitled *"Pithecanthropus erectus*, a Man-like Species of Transitional Anthropoid from Java."* As we noted earlier, the name *"Pithecanthropus"* had been suggested some years before by Haeckel for the transitional form between ape and human. We also noted that the generic term *"Pithecanthropus"* is now included as part of *Homo* (but the species name *erectus* is still used). Haeckel came to the support of Dubois, but the majority of scientists, including Virchow, strongly and often nastily, objected to Dubois' views.

Dubois returned to Europe in 1895 and countered the criticism by elaborating the points briefly covered in his original paper. He also brought along the actual fossil material, which gave scientists an opportunity to directly examine the evidence. As a result, many opponents became more sympathetic to his views, although Virchow remained adamant in his opposition.

However, to this day questions about the finds remain: Does the femur really belong with the skullcap? Did the field crew dig through several layers, thus mixing the faunal remains? Moreover, many anthropologists believe the Trinil femur to be relatively recent and representative of modern *H. sapiens*, not *H. erectus*.

Despite the still-unanswered questions, there is general acceptance that Dubois was correct in identifying the specimen as belonging to a previously undescribed species; that his estimates of cranial capacity were reasonably accurate; that *"Pithecanthropus erectus,"* or *H. erectus* as we call it today, is the ancestor of *H. sapiens*; and that bipedalism preceded enlargement of the brain.

By 1930, the controversy had faded, especially in the light of important new discoveries near Peking (Beijing), China, in the late 1920s (discussed below). Resemblances between the Beijing skulls and Dubois' *"Pithecanthropus"* were obvious, and scientists pointed out that the Java form was not an *apeman*, as Dubois contended, but rather, was closely related to modern *Homo sapiens*.

One might expect that Dubois would welcome the China finds and the support they provided for the human status of *"Pithecanthropus,"* but Dubois would have none of it. He refused to recognize any connection between Beijing and Java and described the Beijing fossils "as a degenerate Neanderthaler" (von Koenigswald, 1956, p. 55). He also refused to accept placing *"Pithecanthropus"* in the same species with von Koenigswald's later Java finds.*

HOMO ERECTUS FROM JAVA

Six sites in eastern Java have yielded all of the *H. erectus* fossil remains found to date on that island. The bulk of the material is found at four sites (Sangiran,† Trinil, Sambungmachan, and Ngandong) along, or close to, the Solo River. There is also a child's calvarium at Modjokerto (Perning) and a mandible fragment, Dubois' first find, at Kedung Brubus.

---

*G. H. R. von Koenigswald worked in Java in the early 1930s and was a friend of Dubois.

†An adult female skull of *H. erectus* was found in May, 1993, near the village of Sangiran, and has been dated to 500,000–700,000 y.a. The skull is more complete than most other Sangiran skulls. As of this writing, a description of the skull has not yet been published (*Science* 261:397, 1993).

The dating of these fossils has been hampered by the complex nature of Javanese geology. It is generally accepted that most, if not all, of the fossils belong in the Middle Pleistocene and are less than 800,000 years old.*

At Sangiran, where the remains of at least five individuals have been excavated, the cranial capacity of the fossils ranges from 813 cm^3 to 1,059 cm^3; at Sambungmachan, the braincase (calvaria) is estimated to represent a cranial capacity of 1,035 cm^3. The increase in brain size suggests either an evolutionary increase in brain size or, perhaps, sexual dimorphism. However, with the lack of postcranial material associated with the skull, it is very difficult to determine the sex of the fossils.

Like Sangiran, Ngandong has also been a fruitful site with remains of 12 crania recovered. The dating here is also confusing, but the Late Pleistocene has been suggested, which may explain the larger cranial measurements of Ngandong as well as features that are more modern than other Javanese crania. Ngandong 6, for example, has a cranial size of 1,251 cm^3, a measurement well within the range of *H. sapiens*.

The Ngandong material shares cranial features with other Javanese specimens, but the supraorbital torus, for example, is not as thick, and there is very little post-orbital constriction (see Fig. 15-5). Nevertheless, taking all features into consideration, most scholars group these remains with *H. erectus*, but seemingly closer to the roots of *H. sapiens*. Another interpretation, favored by some, is simply to classify all the Ngandong remains as *H. sapiens*.

We can say little about the hominid way of life in Java. Very few artifacts have been found and those have come mainly from river terraces, not from primary sites. "... on Java there is still not a single site where artifacts can be associated with *H. erectus*" (Bartstra, 1982, p. 319).

Figure 15-5

Rear view of Ngandong skull. Note that the cranial walls slope downward and outward (or upward and inward), with the widest breadth low on the cranium, giving it a pentagonal form.

PEKING (BEIJING)

The story of Peking *H. erectus* is another saga filled with excitement, hard work, luck, and misfortune. Europeans had known for a long time that "dragon bones," so important to the Chinese for their healing and aphrodisiac powers, were actually ancient mammal bones. In 1917, the Geological Survey of China decided to find the sites where these dragon bones were collected by local inhabitants and sold to apothecary shops. In 1921 a Swedish geologist, J. Gunnar Andersson, was told of a potentially fruitful fossil site in an abandoned quarry near the village of Zhoukoudian. A villager showed Andersson's team a fissure in the limestone wall, and within a few minutes they found the jaw of a pig. "That evening we went home with rosy dreams of great discoveries" (Andersson, 1934, pp. 97–98).

A young Chinese geologist, Pei Wenshong, took over the direction of the excavation in 1929, and concentrated on what is called the lower cave, known as Locality 1. On December 1, Pei began digging out the sediment in one branch of the lower cave, and on the following day he found one of the most remarkable fossil skulls to be recovered up to that time. One of the Chinese workers tells the story:

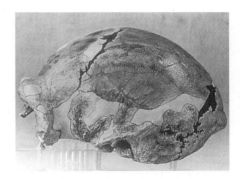

Figure 15-6

H. erectus (*specimen from Zhoukoudian*). *From this view, the supraorbital torus, low vault of the skull, nuchal torus, and angled occiput can clearly be seen.*

---

*The child's calvarium from Modjokerto has just recently been redated by researchers from the Institute of Human Origins to 1.8 m.y.a. If this date is confirmed, it would even predate the Georgian find (p. 409) and require a major reinterpretation of the evolutionary history of *Homo erectus*.

We had got down about 30 meters deep. . . . It was there the skull-cap was sighted, half of it embedded in loose earth, the other in hard clay. The sun had almost set. . . . The team debated whether to take it out right away or to wait until the next day when they could see better. The agonizing suspense of a whole day was felt to be too much to bear, so they decided to go on (Jia, 1975, pp. 12–13).

Pei brought the skull to Dr. Davidson Black, an anatomist at the Peking Union Medical College (see Fig. 15-7). Because the fossil was embedded in hard limestone, it took Black four months of hard, steady work to free it from its tough matrix. The result was worth the labor. The skull, that of a juvenile, was thick, low, and relatively small, but in Black's mind there was no doubt it belonged to an early hominid. The response to this discovery, quite unlike that which greeted Dubois almost 40 years earlier, was immediate and enthusiastically favorable.

Work at Locality 1 continued. Dr. Black maintained a killing schedule, working at night so he would not be interrupted. His health was not robust, and he probably should not have remained in Beijing's harsh climate.

He tried to stick it out but it was too much for him. When his secretary entered his room on March 15, 1934, she found him slumped over his desk, dead from a heart attack, with the beloved skull of Peking Man in his hand (von Koenigswald, 1956, p. 48).

Dr. Franz Weidenreich (Fig. 15-8), distinguished anatomist and well known for his work on European fossil hominids, succeeded Black. Weidenreich left his native Germany because of the academic repression and vicious racial policies of the Nazi regime. In 1935 he was appointed as visiting professor of anatomy at the Peking Union Medical College and honorary director of the Cenozoic Research Laboratory, Geological Survey of China. Excavations at Zhoukoudian ended in 1937, with Japan's invasion of China, but work continued at the Cenozoic Research Laboratory.

As relations between China and Japan deteriorated, Weidenreich decided he had better remove the fossil material from Beijing to prevent it from falling into the hands of the Japanese. Weidenreich left China in 1941, taking excellent, prepared casts, photographs, and drawings of the Peking material with him. After he left, the bones were packed in November, and arrangements were made for the U.S. Marine Corps to take the bones with them when they left Beijing for the United States. The bones never reached the United States and have never been found. To this day no one knows what happened to them, and their location remains a mystery.

Figure 15-7

Dr. Davidson Black, responsible for the study of Zhoukoudian fossils.

Figure 15-8

Dr. Franz Weidenreich. His plan to send Zhoukoudian material to the United States failed.

ZHOUKOUDIAN *HOMO ERECTUS*

In their recent book (1990), Jia and Huang list the total fossil remains of *H. erectus* unearthed at the Zhoukoudian cave as of 1982:

14 skullcaps (only 6 relatively complete)

6 facial bones (including maxillae, palates, and zygomatic bone fragments)

15 mandibles (mostly one side, only one nearly complete, many fragments)

122 teeth: isolated

38 teeth: rooted in jaws

3 humeri: (upper arm bone, only 1 well preserved, the rest in fragments)

Figure 15-9

Zhoukoudian Cave. Grid on wall drawn for purposes of excavation. Entrance to the cave can be seen near grid.

1 clavicle (both ends absent)

1 lunate (wrist) bone

7 femurs (thighbones, only one well preserved)

1 tibia (fragmentary)

(and over 100,000 artifacts)

These remains belong to upwards of 40 male and female adults and children, and constitute a considerable amount of evidence, the largest number of *H. erectus* specimens found at any one site. With the meticulous work by Dr. Weidenreich, the Zhoukoudian fossils have led to a good overall picture of the eastern *H. erectus* of China.

Peking *H. erectus*, like those from Java, possess the typical *H. erectus* fore and aft cranial bulges—the supraorbital torus in front and the nuchal torus behind; the skull is keeled by a sagittal ridge, the face protrudes in alveolar prognathism, the incisors are shoveled, and the molars contain large pulp cavities. Again like the Javanese forms, the skull shows the greatest breadth near the bottom (these similarities were recognized long ago by Black and Weidenreich).

Cultural Remains   More than 100,000 artifacts were recovered from this vast site that was occupied intermittently for almost 250,000 years, which, according to the Chinese (Wu and Lin, 1983, p. 86), "is one of the sites with the longest history of habitation by man or his ancestors. . . ." The occupation of the site has been divided into three cultural stages:

Earliest Stage (460,000–420,000 y.a.)*   The tools are large, close to a pound in weight, and made of soft stone, such as sandstone.

Middle Stage (370,000–350,000 y.a.)   Tools become smaller and lighter (under a pound) and these smaller tools comprise 68% of the total; the large tools make up only 12%.

Final Stage (300,000–230,000 y.a.)   Tools are still smaller, and the tool materials are of better quality. The coarse quartz of the earlier periods is replaced by a finer quartz, sandstone tools have almost disappeared, and flint tools increase in frequency by as much as 30%.

---

*These dates should be considered tentative until more precise chronometric techniques are available.

Quartzite chopper

Flint point

Flint awl

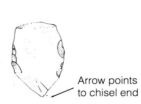

Arrow points
to chisel end

Graver or burin

Figure 15-10

Chinese tools from Middle Pleistocene sites. (Adapted from Wu and Olsen.)

The early tools are crude and shapeless but become more refined over time and, toward the top of Locality 1, there are some finely made tools. Common tools at the site are choppers and chopping tools, but retouched flakes were fashioned into scrapers, points, burins, and awls.

Stone was not the only material selected by Zhoukoudian hominids; they also utilized bone and probably horn. Found in the cave were antler fragments, which had been hacked into pieces. Antler roots might have served as hammers and the sharp tines as digging sticks. Also found in abundance were many skulls of sika and thick-jaw deer, lacking both facial bones as well as antlers, thus leaving only the braincases intact. Jia suggests that since the skulls show evidence of repeated whittling and over 100 specimens were discovered, all similarly shaped, "it is reasonable to infer they served as 'drinking bowls'." He goes on to conjecture that the braincase of the Beijing *H. erectus* fossils "retain similar characteristics and probably served the same purpose." Jia is responding to the claim that whittling away the base of a skull was performed in order to remove the brain for dietary purpose; that is, cannibalism. Alternatively, he suggests the removal of the base of the Zhoukoudian skulls was not for cannibalism, but to produce drinking bowls (Jia, 1975, p. 31; Jia and Huang, 1990, p. 212).

The way of life at Zhoukoudian has traditionally been described as that of hunter-gatherers who killed deer and horses as well as other animals and gathered fruits, berries, and ostrich eggs. Fragments of charred ostrich eggshells, the copious deposits of hackberry seeds unearthed in the cave, and the flourishing plant growth surrounding the cave, all suggest that meat was supplemented by the gathering of herbs, wild fruits, tubers, and eggs. Layers of ash in the cave, over eighteen feet deep at one point, suggest fire and hearths, but whether Beijing hominids could actually *make* fire is unknown. Wu and Lin (1983) state that "Peking Man was a cave dweller, a fire user, a deer hunter, a seed gatherer and a maker of specialized tools"(p. 94).

Did *H. erectus* at Zhoukoudian use language? If by language, we mean articulate speech, it is unlikely. Nevertheless, there are some scholars who believe that speech originated early in hominid evolution. There are others who argue that speech did not originate until up to 200,000 years later in the Upper Paleolithic, with the origin of anatomically modern humans (see Chapter 17). We agree with Falk when she writes, "Unfortunately, what it is going to take to *settle* the debate about when language originated in hominids is a time machine. Until one becomes available, we can only speculate about this fascinating and important question" (1989, p. 141).

Did they wear clothes? Almost surely clothing of some type, probably in the form of animal skins, was worn. Winters in Beijing are harsh today, and appear to have been bitter during the Middle Pleistocene as well. Moreover, at Zhoukoudian awls were found and one of the probable bone tools may be a needle.

Table 15-1 *H. erectus* Fossils of China

Designation	Site	Age* Pleistocene Years	Material	Cranial Capacity (cm³)	Year Found	Remarks
Hexian	Longtandong Cave, Anhui	Middle 250,000	calvarium, skull frag., mandible frag., isolated teeth	1,025	1980/81	First skull found in southern or southwest China
Zhoukoudian (Peking)	Zhoukoudian Cave, Beijing	Middle 500,000–200,000	5 adult crania, skull frags., facial bones, isolated teeth, 40+ individuals	850–1,225; avg: 1,010	1927–ongoing	Most famous fossils in China and some of the most famous in the world
Yunxian	Longgudong Cave, Hubei	Middle ?500,000	isolated teeth		1976–82	
Lantian	Chenjiawo Lantian	Middle 650,000	mandible		1963	Old female
Lantian	Gongwangling, Lantian	Middle 800,000	calvarium, facial bones	780	1964	Female over 30. Oldest *erectus* found so far in China

Sources: Leigh (1992); Wu and Dong (1985); Lisowski (1984); Pope (1984); *Atlas of Primitive Man in China* (1980).
*These are best estimates—authorities differ.

What was the life span of *H. erectus* at Zhoukoudian? Apparently, not very long, and infant and childhood mortality were probably very high. Studies of the fossil remains reveal that almost 40% of the bones belong to individuals under the age of 14, and only 2.6% are estimated to be in the 50–60 age group (Jia, 1975, p. 43).

This picture of Zhoukoudian life has been challenged by archeologist Lewis Binford and colleagues (Binford and Ho, 1985; Binford and Stone, 1986a; Binford and Stone, 1986b). Binford and his colleagues reject the description of Beijing *H. erectus* as hunters and believe the evidence clearly points to them as scavengers. The controversy of early hominids as hunters or scavengers has engaged the attention of paleoanthropologists, taphonomists, archeologists, and other scientists, and the matter is not yet settled. Binford and his colleagues also do not believe that Beijing hominids were clearly associated with fire, except in the later phases of occupation (about 250,000 y.a.). Jia and Huang insist that the Beijing hominids *did* use and control fire. "Peking Man certainly used fire. . . . The fact that some ash substances are found in piles shows that Peking Man knew how to control fire" (Jia and Huang, 1990, p. 79).

OTHER CHINESE SITES

More work has been done at Zhoukoudian than at any other Chinese site. Nevertheless, there are other hominid sites worth noting. Three of the more important sites, besides Zhoukoudian, are Chenjiawo (Lantian), a village in Lantian County; Gongwangling, in the same county; and Lontandong Cave, Hexian County.

At Chenjiawo an almost complete mandible containing several teeth was found in 1963. It is quite similar to those from Zhoukoudian but has been provisionally dated at about 600,000–500,000 y.a. If the dating is correct, this

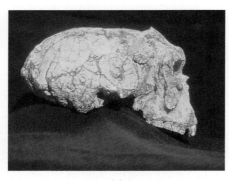

(a)

(b)

Figure 15-11

(a) EV 9002 (Yunxian, China). The skull is in better shape than its companion and its lateral view clearly displays features characteristic of H. erectus: *flattened vault, receding forehead (frontal bone), angulated occiput, supraorbital torus, and alveolar prognathism. (b) EV 9001 (Yunxian). Unfortunately, the skull suffered crushing, but it preserves some lateral facial structures absent in EV 9002.*

Acheulian   A stone tool industry of the Lower and Middle Pleistocene characterized by a large proportion of bifacial (that is, flaked on both sides) tools. Acheulian tool kits are very common in Africa, Southwest Asia, and Western Europe, but are absent elsewhere.

specimen would be older than the Beijing material. The following year a partial cranium was discovered at Gongwangling, not far from Chenjiawo. Dated at 750,000 y.a. (Zhou and Qing, 1989, p. 4), Gongwangling may be the oldest Chinese fossil hominid yet known.

Perhaps the most significant find was made in 1980, at Lontandong Cave (Hexian county) by an IVPP* team, which recovered remains of several individuals. One of the specimens is a well-preserved cranium (with a cranial capacity of about 1,025 cm³) lacking much of its base. Dated roughly at 250,000 y.a., it is not surprising that this Hexian cranium displays several advanced features. The postorbital constriction, for example, is not as pronounced as earlier forms and certain temporal and occipital characteristics are "best compared with the later forms of *H. erectus* at Zhoukoudian . . ." (Wu and Dong, 1985, p. 87).

In June, 1993, Li Tianyuan and Dennis Etler (*Nature*, 357:406, June 4, 1993) reported that two relatively complete skulls were discovered in 1989 and 1990 at the hominid site Quyuanhekou, near the village of Qingqu in Hubei Province. The date given for the site is 350,000 y.a. which, if correct, would make these the most complete crania of this great antiquity in China (Fig. 15-11).

One of the authors had briefly stated the year before (Etler, 1992) that one of the specimens "combines a surprising mix of features." The forehead and brow ridges recall archaic *H. sapiens* and the areas around nose and cheeks "seem to suggest modern humans, especially those from China." Nevertheless, the authors believe the specimens display a number of typical (derived) *H. erectus* features, such as a sharply angulated cranial vault and cranial sides that slope outward toward the bottom of the skull. These traits persuade them the Yunxian skulls belong in the taxon *H. erectus*.

Unfortunately, both skulls are still covered with a hard calcareous matrix, and critics argue that until the skulls are cleaned and the crushed parts properly put together, it is too early to make accurate assessments. In any case, the Yunxian crania will ultimately provide considerable data that will assist in clarifying hominid evolution in China, and perhaps elsewhere in the Old World as well.

In addition to fossil remains, a number of archeological sites have been excavated. Early Paleolithic stone tools have been found in numerous locations in widely separated areas of China. Hand-axes (bifaces) have also been found in several of these sites (Yi and Clark, 1983). At present, there is little reason to believe that *H. erectus* culture in these provinces differed much from that described at Zhoukoudian.

There is, however, dispute on this point. Some scholars (Rightmire, 1981) see almost no detectable changes in cranial dimensions over more than one million years of *H. erectus* evolution. Other researchers (for example, Wolpoff, 1984), who use different methodologies to date and to subdivide their samples, draw a different conclusion—seeing some long-term morphological trends.

The Asian crania from both Java and China are mainly Middle Pleistocene fossils and share many similar features, which may be explained by *H. erectus* migration from Java to China about 800,000 y.a. African *H. erectus* forms are notably older than Asian forms and are not as similar to them as Asian forms (i.e., from Java and China) are to each other.†

---

*The Institute of Vertebrate Paleontology and Paleoanthropology (IVPP). The institute replaced the Cenozoic Research Laboratory.

†Java and China may not be the only areas in Asia that H. erectus inhabited. Remains have been found in Vietnam that may be H. erectus (Olson and Ciochon, 1990:761–788).

EAST AFRICA

Olduvai   Back in 1960, Dr. Louis Leakey unearthed a fossil skull at Olduvai (OH 9) that he identified as *H. erectus*. Skull OH 9 from Upper Bed II has a massive cranium; it is faceless, except for a bit of nose below the supraorbital torus. Estimated at 1,067 cm³, the cranial capacity of OH 9 is the largest brain of all the African *Homo erectus* specimens. Dated at 1.2–1.1 m.y.a., the OH 9 brain case is indeed large for its time period. The browridge is huge, the largest known for any hominid in both thickness and projection, but the vault walls are thin. There appears to be little postorbital constriction nor much of a supratoral sulcus.

Also found at Olduvai, from Bed IV of the Middle Pleistocene (dated at 0.32–0.62 m.y.a.), is a partial skull, OH 12, probably a female. It resembles OH 9, although the cranial capacity is considerably smaller, 700–800 cm³, which may be due to sexual dimorphism. In addition to the skulls, mandibles and postcranial bones have been found.

East Turkana (Koobi Fora)   Some 400 miles north of Olduvai Gorge, on the northern boundary of Kenya, is a finger lake—Lake Turkana. Explored by Richard Leakey and colleagues since 1969, the eastern shore of the lake has been a virtual gold mine for australopithecine, early *Homo*, and *H. erectus* fossil remains.

The most significant *H. erectus* discovery from East Turkana is ER 3733, an almost complete skull, lacking a mandible (Fig. 15-12). Discovered in 1974, the specimen has been given what is considered a firm date of 1.6 m.y.a. The cranial capacity is estimated at 848 cm³, at the lower end of range for *H. erectus*, but this is not surprising considering its date of more than 1.5 m.y.a. The calvarium resembles the Asian *H. erectus* in most features. Another find in the same year, somewhat younger than ER 3733, and at the same site is ER 3883, consisting of a well-preserved braincase and a partial section of the upper face. Quite similar to ER 3733, ER 3883 has a slightly smaller cranial capacity (estimated at 804 cm³).

Not many tools have been found at *H. erectus* sites in East Turkana. Oldowan types of flakes, cobbles, and core tools have been found, and the introduction of **Acheulian** tools about 1.4 m.y.a. replaced the Oldowan tradition.

West Turkana*   In August of 1984, Kamoya Kimeu, a member of Richard Leakey's team, living up to his reputation as an outstanding finder of fossils, discovered a small piece of skull near the base camp on the west side of Lake Turkana. Leakey and his colleague, Alan Walker of Johns Hopkins University, excavated the site known as Nariokotome in 1984 and then again in 1985.

The dig was a resounding success. The workers unearthed the most complete *H. erectus* skeleton yet found (Fig. 15-13). Known properly as WT 15000, the all but complete skeleton includes facial bones and most of the postcranial bones, a rare event indeed for *H. erectus*, since these particular bones are scarce at other *H. erectus* sites. The completeness of the skeleton should help resolve some of the riddles associated with *H. erectus* (see Box 15-1).

Another remarkable feature of the find is its age. Its dating is based on the chronometric dates of the geologic formation in which the site is located and is set at about 1.6 m.y. The fossil is that of a boy about 12 years of age and

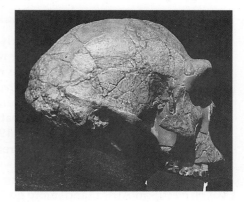

Figure 15-12

ER 3733. One of the most complete East Turkana H. erectus *fossils.*

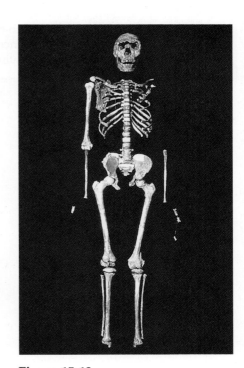

Figure 15-13

WT 15000 from Nariokotome, Kenya. The most complete and oldest H. erectus *specimen yet found.*

---

*WT is the symbol for West Turkana, that is, the west side of Lake Turkana. The east side is symboled as ER—East Rudolf. Rudolf was the former name of the lake (see p. 365).

Box 15-1   The Nariokotome Skeleton—A Boy for All Seasons

The discovery of the spectacularly well-preserved skeleton from Nariokotome on the west side of Lake Turkana has allowed considerable new insight into key anatomical features of *Homo erectus*. Since its recovery in 1984 and 1985, very detailed studies have been undertaken, and recent publication of the results (Walker and Leakey, 1993; Walker, 1993) allows some initial conclusions to be drawn. Moreover, the extraordinary quality of the remains has also allowed anthropologists to speculate on some major behavioral traits of *H. erectus* in Africa (and, more generally, for the entire species).

The remains comprise an almost complete skeleton, lacking only most of the small bones of the hands and feet and the unfused ends of long bones. This degree of preservation is remarkable, and this individual is the most complete skeleton of *any* fossil hominid yet found from before about 100,000 y.a. (after which deliberate burial facilitated much improved preservation). This superior preservation may well have been aided by rapid sedimentation in what is thought to have been an ancient shallow swamp. Once the individual died, his skeleton would have been quickly covered up, but some disturbance and breakage nevertheless did occur—from chewing by catfish, but most especially from trampling by large animals wading in the swamp 1.6 m.y.a.

As we have discussed, the individual was not fully grown when he died. His age (12 ± 1 years—Walker, 1993) is determined by the stage of dental eruption (his permanent canines are not yet erupted) and by epiphyseal union of the ends of long bones (see Appendix B). Moreover, as we have also noted, for his age this young *Homo erectus* male was quite tall (5′3″) and, using modern growth curve approximations, his adult stature would have been over 6 feet (had he lived to full maturity).

More than simply tall, the body proportions of this boy's skeleton are intriguing. Reconstructions suggest he had a linear build with long appendages, thus conforming to predictions of *Allen's rule* for inhabitants of hot climates (see p. 148). Further extrapolating from this observation, Alan Walker also suggests *H. erectus* must also have had a high sweating capacity to dissipate heat (that is, in the modern human fashion) (see pp. 145–147 for a discussion of heat adaptation in humans).

The evidence from limb proportions suggests a quite warm mean annual temperature (90°F; 30°C) in East Africa 1.6 m.y.a. Paleoecological reconstructions

---

5 feet 3 inches tall. Had he grown to maturity, his height, it is estimated, would have been more than 6 feet, taller than *H. erectus* was heretofore thought to be. The postcranial bones appear to be quite similar, though not identical, to those of modern humans. The cranial capacity of WT 15000 is estimated at 880 cm³; the brain was nearly full-grown, so the full adult cranial capacity (had the boy reached maturity) is estimated at 909 cm³ (Begun and Walker, 1993).

Ethiopia   In southern Ethiopia, the 1991 Paleoanthropological Inventory of Ethiopia team of international scientists discovered a site, Konso-Gardula (KGA) containing a remarkable abundance of Acheulian tools, a hominid upper third molar, and an almost complete mandible (Fig. 15-14) with several cheek teeth. Both specimens are attributed to *Homo erectus* "because they lack specialized characteristics of robust *Australopithecus*" (Asfaw et al., 1992).

The mandible is robust and is said to be similar to ER 992, a mandible from Turkana and dated about 1.3 m.y.a. The Acheulian stone tools, mainly bifaces and picks, are made of quartz and quartzite and volcanic rock, from cobbles, blocks, cores, and flakes.

confirm this estimate of tropical conditions (much like the climate today in northern Kenya).

Another fascinating anatomical clue is seen in the beautifully preserved vertebrae. The opening through which the spinal cord passes (the neural canal—see Appendix A) is quite small in the thoracic elements. The possible behavioral corollaries of this reduced canal (as compared to modern *H. sapiens*) are also intriguing. Ann MacLarnan (1993) has proposed that the reduced canal argues for a reduced size of the spinal cord which, in turn, may suggest less control of the muscles between the ribs (the intercostals). One major function of these muscles is the precise control of breathing during human speech. From these data and inferences, Alan Walker has concluded that the Nariokotome youth (and *H. erectus* in general) was not fully capable of human articulate speech. (As an argument regarding language potential, this conclusion will, no doubt, spark considerable debate.)

A final interesting feature can be seen in the pelvis of this adolescent skeleton. It is very narrow and is thus correlated with a narrow bony birth canal. Walker (1993) again draws a behavioral inference from this anatomical feature. He estimates that a newborn with a cranial capacity no greater than a mere 200 cm³ could

have passed through this pelvis. As we showed elsewhere, the adult cranial capacity estimate for this individual was slightly greater than 900 cm³—thus arguing for significant postbirth growth of the brain (exceeding 75% of its eventual size, again mirroring the modern human pattern). Walker speculates that this slow neural expansion (compared to other primates) leads to delayed development of motor skills and thus a prolonged period of infant/child dependency (what Walker terms "secondary altriciality"). Of course, again as with other speculative behavioral scenarios, critics will, no doubt, find holes in this reconstruction as well. One point you should immediately note is that this specimen is the immature pelvis of a male. Thus, the crucial dimensions of an adult female *H. erectus* pelvis remain unknown. Nevertheless, it could not have departed too dramatically from the condition seen at Nariokotome—unless one accepts an extreme degree of sexual dimorphism in this species.

The *Homo erectus* remains from East Africa show several differences from the temporally later fossil samples from Java and China. The African specimens (as exemplified by ER 3733, presumably a female, and WT 15000, presumably a male) are not as strongly buttressed in the cranium (by supraorbital or nuchal tori) and do not have such thick cranial bones as seen in Asian representatives of *H. erectus*. These differences, as well as others observed in the postcranial skeleton, have so impressed some researchers that they, in fact, argue for a *separate* species status for the African *H. erectus* remains (as distinct from the Asian samples). Bernard Wood, the leading proponent of this multiple species solution, has suggested the name *Homo ergaster* be used for the African remains (*H. erectus* would then be reserved solely for the Asian material) (Wood, 1991).

However, this taxonomic division has not been generally accepted, and the current consensus (reflected in this text) is to continue to refer to all these hominids as *Homo erectus*. As with the Plio-Pleistocene samples, we accordingly will have to accommodate a considerable degree of intraspecific variation within this taxon. As Wood has concluded regarding variation within a broadly defined *H. erectus* species: "it is a species which manifestly embraces an unusually wide degree of variation in both the cranium and postcranial skeleton" (Wood, 1992a, p. 329).

SOUTH AFRICA

A mandible was found among fossil remains collected at Swartkrans in South Africa in the 1940s and 1950s. This specimen, SK 15, was originally assigned to "*Telanthropus capensis*," but there is disagreement about its species designation. Rightmire (1990) believes it may be linked with *Homo erectus*, but others are not certain. If it is *H. erectus*, it would demonstrate that *H. erectus* inhabited South, East, and North Africa.

NORTH AFRICA

With evidence from China and Java, it appears clear that *H. erectus* populations, with superior tools and weapons and presumably greater intelligence than their predecessors, had expanded their habitat. The earliest evidence for *H. erectus*, 1.6–1.8 m.y.a., comes from East Africa, and about 1 million years later in eastern Asia. It is not surprising, therefore, that *H. erectus* migrations would have taken them to northwest Africa as well.

North African remains, comprised almost entirely of mandibles or mandible fragments and a partial parietal bone, have been found at Ternifine (now Tighenif), Algeria; and in Morocco, at Sidi Abderrahman and Thomas quarries. The three Ternifine mandibles and parietal fragment are quite robust, and have been dated at early Middle Pleistocene, about 700,000 y.a. The Moroccan material is not as robust as Ternifine, and may be a bit younger, at 500,000 y.a. In addition, an interesting cranium was found in a quarry north of Salé, near Rabat, on the Atlantic Ocean side of Morocco. The walls of the skull vault are thick, and several other features resemble those of *H. erectus*. Some features have suggested that Salé represents a *H. sapiens*, but a date of 400,000 years ago and an estimated cranial capacity of about 900 cm³ appear to nullify that possibility.

(Europe presents a similar situation. At present, many paleoanthropologists believe that early European inhabitants, once assigned to *H. erectus* should now be reassigned to early *sapiens* status, known as "archaic *H. sapiens*." Needless to say, not everyone agrees. These enigmatic archaic *H. sapiens* are discussed in Chapter 16.)

Human Emergence: *Australopithecus* to *Homo erectus*

Surveying hominid evolution of the Early and Middle Pleistocene, we see the disappearance of australopithecines and early *Homo* and the appearance of *H. erectus* populations, who expanded their habitat beyond African boundaries. As we examine *H. erectus*, we find a number of changes that mark human evolution in several directions: *physical, technological*, and *social*.

PHYSICAL TRENDS

From the physical point of view, *H. erectus* is notably similar to modern populations. The *H. erectus* femur/pelvis complex may be somewhat different from our own (Day, 1984; Kennedy, 1984), but if it were possible to observe

H. erectus walking, it is unlikely that we would observe a stride noticeably different from that of modern humans. We would also note *H. erectus* is quite tall, even by modern standards.

However, when we examine the cranium, obvious differences emerge. The vault of the skull is low, not domelike as our own, and the forehead slopes back instead of vertically. The supraorbital torus is a feature remarkably different from *H. sapiens*, as is the prominent projection in the tooth-bearing portion of the face, and the receding chin. At the back of the skull, the occipital bone angles sharply, and the widest part of the skull is much lower than in later hominids.

TECHNOLOGICAL TRENDS

Scholars have noted the remarkable stasis of the physical and cultural characteristics of *Homo erectus* populations, which seemed to change so little in the more than 1.5 m.y. of their existence. Accepting a moderate position, we can postulate there were some changes: the brain of later *H. erectus* was somewhat larger, the nose more protrusive, the body not as robust as in earlier forms. Moreover, there were modifications in stone tool technology.

Expansion of the brain presumably enabled *H. erectus* to develop a more sophisticated tool kit than seen in earlier hominids. The important change in this kit was a core worked on both sides, called a *biface* (known widely as a hand-axe, Fig. 15-14). The biface has a flatter core than, and is a change from, the roundish earlier Oldowan pebble tool. This change enabled the stone-knapper to produce sharper, straighter edges, resulting in a more efficient implement. This *Acheulian* stone tool became standardized as the basic *H. erectus* all-purpose tool (with only minor modifications) for more than a million years. It served to cut, scrape, pound, dig, and more—a most useful tool that has been found in Africa, parts of Asia, and later in western Europe. Like populations elsewhere, *H. erectus* in China manufactured choppers and chopping tools as their core tools, and like other *H. erectus* toolmakers, fashioned scrapers and other small tools, but they did not manufacture bifaces (Fig. 15-15).

In early days, toolmakers employed a stone hammer (simply an ovoid-shaped stone about the size of an egg or a bit larger) to remove flakes from the core, thus leaving deep scars. Later, they used other materials such as wood and bone. They learned to use these new materials in the manufacture

Figure 15-14

Acheulian biface ("hand-axe"), a basic tool of the Acheulian tradition.

Figure 15-15

Small tools of Acheulian industry. (a) Side scraper; (b) point; (c) end scraper; (d) burin.

(a)

(b)

(c)

(d)

Figure 15-16

Acheulian cleaver, possibly a butchering tool.

of softer hammers, which gave them more control over flaking, thus leaving shallow scars, sharper edges, and a more symmetrical form. Toward the end of the Acheulian industry, toolmakers blocked out a core with stone hammers and then switched to wood or bone for refining the edges. This technique produced more elegant-appearing and pear-shaped implements.

Also introduced by *H. erectus* was the cleaver (Fig. 15-16). Instead of coming to a point, like the hand-axe, one end of the cleaver was blunted, giving the appearance of a modern axe head. It was probably used in butchering—chopping and breaking the bones of large animals.

Evidence of butchering is widespread at *H. erectus* sites and, in the past, such evidence has been cited in arguments for consistent hunting. However, this assumption has been challenged, especially by archeologists (p. 342) who believe the evidence does not prove the hunting hypothesis. Instead, they believe that *H. erectus* was primarily a scavenger. However, the scavenger hypothesis has also not yet been proven conclusively, and we thus discuss *H. erectus* as hunter *and* scavenger.

SOCIAL TRENDS

One of the fascinating qualities of *H. erectus* was a penchant for travel. From the relatively close confines of East Africa, *H. erectus* dispersed widely in the Old World, and by the time *H. sapiens* appears, a million years or more later, *H. erectus* had trekked to vast parts of the earth. Within Africa, *H. erectus* had migrated to South and North Africa, and about a million years ago some groups apparently moved from Africa to Asia.

The life of hunter/scavengers is nomadic, and the woodland and savanna that covered the southern tier of Asia, from East Africa to Southeast Asia, would have been an excellent environment for *H. erectus* (as it was similar to the econiche of their African ancestors). As the population grew, small groups budded off and moved on to find their own hunting/scavenging areas. This process, repeated again and again, led *H. erectus* east, crossing the Sunda shelf to Java, arriving there several hundred thousand years later.

Once in Java, it would have been impossible to take a further step east, since there was no land bridge that joined Australia to Java. It was possible, however, to travel north, and by 700,000 y.a., *H. erectus* had also reached China.

Why did *H. erectus* emigrate from Africa? We shall probably never know. It has been suggested that extreme climatic conditions, such as torrential rainfall, may have compelled the inhabitants to leave. However, a recent point has been made concerning the crucial time period: between the glacial episode 2.4–2.8 m.y.a. and the next episode at 0.9–0.7 m.y.a. there were no major global climatic changes (Asfaw et al., 1992). It was during this period, about 1.8 m.y.a., that *H. erectus* first appeared in East Africa. It was also later during this period that *H. erectus* dispersed from Africa. Since there apparently were no major climatic changes in Africa during this time, there were probably no major environmental stimuli that would have motivated *H. erectus* populations to disperse. Therefore, it was apparently something other than gross environmental conditions that caused the emigration.

When we look back at the evolution of *H. erectus*, we realize how significant this early human's achievements were. It was *H. erectus* who increased in body size with more efficient bipedalism; who embraced culture wholeheartedly as a strategy of adaptation; whose brain was reshaped and increased in size to within *H. sapiens'* range; who became a more efficient scavenger and likely hunter with greater dependence on meat; who apparently established more permanent bases; and who probably used fire and may have also controlled it. In short, it was *H. erectus*, committed to a cultural way of life, who transformed hominid evolution to human evolution, or as Foley states, ". . . the appearance and expansion of *H. erectus* represented a major change in adaptive strategy that influenced the subsequent process and pattern of human evolution" (1991, p. 425).

Summary

Homo erectus remains are found in geological contexts dating from about 1.8 million to about 200,000 years ago, a period of more than 1.5 million years. The first finds were made by Dubois in Java, and later discoveries came from China and Africa. Differences from early *Homo* are notable in *H. erectus'* larger brain, taller stature, robust build, and changes in facial structure and cranial buttressing.

The long period of *H. erectus'* existence was marked by a remarkably uniform technology over space and time. Nevertheless, compared to earlier hominids, *H. erectus* introduced more sophisticated tools and probably ate novel and/or differently processed foods, using these new tools and probably fire as well. They were also able to move into different environments and successfully adapt to new conditions.

Originating in East Africa, *H. erectus* migrated in several directions: south and northwest in Africa, and then east to Java and China. The evidence from China, especially Zhoukoudian, supports a *H. erectus* way of life that included scavenging and hunting and controlled use of fire (but note that there is not complete agreement about this archeological reconstruction).

It is generally assumed that some *H. erectus* populations evolved to *H. sapiens*, since many fossils, such as Ngandong (and others discussed in Chapter 16), display both *H. erectus* and *H. sapiens* features. There remain questions about *H. erectus'* behavior (for example, Did they hunt?) and about evolution to *H. sapiens* (Was it gradual or rapid? Which *H. erectus* populations contributed genes to *H. sapiens*?). The search for answers continues.

Questions for Review

1. Describe the Pleistocene in terms of (a) temperature and (b) the dating of fossil hominids.
2. Describe *H. erectus*. How is *H. erectus* anatomically different from early *Homo*? From *H. sapiens*?
3. In what areas of the world have *Homo erectus* fossils been found?
4. In comparing *H. erectus* with earlier hominids, why is it important to *specify* which comparative sample is being used?
5. What was the intellectual climate in Europe in the latter half of the nineteenth century, especially concerning human evolution?
6. Why do you think there was so much opposition to Dubois' interpretation of the hominid fossils he found in Java?
7. Why do you think Zhoukoudian *H. erectus* was enthusiastically accepted whereas the Javanese fossils were not?
8. What questions are still being asked about Dubois' finds? Explain.

9. What new ideas did Dubois suggest about human evolution?
10. How does the Beijing *erectus* physically differ from the Java *erectus*? How do you account for these differences?
11. Describe Beijing *erectus'* way of life as suggested in the text. What disagreements have been voiced about this conjecture?
12. *H. erectus* has been called the first human. Why?
13. What is the *H. erectus* evidence from Africa, and what questions of human evolution does the evidence raise?
14. Cite as many reasons as you can why WT 15000 is important.
15. Can you suggest any reasons why the earliest remains of *H. erectus* have come from East Africa?
16. *H. erectus* migrated to various points in Africa and vast distances to east Asia. What does this tell you about the species?
17. What kinds of stone tools have been found at *H. erectus* sites?

Chapter 16

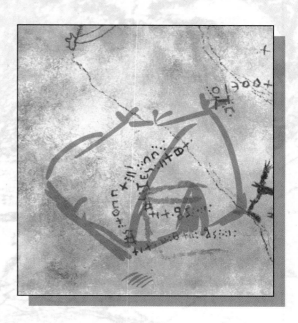

Neandertals and Other Archaic *Homo Sapiens*

Contents

Issue ~~4~~ Did Neandertals Speak?

Actually, no one denies the Neandertal ability to speak. The real question is: Were Neandertals able to use all of the vowels and consonants of modern human languages or were they somehow compromised in their ability to communicate? As with determining the date hominids first controlled fire (Issue, Chapter 15), the pros and cons of this question have been argued for years, and the end is not in sight.

Professor Ralph Holloway, a specialist in the study of fossil brains,* maintains that the Neandertal brain was similar to our own and, on average, slightly larger. Holloway writes, "I believe the Neandertal brain was fully *Homo*, with no essential differences in its organization compared to our own. . . . Neandertals did have language" (1985, p. 320).

Professor Philip Lieberman (1972, 1991), a linguist, argues that the Neandertal larynx was located high in the vocal tract, a position closer in form to *nonhuman* primates than to modern humans. In modern humans, Lieberman states, the larynx is positioned further down in the throat. Furthermore, the size of Neandertal's oral cavity (the distance from the teeth to the back of the mouth) was greater than ours. Following the logic of this reconstruction, had their tongue and vocal tract been configured like modern humans, their larynx, because of the oral cavity's large size, would have been located in their chest! Such a position is unknown in any animal species. Therefore, concludes Lieberman, Neandertals could not have had the same positioning of the tongue and other structures of the vocal tract as seen in modern humans, and this differently arranged vocal tract could not have formed the vowels [i] as in tea; [u], as in too; and [a], as in tall; or the consonants [k] and [g], as in Kate and gate.

Lieberman points out that the skeletal structure of the basicranium (the base of the cranium, especially the portion between the back of the palate and the front of the foramen magnum, which is preserved sometimes in fossils) is a clue to the positioning of the supralaryngeal vocal tract (which does not fossilize): "In brief, flexed basicrania are associated with modern human supralaryngeal vocal tracts, in which the larynx is positioned low in the neck" (Lieberman, 1993, p. 173). Flat basicrania, he contends, are associated with the larynx positioned high in the neck, resulting in limited speech.†

Lieberman claims that the La Chapelle-aux-Saints Neandertal had a flat basicranium, which made for a highly positioned larynx and this individual accordingly would have had a vocal tract unable to produce full articulation.

Lieberman initially collaborated with Professor of Anatomy Edmund Crelin from Yale University. More recently, his ideas have also been supported by another anatomist, Jeffrey Laitman of Mount Sinai School of Medicine in New York City. In fact, Laitman has further argued that Neandertal cranio-facial morphol-

---

*Fossils do not possess brains, of course, since the soft tissue has long since decomposed. It is the endocast—the landscape of the inside surface of the cranium—that is studied for clues to the structure of the brain.

---

†It has been suggested that this communication handicap may have affected Neandertal's ability to survive and led to their extinction. In fact, Lieberman argues, "the extinction of Neandertal hominids was due to the competition of modern human beings who were better adapted for speech and language" (cited in Trinkaus and Shipman, 1992, p. 391). This argument has been used by some paleoanthropologists who believe that Neandertals were not the ancestors of anatomically modern humans in Europe and the Near East, thus supporting the notion they (and other archaic *sapiens*) were replaced by populations presumably migrating out of Africa (this and alternative theories will be discussed in Chapter 17).

With reference to the demise of Neandertals, Professor John Fremlen, of the University of Birmingham, England, wrote the following letter to *Science* (1975, 187, p. 600), wittily demonstrating that even if Neandertals could not use the three vowels noted above, they could, nevertheless, successfully communicate.

Et seems quete prebable thet the Ne'enderthals ked speke less well then ther seccessers, end thet thes wes the resen fer ther demese. But even if we beleve the kempeter resels it seems emprebeble thet ther speech was enedeqwete bekes of the leck of the three vewels seggested. The kemplexete of speech depends en the kensenents, net en the vewels, es ken be seen frem the general kemprehensebelete of thes letter.

ogy (including aspects of the basicranium, nasal area, and sinuses) was specialized for respiration in a cold climate. As a result, Laitman hypothesizes, these upper respiratory specializations, "would have placed limitations on Neandertal vocal modification mechanisms as compared to ours" (Laitman et al., 1993, p. 129).

Are Lieberman and colleagues correct in their interpretations? Perhaps. But, then again, perhaps not. From the earliest publications (1971, 1972), the hypotheses have been vigorously challenged by other anatomists and have been especially strongly critiqued by anthropologists.

The proposed high location of the larynx is criticized by Professor (and anatomist) Dean Falk, who points out that this position is not found in newborn humans, adult humans, or for that matter, in chimpanzees. She concludes that "the statement that Neandertal was less than fully articulate remains unsubstantiated because it rests on a questionable reconstruction of the larynx" (1975, p. 123).* In fact, other anatomists have shown that in the initial reconstruction as proposed by Lieberman and associates, Neandertals would have been unable not only to speak

*Professor Falk was commenting on the 1972 paper by Lieberman et al.; however, her statement equally applies to Lieberman's position as published in 1989 and 1991.

fully, but also would not have been able to swallow or open their mouths!

Professor David Frayer, a paleoanthropologist, notes (1992) that the La Chapelle cranium was recently reconstructed, and the basicranium in the newly constructed version is *flexed*, not flat. La Chapelle's larynx then, according to Lieberman's own hypothesis, should have been positioned low in the throat, like that of modern humans, and be capable of complete articulation. Lieberman's response was that the recent reconstruction of the La Chapelle skull may not have been correct, and he still maintains that Neandertals were probably limited in speech.

Frayer also measured the angle of flexion of the basicrania of skulls from the Upper Paleolithic, the Mesolithic (about 10–15,000 years ago), and from a medieval collection of human remains from Hungary, all of whom presumably possessed modern human speech capabilities. Comparing his results with measurements from a number of Neandertal crania, Frayer found some of the Neandertal basicrania were just as, or even more, flexed than those of anatomically modern humans (that is, some of the modern crania were *flatter* than those of Neandertals). He points out that even if Neandertal basicrania were *flat*, they would have been as capable of unlimited speech as were the modern humans from the three time periods mentioned above.

The matter of Neandertal language capability is not settled. The hypotheses presented by Lieberman

and Frayer cannot both be correct. Although it must be admitted that the consensus among most professionals strongly disagrees with Lieberman. Further research may (or may not) provide confirmation of one or the other hypothesis, or a new one may even be suggested, which is the nature of the scientific process.

SOURCES:

Falk, Dean, "Comparative Anatomy of the Larynx in Man and the Chimpanzee: Implications for Language in Neandertal," *American Journal of Physical Anthropology*, **43**(1975):123–132.

Holloway, Ralph L., "The Poor Brain of *Homo sapiens Neanderthalensis*," in *Ancestors: the Hard Evidence*, Eric Pelson. New York: Alan B. Liss, 1985.

Laitman, J. T. et al., "Neandertal Upper Respiratory Specializations and Their Effect Upon Respiration and Speech," *American Journal of Physical Anthropology*, Supplement 16(1993):129.

Lieberman, Phillip, "On Neanderthal Speech and Neanderthal Extinction," *Current Anthropology*, **33**(1992):409–410.

———, "On the Kebara 2 Hyoid and Neanderthal Speech," *Current Anthropology*, **34**(1994):172–175.

Lieberman, P. and Crelin, E. S., "On the Speech of Neandertal Man," *Linguistic Inquiries*, **2**(1971):203–222.

Lieberman, P. et al., "Phonetic Ability and Related Anatomy of the Newborn and Adult Human, Neanderthal Man, and the Chimpanzee," *American Anthropologist*, **74**(1972):287–307.

Introduction

In Chapter 15, we saw that *H. erectus* was present in Africa at least 1.6 m.y.a. About 800,000 years later, *H. erectus* had reached Java and China. Excepting the new possible find in the Republic of Georgia, we also noted that *H. erectus* fossils thus far have not been found in Europe, although several routes could easily have provided access. A major difficulty in accurately assessing finds is that a number of fossils from Europe—as well as Africa, China, and Java—display *both H. erectus* and *H. sapiens* features.

These particular forms, possibly representing some of the earliest members of our species, fall into the latter half of the Middle Pleistocene, from about 400,000 to 130,000 years ago and are often referred to as **archaic *H. sapiens*** (Fig. 16-1). The term *sapiens* is used, because the appearance of some derived sapient traits suggests they are transitional forms. In most cases, these early archaic *sapiens* also retain some *H. erectus* features mixed with those derived features that distinguish them as *H. sapiens*. However, as they do not possess the full suite of derived characteristics diagnostic of **anatomically modern *sapiens***, we classify them as archaic forms of our species. In general, we see in several different areas of the Old World through time a morphological trend from groups with more obvious *H. erectus* features to later populations displaying more diagnostic *H. sapiens* features.

When we speak of evolutionary trends and transitions from one species to another—for example, from *H. erectus* to *H. sapiens*—we do not wish to imply that such changes were in any way inevitable. In point of fact, most *H. erectus* populations never evolved into anything else. *Some* populations of *H. erectus* did apparently undergo slow evolutionary changes and, thus, some populations of what we call archaic *H. sapiens* emerge as transitional forms. In turn, *some* of these archaic *H. sapiens* populations suggest evolutionary change in the direction of anatomically modern *H. sapiens*.

In this chapter and the next we will attempt, where the data permit, to focus upon those populations that provide clues regarding patterning of hominid evolutionary change. We would like to ascertain *where* such transformations took place, *when* they occurred, and *what* were the adaptive stimuli (both cultural and biological) that urged the process along.

There are still significant gaps in the fossil data, and we certainly do not have a complete record of all the transitional stages; nor are we ever likely to possess anything approaching such a complete record. What we can do is paint the evolution of later hominids in fairly broad strokes to show the general trends.

However, we must again caution the student not to interpret these statements too superficially. Evolution can and *usually* does produce a variety of adaptive responses. Some endure long term; others fade from the scene fairly rapidly. When considering this perspective, we should be careful not to regard various ancient hominids as unsuccessful "dead ends." After all, both the robust australopithecines and *Homo erectus* survived for at least 1.5 million years. Neandertals were on the scene for about 100,000 years. From our narrow, contemporary perspective we should be very cautious about whom we call "successful" or "unsuccessful."

To organize the material covering the several hundred thousand years (or more) of archaic *H. sapiens*, we shall divide them into early archaic forms and late archaic forms (Neandertals). We should also point out that there is a good deal of controversy among paleoanthropologists concerning many of the archaic specimens. The dating is not always clear, the fossil remains are

Archaic *H. sapiens* Earlier forms of *Homo sapiens* (including Neandertals) from the Old World that differ from *H. erectus* but lack the full set of characteristics diagnostic of modern *sapiens*.

Anatomically modern *sapiens* (AMS) Includes all modern humans and some fossil forms, perhaps dating as early as 200,000 y.a. Defined by a set of derived characteristics, including cranial architecture and lack of skeletal robusticity. Usually classified at the subspecies level as Homo sapiens sapiens (see Chapter 15).

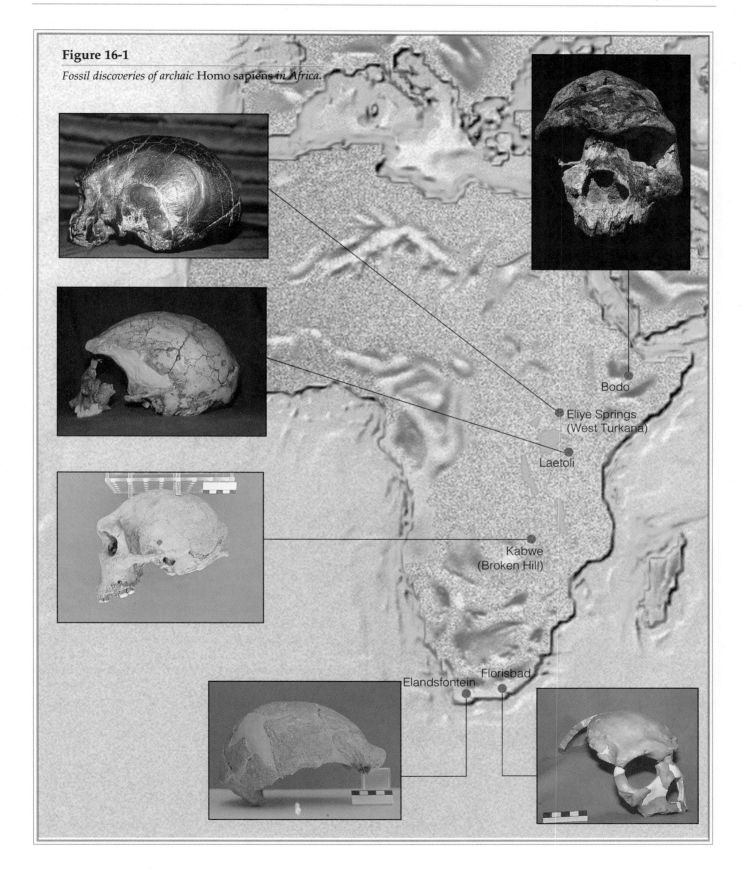

Figure 16-1

Fossil discoveries of archaic Homo sapiens *in Africa.*

Bodo

Eliye Springs
(West Turkana)

Laetoli

Kabwe
(Broken Hill)

Florisbad

Elandsfontein

Box 16-1   Comparison of Anatomically Modern *sapiens* and *H. erectus*

Homo sapiens differs from *H. erectus* in a number of characteristics.* In *H. sapiens sapiens*:

1. The skull is larger, with a 1,350 cm³ mean cranial capacity
2. Muscular ridges in the cranium are not strongly marked
3. The forehead is rounded and vertical
4. The supraorbital ridges are not well developed and do not form a continuous and uninterrupted torus

*For a fuller definition, see Howell, 1978, pp. 201ff.

5. The occipital region is rounded and the nuchal area is relatively small
6. The mastoid process is prominent and of a pyramidal shape (see Appendix A)
7. The calvarium is of maximum width, usually in the parietal region
8. Jaws and teeth are relatively small
9. The maxilla has a concave surface known as a canine fossa
10. The chin is distinct
11. Limb bones are relatively slender and slight

sometimes inadequate for unambiguous analysis, and several hypotheses regarding their species and subspecies designation and their place in human evolution remain to be considered.

In this chapter, then, we shall examine the course of human evolution in the Middle Pleistocene. It is a period of interest and concern to us, for it was during this time that our own species evolved from *H. erectus* to the *sapiens* grade, a time of brain growth and an impressive change in culture.

Early Archaic *H. sapiens*

In many cases, early archaic forms show morphological changes compared to *H. erectus*. These derived changes are reflected in brain expansion; increased parietal breadth (the basal portion of the skull is no longer the widest area and, therefore, the rear view of the skull is no longer pentagonal); some decrease in the size of the molars and increase in the size of the anterior teeth; and general decrease in cranial and postcranial robusticity.

As mentioned, archaic *sapiens* fossils are found on the three continents of Africa, Asia, and Europe. In Europe, the well-known Neandertals are included in this category. (Neandertals are not found anywhere except Europe and western Asia.) Our discussion shall start with the archaic *sapiens* of Africa.

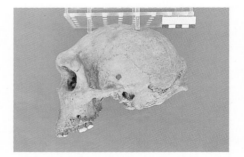

Figure 16-2

Broken Hill (Rhodesian Man), Kabwe. Note very heavy supraorbital torus.

AFRICA

In Africa, the appearance of archaic *sapiens* can be seen at several sites. One of the best known is Broken Hill (Kabwe). Found in a shallow Broken Hill mine shaft, at Kabwe, Zambia, Africa, were a complete cranium and other cranial and postcranial material belonging to several individuals.

A mixture of older and later traits can be seen in this fossil material. The skull's massive supraorbital torus (one of the largest of any hominid), low vault, and prominent occipital torus recall those of *H. erectus*. On the other hand, the occipital is less angulated, the vault bones thinner, and the cranial base essentially modern. A cranial capacity of 1,280 cm^3 is significantly beyond the *erectus* average of about 1,000 cm^3. Dating estimates of Broken Hill have ranged throughout the Middle Pleistocene and Upper Pleistocene, but recent estimates have given dates in the neighborhood of 130,000 y.a.

Discovered in 1976 in northeast Ethiopia, in the general area where Lucy was found (see Chapter 13), is an incomplete cranium (Bodo) dating from the Middle Pleistocene. Like Broken Hill, to which it has been compared, the skull displays a mixture of *H. erectus* and more modern features. Bodo's classification is also murky. It has been called *H. erectus* and also archaic *sapiens*; that is, transitional between *H. erectus* and anatomically modern humans.

There are several interesting points associated with Bodo. Some evidence suggests that animals were butchered at the site. Acheulian tools are associ-

(a)

Figure 16-3

A Middle Pleistocene butchering site at Olorgesailie, Kenya, excavated by Louis and Mary Leakey who had the catwalk built for observers. (b) Is a closeup view of the Acheulian tools, mainly hand-axes, found at the site.

(b)

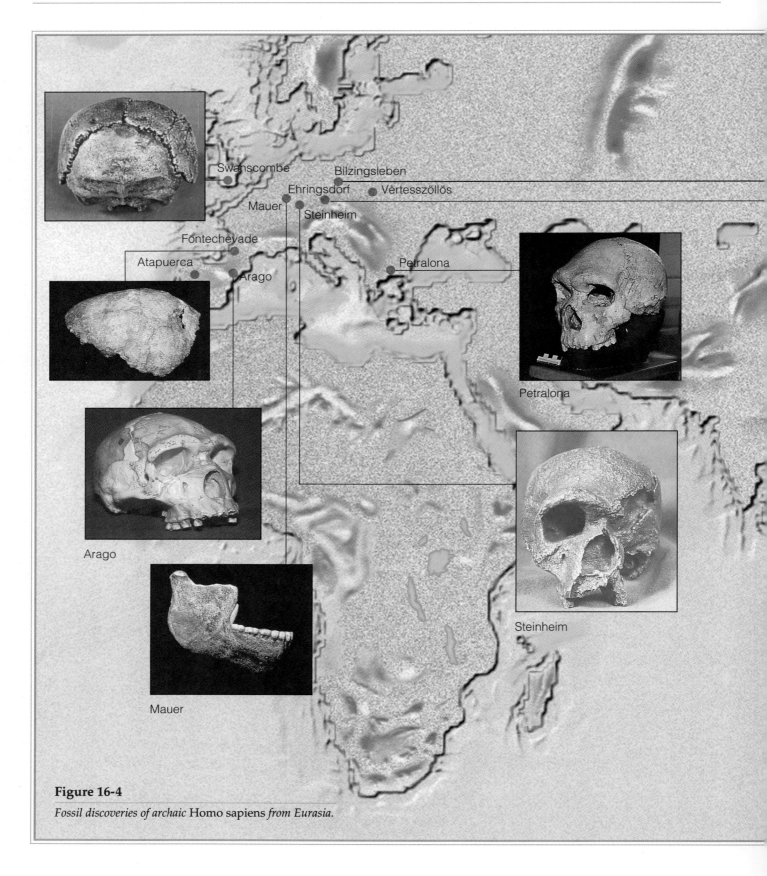

Figure 16-4

Fossil discoveries of archaic Homo sapiens *from Eurasia.*

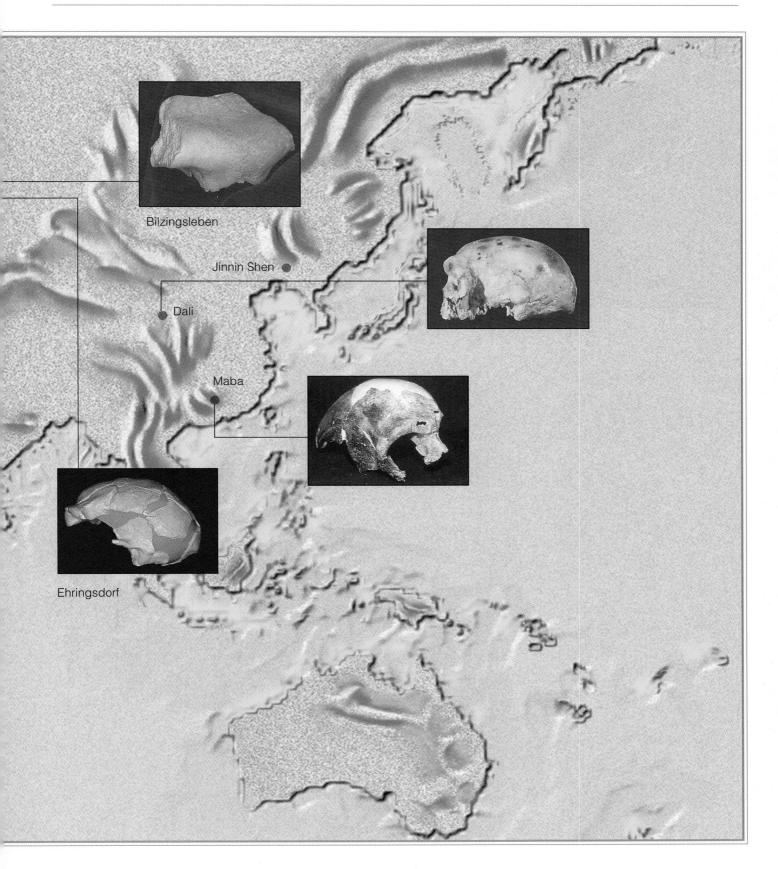

Bilzingsleben

Jinnin Shen

Dali

Maba

Ehringsdorf

Figure 16-5

(a) Bodo. An early archaic sapiens *from Africa. The cranium shows cutmarks around the orbit. (Courtesy of Tim White)*

ated with several hippopotamus skeletons, and cutmarks are found on the human skull (Conroy et al., 1978).

White (1986) examined the skull and counted 17 cutmark areas. These are located in the interorbital area, on the supraorbital torus, cheek bones, and on the posterior parietals. White believes this argues "for a patterned intentional defleshing of this specimen by a hominid(s) with stone tool(s)" (White, 1986, p. 508). That is to say, Bodo was scalped, and this is the earliest solid evidence for deliberate defleshing.

Three other crania plus four more from Elandsfontein (Saldanha), Florisbad from South Africa, Laetoli near Olduvai Gorge, and Eliye Springs from West Turkana also show a combination of *erectus* and *sapiens* characteristics (p. 434), and they are all mentioned in the literature as being similar to Broken Hill. These similarities may signify a close phylogenetic relationship of hominids from East and South Africa. It is also possible that several populations were evolving in a somewhat similar way from *H. erectus* to a more *sapiens*-looking morphology.

We should point out that the evolutionary path of these hominids did not take a Neandertal turn. It seems there were no Neandertals in Africa. Nor were there any in the Far East.

ASIA

China   Like their counterparts in Europe and Africa, Chinese archaic *sapiens** also display both older and later characteristics. Chinese paleoanthropologists believe that archaic *sapiens* traits, such as sagittal keeling, flattened nasal bones, and others, are shared with *H. erectus*, especially those from Zhoukoudian. They also point out that some of these features can be found in modern *H. sapiens* in China today, indicating substantial phylogenetic continuity. That is to say, Chinese researchers suggest anatomically modern Chinese evolved separately from *H. sapiens* in Europe or Africa.

That such regional evolution occurred in many areas of the world or, alternatively, that anatomically modern migrants from Africa displaced local populations is the subject of a major ongoing debate in paleoanthropology. This important controversy will be discussed in Chapter 17.

Dali, the most complete skull of the late Middle or early Upper Pleistocene fossils in China, displays *erectus* and *sapiens* traits and is clearly classified as early *H. sapiens* despite its relatively small cranial capacity of 1,120 cm³. Changyang fragments, Ixujiayao material, and a partial skull from Maba also reflect both earlier and later traits and are placed in the same category as Dali. In addition, the recent (1984) discovery of a partial skeleton from Jinnin Shen in northeast China has been given a provisional date of 250,000 y.a. (Pope, 1992). The cranial capacity is surprisingly large (approximately 1,300 cm³) and the walls of the braincase are thin—both modern features and quite unexpected in an individual this ancient (if the dating estimate does indeed hold up).

According to present dating estimates, early *H. sapiens* lived in China from about 260 to 100 thousand years ago. Studies of the specimens continue, including the dating, which ranges from Middle Pleistocene to early Upper Pleistocene. The evolutionary sequence will be clearer when the fossil dates

---

*Chinese anthropologists prefer the term "early *Homo sapiens*" instead of archaic *H. sapiens*.

are more secure. Nevertheless, what we observed in Africa, the apparent evolution from *H. erectus* to archaic *H. sapiens*, with a mosaic of *erectus* and *sapiens* traits, was also the case in China.

India   In 1982, a partial adult skull was discovered in the Narmada Valley, central India. Associated with this fossil were Acheulian hand-axes, cleavers, flakes, and choppers. This Narmada specimen has been dated as Middle Pleistocene with a probable cranial capacity within the range of 1,155 to 1,421 cm^3. K. A. R. Kennedy (1991), who made a recent study of the fossil, believes Narmada should be viewed as an early example of *H. sapiens*.

EUROPE

Various attempts have been made to organize European archaic *H. sapiens* of the Middle and early Upper Pleistocene in the time range of 250,000 to 105,000 years ago. Because in many cases definite dates or adequate remains (or both) are lacking, it is difficult to be certain which fossils belong where in the evolutionary sequence. *H. erectus* may once have roamed the fields of Europe, but there are no fossils that unequivocally prove it. As we noted, what we find in Europe are fossils, such as those in Africa and China, whose features resemble both *erectus* and *sapiens*. Among some of these earliest archaic *sapiens* from Europe, there are features resembling those of Neandertals, which leads to the possibility that some of these forms were the ancestors of Neandertals.

It may be possible to divide the fossils of the Middle Pleistocene into two groups (see Table 16-1): an older one that tends to be morphologically closer to *H. erectus*; and a later group that shares derived features with Neandertals. However, the morphological differences between the two groups are not always clear-cut.

Earlier archaic *sapiens*' resemblance to *H. erectus* may be seen in the robusticity of the mandible, lack of a chin, thick cranial bones, thick occipital bone, pronounced occipital torus, heavy supraorbital torus, receding frontal bone, marked alveolar prognathism, greatest parietal breadth near base of skull, and large teeth. (They, of course, have one or more *sapiens* characteristics.) Examples of these early archaic forms from Europe include fossils from Steinheim, Swanscombe, and Vértesszöllös (see Table 16-1). Later archaic representatives also possess some *erectus* characteristics, but they also have one or more of the following traits: larger cranial capacity, occipital bun or indications of one, more rounded occipital, nonprojecting middle facial region, parietal expansion, and reduced tooth size.

The later group, essentially from the latter half of the Middle Pleistocene, overlaps to some extent with the older group. From an evolutionary point of view, this later group may have evolved from the earlier one and, displaying traits unique to Neandertals, may in turn, have given rise to the Neandertals. Examples of this somewhat later European transitional group include specimens from Fontechevade (France) and Ehringsdorf (Germany), as well as recent discoveries from Atapuerca, northern Spain. This last site, dated to approximately 300,000 y.a., has yielded the largest sample yet of archaic *Homo sapiens* and includes the remains of at least 24 individuals (among which are several excellently preserved crania) (Arsuaga et al., 1993). Excavations continue at this remarkable site, where bones have somehow accumulated within a deep chamber inside a cave. Provisional descriptions only

Table 16-1   Archaic *sapiens* in Europe*

Name	Site	Date	Human Remains	Associated Finds	Cranial Capacity cm³	Comment
Bilzingsleben	Quarry at Bilzingsleben, near Erfurt, Germany	425–200 k.y.a.†; probably 280 k.y.a.	Skull fragments and teeth	Flake industry, flora and fauna	Insufficient material	Resembles *H. erectus* in some features
La Chaise	Caves of Bourgeois-DeLauny, near La Chaise, Charente, western France	200–150 k.y.a.	Cranial fragments, fragmentary post-cranial bones, teeth	—	Insufficient material	Mandible resembles Neandertal
Petralona	Cave near Petralona, Khalkidhiki, north-eastern Greece	Date uncertain; ?300–200 k.y.a.	Nearly complete skull	No artifacts or faunal remains found with skull	1,190–1,220	Mosaic; some bones resemble Neandertal, Broken Hill, and *H. erectus*
Steinheim	Gravel pit at Steinheim, Germany	Mindel-Riss Interglacial—300–250 k.y.a.; date uncertain	Nearly complete skull, lacking mandible	No artifacts, fauna	1,100	Pronounced supraorbital torus, frontal low, occipital rounded; foramen magnum cut out to remove brain
Swanscombe	Swanscombe, Kent, England	Mindel-Riss Interglacial—300–250 k.y.a.; date uncertain	Occipital and parietals	Middle Acheulian artifacts, animal bones	1,325 (estimate)	Bones thick like *H. erectus*; occipital resembles Neandertal
Vértesszöllös	Near village of Vértesszöllös, 30 miles west of Budapest, Hungary	210–160 k.y.a.; date uncertain	Adult occipital bone, fragments of infant teeth	Flake and pebble tools, animal bones	1,115–1,434 (estimate)	Occipital thick (*H. erectus* trait), but size and angulation suggests *sapiens*

*Non-Neandertal specimens
†k.y.a. stands for "thousand years ago."

have thus far been completed, but the morphology has been interpreted as showing several indications of an early Neandertal-like pattern (arching browridges, projecting midface, and other features).

Middle Pleistocene Evolution

Like the *erectus*/*sapiens* mix in Africa and China, the fossils from Europe exhibit this mosaic of traits from both species. However, it is important to note that the fossils from each continent differ; that is, the mosaic Chinese forms are not the same as those from Africa or Europe. Some European fossils, assumed to be earlier, are more robust and possess more *erectus* than *sapiens* features. The later Middle Pleistocene European fossils appear to be more Neandertal-like, but the uncertainty of dates prevents a clear scenario of the Middle Pleistocene evolutionary sequence.

Table 16-2 A Partial List of Archaic *sapiens*

Name	Site	Date	Human Remains	Associated Finds	Cranial Capacity cm³	Comment
AFRICA						
Bodo	Awash River Valley, Ethiopia	Middle Pleistocene	Incomplete skull, part of braincase	Acheulian artifacts, animal bones	Insufficient remains for measurement	Resembles Broken Hill; first evidence of scalping
Broken Hill (Kabwe)	Cave deposits near Kabwe, Zambia	Late middle Pleistocene; 130 k.y.a.* or older	Nearly complete cranium, cranial fragments of second individual, miscellaneous postcranial bones	Animal bones and artifacts in cave, but relationship to human remains unknown	1,280	Massive brow-ridge, low vault, prominent occipital torus; cranial capacity within range of modern *sapiens*
CHINA						
Dali	Near Jiefang village, Shaanxi Province, north China	Late middle Pleistocene (230–110 k.y.a.)	Nearly complete skull	Flake tools, animal bones	1,120–1,200	Robust supra-orbital ridge, low vault, retreating forehead, canine fossa
Maba	Cave near Maba village, Guangdong Province, south China	Early Upper Pleistocene (140–120 k.y.a.)	Incomplete skull of middle-aged male	Animal bones	Insufficient remains for measurement	Receding forehead, modest keel on frontal bone
EUROPE						
Arago (Tautavel)	Cave site near Tautavel, Verdouble Valley, Pyrenees, southeastern France	500–400 k.y.a.	Face; parietal perhaps from same person; many cranial fragments	Upper Acheulian (or Tayacian) artifacts, animal bones	1,150	Thick supra-orbital torus, pronounced alveolar prognathism; parietal resembles Swanscombe

*k.y.a. stands for "thousand years ago."

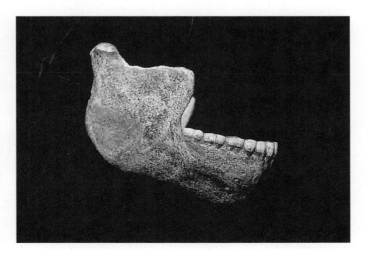

Figure 16-6

Cast of Mauer mandible; note the wide ascending ramus.

The physical differences from *H. erectus* are not extraordinary. Bones remain thick, the supraorbital torus continues to be prominent, and vault height shows little increase. There is, however, a definite increase in brain size and a change in the shape of the skull from pentagonal to globular as seen in a rear view. There is also a trend, especially with the later Middle Pleistocene forms, toward less occipital angulation. It is interesting to note that in Europe the changes move toward a Neandertal *sapiens* pattern, but in Africa and Asia, toward modern *sapiens*.

The lack of classic *H. erectus* remains in Europe is also interesting. There has been more digging and searching for fossils in Europe than anywhere in the world. If the bones were there, it seems plausible that some would have been found by now.

Middle Pleistocene Culture

The Acheulian technology of *H. erectus* persevered in the Middle Pleistocene with relatively little change until near the end of the period, when it became slightly more sophisticated. The hand-axe, absent in China in the Lower Pleistocene, remains absent in the Middle Pleistocene, and choppers and chopping tools continue to be the basic tools. Bone, a very useful tool material, went practically unused by archaic *sapiens*. Flake stone tools similar to those of the earlier era persisted, perhaps in greater variety. Archaic *sapiens* in Africa and Europe invented a method—the Levallois technique—for predetermining flake size and shape (Klein, 1989). This was no mean feat and suggests increased cognitive abilities in late archaic *sapiens* compared to earlier archaic forms.

Archaic *sapiens* continued to live both in caves and open-air sites, but may have increased their use of caves. Did archaic *H. sapiens* control fire? Klein (1989, p. 255) suggests they did. He writes that there was a "concentration of burnt bones in depressions 50–60 cm across at Vértesszöllös . . ." and "fossil hearths have also been identified at Bilzingsleben and in several French caves

Figure 16-7

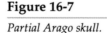

Partial Arago skull.

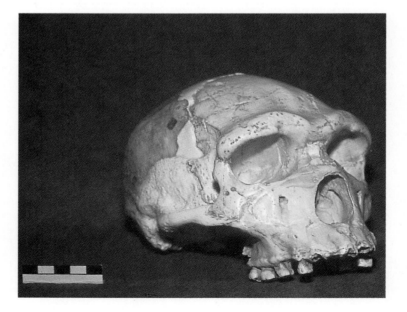

Box 16-2   Arago

Fieldwork at Arago Cave near the village of Tautavel (close to the Spanish border in southeastern France) began in 1964 under the supervision of the husband and wife team, Henry and Marie-Antoinette de Lumley (de Lumley and de Lumley, 1973). A second glaciation (Mindel) date has been suggested, perhaps 400 m.y.a.

In their excavation of the site, the de Lumleys discovered more than 20 occupation levels, each separated by 2 to 7 feet of sterile sand. More than 100,000 Acheulian artifacts have been recovered from the site. Over 50 cranial and postcranial remains of at least 4 adults and 3 children have been recovered. A partial cranium, mostly face and frontal bone, is apparently that of a young male. Like other archaic fossils, Arago displays a mosaic of *erectus* and archaic *sapiens* characters.

that were probably occupied by early *H. sapiens*. . . ." Chinese archeologists insist that many Middle Pleistocene sites in China contain evidence of human-controlled fire. However, not everyone is convinced (see p. 406).

That archaic *sapiens* built temporary structures is revealed by collections of bones, stones, and artifacts at several sites. Here, they manufactured artifacts and exploited the area for food. The stones may have been used to support the sides of a shelter.

In the Lazaret Cave in the city of Nice, southern France, a shelter about 36 feet by 11 feet was built against the cave wall, and skins were probably hung over a framework of poles as walls for the shelter. The base was supported by rocks and large bones, and inside the shelter were two hearths. The hearth charcoal suggests the hominid occupants used slow-burning oak and boxwood, which produced easy to rekindle embers. Very little stone waste was found inside the shelter, suggesting they manufactured tools outside, perhaps because there was more light.

Figure 16-8

Swanscombe, England. Note the depression (suprainiac fossa) in the center of the occiput, above the nuchal torus. This is considered to be a Neandertal trait.

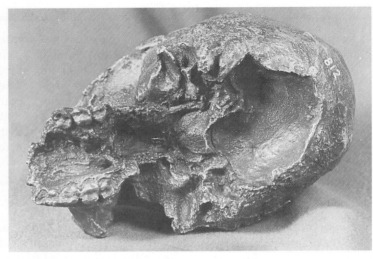

(a)

(b)

Figure 16-9

Cast of Steinheim skull. (a) Frontal view showing warped skull. (b) Basal view, showing how the foramen magnum was enlarged, apparently for removal of the brain—for dietary or ritualistic purposes.

Archeological evidence clearly alludes to the utilization of many different food sources, such as fruits, vegetables, seeds, nuts, bird eggs, and so forth, each in its own season. Marine life was also exploited. From Lazaret and Orgnac (southern France) comes evidence of freshwater fishing for trout, perch, and carp. The most detailed reconstruction of Middle Pleistocene life in Europe comes from evidence at Terra Amata, on the southern coast of France (Villa, 1983; de Lumley and de Lumley, 1973). From this site has come fascinating evidence relating to short-term, seasonal visits by archaic *H. sapiens* who built flimsy shelters, gathered plants, exploited marine resources, and hunted medium-sized and large mammals.

The long period of transitional hominids in Europe, as documented by the fossil and archeological finds discussed above, was to continue well into the Upper Pleistocene (after 125,000 y.a.). However, the evolution of archaic *H. sapiens* was to take a unique turn, with the appearance and expansion of the Neandertals.

Neandertals (130,000–35,000 y.a.)
Late Archaic *Sapiens*

Despite their apparent disappearance about 35,000 y.a., Neandertals continue to haunt the best laid theories of paleoanthropologists. They fit into the general scheme of human evolution, and yet they are misfits. Classified as *H. sapiens*, they are like us and yet different. It is not an easy task to put them in their place.*

Homo sapiens neanderthalensis is the subspecific designation for Neandertals, although not all paleoanthropologists agree with this terminology. The subspecies for anatomically modern *sapiens* is designated as *Homo sapiens sapiens*. *Thal*, meaning valley, is the old spelling and is kept in the species designation. The modern spelling is *tal*, and is now pronounced and spelled this way in Germany; we shall adhere to contemporary usage in the text with the spelling *Neandertal*.

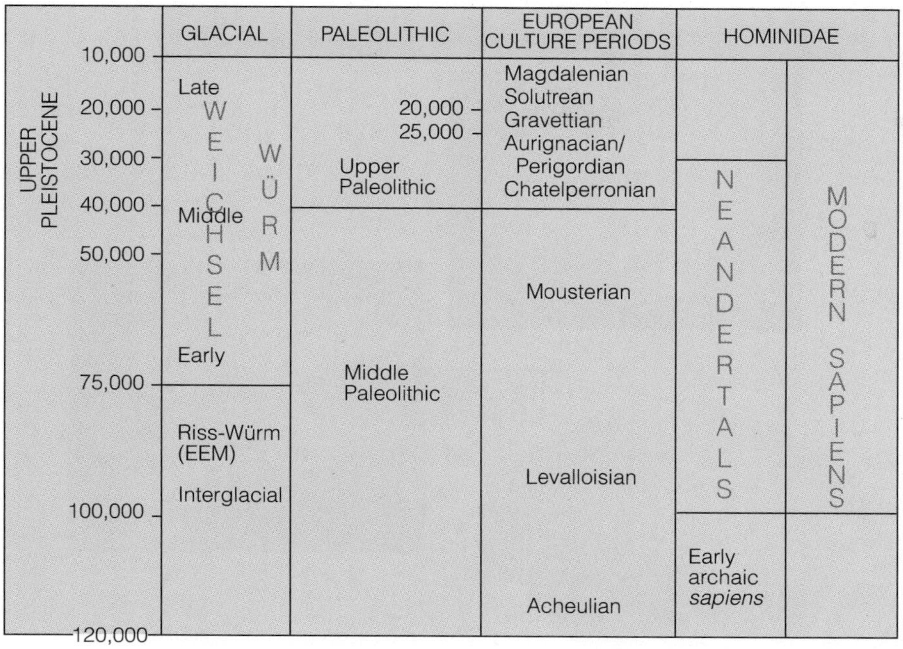

	GLACIAL	PALEOLITHIC	EUROPEAN CULTURE PERIODS	HOMINIDAE	
UPPER PLEISTOCENE 10,000 20,000 30,000 40,000 50,000 75,000 100,000 120,000	Late W E I C H S E L Early Riss-Würm (EEM) Interglacial W Ü R M	20,000 25,000 Upper Paleolithic Middle Paleolithic	Magdalenian Solutrean Gravettian Aurignacian/ Perigordian Chatelperronian Mousterian Levalloisian Acheulian	N E A N D E R T A L S Early archaic *sapiens*	M O D E R N S A P I E N S

Figure 16-10

Upper Pleistocene. Correlation approximations. The culture periods of the Upper Paleolithic are not necessarily sequential as shown. This figure is simply meant to assist the student in organizing Upper Pleistocene data.

In the following discussion of Neandertals, we refer to those who lived especially during the last glaciation, which began about 75,000 y.a. and ended about 10,000 y.a. The majority of fossils have been found in Europe where they have been most studied. Our description of Neandertal, therefore, is based primarily on those specimens from western Europe, who are usually called *classic* Neandertals or late archaic *H. sapiens*. Not all Neandertals—including others from eastern Europe, western Asia, and those from the interglacial that preceded the last glacial—entirely conform to our description of the classic morphology. They tend to be less robust, perhaps because the climate in which they lived was not as cold as western Europe during the last glaciation.

These troublesome hunters (classic Neandertals) are the cave man of cartoonists, walking about with bent knees, dragging a club in one hand and a woman by her hair in the other. They are described as brutish, apelike, and obviously stupid. This image is more than somewhat exaggerated.

While cartoonist's license is not to be denied, the fact remains that Neandertals walked as upright as any of us, and, if they dragged clubs and women, there is not the slightest evidence of it. Nor are they particularly apelike and, in the light of twentieth-century human behavior, we should be careful of whom we call brutish.

As far as intelligence is concerned, Neandertals produced excellent **Mousterian** implements and, in fact, invented a new tool-making technique, the disc-core technique (Campbell, 1976). Neandertals were also clever enough to cope with the severely cold weather of the last glacial period. In addition to open sites, they lived in caves. They wore clothing, built fires, gathered in settlements (some of which extended right up to the Arctic Ocean), hafted* some of their tools, and hunted skillfully. It has also been suggested that Neandertals, especially in western Europe, also were producing artwork and making symbolic images (Marshak, 1989).

Mousterian   The stone tool industry found widespread in Europe and southwest Asia during the Upper Pleistocene. Associated with both Neandertals and modern *sapiens*.

---

*Attaching a handle to a blade.

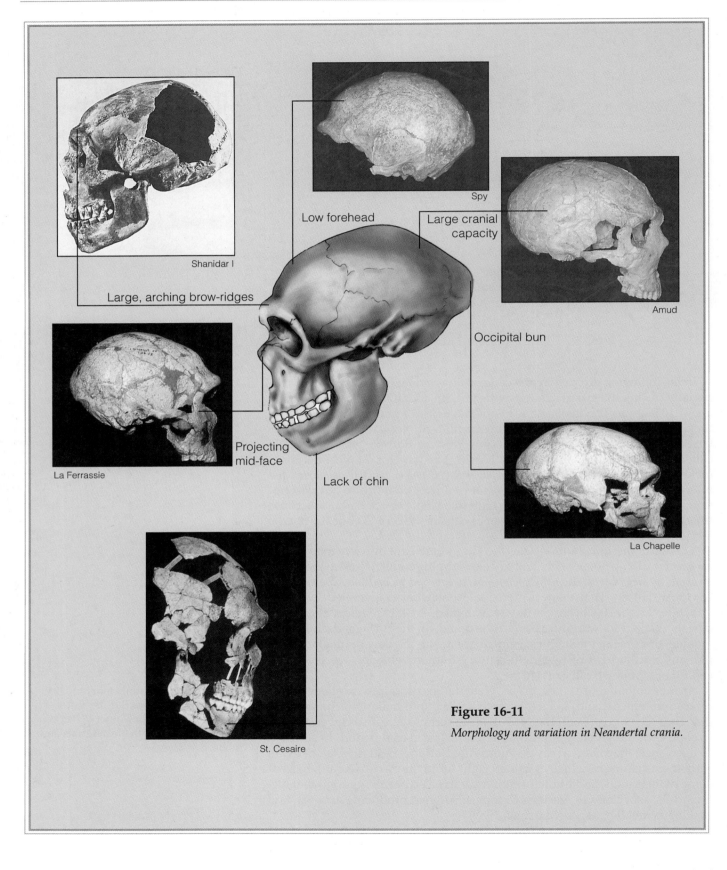

Figure 16-11

Morphology and variation in Neandertal crania.

Neandertals were the first hominids to intentionally bury their dead. Burial of the dead is significant in that it represents special treatment of deceased individuals. In some instances, bodies were found in a tightly flexed position, resembling modern burial practices in many contemporary societies. Several Neandertal burials are associated with various grave goods, including stone tools and animal bones. For example, at Shanidar Cave in Iraq (see p. 455), pollen samples taken from one burial suggest that flowers were placed in the grave of a Neandertal male.

While various interpretations of Neandertal burial practices have been advanced, most scholars see these behaviors as indicative of ritual practices. Ritual treatment of the dead implies, at the very least, a concern and respect for the dead not evidenced by earlier archaic *H. sapiens*. Moreover, some form of belief in an afterlife may be indicated. These behaviors further substantiate the view that Neandertal intellectual abilities and capacity for abstract thought were very similar to our own.

NEANDERTAL MORPHOLOGY

Another feature that argues against the intellectual inferiority of Neandertals is brain size, which in Neandertals actually was larger than that of *H. sapiens* today. The average for contemporary *sapiens* centers around 1,400 cm³ and for Neandertals, 1,520 cm³. The larger size may be associated with the metabolic efficiency of a larger brain in cold weather. The Inuit (Eskimo) brain also averages larger (about that of Neandertals) than other modern world populations.

The classic Neandertal cranium is large, long, low, and bulging at the sides. Viewed from the side, the posterior portion off the occipital bone is somewhat bun shaped, but the marked occipital angle typical of many *H. erectus* crania is absent. The forehead rises more vertically than that of *H. erectus*, and the browridges arch over the orbits instead of forming a straight bar.

Compared to anatomically modern humans, the Neandertal face stands out. It projects, almost as if it were pulled forward. This feature can be seen when the distance of the nose and teeth from the orbits is compared with that of modern *sapiens*. (It would appear that Neandertals were blessed with an extraordinarily large nose which, in the flesh, must have been a monumental sight.)

Postcranially, Neandertals were very robust, barrel-chested, and powerfully muscled. This robust skeletal structure, in fact, dominates hominid evolution from *H. erectus* through archaic *H. sapiens*. We have thus far stressed the differences between Neandertals and anatomically modern humans, but aside from their muscularity, cranial shape, and face, there was not a great deal of difference between "them" and "us."

NEANDERTAL QUERIES

With the onset of the Riss-Würm (Eem) interglacial, about 125,000 y.a., we encounter the complex situation of the Neandertals. For about 100,000 years, Neandertals lived in Europe and western Asia, and their coming and going has raised more questions and controversies than perhaps any other hominid group.

We have traced Neandertal forebears back to the later archaic *H. sapiens*. But these were transitional forms, and it is not until the last interglacial that Neandertals appear. Actually, few Neandertal fossils have been found from

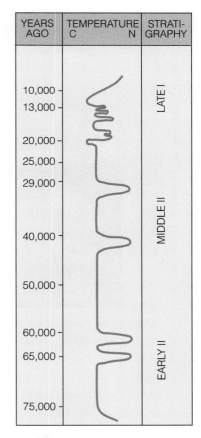

Figure 16-12

The Würm glaciation. During a glacial period, such as the Würm, the temperature—and the presence of ice—varies. The 65,000 years of the Würm were not simply one long cold period.

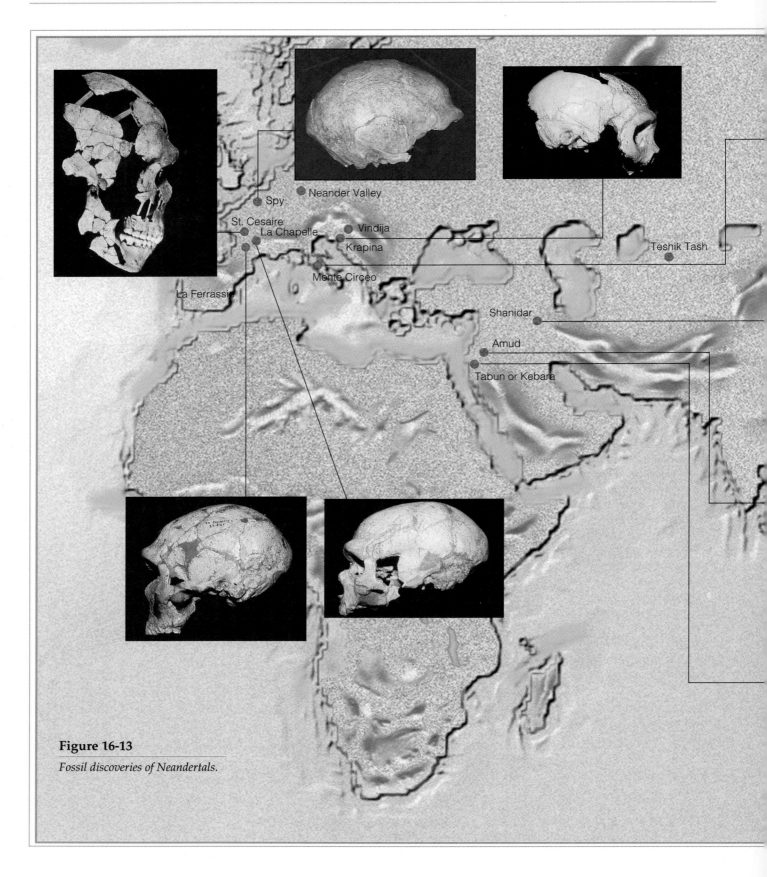

Figure 16-13

Fossil discoveries of Neandertals.

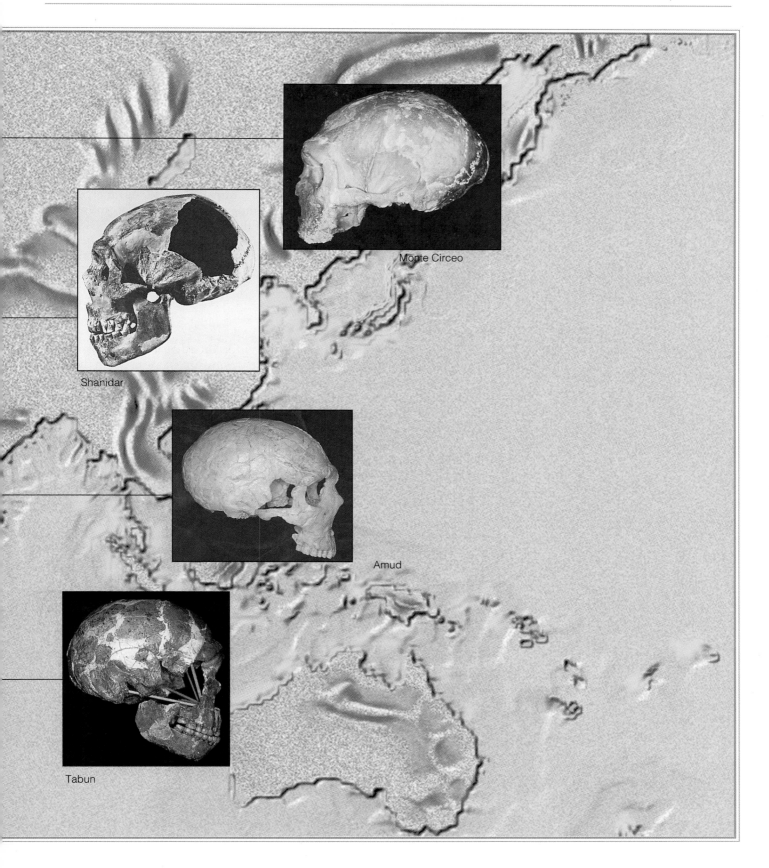

Monte Circeo

Shanidar

Amud

Tabun

this interglacial. It is most especially the Würm glacial that is considered the classic Neandertal period.

There are several basic questions to bear in mind as we examine Neandertal evolution more closely. Did the anatomically modern humans of Europe who succeeded the Neandertals evolve from them? Professor Fred Smith, a specialist in central European hominid evolution, argues that such a continuous evolutionary process is evident in this region; "morphological continuity between Neandertals and the [early modern humans] is clearly documented by the available information" (1984, p. 192).

Perhaps the most intriguing questions remain unanswered, and may be unanswerable: Whatever happened to the Neandertals? Did they merge with some of their anatomically modern contemporaries? Did they become extinct because they could not compete successfully with their neighbors? Did they fade into extinction because of limited speech capability? Did they become extinct for some other reason? In considering these and other questions, we shall start at the beginning.

Neandertal Beginnings

Neandertal takes its name from the Neander Valley near Düsseldorf, Germany (see Box 16-1). In 1856, workmen quarrying limestone caves in the valley came across some fossilized bones. The owner of the quarry believed them to be bear and gave them to a natural science teacher who realized they were not the remains of a cave bear, but rather, of an ancient human. Exactly what the bones represented became a *cause célèbre* for many years, and the fate of "Neandertal Man," as the bones were named, hung in the balance until later finds provided more evidence.

What swung the balance in favor of accepting the Neander Valley specimen as a genuine hominid fossil were other nineteenth-century finds similar to it. What is more important, the additional fossil remains brought home the realization that a form of human different from nineteenth-century Europeans had in fact once existed.

Some of these nineteenth-century finds include a skull, which no one understood, found at Gibraltar in 1848. A decade later the Neander Valley find placed the Gibraltar skull in a more accurate perspective as an early human, a Neandertal.

It was a new Belgian find in 1886 in a cave at Spy (pronounced *Spee*), in Belgium, which provided more confirmation. Two almost complete skeletons, associated with Mousterian tools, were excavated. The Spy skeletons convinced most European scientists that Neandertal was real, that its antiquity was very old, and that it was a human form that existed before the present population.

> It showed without doubt that the remains were "eminently Neandertaloid" and unquestionably old. The excellent documentation of the context in which the remains had been found silenced all argument about antiquity (Trinkaus and Shipman, 1992, p. 128).

Nevertheless, the evolution controversy continued to rage. Not even all scientists were persuaded that evolution was a valid concept, and there remained scientists who were still skeptical of the existence of hominid fossils. (See Chapter 4 for a discussion of the history of evolutionary thought.) Cuvier's dictum, "L'homme fossile n'existe pas" (free translation: there is no such thing as fossil man), was still accepted by many Europeans. The discovery of the La Chapelle-aux-Saints skeleton (discussed below) settled the issue of the existence of fossil hominids once and for all.

LA CHAPELLE-AUX-SAINTS

One of the most important Neandertal discoveries was made in 1908 at La Chapelle-aux-Saints, near Correze in southwestern France. A nearly complete skeleton was found in a Mousterian cultural layer by three French priests who were already known for their archeological research. The body had been buried in a shallow grave and fixed in a flexed position, with several fragments of nonhuman long bones placed over the head and over them, a bison leg. Around the body were flint tools and broken animal bones.

The skeleton was turned over for study to a well-known French paleontologist, Marcellin Boule, who published his analysis in three copious volumes. (It was his exhaustive publication that set the tone for the detailed description of prehistoric humans that survives to this day.) Boule depicted the La Chapelle Neandertal as a brutish, bent-kneed, not fully erect biped. As a result of this exaggerated interpretation, some scholars, and certainly the general public, concluded that all Neandertals were highly primitive apelike creatures.

Why did Boule draw these conclusions from the La Chapelle skeleton? Apparently, he misconstrued the erectness of the spine due to the presence of osteoarthritis in this older male. In addition, and probably more importantly, Boule and his contemporaries found it difficult to accept fully as a human ancestor, an individual who appeared to depart, however slightly, from the modern pattern. "With the over-emphasis of the nonmodern features of the La Chapelle-aux-Saints skeleton, it became a much less likely candidate for the forefather of the succeeding Upper Paleolithic forms" (Brace, 1977, p. 219).

The skull of this male, who was at least 40 years of age when he died, is very large, with a cranial capacity of 1,620 cm^3. As is typical for western European "classic" forms, the vault is low and long, the supraorbital ridges are immense, with the typical Neandertal arched shape, and the forehead is low and retreating. Prognathism in the alveolar area is pronounced, and the face is long and projecting. At the rear of the skull, the occiput is protuberant and bun-shaped. (See Fig. 16-14.)

La Chapelle is not a typical Neandertal, but an unusually robust male and "evidently represents an extreme in the Neandertal range of variation" (Brace et al., 1979, p. 117). Unfortunately, this skeleton, which Boule claimed did not even walk completely erect was widely accepted as "Mr. Neandertal." But not all Neandertals express the suite of "classic Neandertal" traits to the degree seen in La Chapelle.

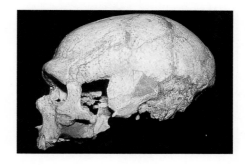

Figure 16-14

La Chapelle-aux-Saints. Note the occiputal bun, facial and alveolar prognathism, and low vault.

Neandertals and Modern *Homo sapiens*

The most recent of the western European Neandertals comes from St. Cesaire, southwestern France, dated at about 35,000 y.a. The bones were recovered from a bed of discarded chipped blades, hand-axes, and other stone tools of a type called *Chatelperronian*, a tool industry of the Upper Paleolithic that is also associated with Neandertals. This site is fascinating for several reasons. Anatomically modern humans were living in western Europe by about 35,000 y.a. or a bit earlier. Therefore, it is possible that Neandertals and

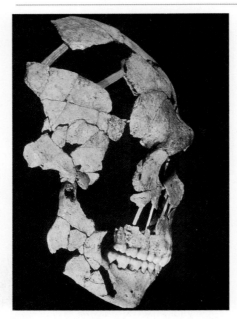

Figure 16-15

St. Cesaire, the "last" Neandertal.

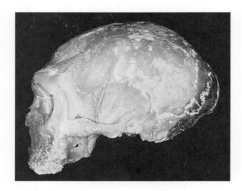

Figure 16-16

Monte Circeo, a more typical Neandertal. Supraorbital torus illustrates Neandertal traits but the occipital area is more modern.

modern *sapiens* were living in close proximity for several thousand years. How did these two groups interact?

Evidence from a number of French sites (Harrold, 1989) indicates that Neandertals borrowed technological methods and tools (such as blades) from the anatomically modern populations and thereby modified their own Mousterian tools, creating a new industry, the Chatelperronian.

However, the *concept* of diffusion does not tell us the *how* of the diffusion process. Did the Neandertals trade, steal, or fight for what they acquired? Did the modern *sapiens* peacefully teach their technology to their neighbors? Did the two groups interbreed? Did the Neandertals become assimilated into the modern population? It would also be interesting to know more precisely how long the coexistence of Neandertal and modern *sapiens* lasted.* No one knows the answers to these questions, but it has been suggested that an average annual difference of 2 percent mortality between the two populations (that is, modern *sapiens* lived longer than Neandertals) would have resulted in the extinction of the Neandertals in approximately one thousand years (Zubrow, 1989).

It should be noted that not all paleoanthropologists agree with the notion of the coexistence of Neandertals and Upper Paleolithic modern humans. For example, in a recent paper, Professor David Frayer, University of Kansas, states: ". . . there is still *no human fossil evidence* which supports the coexistence of Neanderthal and Upper Paleolithic forms in Europe. . . ." (emphasis added) (1992, p. 9).

There are quite a few other western European classic Neandertals and significant finds in central Europe. At Krapina, Croatia, there is an abundance of bones—almost a thousand fragments—adding up to 70 individuals and a thousand stone tools or flakes (Trinkaus and Shipman, 1992). Krapina is an old site, dating back to the early Würm, about 70,000 y.a., and the characteristic Neandertal features of these specimens (although less robust) are very similar to the western European finds. Krapina is also important as a burial site, one of the oldest ones on record.

Another interesting site in central Europe is Vindija, about 30 miles from Krapina. The site is an excellent source of faunal, cultural, and hominid materials stratified in *sequence* throughout much of the Upper Pleistocene. Neandertal fossils were found in level G, consisting of some 35 specimens, tentatively dated at about 42,000 y.a. Even though some of their features approach the morphology of early south-central European modern *sapiens*, the overall pattern is definitely Neandertal. However, these modified Neandertal features, such as smaller browridges and slight chin development, may also be seen as an evolutionary trend toward modern *H. sapiens*.

Professor Fred Smith, at Northern Illinois University, takes the view that variation in Vindija G skull features points to a trend continuing on to the later anatomically modern specimens found in the upper levels of the cave. Does Vindija support the proposition that the origin of *H. sapiens* could have occurred here in central Europe? As we have already mentioned, Smith does not insist upon this interpretation and suggests anatomically modern *sapiens* could have come from elsewhere. But he does believe there is morphological and genetic continuity between the lower and upper levels of the cave.

---

*For a fictionalized account of the confrontation of Neandertals and anatomically modern humans, read Nobel Prize winner William Golding's excellent novel, *The Inheritors*. Several movies have also been made on this theme. Another novel on the subject is Jean M. Auel's *Clan of the Cave Bear*.

WESTERN ASIA

Israel In addition to European Neandertals, there are numerous important discoveries from southwest Asia. Several specimens from Israel display modern features and are less robust than the classic Neandertals of Europe; but again the overall pattern is Neandertal. The best known of these specimens is Tabun (Mugharet-et-Tabun, "Cave of the Oven") at Mt. Carmel, a short drive south from Haifa. Tabun, excavated in the early 1930s, yielded a female skeleton, recently dated by thermoluminescence (TL) at about 90,000 y.a. If this dating proves accurate, it places the Tabun find as clearly contemporary with early modern *sapiens* found in nearby caves. Another Israeli Neandertal was found at Amud in 1961 not far from Lake Kinneret (Lake Tiberias). The Amud specimen resembles classic Neandertals, the cranial capacity is 1,740 cm³, much larger than the average for anatomically modern humans.

A more recent Neandertal burial, discovered in 1983, comes from Kebara, a neighbor of Tabun at Mt. Carmel. The male skeleton is incomplete—the cranium and much of the lower limbs are missing. However, the pelvis, dated at 60,000 y.a., is the most complete Neandertal pelvis so far recovered. This pelvis provides clear evidence that nullifies the prior hypothesis that the Neandertal pelvis differed significantly from the modern form in such a way that gestation took perhaps twelve months instead of the nine required for anatomically modern humans. Also recovered at Kebara was a hyoid bone, the first from a Neandertal, and this find is especially important from the point of view of establishing language capabilities (see Issue, this chapter).

It may seem strange to bury a person minus his head, but it is possible this was a secondary burial. Many societies have had such a ritual, even in recent times, in which the body is removed from the grave, probably washed or defleshed, and then reinterred. If this were so at Kebara, it raises the probability of Neandertal ritual, a notion that remains unsettled.

Iraq A most remarkable site is Shanidar, in the Zagros Mountains of northeastern Iraq, where partial skeletons of 9 individuals—males and females (7 adults and 2 infants)—were found, 4 of them deliberately buried. These are quite typically Neandertal, although the occipital torus is weak, the occiput is quite well rounded, and an incipient chin is present on at least one of the mandibles. Several skulls look deformed, as if their foreheads had been bound when the individuals were children (Trinkaus, 1984b). Such cranial deformation is known from several areas of the world in very recent times.

One of the more interesting individuals is Shanidar 1, a male who lived to be somewhere between 30 and 45 years old, a considerable age for a prehistoric human. His stature is estimated at 5 feet, 7 inches, with a cranial capacity of 1,600 cm³, quite a bit higher than the modern European mean of 1,415 cm³. This individual shows several fascinating features:

> There had been a crushing blow to the left side of the head, fracturing the eye socket, displacing the left eye, and probably causing blindness on that side. He also sustained a massive blow to the right side of the body that so badly damaged the right arm that it became withered and useless; the bones of the shoulder blade, collar bone, and upper arm are much smaller and thinner than those on the left. The right lower arm and hand are missing, probably not because of poor preservation . . . but because they either atrophied and dropped off or because they were amputated (Trinkaus and Shipman, 1992, p. 340).

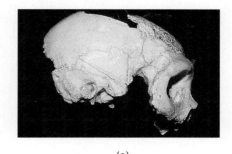

(a)

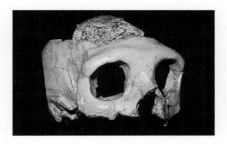

(b)

Figure 16-17

Krapina C. (a) Lateral view showing characteristic Neandertal traits. (b) Three-quarters view.

Figure 16-18

Excavation of the Tabun cave, Mt. Carmel, Israel.

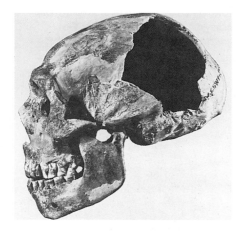

Figure 16-19

Shanidar 1. Does he represent Neandertal compassion for the handicapped?

In addition to these injuries, there was damage to the lower right leg (including a healed fracture of a foot bone). The right knee and left leg show signs of pathological involvement and these changes to the limbs and foot may have left this man with a limping gait.

How such a person could perform normal obligations and customs is difficult to imagine; however, both Dr. Ralph Solecki, who supervised the work at Shanidar Cave, and Erik Trinkaus, who has carefully studied the Shanidar remains, believe that in order to survive he must have been helped by others:

> . . . a one-armed, partially blind, crippled man could have made no pretense of hunting or gathering his own food. That he survived for years after his trauma was a testament to Neandertal compassion and humanity (Trinkaus and Shipman, 1992, p. 341).*

It is also suggested that since the injuries were serious and Shanidar 1 survived for years, the social system to which he belonged was organized, that cooperation and care of the sick and disabled were an important cultural value. Also, as we have already mentioned, intentional burial is evidence of a special attitude toward death and, perhaps, a belief in the supernatural and life after death.

Central Asia

Uzbekistan About 1,600 miles east of Shanidar in Uzbekistan, in a cave at Teshik-Tash, we find the easternmost Neandertal discovery. The skeleton is that of a 9-year-old boy who appears to have been deliberately buried. It was

---

*K. A. Dettwyler believes that Shanidar 1 could have survived without assistance, and that there is no solid evidence that compassion explains this individual's survival (1991).

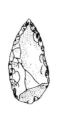

Convex side scraper   Point   Convergent scraper   Levallois flake

Figure 16-20

Mousterian tools (after Bordes).

reported that he was surrounded by five pairs of wild goat horns, suggesting a burial ritual or, perhaps, a religious cult, but this interpretation has also been seriously questioned. The Teshik-Tash individual, like other specimens discussed above from Croatia and southwest Asia, also shows a mixture of Neandertal traits (heavy browridges and occipital bun) and modern traits (high vault and definite signs of a chin).

The Teshik-Tash site represents the easternmost location presently established for Neandertals. Thus, based on current evidence, it is clear that the geographical distribution of the Neandertals extended from France eastward to central Asia, a distance of about 4,000 miles.

Culture of Neandertals

Neandertals, who lived in the culture period known as the Middle Paleolithic, are usually associated with the Mousterian industry (although the Mousterian industry is not always associated with Neandertals). In the early Würm, Mousterian culture extended from the Atlantic Ocean across Europe and North Africa into the former Soviet Union, Israel, Iran, and as far east as Uzbekistan and, perhaps, even to China.

Technology

Mousterian people specialized in the production of flake tools based on the Levallois method, a prepared core technique that originated perhaps as much as 200,000 y.a. In this manufacturing process, a chunk of flint was chipped all the way round and on top, producing a modified core resembling a turtle in form. Lastly, this core was flaked on the side to produce a tool ready for use (Fig. 16-20).

Neandertals improved on the Levallois technique by inventing a variation. They trimmed the flint nodule around the edges to form a disc-shaped core. Each time they struck the edge, they produced a flake, and continued so, until the core became too small and was discarded. Thus, the Neandertals were able to obtain more flakes per core than their predecessors. They then trimmed (retouched) the flakes into various forms, such as scrapers, points, knives, and so on.

Neandertal craftspeople elaborated and diversified traditional methods, and there is some indication of development in the specialization of tools used in skin and meat preparation, hunting, woodworking, and hafting. They may have made some use of new materials, such as antler and bone,

Nodule

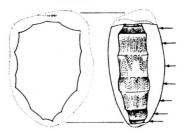

The nodule is chipped on the perimeter.

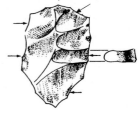

Flakes are radially removed from top surface.

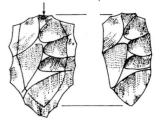

A final blow at one end removes a large flake.

Figure 16-21

The Levallois method.

Figure 16-22

Cutaway of Terra Amata hut. Note the hearth, the workspaces where people sat making tools, the poles that supported the roof, and the stones at the base of the hut supporting the sides. (Adapted from de Lumley, 1969.)

but their specialization and innovation cannot be compared to the succeeding period, the Upper Paleolithic. Nevertheless, Neandertals advanced their technology, which tended to be very similar in basic tool types, over considerable geographic distances, far beyond that of *H. erectus*. It is quite likely that their modifications in technology laid the basis for the remarkable changes of the Upper Paleolithic (discussed in Chapter 17).

Settlements

People of Mousterian culture lived in a variety of open sites, caves, and rock shelters. Living in the open on the cold tundra suggests the building of shelters, and there is some evidence of such structures (although the last glaciation must have destroyed many open sites). At the site of Moldova I, in the Ukraine (now an independent state and neighbor of Russia), archeologists found traces of an oval ring of mammoth bones, enclosing an area of about 26 by 16 feet, which may have been used to weigh down the skin walls of a temporary hut or tent. Inside the ring are traces of a number of hearths, hundreds of tools, thousands of waste flakes, and many bone fragments, quite possibly derived from animals brought back for consumption.

Evidence for life in caves is abundant. Windbreaks of poles and skin were probably erected at the cave mouth for protection against severe weather. Fire was in general use by this time, of course, and was no doubt used for cooking, warmth, and keeping predators at bay.

How large were Neandertal settlements, and were they permanent or temporary? These questions are not yet answered, but Binford (1982) believes the settlements were used repeatedly for short-term occupations.

Symbolism

It has been suggested by some linguists that although Neandertals were capable of speech (symbolic vocal language), they were limited by the anatomy of the vocal tract. A recent discovery of a hyoid bone, mentioned earlier, in the Kebara remains at Mt. Carmel in Israel, may indeed be the first

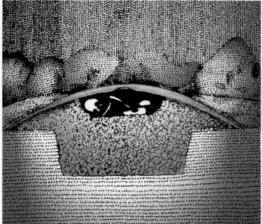

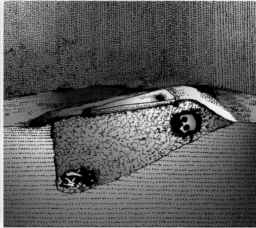

Figure 16-23

La Ferrassie burial.

ever reported from a fossil hominid. Contrary to the expectations of some researchers, the Kebara hyoid bone is very similar to the modern form and, thus, a reanalysis of the Neandertal ability to speak has been suggested (Arensburg et al., 1989).

Regarding symbols, Marshack (1989) suggests that Neandertals produced artwork—pendants and drilled bone objects, which he believes implies symbolism, and may have been the basis for the sophisticated art of the Upper Paleolithic (see p. 482).

It has also been suggested that the Neandertal practice of intentional burial of the dead is a symbol—possibly of belief in a future life, a special attitude toward death, the development of human compassion or, of course, none of these. From a symbolistic point of view, it appears that

> capacities of planning, forethought, abstraction, kinesthetic coordination, learning and other fundamental human characteristics appear well developed during the Middle Paleolithic of Europe" (Hayden, 1993, p. 137).

ECONOMY

Neandertals were successful hunters, as the abundant remains of animal bones at their sites demonstrate. Evidence from Shanidar, for example, suggests they probably gathered as well—berries, nuts, and other plants.

Erik Trinkaus has been a professor in the Department of Anthropology at the University of New Mexico since 1983. He received a Ph.D. in anthropology from the University of Pennsylvania. From 1974 to 1983, he served on the faculty of the Department of Anthropology at Harvard University where he was curator of biological anthropology at the Peabody Museum. In addition, Dr. Trinkaus has been an associate of the Laboratoire d'Anthropologie de l'Université de Bordeaux since 1984.

During the past two to three million years our genus (the genus *Homo*) has evolved from an apelike, but nonetheless bipedal, primate to the wide-spread and (for the time being) successful species we call modern *Homo sapiens*. During this time, there has been a complex evolutionary interaction between human anatomy and physiology on the one hand and human cultural behavior and the environment on the other. If we are to understand what it is that makes us human and evolutionarily successful, what it is in our biology and behavior that has enabled us to become the dominant species on this planet, we have to do that in part by understanding the patterns and processes of human evolution in the past. For whatever we may be doing with our biology and behavior in the modern world, it is in the past that these basic patterns emerged. Moreover, it is apparent that modern humans and our ancestors are/were part of a dynamic evolving world, a world in which we evolved from creatures that were indeed less human and more apelike than ourselves but nonetheless unique and important creatures in their own right.

Through the recognition of these two basic premises and a desire to understand both ourselves and the cultural and biological processes that led to ourselves, I have focused my attention, through studies, research, and teaching, on one of the more interesting periods of human evolution—the emergence of modern humans. The work has involved the study of the remains of early humans, the first representatives of people anatomically very much like ourselves (although they are more robust). It has also concentrated on the fossils of late archaic humans, the most recent representatives of a long lineage of archaic humans leading from early *Homo erectus* up to groups like the Neandertals of Europe and western Asia.

There are several advantages in working on this time period. It represents the last major biological *and* cultural transition in human evolution, since it involved both the biological shift from late archaic to early modern humans and the technological and cultural transition from the Middle to the Upper Paleolithic. It is a time period for which we have abundant and extensively studied archeological remains, so that we understand a lot about the behavioral similarities and differences across this transition. It is a phase of human evolution where we know a considerable amount about the environment and the associated fluctuations in climate and ecological zones through the last few phases of the Pleistocene. It is also a period for which, especially in Europe and western Asia, we have abundant human fossil remains and numerous well-preserved, associated skeletons derived from burials. As a result of all of this, there are many questions regarding the biology and behavior of these late archaic and early modern humans that we can ask of these fossils, questions that remain largely unasked and certainly unanswered for earlier phases of human evolution. The main disadvantage of working on these fossil remains, as opposed to those of earlier humans, is that the differences between groups are mostly very subtle, requiring considerable effort and reasonable numbers of specimens to tease out the important aspects of these prehistoric humans.

Most of the attention that has been paid to the emergence of modern humans has concerned phylogenetic issues, in particular whether regional groups of late archaic humans like the Neandertals were ancestral to modern humans. For many years I avoided that issue, finding it intractable. In the last decade the growing interest in the question has forced me to consider it more closely, and I ended up concluding that both of the extreme positions are undoubtedly inaccurate and that reality lies somewhere in between, in the complex interactions of neighboring populations through time in a changing environment. For this reason, but mostly from my long-standing concern with the past patterns of human evolution and trying to understand the evolutionary origins of what is it that makes us human, I have focused on more "functional" analyses of the human fossil remains.

These functional studies have been based on the premise that the human skeleton, particularly the limbs, acts as a mechanical system that allows certain kinds of movements through joint shape and muscle attachments, and is structurally capable of resisting the mechanical forces placed upon it by muscles and body movement. This is combined with our knowledge of how the body operates in modern humans and other mammals, which has facilitated detailed studies of the upper and lower limbs of Neandertals and early modern humans. In this way, we are beginning to understand what the subtle differences in joint size, shape, and orientation, in muscle attachment size and position, and in long bone shaft size and shape, can tell us about human manipulative behaviors and human locomotion on the landscape. My work in this area started with a doctoral dissertation on the foot bones of Neandertals, since the foot closely reflects how the body moves during walking, and it has progressed up the legs and down the arms to the hands. In part, the research has evolved as each analysis raises as many questions as it answers; many of the same questions are being answered as new and more sophisticated techniques become available and as additional fossils are discovered.

At the same time, examining many of these fossils, I have become aware of the high levels of abnormal lesions on them, from growth defects in tooth enamel to healed broken bones, plus the realization that very few of our Neandertal fossils represent elderly individuals. These have led into the areas of paleopathology and paleodemography, as we have tried to learn more about their levels of stress and what that might tell us about their lifestyles. From this is emerging a better picture of the emergence of modern humans, with tentative answers as to "why" they emerged rather than just "from whom" they evolved.

Ironically, unlike most current specialists in human origins, I had little idea of even who the Neandertals were until I was near the end of my undergraduate years. My interests had been focused on understanding human social processes and how they integrated with more economic and technological aspects of human existence. From that I became interested in archeology and, through that pursuit, I eventually came to realize that many of my interests regarding social and technological processes could be addressed through human skeletal remains. From there, it was a small step to look at these changes on a larger scale and focus upon the Neandertals and modern human origins as an arena for exploring these issues. In this context, it is important to remember that, however detailed and technical the actual analyses on the fossils become, the ultimate questions are ones that derive from looking at humans as biological and cultural creatures who evolved over long periods of time from something less human than ourselves.

It is assumed that, in the bitter cold of the fourth glacial period, Neandertals must have worn clothing, and they may have developed methods of curing skins. But since there is no evidence of sewing equipment, the clothing was probably of simple design, perhaps something like a poncho.

> Overall, the image of Neandertals is one of humans who had made several major adaptive advances over their predecessors, developments that allowed them to exploit previously uninhabitable regions and climates. . . . While on the one hand Neandertals can be seen as the culmination of two million years of evolution since the earliest appearance of *Homo erectus*, on the other hand they were also heralds of a new human biology—one that would be enhanced and exaggerated in millennia to come . . . (Trinkaus and Shipman, 1992, p. 418).

We know much more of European Middle Paleolithic culture than any comparable period, as it has been studied longer by more scholars. In recent years, however, Africa has been a target not only of physical anthropologists, as we have seen copiously documented in earlier chapters, but also of archeologists, who have added considerably to our knowledge of African Pleistocene hominid history. In many instances the technology and assumed cultural adaptations were similar in Africa to those in Europe and southwest Asia. We will see in the next chapter that the African technological achievements also keep pace with (or even precede) those in western Europe.

Conclusion: Evolutionary Trends in the Genus *Homo*

To understand the evolution of the various forms of *Homo sapiens* discussed in this chapter, it is useful to briefly review general trends of evolution in the genus *Homo* over the last 2 million years. In doing so, we see that at least three major *transitions* have taken place. Paleoanthropologists are keenly interested in interpreting the nature of these transitions, as they inform us directly regarding human origins. In addition, such investigations contribute to a broader understanding of the mechanics of the evolutionary process—both at the micro- and macroevolutionary levels.

The first transition of note was that from early *Homo* to *Homo erectus*. This transition was apparently geographically restricted to Africa and appears to have been quite *rapid* (lasting 200,000 years at most, perhaps considerably less time). It is important to recall that such a transition by no means implies that all early *Homo* groups actually evolved into *H. erectus*. In fact, many paleoanthropologists (part of a growing consensus) suggest that there was more than one species of early *Homo*. Clearly, only one could be ancestral to *H. erectus*. Even more to the point, only *some* populations of this one species would have been part of the genetic transformation (speciation) that produced *Homo erectus*.

The second transition is more complex and is the main topic of this chapter. It is the gradual change in several populations of *H. erectus* grading into early *H. sapiens* forms—what we have termed archaic *H. sapiens*. This transition was not geographically restricted, as there is evidence of archaic *sapiens* widespread in the Old World (in East and South Africa, in China and Java, and in Europe). Moreover, the transition appears not to have been rapid, but rather quite slow and uneven in pace from area to area. The complexity of this evolutionary transition creates ambiguities for our interpretations and resulting classifications.

For example, in Chapter 15 we included the Ngandong (Solo) material from Java within *Homo erectus*. However, there are several derived features in many of these specimens which suggest, alternatively, they could be assigned to *Homo sapiens*. The dating (a rough estimate only) of 130,000 y.a. would argue (if this *is* a *H. erectus* group) for a very late remnant, probably isolated, *H. erectus* population surviving in southern Asia at the same time that archaic *sapiens* were expanding elsewhere. Whatever the interpretation of Ngandong—either as a late *H. erectus* or as a quite primitive (that is, not particularly derived) archaic *sapiens*—the conclusion is actually quite arbitrary (after all, the evolutionary process is continuous). We, by the nature of our classifications, have to draw the line *somewhere*. (As a further aside, these largely arbitrary lines determine which specimens are discussed in which chapters!)

Another important ramification of such considerations relates to understanding the nature of the *erectus/sapiens* transition itself. In Java, the transition (with late-persisting *erectus* genetic components) appears slower than, for example, in southern Africa or in Europe. Nowhere, however, does this transition appear to have been as rapid as that which originally produced *H. erectus*. Why should this be so? To answer this question, we must refer back to basic evolutionary mechanisms (discussed in Chapter 4). First, the environments certainly differed from one region of the Old World to another during the time period 350,000–100,000 y.a. And, recall that by the beginning of this time period, *H. erectus* populations had been long established in eastern Asia, southern Asia, North Africa and East Africa. Moreover, by 250,000 years ago *H. erectus* or their immediate descendants had already reached Europe—or soon would do so. Clearly, we would not expect the same environmental conditions in northeast China as we would in Indonesia. Accordingly, natural selection could well have played a *differential* role influencing the frequencies of alternative alleles in different populations—in a pattern similar (but more intensive) to that seen in environmental adaptations of contemporary populations (see Chapter 6).

Second, many of these populations (in Java, southernmost Africa, and glacial Europe) could have been isolated and thus probably quite small. Genetic drift, therefore, also would have played a role in influencing the pace of evolutionary change. Third, advance or retreat of barriers, such as water boundaries or glacial ice sheets, would have dramatically affected migration routes.

Thus, it should hardly come as a surprise that some populations of *H. erectus* evolved at different rates and in slightly different directions from others. Some probably limited migration did almost certainly occur among the various populations. With sufficient gene flow, the spread of those few genetic modifications that distinguish the earliest *H. sapiens* eventually did become incorporated into widely separated populations. This, however, as you can see, was a long, slow, inherently uneven process.

What, then, of the third transition within the genus *Homo*? This is the transition from archaic *sapiens* to anatomically modern *sapiens*—and it was considerably *faster* than the transition we have just discussed. Just how quickly anatomically modern forms evolved and exactly *where* this happened is a subject of much contemporary debate. This topic is the central focus of our next, and concluding, chapter.

Summary

During the Middle Pleistocene, significant changes occurred in *H. erectus* morphology. The changes, especially in cranial traits, led scientists to assign a new species designation to these forms (that is, *Homo sapiens*). Because they exhibited a mosaic of *H. erectus* and sapient characteristics, the term archaic *H. sapiens* is used to indicate that they were forms transitional between *H. erectus* and anatomically modern humans. Some archaic *sapiens* possessed more derived modern traits than others, and these are sometimes referred to as later archaic *sapiens* or early *H. sapiens sapiens*. It has been suggested that some later European archaic forms were directly ancestral to Neandertals.

In addition to morphological changes among archaic forms, there were cultural developments as well. Archaic *H. sapiens* invented new kinds of tools and toolmaking techniques, introduced new foods, built more complex shelters, probably controlled fire, and may have used some form of speech.

In western Europe, archaic *sapiens* evolved a unique form—classic Neandertals, who apparently migrated from Europe to the Near East and then even further into Asia. Neandertals were physically robust and muscular, different from both early archaic forms and modern *H. sapiens*. Their culture was more complex than earlier archaic cultures and, it appears, in Europe and the Near East, they lived in areas also inhabited by modern *sapiens*. Whether modern forms in these areas evolved directly from Neandertals or migrated from Africa (or the Near East) and ultimately replaced Neandertals is one of the important issues currently under active discussion by paleoanthropologists.

Finally, we would emphasize that Neandertals and all humans on earth today belong to the same species, *H. sapiens*. There are physical differences among these forms, of course, and for that reason Neandertals are assigned to the subspecies *H. sapiens neandertalensis*, and anatomically modern forms, the subspecies *H. sapiens sapiens*.

We should point out that this assignment of a *separate* subspecies for the Neandertals emphasizes some reasonably notable degrees of variation—that is, Neandertals are viewed as more different from *any* modern group of *H. sapiens* than these groups differ from one another. Some scholars (still a minority view) would even more dramatically emphasize this variation and thus assign Neandertals to a separate species from *Homo sapiens*.

Neandertals have received a bad press for the past 90 years and are often portrayed as pathological creatures of little skill, grace, or intelligence. Actually, the physical differences between "us" and "them" are relatively minor, but the Neandertal overhanging brow, facial prognathism, and other superficial features could bias our judgment.

Questions for Review

1. In what respect does *H. sapiens* (broadly defined) contrast with *H. erectus*?
2. What is meant by "archaic" *H. sapiens*?
3. How does archaic *sapiens* contrast with anatomically modern *sapiens*?
4. From what areas of the world have archaic *H. sapiens* been discovered? Compare and contrast the finds from two separate areas.
5. What is meant by saying archaic *H. sapiens* specimens are transitional?

6. What differences in culture (and technology) do we see in the later Middle Pleistocene as compared to sites discussed in Chapter 15 (associated with *H. erectus*)?

7. Why have Neandertals been depicted (by the popular press and others) as being primitive? Do you agree with this interpretation? Why or why not?

8. From what general areas of the world have Neandertal fossil remains been discovered?

9. What evidence suggests Neandertals deliberately buried their dead? What interpretations does such treatment of the dead suggest to you?

10. What physical characteristics distinguish the Neandertals from anatomically modern *sapiens*?

11. In what ways does Neandertal culture differ from preceding periods?

12. What two major transitions within the genus *Homo* have been discussed in this chapter and in Chapter 15? Compare these transitions for geographic distribution as well as aspects of evolutionary pace.

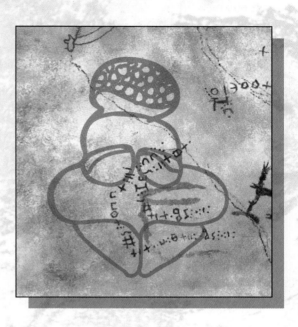

Chapter 17

Contents

Homo sapiens sapiens

In this text, we have presented a great number of varied scenarios, hypotheses, and theories relating to human origins. In the issues, we have also raised numerous controversial ideas, many of which relate to *popular* views of human evolution. Throughout, a major emphasis (beginning with the issue for Chapter 1) is to stimulate you to think *critically*. Of course, as students in an introductory course, you do not possess all the experience and knowledge required to make a definitive judgment on conflicting scientific data, especially when only the bare outlines of the various controversies are presented. Our intent as authors is understandably, then, somewhat more focused. Through the issues and other areas of controversy we raise, we have attempted to: (1) provide a sampling of different professional opinions; (2) provide you with examples of how science works as a tool for rigorously evaluating data; and (3) by so doing, to allow you more comprehensively to perfect critical thinking skills you will be able to apply to a wide range of topics.

In this chapter, we address the last major controversial topic in human evolutionary studies: the nature of the origin and dispersal of anatomically modern human beings. As you will see, there are three main theories that attempt to explain this important evolutionary event. These three views are all sufficiently documented with at least *some* data to qualify as "theories." Nevertheless, as two of these views are quite contradictory on several key points, obviously they both cannot be correct. The third theory is somewhat of a compromise between the other two, but it, too, may prove inadequate.

How do scientists evaluate the relative reliability and utility of differing viewpoints? First of all, the theories must be presented in widely circulated professional publications and stated in comprehensible form. All these views on recent human origins have met this test. Secondly, each theory must clearly define the limits of its current applicability and allow *predictions* of how further (as yet undiscovered) finds will likely fit the established pattern. Lastly, and most obviously, the entire construct should be falsifiable, if adequate contradictory evidence is presented.

An example of a hypothesis that employs new methodologies to explain the dispersal of modern *Homo sapiens* serves to illustrate these points.

For a number of years, biochemists and molecular biologists have sought to use the genetic patterning as determined in *living* animals to investigate the nature and timing of past evolutionary events, in some cases those occurring several million years ago. We introduced such a perspective in Chapter 8 and showed in Chapter 11 how it has provisionally been applied to understanding the initial divergence of hominids. A similar perspective has been attempted in recent years as applied to reconstructing evolutionary events in the last 200,000 years (the time period suggested as central to the initial wide dispersal of modern *H. sapiens*).

The genetic tool that has been used to gain new insights has come from analysis of human mitochondrial DNA (mtDNA). By comparing the mtDNA sequences in various contemporary human populations, a team of researchers (Allan Wilson, Rebecca Cann, and Mark Stoneking),* initially conducting experiments at the University of California, Berkeley, determined that African genetic patterns are much more diverse than any other recent population. Moreover, *all* of the genetic diversity seen in modern human populations (worldwide) must have originated and spread from Africa sometime over approximately the last 200,000 years. Another deduction drawn by the University of California researchers was that there was probably a single maternal lineage in Africa that formed the ancestral basis for all later humans. The popular press misinterpreted this

---

*Allan Wilson passed away in 1991; Rebecca Cann is now at the University of Hawaii; Mark Stoneking is at Pennsylvania State University.

view (which postulated a *population* of individuals) to represent *one* woman. Thus was born the notion of African "Eve." (A cautionary—and encouraging—note should be added here; now that you have just about completed an introductory course dealing in large part with human evolution, you need no longer rely solely upon sensationalized, and often inaccurate, reports from the mass media.)

Popular hyperbole aside, the evidence presented by these molecular biologists was to have a profound impact on the long-established debate among *paleoanthropologists* regarding recent human origins. One school of thought, led by Chris Stringer of the British Museum of Natural History, eagerly supported this new evidence, as the molecular data appeared to confirm their prior views. Another group of scholars, most enthusiastically led by Milford Wolpoff (of the University of Michigan), were caustic critics. The largest group of anthropologists stood somewhere in the middle, impressed by the new genetic methodologies but, nevertheless, suspicious of the extremely broad claims made by its advocates.

A crucial point to this debate (and *all* such scientific controversies) is that the evidence must stand the *test of confirmation*. If presented adequately, as we have noted, the re-sults should be repeatable, should allow predictable expansion, and, failing confirmation, should be falsifiable (and, in the latter event, either rejected outright or, at least, substantially modified).

The acid test of the mitochondrial DNA-based model of modern human origins came as the approach was attempted by other laboratories using similar techniques and statistical treatments. In February, 1992, three different papers were published by different teams of researchers, all of which severely challenged the main tenets of the hypotheses as proposed by Wilson, Cann, and Stoneking. The most serious error was a failure to recognize how many *equally valid* results could be deduced statistically from the *same set* of original data. In science, as we have remarked before, beyond the data themselves, the methodological treatments (especially statistical models) greatly influence both the nature and *confidence limits* of the results.

The central conclusion that Africa alone was the *sole* source of modern humans could still be correct. Yet, now it had to be admitted that dozens (indeed, thousands) of other equally probable renditions could be derived from the supposedly unambiguous mitochondrial data. Thus, barely a few months after the original researchers had proposed their most systematic statement of their hypotheses, the entire perspective (especially its statistical implications) was shaken to its very foundations—and, in many people's eyes, falsified altogether.

An interesting twist regarding this entire reassessment is that the team from Pennsylvania State University that challenged the initial results was joined in its critique by Mark Stoneking, one of the original formulators of the now-questioned hypothesis. A viable scientific perspective, so well illustrated here, is that new approaches (or refined applications) oftentimes necessitate reevaluation of prior hypotheses. It takes both objectivity and courage to admit miscalculations. By so doing, an even more permanent and positive legacy helps contain the inherent personal biases that sometimes have so divided the study of human origins.

Stoneking and some of his colleagues still maintain some of the tenets of their original hypotheses. However, the notion that African *sapiens* ancestors contributed exclusively within the last 200,000 years to *all* later human populations is no longer considered viable by most anthropologists. Moreover, the romanticized image of one female, "Eve," as the sole maternal ancestor of all humans today has been rejected altogether by the scientific community. As a misstated exaggeration promulgated by the popular press, Eve's demise came none too soon; nor will her passing be mourned by well-versed students of human evolution.

Introduction

In this chapter, we come to anatomically modern humans, taxonomically known as *Homo sapiens sapiens*. As we discussed in Chapter 16, in some areas evolutionary developments produced early archaic *H. sapiens* populations exhibiting a mosaic of *H. erectus* and *H. sapiens* traits. In some regions, the trend emphasizing sapient characteristics continued, and possibly as early as 200,000 y.a., transitional forms (between early archaic and anatomically modern forms) appeared in Africa. Given the nature of the evidence and ongoing ambiguities in dating, it is not possible to say exactly when anatomically modern *H. sapiens first* appeared. However, the transition and certainly the wide dispersal of *H. sapiens sapiens* in the Old World appear to have been relatively rapid evolutionary events. Thus, as for the earlier major transitions in human evolution, we can ask several basic questions:

1. **When** (approximately) did *H. sapiens sapiens* first appear?
2. **Where** did the transition take place? Did it occur in just one region, or in several?
3. **What** was the pace of evolutionary change? How quickly did the transition occur?
4. **How** did the dispersal of *H. sapiens sapiens* to other areas of the Old World (outside that of origin) take place?

In a recent paper, evidence was presented that anatomically modern forms first evolved in Africa about 130,000 y.a. (Foley and Lahr, 1992), but whether such humans evolved *solely* in Africa or also evolved from archaic *H. sapiens* in other regions as well, has been a matter of considerable debate for most of the last decade. Opposed to those who believe modern *sapiens* originated in Africa are the regional continuity advocates. As we shall see, there is at present insufficient evidence to prove either case.

We take up these varied hypotheses in this chapter and trace the evolution of anatomically modern human populations. We shall also discuss the culture of the people who lived mainly during the **Upper Paleolithic** age, a time of extraordinary technological change and artistic development.

Upper Paleolithic A culture period composed of various stone tool industries and distinguished by technological innovation. Best known from western Europe, similar industries are also known from central/eastern Europe and Africa.

The Origin and Dispersal of *Homo sapiens sapiens* (Anatomically Modern Human Beings)

As we noted, one of the most puzzling questions debated in paleoanthropology today is the origin of modern humans. There are three basic hypotheses: (1) the Recent African Evolution Model; (2) the African-European *sapiens* hypothesis; and (3) the Multiregional Evolution Model.

THE RECENT AFRICAN EVOLUTION MODEL (COMPLETE DISPLACEMENT)

This hypothesis, developed by Stringer and Andrews (1988), is based on the origin of modern humans in Africa and displacement of populations in Europe and Asia. In brief, anatomically modern populations arose in Africa within the last 200,000 years, then migrated out of Africa, completely *displacing* populations in Europe and Asia. This model thus does not take into account any transition from archaic *H. sapiens* to modern *sapiens* anywhere in the world—except Africa. A critical aspect of the Stringer and Andrews theory is that it considers the appearance of anatomically modern humans as a biological speciation event. Thus, there could be no admixture of migrating African modern *sapiens* with local populations; it would have been impossible, since the African modern humans were a *biologically* different species.

A crucial source of supporting evidence for this African origin hypothesis has come from genetic data obtained from living peoples. Underlying this approach is the assumption that genetic patterning seen in contemporary populations will provide clues to relationships and origins of ancient *Homo sapiens*. However, as with numerous prior attempts to evaluate such patterning from data on human polymorphisms (for example, ABO, HLA—see Chapter 5), the obstacles are enormous.

A recent innovation uses genetic sequencing data derived directly from DNA. The most promising application has come not from the DNA within the nucleus, but from DNA found in the cytoplasm; that is, mitochondrial DNA (mtDNA). Mitochondria are tiny organelles found in the cell, outside the nucleus. They contain a set of DNA, dissimilar from nuclear DNA, inherited only through the mother. Thus, mtDNA does not undergo the genetic recombination that occurs in nuclear DNA during meiosis.

Using mtDNA gathered from a number of different populations, scientists at the University of California, Berkeley, constructed "trees" (something like a family tree) that, they claimed, demonstrated that the entire population of the world today descended from a single African lineage. However, the methodology of these molecular biologists has been faulted (see Box 17-1). Using the same mtDNA material, other scientists constructed many trees that differed from those of the Berkeley group, and some of them are *without African roots* (see *Science*, **255**:686–687, Feb. 7, 1992).

THE AFRICAN-EUROPEAN *SAPIENS* HYPOTHESIS (PARTIAL DISPLACEMENT)

Formulated by Gunter Bräuer of the Institute of Human Biology, University of Hamburg, this model also begins with African early archaic *H. sapiens* from which emerged a late archaic stage. Finally, also in Africa, anatomically modern *sapiens* populations first evolved. Bräuer places the archaic *sapiens* at dates of over 100,000 y.a., and the first modern *sapiens* in South Africa at about 100,000 y.a. He sees the dispersal of *H. sapiens sapiens* out of South Africa as a result of climatic and environmental conditions, and thus as a gradual process. Moving into Eurasia, modern humans hybridized with resident archaic groups, thereby eventually replacing them. The disappearance of archaic humans, therefore, was due to both hybridization and replacement and was a gradual and complex process. This model includes components of regional continuity, hybridization, and replacement, with the emphasis on replacement.

THE MULTIREGIONAL EVOLUTION MODEL (REGIONAL CONTINUITY)

This third model is most closely associated with Milford Wolpoff of the University of Michigan, and his associates (1984), who believe that local populations (not all, of course) in Europe, Asia, and Africa continued their indigenous evolutionary development from archaic *H. sapiens* to *anatomically modern humans*. A question immediately arises: How is it possible for different local populations around the globe to evolve with such similar morphol-

Box 17-1   The Garden of Eden Hypothesis

Gathering samples of mtDNA from placentas of individuals whose ancestors lived in Africa, Asia, Europe, Australia, and New Guinea, biologists from the University of California, Berkeley, postulated a distinctive genetic pattern for each area. They then compared the diversity of the various patterns (Cann et al., 1987).

They found the greatest variation among Africans and therefore postulated Africa to have been the home of the oldest human populations (the assumption is that the longer the time, the greater the accumulation of genetic variation). They also found that the African variants contained only African mtDNA, whereas those from other areas all included at least one African component. Therefore, the biologists concluded, there must have been a migration initially from Africa, ultimately to all other inhabited areas of the world. By counting the number of genetic mutations and applying the rate of mutation, Rebecca Cann and her associates calculated a date for the origin of anatomically modern humans: between 285,000 and 143,000 years ago; in other words, an average estimate of about 200,000 years ago. Indeed, a further contention of the mtDNA researchers is that the pattern of variation argues that all modern humans shared in common a single African female lineage that lived sometime during this time range. Thus was born the popularized concept of "mitochondrial Eve."

Not all scientists, by any means, agree with this scenario. The estimated rate of mutations may be incorrect, and, therefore, the proposed date of migration out of Africa would also be in error. Also, secondary migration, outside Africa, could disrupt the direct inheritance of the African maternal line. Even more troubling are the inherent biases in the statistical technique used to identify the primary population relationships ("trees"). Recent reanalyses of the data suggest the situation is not as nearly clear-cut as originally believed. On the basis of these new studies many have proclaimed that mitochondrial Eve is dead—and perhaps the Out of Africa hypothesis with her. As could be expected, the proponents of the African origin view are not yet ready to bury Eve or significantly alter their confidence in the Out of Africa hypothesis. A representative opinion is voiced by Christopher Stringer of the British Museum of Natural History: "Eve may have had a quick kick in the pants, but the Out of Africa hypothesis certainly isn't dead" (quoted in Gibbons, 1992).

As the debate continues, new lines of evidence and new techniques are being pursued: more ways to sequence both mitochondrial and nuclear DNA; more complete evidence of human polymorphisms; genetic sequence data for the Y chromosome; and, it is hoped, more reliable statistical techniques to interpret these complex data. We discuss in the Issue for this chapter (p. 468) the nature of the scientific pursuit. New ideas, especially controversial ones, stimulate further research. Neither the genetic patterning of contemporary human populations nor the evolutionary history of *Homo sapiens* are particularly simple phenomena. We thus should not expect easily obtained, simple solutions. The scientific search itself is exciting and speaks volumes about the supreme human capacity for rational thought and of our quest for knowledge.

ogy? The multiregional model explains this phenomenon by (1) denying that the earliest modern *sapiens* populations originated in Africa, and refuting the notion of complete displacement; and (2) that some gene flow (migration) between archaic populations was extremely likely and, consequently, modern humans cannot be considered a species separate from archaic forms.

Through gene flow and local selection, according to the multiregional hypothesis, local populations would *not* have evolved totally independently from one another and such mixing would have "prevented speciation between the regional lineages and thus maintained human beings as a *single*, although obviously polytypic, species throughout the Pleistocene" (F. Smith et al., 1989).

The Problems with Interpretation

There are three major problems concerning identification of taxa, archeological associations, and dating control. As we noted, for such subtle distinctions it is not always possible to draw an absolute line between archaic *H. sapiens* and modern humans. This conclusion holds true wherever we find *sapiens*, since some archaic forms may exhibit modern traits, and early modern *sapiens* may display archaic traits.

Paleoanthropologists make taxonomic decisions by looking at the overall configuration of the fossil find, and the more complete the remains, the more valid the conclusion is apt to be. However, there are cases where the skeletal remains (especially crania) are difficult to interpret. Then the decision becomes fairly arbitrary, and the fossil may be placed in one or the other group, depending on a particular scientist's interpretation. This kind of problem with interpretation is especially true in making distinctions among *subspecies* where the biological differences are quite subtle.

Another difficulty concerns the presumed association of anatomically modern humans with the stone tool cultures called the Upper Paleolithic. This notion arose in Europe where the relationship between humans and technology was first noticed in the archeological record. However, this correlation does not necessarily hold in Africa or Asia; nor is the association in Europe absolute. We must also mention that the line between the **Middle Paleolithic** and Upper Paleolithic cannot be clearly drawn.

A third problem, already mentioned, concerns dating techniques (see Chapter 12). The proper way to determine the taxon of a fossil is by its morphology. There are times, however, when a specimen appears to be an anatomically modern form morphologically, but turns out to be dated, for various reasons, far earlier than the appearance of modern *sapiens* elsewhere. The date of the specimen may be questioned. Alternatively, we may have to conclude, if the dates prove correct, that the direction and/or pace of evolutionary change varied from one area to another. Dating techniques have been improving in recent years, and we may look forward to more accurate dating, not only of new fossils, but also the redating of previously discovered finds.

Middle Paleolithic The culture period defined by stone tool industries called Mousterian. Found in Europe and the Near East (where it is associated with Neandertals) and also known from north Africa.

Homo sapiens sapiens Discoveries

Africa

At the present time it appears that the earliest modern *sapiens* fossils have been found in Africa, but not everyone agrees with the dates or designations, or precisely which specimens are modern and which are archaic forms. With this cautionary note, we continue our discussion, but there undoubtedly will be corrections as more evidence is gathered.

In Africa, there are several early fossil finds that have been interpreted as fully anatomically modern forms. These specimens come from the Klasies River Mouth on the south coast (which could be the earliest find), Border Cave to the north, and Omo Kibish 1 in southern Ethiopia, and they have all been dated to about the 100–120,000 y.a. range. Some paleoanthropologists consider these fossils to be the earliest known anatomically modern humans. Problems with dating, **provenience**, and differing interpretations of the evidence have led other paleoanthropologists to question whether the *earliest*

Provenience In archeology, the specific location of a discovery.

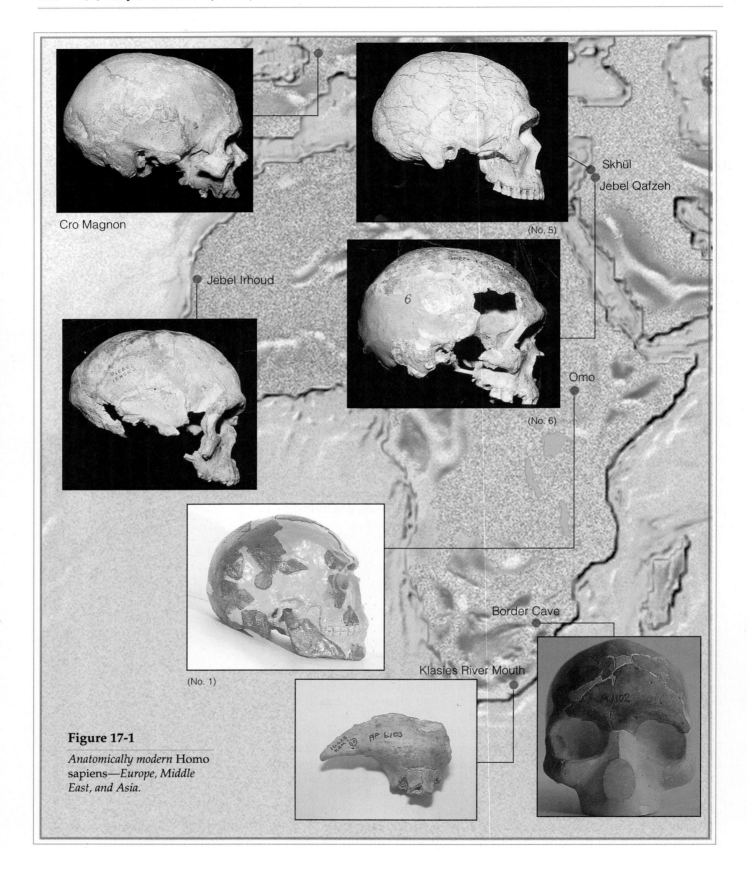

Cro Magnon

Skhül

Jebel Qafzeh

(No. 5)

Jebel Irhoud

6

Omo

(No. 6)

(No. 1)

Border Cave

Klasies River Mouth

Figure 17-1

Anatomically modern Homo sapiens—*Europe, Middle East, and Asia.*

Figure 17-2

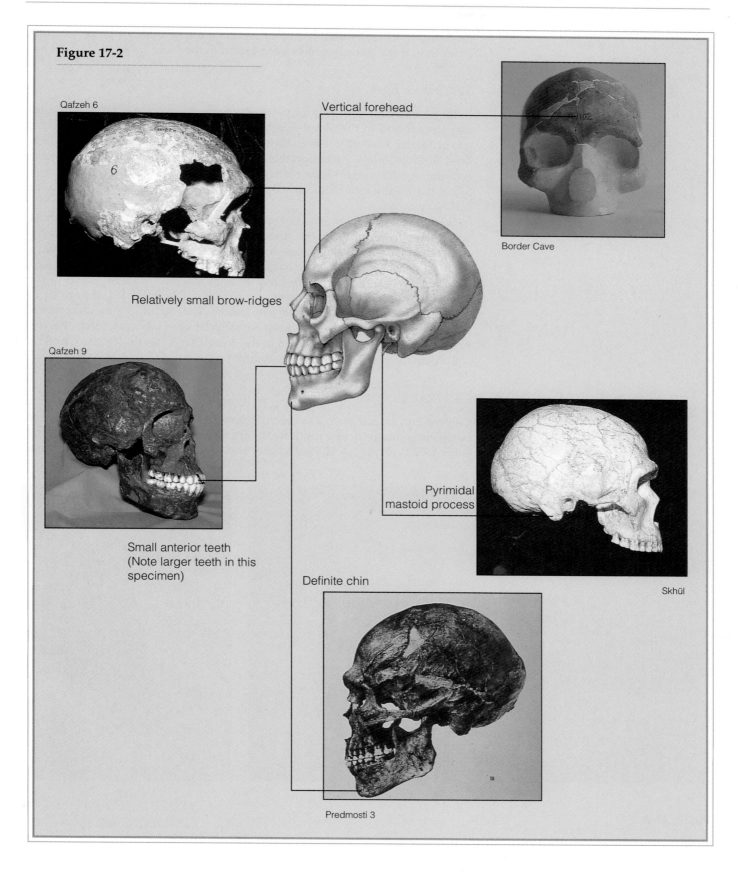

Qafzeh 6

Relatively small brow-ridges

Qafzeh 9

Small anterior teeth
(Note larger teeth in this
specimen)

Vertical forehead

Border Cave

Pyrimidal
mastoid process

Skhül

Definite chin

Predmosti 3

modern forms really did evolve in Africa. Other modern *sapiens*, possibly older than these Africans, have been found in the Near East.

THE NEAR EAST

In Israel, early modern *H. sapiens* fossils (the remains of at least 10 individuals) were found in the Skhūl cave at Mt. Carmel, very near the Neandertal site of Tabun. Also from Israel, the Qafzeh cave has yielded the remains of at least 20 individuals. Although their overall configuration is definitely modern, some specimens show certain archaic (that is, Neandertal) features. Skhūl has been dated to about 90,000 y.a. and Qafzah has been placed in the 100,000 y.a. range.

Such early dates for modern specimens pose some problems for those advocating local replacement (the multiregional model). How early do archaic *sapiens* (Neandertals) appear in the Near East? A recent chronometric calibration for the Tabun cave suggests a date as early as 100,000 years ago. Neandertals thus may *slightly* precede anatomically modern forms in the Near East, but there would appear to be considerable overlap in the timing of occupation by these different *sapiens* forms. And, recall, the modern site at Mt. Carmel (Skhūl) is very near the Neandertal site (Tabun)! Clearly, the dynamics of *Homo sapiens* evolution in the Near East is highly complex, and no simple model may explain it adequately.

CENTRAL EUROPE

Central Europe has been a source of many fossil finds, including numerous fairly early anatomically modern *H. sapiens*. At several sites, it appears that some fossils display both Neandertal and modern features, which supports

(a)   (b)

Figure 17-3

(a) Mt. Carmel, studded with caves, was home to H. sapiens sapiens *at Skhūl (and to Neandertals at Tabun and Kebara);*
(b) Skhūl Cave. The fossils have been dated at 90,000 y.a.

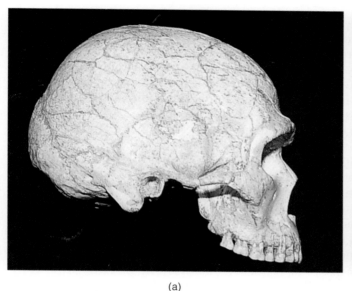
(a)

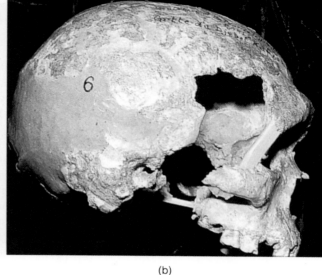
(b)

Figure 17-4

(a) Skhūl 5; (b) Qafzeh 6. These specimens from Israel are thought to be representatives of early modern Homo sapiens. *The vault height, forehead, and lack of prognathism are modern traits.*

the regional continuity (from Neandertal to modern) hypothesis. Such apparently was the case at Vindija (see p. 454).

Smith (1984) offers another example of local continuity from Mladeč in the Czech Republic. Among the earlier European modern *sapiens*, dated to about 33,000 y.a., the Mladeč crania (2 female, 3 male) display a great deal of variation, partly due to sexual dimorphism. Although the crania (except for one of the females) possess a prominent supraorbital torus, they are reduced from the typical Neandertal pattern. Also modern is the reduction of the occipital projection, called a *hemibun*. Reduced midfacial projection, a higher forehead, and postcranial elements "are clearly modern *H. sapiens* in morphology and not specifically Neandertal-like in a single feature" (F. Smith, 1984, p. 174).

Another early modern site is Předmostí, also in the Czech Republic, where remains of nearly 30 individuals were found in a collective grave. The specimens show a diversity of traits, as can be seen in Předmostí 3 with a Neandertal-like browridge (see Fig. 17-6).

Figure 17-5

Mladeč 5. Mladeč in the Czech Republic contains some of the earliest European representatives of modern Homo sapiens.

WESTERN EUROPE

This area of the world and its fossils have received the greatest paleoanthropological attention for several reasons, one of which is probably serendipity. Over the last century and a half, many of the scholars interested in this kind of research happened to live in western Europe, and the southern region of France happened to be a fossil cornucopia. Also, discovering and learning about ancient human ancestors caught the curiosity and pride of the local population.

Because of this scholarly interest a great deal of data were gathered, with little reliable comparative information available from elsewhere in the world. Consequently, theories of human evolution were based almost exclusively upon the western European material. It has only been in recent years with

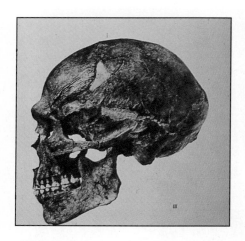

Figure 17-6

Předmostí 3 (Czech Republic). An anatomical modern sapiens *with a few archaic traits.*

growing evidence from other areas of the world and with the application of new dating techniques that recent human evolutionary dynamics have been seriously considered on a worldwide basis.

There are many anatomically modern human fossils from western Europe going back 40,000 years or more, but by far the best known western European *H. sapiens* is from the Cro-Magnon site. Three adult males, one adult female, and four very young children were discovered in 1868 in a rock shelter in the village of Les Eyzies, in the Dordogne of southern France (Gambier, 1989).

Associated with an evolved Aurignacian tool assemblage, an Upper Paleolithic industry, the Cro-Magnon materials, dated at 30,000 y.a., represent the earliest of France's anatomically modern humans. The so-called "Old Man" (Cro-Magnon 1) became the archetype for what is known as the Cro-Magnon, or Upper Paleolithic, "race" of Europe. Actually, of course, there is no such race, and Cro-Magnon 1 is not typical of Upper Paleolithic western Europeans, and not even all that similar to the other two male skulls that were found at the site.

Considered together, the three male crania reflect a mixture of modern and archaic traits. Cro-Magnon 1 is the most gracile of the three—the supraorbital tori of the other two males, for example, are more robust. The most modern-looking is the female cranium which may be a function of sexual dimorphism.

The question of whether continuous local evolution produced anatomically modern groups directly from Neandertals in some regions of Eurasia is far from settled. Variation seen in the Mladeč and Předmostí fossils indicate a combination of both Neandertal and modern characteristics, and may suggest gene flow between the two different *sapiens* groups. However, tracing such relatively minor genetic changes—considering the ever-present problems of dating, lack of fossils, and fragmented fossil finds—may well prove impossible.

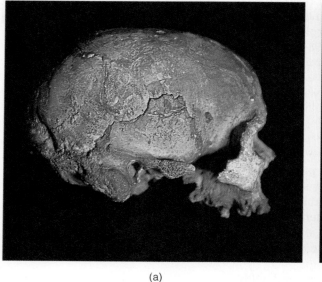
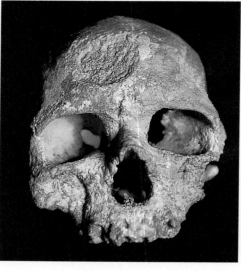

(a)   (b)

Figure 17-7

Cro-Magnon 1 (France). In this specimen, modern traits are quite clear. (a) Lateral view; (b) frontal view. (Courtesy of David Frayer)

ASIA

Bräuer lists six early anatomically modern human localities in China: Upper Cave at Zhoukoudian, Liujiang, Ziyang, Chilinshan, Ordos, and Huanglong. The fossils from these sites are all fully modern, and most are considered quite late Upper Pleistocene. The Upper Cave at Zhoukoudian has been dated between 10,000 and 18,000 y.a. The Ordos find was discovered at Dagouwan, Inner Mongolia, and may be the oldest anatomically modern material from China, perhaps dating to 50,000 y.a. or more (Etler, personal communication).

Chinese paleoanthropologists see a regional continuous evolution from Chinese *H. erectus* to archaic *H. sapiens* to anatomically modern humans. This view is supported by Wolpoff who mentions that materials from Liujiang and Upper Cave at Zhoukoudian "have a number of features that are characteristically regional" and that these features are definitely not African (1989:83).*

In addition to the well-known finds from China anatomically modern remains have also been discovered in southern Asia. At Batadomba Iena in southern Sri Lanka, modern *Homo sapiens* have been dated to 25,500 y.a. (Kennedy and Deraniyagala, 1989).

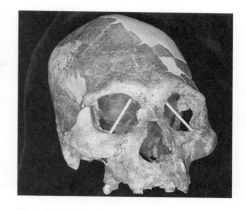

Figure 17-8

Kow Swamp (Australia). Note the considerable robusticity in this relatively late Australian Homo sapiens sapiens *cranium.*

AUSTRALIA

During glacial times, the Indonesian islands were joined to the Asian mainland, but Australia was not. Evidence shows that modern humans did some island hopping to New Guinea and surrounding islands and to Australia; in fact, it is likely that by 40,000 y.a., Sahul—the area including New Guinea and Australia—was inhabited by modern humans. Bamboo rafts may have been the means of crossing the sea between islands, which would not have been a simple exercise (one wonders why they would have even tried). Just where the future Australians came from is unknown, but Borneo, Java, and New Guinea have all been suggested. Modern humans from the Niah Cave in Borneo or Ngandong hominids from Java may have been the Australian ancestors.

Archeological sites in Australia have been dated to at least 55,000 years ago (Roberts et al., 1990), but the oldest human fossils themselves have been dated to about 30,000 y.a. These oldest Australians are from Lake Mungo, where the remains of two burials (one of which was first cremated) date to 25,000 y.a. and at least 30,000 y.a., respectively. Their crania are rather gracile with, for example, only moderate development of the supraorbital torus. The Keilor find (15,000 y.a.), more recent than Lake Mungo, is another gracile cranium that fits in well with the Mungo forms. A modern *sapiens*, Wajak (formerly Wadjak) was found in Java by Dubois, and similarities between Wajak and Lake Mungo and especially Keilor have been noted by a number of researchers. These gracile specimens are quite different from the more robust native Australians of today.

Unlike these more gracile early Australian forms are the Kow Swamp people who are believed to have lived between about 14,000 and 9,000 years ago. The presence of certain archaic traits such as receding foreheads, heavy supraorbital tori, and thick bones are difficult to explain, since these features contrast with their postcranial anatomy, which matches that of recent Australian natives.

---

*Professor Wolpoff's statement supports his belief in regional continuity. His reference to Africa is a criticism of the displacement hypothesis.

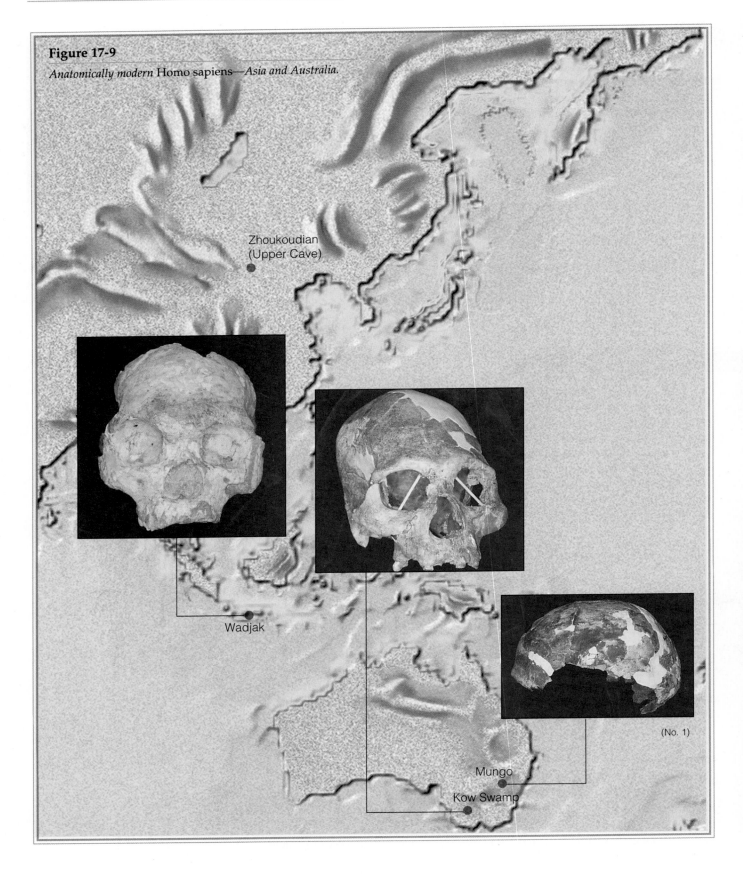

Figure 17-9

Anatomically modern Homo sapiens—*Asia and Australia.*

Zhoukoudian
(Upper Cave)

Wadjak

Mungo

Kow Swamp

(No. 1)

GLACIAL	UPPER PALEOLITHIC (beginnings, thousands of years ago)	CULTURE PERIODS
W Ü R M	17,000 –	Magdalenian
	21,000 –	Solutrean
	27,000 –	Gravettian
	33,000 –	Aurignacian Chatelperronian
	Middle Paleolithic	Mousterian

Figure 17-10

Culture periods of the European Upper Paleolithic and their approximate beginning dates.

Technology and Art in the Upper Paleolithic

EUROPE

The culture period known as the Upper Paleolithic begins in western Europe at approximately 35,000 years ago. Upper Paleolithic cultures are usually divided into five different industries based on stone tool technologies: (1) Chatelperronian (discussed in Chapter 16); (2) Aurignacian; (3) Gravettian; (4) Solutrean; and (5) Magdalenian. Major environmental shifts were also apparent during this period. During the last glacial period, at about 30,000 y.a., a warming trend lasting several thousand years partially melted the glacial ice. The result was that much of Eurasia consisted of tundra and steppe. It was a vast area of treeless country covered with lakes and marshes. In many areas in the north, permafrost prevented the growth of trees but permitted the growth, in the short summers, of flowering plants, mosses, and other kinds of vegetation. This vegetation served as an enormous pasture for herbivorous animals, large and small, and carnivorous animals that fed off the herbivores. It was a hunter's paradise, with hundreds of thousands of animals dispersed across expanses of tundra and grassland, from Spain through Europe and into the Russian steppes.

Large herds of reindeer roamed the tundra and steppes along with mammoths, bison, horses, and a host of smaller animals that served as a bountiful source of food. It was a time of relative affluence, and ultimately Upper Paleolithic people spread out over Europe, living in caves and open-air camps, and building large shelters. Mammoth-bone dwellings with storage pits have been excavated in the former Soviet Union, with archeological evidence of social status distinctions (Soffer, 1985). It was during this period that western Europe (or perhaps portions of Africa) achieved the highest density of population in human history up to that time.

Hunters in Europe continued an older practice of driving animals into bogs and swamps where they could easily be dispatched and butchered. They also used the method of stampeding horses and caribou over cliffs or into canyon cul-de-sacs. Food acquisition was so intense that it has been suggested that the extinction of some of these Pleistocene prey animals was due to overkill. It is also possible that the change of climate was the primary factor leading to numerous extinctions as the glaciers retreated with dramatic effects on vegetation.

The Upper Paleolithic was a technological age and, in its way, can be compared to the past several hundred years in our own history of amazing tech-

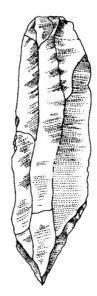

Figure 17-11

Burin. A very common Upper Paleolithic tool.

Figure 17-12

Solutrean blade. This is the best-known work of the Solutrean tradition. Solutrean stonework is considered the most highly developed of any Upper Paleolithic industry.

nological change after centuries of relative technological inertia. It appears that anatomically modern *sapiens* of the Upper Paleolithic not only invented new and specialized tools, they increased the use of, and probably experimented with, new materials, such as bone, ivory, and antler.

Solutrean tools are good examples of Upper Paleolithic skill and, perhaps, esthetic appreciation as well. In this lithic tradition stoneknapping developed to the finest degree ever known. Using a pressure-flaking technique, the artist/technicians made beautiful parallel-sided lance heads, expertly flaked on both surfaces, with such delicate points they can be considered works of art that quite possibly never served, or were intended to serve, a utilitarian purpose.

The last stage of the Upper Paleolithic, known as the **Magdalenean**, was a spectacular period of technological innovation. The spear thrower (Fig. 17-13), a wooden or bone hooked rod (called an *atlatl*), acted to extend the hunter's arm, thus enhancing the force and distance of a spear throw. For catching salmon and other fish, the barbed harpoon is a clever example of the craftsperson's skill. There is also evidence that the bow and arrow may have been used (for the first time) during this period. The introduction of the punch technique (Fig. 17-14) provided an abundance of standardized blank stone flakes that could be fashioned into burins for working wood, bone, and antler; into borers, for drilling holes in skins, bones, and shells; and into blades for knives with serrated or notched edges for scraping wooden shafts into a variety of tools.

The elaboration of many more specialized tools by Upper Paleolithic peoples probably made more resources available to them and may also have had an impact on the biology of these populations. Professor C. Loring Brace of the University of Michigan has suggested that, with more efficient tools used for food processing, anatomically modern *sapiens* would not have required such large front teeth (incisors). With relaxed selection pressures (no longer favoring large anterior teeth), incorporation of random mutations would through time lead to reduction of dental size and accompanying facial features. In particular, the lower face became less prognathic (as compared to archaic specimens) and thus produced the concavity of the cheekbones called a *canine fossa*. Moreover, as the dental-bearing portion of the lower jaw regressed, the buttressing below would have become modified into a *chin*, that distinctive feature seen in anatomically modern *sapiens*.

In addition to their reputations as hunters, western Europeans of the Upper Paleolithic are even better known for their art. Interest in art can be seen throughout the Upper Paleolithic. Fine examples of small sculptures have been excavated in western, central, and eastern Europe. Tools and tool handles, often engraved with elegant and realistic animal carvings, and sculptured figurines can be found in many areas of Europe. In the Aurigna-

Magdalenian The final phase of the Upper Paleolithic in Europe.

Figure 17-13

Spear thrower (atlatl). Note the carving.

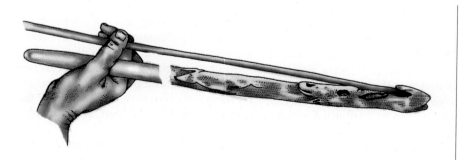

cian stage, sculpture in the round was achieved with surprising grace and style.

Female figurines, known as Venuses, were sculpted not only in western Europe, but in central and eastern Europe, and Siberia as well. Some of these figures were realistically carved, and the faces appear to be modeled after actual women. Other figurines may seem grotesque with sexual characteristics exaggerated, perhaps for fertility or ritual purposes.

It was, however, during the final phases of the Upper Paleolithic, particularly during the Magdalenian, that European prehistoric art reached its climax. In Lascaux Cave of southern France, immense wild bulls dominate what is called the Great Hall of Bulls, and horses, deer, and other animals adorn the walls in black, red, and yellow, drawn with remarkable skill.

Although beautiful artwork is best known in France (at Lascaux and many other sites), it is a cave at Altamira in northern Spain that is perhaps the most exemplary. Superb portrayals of bison in red and black, painted on walls and ceilings, taking advantage of natural bulges to give a sense of relief, fill the cave. It is a treasure of beautiful art whose meaning has never been satisfactorily explained. It could have been religious, magical, a form of visual communication, or art for the sake of beauty.

Ever since cave art was discovered, attempts have been made to interpret the sculptures, paintings, and other graphic material found in the caves or on rocks and tools at open-air archeological sites. One of the early explanations of Upper Paleolithic art emphasized the relationship of paintings to hunting: hunting rituals were viewed as a kind of imitative magic that would increase prey animal populations or help hunters successfully find and kill their quarry. As new hypotheses were published, their applicability and deficiencies were discussed. As many of these new hypotheses faded, others were expounded and the cycle of new hypotheses, critiques, etc., continued.

Among these hypotheses, the association of religious ritual and magic is still considered viable because of the importance of hunting in the Upper Paleolithic economy. Nevertheless, other ideas about these graphics have been widely discussed: the viewing of Upper Paleolithic art from a male/female perspective; the consideration of a prevalent dots and lines motif as a notational system associated with language, writing, or a calendar system (Marshack, 1972, 1976). Other perspectives and ongoing questions include why certain areas of caves were used for painting, but not other similar areas; why certain animals were painted, but not others; why males were painted singly or in groups, but women only in groups; why males were painted near animals, but women never were; and why groups of animals were painted in the most acoustically resonant areas (rituals were perhaps performed in areas in the cave with the best acoustic properties).

Figure 17-14

The punch blade technique.

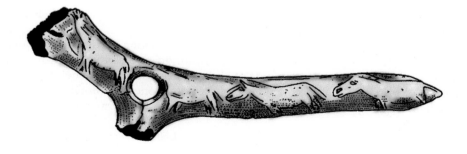

Figure 17-15

Magdalenian bone artifact. Note the realistic animal engraving on this object (the precise function of which is unknown).

(a)   (b)

Figure 17-16

Venus of Brassempouy. Upper Paleolithic artists were capable of portraying human realism (shown here) as well as symbolism (depicted in Fig. 17-17). (a) Frontal view; (b) lateral view.

A recent explanation has been suggested by Lawrence Straus (1991), who considers the severe climatic conditions during the maximum of the Last Glacial, around 20,000 to 18,000 y.a. It was during this period in southwestern France and Iberia (Spain and Portugal) that most of the cave and mobile art was created. Straus points out that wherever there are clusters of living sites, there are cave art sanctuaries and residential sites with abundant mobile art objects. The caves could have been meeting places for local bands of people and loci for group activities. Bands could share hunting techniques and knowledge, and paintings and engravings served as "encoded information" that could be passed on across generations. Such information, Straus argues, would have been crucial for dealing with the severe conditions of the Last Glacial.

THE NEAR EAST

Most of our knowledge of the Upper Paleolithic stems from European studies. There were similar changes in other parts of the world, but they have yet to be as thoroughly examined. In the Near East, engraved pebbles have been found, but the artistic floresence of western Europe is absent.

Figure 17-17

Venus of Willendorf, Austria.

AFRICA

Microliths (thumbnail-sized stone flakes hafted to make knives, saws, etc.) and blades characterize Late Stone Age* technology. There was also much use of bone and antler in central Africa.

Open-air settlements, probably temporary camps for a particular purpose, such as butchering, are well known. Also common, and continuing from the Middle Stone Age, are settlements at springs, caves, and rock shelters. Personal adornment items come into use in the Late Stone Age. Bone beads and shell and stone pendants have a wide distribution, and ochre and other col-

---

*The Late Stone Age in Africa is equivalent to the Upper Paleolithic in Eurasia.

Figure 17-18

Cave painting.

oring materials may have been used for painting the body or decorating clothing. Rock art, some of it quite elaborate, of the Late Stone Age is known from many areas of sub-Saharan Africa.

AUSTRALIA

By the late Pleistocene, the coast, river, and lake areas of Australia were already inhabited. More than 20,000 y.a., Australians had begun grinding stone ax heads, the first ever made anywhere, and a few thousand years later ground stone mortars, pestles, grinders, and grinding slabs had become established. These stone tools suggest the gathering of seeds, roots, and vegetables, and made a semisedentary lifestyle possible.

Panels of hand stencils and areas of red pigment have been found in caves on Tasmania, an island off the coast of Australia. Patterns of incisions and rectilinear lines were made on cave limestone. There are thousands of rock engraving sites in central Australia, consisting of circles and bird tracks, and geometric forms, such as stars and crosses. Anthropomorphic-like creatures, often with complex headdresses, have been found at some sites.

The early Australians buried their dead, and some were perhaps first ritually cremated and then buried. Bone ornaments, such as beads, have been found in southwestern Australia. Rhys Jones, an Australian prehistorian, suggests that "these data may be associated with an aesthetic sense, perhaps social differentiations and beliefs in the religious sphere" (1989, p. 773), a conclusion that could well apply to all Upper Paleolithic peoples.

CHINA

Tools in the Chinese Upper Paleolithic are similar to those on other continents: stone and bone artifacts, flake tools, and cores shaped for reduction and retouching. Typical implements include thumbnail scrapers, projectile points, borers, side scrapers, end scrapers, burins, and backed knives. Bone needles at Upper Cave, Zhoukoudian (the site of the famous *H. erectus* finds discussed in Chapter 15), suggest protective clothing to deal with the harsh climatic conditions. From an archeological locality in north China, remains of at least 130 wild horses and 88 wild asses indicate that large-game hunting was apparently specialized and an important subsistence source.

Cave art like that in western Europe is not found in China, but a number of sites yielded such ornaments as perforated shells, bones, and ostrich egg-shells. Upper Cave also produced perforated marine shells and pebbles, stone beads, and drilled fox teeth.

There is also evidence of ritual burials at Upper Cave, where several skulls and postcranial bones were placed on a layer of hematite (a red iron ore) powder. Also, many of the ornaments in association with the burials were stained red with hematite. It appears that Upper Paleolithic ritual burials with accompanying religious implications were a worldwide phenomenon.

Summary of Upper Paleolithic Culture

As we look back at the Upper Paleolithic, we can see it as the culmination of two million years of cultural development. Change proceeded incredibly slowly for most of the Pleistocene, but as cultural traditions and materials accumulated and the brain (and, we assume, intelligence) expanded and reorganized, the rate of change quickened.

Cultural evolution continued with the appearance of early archaic *sapiens* and moved a bit faster with later archaic *sapiens*. Neandertals in Eurasia, and their contemporaries elsewhere, added ceremonial burials, rituals, techno-logical innovations, and much more.

Building on the existing culture, Late Pleistocene populations attained so-phisticated cultural and material heights in a seemingly short (by previous standards) burst of exciting activity. In Europe and central Africa particularly there seem to have been dramatic cultural innovations that saw big-game hunting, potent new weapons (including harpoons, spear throwers, possibly the bow and arrow), body ornaments, needles, "tailored" clothing, and buri-als with grave goods, which might indicate some sort of status hierarchy.

This dynamic age was doomed, or so it appears, brought on by the cli-matic changes of about 10,000 y.a. As the temperature slowly rose and the glaciers retreated, animal and plant species were seriously affected, and humans were thus affected as well. As traditional prey animals and easy-to-process food were depleted or disappeared altogether, other means of obtaining food were sought.

Grinding hard seeds or roots became important, and as familiarity with vegetation increased, domestication of plants and animals developed. De-pendence on domestication became critical and with it came permanent set-tlements, new technology, and more complex social organization.

The long road from hominid origins, from those remarkable footprints en-graved into the African savanna, has now led by millions of chance evolu-tionary turnings to us, anatomically modern human beings. But this road is not yet finished. We are the inheritors, both biologically and culturally of our hominid forbears. Now, for the first time in human evolution, perhaps we have some choice in the direction our species may take. Knowledge of the past—of human potentials and of human limitations—might well be our best guide in making intelligent choices as individuals and most especially col-lectively as a species. Evolution has endowed us with a marvelous brain, and with it the capacity for great intelligence, artistic achievement and much more. However, wisdom is a hard won treasure to be learned anew every generation.

Summary

The date and location of the origin of anatomically modern human beings have been the subject of a fierce debate for the past decade, and the end is not in sight. One hypothesis (Recent African evolution; complete displacement) claims anatomically modern forms first evolved in Africa more than 100,000 y.a. and then, migrating out of Africa, completely displaced archaic *sapiens* in the rest of the world. Another school (Multiregional evolution; regional continuity) takes a diametrically different view and maintains that, in various geographic regions of the world, local groups of archaic *sapiens* evolved directly to anatomically modern humans. A third hypothesis (African-European *sapiens*; partial displacement) takes a somewhat middle position suggesting an African origin but also accepting some later hybridization outside of Africa.

The Upper Paleolithic was an age of extraordinary innovation and achievement in technology and art. Many new and complex tools were introduced, displaying fine skill in working wood, bone, and antler. It was a period that might be compared, for its time, to the past several hundred years of our own technological advance.

Cave art in France and Spain displays the masterful ability of Upper Paleolithic painters, and beautiful sculptures have been found at many European sites. Cave art has also been found in Africa and Australia. Upper Paleolithic *Homo sapiens* displayed amazing development in a relatively short period of time. The culture produced during this period led the way to still newer and more complex cultural techniques and methods.

Questions for Review

1. What characteristics define anatomically modern *sapiens*?
2. How do these characteristics of modern *sapiens* compare with archaic *sapiens*?
3. What are the three major theories that seek to explain the origin and dispersal of *Homo sapiens sapiens*? Compare and critically discuss these three views.
4. How have data from mitochondrial DNA been used to support an African origin of *H. sapiens sapiens*? How has this evidence been recently challenged?
5. Discuss (and compare) the early evidence of anatomically modern humans from two different regions.
6. It is said that the Upper Paleolithic was a time of technological innovation. Support this statement by using specific evidence and compare with cultural data from earlier in the Pleistocene.
7. From which regions has cave art, dating to the Late Pleistocene, been discovered? Particularly for the cave art of Europe, what explanations of its meaning have been proposed?

Atlas of Primate Skeletal Anatomy

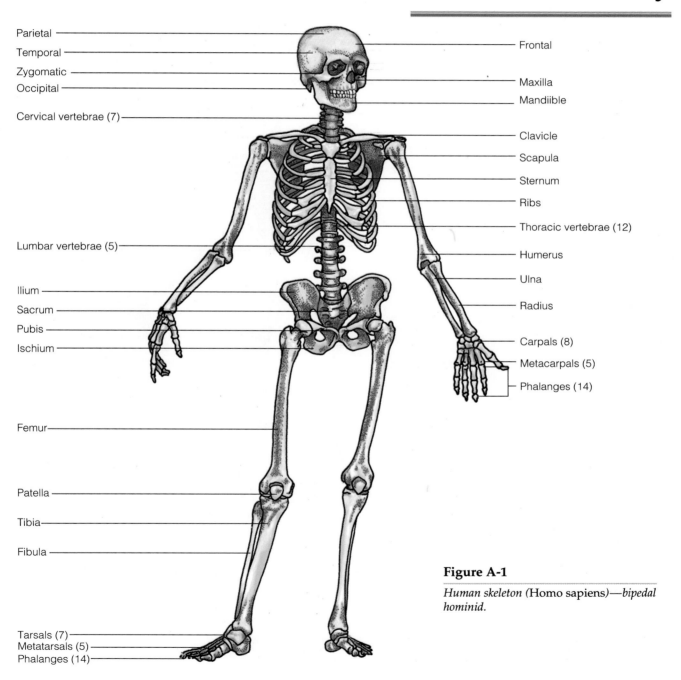

Parietal

Temporal

Zygomatic

Occipital

Cervical vertebrae (7)

Lumbar vertebrae (5)

Ilium

Sacrum

Pubis

Ischium

Femur

Patella

Tibia

Fibula

Tarsals (7)
Metatarsals (5)
Phalanges (14)

Frontal

Maxilla

Mandiible

Clavicle

Scapula

Sternum

Ribs

Thoracic vertebrae (12)

Humerus

Ulna

Radius

Carpals (8)

Metacarpals (5)

Phalanges (14)

Figure A-1

Human skeleton (Homo sapiens)—*bipedal hominid.*

Figure A-2

*Chimpanzee skeleton (Pan troglodytes)—
knuckle-walking pongid.*

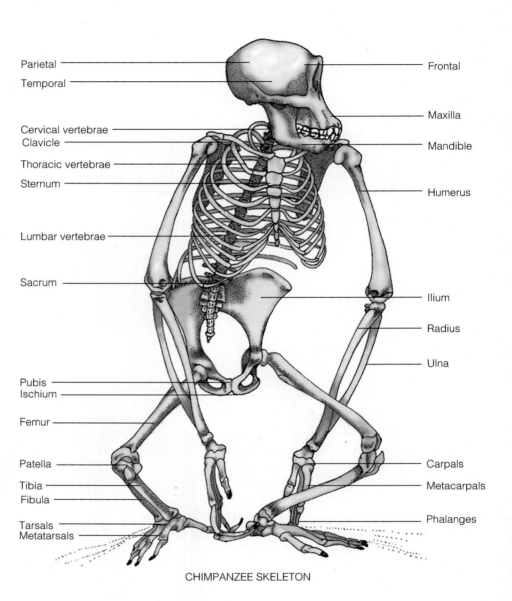

Parietal

Temporal

Cervical vertebrae

Clavicle

Thoracic vertebrae

Sternum

Lumbar vertebrae

Sacrum

Pubis

Ischium

Femur

Patella

Tibia

Fibula

Tarsals

Metatarsals

Frontal

Maxilla

Mandible

Humerus

Ilium

Radius

Ulna

Carpals

Metacarpals

Phalanges

CHIMPANZEE SKELETON

Figure A-3

Monkey skeleton (rhesus macaque; Macaca mulatta*)—A typical quadrupedal primate.*

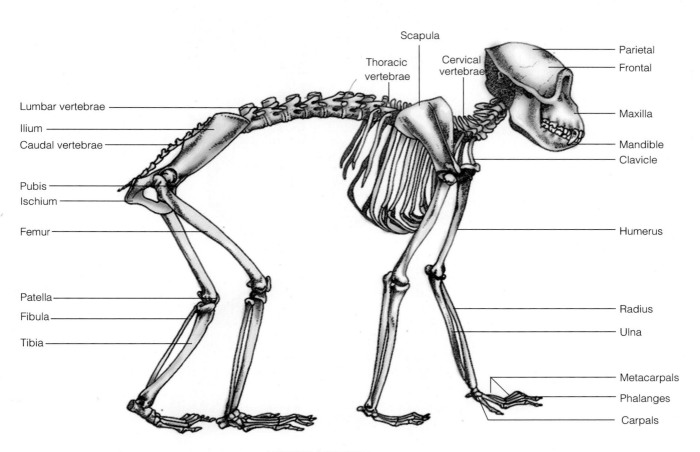

MONKEY SKELETON

Figure A-4

Human cranium.

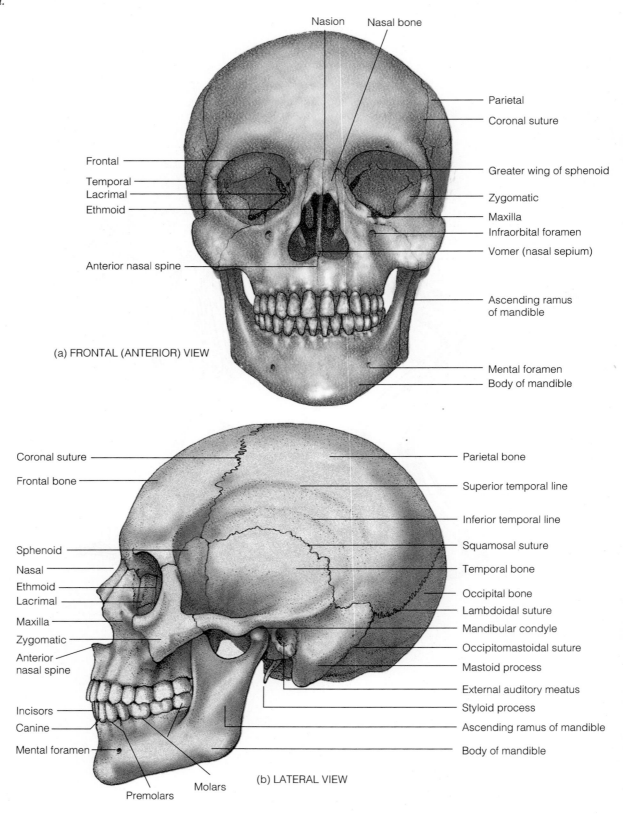

Nasion

Nasal bone

Parietal

Coronal suture

Frontal

Temporal

Lacrimal

Ethmoid

Greater wing of sphenoid

Zygomatic

Maxilla

Infraorbital foramen

Vomer (nasal sepium)

Anterior nasal spine

Ascending ramus
of mandible

(a) FRONTAL (ANTERIOR) VIEW

Mental foramen

Body of mandible

Coronal suture

Frontal bone

Parietal bone

Superior temporal line

Inferior temporal line

Sphenoid

Nasal

Ethmoid

Lacrimal

Maxilla

Zygomatic

Anterior
nasal spine

Squamosal suture

Temporal bone

Occipital bone

Lambdoidal suture

Mandibular condyle

Occipitomastoidal suture

Mastoid process

External auditory meatus

Incisors

Canine

Mental foramen

Styloid process

Ascending ramus of mandible

Body of mandible

Premolars

Molars

(b) LATERAL VIEW

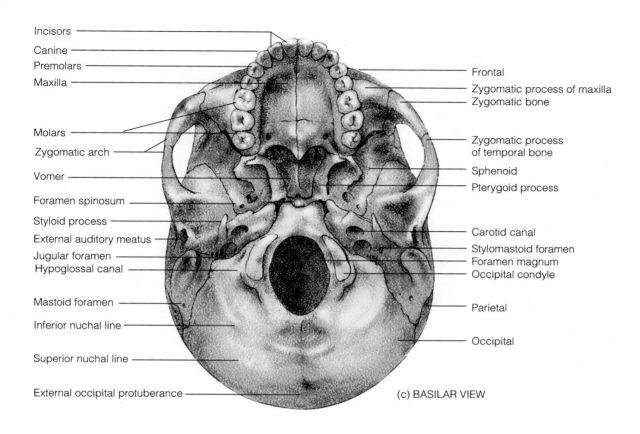

Incisors
Canine
Premolars
Maxilla

Molars
Zygomatic arch

Vomer

Foramen spinosum
Styloid process
External auditory meatus
Jugular foramen
Hypoglossal canal

Mastoid foramen
Inferior nuchal line

Superior nuchal line

External occipital protuberance

Frontal
Zygomatic process of maxilla
Zygomatic bone

Zygomatic process
of temporal bone
Sphenoid
Pterygoid process

Carotid canal
Stylomastoid foramen
Foramen magnum
Occipital condyle

Parietal

Occipital

(c) BASILAR VIEW

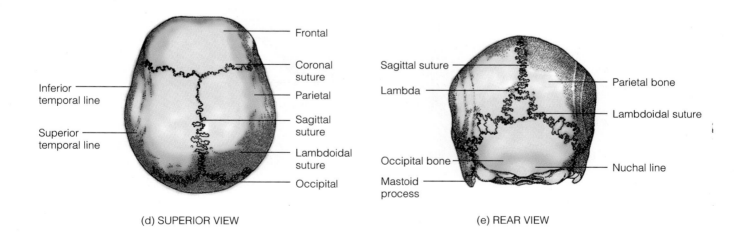

Inferior
temporal line

Superior
temporal line

Frontal

Coronal
suture

Parietal

Sagittal
suture

Lambdoidal
suture

Occipital

(d) SUPERIOR VIEW

Sagittal suture

Lambda

Occipital bone

Mastoid
process

Parietal bone

Lambdoidal suture

Nuchal line

(e) REAR VIEW

Figure A-5

Gorilla crania.

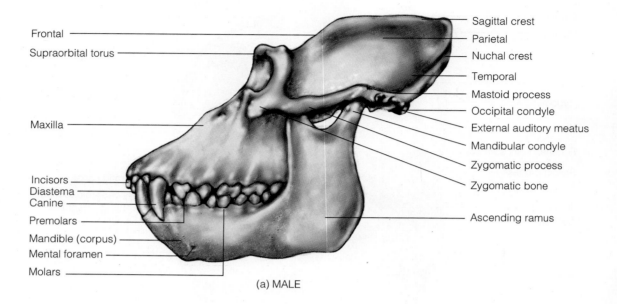

Frontal
Supraorbital torus
Maxilla
Incisors
Diastema
Canine
Premolars
Mandible (corpus)
Mental foramen
Molars

Sagittal crest
Parietal
Nuchal crest
Temporal
Mastoid process
Occipital condyle
External auditory meatus
Mandibular condyle
Zygomatic process
Zygomatic bone
Ascending ramus

(a) MALE

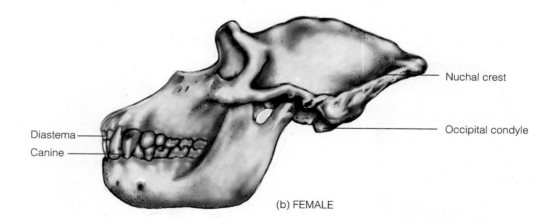

Diastema
Canine

Nuchal crest

Occipital condyle

(b) FEMALE

Figure A-6

Human vertebral column.

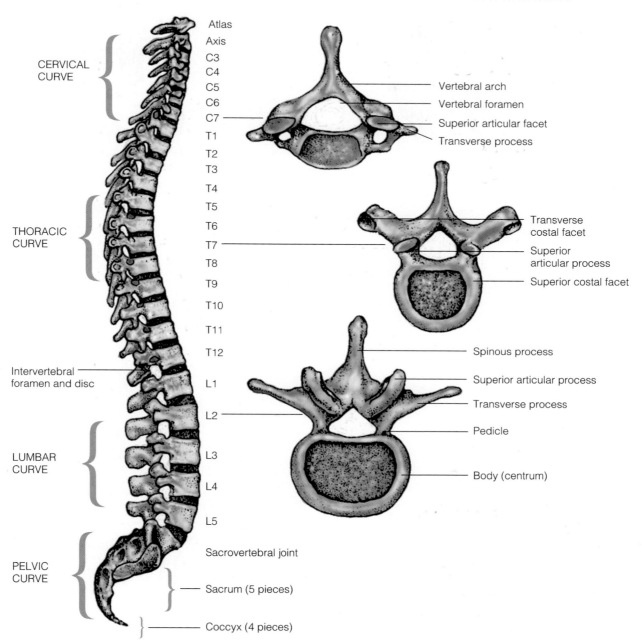

Human vertebral column (lateral view) and representative views of selected cervical, thoracic, and lumbar vertebrae (superior views).

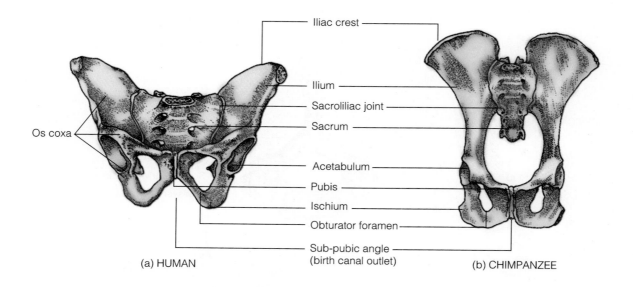

Figure A-7

Pelvic girdles.

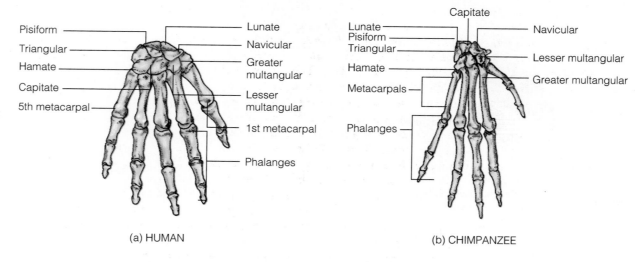

Figure A-8

Hand anatomy.

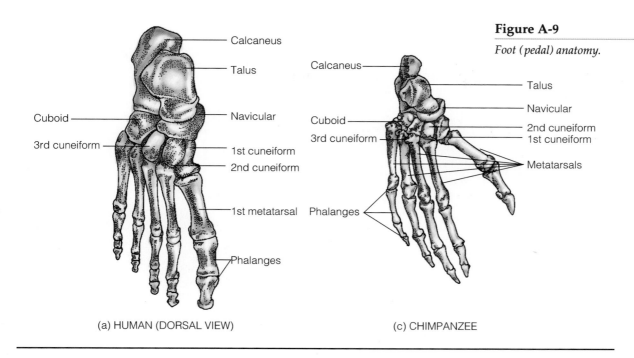

(a) HUMAN (DORSAL VIEW)

(c) CHIMPANZEE

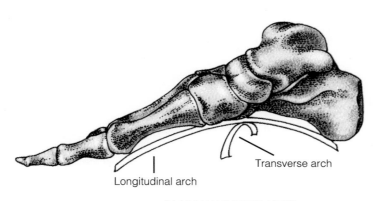

(b) HUMAN (MEDIAL VIEW)

Forensic Anthropology*

It is a fascinating and startling fact that there are hundreds of millions of humans buried around this planet, and often their bones come to light for one reason or another. Indeed, thousands of skeletons have been excavated and are now curated in various natural history and anthropology museums. Skeletal biologists (also called *human osteologists*) are often asked to assist in unearthing these human remains and to perform various specialized analyses on them when prehistoric or, occasionally, historic burial sites are excavated.

Many situations occur in which forensic anthropologists are called upon by the police and other law enforcement agencies to assist in identification by using their knowledge of skeletal biology. Usually, the anthropologist is called upon to provide clues as to the personal identity of a deceased individual or individuals (through analysis of partially skeletalized remains), but is also occasionally asked to perform other tasks. Some examples of these tasks are: to identify skeletal trauma, match remains from a suspected scene of a crime with the corpus delecti, sort human from nonhuman remains, and, sometimes, to either compare a photograph to a living person, or to compare two photographs to determine the identity of the persons pictured. A few case reports will better illustrate the types of problems encountered by a forensic anthropologist. These are based on actual cases, and will be resolved for you at the end of this section.

Case 1: An old plane crash was discovered in the remote mountains of Colorado, and skeletal material was still inside. How many people are represented by this skeletal material, and who were they?

Case 2: A skeleton was discovered by a farmer while plowing his fields before planting. He contacted the local sheriff, who wondered if a past homicide victim could have been buried there.

Case 3: A building has exploded because of a natural gas leak, and five people are thought to have been inside at the time of the explosion and fire. These individuals were: a 23-year-old female and a 24-year-old female, both with no children; a 32-year-old female with three children; a 53-year-old male, and a 54-year-old male. As these remains are almost completely skeletonized, how can they be identified?

Case 4: A very old photograph that bears a striking resemblance to Abraham Lincoln was discovered in the attic of an old house. Tests could be performed by other forensic specialists (questioning documents examiners, for example) to determine the age of the photo-

*This appendix was written by Diane France and Robert Jurmain, with special thanks to George Gill for his contributions.

graphic paper, etc., and, of course, these would aid in discounting a fraudulent claim; but the photograph could still be of the correct age and be of a person other than Lincoln.

The first three cases must begin with a determination of the species represented by the remains. If the bones are not human, the forensic anthropologist's role is usually over, but if they are human, the work has just begun. Even if the police have an idea of who is represented by these remains, the specialist usually begins the investigation with a determination of the basic features: sex, age, race, stature, skeletal pathology, and notation of idiosyncrasies that could aid in final identification (such as healed fractures, prosthetic devices, and so on).

Sexing the Skeleton

Several evolutionary factors have helped us to be able to identify sex in the human skeleton. The pelvic girdles in quadrupeds do not differ greatly between males and females of a species, but in humans the birth canal had a tendency to become smaller with bipedalism. This problem was compounded by the human newborn, whose head was relatively larger than the newborns of other animals, so throughout our evolution modifications were selected for in the female pelvic girdle relating to proportionately larger birth outlets, and these modifications aid in the determination of sex today. This sexual dimorphism (difference in morphology between the sexes) is most reliably diagnosed in the pelvic girdle, as shown below (see Figs. B-1 and B-2).

Pelvic Girdle	Typical Male	Typical Female
Subpubic angle	Less than 90 degrees	More than 90 degrees
Pubic shape	Triangular	Rectangular
Subpubic angle shape (see also Phenice, 1969)	Convex	Concave
Greater sciatic notch	Less than 68 degrees	More than 68 degrees
Sacrum	Smaller and more curved	Larger and straighter

Figure B-1

Male pelvic girdle.

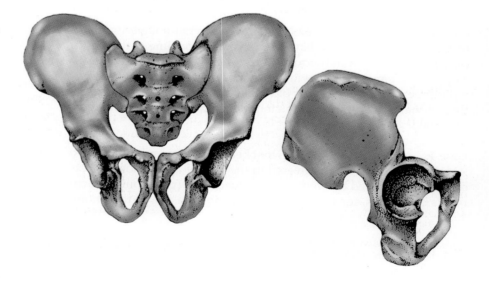

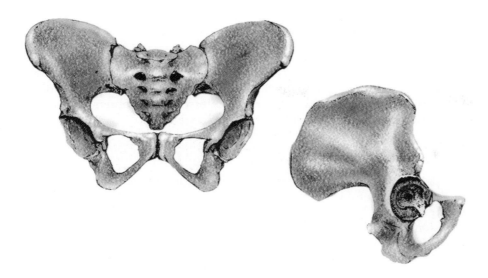

Figure B-2

Female pelvic girdle.

In addition, humans display types of sexual dimorphism also common to most other animals: Males are usually larger and have more rugged areas for muscle attachments than do females of the same species. However, in order to utilize this size difference in sex determination, the researcher must be able to identify the population from which the skeleton was taken, as whole populations differ in skeletal size and robusticity. For instance, Asian Indians are much smaller and more gracile than Australian Aborigines.

After the pelvis, the cranium is the area of the skeleton most commonly used for sex determination. Some of these traits are listed below (see Fig. B-3).

Cranium	Typical Male	Typical Female
Muscle attachment areas (mastoid process, etc.)	More pronounced	Less pronounced
Supraorbital torus (brow-ridges)	More pronounced	Less pronounced
Frontal bone	Slanting	Globular
Supraorbital rim (in eye orbit)	Rounded	Sharp
Palate	Deep	Shallow

Other bones of the body also show secondary sex characteristics, but are often less reliable than those of the cranium, as heavy muscle use affects the size and ruggedness of the muscle attachments, which can then sometimes change the diagnosis of sex. Areas probably not as affected by muscle use are:

Other Bones	Typical Male	Typical Female
Suprascapular notch on scapula	Often present	Often absent
Femur: angle of neck to shaft	Smaller angle	Greater angle

The standards discussed here are for adult skeletons; sexing techniques for pre-adolescents are not as yet widely used.

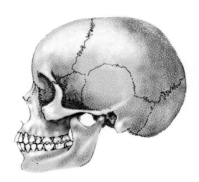

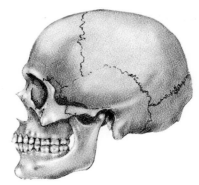

Figure B-3

Cranium and mandible: female (top); *male* (bottom).

Determination of Age

During growth, the skeleton and dentition undergo regular changes that allow the determination of age at death. The age determination in individuals under about 20 years centers on deciduous (baby) and permanent dentition eruption times, on the appearance of ossification centers, and on the fusion of the separate ends of long bones to bone shafts.

DENTAL ERUPTION

The determination of the ages at which the deciduous and permanent dentition erupts is useful in identifying age to approximately 15 years. The third molar (wisdom tooth) erupts after this time, but is so variable in age of eruption (if it erupts at all) that it is not a very reliable age indicator. (See Fig. B-4.)

BONE GROWTH

Postcranial bones are preceded by a cartilage model that is gradually replaced by bone, both in the primary growth centers (the diaphyses) and in the secondary centers (the ends of the bones, or epiphyses). The initial ossification centers are, of course, very small, and are only rarely encountered by a forensic anthropologist. The bone continues to grow until the epiphyses fuse to the diaphyses. Because this fusion occurs at different times in different bones, the age of an individual can be determined by which epiphyses have fused and which have not (see Figs. B-5 and B-6). The characteristic undulating appearance of the unfused surfaces of bone helps differentiate it from the mature long bone (smooth) or merely a broken end of a bone (sharp and jagged).

Figure B-4

Skeletal age: dental development.

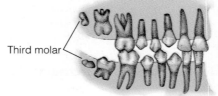

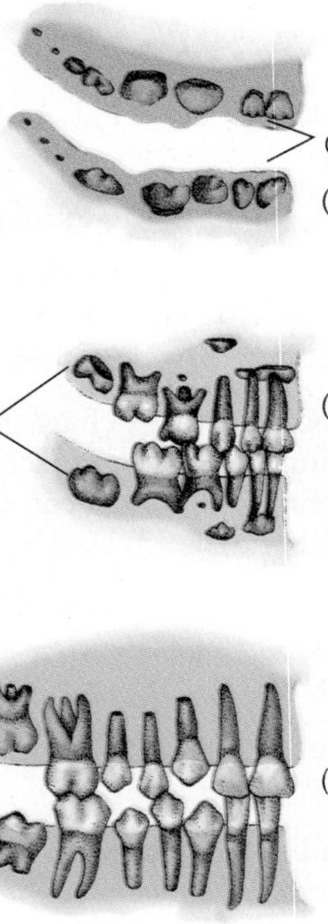

Gumline

(a) Birth: The crowns for all the deciduous (milk) teeth (shown in color) are present; no roots, however, have yet formed.

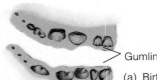

First permanent molar

(b) 2 years: All deciduous teeth (shown in color) are erupted; the first permanent molar and permanent incisors have crowns (unerupted)formed, but no roots.

Third molar

(c) 12 years: All permanent teeth are erupted except the third molar (wisdom tooth).

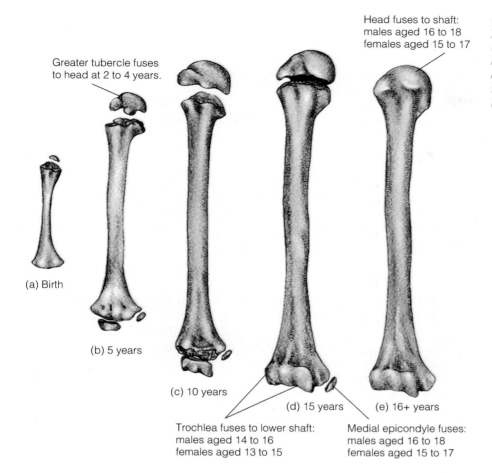

Greater tubercle fuses
to head at 2 to 4 years.

Head fuses to shaft:
males aged 16 to 18
females aged 15 to 17

(a) Birth

(b) 5 years

(c) 10 years

(d) 15 years

(e) 16+ years

Trochlea fuses to lower shaft:
males aged 14 to 16
females aged 13 to 15

Medial epicondyle fuses:
males aged 16 to 18
females aged 15 to 17

Figure B-5

Skeletal age: epiphyseal union in the humerus. Some regions of the humerus exhibit some of the earliest fusion centers in the body, while others are among the latest to complete fusion (not until late ꭓlescence).

Females mature more quickly than males, so a one to two year difference will have to be factored into the age determination (in those cases, of course, where we *can* first determine sex).

Once a person has reached physiological maturity (by the early 20s), the determination of age becomes more difficult. Several techniques are used, including the progressive, regular changes in the pubic symphyseal face (the most common technique), in the sternal ends of the ribs, in the auricular surface of the ilium, in ectocranial (outside the cranium) and endocranial (inside the cranium) suture closures, and in cellular changes determined by microscopic examination of the cross section of various long bones. In addition, degenerative changes, including arthritis and osteoporosis, can aid in the determination of relative age, but should not be used by themselves to determine age, as injury and certain diseases can cause changes that mimic old age in bones.

Pubic Symphyseal Face: The pubic symphyseal face in the young (Fig. B-8) is characterized by a billowing surface (with ridges and furrows) such as seen on a normal epiphysis, but undergoes regular metamorphosis from age 18 onward. Figure B-9 shows a symphyseal face typical of an age in the mid-30s, with a more finely grained face and perhaps still containing remnants of the ridge and furrow system. Figure B-10 is typical of an age in the early 60s, with bony outgrowths often developing on the outer rims of the symphyseal face. The first technique was developed by T. W. Todd (1920, 1921) utilizing dissection room cadavers. McKern and Stewart (1957) developed a technique

Figure B-6

Distal femur.

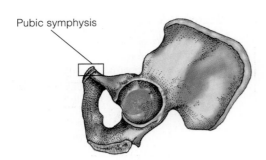

Pubic symphysis

(a) Position of the pubic symphysis. This area of the pelvis shows systematic changes progressively throughout adult life. Two of these stages are shown in (b) and (c).

(b) Age: 21. The face of the symphysis shows the typical "billowed" appearance of a young joint; no rim present.

(c) Age: mid-50s. The face is mostly flat, with a distinct rim formed around most of the periphery.

Figure B-7

Skeletal age: Remodeling of the pubic symphysis.

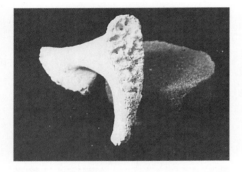

Figure B-8

Pubic symphysis face typical of an age in the late teens or early twenties.

Figure B-9

Pubic symphysis face typical of an age in the mid-thirties.

using American males killed in the Korean War. Both of the samples from which these systems were derived have limitations in that the dissection room sample used by Todd was based on individuals of uncertain age (Brooks, 1985, 1986) and the Korean War dead sample was predominantly young Caucasoid males, with few individuals over age 35.

Recently a system has been developed by J. M. Suchey, D. Katz, and S. T. Brooks based on a large sample (*n* = 739) of males for whom legal documentation of age was provided by death certificates. This autopsy room sample should be more representative of the general population than past samples. The majority of the males were born either in the United States or Mexico. This sample was taken at autopsies involving homicides, suicides, accidents, or unexpected natural deaths.

Determination of Race

When an anthropologist is asked to help in the identification of a parcel of bones, part of that identification must include a statement as to probable race, because society includes race as a part of the personal identity. Racial identification is often difficult, however, as most of the morphological characteristics we use to distinguish race follow a continuum; that is, one trait is more often, but not exclusively, associated with one race. Even skin color, the most noticeable of characteristics, cannot adequately categorize all individuals, for there are dark-skinned Caucasoids and Mongoloids (disregarding the effects of tanning), and light-skinned Negroids. In fact, it can be said that for many traits, there is more variation *within* races than *between* races. (See Chapter 5.)

The races of the world have been divided in different ways in history, but many anthropologists today identify five or six basic groups: Mongoloids (including Japanese, Chinese, and North, Central, and South American Indians), Negroids (including African and U.S. Blacks), Caucasoids (including Europeans, and other people with European ancestry, West Asians, Asian Indians, and some North American peoples), Australoids (Australian Aborigines), and Polynesians. This is not by any means a complete classification scheme, nor is it the only classification scheme used by physical anthropologists today.

The chart below lists some of the differences we usually see in the skulls of three races common to the Western Hemisphere (most of the currently important differences used in the identification of race occurs in the cranium). (See also Brues, 1977; Krogman, 1962; Stewart, 1979; Bass, 1987; and Gill, 1986.)

Feature	Negroid	Caucasoid	Mongoloid
Central incisors (cross section) (Dahlberg, 1951)	Blade	Rarely shoveled	Shoveled
Cranial shape[a]	Dolicocranic (long)	Mesocranic (medium)	Brachycranic (round)
Nasal root (top of nasal bridge)	Wide, rounded	Narrow, pinched	Medium, tented
Nasal aperture[b]	Platyrrhiny (wide)	Leptorrhiny (narrow)	Mesorrhiny (medium)
Zygomatic bone	Medium	Retreating	Projecting
External auditory meatus (ear opening)	Round	Round	Oval
Facial shape	Prognathic (lower face projects forward)	Orthognathic (lower face nonprojecting)	Medium

Figure B-10

Pubic symphysis face typical of an age in the early sixties.

In addition to the standard measurements, indices, and observations discussed here, further methods using skull and face measurements have been developed to aid in race determination. The most widely used of these is a *discriminant function* method (using a set of formulae) developed by Giles and Elliot (1962) for distinguishing Blacks, Caucasoids, and American Indians. Measurements are taken on the cranium of each adult, plugged into the formulae, and the final values plotted on a graph. It must be pointed out that, first, sex must be established (the formulae vary for males and females) and, second, the method is devised to answer only a limited question ("Is the cranium from a Black, from a Caucasoid, or from an American Indian?"). The discriminant function method itself helps address the first point (sex) since the technique has also been used to devise a formula for sex determination (from a few of the same measurements). The problem with this method is not so much the need to determine sex first, or the fact that it answers a limited

[a] The cranial shape is obtained from the Cranial Index, calculated from:

$$\frac{\text{Cranial breadth}}{\text{Cranial length}} \times 100$$

Up to 75 = dolicocrany
75–79.9 = mesocrany
80–84.9 = brachycrany
85 and up = hyperbrachycrany
(Bass, 1987)

[b] The nasal aperture shape is obtained from the Nasal Index:

$$\frac{\text{Nasal breadth}}{\text{Nasal height}} \times 100$$

Up to 47.9 = leptorrhiny
48–52.9 = mesorrhiny
53 and up = platyrrhiny
(Bass, 1987)

question (since most skulls on this continent come from Blacks, Caucasoids, or American Indians), but rather its accuracy. Particularly regarding American Indian specimens from the western United States, the percentage of correct ascertainment is quite low (Birkby, 1966; Gill, 1986). The sexing formula has proven quite accurate, however.

A new metric method developed by Gill and Hughes (Gill et al., 1988) appears to be much more accurate in race determination than the widely used Giles-Elliot approach. With six measurements (and three indices from them), it defines the amount of projection of the mid-face (which is extreme among the sharp-featured Caucasoids). The method does require a specialized (and rather rare) caliper, but is quite reliable in sorting Caucasoids from members of all other populations (in approximately 90 percent of cases). This method is also mathematically simple and can be performed quickly in an autopsy setting. However, it cannot address the problem of sorting Mongoloids from Blacks, since their mid-facial projections are similar.

So, even today, with many new techniques and extensive use of the computer, race determination remains a challenging and somewhat subjective area. It requires the simultaneous use of many approaches rather than any single "foolproof" method. "By definition, race is quantitative [no sharp boundaries]. Perfection can never be attained in defining or diagnosing a condition that does not even exist in absolute form" (Gill, 1986, p. 156).

Estimation of Stature

Formulae for stature reconstruction in unidentified individuals have been developed by measuring the long bones of deceased individuals of known

Figure B-11

Estimating stature: measuring the length of the femur.

Femur Length (MM)*	Stature	
	CM	INCHES
452	169	66
456	170	66
461	171	67
465	172	67
469	173	68

*Note: Data drawn from White males with known statures at time of death.

stature (Genoves, 1967; Trotter and Gleser, 1952). As is true of any statistical approximation of a population, these formulae are applied most reliably to the samples from which they are derived, though they may also be used on wider populations represented by these samples. Because these formulae were derived for each sex of various racial groups, the sex and race of the unknown individual must be known before these formulae can be reliably applied.

Resolution of the Case Studies

Case 1:   Even though the remains were burned, at least two individuals were identified as the pilot and friend who had filed the initial flight plan. It had been suspected at the time of the crash that at least one more person had been aboard, but there was no evidence to support that claim.

Case 2:   The skeleton was human and was determined to be that of an American Indian male. Although often remains of this kind in these circumstances are automatically diagnosed as an archeological burial, the rapid decay rates of flesh and bone in many areas of the United States and other countries will cause the remains to look ancient in a very short time; thus, a forensic anthropologist must be alert to this possibility. In this case, however, further circumstantial evidence suggested that this was archeological, in that a projectile point was found in the tibia at the knee.

Cases of this kind are useful in disputes between American Indian groups about land and resource ownership, for, in increasing numbers, the tribal affinity of remains can be determined. Human identification in these circumstances has far-reaching ramifications.

Case 3:   As noted in the introduction, the ages of two of the females and two of the males were very similar to each other, so that even with the determination of sex and age, the identity of these very fragmentary remains was not easily determined. The 32-year-old female was identified by age determination of the pubic symphysis, and by the evidence on the pelvis that she had had children. There was evidence of at least two other women aside from the 32-year-old female, but because the stature of these other women was very similar, the identification was only tentative. Completely reliable identification was not possible, and it was noted only that there was no evidence that those women were *not* present in the building. The identification of the men was similarly difficult, as they again were about the same age. In addition, though one of the men had a surgical staple in his right knee, which would ordinarily have been evidence for identification, that area of the body was not recovered for either individual. One of the men, however, was over 6 feet tall, while the other was around 5 feet 8 inches tall. Stature reconstruction using the femur, and premortem and postmortem X-rays of the pelvic region of the men were ultimately used for the identification.

Case 4:   Dr. Ellis Kerley (1984) determined, by comparing many features of a known Lincoln photograph to this photograph, that this was of a person other than our sixteenth president.

Photo Superimposition

Employed when a probable identification has been made, the technique of photo superimposition has been used in many cases lately, including the famous case of the identification of the Nazi war-criminal Josef Mengele (presented at the Annual Meeting of the American Academy of Forensic Sciences in New Orleans in 1986). In this and other cases, the skull (or large portions of the skull) are superimposed onto photographs of the known individual. If enough landmarks fall on the same position on the skull *and* on the photograph, the researcher is satisfied that he or she has made the correct identification. (Note: this technique could also have been used to reinforce the decision made in some of the cases outlined above.)

Facial Reconstruction in Human Identification*

Facial reconstruction (also termed *facial reproduction*) is a process used when other identification procedures (including fingerprints and dental matches) have been unsuccessful. Two different methods of producing a face on the skull are employed: a portrait of the individual using clues from the bones of the face; and a more direct, three-dimensional method of applying clay to the skull (or to a plaster cast of the skull). These techniques employ both science and art: The physical anthropologist discovers the age, sex, and race of the skull, but there is no direct evidence from bone that indicates the eye color, hair color and style, lip form, or degree of wrinkling or fleshiness in the individual. Therefore, there is a great deal of subjectivity in the rendering of the finished product; an exact reproduction is not expected, only a general likeness.

The following photographs show a facial reproduction taking shape. Erasers or blocks of clay marking tissue depths (arrived at experimentally from cadavers) are commonly glued to the skull. Clay strips, graduated to the various tissue depths, then "fill in the dots" between erasers, and the face is "fleshed out." The eyes, nose, lips, and sometimes ears are then fashioned according to various guidelines, and a wig is usually added.

Figures i and j show the reproduction of a Caucasoid female, over 60 years old. The first figure shows a nearly complete reproduction, but without the effects of aging, while Fig. j is the finished product, including the features characteristic of a woman of that age.

*Contributed by Diane France and Sandra C. Mays, Supervisor, Crime Laboratory Section, Wyoming State Crime Laboratory. Stages of reconstruction are from both authors; finished reconstruction by Sandra Mays.

Figure B-12

Facial reconstruction from a skull.

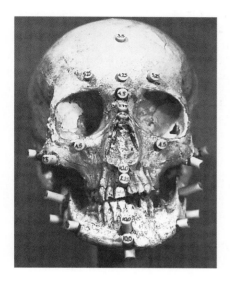

Figure a

Erasers precut to experimentally determined tissue depths are glued to skull.

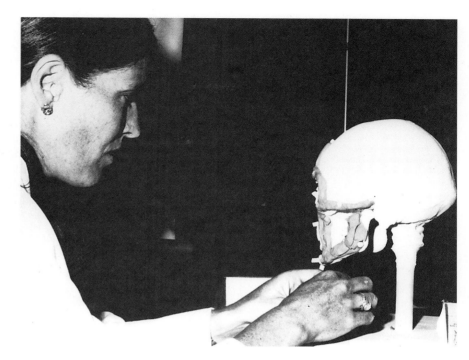

Figure b

Sandra Mays applies strips of clay between erasers, graduated to eraser depths.

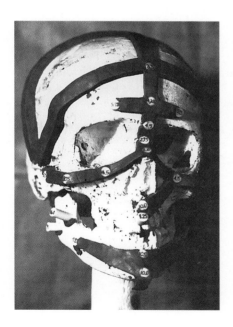

Figure c

Strips of clay connect erasers.

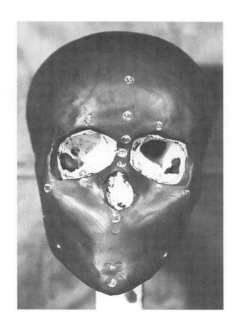

Figure d

Clay is added to "flesh out" the face.

Figures e and f

A nose and lips are added and refined.

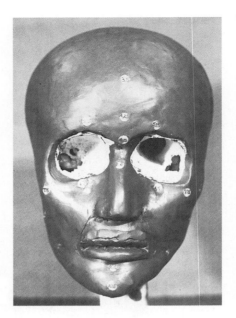
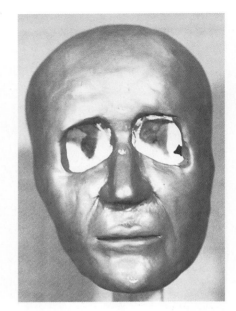

Figures g and h

Glass (or plastic) eyes are placed into orbits, and eyelids are fashioned.

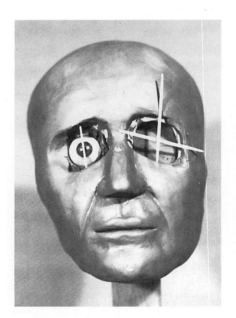
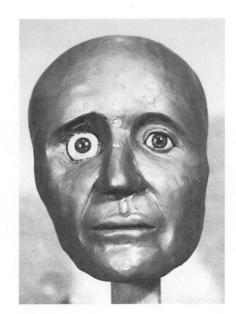

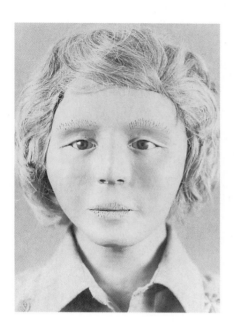
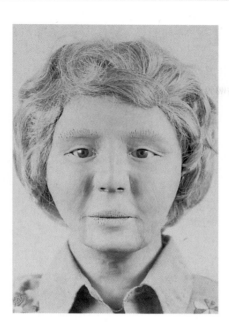

Figures i and j

Completed reproduction. (i) Before adding aging features. (j) After "aging" the face to correspond with aging indicators ascertained from other parts of the skeleton.

Glossary

Acclimatization   Physiological response within individuals to environmental pressure; usually takes a few weeks to a few months.

Acheulian   A stone tool industry of the Lower and Middle Pleistocene characterized by a large proportion of bifacial (that is, flaked on both sides) tools. Acheulian tool kits are very common in Africa, Southwest Asia, and Western Europe, but are absent elsewhere.

Adaptation   Functional response of organisms or populations to the environment. Adaptation results from evolutionary change (specifically, as a result of natural selection).

Adaptive niche   The whole way of life of an organism: where it lives, what it eats, how it gets food, and so forth.

Adaptive radiation   The relatively rapid expansion and diversification of an evolving group of organisms as they adapt to new niches.

Affiliative   Pertaining to amicable associations between individuals. Affiliative behaviors, such as grooming, reinforce social bonds and promote group cohesion.

Allele frequency   The proportion of one allele to all others at a given locus in a population.

Alleles   Alternative forms of a gene. Variants that occur at the same locus.

Alloparent   An individual, other than a parent, who exhibits parental behavior.

Allometry   Also called "scaling," allometry is the differential proportion among various anatomical structures. For example, the relative size of the brain changes during the development of an individual. Moreover, scaling effects must also be considered when comparing species.

Altricial   Dependent at birth. A relative measure. At the other end of the spectrum, we say young are "precocial." Among mammals, primates are relatively altricial.

Altruism   Helping others without direct benefit to oneself.

Amino acids   Small molecules that are the major component parts of proteins.

Analogies   Similarities between organisms based strictly on common function with no assumed common evolutionary descent.

Anatomically modern *sapiens* (AMS)   Includes all modern humans and some fossil forms, perhaps dating as early as 200,000 y.a. Defined by a set of derived characteristics, including cranial architecture and lack of skeletal robusticity. Usually classified at the subspecies level as *Homo sapiens sapiens*.

Anthropoid   A member of the suborder of Primates, the Anthropoidea, including monkeys, apes, and humans.

Anthropometry   Measurement of human body parts, most especially measurement of skeletal elements.

Anthropology   The field of inquiry that studies human culture and evolutionary aspects of human biology; includes cultural anthropology, archeology, linguistics and physical anthropology.

Arboreal   Adapted to life in the trees.

Archaic *Homo sapiens*   Earlier forms of *Homo sapiens* (including Neandertals) from the Old World that differ from *H. erectus*, but lack the full set of characteristics diagnostic of modern *sapiens*.

Artifacts   Traces of hominid behavior; very old ones are usually of stone. The objects either must be consistently modified or transported and collected in some consistent fashion.

Artificially provisioned   Food made available to primates by humans.

Association   What an archeological trace is found with.

Australopithecine   (os-tral-oh-pith´-e-seen) The colloquial name for members of the genus *Australopithecus*.

Autonomic   Autonomic responses are physiological manifestations not under voluntary control. An example in chimpanzees would be the erection of body hair during excitement. An example in humans is blushing. Both convey information regarding emotional states but neither is a deliberate behavior and communication is not intended.

Autosomes   All chromosomes except the sex chromosomes.

Axillae   Armpits.

Balanced polymorphism   The maintenance of two or more alleles in a population due to a selective advantage of the heterozygote.

Biocultural evolution   The mutual, interactive evolution of human biological structure and human culture. The concept that biology makes culture possible and that developing culture further influences the direction of biological evolution. The single most crucial organizing concept in understanding the unique components of human evolution.

Biological determinism   The concept that various aspects of behavior (e.g., intelligence, values, morals) are governed by biological factors (genes). The inaccurate association of various behavioral attributes with certain biological traits, such as skin color.

Biostratigraphy   Dating method based on evolutionary changes within an evolving lineage.

Bipedally   Walking habitually on two legs—the single most distinctive feature of the Hominidae.

Brachycephalic   Having a broad head or a skull in which the width is 80% or more of the length.

Breeding isolates   Populations geographically (and/or socially) separate and, therefore, easy to define.

Carcinogen An agent that promotes cancer (often a mutagen as well).

Carrier In recessive inheritance, a person who *carries* a recessive allele in single dose (that is, heterozygous). Thus, a carrier does not express the recessive trait in the phenotype.

Catarrhine The group (infraorder) comprising all Old World anthropoids, living and extinct.

Centromere The constricted portion of a chromosome. After replication, the two strands of a double-stranded chromosome are joined at the centromere.

Cerebrum The outer portions of the brain; in vertebrates, divided into right and left hemispheres.

Chordata (Chordates) The phylum of the Animal Kingdom that includes vertebrates.

Chromatin The loose, diffuse form of DNA seen during interphase. When condensed, chromatin forms into chromosomes.

Chromosomes Discrete structures composed of DNA and protein found only in the nuclei of cells. Chromosomes are only visible under magnification during certain portions of cell division.

Chronometric chrono: time; metric: measure. A dating technique that gives an estimate in actual numbers of years.

Cladistics The school of evolutionary biology that seeks to make hypotheses through interpreting patterns of primitive/derived characteristics.

Classification The ordering of organisms into categories, such as phyla, orders, families, to show evolutionary relationship.

Cline A distribution of allele frequencies over space. Actually, the depiction of frequencies by connecting lines of equal frequency (an isopleth), as in temperature indicators on a weather map. See Figures 5-1 and 5-2, for examples.

Codominance Refers to the expression of two alleles in the heterozygote. In this situation, neither allele is dominant or recessive, so that both are expressed in the phenotype.

Codons The triplets of messenger RNA bases that code for a specific amino acid during translation.

Communication Any act that conveys information, in the form of a message, to another. Frequently, the result of communication is a change in the behavior of the recipient. Communication may not be deliberate in that it may be the result of involuntary processes or a secondary consequence of an intentional action.

Complementary Refers to the highly specific manner in which DNA bases bond with one another. Complementary base pairing is the structural basis for DNA replication.

Consortship Exclusive relationship of one adult male and one adult female (usually, but not always, in estrus).

Conspecifics Members of the same species.

Context The environmental setting where an archeological trace is found.

Continental drift The movement of continents on sliding plates of the earth's surface. As a result, the position of large land masses has shifted dramatically in the last 250 million years.

Continuum A set of relationships in which all components fall along a single integrated spectrum. All life reflects a single *biological* continuum.

Core area The portion of a home range containing the highest concentration and most reliable supplies of food and water. The core area is frequently the area that will be defended.

Crepuscular (kre-pus´-kew-ler); creper: dark, dusty Active at twilight or dawn.

Culture Culture involves all aspects of human adaptation, including technology, traditions, language, social roles, and so forth. Culture is learned and transmitted from one generation to the next by nonbiological means.

Cytoplasm The portion of the cell contained within the cell membrane, excluding the nucleus. The cytoplasm consists of a semifluid material and contains numerous structures involved with cell functions.

Dendogram (tree diagram) A diagrammatic presentation of population relationships using several genetic traits simultaneously.

Deoxyribonucleic acid (DNA) The double-stranded molecule that contains the genetic code. DNA is the main component of chromosomes.

Derived Relating to a character state that reflects a more specific evolutionary line, and thus more informative of precise evolutionary relationships.

Derived Character state found only in particular lineages—and thus indicative of forms *after* a divergence.

Diploid The full complement of chromosomes. Two of each pair.

Displays Sequences of stereotyped behaviors that serve to communicate emotional states. Nonhuman primate displays are most frequently associated with reproductive or agonistic behavior.

Diurnal Active during daylight hours.

Dolicocephalic Having a long, narrow head. A skull in which the width is less than 75% of the length.

Dominance Also referred to as *dominance hierarchy* and *status* rank. The domination of some members of a group by other members. A hierarchy of ranked statuses sustained by hostile, or threat of hostile, behavior, which may result in greater access to resources, such as sleeping sites, food, and mates.

Dominant A trait governed by an allele that can be expressed in the presence of another, different allele (that is, heterozygotes). Dominant alleles prevent the expression of recessive alleles in heterozygotes.

Ecological niche Specific environmental setting to which an organism is adapted.

Encephalization The proportional size of the brain relative to some other measure, usually some estimate of overall body size.

Endocast An endocast is a solid (in this case, rock) impression of the inside of the skull showing the size, shape, and some details of the surface of the brain.

Enzymes Specialized proteins that initiate and direct chemical reactions in the body.

Epochs A category of the geological time scale; a subdivision of period. In the Cenozoic, epochs include: Paleocene, Eocene,

Oligocene, Miocene, Pliocene (from the Tertiary), and the Pleistocene and Recent (from the Quaternary).

Ethnography   The study of a human society. In cultural anthropology, ethnography is traditionally the study of non-Western societies.

Ethology   The study of the behavior of nonhuman animals.

Eugenics   The science of race improvement through forced sterilization of members of some groups and encouraged reproduction among others. An overly simplified, often racist view—now discredited.

Evolutionary trends   General structural and behavioral traits that are commonly shared by a related group of organisms.

Exogamous   *Exogamy* is a mating system whereby individuals find mating partners from outside their natal group. When applied to humans, the term may refer to marriage rules that dictate marriage with partners from another social grouping (for example, village, kinship group, or clan).

Fixity of species   The notion that species, once created, never change. An idea diametrically opposed to theories of biological evolution.

Free-ranging   Applied to animals living in their natural habitat.

Frugivorous   (fru-give'-or-us) Having a diet composed primarily of fruit.

Genetics   The study of gene structure and action and the patterns of inheritance of traits from parent to offspring. Genetic mechanisms are the underlying foundation for evolutionary change.

Genome   The entire genetic complement of an individual or that characteristic of a whole species.

Eukaryotic   Cells with nuclei, as seen in many single-celled organisms and all multicelled organisms.

Forensic anthropology   An applied anthropological approach dealing with matters of law. Physical anthropologists use their expertise to assist coroners and others in the analysis and interpretation of human remains.

Founder effect   Also called the *Sewall Wright effect*. A type of genetic drift in which allele frequencies are altered in small populations that are nonrandom samples of larger ones.

Gametes   Reproductive cells (eggs and sperm in animals) developed from precursor cells (primary sex cells) in the ovaries or testes.

Gene   The colloquial term referring to a segment of genetic material. Technically, this term has two different meanings (see *locus* and *allele*).

Gene pool   The total complement of genes in a population.

Genetic adaptation   Genetic changes within populations in response to selection (environmental) pressure; usually takes many generations.

Genetic drift   Evolutionary changes produced by random factors.

Genotype   The genetic makeup of an individual. *Genotype*

can refer to an organism's entire genetic makeup, or to the alleles at a particular locus.

Geological Time Scale   The organization of earth history into eras, epochs, and periods. Commonly used by geologists and paleoanthropologists.

Grooming   Cleaning through the hair and fur.

Half-life   The amount of time it takes a radioactive isotope to change half its initial (or remaining) amount to a by-product. If ^{238}U changes to lead with a half-life of 4.5 billion years, that means it takes this amount of time to convert half the ^{238}U to lead.

Haploid   A half-set of chromosomes; one of each pair. Haploid complements are found in gametes.

Hardy-Weinberg equilibrium   The mathematical relationship expressing—under ideal conditions—the predicted distribution of genes in populations; the central theorem of population genetics.

Hederodontism   Having different teeth. Characteristic of mammals whose teeth consist of incisors, canines, premolars, and molars.

Hemizygous   *Hemi* means half. The condition in males for an allele on the X chromosome. As males have only one X chromosome, the allele is always expressed.

Heterozygous   Having different alleles at the same locus on both members of homologous chromosomes.

Home range   The area exploited by an animal or social group. Usually given for one year—or the lifetime of an animal.

Hominidae   The taxonomic family to which humans belong; also includes other, now extinct, bipedal relatives.

Hominids   Members of the family Hominidae.

Hominoid   A member of the superfamily, Hominoidea. The group includes apes and humans.

Homoiothermic (Homoiothermy)   The ability to maintain a constant, internal body temperature through physiological means, independent of environmental factors. Whereas reptiles today rely upon exposure to the sun to raise energy levels and body temperature, birds and mammals do not. Some dinosaurs also appear to have been homoiothermic.

Homologies   Similarities between organisms based on descent from a common ancestor.

Homology   Similarities between organisms based on common evolutionary descent.

Homologous   Refers to members of chromosome pairs. Homologous chromosomes carry genes that govern the same traits. During meiosis, homologous chromosomes pair and exchange segments of DNA. They are alike with regard to size, position of centromere, and banding pattern.

Homozygous   Having the same allele at the same locus on both members of a pair of homologous chromosomes.

Homozygous recessive   A genotype that contains two recessive alleles at the same locus. Only in this genotype will recessive phenotypes be expressed.

Hormones   Proteins produced by specialized cells that travel to other parts of the body where they influence chemical reactions.

Hybrid   Offspring of mixed ancestry.

Inheritance of acquired characteristics   The theory that traits acquired by an individual during its lifetime are passed on to offspring. As demonstrated by modern genetics, this idea is now known to be invalid.

Interphase   That portion of the cell cycle when visible division is not obvious (that is, chromosomes cannot be seen). However, DNA and all other structures assorted in cell division are replicated during interphase.

Interspecific   Between two or more species.

Intraspecific   Within one species.

Immunity   An organism's ability to recognize and deactivate foreign antigens very quickly as a consequence of earlier (mild) exposure (for example, through vaccination).

Ischial callosities   Patches of tough, hard skin on the rear ends of Old World monkeys and chimpanzees.

Karyotype   The chromosomal complement of an individual or that typical for a species. Usually displayed as a photomicrograph, often using special stains to highlight the bands or centromeres.

Law of Independent Assortment   Mendel's second law which states that the units (what we call, "alleles") that govern one trait assort independently of the units that govern other traits.

Law of Segregation   Genes occur in pairs (because chromosomes occur in pairs). During gamete production (meiosis), the members of each gene pair separate so that each gamete contains one member of each pair. During fertilization, the full number of chromosomes is restored and members of gene pairs are reunited.

Life history   Basic components of an animal's development and physiology, viewed from an evolutionary perspective. Such key components include body size, proportional brain size, metabolism, and reproduction.

Locus   That portion of a chromosome responsible for the production of a polypeptide chain.

Macroevolution   Large changes produced only after many generations.

Magdalenian   The final phase of the Upper Paleolithic in Europe.

Major histocompatibility complex (MHC)   The large genetic complex (located in humans on chromosome #6) that plays a central part in immune response—recognition of foreign antigens and production of specialized cells to deactivate them.

Malnutrition   A diet insufficient in quality (that is, lacking in some essential component) to support normal health.

Marker   A clearly identifiable trait that can be easily traced in pedigrees. Most markers are now ascertained at the DNA level and are mapped to specific human chromosomes. In this way, other traits (controlled by other loci) that correlate with the marker in pedigrees can also be (approximately) mapped as well.

Material culture   The physical manifestations of human activities; includes tools, house structures, etc. As the most durable aspects of culture, material remains make up the majority of archeological evidence of past societies.

Meiosis   Specialized cell division in the reproductive organs (in animals, ovaries or testes) which produces gametes. These daughter cells contain half the number of chromosomes of the parent cells and are not identical.

Mendelian traits   Traits that are under the influence of one genetic locus; also called *simple traits*.

Messenger RNA   A form of RNA that is formed on one side (one strand) of the DNA molecule. It carries the DNA code from the nucleus (after processing) to the cytoplasm, where protein synthesis takes place.

Metazoa   Multicellular animals. A major division of the Animal Kingdom.

Microevolution   Small, short-term changes occurring over just a few generations.

Middle Paleolithic   The culture period defined by stone tool industries called Mousterian. Found in Europe and the Near East (where it is associated with Neandertals) and also known from north Africa.

Migration   Movement of genes between populations.

Mitosis   Simple cell division; the process by which somatic cells divide to produce two identical daughter cells.

Monogenism   The nonevolutionary theory that all human races are descendants of one pair (Adam and Eve).

Monophyletic   A grouping of organisms (a taxon) that share a common ancestor.

Morphology   morph: form
The study of the structure of organisms.

Mosaic evolution   Rate of evolution in one functional system varies from other systems.

Mother-infant attachment   The attachment between mother and her offspring. One of the most basic themes running through primate social relations.

Motor cortex   The *cortex* of the brain, the outer layer, is composed of nerve cells or neurons. The *motor cortex* is that portion pertaining to outgoing signals involved in muscle use.

Mousterian   The stone tool industry found widespread in Europe and southwest Asia during the Upper Pleistocene. Associated with *both* Neandertals and modern *sapiens*.

Mutagen   An agent that mutates (alters) the DNA of a cell.

Mutation   An alteration in the genetic material (a change in the base sequence of DNA).

Natural selection   The evolutionary factor (first articulated by Charles Darwin) that causes changes in allele frequencies in populations due to differential net reproductive success of individuals.

Neocortex   The outer (cellular) portion of the cerebrum, which has expanded through evolution, particularly in primates, and most especially in humans. The neocortex is associated with higher mental function.

Nocturnal   Active at night.

Nucleotides   The basic subunit of DNA. Each nucleotide contains one sugar, one phosphate, and one of the four DNA bases.

Nucleus   A structure (organelle) found in all eukaryotic cells. The nucleus contains chromosomal DNA.

Nulliparous   null: none, not any; parous: birth. Never having given birth.

Osteology   The study of skeletons. Human osteology focuses on the interpretation of the skeletal remains of past groups. The same techniques are used in paleoanthropology to study early hominids.

Paleoanthropology   The interdisciplinary approach to the study of earlier hominids—their chronology, physical structure, archeological remains, habitats, etc.

Paleoecological   paleo: old
ecological: environmental setting
The study of ancient environments.

Paleomagnetism   Dating method based on shifting magnetic poles.

Paleopathology   The branch of osteology that studies the traces of disease and injury in human skeletal (or, occasionally, mummified) remains.

Paleospecies   A group of organisms from different periods classified within the same species.

Pangenesis   An early belief that contributions to reproductive cells came from particles within different body parts.

Parallel evolution   Independent evolution of similar structures from evolutionary distinct ancestors.

Pedigree   A diagram showing family relationships in order to trace the hereditary pattern of particular genetic (usually Mendelian) traits.

Pedologist   pedon: ground, soil
An expert in the study of soil.

Petrologist   petr: rock
An expert in the study of rocks and minerals.

Phenotype   The observable or detectable physical characteristics of an organism; the detectable expression of the genotype.

Phenotypic ratio   The proportion of one set of phenotypes to other phenotypes in a specific sample. For example, Mendel observed that there were approximately three tall plants for every short plant in the F_2 generation. This situation is expressed as a phenotypic ratio of 3:1.

Philopatric   *Philopatry.* Refers to remaining in one's natal group or home range as an adult. In most species, members of one sex disperse from their natal group as young adults, and members of the philopatric sex remain. In the majority of nonhuman primates, the philopatric sex is female.

Phylogeny   A schematic representation showing ancestor-descendant relationships usually in a chronological framework.

Pleistocene   The epoch of the Cenozoic from 1.8 m.y.a. until 10,000 y.a. Literally, meaning "ice age." This epoch is associated with continental glaciations in northern latitudes.

Polar body   A nonviable product of female meiosis (öogenesis), as it contains no cytoplasm.

Point mutation   The change in a single base of a DNA sequence.

Polyandrous   poly: many
androus: males
Two or more males mating with one female.

Polygenic   *Poly* means many; *genic* represents genes (that is, loci). Refers to traits that are influenced by two or more loci.

Polygenism   Another nonevolutionary theory that states human races are not all descended from Adam and Eve and therefore are not all members of the same species.

Polymorphism   *poly*: many;
morph: form
A genetic locus with two or more alleles in appreciable frequency.

Polypeptide chain   A sequence of amino acids that may act alone (or in combination) as a functional protein.

Polytypic   Refers to species composed of several populations that differ from each other with regard to certain physical traits.

Population   Within a species, a community of individuals where mates are usually found.

Population   A group of individuals from which mates are usually found. A population shares a common gene pool.

Postorbital bar   The bony element that closes in the outside of the eye orbit—a characteristic of primates.

Prehensility   Adapted for grasping.

Primate   The order of mammals that includes prosimians, monkeys, apes, and humans.

Primitive   Relating to a character state that reflects an ancestral condition, and thus not diagnostic of those derived lineages usually branching later.

Primitive   A character state of an organism that is inherited from an ancestor (before a divergence) when comparing with another lineage.

Prokaryotic   Cells without nuclei, as found in bacteria and blue-green algae.

Prosimian   A member of the suborder of Primates, the Prosimii, traditionally including lemurs, lorises, and tarsiers.

Protein synthesis   The assembly of chains of amino acids into functional protein molecules. The process is directed by DNA.

Provenience   In archeology, the specific location of a discovery.

Punctuated equilibrium   The concept that evolutionary change proceeds through long periods of stasis, punctuated by rapid periods of change.

Random assortment   The random distribution of chromosomes to daughter cells during Meiosis I. Along with recombination, the source of variation resulting from meiosis.

Recessive   A trait that is not phenotypically expressed in heterozygotes. Also refers to the allele that governs the trait. In order for the trait to be expressed, there must be two copies of the allele (that is, the individual must be homozygous).

Recombination (crossing-over)   The exchange of genetic material between homologous chromosomes during Meiosis I.

Rhinarium   (rine-air′-ee-um) The moist, hairless pad at the end of the nose seen in most mammalian species. The rhinarium enhances an animal's ability to smell.

Ribonucleic acid (RNA)   A single-stranded molecule, similar in structure to DNA. The three types of RNA are essential to protein synthesis.

Ribosomes   Structures (organelles) in the cytoplasm, made up of RNA and proteins, where protein synthesis takes place.

Ritualized behavior Ritualized behaviors are exaggerated and removed from their original context to convey information.

Sagittal crest Raised ridge along the midline of the cranium where the temporal muscle (used to move the jaw) is attached.

Sex cells Those reproductive cells that produce gametes. Gametes are also sometimes referred to as sex cells.

Sex chromosomes In animals, those chromosomes involved with primary sex determination. The X and Y chromosomes.

Shared derived Relating to specific character states shared in common between two forms and considered the *most* useful for making evolutionary interpretations.

Sickle-cell anemia A severe inherited disease that results from a double dose of a mutant allele, which in turn results from a single base substitution at the DNA level.

Sociobiology An evolutionary approach to the explanation of behavior, emphasizing the role of natural selection.

Socioecology The study of primates and their habitats; specifically, attempts to find patterns of relationship between the environment and primate social behavior.

Somatic cells Basically, all the cells in the body, except those involved with primary reproduction.

Speciation The process by which new species are produced from earlier ones. The most important mechanism of macroevolutionary change.

Species A group of interbreeding organisms that is reproductively isolated from other such groups.

Stratigraphy Sequential layering of deposits.

Substrate The surface on which an animal moves or rests.

Sympatric Animals living in the same area. Two or more species whose habitats partly or largely overlap.

Taphonomy *taphos*: dead
The study of how bones and other materials come to be buried in the earth and preserved as fossils. A taphonomist studies such phenomena as the processes of sedimentation, action of streams, preservation/chemical properties of bone, and carnivore disturbance factors.

Taxon (pl. Taxa) A population (or group of populations) that is judged to be sufficiently distinct and is assigned to a separate category (such as genus or species).

Tectonic movements Movements of the earth's plates that produce mountain building, earthquakes, volcanoes, and rifting.

Teratogen An agent that disrupts development.

Territories The territory is that portion of an individual's or a group's home range actively defended against intrusion, particularly by conspecifics.

Transcription The formation of a messenger RNA molecule on a DNA template.

Transfer RNA The type of RNA that binds to specific amino acids and, during translation, transports them to the ribosome in sequence.

Translation The process of sequencing amino acids from a messenger RNA template into a functional protein or a portion of a protein.

Tuff A geological deposit resulting from volcanic ash (either windblown or waterlaid).

Typology The sorting of phenomena into simple types. Traditional racial classifications were largely based on typological thinking.

Undernutrition A diet insufficient in quantity (calories) to support normal health.

Uniformitarian Also called uniformitarianism. The view that the same processes shaping the earth's surface today have also acted in the past.

Upper Paleolithic A culture period composed of various stone tool industries and distinguished by technological innovation. Best known from western Europe, similar industries are also known from central/eastern Europe and Africa.

Variation (genetic) Inherited differences between individuals. The basis of all evolutionary change.

Vertebrates Animals with bony backbones. Includes fishes, amphibians, reptiles, birds, and mammals.

Vivaparous Giving birth to live young.

Zygote A fertilized egg. The cell immediately following conception, containing the full set of chromosomes.

Bibliography

Aiello, L. C.
  1992 "Body Size and Energy Requirements." *In: The Cambridge Encyclopedia of Human Evolution*, J. Jones, R. Martin and D. Pilbeam, (eds.), Cambridge, England: Cambridge University Press, pp. 41–45.
Alland Jr., Alexander
  1971 *Human Diversity*. New York: Anchor Press/Doubleday.
Altman, I.
  1978 "Crowding: Historical and Contemporary Trends in Crowding Research." *In: Human Response to Crowding*, A. Baum and Y. M. Epstein (eds.), New York: John Wiley & Sons.
Altmann, Jeanne
  1981 *Baboon Mothers and Infants*. Cambridge: Harvard University Press.
Altmann, Stuart A. and Jeanne Altmann
  1970 *Baboon Ecology*. Chicago: University of Chicago Press.
Ames, Bruce N.
  1983 "Dietary Carcinogens and Anticarcinogens." *Science*, **21**: 1256–1264.
Amos, D. Bernard and D. D. Kostyu
  1980 "HLA—A Central Immunological Agency of Man." *In: Advances in Human Genetics* (Vol. 10), H. Harris and K. Hirschhorn (eds.), New York: Plenum Press, pp. 137–208.
Andersson, J. Gunnar
  1934 *Children of the Yellow Earth*. New York: Macmillan.
Andrews, Peter
  1985 "Family Group Systematics and Evolution among Catarrhine Primates." *In: Ancestors: The Hard Evidence*, E. Delson (ed.), New York: Alan R. Liss, pp. 14–22.
Andrews, Peter and Jens Lorenz Franzen (eds.)
  1984 *The Early Evolution of Man*. Frankfurt: Cour. Forsch.-Inst. Seckenberg.
Anthrop, Donald F.
  1973 *Noise Pollution*. Lexington, Mass.: D. C. Heath & Co.
ApSimon, Helen and Julian Wilson
  1986 "Tracking the Cloud from Chernobyl." *New Scientist*, July 17, 1986: pp. 42–45.
Ardrey, Robert
  1976 *The Hunting Hypothesis*. New York: Atheneum.
Arensburg, B., L. A. Schepartz, et al.
  1990 "A Reappraisal of the Anatomical Basis for Speech in Middle Paleolithic Hominids." *American Journal of Physical Anthropology*, **83**(2):137–146.
Arensburg, B., A. M. Tillier, et al.
  1989 "A Middle Paleolithic Human Hyoid Bone." *Nature*, **338**: 758–760.
Aronson, J. L., R. C. Walter, and M. Taieb
  1983 "Correlation of Tulu Bor Tuff at Koobi Fora with the Sidi Hakoma Tuff at Hadar." *Nature*, **306**:209–210.
Arsuaga, Juan-Luis, et al.
  1993 "Three New Human Skulls from the Sima de los Huesos Middle Pleistocene Site in Sierra de Atapuarca, Spain." *Nature*, **362**:534–537.

Asfaw, Berhane
  1992 "New Fossil Hominids from the Ethiopian Rift Valley and the Afar." Paper presented at the Annual Meeting, American Association of Physical Anthropologists.
Avery, O. T., C. M. MacLeod, and M. McCarty
  1944 "Studies on the Chemical Nature of the Substances Inducing Transformation in Pneumoccal Types." *Journal of Experimental Medicine*, **79**:137–158.

Badrian, Alison and Noel Badrian
  1984 "Social Organization of *Pan paniscus* in the Lomako Forest, Zaire." *In: The Pgymy Chimpanzee*, Randall L. Susman (ed.), New York: Plenum Press, pp. 325–346.
Baker, Paul T. and Michael A. Little
  1976 "Environmental Adaptations and Perspectives." *In: Man in the Andes*, P. T. Baker and M. A. Little (eds.), Stroudsburg, Penn.: Dowden, Hutchinson, and Ross, pp. 405–428.
Barash, David
  1982 *Sociobiology and Behavior*. (2nd Ed.) New York: Elsevier.
Barnes, Deborah M.
  1986 "Grim Projections for AIDS Epidemic." *Science*, **232**: 1589–1590.
Bartholomew, C. A. and J. B. Birdsell
  1953 "Ecology and the Protohominids." *American Anthropologist*, **55**:481–498.
Bartstra, Gert-Jan
  1982 "*Homo erectus erectus*: The Search for Artifacts." *Current Anthropology*, **23**(3):318–320.
Barzun, Jacques
  1965 *Race: A Study in Superstition*. New York: Harper & Row.
Bass, W. M.
  1987 *Human Osteology: A Laboratory and Field Manual* (3rd Ed.). Columbia, Mo.: Missouri Archaeological Society Special Publication No. 2.
Begun, D. and A. Walker
  1993 "The Endocast of the Nariokotome Hominid." *In*: A. Walker and R. E. Leakey (eds.), q.v.
Behrensmeyer, Anna K. and Andrew P. Hill
  1980 *Fossils in the Making: Vertebrate Taphonomy and Paleoecology*. Chicago: University of Chicago Press.
Bernor, R. L.
  1983 "Geochronology and Zoogeographic Relationships of Miocene Hominoidea." *In*: R. L. Ciochon and R. S. Corruccini (eds.), q.v., pp. 21–66.
Binford, Lewis R.
  1981 *Bones. Ancient Men and Modern Myths*. New York: Academic Press.

  ——
  1983 *In Pursuit of the Past*. New York: Thames and Hudson.

  ——
  1985 "Ancestral Lifeways: The Faunal Record." *AnthroQuest*, **32**, Summer, 1985.

Binford, Lewis R. and Chuan Kun Ho
1985   "Taphonomy at a Distance: Zhoukoudian, 'The Cave Home of Beijing Man'?" *Current Anthropology*, 26:413–442.
Binford, Lewis R. and Nancy M. Stone
1986a   "The Chinese Paleolithic: An Outsider's View." *AnthroQuest*, Fall 1986(1):14–20.

——— 1986b   "Zhoukoudian: A Closer Look." *Current Anthropology*, 27(5):453–475.
Birdsell, Joseph B.
1981   *Human Evolution*. (3d Ed.). Boston: Houghton Mifflin.
Birkby, W. H.
1966   "An Evaluation of Race and Sex Identification from Cranial Measurements." *American Journal of Physical Anthropology*, 24:21–28.
Boaz, N. T., F. C. Howell, and M. L. McCrossin
1982   "Faunal Age of the Usno, Shungura B and Hadar Formation, Ethiopia." *Nature*, 300:633–635.
Bodmer, W. F. and L. L. Cavalli-Sforza
1976   *Genetics, Evolution, and Man*. San Francisco: W. H. Freeman and Company.
Boesch, Christopher and H. Boesch
1989   "Hunting Behavior of Wild Chimpanzees in the Tai National Park." *American Journal of Physical Anthropology*, 78:547–573.
Bogaarts, John
1980   "Does Malnutrition Affect Fecundity? A Summary of Evidence." *Science*, 208:564–569.
Boggess, Jane
1984   "Infant Killing and Male Reproductive Strategies in Langurs (*Presbytis entellus*)." *In*: G. Hausfater and S. B. Hrdy (eds.), q.v., pp. 280– 310.
Bolton, Ralph
1973   "Aggression and Hypoglycemia among the Qolla; a Study in Psychological Anthropology." *Ethnology*, 12:227–257.

——— 1984   "The Hypoglycemia–Aggression Hypothesis: Debate versus Research." *Current Anthropology*, 25:1–53.
Bordes, François
1968   *The Old Stone Age*. New York: McGraw-Hill Book Co.
Bowler, Peter J.
1983, 1989   *Evolution: The History of an Idea*. Berkeley: University of California Press.

——— 1988   *The Non-Darwinian Evolution: Reinterpreting a Historical Myth*. Baltimore: Johns Hopkins University Press.
Brace, C. L. and Ashley Montagu
1977   *Human Evolution* (2nd Ed.). New York: Macmillan.
Brace, C. Loring, H. Nelson, and N. Korn
1979   *Atlas of Human Evolution* (2nd Ed.). New York: Holt, Rinehart & Winston.
Brain, C. K.
1970   "New Finds at the Swartkrans Australopithecine Site." *Nature*, 225:1112–1119.

——— 1981   *The Hunters or the Hunted? An Introduction to African Cave Taphonomy*. Chicago: University of Chicago Press.
Bramblett, Claud A.
1994   *Patterns of Primate Behavior* (2nd Ed.). Prospect Heights, IL: Waveland Press.
Bräuer, Gunter
1984   "A Craniological Approach to the Origin of Anatomically Modern *Homo sapiens* in Africa and Implications for the Appearance of Modern Europeans." *In*: F. H. Smith and F. Spencer (eds.), q.v., pp. 327–410.

——— 1989   "The Evolution of Modern Humans: A Comparison of the African and Non-African Evidence." *In*: Mellars and Stringer (eds.), q.v.
Brock, A., P. L. McFadden and T. C. Partridge
1977   "Preliminary Paleomagnetic Results from Makapansgat and Swartkrans." *Nature*, 266:249–250.
Bromage, Timothy G. and Christopher Dean
1985   "Re-evaluation of the Age at Death of Immature Fossil Hominids." *Nature*, 317:525–527.
Brooks, S. T.
1985   Personal Communication.

——— 1986   "Comments on 'Known' Age at Death Series." Presented in conjunction with "Skeletal Age Standards Derived from an Extensive Multi-Racial Sample of Modern Americans," by J. Suchey and D. Katz, at the Fifty-Fifth Annual Meeting of the American Association of Physical Anthropologists, Albuquerque, New Mexico.
Brose, David and Milford H. Wolpoff
1971   "Early Upper Paleolithic Man and Late Middle Paleolithic Tools." *American Anthropologist*, 73:1156–1194.
Brown, B., A. Walker, C. V. Ward and R. E. Leakey
1993   "New *Australopithecus boisei*: Calvaria from East Lake Turkana, Kenya." *American Journal of Physical Anthropology*, 91:137–159.
Brown, F. H.
1982   "Tulu Bor Tuff at Koobi Fora Correlated with the Sidi Hakoma Tuff at Hadar." *Nature*, 300:631–632.
Brown, T. M. and K. D. Rose
1987   "Patterns of Dental Evolution in Early Eocene Anaptomorphine Primates Comomyidael from the Bighorn Basin, Wyoming." *Journal of Paleontology*, 61:1–62.
Brues, Alice M.
1959   "The Spearman and the Archer." *American Anthropologist*, 61:457–469.

——— 1990   *People and Races* (2nd Ed.). Prospect Heights, IL: Waveland Press.

——— 1991   "The Objective View of Race." Paper presented at American Anthropological Association 90th Annual Meeting. Chicago, Nov.
Buffon, George Louis Leclerc, Compte de
1860   "Histoire Naturelle Generale et Particuliere." Translated by Wm. Smellie. *In*: *The Idea of Racism*, Louis L. Snyder, New York: Van Nostrand Reinhold, 1962.
Bugliarello, G., A. Alexander, J. Barnes and C. Wakstein
1976   *The Impact of Noise Pollution: A Sociotechnological Introduction*. New York: Pergamon Press.
Bunn, Henry T.
1981   "Archaeological Evidence for Meat-eating by Plio-Pleistocene Hominids from Koobi Fora and Olduvai Gorge." *Nature*, 291:574–577.
Burkhardt, Richard W., Jr.
1984   "The Zoological Philosophy of J. B. Lamarck. (Introduction) *In*: Lamarck, q.v.
Butzer, Karl W.
1974   "Paleoecology of South African Australopithecines: Taung Revisited." *Current Anthropology*, 15:367–382.

Campbell, Bernard
1976   *Humankind Emerging*. Boston: Little, Brown and Co. (4th Ed., 1984).

Cann, R. L., M. Stoneking and A. C. Wilson
1987 "Mitochondrial DNA and Human Evolution." *Nature*, **325**: 31–36.
Carrol, Robert L.
1988 *Vertebrate Paleontology and Evolution.* New York: W. H. Freeman and Co.
Cartmill, Matt
1972 "Arboreal Adaptations and the Origin of the Order Primates." *In: The Functional and Evolutionary Biology of Primates*, R. H. Tuttle (ed.), Chicago: Aldine-Atherton, pp. 97–122.

1992 *Evolutionary Anthropology*, **1**:105–111.
Chagnon, N. A.
1979 "Mate Competition Favoring Close Kin and Village Fissioning among the Yanomamo Indians." *In: Evolutionary Biology and Human Social Behavior: An Anthropological Perspective*, N. Chagnon and W. Irons (eds.), North Scituak, MA: Duxbury Press, pp. 86–132.

1988 "Life Histories, Blood Revenge, and Warfare in a Tribal Population." *Science*, **239**:985–992.
Chard, Chester S.
1975 *Man in Prehistory.* New York: McGraw-Hill.
Charteris, J., J. C. Wali, and J. W. Nottrodt
1981 "Functional Reconstruction of Gait from Pliocene Hominid Footprints at Laetoli, Northern Tanzania." *Nature*, **290**:496–498.
Cheney, Dorothy L.
1987 "Interaction and Relationships Between Groups." *In:* B. Smuts et al. (eds.), q.v., pp. 267–281.
Ciochon, R. L., and A. B. Chiarelli (eds.)
1980 *Evolutionary Biology of the New World Monkeys and Continental Drift.* New York: Plenum Press.
Ciochon, Russel L. and Robert S. Corruccini (eds.)
1983 *New Interpretations of Ape and Human Ancestry.* New York: Plenum Press.
Clark, W. E. LeGros
1967 *Man-apes or Ape-men?* New York: Holt, Rinehart & Winston.
1971 New York Times Books (3rd Ed.).
Clarke, R. J.
1985 "*Australopithecus* and Early *Homo* in Southern Africa." *In: Ancestors: The Hard Evidence*, E. Delson (ed.), New York: Alan R. Liss, pp. 171–177.
Cleveland, J. and C. T. Snowdon
1982 "The Complex Vocal Repertoire of the Adult Cotton-top Tamarin (*Saguinus oedipus oedipus*)." *Zeitschrift Tierpsychologie*, **58**:231–270.
Clutton-Brock, T. H. and Paul H. Harvey
1977 "Primate Ecology and Social Organization." *Journal of Zoological Society of London*, **183**:1–39.
Conroy, G., C. J. Jolly, D. Cramer and J. E. Kalb
1978 "Newly Discovered Fossil Hominid Skull from the Afar Depression." *Nature*, **276**:67–70.
Conroy, G. C., M. Pickford, B. Senut, J. van Couvering, and P. Mein
1992 "*Otavipithecus namibiensis*, First Miocene Hominoid from Southern Africa." *Nature*, **356**:144–148.
Coon, C. S., S. M. Garn and J. B. Birdsell
1950 *Races—A Study of the Problems of Race Formation in Man.* Springfield, Ill.: Charles C Thomas.
Corruccini, R. S. and H. M. McHenry
1980 "Cladometric Analysis of Pliocene Hominids." *Journal of Human Evolution*, **9**:209–221.

Cronin, J. E.
1983 "Apes, Humans, and Molecular Clocks. A Reappraisal." *In:* R. L. Ciochon and R. S. Corruccini (eds.), q.v., pp. 115–150.
Crook, J. H.
1970 "Social Organization and Environment: Aspects of Contemporary Social Ethology." *Animal Behavior*, **18**:197–209.
Crook, J. H. and J. S. Gartlan
1966 "Evolution of Primate Societies." *Nature*, **210**:1200–1203.
Cummings, Michael
1991 *Human Heredity* (2nd Ed.). St. Paul: West Publishing Co.

Dalrymple, G. B.
1972 "Geomagnetic Reversals and North American Glaciations." *In: Calibration of Hominoid Evolution*, W. W. Bishop and J. A. Miller (eds.), Edinburgh: Scottish Academic Press, pp. 303–329.
Damon, Albert
1977 *Human Biology and Ecology.* New York: W. W. Norton and Co.
Dart, Raymond
1959 *Adventures with the Missing Link.* New York: Harper & Brothers.
Darwin, Charles
1859 *On the Origin of Species.* A Facsimile of the First Edition, Cambridge, Mass.: Harvard University Press (1964).
Darwin, Francis (ed.)
1950 *The Life and Letters of Charles Darwin.* New York: Henry Schuman.
Day, M. H. and E. H. Wickens
1980 "Laetoli Pliocene Hominid Footprints and Bipedalism." *Nature*, **286**:385–387.
Day, Michael
1986 *Guide to Fossil Man* (4th Ed.), Chicago: University of Chicago Press.
Deacon, T. W.
1992 "The Human Brain." *In: The Cambridge Encyclopedia of Human Evolution*, S. Jones, R. Martin, and D. Pilbeam (eds.), Cambridge, England: Cambridge University Press, pp. 115–123.
Dene, H. T., M. Goodman and W. Prychodko
1976 "Immunodiffusion Evidence on the Phylogeny of the Primates." *In: Molecular Anthropology*, M. Goodman, R. E. Tashian and J. H. Tashian (eds.), New York: Plenum Press, pp. 171–195.
Desmond, Adrian and James Moore
1991 *Darwin.* New York: Warner Books.
Dettwyler, K. A.
1991 "Can Paleopathology Provide Evidence for Compassion?" *American Journal of Physical Anthropology*, **84**:375–384.
De Vos, J.
1985 "Faunal Stratigraphy and Correlation of the Indonesian Hominid Sites." *In: Ancestors: The Hard Evidence*, E. Delson (ed.), New York: Alan R. Liss, pp. 215–220.
de Waal, Frans
1982 *Chimpanzee Politics.* London: Jonathan Cape.

1987 "Tension Regulation and Nonreproductive Functions of Sex in Captive Bonobos (*Pan paniscus*)." *National Geographic Research*, **3**:318–335.

1989 *Peacemaking among Primates.* Cambridge: Harvard University Press.
Draper, Patricia
1973 "Crowding among Hunter-Gatherers: The !Kung Bushmen." *Science*, **182**:301–303.

Duchin, Linda E.
1990 "The Evolution of Articulate Speech." *Journal of Human Evolution*, **19**:687–697.

Dumont, R. and B. Rosier
1969 *The Hungry Future*. New York: Praeger.

Dunbar, I. M.
1988 *Primate Social Systems*. Ithaca: Cornell University Press.

Durham, William
1981 Paper presented to the Annual Meeting of the American Anthropological Association, Washington, D.C., Dec. 1980. Reported in *Science*, **211**:40.

Eisenberg, J. F., N. A. Muckenhirn, and R. Rudran
1972 "The Relation Between Ecology and Social Structure in Primates." *Science*, **176**:863–874.

Eiseley, Loren
1961 *Darwin's Century*. New York: Anchor Books.

Eldredge, Niles and Joel Cracraft
1980 *Phylogenetic Patterns and the Evolutionary Process*. New York: Columbia University Press.

Etler, Denis
1992 Personal communication.

Falk, Dean
1980 "A Reanalysis of the South African Australopithecine Natural Endocasts." *American Journal of Physical Anthropology*, **53**:525–539.

——— 1983 "The Taung Endocast: A Reply to Holloway." *American Journal of Physical Anthropology*, **60**:479–489.

——— 1987 "Brain Lateralization in Primates and Its Evolution in Hominids." *Yearbook of Physical Anthropology*, **30**:107–125.

——— 1989 "Comments." *Current Anthropology*, **30**:141.

Fedigan, Linda M.
1982 *Primate Paradigms*. Montreal: Eden Press.

——— 1983 "Dominance and Reproductive Success in Primates." *Yearbook of Physical Anthropology*, **26**:91–129.

——— 1986 "The Changing Role of Women in Models of Human Evolution." *Annual Review of Anthropology*, **15**:25–66.

Fisher, R. A.
1930 *The Genetical Theory of Natural Selection*. Oxford: Clarendon.

Fleagle, J. G.
1983 "Locomotor Adaptations of Oligocene and Miocene Hominoids and Their Phyletic Implications." *In*: R. L. Ciochon and R. S. Corruccini (eds.), q.v., pp. 301–324.

——— 1988 *Primate Adaptation and Evolution*. New York: Academic Press.

Fleagle, J. G., and R. F. Kay
1983 "New Interpretations of the Phyletic Position of Oligocene Hominoids." *In*: R. L. Ciochon and R. S. Corruccini (eds.), q.v., pp. 181–210.

Fleischer, R. C., and H. R. Hart, Jr.
1972 "Fission Track Dating, Techniques and Problems." *In*: *Calibration of Hominoid Evolution*, W. W. Bishop and J. A. Miller (eds.), Edinburgh: Scottish Academic Press, pp. 135–170.

Foley, R. A. and M. M. Lahr
1992 "Beyond 'Out of Africa.' " *Journal of Human Evolution*, **22**: 523–529.

Fossey, Dian
1983 *Gorillas in the Mist*. Boston: Houghton Mifflin.

Fouts, Roger S., D. H. Fouts and T. T. van Cantfort
1989 "The Infant Loulis Learns Signs from Cross-Fostered Chimpanzees." *In*: R. A. Gardner et al., q.v., pp. 280–292.

Francoeuer, Robert T.
1965 *Perspectives in Evolution*. Baltimore: Helicon.

Frayer, David
1980 "Sexual Dimorphism and Cultural Evolution in the Late Pleistocene and Holocene of Europe." *Journal of Human Evolution*, **9**:399–415.

——— 1992 "Evolution at the European Edge: Neanderthal and Upper Paleolithic Relationships." *Prehistoire Europeenne*, **2**:9–69.

——— n.d. "Language Capacity in European Neanderthals."

Friedman, Milton J. and William Trager
1981 "The Biochemistry of Resistance to Malaria." *Scientific American*, **244**:154–164.

Frisancho, A. R.
1978 "Nutritional Influences on Human Growth and Maturation." *Yearbook of Physical Anthropology*, **21**:174–191.

——— 1981 *Human Adaptations: A Functional Interpretation*. Ann Arbor: University of Michigan Press.

Froelich, J. W.
1970 "Migration and Plasticity Physique in the Japanese-Americans of Hawaii." *American Journal of Physical Anthropology*, **32**:429.

Galdikas, Biruté M.
1979 "Orangutan Adaptation at Tanjung Puting Reserve: Mating and Ecology." *In*: *The Great Apes*, D. A. Hamburg and E. R. McCown (eds.), Menlo Park, Ca.: Benjamin/Cummings Publishing Co., pp. 195–233.

Gambier, Dominique
1989 "Fossil Hominids from the Early Upper Palaeolithic (Aurignacian) of France." *In*: Mellars and Stringer (eds.), q.v.

Gardner, R. Allen, B. T. Gardner and T. T. van Cantfort (eds.)
1989 *Teaching Sign Language to Chimpanzees*. Albany: State University of New York Press.

Garn, Stanley M.
1965, 1969 *Human Races*. Springfield, Ill.: Charles C. Thomas.

Gates, R. R.
1948 *Human Ancestry*. Cambridge: Harvard University Press.

Gavan, James
1977 *Paleoanthropology and Primate Evolution*. Dubuque, Iowa: Wm. C. Brown Co.

Genoves, S.
1967 "Proportionality of Long Bones and Their Relation to Stature among Mesoamericans." *American Journal of Physical Anthropology*, **26**:67–78.

Gerson, Donald
1977 "Radiation in the Environment." *In*: A. Damon (ed.), q.v., pp. 246–265.

Ghiselin, Michael T.
1969 *The Triumph of the Darwinian Method*. Chicago: University of Chicago Press.

Gibbons, Ann
1992 "Mitochondrial Eve, Wounded but Not Dead Yet." *Science*, **257**:873–875.

Gighlieri, Michael P.
1984 *The Chimpanzees of Kibale Forest*. New York: Columbia University Press.

Giles, E., and O. Elliot
1962 "Race Identification from Cranial Measurements." *Journal of Forensic Sciences*, **7**:147–157.

Gill, G. W.
1986 "Craniofacial Criteria in Forensic Race Identification." *In*: *Forensic Osteology: Advances in the Identification of Human Remains*, K. J. Reichs (ed.), Springfield: Charles C. Thomas.

Gill, G. W., S. S. Hughes, S. M. Bennett, and B. M. Gilbert
1988 "Racial Identification from the Mid-facial Skeleton with Special Reference to American Indians and Whites." *Journal of Forensic Sciences*, **33**(1).

Gingerich, Phillip D.
1985 "Species in the Fossil Record: Concepts, Trends, and Transitions." *Paleobiology*, **11**:27–41.

Goldizen, Anne Wison
1987 "Tamarins and Marmosets: Communal Care of Offspring." *In*: Smuts et al. (eds.), q.v., pp. 34–43.

Goldstein, M., P. Tsarong and C. M. Beall
1983 "High Altitude Hypoxia, Culture, and Human Fecundity/Fertility: A Comparative Study." *American Anthropologist*, **85**:28–49.

Goodall, Jane
1986 *The Chimpanzees of Gombe*. Cambridge: Harvard University Press.

——— 1990 *Through a Window*. Boston: Houghton Mifflin.

Goodman, M., M. L. Baba and L. L. Darga
1983 "The Bearing of Molecular Data on the Cladogenesis and Times of Divergence of Hominoid Lineages." *In*: R. L. Ciochon and R. S. Corruccini (eds.), q.v., pp. 67–86.

Gossett, Thomas F.
1963 *Race, the History of an Idea in America*. Dallas: Southern Methodist University Press.

Gould, Stephen Jay
1981 *The Mismeasures of Man*. New York: W. W. Norton.

——— 1987 *Time's Arrow Time's Cycle*. Cambridge: Harvard University Press.

Gould, S. J. and N. Eldredge
1977 "Punctuated Equilibria: The Tempo and Mode of Evolution Reconsidered." *Paleobiology*, **3**:115–151.

Gould, S. J. and R. Lewontin
1979 "The Spandrels of San Marco and the Panglossian Paradigm: A Critique of the Adaptionist Programme." *Proceedings of the Royal Society of London*, **205**:581–598.

Gowlett, John
1984 *Ascent to Civilization*. New York: Alfred A. Knopf.

Greenberg, Joel
1977 "Who Loves You?" *Science News*, **112** (August 27):139–141.

Greene, John C.
1981 *Science, Ideology, and World View*. Berkeley: University of California Press.

Greenfield, L. O.
1979 "On the Adaptive Pattern of *Ramapithecus*." *American Journal of Physical Anthropology*, **50**:527–548.

Grine, Frederick E. (ed.)
1988a *Evolutionary History of the "Robust" Australopithecines*. New York: Aldine de Gruyter.
1988b "New Craniodental Fossils of *Paranthropus* from the Swartkrans Formation and Their Significance in "Robust" Australopithecine Evolution." *In*: F. E. Grine (ed.), q.v., pp. 223–243.

Haldane, J. B. S.
1932 *The Causes of Evolution*. London: Longmans, Green (reprinted as paperback, Cornell University Press, 1966).

Hamilton, W. D.
1964 "The Genetical Theory of Social Behavior: I and II." *Journal of Theoretical Biology*, **7**:1–52.

Hanna, Joel M. and Daniel A. Brown
1979 "Human Heat Tolerance: Biological and Cultural Adaptations." *Yearbook of Physical Anthropology*, 1979, **22**:163–186.

Harlow, Harry F.
1959 "Love in Infant Monkeys." *Scientific American*, **200**:68–74.

Harlow, Harry F. and Margaret K. Harlow
1961 "A Study of Animal Affection." *Natural History*, **70**:48–55.

Harrold, Francis R.
1989 "Mousterian, Chatelperronian and Early Aurignacian in Western Europe: Continuity or Discontinuity." *In*: *The Human Revolution*, P. Mellars and C. Stringer, Princeton, N.J.: Princeton University Press, pp. 212–231.

Hartl, Daniel
1983 *Human Genetics*. New York: Harper & Row.

Harvey, Paul H., R. D. Martin and T. H. Clutton-Brock
1987 "Life Histories in Comparative Perspective." *In*: Smuts et al. (eds.), q.v., pp. 181–196.

Hausfater, Glenn
1984 "Infanticide in Langurs: Strategies, Counter Strategies, and Parameter Values." *In*: G. Hausfater and S. B. Hrdy, (eds.), q.v., pp. 257–281.

Hausfater, Glenn and Sarah Blaffer Hrdy (eds.)
1984 *Infanticide. Comparative and Evolutionary Perspectives*. Hawthorne, New York: Aldine de Gruyter.

Hayden, Brian
1993 "The Cultural Capacities of Neandertals: a Review and Re-Evaluation." *Journal of Human Evolution*, **24**:113–146.

Henson, Robert
1992 "Ugly Human at Two O'clock." *Discover*, **13**(6):18.

Hiernaux, Jean
1968 *La Diversité Humaine en Afrique subsahariénne*. Bruxelles: L'Institut de Sociologie, Université Libre de Bruxelles.

Hill, A., S. Ward, A. Deino, G. Curtis, and R. Drake
1992 "Earliest *Homo*." *Nature*, **355**:719–722.

Hill, Andrew, and Steven Ward
1988 "Origin of the Hominidae: The Record of African Large Hominoid Evolution Between 14 my and 4 my." *Yearbook of Physical Anthropology*, 1988, **31**:49–83.

Hinde, Robert A.
1987 "Can Nonhuman Primates Help Us Understand Human Behavior?" *In*: B. Smuts et al. (eds.), q.v., pp. 413–420.

Hoffstetter, R.
1972 "Relationships, Origins, and History of the Ceboid Monkeys and the Caviomorph Rodents: A Modern Reinterpretation." *In*: *Evolutionary Biology* (Vol. 6), T. Dobzhansky, T.M.K. Hecht, and W. C. Steere (eds.), New York: Appleton-Century-Crofts, pp. 323–347.

Holloway, Ralph L.
1969 "Culture: A Human Domain." *Current Anthropology*, **10**:395–407.

——— 1981 "Revisiting the South African Taung Australopithecine Endocast: The Position of the Lunate Sulcus as Determined by the Stereoplotting Technque." *American Journal of Physical Anthropology*, **56**:43–58.

——— 1983 "Cerebral Brain Endocast Pattern of *Australopithecus afarensis* Hominid." *Nature*, **303**:420–422.

Hooton, E. A.
    1926   "Methods of Racial Analysis." *Science*, **63**:75–81.
Howell, F. Clark
    1978   "Hominidae." *In*: *Evolution of African Mammals*, V. J. Maglio and H. B. S. Cooke (eds.), Cambridge: Harvard University Press, pp. 154–248.

    1988   "Foreword." *In*: Grine (ed.), q.v., pp. xi–xv.
Howells, W. W.
    1973   *Evolution of the Genus* Homo. Reading, Mass.: Addison-Wesley.

    1980   "*Homo erectus*—Who, When, Where: A Survey." *Yearbook of Physical Anthropology*, **23**:1–23.
Hrdy, Sarah Blaffer
    1977   *The Langurs of Abu*. Cambridge, Mass.: Harvard University Press.

    1984a   "Assumptions and Evidence Regarding the Sexual Selection Hypothesis: A Reply to Boggess." *In*: G. Hausfater and S. B. Hrdy (eds.), q.v., pp. 315–319.

    1984b   "Female Reproductive Strategies." *In*: M. Small (ed.), q.v., pp. 103–109.
Hull, David L.
    1973   *Darwin and His Critics*. Chicago: University of Chicago Press.

The Institute of Vertebrate Paleontology and Paleoanthropology, Chinese Academy of Sciences
    1980   *Atlas of Primitive Man in China*. Beijing: Science Press (Distributed by Van Nostrand, New York).
Isaac, G. L.
    1971   "The Diet of Early Man." *World Archaeology*, **2**:278–299.

    1975   "Stratigraphy and Cultural Patterns in East Africa During the Middle Ranges of Pleistocene Time." *In*: *After the Australopithecines*, K. W. Butzer and G. L. Isaac (eds.), Chicago: Aldine Publishing Co., pp. 495–542.

    1976   "Early Hominids in Action: A Commentary on the Contribution of Archeology to Understanding the Fossil Record in East Africa." *Yearbook of Physical Anthropology*, 1975, **19**:19–35.
Izawa, K., and A. Mizuno
    1977   "Palm-Fruit Cracking Behaviour of Wild Black-Capped Capuchin (*Cebus apella*). *Primates*, **18**:773–793.

Jensen, Arthur
    1969   *Environment, Heredity, and Intelligence*. Cambridge, Mass.: Harvard Educational Review.
Jerison, H. J.
    1973   *Evolution of the Brain and Behavior*. New York: Academic Press.
Jia, L. and Huang Weiwen
    1990   *The Story of Peking Man*. New York: Oxford University Press.
Jia, Lan-po
    1975   *The Cave Home of Peking Man*. Peking: Foreign Language Press.
Johanson, D. C. and T. D. White
    1979   "A Systematic Assessment of Early African Hominids." *Science*, **203**:321–330.
Johanson, Donald and Maitland Edey
    1981   *Lucy: The Beginnings of Humankind*. New York: Simon & Schuster.

Johanson, Donald, F. T. Masao et al.
    1987   "New Partial Skeleton of *Homo habilis* from Olduvai Gorge, Tanzania." *Nature*, **327**:205–209.
Johanson, Donald C. and Maurice Taieb
    1976   "Plio-Pleistocene Hominid Discoveries in Hadar, Ethiopia." *Nature*, **260**:293–297.

    1980   "New Discoveries of Pliocene Hominids and Artifacts in Hadar." International Afar Research Expedition to Ethiopia (Fourth and Fifth Field Seasons, 1975–77). *Journal of Human Evolution*, **9**:582.
Jolly, Alison
    1984   "The Puzzle of Female Feeding Priority." *In*: M. F. Small (ed.), q.v., pp. 197–215.

    1985   *The Evolution of Primate Behavior* (2nd Ed.), New York: Macmillan.
Jones, Rhys
    1990   East of Wallace's Line: Issues and Problems in the Colonization of the Australian Continent." *In*: *The Human Revolution*, P. Mellars and C. Stringer (eds.), Princeton, N.J.: Princeton University Press, pp. 743–782.
Jungers, W. L.
    1982   "Lucy's Limbs: Skeletal Allometry and Locomotion in *Australopithecus afarensis*." *Nature*, **297**:676–678.

    1988   "New Estimates of Body Size in Australopithecines." *In*: F. E. Grine (ed.), q.v., pp. 115–125.

Kay, R. F., J. G. Fleagle and E. L. Simons
    1981   "A Revision of the Oligocene Apes of the Fayum Province, Egypt." *American Journal of Physical Anthropology*, **55**:293–322.
Kelly, Mark and David Pilbeam
    1986   "The Dryopithecines: Taxonomy, Comparative Anatomy, and Phylogeny of Miocene Large Hominoids." *In*: *Comparative Primate Biology*. Vol. 1, *Systematics, Evolution, and Anatomy*, D. R. Swindler and J. Erwin (eds.), New York: Alan R. Liss, pp. 361–411.
Kennedy, G. E.
    1983   "A Morphometric and Taxonomic Assessment of a Hominid Femur from the Lower Member, Koobi Fora, Lake Turkana." *American Journal of Physical Anthropology*, **61**:429–436.
Kennedy, K.A.R.
    1991   "Is the Narmada Hominid an Indian *Homo erectus*?" *American Journal of Physical Anthropology*, **86**:475–496.
Kennedy, Kenneth A. R. and S. U. Deraniyagala
    1989   "Fossil Remains of 28,000-Year-Old Hominids from Sri Lanka." *Current Anthropology*, **30**:397–399.
Kimbel, William H.
    1988   "Identification of a Partial Cranium of *Australopithecus afarensis* from the Koobi Fora Formation, Kenya." *Journal of Human Evolution*, **17**:647–656.
Kimbel, William H., Tim D. White and Donald C. Johanson
    1988   "Implications of KNM-WT-17000 for the Evolution of 'Robust' *Australopithecus*." *In*: F. E. Grine (ed.), q.v., pp. 259–268.
Klein, R. G.
    1989   *The Human Career. Human Biological and Cultural Origins*. Chicago: University of Chicago Press.

    1992   "The Archeology of Modern Human Origins." *Evolutionary Anthropology*, **1**:5–14.
Kramer, Andrew
    1986   "Hominid-Pongid Distinctiveness in the Miocene-Pliocene

Fossil Record: The Lothagam Mandible." *American Journal of Physical Anthropology*, **70**:457–473.

——— 1993   "Human Taxonomic Diversity in the Pleistocene: Does *Homo erectus* Represent Multiple Hominid Species?" *American Journal of Physical Anthropology*, **91**:161–171.

Kroeber, A. L.
1928   "Sub-human Cultural Beginning." *Quarterly Review of Biology*, 3:325–342.

Krogman, W. M.
1962   *The Human Skeleton in Forensic Medicine*. Springfield: C. C. Thomas.

Kummer, Hans
1971   *Primate Societies*. Chicago: Aldine-Atherton, Inc.

Lack, David
1966   *Population Studies of Birds*. Oxford: Clarendon.

Lamarck, Jean Baptiste
1809, 1984   *Zoological Philosophy*. Chicago: University of Chicago Press.

Lancaster, Jane B.
1975   *Primate Behavior and the Emergence of Human Culture*. New York: Holt, Rinehart & Winston.

Landau, M.
1984   "Human Evolution as Narrative." *American Scientist*, **72**:262-268.

Lasker, Gabriel W.
1969   "Human Biological Adaptability: The Ecological Approach in Physical Anthropology." *Science*, **166**:1480–1486.

Latimer, Bruce
1984   "The Pedal Skeleton of *Australopithecus afarensis*." *American Journal of Physical Anthropology*, **63**:182.

Leakey, L.S.B., J. F. Everden and G. H. Curtis
1961   "Age of Bed I, Olduvai Gorge, Tanganyika." *Nature*, **191**:478–479.

Leakey, L.S.B., P. V. Tobias and J. R. Napier
1964   "A New Species of the Genus *Homo* from Olduvai Gorge." *Nature*, **202**:7–10.

Leakey, M. D.
1971   "Remains of *Homo erectus* and Associated Artifacts in Bed IV at Olduvai Gorge, Tanzania." *Nature*, **232**:380–383.

Leakey, M. D., and R. L. Hay
1979   "Pliocene Footprints in Laetolil Beds at Laetoli, Northern Tanzania." *Nature*, **278**:317–323.

Leakey, R.E.F. and M. D. Leakey
1986   "A New Miocene Hominoid from Kenya." *Nature*, **324**:143–146.

Lerner, I. M. and W. J. Libby
1976   *Heredity, Evolution, and Society*. San Francisco: W. H. Freeman and Company.

Lewellen, Ted C.
1981   "Aggression and Hypoglycemia in the Andes: Another Look at the Evidence." *Current Anthropology*, **22**:347–361.

Lewontin, R. C.
1972   "The Apportionment of Human Diversity." *In: Evolutionary Biology* (Vol. 6), T. Dobzhansky et al. (eds.), New York: Plenum, pp. 381–398.

Li, Wen-Hsiung and Masako Tanimura
1987   "The Molecular Clock Runs More Slowly in Man than in Apes and Monkeys." *Nature*, **326**:93–96.

Lieberman, Daniel, David R. Pilbeam and Bernard A. Wood
1988   "A Probalistic Approach to the Problem of Sexual Dimorphism in *Homo habilis*: A Comparison of KNM-ER-1470 and KNM-ER-1813." *Journal of Human Evolution*, **17**:503–511.

Linnaeus, C.
1758   *Systema Naturae*.

Lisowski, F. P.
1984   "Introduction." *In: The Evolution of the East African Environment*. Centre of Asian Studies Occasional Papers and Monographs, No. 59, R. O. Whyte (ed.), Hong Kong: University of Hong Kong, pp. 777–786.

Livingstone, Frank B.
1964   "On the Nonexistence of Human Races." *In: Concept of Race*, A. Montagu (ed.), New York: The Free Press, pp. 46–60.

——— 1969   "Polygenic Models for the Evolution of Human Skin Color Differences." *Human Biology*, **41**:480–493.

——— 1980   "Natural Selection and the Origin and Maintenance of Standard Genetic Marker Systems." *Yearbook of Physical Anthropology*, 1980, **23**:25–42.

Lovejoy, C. O.
1988   "Evolution of Human Walking." *Scientific American*, **259**(Nov.):118–125.

Lovejoy, C. O., G. Kingsbury, G. Heiple and A. H. Burstein
1973   "The Gait of *Australopithecus*." *American Journal of Physical Anthropology*, **38**:757–780.

Lovejoy, Thomas E.
1982   "The Tropical Forest—Greatest Expression of Life on Earth." *In: Primates and the Tropical Forest*, Proceedings, California Institute of Technology and World Wildlife Fund—U.S., pp. 45–48.

MacKinnon, J. and K. MacKinnon
1980   "The Behavior of Wild Spectral Tarsiers." *International Journal of Primatology*, **1**:361–379.

MacLarnon, Ann
1993   "The Vertebral Canal of KNM-WT 15000 and the Evolution of the Spinal Cord and Other Canal Contents." *In*: A. Walker and R. E. Leakey (eds.), q.v.

Manson, J. H. and R. Wrangham
1991   "Intergroup Aggression in Chimpanzees and Humans." *Current Anthropology*, **32**:369–390.

Marshack, A.
1972   *The Roots of Civilization*. New York: McGraw-Hill Publishing Co.

——— 1989   "Evolution of the Human Capacity: The Symbolic Evidence." *Yearbook of Physical Anthropology*, 1989, **32**:1–34.

Masserman, J., S. Wechkin, and W. Terris
1964   " 'Altruistic' Behavior in Rhesus Monkeys." *American Journal of Psychiatry*, **121**:584–585.

Mayr, Ernst
1962   "Taxonomic Categories in Fossil Hominids." *In: Ideas on Human Evolution*, W. W. Howells (ed.), New York: Atheneum, pp. 242–256.

——— 1970   *Population, Species, and Evolution*. Cambridge: Harvard University Press.

——— 1991   *One Long Argument*. Cambridge: Harvard University Press.

McGrew, W. C.
1992   *Chimpanzee Material Culture. Implications for Human Evolution*. Cambridge: Cambridge University Press.

McGrew, W. C. and E. G. Tutin
1978   "Evidence for a Social Custom in Wild Chimpanzees?" *Man*, **13**:234–251.

McHenry, Henry
1983   "The Capitate of *Australopithecus afarensis* and *A. africanus.*" *American Journal of Physical Anthropology*, **62**:187–198.

──────   1988   "New Estimates of Body Weight in Early Hominids and Their Significance to Encephalization and Megadontia in 'Robust' Australopithecines." *In:* F. E. Grine (ed.), q.v., pp. 133–148.

──────   1992   "Body Size and Proportions in Early Hominids." *American Journal of Physical Anthropology*, **87**:407–431.

McKern, T. W., and T. D. Stewart
1957   "Skeletal Age Changes in Young American Males, Technical Report EP-45." Natick, MA: U.S. Army Quartermaster Research and Development Center.

McKusick, Victor
1990   *Mendelian Inheritance in Man.* (9th Ed.) Baltimore: Johns Hopkins Press.

Mellars, P. and C. Stringer (eds.)
1989   *The Human Revolution.* Princeton, N.J.: Princeton University Press.

Mittermeir, R. A.
1982   "The World's Endangered Primates: An Introduction and a Case Study—The Monkeys of Brazil's Atlantic Forests." *In: Primates and the Tropical Rain Forest*, Proceedings, California Institute of Technology, and World Wildlife Fund—U.S., pp. 11–22.

Mittermeir, R. A. and D. Cheney
1987   "Conservation of Primates in Their Habitats." *In:* B. B. Smuts et al., (eds.), q.v., pp. 477–496.

Moore, Lorna G. and Judith G. Regensteiner
1983   "Adaptation to High Altitude." *Annual Reviews of Anthropology*, **12**:285–304.

Morbeck, M. E.
1975   "*Dryopithecus africanus* Forelimb." *Journal of Human Evolution*, **4**:39–46.

──────   1983   "Miocene Hominoid Discoveries from Rudabánya. Implications from the Postcranial Skeleton." *In:* R. L. Ciochon and R. S. Corruccini (eds.), q.v., pp. 369–404.

Morgan, Elaine
1972   *The Descent of Women.* New York: Stein and Day.

Morris, Desmond
1967   *The Naked Ape.* New York: McGraw-Hill.

Mourant, A. E., A. C. Kopec, and K. Sobczak
1976   *The Distribution of the Human Blood Groups.* Oxford: Oxford University Press.

Mueller, William H., et al.
1979   "A Multinational Andean Genetic and Health Program. VIII. Lung Function Changes with Migration between Altitudes." *American Journal of Physical Anthropology*, **51**:183–196.

Napier, J. R. and P. H. Napier
1967   *A Handbook of Living Primates.* New York: Academic Press.

──────   1985   *The Natural History of the Primates.* London: British Museum (Natural History).

Napier, John
1967   "The Antiquity of Human Walking." *Scientific American*, **216**: 56–66.

Nature
1986   "Chernobyl Report." *Nature*, **323**:26–30.

Newman, Marshall T.
1975   "Nutritional Adaptation in Man." *In: Physiological Anthropology*, Albert Damon (ed.), New York: Oxford University Press, pp. 210–259.

Newman, Russell W.
1970   "Why Man Is Such a Sweaty and Thirsty Naked Animal: A Speculative Review." *Human Biology*, **42**:12–27.

Newman, Russell W. and Ella H. Munro
1955   "The Relation of Climate and Body Size in U.S. Males." *American Journal of Physical Anthropology*, **13**:1–17.

Nishida, T.
1991   Comments. *In:* J. H. Manson and R. Wrangham, q.v.

Nishida, T., M. Hiraiwa-Hasegawa, T. Hasegawa, and Y. Takahata
1985   "Group Extinction and Female Transfer in Wild Chimpanzees in the Mahale National Park, Tanzania." *Zeitschrift Tierpsychologie*, **67**:284–301.

Nishida, T., H. Takasaki, and Y. Takahata
1990   "Demography and Reproductive Profiles." *In: The Chimpanzees of the Mahale Mountains*, T. Nishida (ed.), Tokyo: University of Tokyo Press, pp. 63–97.

Nishida, T., R. W. Wrangham, J. Goodall, and S. Uehara
1983   "Local Differences in Plant-feeding Habits of Chimpanzees between the Mahale Mountains and Gombe National Park, Tanzania." *Journal of Human Evolution*, **12**:467–480.

Oakley, Kenneth
1963   "Analytical Methods of Dating Bones." *In: Science in Archaeology*, D. Brothwell and E. Higgs (eds.), New York: Basic Books, Inc.

Olson, John W. and R. Ciochon
1990   "A Review of the Evidence for Postulated Middle Pleistocene Occupation in Viet Nam." *Journal of Human Evolution*, **19**: 761–788.

Ortner, Donald J.
1981   "Biocultural Interaction in Human Adaptation." *In: How Humans Adapt.* Donald J. Ortner, ed. Washington, D.C.: Smithsonian Institution Press.

Pickford, M.
1983   "Sequence and Environments of the Lower and Middle Miocene Hominoids of Western Kenya." *In:* R. L. Ciochon and R. S. Corruccini (eds.), q.v., pp. 421–439.

Pilbeam, David
1972   *The Ascent of Man.* New York: Macmillan.

──────   1982   "New Hominoid Skull Material from the Miocene of Pakistan." *Nature*, **295**:232–234.

──────   1986   "Distinguished Lecture: Hominoid Evolution and Hominoid Origins." *American Anthropologist*, **88**:295–312.

──────   1988   "Primate Evolution." *In: Human Biology*, G. A. Harrison et al., (eds.), New York: Oxford University Press, pp. 76–103.

Pope, G. G.
1984   "The Antiquity and Paleoenvironment of the Asian Hominidae." *In: The Evolution of the East Asian Environment.* Center of Asian Studies Occasional Papers and Monographs, No. 59, R. O. Whyte (ed.), Hong Kong: University of Hong Kong, pp. 822–847.

──────   1992   "Craniofacial Evidence for the Origin of Modern Humans in China." *Yearbook of Physical Anthropology*, 1992, **35**:243–298.

Popp, Joseph L. and Irven DeVore
1979   "Aggressive Competition and Social Dominance Theory." *In: The Great Apes*, D. A. Hamburg and E. R. McCown (eds.),

Menlo Park, Ca.: Benjamin/Cummings Publishing Co., pp. 317–318.

Post, Peter W., Farrington Daniels, Jr. and Robert T. Binford, Jr.
1975 "Cold Injury and the Evolution of 'White' Skin." *Human Biology*, **47**:65–80.

Potts, R.
1984 "Home Bases and Early Hominids." *American Scientist*, **72**: 338–347.

Potts, Richard and Pat Shipman
1981 "Cutmarks Made by Stone Tools from Olduvai Gorge, Tanzania." *Nature*, **291**:577–580.

Proctor, Robert
1988 "From Anthropologie to Rassenkunde." *In: Bones, Bodies, Behavior. History of Anthropology* (Vol. 5), 6. W. Stocking, Jr. (ed.), Madison: University of Wisconsin Press, pp. 138–179.

Pusey, Anne E. and Craig Packer
1987 "Dispersal and Philopatry." *In*: B. B. Smuts et al. (eds.), q.v., pp. 250–266.

Quinn, Thomas C., J. M. Mann, J. W. Curran and P. Piot
1986 "AIDS in Africa: An Epidemiologic Paradigm." *Science*, **234**: 955–963.

Radinsky, Leonard
1973 "*Aegyptopithecus* Endocasts: Oldest Record of a Pongid Brain." *American Journal of Physical Anthropology*, **39**:239–248.

Rak, Y.
1983 *The Australopithecine Face*. New York: Academic Press.

Richard, A. F.
1985 *Primates in Nature*. New York: W. H. Freeman and Co.

Richard, A. F. and S. R. Schulman
1982 "Sociobiology: Primate Field Studies." *Annual Reviews of Anthropology*, **11**:231–255.

Rightmire, G. P.
1981 "Patterns in the Evolution of *Homo erectus*." *Paleobiology*, **7**: 241–246.

——— 1990 *The Evolution of* Homo erectus. New York: Cambridge University Press.

Roberts, D. F.
1973 *Climate and Human Variability*. An Addison-Wesley Module in Anthropology, No. 34. Reading, Mass.: Addison-Wesley.

Roberts, Richard, Rhys Jones, and M. A. Smith
1990 "Thermoluminescence Dating of a 50,000-Year-Old Human Occupation Site in Northern Australia," *Nature*, 345:153–156.

Robinson, J. T.
1972 *Early Hominid Posture and Locomotion*. Chicago: University of Chicago Press.

Rose, M. D.
1991 "Species Recognition in Eocene Primates." *American Journal of Physical Anthropology*, Supplement 12, p. 153.

Ruff, C. B. and Alan Walker
1993 "The Body Size and Shape of KNM-WT 15000." *In*: A. Walker and R. Leakey (eds.), q.v.

Rumbaugh, D. M.
1977 *Language Learning by a Chimpanzee: The Lana Project*. New York: Academic Press.

Sachick, Kathy B. and Dong Zhuan
1991 "Early Paleolithic of China and Eastern Asia." *Evolutionary Anthropology*, **2**(1):22–35.

Sarich, Vincent
1971 "A Molecular Approach to the Question of Human Origins." *In: Background for Man*, P. Dolhinow and V. Sarich (eds.), Boston: Little, Brown & Co., pp. 60–81.

Schaller, George B.
1963 *The Mountain Gorilla*. Chicago: University of Chicago Press.

Scheller, Richard H. and Richard Axel
1984 "How Genes Control Innate Behavior." *Scientific American*, **250**:54–63.

Schull, William J., M. Otuke and J. V. Neel
1981 "Genetic Effects of the Atomic Bombs: A Reappraisal." *Science*, **213**:1220–1227.

Senut, Brigette and Christine Tardieu
1985 "Functional Aspects of Plio-Pleistocene Hominid Limb Bones: Implications for Taxonomy and Phylogeny." *In: Ancestors: The Hard Evidence*, E. Delson (ed.), New York: Alan R. Liss, pp. 193–201.

Seyfarth, Robert M., Dorothy L. Cheney, and Peter Marler
1980a "Monkey Responses to Three Different Alarm Calls." *Science*, **210**:801–803.

——— 1980b "Ververt Monkey Alarm Calls." *Animal Behavior*, **28**:1070–1094.

Shipman, P. L.
1983 "Early Hominid Lifestyle. Hunting and Gathering or Foraging and Scavenging?" Paper presented at 52nd Annual Meeting, American Association of Physical Anthropologists, Indianapolis, April.

——— 1987 "An Age-Old Question: Why Did the Human Lineage Survive?" *Discover*, **8**:60–64.

Sibley, Charles and Jon E. Ahlquist
1984 "The Phylogeny of the Hominoid Primates as Indicated by DNA-DNA Hybridization." *Journal of Molecular Evolution*, **20**:2–15.

Simons, E. L.
1969 "The Origin and Radiation of the Primates." *Annals of the New York Academy of Sciences*, **167**:319–331.

——— 1972 *Primate Evolution*. New York: Macmillan.

——— 1985 "African Origin, Characteristics and Context of Earliest Higher Primates." *In: Hominid Evolution: Past, Present, and Future*. P. Tobias (ed.), New York: Alan R. Liss, pp. 101–106.

Simpson, G. G.
1945 "The Principles of Classification and a Classification of Mammals." *Bulletin of the American Museum of Natural History*, **85**:1–350.

Simpson, G. G., C. S. Pittendright and L. H. Tiffany
1957 *Life*. New York: Harcourt, Brace and Co., Inc.

Skelton, R. R., H. M. McHenry and G. M. Drawhorn
1986 "Phylogenetic Analysis of Early Hominids." *Current Anthropology*, **27**:1–43; 361–365.

Small, Meredith F. (ed.)
1984 *Female Primates. Studies by Women Primatologists*. Monographs in Primatology, Vol. 4. New York: Alan R. Liss.

Smith, Fred H.
1984 "Fossil Hominids from the Upper Pleistocene of Central Europe and the Origin of Modern Europeans." *In*: F. H. Smith and F. Spencer (eds.), q.v., pp. 187–209.

Smith, Fred H., A. B. Falsetti and S. M. Donnelly
1989 "Modern Human Origins." *Yearbook of Physical Anthropology*, 1989, **32**:35–68.

Smith, Fred H. and Frank, Spencer (eds.)
1984 *The Origins of Modern Humans*. New York: Alan R. Liss, Inc.

Smuts, Barbara
1985   *Sex and Friendship in Baboons.* Hawthorne, N.Y.: Aldine de Gruyter.
Smuts, Barbara B. et al. (eds.)
1987   *Primate Societies.* Chicago: University of Chicago Press.
Soffer, Olga
1985   *The Upper Paleolithic of the Central Russian Plain.* New York: Academic Press.
Solecki, Ralph
1971   *Shanidar, The First Flower People.* New York: Alfred A. Knopf.
Stanyon, Roscoe and Brunetto Chiarelli
1982   "Phylogeny of the Hominoidea: The Chromosome Evidence." *Journal of Human Evolution,* 11:493–504.
Steegman, A. T., Jr.
1970   "Cold Adaptation and the Human Face." *American Journal of Physical Anthropology,* 32:243–250.

1975   "Human Adaptation to Cold." *In: Physiological Anthropology,* A. Damon (ed.), New York: Oxford University Press, pp. 130–166.
Stern, Jack T. and Randall L. Susman
1983   "The Locomotor Anatomy of *Australopithecus afarensis.*" *American Journal of Physical Anthropology,* 60:279–317.
Stewart, T. D.
1979   *Essentials of Forensic Anthropology: Especially as Developed in the United States.* Springfield: C. C. Thomas.
Stiner, Mary C.
1991   "The Faunal Remains from Grotta Guatari." *Current Anthropology,* 32(2)April:103–117.
Strauss, Lawrence Guy
1993   "Southwestern Europe at the Last Glacial Maximum." *Current Anthropology,* 32:189–199.
Stringer, C. B. (ed.)
1985   "Middle Pleistocene Hominid Variability and the Origin of Late Pleistocene Humans." *In: Ancestors: The Hard Evidence,* E. Delson (ed.), New York: Alan R. Liss, pp. 289–295.

1993   "Secrets of the Pit of the Bones." *Nature,* 362:501–502.
Stringer, C. B. and P. Andrews
1988   "Genetic and Fossil Evidence for the Origin of Modern Humans." *Science,* 239:1263–1268.
Struhsaker, T. T.
1967   "Auditory Communication among Vervet Monkeys (*Cercopithecus aethiops*)." *In: Social Communication Among Primates,* S. A. Altmann (ed.), Chicago: University of Chicago Press.

1975   *The Red Colobus Monkey.* Chicago: University of Chicago Press.
Struhsaker, Thomas T. and Lysa Leland
1979   "Socioecology of Five Sympatric Monkey Species in the Kibale Forest, Uganda." *Advances in the Study of Behavior,* Vol. 9, New York: Academic Press, pp. 159–229.

1987   "Colobines: Infanticide by Adult Males." *In: B. B. Smuts et al. (eds.), q.v., pp. 83–97.
Sumner, D. R., M. E. Morbeck and J. Lobick
1989   "Age-Related Bone Loss in Female Gombe Chimpanzees." *American Journal of Physical Anthropology,* 72:259.
Suomi, Stephen J., Susan Mineka and Roberta D. DeLizio
1983   "Short- and Long-Term Effects of Repetitive Mother-Infant Separation on Social Development in Rhesus Monkeys." *Developmental Psychology,* 19(5):710–786.
Susman, Randall L.
1988   "New Postcranial Remains from Swartkrans and Their Bear-

ing on the Functional Morphology and Behavior of *Paranthropus robustus.*" *In:* F. E. Grine (ed.), q.v., pp. 149–172.
Susman, Randall L., Jack T. Stern and William L. Jungers
1985   "Locomotor Adaptations in the Hadar Hominids." *In: Ancestors: The Hard Evidence,* E. Delson (ed.), New York: Alan R. Liss., pp. 184–192.
Suzman, I. M.
1982   "A Comparative Study of the Hadar and Sterkfontein Australopithecine Innominates." *American Journal of Physical Anthropology,* 57:235.
Szalay, Frederick S. and Eric Delson
1979   *Evolutionary History of the Primates.* New York: Academic Press.

Tattersal, Ian, Eric Delson, and John Van Couvering
1988   *Encyclopedia of Human Evolution and Prehistory.* New York: Garland Publishing.
Teleki, G.
1986   "Chimpanzee Conservation in Sierra Leone—A Case Study of a Continent-wide Problem." Paper presented at Understanding Chimpanzees Symposium, Chicago Academy of Sciences, Chicago, Nov. 7–10, 1987.
Tenaza, R. and R. Tilson
1977   "Evolution of Long-Distance Alarm Calls in Kloss' Gibbon." *Nature,* 268:233–235.
Tobias, Phillip
1971   *The Brain in Hominid Evolution.* New York: Columbia University Press.

1983   "Recent Advances in the Evolution of the Hominids with Especial Reference to Brain and Speech." Pontifical Academy of Sciences, *Scrita Varia,* 50:85–140.

1991   *Olduvai Gorge, Volume IV. The Skulls, Endocasts and Teeth of Homo habilis.* Cambridge: Cambridge University Press.
Todd, T. W.
1920–21   "Age Changes in the Pubic Bone." *American Journal of Physical Anthropology,* 3:285–334; 4:1–70.
Trinkaus, E.
1983   *The Shanidar Neandertals.* New York: Academic Press.

1984   "Western Asia." *In:* F. H. Smith and F. Spencer (eds.), q.v., pp. 251–293.
Trinkaus, E. and W. W. Howells
1979   "The Neandertals." *Scientific American,* 241(6):118–133.
Trinkaus, Erik and Pat Shipman
1992   *The Neandertals.* New York: Alfred A. Knopf.
Trivers, R. L.
1971   "The Evolution of Reciprocal Altruism." *Quarterly Review of Biology,* 46:35–57.

1972   "Parental Investment and Sexual Selection." *In: Sexual Selection and the Descent of Man,* B. Campbell (ed.), Chicago: Aldine, pp. 136–179.
Tuttle, Russell H.
1990   "Apes of the World." *American Scientist,* 78:115–125.

Van Couvering, A. H. and J. A. Van Covering
1976   "Early Miocene Mammal Fossils From East Africa." *In: Human Origins,* G. Isaac and E. R. McCown (eds.), Menlo Park, Ca.: W. A. Benjamin, pp. 155–207.
Villa, Paola
1983   *Terra Amata and the Middle Pleistocene Archaeological Record of Southern France.* University of California Publications in

Anthropology, Vol. 13. Berkeley: University of California Press.

Visalberghi, E.
1990   "Tool Use in *Cebus*." *Folia Primatologica*, **54**:146–154.

Vogel, F.
1970   "ABO Blood Groups and Disease." *American Journal of Human Genetics*, **22**:464–475.

Vogel, F., M. Kopun and R. Rathenberg
1976   "Mutation and Molecular Evolution." *In*: *Molecular Anthropology*, M. Goodman et al. (eds.), New York: Plenum Press, pp. 13–33.

Von Koenigswald, G.H.R.
1956   *Meeting Prehistoric Man*. New York: Harper & Brothers.

Walker, A.
1976   "Remains Attributable to *Australopithecus* from East Rudolf." *In*: *Earliest Man and Environments in the Lake Rudolf Basin*, Y. Coppens et al. (eds.), Chicago: University of Chicago Press, pp. 484–489.

———   1991   "The Origin of the Genus *Homo*." *In*: S. Osawa and T. Honjo (eds.), *Evolution of Life*. Tokyo: Springer-Verlag, pp. 379–389.

———   1993   "The Origin of the Genus *Homo*." *In*: D. T. Rasmussen (ed.), *The Origin and Evolution of Humans and Humaness*. Boston: Jones and Bartlett, pp. 29–47.

Walker, Alan and R. E. Leakey
1993   *The Nariokotome* Homo erectus *Skeleton*. Cambridge: Harvard University Press.

Walker, Alan and Mark Teaford
1989   "The Hunt for *Proconsul*." *Scientific American*, **260**(Jan.):76–82.

Walters, Jeffrey and Robert Seyfarth
1987   "Conflict and Cooperation." *In*: B. B. Smuts, et al. (eds.), q.v., pp. 306–317.

Ward, S. C. and D. R. Pilbeam
1983   Maxillofacial Morphology of Miocene Hominoids from Africa and Indo-Pakistan." *In*: R. L. Ciochon and R. S. Corruccini (eds.), q.v., pp. 211–238.

Ward, Steven and William H. Kimbel
1983   "Subnasal Alveolar Morphology and the Systematic Position of *Sivapithecus*." *American Journal of Physical Anthropology*, **61**:157–171.

Washburn, S. L.
1963   "The Study of Race." *American Anthropologist*, **65**:521–531.

———   1971   "The Study of Human Evolution." *In*: P. Dolhinow and V. Sarich (eds.), *Background for Man: Readings in Physical Anthropology*, Boston: Little, Brown, pp. 82–121.

Watson, J. B., and F. H. C. Crick
1953a   "Genetical Implications of the Structure of the Deoxyribonucleic Acid." *Nature*, **171**:964–967.

———   1953b   "A Structure for Deoxyribonucleic Acid." *Nature*, **171**:737–738.

Weiner, J. S.
1954   "Nose Shape and Climate." *American Journal of Physical Anthropology*, **12**:615–618.

———   1955   *The Piltdown Forgery*. London: Oxford University Press.

———   1977   "Human Ecology." *In*: *Human Biology*, G. A. Harrison et al. (eds.), New York: Oxford University Press, pp. 387–483.

Weiss, K. M., K. K. Kidd, and J. R. Kidd
1992   "A Human Genome Diversity Project." *Evolutionary Anthropology*, **1**:80–82.

White, T. D.
1980   "Evolutionary Implications of Pliocene Hominid Footprints." *Science*, **208**:175–176.

———   1983   Comment Made at Institute of Human Origins Conference on the Evolution of Human Locomotion (Berkeley, Ca.).

White, T. D. and J. M. Harris
1977   "Suid Evolution and Correlation of African Hominid Localities." *Science*, **198**:13–21.

White, Tim D. and Donald C. Johanson
1989   "The Hominid Composition of Afar Locality 333: Some Preliminary Observations." *Hominidae*, Proceedings of the 2nd International Congress of Human Paleontology, Milan: Editoriale Jaca Book, pp. 97–101.

White, T. D., D. C. Johanson and W. H. Kimbel
1981   "*Australopithecus africanus*: Its Phyletic Position Reconsidered." *South African Journal of Science*, **77**:445–470.

Whyte, Robert Orr (ed.)
1984   "The Evolution of the East Asian Environment." Centre of Asian Studies Occasional Papers and Monographs, No. 59. Hong Kong: University of Hong Kong.

Williams, G. C.
1966   *Adaptation and Natural Selection: A Critique of Some Current Evolutionary Thought*. Princeton: Princeton University Press.

Williams, Robert C.
1985   "HLA II: The Emergence of the Molecular Model for the Major Histocompatibility Complex." *Yearbook of Physical Anthropology*, 1985, **28**:79–95.

Wilson, E. O.
1975   *Sociobiology, The New Synthesis*. Cambridge: Harvard University Press.

Wolf, Katherine, and Steven Robert Schulman
1984   "Male Response to 'Stranger' Females as a Function of Female Reproduction Value among Chimpanzees." *The American Naturalist*, **123**:163–174.

Wolpoff, Milford H.
1983a   "Lucy's Little Legs." *Journal of Human Evolution*, **12**:443–453.

———   1983b   "*Ramapithecus* and Human Origins. An Anthropologist's Perspective of Changing Interpretations." *In*: R. L. Ciochon and R. S. Corruccini (eds.), q.v., pp. 651–676.

———   1984   "Evolution in *Homo erectus*: The Question of Stasis." *Paleobiology*, **10**:389–406.

———   1989   "Multiregional Evolution: The Fossil Alternative to Eden." *In*: P. Mellars and C. Stringer, q.v., pp. 62–108.

Wolpoff, Milford H., et al.
1981   "Upper Pleistocene Human Remains from Vindija Cave, Croatia, Yugoslavia." *American Journal of Physical Anthropology*, **54**:499–545.

Wolpoff, M., Wu Xin Chi, and Alan G. Thorne
1984   "Modern *Homo sapiens* Origins." *In*: Smith and Spencer (eds.), q.v., pp. 411–483.

Wood, Bernard
1991   *Koobi Fora Research Project IV: Hominid Cranial Remains from Koobi Fora*. Oxford: Clarendon Press.

———   1992a   "Origin and Evolution of the Genus *Homo*." *Nature*, **355**:783–790.

1992b "A Remote Sense for Fossils." *Nature*, **355**:397–398.

Wrangham, Richard
1980 "An Ecological Model of Female-Bonded Primate Groups." *Behavior*, **75**:262–300.

Wu, Rukang and S. Lin
1983 "Peking Man." *Scientific American*, **248**(6):86–94.

Wu, Rukang and C. E. Oxnard
1983 "Ramapithecines from China: Evidence from Tooth Dimensions." *Nature*, **306**:258–260.

Wu, Rukang and Xingren Dung
1985 "*Homo erectus* in China." *In*: *Palaeoanthropology and Palaeolithic Archaeology in the People's Republic of China*, R. Wu and J. W. Olsen (eds.), New York: Academic Press, pp. 79–89.

Yi, Seonbok and G. A. Clark
1983 "Observations on the Lower Palaeolithic of Northeast Asia." *Current Anthropology*, **24**:181–202.

Yunis, Jorge J. and Om Prakesh
1982 "The Origin of Man: A Chromosomal Pictorial Legacy." *Science*, **215**:1525–1530.

Zhou Min Zhen and Wang Yuan Quing
1989 "Paleoenvironmental Contexts of Hominid Evolution in China." *Circum-Pacific Prehistory Conference*, Seattle: University of Washington Press.

Zubrow, Ezra
1990 "The Demographic Modeling of Neanderthal Extinction." *In*: *The Human Revolution*, P. Mellars and C. Stringer, Princeton, N.J.: Princeton University Press, pp. 212–231.

Index

(continued from copyright page)

Chapter 4: Fig. 4-2 Bettmann Archive; Fig. 4-3 Bettmann Archive; Figs. 4-4, 4-5 American Museum of Natural History; Fig. 4-6 Bettmann Archive; Fig. 4-7 Bettmann Archive; Figs. 4-8, 4-9, 4-11 American Museum of Natural History; Fig. 4-14 Harry Nelson; Fig. 4-15 Library, N.Y. Academy of Medicine; Box, p. 91, Courtesy, *Annual Review of Genetics*; Fig. 4-16 Michael Tweedie/ Photo Researchers; Breck P. Kent/Animals, Animals.

Chapter 6: Fig. 6-1 Norman Lightfoot/Photo Researchers; Fig. 6-3 Renee Lynn/Photo Researchers; George Holton/Photo Researchers; Fig. 6-5 Reprinted with permission from *Man in the Andes: A Multidisciplinary Study of High Altitude Quechua*, Edited by Baker and Little; Fig. 6-6 Wide World; Fig. 6-7 Wide World; Fig. 6-8 Wide World; Fig. 6-9 John Elk/Stock, Boston.

Chapter 7: Fig. 7-8 Hansejudy Beste/Animals, Animals; Fig. 7-9 J. C. Stevenson/Animals, Animals; p. 193 (Fig. 4) Dian Fossey; (Fig. 5) Lynn Kilgore.

Chapter 8: Figs. 8-11, 8-12 Courtesy Fred Jacobs; Fig. 8-13 Courtesy, San Francisco Zoo; Fig. 8-15 Courtesy Bonnie Pedersen/Arlene Kruse; Fig. 8-17 David Haring, Duke University Primate Center; Fig. 8-19 San Diego Zoo; Fig. 8-20 Raymond Mendez/Animals, Animals; Figs. 8-22, 8-23 R. Jurmain; Figs. 8-25(a), (b) Lynn Kilgore; Fig. 8-26 Hans Kummer; Fig. 8-27 R. Jurmain; Fig. 8-31 Lynn Kilgore; Fig. 8-32 R. Jurmain, Photo by Jill Matsumoto/Jim Anderson; Figs. 8-33(a), (b) Lynn Kilgore; Figs. 8-35(a), (b) R. Jurmain, Photo by Jill Matsumoto/Jim Anderson; Fig. 8-36 Courtesy, Ellen Ingmanson; Fig. 8-37 R. Jurmain, Photo by Jill Matsumoto/Jim Anderson.

Chapter 9: Fig. 9-1 Lynn Kilgore; Fig. 9-2 Bonnie Pedersen; Fig. 9-3 Courtesy John Oates; Fig. 9-4 Courtesy, Jean DeRousseau; Fig. 9-5 Courtesy, John Oates; Fig. 9-6(a) Lynn Kilgore; (b), (c) R. Jurmain; (d) Arlene Kruse/Bonnie Pedersen; Fig. 9-7(a) San Diego Zoo; (b) Harry Nelson; Fig. 9-8(a) Harry Nelson; (b) Arlene Kruse/Bonnie Pedersen; Fig. 9-9 Harry Harlow, University of Wisconsin, Primate Laboratory; Figs. 9-10, 9-11 Lynn Kilgore; Fig. 9-12 Joe MacDonald/Animals, Animals; Fig. 9-13(a) Maseo Kauakii; (b) Porter Zoo, Brownsville, Texas; p. 261 Peter Weit/ Sygma.

Chapter 10: Fig. 10-1 Courtesy, Meredith Small; p. 266, p. 267, Figs. 1, 2, 3, 4 R. Jurmain; Fig. 10-2(a) Lynn Kilgore; (b) Baron Hugo van Lawick, © National Geographic Society; Fig. 10-4 Harry Nelson; Figs. 10-5, 10-6 Lynn Kilgore; Fig. 10-7 Beatrice Gardner; Fig. 10-10(a) Courtesy, The Jane Goodall Institute; (b) Courtesy, Carol Lofton, Distinctive Images.

Chapter 11: Figs. 11-5(a), (b) Courtesy Elwyn Simons; Fig. 11-8 R. Jurmain; Figs. 11-10, 11-11 Courtesy, David Pilbeam.

Chapter 12: Figs. 12-1, 12-4 R. Jurmain; p. 333 David Siddon, L. S. B. Leakey Foundation; Fig. 12-6 R. Jurmain; p. 336 R. Jurmain; Fig. 12-7 Harry Nelson; Figs. 12-11, 12-12 R. Jurmain.

Chapter 13: Fig. 13-5 Harry Nelson; Fig. 13-6 Courtesy, Peter Jones; Figs. 13-7, 13-8, 13-9(a), (b), 13-10, 13-11 Institute of Human Origins; Fig. 13-12 National Museums of Kenya; Fig. 13-13 Reprinted with permission of the National Museums of Kenya, Copyright reserved, Courtesy of Alan Walker; Fig. 13-14 Institute of Human Origins; Fig. 13-15 Reproduced with permission of the National Museums of Kenya, Copyright reserved; Fig. 13-17 National Museums of Kenya; Fig. 13-18 Courtesy of Raymond Dart, Photo by Alun Hughes; Fig. 13-19(a) Photo by Alan Hughes, reproduced by permission of Professor Phillip V. Tobias; Fig. 13-20 Courtesy, Ellen Ingmanson; Fig. 13-21 Wide World; Fig. 13-23 Transvaal Museum, South Africa (also source of specimen); Fig. 13-24 Bettmann Archive.

Chapter 15: Fig. 15-3 Harry Nelson; Fig. 15-4 Courtesy of New York Academy of Medicine Library; Figs. 15-5, 15-6 Kindness of S. Sartono; Fig. 16-7 Courtesy of New York Academy of Medicine Library; Figs. 15-8, 15-9 Courtesy of American Museum of Natural History; Fig. 15-11 Courtesy of Denis Etler; Fig. 15-12 Harry Nelson; Fig. 15-13 Reproduced with permission of the National Museum of Kenya. Copyright reserved.

Chapter 16: Fig. 16-2 Harry Nelson; Fig. 16-3 R. Jurmain; Fig. 16-5 Tim D. White; Fig. 16-6 Harry Nelson; Fig. 16-7 Courtesy of H. De Lumley; Fig. 16-9 Harry Nelson; Figs. 16-14, 16-15, 16-16, 16-17 Fred Smith; Figs. 16-17, 16-18 Harry Nelson.

Chapter 17: Figs. 17-3, 17-4 David Frayer; Fig. 17-5 Fred Smith; Figs. 17-7(a), (b) David Frayer.

Composite Illustrations

Chapter 13-17:   ER-1813, ER-1470, Reproduced with permission of the National Museums of Kenya, copyright reserved. OH24, Tim White. OH7, H. Nelson. Stw 53, courtesy of P. V. Tobias (reconstruction by Ronald J. Clark).

Chapter 13-25:   "Zinj," H. Nelson. Taung, courtesy of P. V. Tobias; photo by Alun Hughes. Sts 5, Sk 48, Transvaal Museum, South Africa. LH 4, Lucy, Institute of Human Origins. WT-17,000, Reproduced with permission of the National Museums of Kenya, copyright reserved; courtesy Alan Walker.

Chapter 14-4:   ER-406, ER-732, ER-729, Reproduced with permission of the National Museums of Kenya, copyright reserved. SK 48, Transvaal Museum, South Africa. WT-17,000, Reproduced with permission of the National Museums of Kenya, copyright reserved; courtesy Alan Walker.

Chapter 15-1:   ER-3733, Reproduced with permission of the National Museums of Kenya, copyright reserved. Salé, courtesy J. J. Bublin, WT-15,000, Reproduced with permission of the National Museums of Kenya, copyright reserved. OH 9, Hexian, Lantian, H. Nelson. Sangiran 17, Ngandong, courtesy S. Sartono.

Chapter 15-2:   *Upper center, upper right, and upper left*, H. Nelson. *Center left*, From Franz Weidenreich, "Morphology of Solo Man," Anthropology Papers of the American Meusum of Natural History, Vol. 43, part 3, 1951. Courtesy Public Affairs Department, The American Museum of Natural History. *Lower right*, courtesy S. Sartono. *Upper right,* Robert Jurmain.

Chapter 16-1:   Eliye Springs, Laetoli 18, Florisbad, courtesy Güunter Bräuer. Kabwe, courtesy Fred Smith. Bodo, Elandsfontein, courtesy T. D. White.

Chapter 16-4:   Swanscombe, H. Nelson. Fontechevade, Petralona, Ehringsdorf, courtesy Fred Smith. Arago, courtesy H. DeLumley. Mauer, H. Nelson. Steinheim, H. Nelson. Maba, Dali, courtesy Wu Xinzhi. Bilzingsleben, courtesy Milford Wolpoff.

Chapter 16-11:   Spy, courtesy Milford Wolpoff. Shanidar, H. Nelson. La Ferrassie, La Chapelle, St. Cesaire, Amud, courtesy Fred Smith.

Chapter 16-13:   La Ferrassie, La Chapelle, St. Cesaire, courtesy Fred Smith. Krapina, Spy, courtesy Milford Wolpoff.

Chapter 17-1:   Cro Magnon, courtesy David Frayer. Jebel Irhoud, Omo, Klasies River Mouth, Border Cave, Jebel Wafzah, Skhūl, courtesy Fred Smith.

Chapter 17-2:   Qafzeh 6, 9, Skhūl 5, Border Cave, courtesy Fred Smith. Predmostí 3, H. Nelson.

Chapter 17-8:   Wadjak, Mungo, Kow Swamp, courtesy Milford Wolpoff.